CHINESE SOCIETY IN THAILAND:

An Analytical History

Publication of this book has been made
possible by a grant from the Hull Memorial
Publication Fund of Cornell University.

Thailand, showing regions and major towns

CHINESE SOCIETY
IN THAILAND:
An Analytical History

By G. WILLIAM SKINNER

Professor of Anthropology and Asian Studies

Cornell University

CORNELL UNIVERSITY PRESS

Ithaca, New York

CORNELL UNIVERSITY PRESS

LONDON: OXFORD UNIVERSITY PRESS

First published 1957
Second printing 1962

PRINTED IN THE UNITED STATES OF AMERICA

Preface

WITH the demise of Western colonialism in Southeast Asia, the overseas Chinese have assumed greater importance for the future of that region. China's recent emergence as a major Communist power, too, has added a new dimension to their potential influence. Centuries before these developments, however, overseas Chinese were already playing an important role in the economic development and social evolution of the major Southeast Asian countries. It is no exaggeration to say that the central current of Thai history in recent centuries cannot be properly understood or analyzed apart from the changing position of the overseas Chinese. Yet Western and Thai historians alike have paid them scant attention. It is hoped that the present volume will help rectify the comparative disregard of the overseas Chinese characteristic in historical works on Thailand and provide background necessary for an understanding of the Chinese role at the present time.

In fact, it was the need for historical depth in analyzing field data on contemporary Chinese society in Thailand that prompted me to undertake a diachronic inquiry. What began as an investigation into the genesis of the "Chinese problem" in Thailand developed into a more extensive study as I became increasingly interested in the subject matter and more convinced of its importance. The major emphasis of the present work, however, reflects the initial interest in societal development. As a history, therefore, it is somewhat untraditional, both in organization and in treatment of the subject matter. The approach is analytical rather than narrative, and it is oriented more to the objectives of the social sciences than to those of the humanities. It should also be noted that the later chapters are based as much on material collected by methods traditional to anthropological field work as on that found in bibliographical records. Finally, because no adequate survey of the current position of the Chinese in Thailand is available in the published literature, the final chapter includes a general description of contemporary Chinese society in Thailand.

The Transcription of Chinese and Thai

Chinese names and other terms have been transcribed according to the simplified Wade-Giles system used in C. H. Fenn's *Five Thousand Dictionary,* except for the omission of tone numerals. Items for which character identification appeared to be useful are indicated in the text by a number preceded by C in parentheses, e.g., (C 107). These C numbers refer to the character list beginning on page 439. Chinese characters for place names in south China are not included in the character list but instead are shown on Maps 2, 3, and 4. The names of Chinese provinces and of the better known cities are spelled in the usual form established in the *Postal Atlas of China,* e.g., Kwangtung, Fukien, Swatow, Canton, Amoy.

For Thai names and terms, I have used a phonetic system of romanization based on that recommended by the Royal Institute of Thailand in 1939 and outlined in the *Journal of the Thailand Research Society* of March 1941. Since several changes have been made in order to eliminate special letters and diacritical marks, the orthography followed will be briefly described here. The voiced stops, occurring only in initial position, are written *b* and *d;* the voiceless, unaspirated stops are written *p, t, j* (palatal stop), and *k,* while the voiceless aspirated stops are written *ph, th, ch,* and *kh.* The glottal stop is not transcribed. The voiceless spirants are written *f, s,* and *h,* and the voiced nasals, *m, n,* and *ng.* The nine vowels are written as follows: front unrounded, *i, e, ae;* central unrounded, *ue, oe, a;* back rounded, *u, o, ǫ* [ɔ]. Homophonous vowel clusters (long vowels) are not distinguished from unlengthened or short vowels, but the three heterophonous vowel clusters which occur are, of course, indicated: *ia, uea, ua.* In initial position, the voiced semivowels are written *y* and *w.* In final position, the former is written *i* and the latter *o* when following *a* or *ae,* but *w* when following *i.*

The use of a phonetic romanization for Thai, while increasingly preferred by scholars and laymen alike, is by no means universal. Many writers on Thailand employ with more or less consistency systems based on a transliteration of the Thai spelling, whereby, for instance, "Phahon" becomes "Bahol" or "Suratthani" becomes "Surashtra Dhani"—forms which are of little assistance in approximating the Thai pronunciation of the names in question. The most common variant transcriptions of Thai proper names will be found in the index.

Chinese and Thai Territorial Units

During the Ming and Ch'ing dynasties in China, the *fu* or prefecture was a large and important administrative area embracing one or more dependent *chou* or departments. There were also independent *chou* under the direct jurisdiction of the provincial governments. A *chou*, in turn, embraced several *hsien* or counties. Shortly after the Chinese revolution, both *chou* and *fu* were abolished as administrative units, but the former groupings of *hsien* under their old *chou* and *fu* names are still current in the popular mind. The word *hsiang*, when used to refer to an administrative unit, signifies a rural township, usually containing at least one market town and several villages. There are ordinarily several tens of *hsiang* in a *hsien*. The unitalicized forms, fu, chou, hsien, and hsiang, are used in the text to mean Chinese prefectures, departments, counties, and rural townships, respectively.

Between 1894 and 1932, Thailand was divided into between ten and eighteen *monthon* or circles, each made up of several *jangwat* or provinces. In 1932, *monthon* administrations were abolished. (In 1952, the various *jangwat* were regrouped under nine *phak* or regions, but these groupings are not referred to in this volume.) Each *jangwat*, of which there are seventy-one at present, is subdivided into *amphoe* or districts, each in turn made up of several *tambon* or communes. In rural areas the *tambon* ordinarily comprises several villages. The unitalicized forms, monthon, jangwat, amphoe, and tambon, are used in the text to mean the Thai circles, provinces, districts, and communes, respectively.

A word should also be said about the name of the country itself. For centuries the Thai have called their kingdom Mueang Thai, i.e., Thailand. Westerners, however, have until recently referred to the country as Siam. In modern times, the official name was Siam up to 1939 and again between 1945 and 1948. The present official name, Thailand, is now generally used by serious scholars, British writers aside, when referring to contemporary affairs. In discussing the recent period I have ordinarily used Thailand, but for the rest both names have been employed indiscriminately for the sake of variety.

Regions of Thailand

For the purposes of this study, Thailand has been divided into seven regions: North Siam, Middle Siam, Northeast Siam, Southeast Siam, Lower Siam, Southwest Siam, and South Siam. The regional boundaries used were chosen to coincide with administrative boundaries which have not been appreciably changed during the present century. In other words, certain boundaries of the former monthons which coincide with present-day jangwat boundaries have been taken to define the seven regions used. This procedure allows historical comparison of Thai statistics for the various administrative areas when these are grouped according to the seven regions here defined. The disadvantage inherent in this definition of regions is that in many cases the precise placement of the boundaries is arbitrary in terms of "natural" geography.

The seventy-one jangwats are given below in the orthography used here, alphabetically arranged under their respective regions. This list is meant to serve both as a reference and to define the seven regions used in the present study (see also the frontispiece map).

North Siam

Chiangmai
Chiangrai
Lampang
Lamphun
Maehongson
Nan
Phrae

Northeast Siam

Buriram
Chaiyaphum
Kanlasin
Khonkaen
Loei
Mahasarakham
Nakhonphanom
Nakhonratchasima
Nongkhai
Roi-et
Sakonnakhon
Sisaket

Surin
Ubonratchathani
Udonthani

Middle Siam

Chainat
Kamphaengphet
Nakhonsawan
Phijit
Phitsanulok
Phetchabun
Sukhothai
Tak
Uthaithani
Uttaradit

Lower Siam

Angthong
Ayutthaya
Lopburi
Nakhonpathom
Nonthaburi
Phranakhon

Prathumthani
Saraburi
Singburi
Samutprakan
Samutsakhon
Suphanburi
Thonburi

Southeast Siam

Chachoengsao
Chonburi
Janthaburi
Nakhonnayok
Prajinburi
Rayong
Trat

Southwest Siam

Kanjanaburi
Prajuapkhirikhan
Phetchaburi
Ratchaburi
Samutsongkhram

South Siam	Pattani	Satun
Chumphǫn	Phangnga	Songkhla
Krabi	Phatthalung	Suratthani
Nakhǫnsithammarat	Phuket	Trang
Narathiwat	Ranǫng	Yala

Reign Periods of Thai Kings

The reign periods of the Chinese emperors mentioned in the text are available in numerous standard reference works, but those for Thai kings are not equally accessible or well known. Accordingly, a reference list of the early Thai kings mentioned in the text and of all kings since 1767 is given below:

SUKHOTHAI PERIOD (Incomplete)

Ramkamhaeng . . . . 1275?–1317?

AYUTTHAYAN PERIOD (Incomplete)

Baromarat II	1424–1448
Ekathotsarot	1605–1620
Sisaowaphak	1620–1620
Songtham	1620–1628
Prasat Thǫng	1629–1656
Narai	1657–1688
Thaisa	1709–1733
Baromakot	1733–1758

THONBURI PERIOD

Taksin 1767–1782

BANGKOK PERIOD (Jakkri Dynasty)

Rama I	Yǫtfa	1782–1809
Rama II	Loetla	1809–1824
Rama III	Nangklao	1824–1851
Rama IV	Mongkut	1851–1868
Rama V	Julalongkǫn	1868–1910
Rama VI	Wachirawut	1910–1925
Rama VII	Prachathipok	1925–1935
Rama VIII	Ananda Mahidon	1935–1946
Rama IX	Phumiphon Adunladet	1946–

With regard to the reign dates of the early seventeenth-century kings, attention should be called to corrections of the usual chronology which were suggested by Giles (1938, 167) and have been accepted here.

Thai Dates

The Buddhist era (B.E.), as used in Thailand, starts 543 years earlier than the Christian era. Prior to 1940, the Thai year officially began on April 1 rather than January 1. By royal decree, the year B.E. 2483 (1940) was only nine months long (April 1 to December 31), thus making the Thai year coincide with our own. In order to avoid confusion, all Thai dates in this book have been converted into Christian era dates by subtracting 543 years. It is customary in the case of dates prior to 1940 to indicate B.E. years with the use of a slash. Thus B.E. 2480 would be written 1937/38, by which is meant the Buddhist year which began April 1, 1937, and ended March 31, 1938.

Certain Thai statistics around the turn of the century were compiled according to the Western year beginning January 1, presumably because of the influence of foreign advisors. Annual statistics in these series were changed to accord with the Thai year in 1906. In tables and charts, the precise period covered by "annual" statistics is indicated.

Thai Currency

The unit of Thai currency is the *baht,* often called *tical* by Westerners. The conventional English spelling of the Thai word, *baht,* is used here rather than either the romanization according to the orthography otherwise adhered to in this study, *bat,* or the word *tical.* The baht is divided into 100 *satang.* Prior to World War II, the exchange rate of the baht was fairly steady at about 2.0 to 2.5 to the U.S. dollar, but wartime inflation drastically altered the rate. Since 1949, free market rates have fluctuated between 17 and 23 baht to the U.S. dollar, with an average of about 20.

References and Bibliography

In order to minimize the space devoted to notes, references are given in brief form according to a standardized system. Reference notes are of three types: (1) Works by known authors are cited by the last name of the author and the date of completion or publication of the book or article. Different authors of the same surname are distinguished by the initial(s) of their given names. (2) Unsigned articles are cited by the title of the article in quotation marks and the date of publication. (3) Serials (newspapers, journals, yearbooks, annual reports, and so on) and all other works are cited by italicized title, often abbreviated, and the date. In the case of annual reports and yearbooks, the date given is that of the year to which the report of the book pertains, even when it differs from the date of publication. The Reference Bibliography gives the full bibliographical citation of all publications mentioned in the text and notes. Entries in the Bibliography for Chinese-language works include C numbers, which refer to the list of Chinese characters mentioned above.

Acknowledgments

It is not possible to name or express adequate gratitude to the many individuals in Thailand whose assistance facilitated the collection of material used in this study. I should like to acknowledge co-operation from officials in the following agencies of the Thai government: the National Library, the Central Statistical Office, the Alien Division of the Police Department, the Private Schools Division of the Ministry of Education, and the Krungthep and Thonburi Municipal Offices. The United States Information Service, the British Information Service, and E.C.A.F.E. were also of considerable assistance, as were the officers and staff members of the major Chinese associations in Bangkok. Most of the persons associated with the Cornell Research Center contributed in one way or another to the present study, in particular Robert B. Textor, Loebongs Sarabhayavanija, Lerchiew Wong, Er Siak Hong, Dalton T. Djang, Liang Mang Soon, and Vichitr Saengmani. I should like to pay special tribute to the intelligence, scholarship, and diligence of my research associate, James T. Peng, whose assistance was substantial and always invaluable. Appreciation is expressed both to Mr. Peng and to Phraya Anuman Rajathon of the Royal Institute of Thailand for reading a preliminary draft of this study and for making helpful suggestions.

I am also grateful to Hsin-min Wu (Mrs. John F. Brohm) for her expert assistance in translating Chinese materials and for writing the character reference list; to Mrs. Cynthia Wellenkamp for her gracious co-operation and help with the preliminary draft of this study; and to Mrs. Warren E. Harrison for typing the final manuscript. Above all, I want to thank my wife, Carol, for her manifold and indispensable contributions at every stage of this study, and in particular for drawing the maps and charts included in the present volume.

My indebtedness to Professor Lauriston Sharp and Professor Knight Biggerstaff of Cornell University is for much more than their invaluable

[*Preface*]

advice and guidance relative to the present study. This acknowledgment cannot convey my appreciation of their friendship and counselorship through the years. Warm gratitude is also expressed to Professor Charles F. Hockett of Cornell University for his encouragement and suggestions.

Finally, I gratefully acknowledge a travel grant from the Social Science Research Council and the long-term financial support from the Cornell Southeast Asia Program which made the present study possible.

G. William Skinner

Djakarta, Indonesia
November 1956

Contents

[Contents]

Tables

[Tables]

Charts

Maps

CHINESE SOCIETY IN THAILAND:

An Analytical History

THE EARLY CENTURIES:

The Chinese in Old Siam

A. *Sino-Thai Relations up to the Seventeenth Century*

SOME of the finest bas-reliefs in Khmer art are to be found in the
Bayon, the temple at the center of Jayavarman VII's city, Angkor
Thom, which was completed not later than the first decade of the
thirteenth century. One of the tableaux of the outer gallery of that
temple depicts in minute detail a Chinese junk, manned by an obviously non-Khmer crew. The junk resembles in almost every structural
particular the type built by the Chinese in Siam and used by them
for trade within the Gulf of Siam in recent centuries.[1] This discovery
lends strong support to the belief of several German scholars [2] that
Chinese traders were already established in the markets and ports
of the Gulf of Siam when the Thai reached the Jaophraya Delta and
the Malay Peninsula in the thirteenth century.

In the last decade of that century, Chou Ta-kuan (C 1) found
Chinese engaged in business at Angkor Thom and reported that Chinese constantly came to Cambodia.[3] According to old Thai records,
the Malay Peninsula was the first part of Siam to which Chinese and
other foreign traders were attracted. Every year a fleet of junks from
China called at the various ports and settlements on the east side of
the peninsula.[4] There is some evidence that in the thirteenth and fourteenth centuries Chinese traders with goods destined for India and
further west may have gone, with the northeast monsoon, only as far

as Chumphǫn, Suratthani (Bandǫn), or Nakhǫnsithammarat (Ligor), where their cargoes were unloaded for transshipment overland in time for the traders to return to China with the opening southwest monsoon.[5]

In fact, the most plausible explanation of how the Chinese discovered the tin deposits of South Siam assumes that Chinese traders themselves took part in this transpeninsular traffic. It is probable that Chinese came across the ore deposits in traveling, say, from Nakhǫnsithammarat on the Gulf of Siam to Trang on the Bay of Bengal, and smelted a small quantity on the spot for their own use.[6] Other Chinese traders who ventured through the Straits of Malacca may have made similar discoveries in Phuket. Credner and Helbig [7] believe that these discoveries had been made and mining begun by Chinese prior to the fourteenth century, while other writers [8] suggest the following century. In any case, Chinese tin miners were well established in South Siam when the first Westerners penetrated the area.[9]

The Thai kingdom of Sukhothai was established in the mid-thirteenth century, and the Mongol court sought in the latter part of that century to enroll the kingdom, called Hsien (C 2) by the Chinese, as a tributary state. Chinese emissaries were sent in 1282, 1293, and 1294, in the last case bearing a summons to the Sukhothai king, Ramkamhaeng, to go to the imperial court.[10] Ramkamhaeng finally sent tributary missions to Peking in 1296, 1297, and 1299.[11] Further tributary missions followed in 1314, 1319, and 1323, after which Sukhothai missions to Peking came to an end.[12] Nonetheless, private Chinese traders, so far as is known, continued their commerce with Thai ports right up to the end of the Yüan dynasty.

The collapse of Mongol power in China, however, brought about internal disorder which paralyzed foreign commerce for several decades after 1368, and there is no evidence that Chinese trade with Siam flourished to any degree during the first few decades of the Ming dynasty.[13] It is at just this period, however, that regular tributary missions began from Ayutthaya to the Ming capital, Nanking. It may be that the taste for Chinese goods acquired by the Thai rulers prior to the decline in Chinese trade around 1368 lent a commercial motive to the tribute missions to China in the early Ming period. In any case the Ming emissary to Siam in 1370 met with a favorable response, the more so since the edict he carried was addressed to Hsien-lo. Since Hsien was the Chinese name for Sukhothai and Lo-hu (C 3) that for the Kingdom of Louvo or Lopburi,[14] the use of the combined term by the Chinese court in effect recognized Ayutthaya as the legitimate successor to the earlier states and accepted the sub-jugation of Sukhothai by Ayutthaya. It was very much to the interests of the Ayutthayan king to obtain from Nanking investiture as the King (Wang) of Hsien-lo, which in fact was shortly forthcoming.[15] A series of frequent Thai tribute missions and state visits followed, lasting well beyond the era of the famous Ming maritime expeditions carried out by Cheng Ho (C 4) between 1405 and 1433. It cannot be shown that Cheng Ho himself ever went to Ayutthaya, but certainly the capital and probably other parts of Siam were visited by several important members of his suites, including Ma Huan (C 5), Hung Pao (C 6), and Fei Hsin (C 7).[16]

Both Ma Huan and Fei Hsin were greatly impressed by the inde-pendent status of Siamese women, and above all by their predilection for Chinese men. According to Fei, "whenever [a Siamese woman] meets a Chinese man, she is greatly pleased with him, and will in-variably prepare wine to entertain and show respect to him, merrily singing and keeping him overnight." The husband in such a case, according to Ma, is not perturbed but flattered that his wife should be beautiful enough to please the Chinese.[17] From this idyllic account, it would appear that the Chinese had other reasons than trade for resorting to Siam. In any case, the fabulous stories told by the expedi-tionaries after their return to China greatly stimulated trade and emigration to Nan-yang.

The situation described by the early fifteenth-century expedition-aries may well have led to the first of Siam's *lukjin*,[18] i.e., children of Chinese fathers and Thai mothers. A Chinese source of the following century indicates clearly that Chinese had been settled for several generations:[19] "In this country, people have no surnames. The Chi-nese at first retain their own surnames, but give them up after a few generations." In view of the fact that Chinese women never emi-grated in those days, this description attests Chinese intermarriage with Thai women and rapid assimilation of their lukjin offspring. The same passage mentions "a certain . . . street where the Chinese live," suggesting that there was already in the early sixteenth century a Chinese quarter in Ayutthaya.

There is also indirect evidence of Chinese settlement and assimila-tion in Siam well before the fifteenth century. According to Thai tradi-tions, Ramkamhaeng's final mission to China brought Chinese potters to Sukhothai in 1300. The new type of pottery manufactured shortly thereafter at Sukhothai and the celedon wares later produced at the Sawankhalok kilns are of Chinese design and technique.[20] Le May [21] has demonstrated that the Chinese influence in Sawankhalok pottery decoration died out by the first half of the fifteenth century, which suggests that the descendants of the immigrant potters had by that time been assimilated. Chinese political refugees were also among the earliest immigrants to Siam. The first authenticated case of this kind is that of Ch'en Yi-chung (C 11), who fled from Kwangtung to Champa when the Mongols conquered south China from the Sung rulers, and then, on the sack of the Cham capital by the Mongols in 1283, went to Siam, where he later died.[22] Enemies of the Ming court, including Ho Pa-huan (C 12), fled to Siam at the beginning of the fifteenth century, though they were extradited by the Ayutthayan king at the request of Emperor Yung-lo.[23] Chinese annals also record the earliest known example of a Chinese becoming an official of the Thai government: somewhat before 1480, Hsieh Wen-pin (C 13), a native of T'ing-chou (Fukien) who "drifted" to Siam while peddling salt, became an official with the rank of Okkhun.[24]

ᵢ In the latter part of the sixteenth century occurred an intriguing episode in the history of Pattani—one which points to considerable settlement of Chinese in that part of Siam. During the 1560's and 1570's, one of the most notorious sea pirates and bandits in Kwangtung and Fukien was Lin Tao-ch'ien (C 14). After narrowly escaping death more than once, he fled with his men to Nan-yang, looking for a permanent place to stay. After stopping at Pulo Condore, "he went to Ta-nien [Tani, short for Pattani], a country in the southwestern part of Siam. He attacked this country and got it. The present king of Ta-nien is his descendant." [25] This occurred early in the reign of Wan-li (1573–1620), probably between 1578 and 1580. The evidence is contradictory as to whether Lin was himself a Teochiu or a Hokkien, but he clearly came to Nan-yang from Fukien, and probably most of his followers were Hokkien. One section of the Ming History [26] suggests that the men who went with him numbered over two thousand.

The local Chinese in Pattani still keep the story of Lin Tao-ch'ien very much alive. According to their version, Lin, a hero from Fukien during the Ming dynasty, arrived in Pattani in a warship with a large army. He occupied the capital after one engagement, and the terrified Malay ruler gave his daughter to him in marriage and made him heir to the throne. The Annals of Pattani, however, state that Lin was simply a Hokkien arsenal foreman who married a Malay woman, settled at Kase, and was naturalized; he made three cannon for the Queen of Pattani and was killed while attempting to fire one. This version goes on to state that the Malays in Kase all say that Lim To Khiam (Lin Tao-ch'ien) was the ancestor of their families.[27] It is most likely true that Lin's men as well as he himself also figured among their ancestors. Hsü Yün-ch'iao makes a case that Lin married the daughter of the Malay ruler, took over the throne and ruled until the cannon accident, after which his wife became the first Queen of Pattani. It is not necessary to accept this rather contrived interpretation, however. Lin probably "lived like a king" as chieftain of his men and their families at Kase, and, as something of a culture hero, his position has been exaggerated in more recent accounts.[28] The Chinese in Pattani also believe that Lin's younger sister, Lin Ku-niang, followed him to Pattani and tried in vain to persuade him to return to China. She is still worshipped in Pattani as a symbol of fervent Chinese patriotism.

The episode of Lin Tao-ch'ien, along with Pattani's position as a thriving port, may help account for the large Chinese population with which Pattani was credited by writers in the early 1600's. It may even be that three Chinese who served as officials in the Pattani government around 1600 were Lin Tao-ch'ien's men or their descendants. One of these was a native of Chang-chou named Chang, who served in the government both before and after the first Queen of Pattani; his son was also made an official on his death. The other two were Li Kuei (C 16) and Lin Yin-lin (C 17), who, from official letters addressed to them by Japanese officials in 1599 and 1602 respectively, were apparently high in the service of the Queen of Pattani.[29]

In reviewing the tantalizing bits of information available about individual Chinese who were living but not trading in Siam in the early centuries, it should be remembered that they were mentioned in official annals and records only because of their exceptional nature. The bulk of Chinese immigrants were certainly anonymous Chinese traders. To obtain a somewhat clearer picture of the growth of Chinese society in Siam it is necessary to look however briefly at the patterns of trade and tribute between Siam and China.

The frequency of Siamese tribute missions to China during the first 250 years of the Ming dynasty (i.e., through the reigns of Wan-li in

China and of King Ekathotsarot in Siam) [30] presents a significant pattern:

Period	No. of yrs.	No. of tribute missions	Frequency of missions (no. per decade)
1368–1404	37	14	3.9
1405–1433	29	8	2.8
1434–1499	66	12	1.8
1500–1579	80	9	1.1
1580–1619	40	3	0.8
Total	252	46	1.8

It will be noted that Siam allowed the number of tributary missions to decrease steadily during the entire period of over two and a half centuries. Equally significant is the fact that Cheng Ho's maritime expeditions (1405–1433) did not alter the downward trend in any way: the tributary missions were less frequent after his expeditions than before. Private Chinese trade with Siam, on the other hand, expanded steadily during the period. Thus, if the expeditions of Cheng Ho were in part an attempt to bring the sources of Chinese overseas commerce into the tributary structure, as Fairbank and Teng suggest,[31] they were notably unsuccessful.

It would appear that the tributary system held both political and economic advantages for the Siamese rulers. It could be used to affirm the legitimacy of an incumbent Thai king or ruling house, and it was a means for acquiring Chinese goods and revenue from the China trade. If this assumption is reasonable, then two theses suggest themselves: (1) During periods early in the era of a Thai ruling house, Siamese tributary missions should be more frequent than later, after its tenure is secured. (2) During periods of free trade (i.e., no monopolistic state trading), the frequency of tributary missions should be inversely proportional to the activity of private traders in supplying desired imports from China, the theory being that if private traders supply the needed merchandise and pay taxes on their imports into the royal treasury, the economic function of tribute missions is more or less obviated.

These relationships would seem to be borne out in general by such information as we have on Sino-Thai relations prior to 1620. Tribute missions lapsed early in the fourteenth century as private Chinese trade with Siam increased. When the supply of Chinese goods was interrupted after the Chinese dynastic change in 1368, tributary missions were resumed at a rate of 3.9 per decade, decreasing in frequency during the following two centuries as the Sino-Thai trade in Chinese hands increased and as the position of the kingdom of Ayutthaya and its kings became more secure. The significance of all this for Chinese immigration lies in the fact that tribute missions were forbidden by the Chinese court to carry Chinese passengers back with them. When in 1480, for instance, a Siamese mission secretly brought back some Chinese passengers, the emperor sent officials to Ayutthaya to administer severe reproaches.[32] Thus Chinese overseas emigration could be carried out only via Chinese junks, and so would presumably fluctuate according to the volume of the trade with Siam carried on by Chinese merchants.

The growth in the number of Chinese traders in Siam and of the volume of the trade they carried on between China and Siam during the Ming dynasty is not easily documented, but the general trend is clear. The trade disrupted in 1368 was certainly under way again by the beginning of the fifteenth century. Ma Huan, for instance, wrote that Chinese vessels went to Siam to trade, and a century later, when Albuquerque wanted to send an envoy to Siam from Malacca in 1511, he had to enlist the services of some Chinese junks which were about to leave for Ayutthaya.[33] De Campos, after a survey of sixteenth-century Portuguese accounts of Siam,[34] mentions Chinese merchants as being "everywhere established in Thailand," which is to say everywhere the Portuguese went. Where there were traders in the sixteenth century, there were generally also pirates, and the Chinese records provide several examples of Chinese freebooters with headquarters in South Siam. In 1540, the notorious Hsü brothers (C 18) were in Pattani and enticed Portuguese traders there to prepare raids on the Fukien coast.[35] In 1554, two other formidable pirates, Ho Ya-pa (C 19) and Cheng Tsung-hsing (C 20), were also stationed at Pattani, from which port they led raids on the China coast.[36] The Chinese pirates who plied a more modest trade in the Gulf of Siam went unrecorded in the Chinese histories.

By the early seventeenth century, the position of Chinese traders in Siam was much more substantial. (These examples are all taken from the reign of King Ekathotsarot, 1605–1620.) In 1616, the Dutch Resident at Pattani wrote that the Chinese far outnumbered the native population there.[37] A Chinese source published the following year, in detailing business conditions at Pattani, stated that "Chinese residents are numerous, their toes following one another's heels. . . . When goods are sold, they [the authorities] do not dare impose any duties [on us]." [38] The Chinese position at Nakhǫnsithammarat was equally favorable: In discussing a possible Dutch treaty with the king of that Thai dependency, van Nyenrode wrote in 1612 that according to the draft the Chinese would have to pay only the ordinary tolls and duties, "nobody being allowed to do them any harm or cause them any trouble." [39] The Chinese trading community of Nakhǫnsithammarat was extensive enough to warrant a special trip there in 1620 by an English trader desiring to establish commercial relations with it.[40] According to van Vliet, Chinese from southern Fukien at that time annually brought "pretty large cargoes of all kinds of Chinese goods to this country [Siam] and returned with big loads of sapanwood, lead and other merchandise." [41] It was during Ekathotsarot's reign that a Chinese writer stated: "The inhabitants [of Siam] accept the Chinese very cordially, much better than do the natives of any other country; therefore Siam is a country that is really friendly to the Chinese." [42]

The general trend during the first two and a half centuries of the Ming dynasty, then, is clear: steadily decreasing tribute missions from Siam accompanied by steadily increasing private Chinese trade and Chinese immigration. The 1620's, however, saw a reversal of the patterns of Sino-Thai trade and tribute. In 1620, King Sisaowaphak came to the Thai throne, and a letter written in that year by van Hasell at Songkhla complained that the new king was incapable of controlling the Siamese officials and noblemen, which in turn led to the deterioration of the Chinese trade.[43] This remark is amplified by van Vliet [44] who stated that "the Chinese from Chinseeuw [Bay of Amoy] who used to appear every year in Siam with their junks and various cargoes, were detained by the deceit of the [Siamese] mandarins, apparently with the knowledge of the king." Chinese traders were also adversely affected in the 1620's by Japanese competition. Japanese influence had become important during Ekathotsarot's reign, when a considerable colony of Japanese traders settled in Ayutthaya and other ports. During the reign of King Songtham (1620–1628), however, Japanese influence reached unprecedented proportions. The king maintained very close relations with Japan, exchanged several embassies with the Shogun, and maintained a personal Japanese bodyguard, while the Japanese adventurer Yamada became a significant power in Siamese politics. By the late 1620's, the trade between Siam and Japan was probably more important than the combined trade between Siam and other foreign countries. In these circumstances, the

Sino-Thai trade in Chinese hands suffered greatly—Chinese-type imports now came from Japan—although Chinese traders had a substantial part in the Japan-Siam trade.[45]

Moreover, when King Prasat Thọng came to the throne in 1629, he inaugurated royal trade monopolies which severely challenged established Chinese interests.[46] Chinese and other traders to the ports of Southwest Siam had to obtain permits from the king, while tin and lead had now to be delivered to the king's warehouse in Ayutthaya before export.[47] In van Vliet's words:

> The Chinese from Chincheeu [Bay of Amoy] and Cochinchina were trading in former days to a greater extent to Siam than at present. . . . By the trade of these nations to Siam the income of the king and the welfare of the people increased and trade flourished. But as the present king [Prasat Thọng] preferred to force the market by his factors, the prices of the goods which are imported by the Moors [i.e., Indians, Arabs, and Persians] the Chinese, etc., and further lays taxes upon them and does not pay market prices, nobody comes to Siam unless compelled to do so . . .
>
> Through the strange actions of the king and many vexations, many foreign merchants left the country; while some of them were sent away or expelled, so that at present there are in Siam only a few rich merchants (two or three rich Moors and a few rich Chinese).[48]

King Prasat Thọng and his brother annually sent one ship to Canton and two or three junks to other Chinese ports, one ship to the Choromandel Coast, and occasional junks to other Southeast Asian ports.[49]

The situation of Chinese traders in Siam, then, reached a nadir during roughly the period 1620–1632, essentially the reign of King Songtham and the first three years of Prasat Thọng's reign. From then on, the position of Chinese traders steadily improved for the remainder of the Ayutthayan period (to 1767). During Prasat Thọng's reign two developments were to the advantage of Chinese traders. The king was a usurper who seized power against the desires of the influential Japanese element at court, and in 1632, fearing a plot against him, he massacred the Japanese colony in Ayutthaya and drove most of the Japanese out of the country. As a result the Siam-Japan trade passed almost entirely into Chinese hands. Even the king's merchandise was exported to Japan on Chinese junks, since Thai supercargoes were not allowed to land in Japan. After 1636, Japan was virtually closed to all foreigners *except* the Chinese.[50]

The second development was the quick adaptation of Chinese traders to the new system of royal trading monopolies and the realization of the king that greater profits would be realized in the royal trade if he used Chinese traders, who were the most experienced seamen to be found and who alone had access to the majority of Chinese ports. In consequence, the Chinese came to be well regarded by Prasat Thọng, and some of them were "considered the best factors, traders and sailors" while others were "appointed to high positions and offices." [51] Mandelslo, writing of 1639, stated specifically that the king's factors, warehousemen, and accountants abroad were Chinese.[52] Furthermore, Chinese traders could still carry on some trade of their own, and in spite of Prasat Thọng's "vexations" every year two or three junks came to Ayutthaya from southern Fukien, and one to three Chinese-owned junks were sent from Ayutthaya to Cochinchina.[53] As van Vliet summed up the situation in 1638: [54] "In the kingdom of Siam many Chinese are still living who enjoy reasonable freedom in trade throughout the whole country . . ."

Both the British and the Dutch began trading in Siam early in the seventeenth century, but during Prasat Thọng's reign only the Dutch provided any real competition for the Chinese traders.[55] Ill feeling between the Dutch and Chinese, arising from trading competition, reached a peak in 1663, during the reign of King Narai, when armed Chinese beseiged the Dutch factory at Ayutthaya and forced the Resident to flee with all his men and goods.[56] It has been suggested that certain of the king's officials incited the Chinese to this action. In any case the Dutch retaliated with a show of force, and managed to conclude in 1664 a very one-sided treaty with King Narai—a treaty which gravely prejudiced Chinese interests. One article confirmed Dutch monopoly rights in the deerskin and cowhide trade, while another stipulated that

neither now nor hereafter shall his Majesty the King or his subjects, of whatever station they may be, have the power to place any Chinese . . . on their junks, ships or smaller vessels, much less to endeavour to introduce men of that nation within their boundaries; [and] that all junks and ships on which natives of that country shall be found, if met by ours at sea, shall be seized as prizes, and the [Dutch] Company shall not be bound at any time to make any retribution.[57]

This treaty was a bold attempt on the part of the Dutch to secure for their Company the whole of Siam's trade with China and Japan, for the greatest part of the trade was carried by Chinese or Siamese ships, both with Chinese crews, and it would have been exceedingly difficult if not impossible to recruit crews among the Thai. The attempt failed, however, not only because it was opposed to the vested interests of the king and all the established traders in Siam, but also because the Dutch were reluctant to antagonize the Chinese Empire. Later in Narai's reign, French visitors at the Thai capital recorded that the king sent annually to Japan several ships manned by Chinese.[58] Indeed, a comprehensive report on the trade of Siam in 1678 [59] affirmed that all the king's maritime and mercantile affairs were managed by Chinese, both in Siam and abroad.

During Narai's reign, the Chinese were also supreme among private traders at Ayutthaya. Both Gervaise and Tachard state specifically that the Chinese had the biggest share of the trade at Ayutthaya, both with China and with Japan [60]—this in spite of the inroads of the British and French. The death of King Narai and the anti-Western revolution in 1688 spelled the end of French and British trade in Siam for well over a century. By this time, too, Portugal had lost all commercial and political importance in the country, and only the Dutch, among the Europeans, emerged from the disorders with their monopolies intact. However, they ran into severe trouble in 1705, and Dutch participation in the Siamese trade was sporadic thereafter.[61] The net result of the revolution of 1688 was that the European share of Siam's trade with East Asian countries fell to the Chinese, who were in no wise excluded by the successors of King Narai.

The general course of events, then, favored the Chinese. The Portuguese, Japanese, English, French, and Dutch, each in turn, stimulated trade in Siam for their own benefit, but each in the end was forced to quit, leaving what remained to the Chinese. The latter fared well for the simple reason that they were never considered foreigners by the Thai.[62] Likewise the royal state trading of Kings Prasat Thong, Narai, and their successors provided lucrative employment for Chinese as factors, warehousemen, accountants, and seamen—and without precluding Chinese private trade. As a result of these developments, and in spite of certain restrictions imposed on overseas trade and emigration by the authorities in China,[63] Chinese immigrants were attracted to Siam in ever greater numbers throughout the sixteenth and seventeenth centuries.

The Manchu conquest of south China after 1645 was a further impetus to emigration from China. Opposition to the alien invaders was especially strong in Fukien and Kwangtung, and it is well known that thousands from Canton, Ch'ao-chou and Ch'üan-chou fled overseas to Taiwan and Nan-yang.[64] Tradition among the Chinese in Bangkok today has it that two main groups of refugees from the Manchus came to Siam: those from Ch'ao-chou (Teochius) to Southeast Siam, centering on Bangplasoi, and those from southern Fukien (Hokkiens) to South Siam, centering at Songkhla.

If now, we turn to Siamese tribute missions to China during the period just reviewed (1620–1709, i.e., from the reign of Sisaowaphak up to, but not including Thaisa), the relationship between trade and tribute posited earlier appears to be confirmed again. The number and frequency of Siamese tribute missions to China during the period, subdivided according to Thai reign periods, is as follows: [65]

Period	No. of years	No. of missions	Frequency of missions (no. per decade)
1620–1655	36	7	1.9
1656–1688	33	5	1.5
1689–1709	21	1	0.5
Total	90	13	1.4

It will be noted, first of all, that the average frequency of missions for the whole period is lower than the average frequency for the era summarized earlier (1.4 for 1620–1709 as against 1.8 for 1368–1619). This situation accords with the thesis suggested, for, generally speaking, private Chinese trade with Siam flourished to a greater extent during 1620–1709 than during the preceding era. Furthermore, the downward trend in frequency of missions apparent during the 250 years prior to 1620 was reversed in the 1620–1655 period (0.8 per decade for 1580–1619 as against 1.9 for 1620–1655), and it was precisely that period during which Chinese traders received the worst setback suffered by them during the entire Ayutthayan period, as described above. From the 1630's on, the position of Chinese traders in Siam steadily improved as the rigors of the royal monopoly were relaxed, as Chinese traders were absorbed into the state trading system, and as competitors of other foreign nations were eliminated one by one. Accordingly, the frequency of Siamese tribute missions steadily decreased during this period.[66]

B. Seventeenth-Century Chinese Society

From the accounts of the many travelers, traders, missionaries, and diplomatic emissaries who visited Siam in the seventeenth century, it is possible to reconstruct something of the society of the Chinese in Siam. Fortunately it is the most accurate of the visitors, van Vliet and de la Loubère, who give the most detailed information. De la Loubère estimated that there were three or four thousand Chinese "at Siam." However, it is clear that by "Siam" he meant the city of Ayutthaya, since the statement occurs in a section descriptive of the city, while elsewhere in his work he refers to the capital city as Siam, e.g., in his remark that the people of different nations "inhabit different quarters in the City and Suburbs of Siam." Even in de la Loubère's map of the lower Jaophraya valley, Ayutthaya is labeled "Siam." [67] Further-more Hutchinson [68] has called attention to the fact that Ayutthaya was frequently called "Siam" by Europeans in the seventeenth century. The point is labored here because every writer who has since dealt with the subject has misinterpreted de la Loubère's estimate as re-ferring to the entire country.[69] In view of the numerous, and in some cases populous, Chinese settlements in ports all around the Gulf of Siam in the seventeenth century,[70] we might estimate the Chinese population in all parts of the country outside the capital to have been at least twice that of Ayutthaya itself. We may assume, then, a mini-mum of ten thousand Chinese in Siam during the latter half of the seventeenth century. It is unlikely, however, that the Chinese formed as much as one per cent of the total population of the country.[71]

The Chinese of Ayutthaya lived both within and without the city walls. The city proper was completely surrounded by water. Boats arriving at the capital docked in the Chinese quarter at the southeast corner of the city, at the foot of an east-west street called by English writers "China Row." The other major street ran northward, in the heart of the city, from China Row to the royal palace. It contained the major public market as well as the shops of artisans and traders. These two streets were the finest in the city; along them were more than one hundred two-story houses, built of stone or brick and roofed with flat tiles, which belonged to Chinese and "Moors," i.e., Indian, Arab, and Persian merchants. The other dwellings of the city, except for the few European residences, were poor cottages built of bamboo and planks.[72] Outside the city, the Chinese quarters lay across the canals and river to the south and east.[73] It should be noted that only the "Moors" and Chinese had extensive settlements within the city walls, though before 1688 the French, English, and Dutch also had a few scattered resi-dences in the city proper. All other peoples, including the Portuguese, Japanese, Cochinchinese, Malays, Macassars, and Peguans (Mons), were relegated to the environs, each nation in its own quarter or camp.[74]

Each of these national settlements had its own official or officials,

ment "shall request foreign governments to have those Chinese who have been abroad repatriated so that they may be executed." [91] It is improbable that any such request was ever put to the Siamese, if for no other reason than that no formal intercourse between the two countries was recorded between 1708 and 1722. The reasons why K'ang-hsi took a dim view of the Nan-yang trade are not hard to find. The Chinese colonies which it inevitably fostered were hotbeds of anti-Manchu elements, organized by refugees and their indoctrinated descendants into secret societies whose aim was to restore the Ming dynasty. Especially in Siam and Annam there were thousands of Chinese who had not given up their opposition to the Manchus. [92]

In 1717, K'ang-hsi embarked on a new policy designed to lure the overseas Chinese back. All were invited to return, and those who had gone abroad before the beginning of his reign (i.e., fifty-six years previously) were expressly pardoned. [93] Decrees during the remainder of the century blew hot and cold, some enticing, some punitive. Yung-cheng in 1729, "believing that those who do business abroad are usually undesirable persons and that their number is likely to increase in the course of the years if they are allowed freely to come and go," decreed that "a date must be set for their return, after which they shall not be allowed to come home." [94] During the following two decades, dates were set and then extended, enticements were made to certain groups of emigrants to return, threats were specified, and examples made of exceptional cases of returned overseas Chinese, but nonetheless throughout the second quarter of the century "the movement of traders from the interior [i.e., China] abroad increased as the welling of a spring." [95] An especially attractive offer was made by the governor of Fukien in 1754. His notice, following imperial approval of his memorial, gave permission to all "good" Chinese subjects trading in foreign states to return provided that "their real reason for not returning within the time allowed was their inability to close their accounts." Such overseas Chinese were assured that the authorities of their home districts would not be allowed to make their past absence "a pretext for extorting from them the money or goods they may bring with them" and that they would be permitted to bring their foreign wives and children with them. [96]

From the Ch'ing directives of the first half of the eighteenth century, several conclusions can be drawn that are pertinent here. First, that the imperial government did not want to stop the trade with Nan-yang (a) because it was so closely tied up with the tributary system,

(b) because the government was coming to need certain Nan-yang products, and (c) because south Chinese merchants put pressure on, and paid bribes to, Kwangtung and Fukien officials to maintain the trade. Second, that the Ch'ing court recognized the danger to its security inherent in the anti-Manchu activities of the overseas communities. Third, that the imperial government was nevertheless powerless to prevent the ever increasing exodus of Chinese to Nan-yang. And fourth, that the return of overseas Chinese, so desired by the government, was hindered by rapacious officials who relied on the letter of restrictive laws to extort wealth from returnees. The Manchu government's aims—expanded trade with Nan-yang, within the tribute system, but with no Chinese permanently residing abroad—were self-contradictory.

Siam provides one of the most interesting illustrations. At the end of his reign, K'ang-hsi was intrigued by reports from King Thaisa's first tributary mission that rice was plentiful and cheap in Siam, especially in view of recurring famine conditions in south China, and in 1722 he issued the following imperial edict to the Grand Secretary:

The Hsien-lo people say that rice is plentiful in their land and two or three ounces of silver can buy one picul of paddy. We have given orders to have rice transported to Fukien and other places. It would be very beneficial to those places. These 300,000 piculs are transported for official purposes and they are to be exempt from taxes.[97]

King Thaisa of Siam welcomed this new market; supplies continued to be sent, and in 1724 a tribute mission was sent to Yung-cheng in Peking. However, ninety-six of the seamen manning the Thai tribute vessel were originally Chinese and had to request imperial permission not to be detained in China. The emperor's edict pointedly commended the obedience of the Thai envoys and permitted the Chinese sailors "to absent themselves from their native places to demonstrate our magnanimity." [98] When another mission was sent in 1729, the emperor issued an edict "to show our kindness to our distant vassals by reducing the amount of . . . tribute. . . . Among the tribute articles, the following can be spared: thorn-incense, gum benzoin, and muslin." [99] Relations between the two countries continued close for several decades; tributary missions were sent by Siam, and trade flourished. Rice was regularly shipped to Fukien under special duty restrictions decreed by Ch'ien-lung.[100] In 1747, the governor of Fukien

city live along the canals in what were during the seventeenth and eighteenth centuries China Row, the Dutch compound, and the Chinese camps in the environs of the old city.[113]

D. The Chinese under King Taksin and the Early Jakkri Dynasty

With the fall of Ayutthaya to the Burmese, the future of the nation as well as of the Chinese position in Siam hinged on the colorful figure of Phraya Tak. Taksin, as he is often called, was born in 1734 of a Chinese father and Thai mother. His father had migrated to Ayutthaya from his native village of Hua-fu (C 24) in Ch'eng-hai hsien in Ch'ao-chou; he was therefore a Teochiu. His father's surname was Cheng, and his earlier given names were Ta (C 25) and Hai-feng (C 26), but in Siam he assumed the given name Yung (C 27). Just when he migrated to Ayutthaya is unknown, but he prospered there and eventually held the gambling monopoly (farm) in Ayutthaya, wherefore he was given the noble name of Khun Phat.[114] Cheng Yung was married to a Thai woman named Nok-iang, who was the mother of the future king.[115] The family lived across the street from the residence of a Thai nobleman, and this gentleman eventually adopted him.[116] The child was given the Thai name of Sin ("wealthy"), reared as a noble's son, and introduced into the court in adolescence as a royal aide. There he had the inclination and opportunity to learn Chinese as well as Malay and Annamese. In 1764, as a man of only thirty years, he was appointed governor of Tak (Rahaeng). Just before the Burmese invasion he was promoted to the governorship of the more important Kamphaengphet, which office he never assumed, being requested to help defend Ayutthaya against the Burmese. The name, Phraya Tak, or Jao Tak, is, of course, the title he held while governor of that province, while the name which Thai historians often use, Taksin, signifies "that particular governor of Tak whose personal name was Sin."

This is not the place to detail the story of how Taksin escaped with his followers to Southeast Siam (where, incidentally, was found the major concentration of Teochiu Chinese in Siam), there rallied opposition to the Burmese, decisively defeated them at Ayutthaya, was proclaimed king, and eventually brought the entire country under his control. It is, however, important to know that the son of a Chinese, master of both the Thai and Chinese languages, ruled Siam for over fourteen years (1767–1782).[117] Taksin established his capital at Thonburi, on the west bank of the Jaophraya River, in what is today included in the metropolitan area of Bangkok.

Whether Chinese had settled in the Bangkok area before 1767 is not known for certain, but it is very possible that a Chinese settlement was there as early as the first half of the seventeenth century.[118] In any case, during Taksin's reign a large Chinese settlement and market serving the capital grew up on the east bank of the river, centered at Thatian, near the site of the present royal palace. It was perhaps only natural that under Taksin the Chinese increased and prospered. Turpin, writing in 1770 on the basis of eyewitness accounts of the first years of Taksin's reign,[119] states: "The Chinese colony is the most numerous and flourishing, by the extent of its commerce and by the privileges which it enjoys." Crawfurd, one of the first Europeans to visit the country after Taksin reigned, wrote:

It was through the extraordinary encouragement which he [Taksin] gave to his countrymen that they were induced to resort to the country and settle it in such numbers. This extraordinary accession of Chinese population constitutes almost the only great and material change which has taken place in the state of the kingdom during many centuries.[120]

It was equally natural that Taksin should have especially favored Chinese of his own speech group, the Teochius. During his reign they were known as *jin-luang*, "royal Chinese." [121] Taksin's policies doubtless attracted many Teochius to Bangkok, where they predominate today.

According to a French Catholic missionary in Siam at the time, the rapid rehabilitation of the Siamese economy after the Burmese sack of Ayutthaya was made possible by the local Chinese.[122] In 1768–1769, the Chinese in Ayutthaya went through the ruins with a fine-toothed comb and recovered uncounted treasures from the debris and interiors of pagodas.

The Chinese have put gold and silver into circulation in Siam; it is to their industry that one owes the prompt recovery of this kingdom. If the Chinese were not so eager for gain, there would today be neither silver nor money in Siam.

Early in his reign, King Taksin was instrumental in embarking one of the most remarkable Chinese families in Thai history on a long record of governmental service in southern Siam.[123] The founder of the family, Wu Yang (C 28), was a Hokkien from Hsi-hsing village (C 29) in Chang-chou. He came to Songkhla by junk from Fukien in

herents. Jaophraya Jakkri, known to posterity by part of his posthumous name, Yǫtfa, or as Rama I, was the founder of the present Jakkri
dynasty. He established a new capital in Bangkok, across the river
from Taksin's palace, on the site of the Chinese port and trading
center which had developed during the 1770's. The Chinese market
was moved bodily to the Wat Sampluem area outside the southeast
gate of the royal city.[128] This newly located market came to be called
Sampheng, and that quarter today is still the Chinese center of Bangkok. Thus it was that the new capital, destined to grow into the
greatest metropolis ever seen in Siam, had from the beginning a strong
Chinese element.

Chinese histories record a tribute mission from Siam to China in
1782. It could have been dispatched by Phraya Sankhaburi during his
brief period in power during March and April. However, in view of
the fact that missions were usually dispatched from Siam on the southwest monsoon, which begins in the summer, the mission was most
probably that of Rama I, in which case he was unusually prompt in
reporting to the emperor. The reply was cool, the new king being
directed to send full particulars and a formal request for investiture.[129]
In 1784, Rama I again sent tributary envoys, this time with a personal
application for a patent of authority as well as a request for two
thousand copper shields for use in defense against the Burmese.[130]
This startling request—the purchase of copper by foreigners was expressly banned by Ch'ing statutes [131]—apparently gave Ch'ien-lung
second thought, and only in 1786, when Rama I sent another tribute
mission, did the new king receive investiture.

Surprisingly enough, Rama I was invested under an authentic Chinese name, Cheng Hua (C 33), and as the son of Cheng Chao (Taksin). The imperial edict to Siam in 1786 said: "We see that the present
head of their state has succeeded to his father's estates and aspirations.
He has sent envoys to pay tribute and his sincerity is commend-
able." [132] It may have been that Rama I's message contained a royal
fib, or that a translator erred in making "son" out of "son-in-law."
According to Cheng Tze-nan,[133] the name, Cheng Hua, was given to
Rama I at the time of his marriage to Taksin's daughter. Hsieh Yu-
jung,[134] on the other hand, considers Cheng Hua a mistaken transliteration of Jaofa, meaning "crown prince." In any case the Jakkri kings
were recorded in Peking under Taksin's surname, Cheng, as long as
Siam sent tribute.[135]

The first two Jakkri kings developed state trading and royal monopolies to an unprecedented degree. In order to increase the production of Siam's exports and provide crews for their royal ships, they encouraged Chinese immigration. Even the ships belonging to the kings brought back Chinese passengers, in direct violation of Manchu tributary and trading regulations.[136] Writing in 1822, Finlayson stated that, because the king and his ministers wished to increase the produce of the country, "Chinese emigrants were . . . encouraged beyond all former example." [137] From this we may assume that the upward trend in Chinese immigration, begun in King Taksin's reign, continued without break into the nineteenth century.

Between 1782, the beginning of the Jakkri dynasty, and 1854, the last year of royal state trading in Siam, thirty-five tribute missions were sent to China, for an average of 4.9 per decade, an all-time high. Such frequent missions were obviously prompted by commercial motives.[138] In developing state trading, the first Jakkri kings took full advantage of the commercial possibilities of the tribute system. The Ch'ien-lung edition of the *Collected Statutes* (1754), which were in force throughout Rama I's reign, included the following provisions: Siam was to send missions ordinarily every three years via Canton. The suite could contain as many as three vessels, each with up to one hundred men, and there was no limitation on the amount of merchandise that could be carried into China duty-free. These goods could be sold to the merchants' hongs in Canton or transported to the capital and marketed at the Residence for Tributary Envoys. The mission could buy in China anything desired, with the exception of those items which might weaken the defense of the Empire—e.g., weapons, copper, saltpeter, and historical works. In addition, "barbarian merchants" from "countries beyond the seas" could come to trade at Canton every summer.[139]

When Rama I took advantage of the last provision, he made use of the Chinese merchants in Bangkok, and toward the end of his reign he was notified that if he wished to trade with China he must send certified Siamese agents and not Chinese traders as supercargoes.[140] The major difficulties encountered by the early Jakkri kings came from their eagerness to send tribute too often and too lavishly.[141] The Siamese case clearly bears out the following conclusion of Fairbank and Teng:

If . . . our suggestion is correct, that embassies grew more frequent in the early nineteenth century in order to facilitate a generally expanded trade in

2

OPEN DOORS
AND OPEN SPACES:
Chinese Migration and
Population Growth to 1917

A. The Background of Immigration

CHINESE immigration to Siam arose out of the Chinese junk trade with Nan-yang. Consequently, the reasons why the Chinese immigrants to Siam come almost entirely from Fukien and Kwangtung can be approached by answering the question: Why was it the natives of Fukien and Kwangtung, in particular, who developed maritime skills and commercial relations with Nan-yang?

There are, naturally, many facets to the answer. The modern "Chinese" population of these coastal provinces is descended from migrants originating in the Yangtze valley and further north. The processes of migration and Sinification were well underway in south China during the Han dynasty. As these "Chinese" populations developed and grew in the coastal valleys of Fukien and Kwangtung, there were several compelling reasons for turning to the sea. Contact with the national base in the river valleys of central and north China was easy by sea and extremely difficult by land. The mountains of south China made overland transport arduous and inland water transport to the north impossible. As Lattimore has suggested,[1] the impossibility of extending

the Grand Canal to the south forced the development of coastal shipping in the southern provinces. The junk trade with Nan-yang which
followed was, in fact, merely an extension southward of coastal shipping. (Chinese mariners could, and those sailing the smaller junks
generally did, sail to Siam without ever losing sight of land.) The
possibilities of overseas trade were borne in upon the southern Chinese by the Arab and Malay traders who early came to Canton and
later Ch'üan-chou (Zaitun). The choice of these ports by foreign
traders was natural since they came from the south, and later the
imperial government restricted trade to particular southern ports.

The migration of Chinese southward to Kwangtung and Fukien
did not stop at the sea. Fishermen and coastal traders showed the
way, and by reason of politics or natural disaster, the movement of
the Chinese population continued overseas, first to Hainan and later
to Taiwan. By Ming times the great majority of the populations of
mainland Kwangtung and Fukien were Sinified, but the same could
not be said of Hainan and Taiwan before the late eighteenth or early
nineteenth century. The Hainanese "Chinese" were from the beginning
a seagoing people; they had arrived by sea, and, faced with an in-
hospitable mountainous interior and hostile aborigines, they maintained
their maritime orientation. When, in the nineteenth century, stability
and economic development became the order of the day in Nan-yang,
the general southward migration quite naturally continued in considerable number to Southeast Asia. That some of this migration
should be directed towards Siam was hardly remarkable in view of
the general similarity of climate and culture; it was easy for Chinese
to adjust in a Buddhist country where rice and fish were the staple
foods.

Overpopulation and underpopulation, of course, are not in themselves causes of emigration and immigration. In this regard, however,
a brief review of the recent demographic history of south China and
of Siam is instructive.[2] Early Chinese contact with Europeans in south
China led to the introduction of sweet potatoes and peanuts by the
beginning of the seventeenth century.[3] These nutritious crops could
be grown on the abundant infertile hilly land of Kwangtung and
Fukien—land unsuitable for rice cultivation. The peace and order
which followed the consolidation of the Manchu victory, in addition to
the added productivity provided by the new crops, led to rapid population increases, which continued up to the early nineteenth century.
By that time, the sweet potato was an essential in the diet, a staple

(for reasons to be discussed later) to provide most of the other labor and services also essential to the economic progress of the period. Thus, labor was in great demand for the prospering tin mines of South Siam, for the expanding steam rice mills and power sawmills, for the lighters and docks in the booming port of Bangkok, and for the construction of canals and railroads; wages became higher in Bangkok than in any other part of the Far East. The growth of the country's population (from over five to over nine millions between 1850 and 1917) meant an increasing demand for the services which Chinese could best provide—for the production of pork and vegetables, the provision of artisan and personal services, and the performance of retailing and middlemen's functions. The development of trade opened new opportunities in shipping and wholesaling and created a growing demand for Chinese tradesmen, compradores, and clerks. During the period 1850–1917, Siam entered the stream of modern world trade; in fact she entered the modern world. The development in Siam attracted and, indeed, was to a large degree made possible by, emigrants from south China.

Furthermore, the process of migration was greatly facilitated during the period in question. Between 1865 and 1886, steamships gradually took over the bulk of passenger traffic between south China and Siam. Safety was greatly increased and fares considerably reduced. This development, as will become evident in the section immediately following, was a crucial turning point in the increase of emigration. In addition, recruitment of emigrants in China in co-operation with agents in Siam became regularized in the 1880's, while malpractices in the various China ports with regard to the passenger traffic were gradually reformed from the late 1880's on. The Manchu government's ban on emigration was by degrees withdrawn during this period, the first step being the legalization of emigration under European auspices provided by the Treaty of Peking in 1860, and the last being the promulgation of the new Ch'ing Code sans ban in 1910.[8]

When the various "reasons" for immigration to Nan-yang generally and to Siam in particular are juxtaposed, one wonders indeed why a really mass movement did not arise sooner—why the Thai were not completely swamped by hordes of starving Chinese immigrants. It is important, in this regard, not to lose sight of the culture of the would-be emigrants. The attachment of the average Chinese to his native soil and village, his strong kin ties, his duties with regard to the ancestor cult, constitute a formidable and integrated obstacle to emigra-

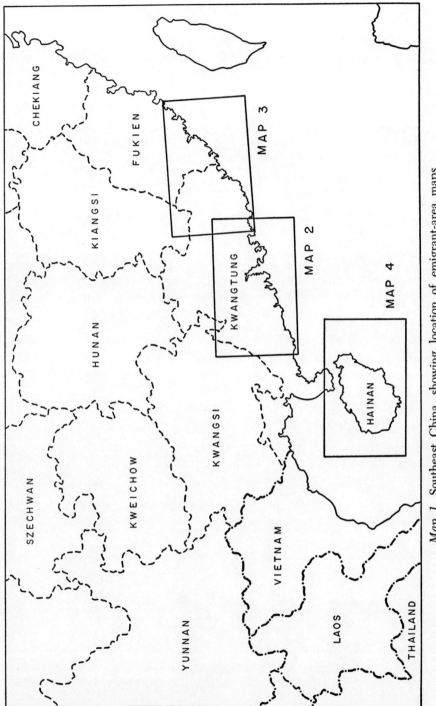

Map 1. Southeast China, showing location of emigrant-area maps

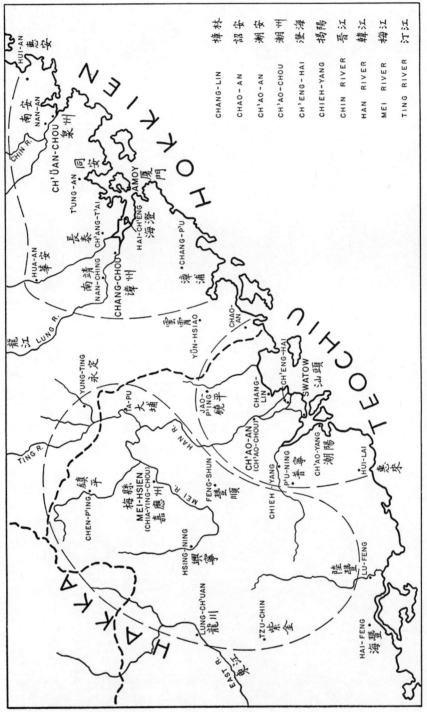

Map 3. Teochiu, Hakka, and Hokkien emigrant areas

centrated in seven hsien [13] in what was the old prefecture, Kuang-chou-fu (see Map 2), but Cantonese emigrants also came from other hsien in that prefecture, from Chao-ch'ing-fu, and, more rarely, from other parts of the province. In Siam today, Cantonese call themselves *kuang-fu-jen,* "people of Kuang-chou prefecture," or *kuang-tung-jen,* "people of Kuangtung province," and in addition they are occasionally called *kuang-chou-jen* by Teochius. We will call them Cantonese, although "Kwongfu" and "Punti" also have some currency in Western literature.

The Hokkiens populate that part of Fukien province south of the Northern Min speech area and east of the Hakka speech area. The name, Hokkien (Hokkian) is simply the pronunciation in that dialect of the province name, and the Hokkiens are known to all other speech groups by various pronunciations of *fu-chien-jen,* i.e., Fukienese.[14] The Hokkien emigrant communities are concentrated in the old prefectures of Ch'üan-chou and Chang-chou (see Map 3).

The Teochius are located in and around the delta of the Han River in northeastern Kwangtung. They moved into this area from southern Fukien, probably in several waves, between the ninth and fifteenth centuries, and other speech groups still often refer to them as *fu-lao* (C 37) (Hok-lao, Hokklo, Hoklo, Holo), i.e., "People of Fukien." [15] The name, Teochiu (Tiechiu, Tiochiu, Tewchew, Taechew, Tio-tsjoe, Tia-chu, Ta-chu, etc.), represents the pronunciation in that dialect of the name of the prefecture in which most Teochius in China live, Ch'ao-chou.[16] The Teochiu emigrant communities are concentrated in six hsien,[17] especially in the coastal regions and the Han Delta itself (see Map 3). p

Hakkas have been a migratory people for centuries. They appear to have originated as a separate group in the Yellow River valley, whence in the fifth century they began migrating southward in several stages. By the thirteenth century, a large group of Hakkas had settled in what became known as Chia-ying-chou, to the northwest of Ch'ao-chou in Kwangtung. In time they occupied a fairly connected area extending from the southwestern tip of Fukien, across northern Kwangtung west of the Teochiu speech area, to eastern Kwangsi, and including the southernmost parts of Kiangsi and Hunan. In addition to expanding in this area, the Hakkas had, by the nineteenth century, established "colonies" all over Kwangtung province, as far west as Szechwan, and even in the offshore islands of Taiwan and Hainan. At the present time their distribution in China is very complex: in some

ch'ang and Ch'iung-shan in the northeastern part of the island (see Map 4).

Each of these five speech groups has been emigrating to Southeast Asia for at least two centuries. Ch'üan-chou (Zaitun) and Canton had been important ports long before the Ming dynasty, and up to the middle of the eighteenth century Hokkiens and Cantonese were predominant among Nan-yang immigrants. It would appear, furthermore, that Hokkiens greatly outnumbered Cantonese as emigrants.[19] The reason for the Hokkien predominance would seem, paradoxically, to lie in the usual restriction of trade by foreigners to Canton. Foreigners were never allowed to trade indiscriminately with China, but were generally restricted to southern ports. Prior to the Manchu dynasty, one or more of the Fukien ports of Ch-üan-chou, Chang-chou, and Amoy were often but by no means always open to foreigners' trade, while by Ming times, if any port was open to the trade of foreigners, Canton always was. While Canton was the most consistently "open" port before the Ch'ing dynasty (prior to 1644), during that dynasty (up to 1842), it was usually the only port open to foreigners, as well as the port to which Nan-yang tribute missions had first to repair. The hypothesis suggested here is that trade with Nan-yang by *Chinese* merchants in *Chinese* junks was never stimulated at Canton to the extent it was at the Fukien ports. At Canton, foreign ships—Arab, Malay, Siamese, European, and others—came regularly, so that Cantonese merchants were not especially diligent in expanding the entirely Chinese part of the trade. At the Fukienese ports, on the other hand, foreigners could sometimes trade and sometimes not, so that the mercantile ambitions of Hokkiens were stimulated but not regularly satisfied. After the Manchus came to power, foreigners were discouraged and usually forbidden from trade in Fukien, and so all the Fukien trade came to be carried by Chinese, for the most part in their own junks.[20] Prior to the nineteenth century emigrants from China were carried almost solely in Chinese junks, and usually went to Nan-yang in the first place to engage in commercial activities connected with the home-port trade. As the *Chinese* trade (as opposed to foreigners' trade) of the Hokkiens increased vis-à-vis the Cantonese, especially during the seventeenth and eighteenth centuries, for reasons suggested above, naturally the porportion of Hokkien immigrants increased. In any case, in the eighteenth century, Hokkiens were unquestionably the principal speech group in Siam.[21]

The century after the fall of Ayutthaya, however, saw radical changes

not only in the size but also in the composition of the Chinese population in Siam. By the late nineteenth century, Hokkiens and Cantonese
had been relegated to fourth and fifth place, respectively, among the
Chinese speech groups in all of Siam except the South. In central and
upcountry Thailand, with Bangkok as its chief port of entry, the
period from 1767 through the nineteenth century saw a spectacular
increase in the proportion of Teochius and large increases in the
proportion of Hainanese and Hakkas, coupled with a sharp decrease
in the proportion of Hokkiens and a milder relative decrease in the
proportion of Cantonese. The new pattern of things was well established prior to the 1880's and was confirmed during that decade as *the*
future pattern for Siam. The unfolding of the new migration patterns
set in the nineteenth century has yielded the speech-group composition of the present-day Chinese population.

Before tracing these changes and pointing to some of their major
determinants, it will be helpful to review the rise and fall of various
south China ports and the process by which steamers replaced junks
in the emigration traffic. During the first half of the nineteenth century, Siam, through the stimuli provided by its "merchant-kings,"
carried on a booming trade, primarily with China and conducted
mainly by Chinese. According to Gutzlaff in the early 1830's, "no
place south of China is the rendezvous of so many Chinese junks as
Siam." [22] Bangkok, in fact, was something of an entrepôt in the China–
Southeast Asian trade. Both South Asian goods and European products were collected at Bangkok—not only from Gulf of Siam ports
but also from those on the Bay of Bengal and in Malaya and Indonesia
—for shipment to China, while Chinese goods were distributed to
these ports from Bangkok.[23] Up to the 1830's the trade was almost entirely in Chinese-style junks, whether Chinese-owned or not. The
junks used in this trade were built sometimes in China, but usually on
the banks of the Jaophraya River in Lower Siam.[24]

In the heyday of the junks, the major south China ports tended to
be inland.[25] Passage up the lower reaches of the rivers offered few
problems to shallow-draft junks, while inland anchorages provided
better protection against pirates and bad weather. There were exceptions, of course, even before 1800 (e.g., Amoy), and during the
nineteenth century most of the inland ports declined in importance.
Around 1825, however, prior to the main shift, the major ports in
Kwangtung and Fukien from which trade was carried on with Siam
(see Maps 2, 3, 4) were (1) Canton and Chiang-men in the Cantonese

venture, one of the most significant in the history of Chinese immigration to Siam, was an immediate success, for Bangkok had for years been the only important immigration port not served by direct steamers from China ports. During the first two years of operation, steamer departures for Bangkok from Swatow averaged one a week; steamer immigration to Bangkok began at the brisk rate of ten thousand annually.[37]

Shipping was also an important determinant of the development of the Hainanese immigration to Siam and their eventual position in the country. The Hainanese trade with Siam must have developed in the eighteenth century. There is practically no mention of the island or its inhabitants in the literature on Siam prior to the early nineteenth century, when several writers describe a full-blown Hainanese trade with Bangkok of forty to fifty junks annually.[38] The Hainanese trading junks were smaller than those used for overseas shipping from other Chinese ports. Hainanese mariners, therefore, could only rarely risk a trip across the open sea to, say, the Philippines or Malaya,[39] much less to more distant places in Nan-yang. Their major trade, therefore, aside from that with the immediately adjacent shores of Kwangtung and Tongking, developed with Cochinchinese, Cambodian, and Siamese ports on the upper Gulf. In fact the Bangkok trade was a natural one for Hainanese junks. Because of the island's southerly position, they could leave port early in the northeast monsoon and reach Bangkok every year ahead of junks from any other part of China.[40] The distance was just about right for an annual round trip, leaving plenty of time to trade in Bangkok. Furthermore the Hainanese sailors could easily pick up timber as they coasted along Southeast Siam and build a junk within two months' time while disposing of the rest of their cargo at Bangkok. In view of the poor development of agriculture on Hainan, Thai rice, raw cotton, and bone for fertilizer, in addition to timber, were especially welcome as cargo for the return trip.[41] As the interior of Thailand began to open up and the demand for manual labor and domestic service grew in Bangkok, a regular emigration junk traffic developed between Hainan and Bangkok. Hainanese ports other than Hai-k'ou began to lose ground after 1876, when Ch'iung-chou (which Hai-k'ou serves) was opened as a treaty port. So far as emigration goes, however, only indirect traffic via Hongkong was diverted to Hai-k'ou prior to the establishment of direct steamer service to Bangkok. The major port for the Bangkok trade and emigration in the 1870's was P'u-ch'ien, thirty miles east of Hai-k'ou.[42]

The same British shipping company in Bangkok which inaugurated direct steamship traffic to Swatow [43] began direct service to Hai-k'ou in 1886, and doubtless in response to similar motives and pressures.[44] With the opening up of Hainan, the Hainanese were proving a valuable source of immigrant man power, and their ties with Bangkok were as close as those with any other part of Nan-yang. This service, which continued for the remainder of the period under review, was crucial in stimulating Hainanese emigration to Siam and assuring them an important position among the Chinese speech groups in that country.

In spite of the direct steamer service between Bangkok and Hai-k'ou, the Hainanese junk trade with Siam died a slow death. All through the remainder of the nineteenth century, it is reported that a large number of emigrants still traveled by junk, while the British Consul at Ch'iung-chou stated as late as 1909 that emigrants were returning by junk to Hainanese ports other than Hai-k'ou.[45] A native of Hainan has written that, even a few years after that, junks were still going to Nan-yang from Ch'ing-lan.[46] This situation meant, of course, that the official customs figures for emigration from Hai-k'ou to Bangkok considerably understate the total traffic between Hainan and Siam throughout the period under review.

The junk traffic with the mainland Chinese ports also never completely died. Square-rigged vessels had all but disappeared from Bangkok by 1907,[47] and the once proud Thai fleet of sailing ships had disintegrated long since,[48] but the Chinese seagoing trading junk remained a prominent feature of Bangkok harbor until the First World War. Nevertheless, from all accounts, after the turn of the century, Chinese immigration by junk was negligible for all but the Hainanese traffic.

The foregoing survey of the changing patterns of shipping during the nineteenth century makes possible now a systematic exposition of the developments which so drastically altered the relative proportions of the speech groups among immigrants to Siam:

1. From 1767 to 1782, the king of Siam was a Teochiu. His benevolent attitude toward those of his own speech group stimulated Teochiu immigration to Siam. Moreover, since he was the first king to reign from a capital in the vicinity of Bangkok, his encouragement gave Teochius a favored start in the modern "Bangkok Era" of Thai history. Since Bangkok thereafter became Thailand's chief port of entry, the Teochius who settled there during Taksin's reign were also a most

strategically placed nucleus to stimulate further immigration from their home areas.

2. The commercial co-operation which members of the Thai elite developed with Chinese shippers and traders during the early Jakkri reigns was in fact primarily a Teochiu-Thai phenomenon. This situation is explained in part by the first point above, for the aristocracy and nobility centered their trading operations in Bangkok, where Teochius were at their strongest. During the Taksin period, too, Teochius were in a more favorable position than other speech groups to become acquainted and work with Thai nobles and aristocrats. Finally, the Thai kings and nobles, comparatively unhampered by considerations of capital, could afford to and preferred to buy and operate the largest junks. Of all the junk types in Kwangtung and Fukien, the Ch'ao-chou Trader, built and manned by Teochius, was the biggest and sturdiest ship; and this was the type most often owned by the Thai trader-officials.[49] The Teochiu-Thai co-operation in the China trade, which lasted through the third reign, put comparatively more capital at the disposal of Teochiu traders and naturally tended to favor the development of Bangkok's trade with Ch'ao-chou ports.

3. A traditional Teochiu specialization in plantation agriculture is doubtless another factor in their rapid rise in Siam. The growing demand in world markets for sugar, pepper, and other agricultural products led to the development, early in the nineteenth century, of plantation agriculture in Southeast and Lower Siam. Around 1810, sugar cane was introduced in Siam by Chinese settlers,[50] and within a few years it became one of the most important export crops, increasing in volume and value till about 1860.[51] The cultivation of pepper was also an increasingly important Chinese undertaking, especially in Southeast Siam, during the first two-thirds of the nineteenth century. Now, as Gutzlaff tells us,[52] the Teochius in Siam in the 1830's were "mostly agriculturalists," and according to reports from other parts of Southeast Asia Teochius were the agriculturalists and plantation workers par excellence. In Singapore in the 1840's, for instance, the vast majority of general agriculturalists and gambier and pepper planters were Teochius.[53] Furthermore, during the nineteenth century the Teochiu region in China was known for its production of sugar for export.[54] It would seem safe to hypothesize, then, that the great expansion in the production of sugar, pepper, and other agricultural products grown by the Chinese in central Siam during the first half of the nineteenth century attracted an increasing and disproportionate

number of Teochius to Bangkok and the areas around the upper Gulf. The development of cotton culture in Siam somewhat later in the nineteenth century [55] by the same token attracted Hainanese, who specialized in cotton growing both in Hainan and Nan-yang.

4. The establishment of Hongkong in 1842 meant that longer-distance shipping from all Cantonese ports decreased in favor of the new colony. Hongkong, with its far-flung trade connections, channeled Cantonese into the most distant emigration traffic—that to the Western hemisphere, Australia, and New Zealand, thus reducing the number of Cantonese immigrants to Siam.

5. The fact that from 1842 to 1858 Amoy and Canton were treaty ports open to foreign shipping while Swatow and Hainanese ports were not meant that patterns of emigration from the Hokkien and Cantonese areas to European colonies in Southeast Asia were well established before the pool of Teochiu, Hakka, and Hainanese emigrants became available for exploitation in areas of European control. The general predominance of Hokkien or Cantonese or both in Southeast Asia was thus continued and intensified everywhere except Siam and Cambodia.

6. The Thai merchant marine was modernized and approaching its heyday just as Swatow was opened as a treaty port. Siam's fleet of merchant steamers was just being built up in 1858 and reached its maximum size in the 1860's; the peak of Thai-flag shipping with China was in 1868.[56] Thus the serious entry into the China trade of the new and formidable Thai merchant marine came late enough for Swatow—the source of Teochiu and Hakka emigrants—to be at an equal advantage with Amoy and Canton in the development of Thai shipping with China.

7. The frequent Thai tributary and trading missions to China via Canton ceased in 1853, after King Mongkut came to the throne. The decline of the overseas junk trade at such ports as Chiang-men had already forced Cantonese emigrants for Siam to rely increasingly on the Siamese ships returning from tribute and trading missions at Canton. The demise of these missions thus entailed a further decrease in Cantonese immigration to Siam. A contemporary estimate in the records of the Cantonese Association in Bangkok placed the total number of Cantonese in the city and environs at only two thousand in 1877.[57]

8. Hainan's closure to foreign shipping during the first three-quarters of the nineteenth century favored Hainanese emigration to

those countries which could be reached by small junks sailing near to the land. Thus a special aspect of Hainanese technology (very small junk types), plus geography (which placed Hainan at just the right distance from Bangkok to suit the product of this technology), plus the history of Western expansion in China (which got around to such small plums as Hainan only relatively late) conspired to strengthen the ties which Hainanese shippers and traders had with Bangkok and establish Siam as the chief destination for Hainanese emigrants prior to 1876.

9. Hakka migration to Siam followed directly from the fact that Swatow was the nearest port of departure for most Hakka emigrants. The combined effect of factors 2, 3, and 6 above favored the development of close trading and shipping connections between Swatow and Bangkok. From the 1860's to the end of the century, exports from Swatow to Siam showed a tendency to increase, while exports from Amoy to Siam, by contrast, steadily decreased.[58] This reflects the growing importance of Swatow as a port, but in particular the increasing preference of ships going to Bangkok to make Swatow the last port of call. As prospective Hakka emigrants poured into Swatow, their choice of destination in Nan-yang was naturally conditioned by available shipping and knowledge about the various Southeast Asian ports, and in both regards Bangkok had an advantage in Swatow. A Chinese customs report in 1879 [59] gives a complete breakdown by native hsien of the 17,215 emigrants from Swatow in that year. With information as to which hsiens are populated by Teochius and which by Hakkas and which by both in what proportions, it is possible to calculate that Hakkas must have formed 27 per cent to 29 per cent of the total emigrants.[60]

10. The fact that regular and direct passenger traffic by steamer was begun by 1870 from Amoy to Singapore and Manila but not from Amoy to Bangkok meant that Hokkien emigrants were again disproportionately directed to the Philippines and the areas served by Singapore (Malaya and South Siam, Java, Sumatra and Burma) as opposed to central Siam.

11. The timing of the main switch from sail to steam in the three ports of Amoy, Swatow, and Hai-k'ou also favored the migration of Teochius, Hakkas, and Hainanese to Bangkok, as opposed to Hokkiens. The main change from sail to steam in the emigration traffic took place in Amoy not later than 1870, i.e., before Bangkok had any

regular steamer connections even with Hongkong; while the switch in Swatow and Hai-k'ou (1875 and 1876, respectively) occurred just when a regular two-steamer run was begun between Bangkok and Hongkong. Thus as soon as most emigrants from Swatow and Hainan were departing by steamer, they were not handicapped, as the Hokkiens had been earlier, in getting to Siam all the way by steamer via Hongkong.

The combined effect of several of the factors already mentioned seems to have shifted the balance for Siam (except the South) between emigrants from Amoy and those from Swatow well before 1876. For four years (1877–1879 and 1881), reliable statistics are available for the direct passenger traffic in foreign bottoms from both ports to Bangkok.[61] They show that departures from Amoy for Bangkok amount to just 50 per cent of the departures from Swatow for Bangkok. Furthermore for these years, direct arrivals in Amoy from Bangkok were 52 per cent of departures, while in the case of Swatow direct arrivals were only 12 per cent of departures. Part of this disparity can be explained by the fact that ships from Bangkok to China more often called at Amoy before Swatow, but these figures may also be interpreted as additional indication that the Hokkien immigration to Siam had already declined from what had previously been a higher rate. The relatively high proportion of returnees from Bangkok to Amoy indicates that the Hokkien preference was already established for residence in Nan-yang elsewhere than in Siam.

12. The final determinant of the predominance of Teochius, Hakkas, and Hainanese in the Chinese immigration to Siam was the establishment of regularly scheduled and frequent passenger steamer traffic from Bangkok to Swatow in 1882 and to Hai-k'ou in 1886. It is obviously crucial that Bangkok's first regular passenger traffic direct to any port in any Chinese emigrant area was with Swatow, that its second such service was with Hai-k'ou, and that these were the only ports so connected with Bangkok for over half a century thereafter. However, if the above analysis is correct, then the British shipping firm at Bangkok, in choosing to establish it's regular runs with Swatow and Hainan, made the only sensible decision in view of already existing patterns. Thus the regular steam passenger services begun in the 1880's were partly a response to the speech-group immigration patterns already set in Siam by 1875, and in turn confirmed and intensified them. Only if these patterns are demonstrated for a given period,

can the pat statement, so often met in the literature on the subject, that Chinese emigrants go where their friends and relatives are, help explain migration trends.

Swatow and Hai-k'ou continued to supply an increasingly large proportion of emigrants to Bangkok after the 1880's. The recorded statistics on direct immigration to Bangkok from Swatow and from Hai-k'ou are given in Table 1. The average rate of 1882–1892 when

Table 1. Direct departures from Swatow and Hai-k'ou for Bangkok, as recorded by Chinese Customs, by periods, 1882–1917 °

Period	From Swatow		From Hai-k'ou	
	Annual average	Total	Annual average	Total
1882–1892	8,381	92,196	1,186	13,047
1893–1905	20,483	266,278	4,979	64,724
1906–1917	48,538	582,456	8,796	105,548
Total		940,930		183,319

° Source: *China Trade Returns* 1882–1917; *Chinese Customs Decennial Reports* 1892–1901, 1902–1911, 1912–1921.

compared with that for 1906–1917 shows a 5.7-fold increase for direct Swatow emigrants and a 7.4-fold increase for direct Hainanese emigrants. On the other hand, a comparison of the estimated average annual arrivals in Siam for the same periods for all Chinese immigrants shows only a 4.2-fold increase (see Table 2 below). While this comparison leaves out of account the indirect traffic and the differences in rate of return, it nonetheless provides evidence of the increasing proportion of immigrants from Swatow and Hainan among all Chinese immigrants to Siam after 1882. From the writer's tabulation of the total passenger traffic of Swatow for the period after 1874, it is clear that an increasing proportion of the total departures from Swatow for all Southeast Asian destinations went to Siam. For 1874–1881, about 15 per cent of all Swatow emigrants went to Siam, for 1882–1892 about 20 per cent, for 1893–1905 about 33 per cent, and for 1906–1917 about 50 per cent. The preference of Teochiu and Hakka emigrants for Siam grew steadily more marked until approximately half of all Swatow emigrants were going to Siam.

Cantonese emigration to Siam apparently had something of a resurgence near the end of the nineteenth century. When the emigration through Hongkong and Macao to Peru, Cuba, the United States, the Hawaiian Islands, Australia, and other distant lands was severely restricted or stopped—the effects of which were felt most strongly from 1882 on—the stream of Cantonese immigration was in larger part directed to Southeast Asia.[62] It is extremely difficult to distinguish Cantonese immigrants in the general traffic statistics for Hongkong, and so impossible to document any trends. From what informants in Bangkok say, however, it appears that the rate of Cantonese immigration to that port was increasing around the turn of the century and remained fairly high during the first decade at least.

The trend in Hokkien migration to Bangkok continued downward after 1875. Regular steamer traffic from Amoy to Bangkok was in fact never established, and when occasional passenger steamers from Amoy to Bangkok became available, the Hokkiens showed practically no interest in emigrating directly to central Siam.[63]

Their migration to South Siam, however, continued at a moderate level on into the twentieth century. Prior to the establishment of good overland communication between Bangkok and South Siam, Chinese immigrants to the lower peninsula came either directly to such southern ports as Songkhla or indirectly via Singapore and Penang. The so-called Chinese rajahs of South Siam—of whom Wu Yang and his descendants in Songkhla provide only one of the more outstanding examples—were practically all of Hokkien extraction and so tended to encourage the immigration of Hokkiens over other speech groups. The direct traffic from China to South Siam apparently lasted well into the twentieth century and consisted primarily of junks from Hokkien, Hainanese, and Cantonese ports, in that order.[64] Especially during the decades prior to 1890, immigration to South Siam was high. Writing of this period, Smyth says that "the peninsula States [of Siam] received some thousands [of Chinese] every year, on the east by junk direct, on the west via the Straits." [65] Throughout most of the period up to 1917, Hokkiens were the dominant speech group among the immigrants to the Straits Settlements, and this was reflected in the immigrant population at Phuket, Trang, Ranong, and other centers in the Siamese part of the peninsula.[66] However, just as the Straits Settlements acquired a strongly heterogeneous Chinese population because of their early steamer connections with all south China ports, so the Chinese population of South Siam came to include increasingly large minorities of non-Hokkiens after the 1880's. Between 1881 and

1915, Chinese migration to Penang was fairly steady at an average of about 47,700 annually; [67] it is probable that at least 5 per cent and possibly 10 per cent of these ended up in Siamese territory.

The many variables involved and the incomplete data make it impossible to calculate with any assurance the proportion of the various speech groups among the immigrants to Siam prior to 1917. The only estimate in the literature is that of Raquez, who concluded that about 50 per cent of the total resident Chinese in the country were Teochius and Hakkas, about 14 per cent Hainanese, with the rest Hokkiens and Cantonese.[68] If Hokkiens and Cantonese together formed a third of the population, however, then one or both must have outnumbered the Hainanese, which was certainly not the case. An inscription on a stone tablet erected in 1908 by Cantonese in Bangkok gives a clearer picture of the relative strength of all but the Hokkiens: [69] "Most of the Chinese in Siam come from Ch'ao-chou and Ch'iung-chou [Hainan]. The third largest group of Chinese in Siam come from Hakka [areas]. Cantonese are far fewer in number than the three above groups." By the end of the period under review, this writer would estimate the proportions in the whole country as follows: Teochius 40 per cent, Hainanese 18 per cent, Hakka and Hokkien 16 per cent each, and Cantonese 9 per cent.

C. Immigration Practice and Procedure

During the first half of the nineteenth century, immigration to Siam was perforce seasonal. The junks arrived on the northeast monsoon from January to April and departed on the southwest monsoon in June and July.[70] With the growth of the Chinese emigration traffic, special passenger junks were evolved,[71] and according to Crawfurd a single one of these was known to have brought twelve hundred immigrants to Bangkok in the 1820's.[72] Probably the bulk of the immigrants, however, came in regular trading junks as yet an additional item of cargo. Gutzlaff's description of conditions is particularly graphic:

The junks which transport them [Chinese emigrants] in great numbers remind one of an African slaver. The deck is filled with them, and there the poor wretches are exposed to the inclemency of the weather and without any shelter, for the cargo fills the junk below. Their food consists of dry rice and an allowance of water; but when the passages are very long, there is often a want of both, and many of them actually starve to death.[73]

Fares for such a trip were $8 (Spanish dollars) from Amoy to Bangkok, and $6 from Chang-lin (in Ch'ao-chou) to Bangkok.[74]

Chinese emigrants during the nineteenth century are often classified as "contract" or "indentured," "credit-ticket" and "free" emigrants. So far as is known, contract immigration never existed to any extent in Siam; it is associated especially with the "coolie traffic" of the nineteenth century to the West Indies and Peru, and to the areas in the Dutch East Indies and Malaya with a European-developed plantation economy. It was only a thinly disguised slave trade; Siam was fortunate to have avoided an economic development leading to widespread indentured labor. The credit-ticket system, however, was fairly widespread in Siam throughout most of the nineteenth century. As the name implies, the emigrant obtained his passage on credit, the ship's captain to be reimbursed on arrival in Siam either by friends or relatives of the emigrant or by an employer, for whom the *hsin-k'e* (Sin Kheh: "newcomer") had to work until his debt was paid off. The system had its abuses as early as 1830, as Gutzlaff's description indicates:

The condition of the emigrants in general is most miserable, without clothing, or money for one day's subsistence. Sometimes they have not money enough to pay their passage from home . . . and they become bondmen to anybody who pays this sum for them, or fall prey to extortioners, who claim their services for more than a year.[75]

With the greatly increased demand for Chinese labor in all of Nanyang—in Siam particularly after the 1860's—organized recruitment of emigrants became universal in the mainland emigrant areas. Unfortunately organized extortion became widespread as well, especially in Ch'ao-chou. There was first of all, the heavy squeeze demanded by the Chinese officials even to permit the emigration, which was technically illegal; the bribes became regularized in Swatow at about 500 to 600 piastres per passenger vessel.[76] Then there developed an extortion racket on the part of certain clan villages near Swatow. The amount charged for merely landing Chinese passengers amounted to $10 per head. "The desire to possess the power of levying blackmail at Swatow itself rose to such a height in 1864 that the surrounding villages engaged in warfare to obtain this end during the whole year. On the arrival of steamers or ships with Chinese passengers, these, on leaving their vessels, have been fought for in the harbor among the shipping, and fire arms discharged most indiscriminately." [77] This situation was not brought under control until 1869 or 1870, when a particularly ruthless Teochiu, General Fang, forcefully brought an end to anarchy in the department.[78]

The squeeze continued as long as emigration was under ban (until 1910), but the abuses of recruitment and private extortion were probably fewer in Swatow for the rest of the century after 1870 than in most other emigration ports. Huber's account of the recruiting system in Ch'ao-chou, written in 1871, is the best of those pertaining to the emigration from Swatow to Bangkok:

In almost all the towns of . . . [Ch'ao-chou and Chia-ying-chou] prefectures, there are emigration brokers called in Chinese k'e-t'ou [literally "head of the guests," i.e., headman of the emigrants] who, each year when the monsoon changes at the end of summer, go into the surrounding villages to recruit passengers. They are generally old emigrants who returned with a little money, and are doing a petty trade in the neighboring town. They have connections with the agents in Swatow of the commercial houses of . . . Bangkok . . . and are authorized to promise employment to the emigrants as soon as they arrive at their destination. Since they are known persons, established nearby indigents and vagabonds approach them without hesitation and accept with confidence their word. . . . The emigrants can either wait in their village until the broker lets them know the day of departure of the ship which will take them, or they can live until then with the broker himself who generally has several free rooms in his house for this purpose. . . .

When the brokers have thus gathered together thirty or forty free emigrants they so notify the agents of the commercial houses with which they have connections. They [the Swatow agents] then charter a ship, and when the cargo is on board . . . they inform the brokers who arrive in Swatow with the passengers they have recruited. They [the brokers] pay the total fares to the ship-owner and receive in return a ticket . . . for each of the emigrants, who can then embark. The fare is, on the average, . . . $6.50 for Bangkok. If the passenger or emigrant cannot procure the sum necessary to pay the fare before leaving, the broker will generally advance it to him and this money is reimbursed, with an allowance of 20 per cent as interest, by the farmer or entrepreneur who engages the emigrant on his arrival at his destination. If the broker cannot make this advance, the shipowner often makes it himself. . . . The sums advanced must be paid before the emigrant can disembark, and the farmer then has a lien on his wages. The shipowner returns to the broker a bonus of 3 per cent of the fare of the emigrants he recruits. This is about all the salary the broker receives for his pains. . . . Vagabonds, unemployed and indigents, especially in the towns, often themselves go to the brokers or Agents of the commercial houses to solicit a passage reimbursable at destination. . . .

Transport of emigrants takes place only during the north monsoon, that is, from October to April. During this period the crossing is generally easy and lasts only on the average . . . fifteen to twenty-five days for Bangkok [this most probably for square-rigged vessels, not junks].

As a rule the free emigrants embark with the idea of returning. Their aim is to go and acquire abroad the means of returning to their native country. . . . Their salaries . . . per month during the first year . . . in Bangkok . . . are from $3.00 to $4.00. From this sum must be deducted the price of the passage which has been reimbursed by the farmer.[79]

Before developing certain aspects of Huber's account, the rather rosy emigration picture he saw in Swatow should be balanced by accounts of the conditions during the voyages themselves. One first-hand account is that obtained by Chen Ta in 1940 from an eighty-three-year-old informant in Swatow; it also pertains to the period around 1870:

When I was a boy, our village had eight sea-going junks. . . . On their southward voyages they usually went to Bangkok, carrying beans, tea, and silk as their major cargoes. The largest junk carried over two hundred passengers. Usually a passenger took with him a water jar of local pottery, two suits of summer clothes, a round straw hat, and a straw mat. The voyage from Swatow to Bangkok often took a month. After setting foot on the junk, . . . we could do little but trust Heaven as to our safety during the voyage.[80]

The *Siam Repository* for 1870 records that a Siamese ship arriving from Swatow came with a thousand or more Chinese passengers:

They must have been inadequately provided for. We hear that when a party of those immigrants were put on board of the steam-tug Johore to be conveyed to Bangkok, the entire party were famishing with thirst. When the cabin-boy was bringing a brass wash basin of water to the cabin, the immigrants made a rush for the basin, seized it and drank. The Captain of the steamer supplied the poor thirsty mortals til there was no more water in the steam tug to give.[81]

Time and again Bangkok sources record that ships—junks, square-riggers, and steamers, Chinese, British, German, and Siamese—arrived overcrowded with immigrants. "One batch of these immigrants [in 1873] say that the vessel in which they came had over 800 passengers, that on the passage out they were put on short allowance, and suffered not a little from hunger." [82] The crusading Samuel J. Smith, a former

American missionary in Siam, editorialized frequently on the subject: He maintained:

A vessel that cannot accommodate passengers has no business to take passengers, or at least she should not take them without having made necessary arrangements to supply them with wholesome and sufficient food, and making some provision for their cleanness and health. They ought to have room enough to sleep. There ought to be a physician on hand to look after the sick, and such conditions as will tend to the health of large companies of people. . . . Siamese ships are subject to Siamese law. It is high time the Siamese had laws on this subject.[83]

His zeal, however, was in vain, for Siam never regulated the immigrant traffic during the period to 1882 when it was most necessary. The British, for their part, first limited the number of passengers according to the tonnage of the ship in 1855, and later strengthened these regulations. The Germans finally did likewise in 1876, and inasmuch as the British and German share of the passenger traffic to Bangkok steadily increased, conditions on emigrant ships showed some improvement.[84] The situation was remedied, however, only when direct regular steamer traffic was introduced. After 1882, the British Consul in Swatow could write: "The passengers are well looked after, and the steamers employed in the service are some of the finest in the world." [85]

To return to the credit-ticket system described by Huber above, the "farmers and entrepreneurs" mentioned were almost exclusively Chinese—the operators of rice mills and sawmills or of plantations requiring manual labor. By farmer is meant those who have purchased monopoly rights ("farms") from the Crown—rights to operate gambling establishments, to import opium, to collect duties on particular imports, to levy various taxes, and so on. The farmers, who were almost always Chinese, usually had to employ extensive staffs to run their monopolies.

A report of the British Consul in Bangkok for 1884 sheds still further light on the system:

The agents of the Chinese firms [in the south China ports] go about and pick up such as they think will make suitable immigrants and, paying the passage and the cost of their food consign them to their agents in Bangkok. If the immigrant has any friends or relatives already there, the latter will repay the agent the sum he has laid out, with an additional bonus of some 50 per cent. in all, generally some 15 dollars, and the man is set at liberty. If he has no friends who will help him, the Chinese sugarcane or betelnut growers will pay the agent a sum of about double what the immigrant has cost him, and will take him away to work off his debt upon their plantations. The coolies seem well treated on these plantations, as no complaints are heard.[86]

It will be noted that while Huber in 1870 speaks of the credit-ticket system as rather an occasional resort, this account, written after regular steam traffic had begun with Swatow, speaks of it as the usual procedure. In point of fact, in order to insure full loads for every trip, the steamship companies induced their agents in China to obtain passengers at all costs; recruitment became more aggressive and the credit-ticket system more widespread. It also gave rise to kidnapping and nonvoluntary emigration in other guises.

Finally, the Ch'ao-chou war-lord, General Fang, cracked down. In January 1888, he ordered the abandonment of the credit-ticket system, and later in the year reinforced his opposition to the irregular practices by publicly trying, torturing, and decapitating a broker accused of kidnapping emigrants. The event caused panic among the emigration agents and prompted the foreign consuls, in the interests of their nationals' lucrative passenger trade, to work out with Chinese administrative authorities a set of regulations designed to end nonvoluntary emigration of all kinds.[87] The credit-ticket system remained under ban for several years, but in 1890 it was reported that "the use of such tickets is winked at by the local officials for a money consideration." [88] The regulations remained in effect, however, throughout the period under review. Though somewhat laxly enforced at times, they were strengthened in 1908 by a decree which reaffirmed that emigrants must pay their passage entirely on their own.[89]

With the continued growth of emigration, the emigration firms and agencies multiplied and expanded. During the period before World War I, each main agency in Swatow had contacts with several sub-agencies (the so-called "coolie-hongs"), nominally independent but actually under the direction of the compradore of the main firm. The Chinese officials in charge of emigration got certain sums when a hong was first established, and the main agency was in effect responsible for keeping its hongs within the law. Connected with the larger hongs were lodging houses for the emigrants awaiting departure. The owners of the hongs and the *k'e-t'ou* (emigrants' headmen) kept in close touch with their correspondents in Bangkok and were apprised from time to time of the number of workers needed. The hong owners then ordered a corresponding number of steamship tickets from their main firm, and sent their agents out to round up that many emigrants.

The hongs got a commission of from $20 to $50 per emigrant, according to his health and sturdiness, but from that the hong owner usually had to make money gifts to the emigrant's family and feed the emigrant until "delivery" to the ship.[90]

It was a lucrative business all around. The transport itself was so profitable during the first decade of this century that the company which dominated the Bangkok run, the Nord-Deutscher Lloyd (which had bought out the British shipping firms at the turn of the century), was willing to transport passengers for almost nothing to drive would-be competitors out of business.[91] In 1908, a year when it monopolized the run, Nord-Deutscher Lloyd transported some 74,574 immigrants from Swatow alone, at a net profit of over $5 per head.[92]

Smyth caught the commercial flavor of the emigrant traffic in his cynical remark: "Of raw imports to Siam the Chinaman certainly heads the list." [93]

D. The Magnitude of Chinese Immigration

It is not easy to estimate the magnitude of Chinese immigration prior to the last quarter of the nineteenth century. According to Crawfurd in 1830,[94] passengers formed "the most valuable importation from China into Siam," the annual immigration coming to about 7,000. For roughly the same time (1825–1830), however, Burney estimates the annual Chinese immigration at 2,000 to 3,000,[95] while Malloch puts it at somewhat over 2,000 in one document [96] and 12,000 in another.[97] To this writer, 6,000 to 8,000 would seem the most probable range for immigration during the first part of the third reign.

In 1839, Malcom [98] cites 1,000 as the annual immigration rate, a figure obviously too small even to maintain the China-born Chinese population of Bangkok, which all observers agreed was increasing. On the other hand, Malloch's figures for around 1850, 15,000,[99] would seem rather high in view of more reliable figures for years several decades later. The scattered emigration statistics for various south China ports afford little basis prior to 1882 for estimating the total emigration to Siam. For the period, 1882–1892, Chinese immigrants were arriving in Siam at an annual rate of slightly over 16,000 according to estimates based on emigration statistics for the ports of Swatow, Hai-k'ou and Amoy. From a study of available data, this writer believes that annual figures as high as 16,000 were not reached before 1882, and that the rate of Chinese immigration increased gradually from around 7,000 annually during the third decade of the century, until it had doubled by about 1870, thereafter showing a slight decline until the big jump in 1882.

It is impossible to determine with any degree of accuracy the fate, demographically speaking, of these early immigrants. Several nineteenth-century writers estimated the proportion of Chinese immigrants to Siam that eventually returned to China, but these guesses varied from "not more than ten per cent" to "almost all." A tabulation of passenger traffic to and from Swatow made by this writer for various periods after 1874 shows that the proportion of arrivals from Southeast Asia to departures for Southeast Asia tended to increase throughout the period 1874 to 1917 (i.e., an increasingly large proportion of emigrants returned). For 1874–1881, the proportion averaged approximately 51 per cent. Inasmuch as the largest group of emigrants to Siam came from the Swatow area, it is not unreasonable to project the Swatow findings backwards and apply them to Siamese immigration. If this is done, then the assumption is that the rate of return from Siam to China was somewhat less than half the rate of arrivals at mid-century, increasing to slightly over 50 per cent by the 1874–1881 period. This reasoning leads to the conclusion that the annual Chinese immigration surplus may have been somewhat over 3,000 in the 1820's, increasing gradually to approximately 7,000 by around 1870.

Beginning in 1882, calculations of the magnitude of immigration can be based on firmer ground. In the early years, Chinese customs migration statistics gave returns limited largely to the traffic in foreign (i.e., non-Chinese) bottoms. As of 1882, the great majority of passengers for Siam began traveling on steamers under European flags. This development meant that the Chinese customs returns for each of the south China ports became much more complete at that time. In the late 1880's the port of Bangkok began recording immigration figures, and after 1899 returns for the total deck-passenger traffic between Bangkok and Eastern ports were reported regularly. On the basis of these various statistical series, and of statements in the literature pertinent to migration in Siam aside from Bangkok, this writer has prepared estimates of the annual arrivals and departures of Chinese in Siam for the period beginning in 1882, which material is presented in Table 2. The estimates for arrivals in Siam are more accurate than those for departures. It is believed that the maximum probable error for the *annual* arrival figures approximates 10 per cent for 1882–1892, 7.5 per cent for 1893–1905, and 5 per cent for 1906–1917; while for the annual departure figures, it would be about 18 per cent for 1882–1892, 13 per cent for 1893–1905, and 9 per cent for 1906–1917. The maximum probable errors for the total arrivals and departures *by periods,* however, is much lower, and these figures shall be referred to in the brief analysis to follow.

It should be noted, first of all, that the figures include all ethnic Chinese, including those born in Siam. If, then, as rarely happened, a Siam-born Chinese returned to China and remained there for the rest of his life, he would appear in the figures only once, as a departure. It is still more important to realize that the number of different individuals who arrived in Siam was less than the total arrivals given—and the same is true for departures—because the same individual sometimes traveled back and forth several times during one ten- or fifteen-year period. It can safely be assumed, however, that the overwhelming majority of the 177,000 arrivals during 1882–1892 were first-time arrivals, and that even by 1906–1917 well over half the immigration consisted of first-time arrivals.

There was, to summarize Table 2, a marked increase in the average number of arrivals and departures. The departure rate, however, increased more rapidly with each succeeding period than did the arrival rate. Perhaps the principal reason for this phenomenon is to be found in the increasing proportion of laborers among the arrivals, for more laborers than merchants returned to China permanently after a shorter stay. The three migration periods reviewed here also saw the gradual relaxation of emigration restrictions on the part of the Chinese government. This legalization, paradoxically, facilitated immigration to China (i.e., the return of emigrants) even more than emigration. Emigrants, after all, in committing their crime escaped the reach of Chinese authority, while returnees were *ipso facto* criminals and subject to extortion. In consequence of the proportionally higher rate of return, then, the average annual surplus of Chinese immigrants in Siam increased from one period to the next far less rapidly than did the total migration.

The significance of the total surplus of arrivals should be made clear. The total figure for each period is the number of *actual individuals* added to the Chinese population by immigration, deaths aside. No matter how much the total immigration and emigration figures may have been inflated by individuals traveling back and forth, the difference between them, or surplus, represents discrete individuals. While some Siam-born Chinese returned to China, the vast majority

Table 2. Estimated total arrivals and departures (in thousands) of ethnic Chinese, all Thailand, annually and by periods, 1882–1917 *

Year	Arrivals	Departures	Year	Arrivals	Departures	Year	Arrivals	Departures
1882	17.3	9.3	1893	27.7	11.2	1906 (¼ yr.)	13.1	10.6
1883	18.0	9.9	1894	33.8	16.1	1906/07	68.0	38.9
1884	13.1	8.4	1895	29.0	17.3	1907/08	90.3	53.0
1885	13.9	7.8	1896	27.8	18.2	1908/09	61.6	49.2
1886	14.2	7.9	1897	31.0	18.6	1909/10	66.8	57.4
1887	15.0	9.2	1898	33.6	19.1	1910/11	80.8	73.0
1888	15.7	7.9	1899	33.7	20.7	1911/12	76.7	63.9
1889	18.3	10.1	1900	27.3	19.0	1912/13	72.8	60.5
1890	18.9	10.4	1901	30.4	19.3	1913/14	73.3	57.2
1891	16.0	9.1	1902	36.5	18.8	1914/15	60.1	56.8
1892	17.1	9.4	1903	54.5	29.9	1915/16	69.2	47.1
			1904	44.0	23.7	1916/17	53.4	40.3
			1905	45.8	30.0	1917 (¾ yr.)	29.6	27.6
Total	177.5	99.4	Total	455.1	261.9	Total	815.7	635.5

Period	Total arrivals	Total departures	% Departures of arrivals	Avg. ann. arrivals	Avg. ann. departures	Total surplus of arrivals	Avg. ann. surplus of arrivals
1882–1892	177.5	99.4	56	16.1	9.0	78.1	7.1
1893–1905	455.1	261.9	58	35.0	20.1	193.2	14.9
1906–1917	815.7	635.5	78	68.0	53.0	180.2	15.0

* Based primarily on statistics given in the following serial publications: Amoy Consular Reports 1882–1893; China Trade Returns 1882–1917; Chinese Customs Decennial Reports 1892–1901, 1902–1911, 1912–1921; Kiungchow Consular Reports 1872–1914; Siam Consular Reports 1882–1913; Siam Trade Statistics 1899–1906; Swatow Consular Reports 1882–1914; Thai Customs Statements 1906/07–1917/18; Thailand Statistical Year Books 1916–1923.

also eventually went back to Siam and so do not enter the surplus figures. For all intents and purposes then, the migration surplus for each period represents the net increment (deaths aside) to the population of *China-born* Chinese in Siam during that period.

E. Factors Affecting Migration Rates

Using data concerning the Swatow-Bangkok and Hai-k'ou-Bangkok migrations, it will be attempted here to account for the changes in the rate of migration to and from Siam between 1882 and 1917.[100] In addition to elucidating the reasons why Chinese migrated to, and stayed or did not stay in Siam, this brief survey should demonstrate that, in the last analysis, specific historical events, and not abstract "causes," determine specific trends and the relative magnitude of Chinese migration. The general picture outlined in the previous sections will be assumed rather than belabored. Reference should be made throughout to Chart 1, which graphs the estimated total arrivals and departures of Chinese in Siam for the period in question.

The initial increase in 1882 both in arrivals and departures resulted, of course, from the inauguration of scheduled passenger steam service between Bangkok and Swatow, and the sharp reduction in fares. In 1882–1883, there was competition among various shipping companies in the passenger traffic from Swatow to the Straits, with the consequence for Siam that in order to compete in attracting emigrants the Bangkok Passenger Steamer Company had to advertise fares as low as $1.40.[101] At the end of 1883, however, competition was limited to a few regular lines which colluded in setting fares, so that by the beginning of 1884 the Swatow to Bangkok fare rose to $6, with the consequent decrease in migration.[102] Another important cause of the sharp decline in 1884 was the outbreak of Sino-French hostilities, which especially hindered the immigration from Hainan and led to recruitment in Ch'ao-chou for an army to fight the French.[103] The immigration rate during 1884–1888 was low in comparison with the two previous years in part because the labor market was somewhat flooded after the first rush to Bangkok when steamer service began.[104] The ban on the credit-ticket system at Swatow early in 1888 caused a reduction in immigration from Swatow, but this was compensated for by a tremendous relative increase from Hainan during that year, when steamer passage to Bangkok really got underway.[105]

The rather marked increase of emigration in 1889 reflects the comparatively lax enforcement of the credit-ticket ban in Swatow and the

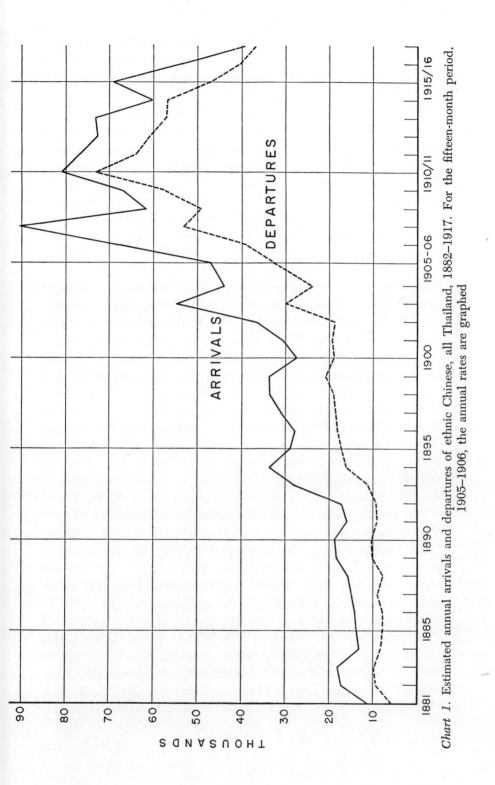

Chart 1. Estimated annual arrivals and departures of ethnic Chinese, all Thailand, 1882–1917. For the fifteen-month period, 1905–1906, the annual rates are graphed

further increase in Hainanese migration.[106] The sharp drop in immigration in 1891 resulted from a business depression in Bangkok, during which many Chinese firms failed and the demand for agricultural and mill labor was depressed.[107]

The spectacular increase in arrivals during 1893–1894 resulted from a coincidence of many factors. First of all, because of heavy frosts in 1893 there was a complete failure of the sweet-potato crop (a major staple for poor peasants) in Ch'ao-chou coupled with poor yields of other agricultural products. Second, construction of the railway between Bangkok and Ayutthaya began in 1892 and required thousands of laborers during the immediately following years; wages for work on the construction gangs—almost all Chinese—were high and rising. Third, the outbreak of bubonic plague in Hongkong in 1894 led to a sharp reduction in emigration from both Hainan and Swatow to Singapore, where emigration from Chinese ports was completely stopped by health officers for several months. At Bangkok, however, there was only a routine medical examination, so many would-be emigrants to Malaya went to Bangkok instead.[108] Finally an eighteenth-century Chinese edict prohibiting emigration and return was repealed in 1893, thus forcing the extortionists in the migration racket onto more tenuous grounds. The sharp rise in departures from Siam may in all probability be attributed to this repeal, inasmuch as extortionists especially belabored the returnees.[109] A decline in arrivals at Siam during 1895 followed the suppression of the plague in Hongkong and the resumption of full-scale emigration from China to the Straits and Deli, while the slight decline the following year must be attributed to the same negative factors plus an excellent crop year in Ch'ao-chou.[110]

The gradual increase in the immigration rate beginning in 1897 was primarily a response to the increasing demand for labor in Siam—for railroad and canal construction and the fast growing number of processing mills—and the consequent increase in wages.[111] There was a spectacular rise in Hainanese immigration in 1898–1899 due to poor crops and high food prices in Hainan during both years.[112] The high immigration rate was abruptly reversed in 1900 because of a coincidence of plague epidemics in both Swatow and Hai-k'ou. This time there were quarantine restrictions on all vessels arriving in Bangkok, with a consequent reduction in the number of direct immigrants to Bangkok from Hai-k'ou of 55 per cent, and from Swatow of 19 per cent.[113] The British Consul at Bangkok in his report for

1900 said that the Chinese secret societies in Siam were supposedly using their influence to keep down the number of immigrating laborers in order to maintain and increase wage rates; [114] but this supposition could hardly be verified even at the time and is quite unnecessary to account for the decrease in immigration recorded for 1900.

The recovery of immigration in 1901 followed the suppression of the plague outbreaks, while the steeper rise in immigration in 1902 was caused mainly by food shortages in Swatow and dire distress in Hainan. In Ch'ao-chou that year crops were poor and rice prices reached unprecedented heights, resulting in a rice shortage at Swatow. At Hainan there was a severe drought throughout the year, and the crop failures forced heavy rice imports at high prices. In consequence there was a 57 per cent increase in the direct emigration from Hai-k'ou to Bangkok. It will be noted that there was no similar increase during 1901–1902 in *departures* from Siam, and the reason would seem to lie in the recrudescence of clan fighting and extortion of returnees at Swatow during those years. [115] The spectacular one-shot increase in both arrivals and departures for 1903 has a simple explanation. Ever since the Scottish Oriental Steamship Company sold its steamers to Nord-Deutscher Lloyd in 1899, the latter company had had a monopoly of the Swatow passenger traffic with Bangkok. In July 1903, however, in the words of the British Consul at Swatow, "a fleet of five steamers, belonging to Messrs. Rickmers and Co., of Bremen, were placed on the Swatow-Bangkok run, and a determined fight ensued, greatly to the advantage of the Swatow coolie, who for some months was able to emigrate at an infinitesimal cost. At one time I believe the fare was 50¢ only, with free food and free barbers, the latter a much appreciated luxury." [116] The ridiculously cheap passage was ended as soon as Nord-Deutscher Lloyd incorporated the rival fleet four months after the competition began. By 1904, fares approximated the old level, and the migration decreased accordingly.

The even more abrupt increase in migration during 1906/07–1907/08 is, against the general background of boom conditions in Bangkok, also attributable to competition on the Swatow-Bangkok passenger run. From June 1906 to January 1908, the Japanese company, Nippon Yusen, entered a fleet and fought hard with Nord-Deutscher Lloyd for the lucrative trade. Both companies carried passengers at a loss—a situation much to the liking of the thrifty Chinese—until after considerable losses an agreement was reached whereby the Japanese firm withdrew. Thereafter fares rose and the migration rates dropped. The drop in immigration for 1908/09 was particularly marked because of excellent rice harvests throughout Ch'ao-chou.[117]

The strong increase in both rates for 1909/10, and the even stronger one in 1910/11 resulted from several concomitant developments. First of all, 1910 was a disastrous crop year in Hainan, and saw a consequent 33 per cent increase in the direct emigration from Hai-k'ou to a prewar high of over 12,000.[118] Then, competition with Nord-Deutscher Lloyd on the Swatow run was renewed early in 1909, when a Bangkok firm with heavy Chinese interests, the Chino-Siam Steam Navigation Company, began operation with six chartered steamers. Another fare war ensued, relieved only in late 1910 when, with the failure of negotiations between the competing companies, Nord-Deutscher Lloyd withdrew several steamers.[119] The complete removal of all legal obstacles to emigration from China provided by the new Ch'ing Code of 1910 [120] may also have contributed to the especially sharp increase in departures recorded for 1910/11. Certainly the imposition of an annual instead of triennial tax on Chinese in Siam—which became known to the Chinese in 1910—and the failure of the consequent Chinese general strike in June of that year led many to return to China, thus contributing to the prewar high in the departure rate reached in 1910/11.

The new annual tax and the eruption of ill-feeling between Chinese and Thai—to be discussed in a later chapter—must also be considered in interpreting the fact that beginning in 1910/11 departures were maintained for several years at an unprecedentedly high proportion of arrivals, as well as in explaining the decline in the rate of arrivals in Siam following 1911. Another, more specific cause of the fall in immigration during 1911/12–1912/13 was the improved crop conditions in Hainan, 1912 bringing the best rice harvest seen in that island in twenty years.[121]

The sharp fall in immigration for 1914/15 was consequent on the withdrawal of the Nord-Deutscher Lloyd and other German shipping after the outbreak of the First World War. Eventually British companies were able to fill a good part of the void in the passenger shipping, and every British ship returning to China was filled with returning Chinese wanting to take advantage of what might be a last chance to get home—thus accounting for the pause in the decline of the departure rate in 1914/15.[122] The rise in immigration 1915/16 is somewhat surprising, but it should be remembered that Siam's economy during the first years of the war was much less dislocated than those of the European colonies in Southeast Asia. Transportation was adequate until the last two years of the war when the demand on British ships for troop transport increased. Furthermore, from May 1915 to March 1916 (almost precisely the Siamese year 1915/16), there was a complete breakdown of social order in Ch'ao-chou and Mei hsien in the interval between the death of General Wu, the old war-lord, and the final success, after considerable fighting, of General Ma. In Hainan, too, there were insurrections, banditry and piracy on an unprecedented scale, which reached a peak in 1916.[123] For the last two years under review, migration rates plummeted, primarily because of the shortage of shipping which became acute in 1917. Furthermore, exchange rates unfavorable to the Chinese emigrants decreased the economic advantage of going abroad.[124]

From this survey, it is apparent, first of all, that the immigration rate was very responsive to specific changes in the prosperity of the emigrant areas in China and of Siam. Of all conditions in the emigrant areas, the state of the crops (in turn dependent mainly on the weather) seems to be the most important single factor, while for Siam, more generalized economic conditions, as reflected in the demand for labor, were of primary importance. Second, rates of both arrivals and departures were especially sensitive to major fluctuations in fare. It will be noted that when the passenger traffic to and from Siam began to take on really mass proportions early in the twentieth century, competition for the extremely lucrative traffic became intermittently intense. The three peaks in both rates (1903, 1907/08, and 1910/11) were the years of lowest fares. It is probably safe to surmise that, in the absence of competition to Nord-Deutscher Lloyd during the first decade of this century, the total migration to Siam prior to 1917 would have been considerably lower. Third, the rate of departures from Siam was less responsive to specific events and conditions in Siam and China than was the arrival rate. Except for the three peaks due to cheap fares, the departure rate generally tended to follow along after the arrival rate, but with fewer sharp fluctuations.

The first two of these conclusions lend support to the generalized statement that the bulk of the immigrants to Siam were poor, had been agricultural workers or peasants in China, and came to Siam to work initially as common laborers, and above all to the contention that the desire for economic improvement was the chief motivation for emigration from China to Siam during this period.

F. The Growth of the Chinese Population in Siam

Available estimates and statistics of the population of overseas Chinese in Southeast Asia are, in general, somewhat less than satisfactory. They are perhaps least trustworthy in the case of Siam. This state of affairs is made worse by the fact that the most widely quoted of the earlier estimates of the number of Chinese in Siam are in all probability the least accurate of those available. In any case, the literature abounds with estimates relative to the ethnic composition of Siam's population, and there were even a few attempts at census taking prior to the First World War. Since the available figures are extremely divergent and contradictory, it is misleading at best to quote only two or three of the more accessible statistics with no attempt at reconciliation or appraisal. The attempt is made here, on admittedly inferior data, to define probable limits to the size of the Chinese population in Siam from the beginning of the third reign to 1917. This undertaking should not only help in understanding the growth and development of Chinese society in Thailand but also provide some of the "first facts" necessary in treating problems of more theoretical interest. In all considerations of acculturation and assimilation, for instance, the size of the various societies in contact and the relative proportion of the carriers of different juxtaposed cultures are of utmost importance.

Of the many estimates of the Chinese population of Siam for years prior to 1917, those worthy of any consideration are given in Table 3. The results of the various "censuses" taken during the first decade of the twentieth century are not given in this table but will be brought into the discussion to follow.

Table 3. Selected estimates of the Chinese and total populations of Thailand prior to 1917 *

Approx. year	Chinese	Total (all races)	Source
1822	440,000	2,790,500	Crawfurd 1830, II, 224 †
1827	800,000	3,252,650	Malloch 1852, 73 ‡
1835	500,000	3,620,000	Edmund Roberts, from Malcom 1839, 146
1839	450,000	3,000,000	Malcom 1839, 145
1849	1,100,000	3,653,150	Malloch 1852, 73
1854	1,500,000	6,000,000	Pallegoix 1854, I, 8
1858	—	5,000,000	Auguste Heurtier, from Girard 1860, 5

Approx. year	Chinese	Total (all races)	Source
1862	1,750,000	7,000,000	Werner 1873, 259 §
1864	—	4,000,000	*Siam Consular Report* 1864
1878	1,750,000	7,750,000	Rousset 1878, 106 ‖
1885	1,500,000	5,900,000	Rosny 1885, 116
1890	3,000,000	10,000,000	Gaston Rautier, from Hallett 1890, 461
1891	500,000	—	Gordon 1891, 289
1892	1,500,000	5,900,000	Hoeylaerts 1892, 10
1894	900,000	9,000,000	*Directory for Bangkok and Siam* 1894, 8
1900	400,000	—	Campbell 1902, 268 #
1900	600,000	—	Raquez 1903, 434
1903	700,000	5,000,000	Little 1903, 261
1903	2,000,000	6,300,000	Mury 1903, 54
1903	2,500,000	—	Gottwaldt 1903, 75, 89
1903	480,000	5,029,000	*Directory for Bangkok and Siam* 1903, 119 **
1907	1,400,000	6,000,000	*Siam Free Press* 1907 ††
1907	2,755,807	—	"Statistik der Chinesen im Auslande" 1907–1908, 277
1910	1,200,000	—	*Survey of Chinese Industry and Commerce* 1951 ‡‡
1912	400,000	6,020,000	Graham 1912, 109
1912	650,000	—	*China Year Book* 1912, 35
1916	1,500,000	—	*China Year Book* 1916, 37

* Extremely deviant estimates, such as that of Bacon's—35 million for Siam proper without dependencies (Bacon 1892, 15)—have not been included. The many estimates in the literature which merely accept some other authority's earlier figures have also been omitted. In this category, for instance, fall the figures of Bowring.

† Crawfurd made an earlier estimate—700,000 Chinese out of a total population of 5.1 million—which he later revised to the figures shown above. Crawfurd 1823, 102–103.

‡ Malloch earlier made another estimate for 1827—1.5 million Chinese out of a total population of 5.0 million—which he later discarded. Malloch 1827, 232.

§ Werner estimated the population of the whole country at 7–8 million, of which one-quarter were Chinese.

‖ Rousset estimated the indigenous population at 6 million, plus 1.5 million Chinese and 250,000 Sino-Siamese métis.

The 400,000 figure is based on the estimated number of Chinese paying the poll tax in 1900. The estimate is not Campbell's own but that of an anonymous authority in whom Campbell is "loath not to place implicit credence."

** This estimate is for only certain of the monthon, but of the excluded monthon only Nakhonsithammarat has any appreciable Chinese population. See below in the text.

†† Quoted in "L'émigration Asiatique" 1907, 490.

‡‡ *T'ai-kuo hua-ch'iao kung-shang-yeh ch'üan-mao* 1951.

To consider first and very briefly the total population of Siam, the Central Statistical Service of the Thai Government has computed estimates for most years since 1902, based on the national censuses reworked for the earlier years.[125] The rate of natural increase was lower in the nineteenth century than in the first decades of the twentieth for at least two reasons: (1) the annual increase through immigration was smaller, (2) the death rate was considerably higher, inasmuch as public health, the control of epidemic diseases in particular, advanced only in the first decades of the twentieth century. On the basis of statements in the literature on nineteenth-century conditions and the twentieth-century estimates by the Central Statistical Service, this writer estimates the total population of Siam to be approximately as follows:

1825	4,750,000	1900	7,320,000
1850	5,200,000	1910	8,305,000
1875	5,950,000	1917	9,232,000

The three nineteenth-century figures given here may be considered too high, especially in view of the earliest estimates shown in Table 3. But to accept such figures as Crawfurd's or Malcom's requires the admission of a natural-increase rate wholly improbable for premodern Siam. One is forced to the conclusion that the contemporary estimates for the first half of the nineteenth century are almost certainly too low. Those for the second half, on the other hand, with the two obvious exceptions, are at least within the realm of possibility.

In the case of contemporary estimates of the Chinese population of Siam, most observers erred on the high side. It will be instructive to examine the estimates of Crawfurd and Malloch in particular, since they present the most complete data. According to Crawfurd:

The whole number [of Chinese] assessed to the capitation tax within the Siamese territory, Malayan States excluded, was given to us at one hundred thousand. Were the Chinese population of Siam, *which they are not,* constituted as under ordinary circumstances, this would make their whole number amount to about four hundred and twenty thousand. . . . The Chinese settlers within the tributary Malay States, engaged in traffic, or in working gold and tin, have been estimated at twenty thousand.[126]

The concrete data that Crawfurd gathered, then, were that there were about 20,000 Chinese altogether in the Siamese Malay States and 100,000 tax-paying Chinese in the rest of Siam. The Chinese head tax was paid by all males over twenty years of age[127] who wore the queue, i.e., who still considered themselves Chinese. It is reasonable to conclude, then, that there were not more than 100,000 China-born Chinese in all Siam at that time. The number of local-born Chinese, i.e., individuals born of a Chinese father who still considered themselves Chinese, could under no circumstances have numbered 320,000. Crawfurd himself, by qualifying his calculation with the clause in italics, admitted that it was foolish to multiply 100,000 by 4.2, his guess as to the average family size in Siam; yet for some reason he persisted in the final estimate of 440,000 Chinese in Siam. Actually, of course, there were *very* few China-born Chinese women in Siam; most of the roughly 100,000 Chinese males over twenty were unmarried or married to Thai women. Of the offspring of Sino-Thai marriages (lukjin), the majority remained Chinese, granted, but many discarded the queue and became Thai. Those male lukjin over twenty who kept the queue were required to pay the tax and so must have been included in the original estimate of 120,000. Consequently, to obtain the total Chinese population one must add to 120,000 an estimate of all unassimilated female lukjin and of unassimilated male lukjin under twenty. A figure of not more than 80,000 should certainly cover this group. Making allowances for tax evasion and the many other possible errors, the total Chinese population in Siam, circa 1822, could not have surpassed 250,000, and was probably closer to 200,000.

Malloch's figure for 1849 (1,100,000) is even more obviously inflated. In an appendix he gives the population by race of over eighty cities and towns in Siam, and the list includes every town of any importance.[128] Excluding from this list towns outside the borders of present-day Thailand, i.e., those in what is now the Federation of Malaya, Cambodia, or Laos, the total estimated urban Chinese population of Siam in 1849, according to Malloch, was 199,344. The figures given for most of the towns far upcountry from Bangkok are clearly inflated (Lamphun, for instance, is shown to have a population of 48,050, of whom 6,050 were supposedly Chinese, while even today Lamphun is a town of less than 10,000), such that the total of Malloch's figures is unquestionably an overestimate. Taking it at its face value, however, the question arises where the other 900,000 Chinese in Malloch's estimate of 1,100,000 lived. Surely in the Siam of 1850 there were more Chinese living in cities and towns than in rural areas. Even allowing another 125,000 for the agricultural Chinese in the Gulf region, the total Chinese population a hundred years ago, as of present-day boundaries, could not have exceeded 325,000. It will be seen that Malloch's total estimate bears no recognizable relationship to the specific figures he also included.

The reason for the overestimations made by Crawfurd, Malloch, and most of the other nineteenth-century "authorities" is not hard to find. They spent most of their time in Bangkok; excursions elsewhere, if any, were to towns in Lower Siam and along the Gulf. The Chinese, of course, were concentrated in Bangkok and in other towns of Lower Siam and the Gulf coast; a fairly accurate estimation of the proportion of the Chinese in these areas applied to the whole country led naturally to gravely inflated estimates of the total Chinese population. Ratzel was the first observer to suspect that these estimates were inflated, pointing out that visitors to Bangkok were probably overly impressed by the numbers and industriousness of the Chinese there.[129] Graham in 1912 gave Ratzel what was perhaps an overenthusiastic second, in these words:

The number of Chinese has been much exaggerated. Pallegoix estimated it at 1,500,000 and more recent observers have gone further, some of them not hesitating to state that half the population of the country is Chinese. Such estimates, however, have usually been based upon the number of Chinese to be seen in the streets of Bangkok where the Chinese element is at its strongest, and it has too often been taken for granted that because every other man encountered in the streets of the capital wears a pigtail, therefore the Celestial must be equally prevalent in other parts of the country. As a matter of fact the Chinese number about a quarter of the inhabitants of Bangkok, but this proportion diminishes rapidly as the distance from the capital increases and, except where the tin-mining and rice-milling industries have caused the formation of separate colonies as at Puket and Petriu, is an almost negligible quantity in most of the rural districts.[130]

This argument is certainly somewhat overstated, but it should suffice to remove the figures of Pallegoix, Werner, Rousset, Rosny, Rautier,[131] Mury, and Gottwaldt from those deserving serious consideration. The 1907 statistic in seven significant figures, given in all seriousness in the pages of a German learned journal, can only have been the wish-fulfillment fantasy of a frustrated pedant.

Gordon, writing in 1891, was another of the more acute observers who felt that "the number of Chinese are apt to be exaggerated."[132] He stated flatly, "It is impossible that there can be more than 500,000 Chinese in Siam," a figure, indeed, that seems highly probable. Campbell's anonymous authority, basing his estimate on the number of Chinese paying the poll tax in 1900, arrived at 400,000 for the whole country, but Campbell, according to his own experience, thought this an understatement.[133] Raquez's estimate for the same year (600,000) is in all probability nearer the correct figure, especially since, when he was in Siam, he paid close attention to matters of population and talked with Chinese leaders.

The first Thai census attempts were piecemeal. The census of 1904 covered only twelve monthon plus the nonurban part of Krungthep monthon. The census of 1909 covered the urban part of Krungthep, i.e., Bangkok. Other monthon were covered for the first time in the 1919 census. The 1904 and 1909 censuses, however, are of special interest here because of the definition of Chinese adhered to:

In taking the census with respect to the Chinese element in the population, the plan adopted has been to go by the fashion of wearing the hair and the dress of the individual, and to categorize all males who wear the queue, whatever degree, as "Chinese," and all females who dress in the Siamese fashion as "Siamese," with the exception of those who dress in the Chinese fashion and come from China.[134]

The census takers, then, attempted to record as Chinese all who showed by outward appearance that they considered themselves Chinese. Chinese population as recorded in the 1904 and 1909 censuses for 13 monthons are given in Table 4. Fortunately, as will be seen, the monthons not included in the census were those with small Chinese populations. By estimating what the census would have found in those monthon (i.e., by taking proportions of the 1919 census figures for those monthon similar to the proportion of the 1904–1919 census figures for the other monthon), it is possible to conclude that the total count for the Chinese in Siam, according to the 1904 census, would have been somewhat less than 400,000 (see the second column of figures in Table 4).

The 1904 census results, assuming that the aim was to record as Chinese all those who considered themselves Chinese, was certainly an undercount for several reasons. First of all, the criterion of "Chineseness" quoted above is not adequate to decide the "race" of children and adolescents. Chinese children of both pure and mixed marriages usually did not wear clothing or headdresses to distinguish them from Thai children, and so in most cases they were probably recorded as Thai. Second, in most cases, the census was conducted by amphoe officers who knew no Chinese; the coverage of many Chinese house-

Table 4. Population of Chinese in Thailand, by monthon, 1904

Region and monthon °	1904 census †	Rounded and complete estimates, 1904	% of total Chinese in each region
Lower Siam			
Nakhonchaisi	33,992	34,000	
Auytthaya	18,615	18,600	
Krungthep	197,918	185,000 ‡	
Total		237,600	59.8 (Lower)
Middle Siam			
Nakhonsawan	6,283	6,300	
Phitsanulok	4,442	4,450	
Phetchabun	136	150	
Total		10,900	2.7 (Middle)
North Siam			
Phayap	—	5,000 §	1.3 (North)
Northeast Siam			
Nakhonratchasima	2,431	2,450 §	
Isan	—	3,000 §	
Udonthani	—	1,500 §	
Total		6,950	1.7 (Northeast)
Southeast Siam			
Prajinburi	35,912	35,950	
Janthaburi	10,080	10,100	
Total		46,050	11.6 (Southeast)
Southwest Siam			
Ratchaburi	38,767	38,750	9.8 (Southwest)
South Siam			
Chumphon	3,129	3,150	
Nakhonsithammarat	9,303	9,300	
Phuket	32,408	32,400	
Saiburi (part)	—	7,000 §	
Total		51,850	13.1 (South)
Total, all Siam (post-1907 boundaries)		397,100	100.0

° Monthons most of which were ceded to France or Britain in 1907 are not included. The estimate for Saiburi is only for that part of the monthon not ceded to

holds was therefore probably less complete than that of Thai house-holds. Third, the traditional Chinese avoidance of government officers in all probability entailed a proportionately greater avoidance of the census takers on the part of the Chinese than of the Thai. The fact that the same official to whom Chinese paid the triennial head tax took the census certainly reinforced the Chinese tendency toward evasion.

There is no reason to assume a geographical differential for these factors, however, and so the percentage distribution of the Chinese by region (see the last column of Table 4) presents a fairly reliable picture of the regional distribution of the Chinese population in Siam. It will be noted that some 94 per cent of the Chinese in 1904 lived in the four regions bordering the Gulf of Siam, the majority in Lower Siam with a secondary concentration in South Siam.

Revenue from the Chinese head tax could also provide a clue as to the size of the Chinese population in Siam up to 1909, were figures available. While unofficial estimates of the revenue are reported for several years, they are too unreliable to serve any purpose in this regard. Actual revenues are not reported in any of the accessible literature, but expected revenues according to the official budget are available for 1903 and 1909; the figures respectively are 792,411 baht and 980,600 baht.[135] The tax was 4 baht and with .25 baht administration fees. This writer's impression is that the fees were included in the income of the various amphoe offices and not sent in as poll-tax revenues. If this were true, then the number officially estimated to pay the tax in cash was 198,102 in 1903, and 245,150 in 1909. Only men over twenty paid the tax, and some of these may still have been paying in kind as of these years; tax evasion was also prevalent. While these figures include some local-born Chinese men, they exclude all China-born women and children and such of the China-born men who managed to evade the tax. They may be taken, then, as *minimum* figures for the number of China-born Chinese in those years.

Britain in 1907. The total figures, then, are for Siam in 1904 as of the post-1907 boundaries.

† Source: Collet 1911, 61–63; also in *Directory for Bangkok and Siam* 1907, 113; 1910, 158. The figure for Krungthep monthon is composed of the census results for the city of Bangkok as of 1909 plus those for the remainder of the monthon for 1904. The breakdown is not available.

‡ The combined 1904–1909 census figure has here been adjusted to apply to 1904.

§ Estimates by the writer based, proportionally according to the other figures, on the 1919 census results by monthon.

There remain the migration statistics to take into account. From the discussion earlier in this chapter it should be apparent that the surplus of Chinese immigration or emigration is approximately equal in size to the addition of China-born Chinese to the population of Thailand. Estimates of the number of China-born Chinese for every year following 1882 can be made, then, given an original estimate as to the size of the China-born Chinese population of Siam at the beginning of 1882 and given death-rate estimates. Additions to the China-born population can be made only by immigration, subtractions only by emigration or death. This writer has attempted a model of the growth of the China-born Chinese population of Siam from 1882 on; the results are graphed in Chart 2.

There is not space here to describe in any detail the assumptions made and steps taken in constructing this model. Briefly, however, upper and lower limits of possible death rates were estimated for the various periods, and the necessary calculations made for the period 1825–1955 assuming a China-born population of 100,000 in 1825, using different series of death rates within the limits of possibility. The resulting series that most closely conformed to a considered adjustment of all reliable estimates and census results throughout the period was selected as the most probable model. It should be pointed out that the decisive variables are the immigration surplus and the death rate. The precise figure used as the China-born Chinese population in 1825 is unimportant for the model after 1882, since the great majority of the China-born Chinese living in 1825 were dead by 1882.

Immigration figures have already been discussed, and so it remains to say a word about the assumptions involved in estimating death rates prior to 1917. It was assumed, first of all, that the China-born Chinese death rate for each age group was higher than the Thai death rate because (1) the China-born Chinese were, in Siam, predominantly urban while the Thai were predominantly rural, so that the Chinese were more susceptible to diseases of high incidence in cities and towns (e.g., tuberculosis, cholera, plague), and (2) the China-born Chinese, as newcomers to Siam, had not developed antibodies or resistance to diseases common in Thailand but rare in China (e.g., malaria, dengue fever, cholera). There is no question but that the various epidemics of plague and cholera during the period under review hit the China-born population in Thailand harder than the local-born population.[136]

The other major factor to be considered is age distribution. At all times, but especially prior to 1917, the bulk of the China-born popula-

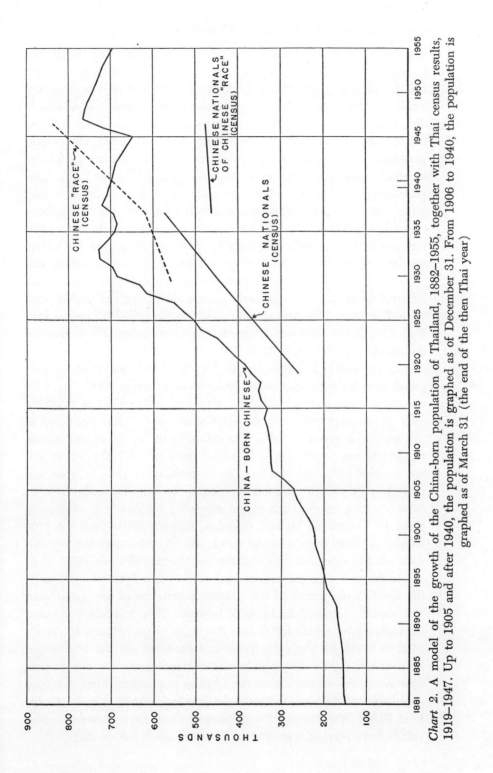

Chart 2. A model of the growth of the China-born population of Thailand, 1882–1955, together with Thai census results, 1919–1947. Up to 1905 and after 1940, the population is graphed as of December 31. From 1906 to 1940, the population is graphed as of March 31 (the end of the then Thai year)

tion consisted of men between the ages of 20 and 50. The proportion of children was extremely small when compared with that of the general population, while the number of old people was comparatively small, too, because of the Chinese practice of returning to China to die. Therefore, the impact of the highest age-specific death rates—infant mortality and old age—was much less than among the general population. On the other hand, the low rates for the late childhood and early adolescent years also were less applicable to the China-born population than to the whole population. On the whole, it would seem that age distribution rather strongly favored the China-born Chinese, i.e., led to a lower total death rate than would have been the case with a normally distributed population, in spite of the higher median age for the China-born population. A balancing out of differential factors leaves little basis for assuming death rates much different from that of the general population during the period prior to 1917, at least. The rates actually used for the 1882–1917 period vary from 35 to 28 per 1000, with a general downward trend. The average of the annual rates used was 31.9.

It is impossible to calculate the growth of the local-born Chinese population, for the many rates involved—of marriage, birth, assimilation, death, and so on—cannot be estimated on the basis of available data. A probable series of estimates, based on the data evaluated in this section, is given in Table 5 to complete the model of the growth of the Chinese population in Thailand prior to 1917. The writer will not attempt a defense of these figures here, other than to point out that (1) they yield totals for every period similar to those shown to be most probable on the basis of the foregoing analysis of the estimates given by Crawfurd, Malloch, Gordon, Raquez, Little, and the 1904 census, (2) they form a *logical series*, and (3) this series is congruent with reliable estimates and statistics for the period since 1917.

The foregoing considerations and calculations "prove" little as to the absolute magnitude of the Chinese population in any given year. The model presented in Table 5, however, does indicate at various intervals figures which fall within the range of probability; the range itself is broad for the early years and narrower for the later years. Seen in this light a few conclusions can confidently be drawn even concerning the magnitude of the Chinese population. First, the total population of Chinese cannot have reached a million prior to the First World War. Second, the number of China-born Chinese in Siam cannot have reached a quarter of a million much before 1900.

Table 5. A probable model of the growth of the Chinese population in Thailand, 1825–1917 (in thousands)

Year	Est. total of China-born Chinese	Decennial rate of increase since previous date	Est. total of local-born Chinese	Decennial rate of increase	Est. total of all Chinese	Decennial rate of increase	Est. total population of Siam	% China-born Chinese of total	% all Chinese of total
		%		%		%			
1825	100		130		230		4,750	2.10	4.8
1850	110	3.9	190	16.2	300	11.6	5,200	2.12	5.8
1860	118	7.3	219	15.3	337	12.3	5,450	2.17	6.2
1870	131	11.0	252	15.1	383	13.6	5,775	2.27	6.6
1880	146	11.5	289	14.7	435	13.6	6,200	2.35	7.0
1890	166	13.7	331	14.5	497	14.3	6,670	2.49	7.5
1900	222	33.7	386	16.6	608	22.3	7,320	3.03	8.3
1910	325	46.4	467	21.0	792	30.3	8,305	3.91	9.5
1917	349	10.2	557	27.4	906	20.6	9,232	3.78	9.8

The model is most useful, however, in indicating trends. This writer is fairly confident that no model congruent with the available data (however different in absolute figures), could show significantly different trends in the growth of the Chinese population. Among the conclusions which might be drawn concerning the growth of the Chinese population in Siam beginning with the second quarter of the nineteenth century up to the end of the "natural" migration period towards the end of the First World War are the following. (1) The number of all Chinese in Siam steadily increased throughout the period. (2) The rate of increase in the Chinese population was consistently higher than the rate of increase in the total population of Siam throughout the period, so that the proportion of Chinese steadily increased. (3) The rate of increase in the China-born population increased, decade by decade but only until about 1910, when the rate began to decline. (4) The proportion of China-born Chinese in the total population increased steadily, decade by decade, until about 1910, when the proportion began to fall off. (5) The *rate* of increase in the local-born Chinese population began to increase only after the effect of the mass migration beginning in 1882 was felt, but then continued to the end of the period.

G. The Expansion of Chinese Settlement

At the beginning of the nineteenth century, the Chinese population in Siam was almost entirely confined to the coastal regions and the lower reaches of the major rivers. There were Chinese settlements in virtually every town along the Gulf coast from Trat (then known as Thungyai) in the far southeast on around to Saiburi in the far south. In central Siam there were Chinese settlements up the Bangpakong River as far as Prajinburi, up the Jaophraya and Thajin rivers as far as Paknampho, and up the Maeklǫng River somewhat beyond Kanjanaburi. There is no reason to doubt that some overseas Chinese traders had penetrated the north and northeast and were engaged to some extent in the interregional caravan trade. But neither material remains nor local documentation are found any place in Thailand north or east of Paknampho which indicate a permanent Chinese settlement in the upcountry region as early as Rama I's reign.[137] The overland trade from the north was, during the nineteenth century, in the hands of Yunnanese, whose caravans not only connected the Lao principalities with southwest China but also with one another.[138] The Yunnanese or "overland Chinese" are distinguished in the colloquial

Thai language from the overseas Chinese, the former being called
Hǫ and the latter Jek.

Within the region of overseas Chinese settlement, Bangkok was
clearly the chief center of Chinese concentration. The Chinese probably constituted over half the population in the capital throughout
the first half of the nineteenth century. Happily, outside observers
during this period are in fairly close agreement as to the size of the
Chinese population of Bangkok. Various estimates follow:

Year	Chinese Population	Total Population	Source	
1822	31,000	50,000	Crawfurd	(1830, II, 121, 215)
1826	60,700	134,090	Malloch	(1852, 70)
1828	36,000	77,300	Tomlin	(1844, 184)
1839	60,000	100,000	Malcom	(1839, 139)
1843	70,000	350,000	Neale	(1852, 29)
1849	81,000	160,154	Malloch	(1852, 70)
1854	200,000	404,000	Pallegoix	(1854, I, 60)
1855	200,000	300,000	Bowring	(1857, I, 85, 394)

The figures given by Tomlin actually totaled 401,300 for the city,
of which no less than 360,000 were supposedly Chinese.[139] Tomlin
explained that he obtained a copy of a "census" of the city conducted
in 1828 by the government and that "at first sight of it we were quite
astounded," as indeed all subsequent readers have been. A summary of
his figures follows:

	Tomlin's figures as given	The same, corrected
Chinese (paying tax)	310,000	31,000
Descendants of Chinese	50,000	5,000
Laos	16,000	16,000
Siamese	8,000	8,000
Peguans	5,000	5,000
Others	12,300	12,300
Total	401,300	77,300

The fact that Crawfurd mentions 31,000 tax-paying Chinese for Bangkok at roughly the same period [140] makes it fairly obvious that Tomlin's
"astounding" figures resulted from a copyist's error, namely the addition of an extra zero to each of the first two figures. The corrected
series—36,000 Chinese, 24,000 Thai and 17,300 others—makes eminent
sense and, in fact, forms the best breakdown available for the first
half of the nineteenth century. Neale's figure for the total population
of the city is clearly inflated, as are Pallegoix's and Bowring's estimates

for both the Chinese and the total population. And although Malloch estimated in 1852 that the total 1826 population was 134,090, earlier he had estimated the 1827 population at 100,000, the "greater part" Chinese.[141] It is perhaps reasonable to conceive of Bangkok's Chinese population as increasing from less than 25,000 to 70,000 or more during the first half of the nineteenth century.

It may seem strange that the Chinese outnumbered the Thai in the Thai capital city, but most nineteenth-century observers attest the fact. For the 1820's, Finlayson wrote: "In the most populous parts of . . . [Bangkok, the Chinese] would appear to constitute at least three-fourths of the whole population. . . . There are but very few parts of Bangkok where the Chinese do not appear to exceed the natives in number. . . ."[142] Crawfurd, too, stated: "It is commonly computed that one-half of the population of the capital is composed of Chinese; a statement which, from what we observed ourselves, I do not consider exaggerated."[143] Malloch's figures for 1826 show 45 per cent of Bangkok's population to be Chinese,[144] while the American missionaries resident in the city in 1835 estimated that the majority of the population of Bangkok and vicinity were Chinese.[145] In 1839, Malcom, who "took some pains on the subject [of the Bangkok population], inquiring of the chief men, counting the houses in some sections, ascertaining the real number of priests, etc.," was of the opinion that Bangkok and the immediate vicinity contained a population of 100,000 of whom 60,000 were "Chinese and descendants."[146] Malloch's statistics for 1849 gave slightly over 50 per cent of the population as Chinese and under 35 per cent Thai,[147] while Pallegoix's for about the same time showed 49.5 per cent Chinese and 35.9 per cent Thai.[148]

The consensus in this regard of all writers on Siam during the first three reigns cannot be questioned. Most premodern oriental capitals consisted of the court and a surrounding host providing services of all kinds for the court. The members of the court itself—the king and his household, the aristocracy and bureaucracy serving in the central government—and many of their immediate retainers were Thai; but most of the slaves serving the court were non-Thai war prisoners and descendants—Burmese, Mons, Cambodians, Malays, and so on. Physicians, astrologers, artisans, and others providing skilled services were mainly foreigners of one ethnic group or another, Chinese predominating. Bangkok, furthermore, because of the heavy mercantile interests of the first three Jakkri kings, was somewhat peculiar among oriental capitals in having a large commercial sector in its population, and the great bulk of this group was Chinese. The Thai, of course, were not free to move to the capital, even if attracted. The great majority of their number were clients or retainers and slaves of patrons and masters in the elite class. Even the freemen attached to those aristocrats and nobles with duties in the capital were mainly left on the landed estates of their patrons in the provinces. Under these circumstances, Chinese immigrants, whose main port of entry was Bangkok and who remained entirely outside the systems of patronage, corvée, and slavery, readily filled most of the demands of the court and of the capital's trade.

Contemporary reports in the 1830's agree that Teochius were the largest of the Chinese speech groups in Bangkok. One writer called them "much the most numerous"; [149] another stated that "the Chinese residents [of Bangkok] are chiefly from Teo-chew." [150] Hokkiens were the next most numerous speech group in the capital. It is significant that in Bangkok the first Protestant missionaries to work among the Chinese, the Baptists, chose the Teochius, while the second Protestant group, that of the American Board of Commissioners for Foreign Missions, chose the Hokkiens. [151] In 1836, Mr. Johnson of the latter mission estimated the number of Hokkiens in Bangkok and vicinity at 20,000 to 50,000. [152] The great majority of the Chinese temples in Bangkok dating back to the first half of the nineteenth century are Teochiu and Hokkien. It is clear, however, that by the 1830's the proportion of Teochius was increasing as against that of Hokkiens in the city's population. Gutzlaff stated that Chinese "come in great numbers from Chao-chow-fu [Ch'ao-chou]" while "emigrants from Tang-an [T'ung-an] district in Fuhkeen are few, mostly sailors or merchants." [153] Next in numerical importance after the Teochius and Hokkiens came the Hainanese and Cantonese, with the Hakkas in last place. For an eleven-month period in 1835–1836, Dr. Daniel B. Bradley kept a record of the speech group of the 934 Chinese treated at a missionary hospital in Bangkok, and of these 713 were Teochius, 150 Hokkiens, 51 Hainanese, 15 Cantonese, and 5 Hakkas. [154] These proportions are indicative, though hardly conclusive for obvious reasons.

Perhaps as early as the first decade of the nineteenth century, Teochiu agriculturalists began to settle in rural areas back from the seaports and river towns. As plantation agriculture expanded, the rural Teochiu population increased, but this settlement was for the most part limited to the areas around the earlier settlements of

Chinese traders. The most rapid rural development was in the valleys of the Janthaburi, Bangpakong, lower Jaophraya, Thajin, and Mae-klǫng rivers.

When Dr. Bradley made a trip to Southeast Siam in 1836, he was "thronged with wondering multitudes . . . [of] Tachu and Hokian-Chinese" in Janthaburi town, while up-river in a rural area he found the land "almost wholly occupied by Tachu-Chinese, [who] . . . raise chiefly sugar-cane, pepper and tobacco." [155] It is typical of the upper Gulf region during the nineteenth century that Hokkiens almost never moved out of the major trading towns, while Teochius were found in both towns and their rural hinterland. Hokkiens were, as Gutzlaff remarked, almost exclusively merchants and sailors. Most of the Hokkien temples in Siam are dedicated to T'ien-hou Sheng-mu (C 39), the Holy Mother and Empress of Heaven, who is the patron deity of sailors. Old Hokkien temples are still standing all around the Gulf and in trading towns of the river deltas, but not a single Hokkien temple is to be found in Siam farther north than Ayutthaya. The Cantonese, while lacking the more exclusively seafaring orientation of the Hokkiens, seldom settled outside the major towns because of their occupational specialization in artisan and mechanical trades.

It was, in fact, neither the Teochius nor the Hokkiens or Cantonese who were the real pioneers in upcountry Siam, but rather the Hainanese. The oldest Chinese temples in Paknampho and everywhere north and east of that communications center are those dedicated to Shui-wei Niang (C 40), the Hainanese deity par excellence. In Khorat in the northeast and in numerous towns on the Nan, Yom and Wang rivers in Middle and North Siam are found nineteenth-century temples to this goddess. It is perhaps significant that the oldest and largest Hainanese temple in Bangkok is located in Samsen near the old wharf from which all upriver traffic began. By the wording on the tablets and inscriptions in upcountry Hainanese temples, it is clear that they are offshoots of the "mother" temple in Samsen. The major area of Hainanese settlement was the Yom and Nan River valleys above Paknampho (see Map 5). The stories told about the days of their parents and grandparents by old Chinese still living substantiate other indications that every town along the Nan River from Phijit up to Nan and on the Yom River from Sukhothai up to Phrae were first settled by Hainanese. Some of these towns were completely new settlements made by Hainanese pioneers, e.g., Khlǫngtan (also known as Sisamrong, in jangwat Sukhothai on the Yom River) and Thalǫ

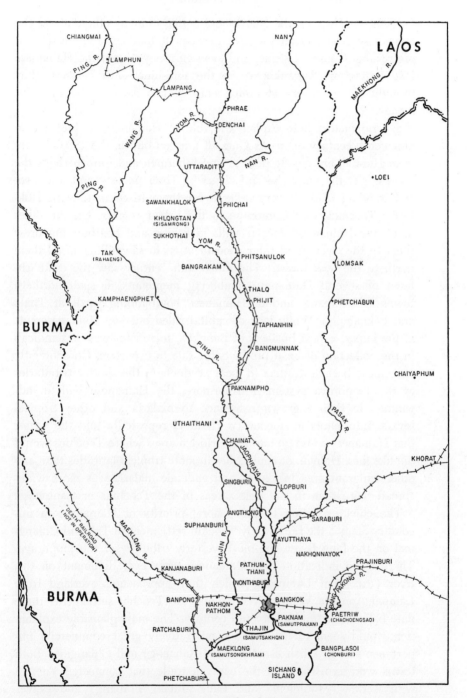

CHIANGMAI
PING R.
LAMPHUN
LAMPANG
PHRAE
DENCHAI
YOM R.
UTTARADIT
NAN R.
PING R.
SAWANKHALOK
KHLONGTAN
(SISAMRONG)
SUKHOTHAI
PHICHAI
WANG R.
YOM R.
TAK
(RAHAENG)
BANGRAKAM
PHITSANULOK
KAMPHAENGPHET
THALO
PHIJIT
NAN
LAOS
MAEKHONG R.
•LOEI
LOMSAK
•PHETCHABUN
BURMA
PING R.
•TAPHANHIN
•BANGMUNNAK
CHAIYAPHUM
PAKNAMPHO
PASAK R.
UTHAITHANI •
CHAINAT
KHORAT
SINGBURI
CHAOPRAYA R.
LOPBURI
"DEATH" RAILROAD
(NOT IN OPERATION)
MAEKLONG R.
ANGTHONG
SUPHANBURI
THAJIN R.
SARABURI
AYUTTHAYA
NAKHONNAYOK•
PRAJINBURI
KANJANABURI
PATHUM-
THANI
NONTHABURI
BANGPAKONG R.
BURMA
BANPONG
NAKHON-
PATHOM
BANGKOK
PAKNAM
(SAMUTPRAKAN)
PAETRIW
(CHACHOENGSAO)
RATCHABURI
THAJIN
(SAMUTSAKHON)
BANGPLASOI
(CHONBURI)
MAEKLONG
(SAMUTSONGKHRAM)
SICHANG
ISLAND
PHETCHABURI

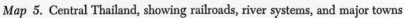

Map 5. Central Thailand, showing railroads, river systems, and major towns

(in jangwat Phijit on the Nan River), while in many others it was the Hainanese who started the first permanent markets and introduced pig raising, Chinese cuisine, and even currency. When the Hainanese first arrived in Sawankhalok in the mid-nineteenth century, they brought along pottery gambling chips which came to be used for money.

Several factors help explain the role of Hainanese as pioneers in nineteenth-century Siam. As Gutzlaff pointed out, in the 1830's "those from Hai-nan are chiefly pedlars and fishermen and form perhaps the poorest, yet the most cheerful class." [156] Their poverty and lowly social standing made it very difficult for them to compete with Hokkiens, Teochius, and Cantonese in the urban centers. On the other hand, the Hainanese' special skills in fishing and boatbuilding drew them to the rivers, and their specialization in sawmilling lured them north to the teak forests. The nineteenth century saw the establishment of several Hainanese lumbering merchants in such northern towns as Lampang, and of Hainanese boatbuilding yards at Thalǫ and Paknampho. While lack of capital ruled out any Hainanese role in the import-export business of Bangkok, this factor was no handicap in the collection of local products for sale to exporters. Consequently Hainanese became traders in local products in the shorter tributaries of the Jaophraya system. Furthermore, the Hainanese had an advantage in their ingrown resistance to malaria and other tropical fevers. Informants in upcountry Thailand repeatedly told the writer that Hainanese could go into fever-ridden areas where Teochius would die like flies. Hainan, of course, lies in more tropical latitudes than any other emigrant area in China, and endemic malaria was more widespread there than in the delta areas of the Teochius or Cantonese.

The chief exception to the general priority of Hainanese in upcountry Siam is the fairly early Teochiu settlement in Tak and Chiangmai on the Ping River, the most westerly tributary of the Jaophraya. There is no indication that Hainanese were ever dominant on this river (except at Lamphun, which they approached overland from Lampang on the Wang River), while the Teochiu settlements there date back to the mid-nineteenth century. The most plausible explanation would seem to lie in the comparatively great commercial importance of Tak (then usually called Rahaeng) and Chiangmai. Both towns were crossroads in the caravan trade that connected Yunnan with Burma (Moulmein) and Laos (Luang Prabang) and Lower Siam (by river to Paknampho). As such, they attracted Teochiu and

Hokkien merchants from Lower Siam and lower Burma, who traded in foreign goods imported via Bangkok and Rangoon and in the products of southwest China. This commerce was quite different from the petty trading in local products in which Hainanese for the most part engaged.

As of the mid-nineteenth century, Malloch reported sizable Chinese populations in more than sixty towns within the present-day boundaries of Siam.[157] These included ten along the Jaophraya River up to Paknampho, six on the Ping-Wang River system and nine on the Yom-Nan tributary system, three each on the Thajin and Maeklong rivers, and two on the Pasak River. Except for six localities in the northeast, all the other towns shown in Malloch's list as having sizable Chinese populations were seaports.[158] This presents striking testimony of the water's-edge nature of Chinese settlement at that time.

The expansion of the Thai economy which came in the wake of the Bowring treaty of 1855 quite naturally altered the settlement patterns of the Chinese. While Bangkok itself absorbed ever increasing numbers of Chinese, their proportion in the city, if anything, declined. During the last quarter of the nineteenth century, the Thai were progressively released from corvée duties, patronage ties, and slavery, and with their new freedom of movement they migrated into Bangkok in ever greater numbers, even as the Chinese. In 1875, Ratzel estimated the Chinese population of Bangkok at 80,000 to 100,000.[159] Thereafter the Thai population grew apace with the Chinese, and up until the First World War the number of Thai were equal or close to that of the Chinese. Bacon in 1893, McCarthy in 1900, and the *Siam Free Press* in 1907 were agreed that Chinese formed about half the total population of the capital.[160]

Other earlier twentieth-century estimates of the proportion of Chinese in Bangkok are almost all too low because they were based on the number of tax-paying Chinese or the 1909 census. In 1900, 65,345 male adult Chinese paid the poll tax in Bangkok,[161] but this figure, for reasons mentioned above (see p. 75), gives no idea of the true magnitude of the total Chinese population. The 1909 census showed 197,918 Chinese out of a total of 867,457 for the whole monthon of Krungthep (containing Bangkok)—22.8 per cent Chinese.[162] However, the urban concentration of Chinese within the monthon would bring the percentage of Chinese in Bangkok proper well over one-quarter, and the census itself seriously undercounted the Chinese, as indicated in the preceding section. Thus the estimates of the Chinese proportion at around one-quarter given by Graham and Prince Damrong [163] must be too low, if taken to apply to local-born as well as China-born Chinese. In fact, Graham himself admitted in 1912, as quoted before, that "every other man encountered in the streets of the capital wears a pigtail." Garnier, writing in 1911, facetiously complained that on arriving in Bangkok "one's first desire is to see the Siamese people, and one's last regret on leaving is that of not having found them." [164] Bangkok had the stamp of a Chinese city.

More and more towns in the interior of Thailand, too, took on a Chinese cast during the latter half of the nineteenth century. As an exchange economy spread upcountry, minor towns developed into commercial centers and attracted merchants and shopkeepers from Bangkok. The main street in Lampang was in the late nineteenth century called "Chinese Road," and such other trading centers as Sukhothai, Tha-it (Uttaradit), Phitsanulok, Phijit, and Khorat swelled with the influx of Chinese. This new movement included a much higher proportion of Teochius and Hakkas. In the words of Raquez in 1903:

Established first in Bangkok, they [the people of Ch'ao-chou] expanded little by little into the environs, choosing by preference the intersections of roads and canals. Up until recent years, they had not gone beyond a radius of 100 kilometers from Bangkok. Toward the north, Uttaradit and Paknampho were their extreme points. Never did they dare attack the teak regions where the first pioneers had left their bones.[165]

When Raquez wrote, however, the major movement upcountry of Teochius and Hakkas was just getting under way. It began in 1897 with the completion of the railway as far as Kaengkhoi on the Pasak River, and continued northward with the railroad throughout the first decade of the century.[166] The present dominant position of Teochius and Hakkas in the major towns of upcountry Siam dates in most cases only to the arrival of the railroad. The northeast line was completed to Khorat in 1900. North of Paknampho, the line was built along the Nan River, reaching Uttaradit in 1908. Before the war, it was completed as far as Denchai, south of Phrae (on the Yom River), and a spur was also built from the main line to Sawankhalok on the Yom River. Thus the northern line was built squarely through the region originally settled by the Hainanese. By 1917, Phijit, Phitsanulok, and Sawankhalok were already dominated by Teochius. The old Tha-it was superseded by new trading centers at the railway stations just north and south of it (Thasao and Banpho, respectively, the latter being the

Uttaradit station proper), and these were Teochiu-dominated from the start. Similarly the town of Denchai was a Teochiu and Hakka creation which developed at the railway station nearest to Phrae and Nan. Within a year or two after the railroad reached Denchai, a road was completed to Phrae, and the Teochiu-Hakka expansion extended to that town.

Several factors help explain the Hainanese' loss of predominance in the largest of the new railroad towns. For one thing, the railroad was built out from Bangkok, where Teochius and Hakkas formed an ever increasing majority. Secondly, for all sections above Chumsaeng (in jangwat Nakhonsawan), the contractors for supplying rock, building the roadbed, and laying the ties were either Teochius or Hakkas or Cantonese, never Hainanese. This meant that Hainanese were disfavored in the recruitment of laborers. In consequence, most of those who quit their railroad construction jobs to settle in the new or newly important towns were of speech groups other than Hainanese. Oldtimers who remember when the railroad was being built from Chumsaeng to Denchai specify that Teochius were dominant among the labor gangs, followed by Cantonese and Hakkas. The explanation for the strong Hakka dominance in the town of Huadong (jangwat Phijit), for instance, is that the concessionaire for blasting roadbed rock at the quarry nearby was a Mei-hsien Hakka. Third, the new commercial importance attained by the major towns with the advent of the railway put them in the same class as Chiangmai and Tak with regard to volume and quality of trade and gave them a similar appeal for Teochiu traders. Finally, with the growth of the larger towns, sanitation was improved, and health conditions became more amenable to the less hardy Teochius and Cantonese. The increased size of such towns as Phitsanulok and Uttaradit also made it worthwhile for artisan specialists—who were mainly Cantonese and Hakkas—to set up shop.

As the Teochius and others settled the larger railway towns, Hainanese showed a tendency to move on out to smaller localities within the region or into virgin territory. As one old informant in Phijit put it: "In general, the Hainanese were the first to come upcountry. When the Teochius came, however, they won out over the Hainanese because of their willingness to do business on a minimal margin. So the Hainanese moved on to more remote areas. The Teochius are shrewder in business, but the Hainanese are more adventurous." Thus the smaller towns in between Uttaradit, Phitsanulok, and Phijit remained chiefly Hainanese even as the Teochius won out in the jangwat capitals.

Similarly the Yom River towns and Lampang (not yet reached by the railway) remained predominantly Hainanese longer than those on the Nan River. Early in the twentieth century, the Hainanese continued to push on into the wilder, malarial regions of jangwats Chiangrai, Nan, Loei, and Chaiyaphum.

The completion of the line to Khorat soon reduced the Hainanese there to a small minority. The generally sparse Chinese settlement of the northeast, however, was not materially changed during the period under review, because no new lines were built in the region until after the First World War. The rail lines constructed in central and southern Siam prior to the First World War also facilitated the rapid growth of the Chinese population in regions outside Bangkok. The eastern line was completed as far as Chachoengsao (Paetriw) in 1908, while the southern line, completed to Phetchaburi in 1903, slowly progressed southward after 1909, reaching the Malayan border by 1917. The latter line had already begun to affect the speech-group distribution in the south before the First World War, as Teochius, Hakkas, and Hainanese moved southward into areas that had previously been dominated by Hokkiens and Cantonese.

The new overland transportation facilities constructed after 1897 thus had a manifold effect on Chinese settlement, which had theretofore been conditioned largely by the structure of natural waterways. There was a rapid increase in the Chinese population in all regions, but especially Middle Siam, together with settlement of areas in the far north and northeast that had never before been penetrated by Chinese. In addition, the railroads brought about an equalization of speech-group distribution in the direction of the Bangkok pattern. The Teochiu dominance in immigration achieved in the 1870's had by the second decade of the twentieth century made itself felt all over Thailand, except for the most remote parts of the north and northeast and the far south.

LIVELIHOOD IN A NEW LAND:

The Chinese Position in the Thai

Economy through the Fifth Reign

A. *Antecedents of an Ethnic Division of Labor*

ONE of the most important factors in the development of the Thai economy during the nineteenth and twentieth centuries has been the persistent tendency toward specialization along ethnic lines. The Thai have consistently preferred agriculture, governmental service, and self-employment in general to other occupations, while Chinese immigrants and their descendants have shown an equally strong preference for commercial activities of all kinds, industry, finance, mining, and wage labor in general. Most of the nineteenth-century writers who noted this ethnic division of labor related it to the differences in character between these two peoples, which they generally remarked in Siam. The Chinese were characterized as displaying extreme industriousness, willingness to labor long and hard, steadiness of purpose, ambition, desire for wealth and economic advancement, innovativeness, venturesomeness, and independence. The Thai, by comparison, were generally said to be indolent, unwilling to labor for more than immediate needs, contented with their lot, uninterested in money or economic advancement, conservative, and satisfied with a dependent status. Insofar as these contrasting characterizations have any validity, they should be considered and explained in terms of the distinctive cultures of the two peoples as formed by two unique and largely independent historical processes. It is proposed in this section to outline briefly some of the cultural and historical factors relevant to the development in Siam of occupational specialization by ethnic group.

The complementary preferences of the Chinese and Thai in Siam are especially striking because the great majority of the population in south China, as well as Siam, is rural, agricultural, and village-centered. This was truer still in the early nineteenth century, by which time the occupational patterns in Siam were fairly well set. Moreover, these patterns were not significantly altered after the last decades of the nineteenth century, when Chinese immigration took on the character of a mass movement of *peasants*. Clearly, it would be worthwhile to look for significant contrasts in the village life or rural culture of south China and Siam.

Of primary importance perhaps is the fact that the south Chinese peasant lived in a grimly Malthusian setting where thrift and industry were essential for survival. Characteristics that may have arisen from necessity through the centuries came, in time, to be cultural imperatives. The Thai peasant, for reasons suggested earlier, lived in an underpopulated and fertile land where the requirements for subsistence were modest and easily obtained. In premodern times, moreover, he could be (and was) more self-sufficient economically than his Chinese counterpart. Under these circumstances, thrift as such was of limited value, and work for its own sake simply senseless. In the Thai universe, consumption and enjoyment were the immediate stuff of living itself—never postponed, ultimate ends. The Thai learned to enjoy life and live it in the present; there was no pressure to do otherwise.[1] The Chinese peasant, however, had every practical reason for frugality and thrift: consumption had to be limited in the present in hopes of assuring future survival; enjoyment had to be sacrificed for work. Under these circumstances protracted labor in the interests of the future became a value in itself.

But this is only part of the picture, for the industriousness and thrift of the Chinese peasant served cultural goals absent in Thai rural culture. The Chinese peasant had a definite place in a temporal continuum of kin. Within the extended kin groups—dead, living, and yet to be born—he looked to the past as well as to the future: he was not only grateful to his ancestors for what his immediate family had, but was responsible to them for what he did to further the fortune of his family and lineage. His world view was, thus, historical and kin-centered, and in this context his industriousness and thrift served ends transcending his individual life. His primary goal was not individual salvation, but lineage survival and advancement. Protracted labor and extreme thrift were the means to these strongly sanctioned ends.

This ambition of the Chinese peasant for family advancement was especially marked because values in Chinese society were elite-centered. All the highly valued goals, systematized and popularized in the Confucian ethic, were attainable in full only by achieving elite status. Thus scholarship, government position, the extended family under one roof, proper homage and honors to ancestors—to mention certain of the more important—were possible only as a family rose from mass to elite status. And yet as ideals, these values permeated the whole society, including the peasant masses. The road to success was simple: hard work, thrift, and mutual help among kin. Any upward change in status, however small, was a success that could with pride be reported to the ancestors and that made possible a closer approximation to cultural ideals. There were always a few peasant families who, through sacrifice in the traditional manner, made the grade, and there was always the odd case of an outstanding peasant son who, given a classical education at lineage expense, provided an entering wedge into the elite scholar-official class for his family and lineage. While such instances were rare, they were sufficiently tantalizing to freshen the ambition of the average peasant and his kin groups.

The contrast provided by Thai rural culture is striking. The peasant had no place in an historical continuum of kin; the Thai did not even use surnames. Immediate ancestors were honored by cremation and then usually forgotten; there was no ancestral cult, no kin responsibility outside the immediate or extended family. The religion of the Thai peasant emphasized individual merit-making and salvation and con-demned as worldly any excessive concern for the material advance-ment of self and family. Furthermore, values for the Thai masses were much less elite-centered than for the Chinese. The Thai peasant could obtain prestige and come closest to achieving his spiritual ends by entering the Buddhist priesthood, a step taken by a large proportion of men in the society and one which in itself involved no upward mobility. Certainly hard labor and thrift were of little avail in achieving his ends. There was, in contrast to the Chinese, little in the kinship system or religion of the Thai peasant to encourage the development of a Protestant-type ethic. In this regard, then, the victory of Hinayana Buddhism in Siam and of the Mahayana type in China (plus its transformation in accordance with Confucianism) may be considered extremely important historical antecedents of the "Chinese problem" in Thailand today.

Given the value orientation of the Chinese masses and the fact that fulfillment of cultural ideals was inhibited almost solely by poverty, it is hardly surprising that money-making activities of all kinds were turned to as secondary means to upward mobility. Merchants engaging in internal trade and artisan-craftsmen of all kinds have had an important place in Chinese society for centuries; witness the often underrated place of market towns in the rural landscape of China. It was the development of foreign trade in south China, however, which more than anything else lent a mercantile, money-conscious and slightly urbanized distinctiveness to the subculture of that region. Wealth from trade, gained by hard work and saved through frugal habits, was as useful in the achievement of cultural objectives as that garnered through the application of the same virtues in agriculture. Merchants could hire tutors for their children so that they might gain entry into officialdom; should they fail the examinations, the wealthier of their fathers could at certain periods buy for them official positions and dignities at court. True enough, merchants were looked down on in the Confucian-inspired occupational ranking,[2] but the profits from foreign trade soon led to collusion between officials and merchants.[3] At least for those parts of Kuangtung and Fukien later to become emigrant areas, mercantile endeavor became an extremely important means of ensuring family survival and advancement.

The development of foreign trade at Canton, Ch'üan-chou, and the lesser ports discussed in the preceding chapter, led to the rise of a new type of urban community. Up to that time, the usual Chinese city was a government center; the bulk of its population served the bureaucracy in one capacity or another—as attendants, servants, artisans, traders. The new south China ports on the other hand were largely trade-centered; the mass of their populations came to be clerks, accountants and laborers for the commercial hongs, dock workers and porters, artisans and other purveyors of services for the wealthy merchants, and above all, tradesmen, large and small. Peasants from the surrounding areas were attracted to the port cities by the new opportunities. South China's monopoly of foreign trade, which persisted for hundreds of years up to the nineteenth century, gave the peoples of the southern ports and immediate hinterlands ample time and opportunities to gain a commercial and financial know-how superior to that of most other Far Eastern peoples.

From these ports, then, came the first emigrants to Nan-yang. They had all the drive, industriousness, and thrifty habits of the Chinese peasant and, in addition, commercial experience and a heightened appreciation of the value of money. In all probability, the more trenchant of the Chinese proverbs concerning wealth originated in south China; they are certainly current today among the emigrants from that area: "Money can do all things." "Wealth begets wealth." "Money makes possible communion with the Gods." "With money, you can get the devil himself to push your cart." For the Thai, such sayings represent the crassest materialism. Typical of their maxims with regard to wealth are these three, attributed to the culture hero Phra Ruang: "Do not long for more than your own share." "Sacrifice wealth rather than honor." "Love thyself more than treasures." [4]

The analysis thus far only indirectly accounts for the willingness of an immigrant of peasant stock to engage in nonagricultural labor in Siam or for the venturesome and innovative aspect of the Chinese character in Siam. In this regard it must be kept in mind that the motivation for leaving his village in the first place was for the Chinese peasant primarily economic. Poverty forced him to go to the coastal ports, and there he was willing to accept any kind of work. Whether he apprenticed to a commercial hong, a craftsman's shop, or went to work as a menial laborer, the change from agricultural employment was already made. As Pelzer points out, a proletariat grew up in the south China cities willing to go wherever work and good wages could be found [5]—which increasingly meant Nan-yang. For many emigrants, then, the initial process in urbanization of occupation took place in China prior to emigration.

It is quite probable, furthermore, that emigration was a selective process, and not only with regard to age and sex. The emigrants were almost exclusively young and male; they doubtless also included a disproportionate number of the most *venturesome* young men. Kulp's analysis of the causes of emigration from a Teochiu village stresses first of all "the achievement of security by the improvement of the family fortunes economically," as we have here, but also points out that "for the young man, the wish for new experience might easily be more dominant than the wish for security." [6] The villagers recognized a selectivity on the basis of venturesomeness by calling the emigrants "galloping guests" and the stay-at-homes "who lacked the courage to break away," "ricepot-keeping turtles."

To complete the picture of the situation in which ethnic occupational specialization arose, it is necessary to look at the social structure of premodern Thai society and at the policy of the Thai government during the first five reigns of the Jakkri dynasty. In the early nineteenth century, the basic division in Thai society was that between the elite and the masses.[7] The king and the royal aristocracy together with the bureaucratic nobility wielded full economic and political power. Beneath these strata were the masses, the great majority of whom were either freemen or slaves. Within this hierarchic system, each individual had a fixed (though not unchangeable) status with clear-cut responsibilities and rights toward individuals above and below him. Every freeman was in theory the client or retainer of a person in the upper strata, while every slave was the property of an elite individual or family. The great majority of the freemen were agriculturalists, but not serfs; they were attached not to the land but to the patron, and in certain circumstances could transfer patrons. The client-patron relationship was paternalistic and interdependent; the freeman got security and care in return for his customary services. Freemen, however, as well as slaves, were not permitted to flee or leave the purview of their patrons and owners. In addition, all male freemen within certain age limits and many classes of slaves were liable to public service in the king's name for four months of each year [8]—this obligation being the basis of the corvée system. Public works of all kinds—temples, canals, fortifications—were built by corvée labor, while the army was manned by conscripts and slaves. Patrons were responsible, when requested, for supplying a certain number of their clients in a corvée capacity to specified government departments.

This description, though brief and somewhat oversimplified, suffices to show that the institutionalized status of the Thai masses precluded the personal freedom and geographical mobility necessary for competition in new economic ventures. Moreover, the system discouraged even the further development of Thai craftsmanship and special skills. "Talent was rewarded by forced service in the patron's household, under disadvantageous economic and social conditions." [9] Agriculturalists had fewer obligations and a less coerced life than artisans, who when especially skilled could be forced into royal service for life. Under these circumstances, Thai initiative and creativity were stifled.[10]

The position of the Chinese in Siam throughout the nineteenth century was in marked contrast to that of the Thai masses. Chinese, alone of Asian foreigners, were exempt from corvée and from the requirement to attach themselves to a patron or government master. They almost entirely escaped slavery, for no Chinese was ever brought to Siam as a war prisoner, and voluntary sale into slavery was utterly repugnant to the Chinese. The Chinese were also free to travel and settle anywhere in the kingdom without restrictions.[11] The favoritism shown the Chinese by the Thai government in the nineteenth century was not unconscious. The first Jakkri kings encouraged Chinese immigration for specific purposes connected with the royal trade. The Chinese were to provide manpower for the commercial agriculture necessary to supply exportable products and for the trading, shipping, and navigating functions themselves. The Chinese were needed, then, for the expansion of trade designed to swell governmental and royal revenues. To serve this purpose, they had to be given freedom unthinkable for the Thai masses of the time. Instead of corvée and in keeping with the royal purposes, the Chinese were charged a head tax large enough to be a sizable source of revenue but not so large as to discourage immigration.

If most aspects of Thai culture and society militated against the masses' taking up nonagricultural pursuits, there still remains the question as to why the Chinese declined to take up subsistence farming and rice cultivation in competition with the Thai. It has been suggested above that a good proportion of the Chinese immigrants were at least partly urbanized and commercialized before leaving China. But this does not alter the fact that an increasing number of the Chinese emigrants, especially after recruitment became regularized in the 1870's, came to Siam almost straight from the farm. The answer lies, primarily it would seem, in the aims and motivation of the emigrants. Their intention was not to establish a copy of Chinese society abroad; their roots were in China, and they left wives and families behind. Their aim, rather, was to escape poverty, to acquire money with which they could return and raise the status of their family. With this motivation, they turned to those jobs and occupations that paid best. The preference of the Thai for rice farming and village life meant a scarcity of labor in all pursuits of an urban nature as well as in specialized commercial agriculture and led to relatively high wages in Siam throughout the period under review.[12] The Chinese immigrant who had been a peasant at home, then, became a wage laborer either on plantations or in the cities and towns and did so for the simple reason that such work paid better than rice cultivation. It should be made explicit that the Chinese were in no wise restricted in the acquisition of uncultivated land. They *could* undertake rice farming or subsistence agriculture more freely even than the Thai. They *did not* to any extent because they could make more money faster in other ways.

The revolutionary changes in Thai society and economy during the reigns of Mongkut and Julalongkǫn served only to strengthen the occupational patterns already set. Corvée was gradually weakened during the second half of the nineteenth century through cash exemption and state employment of wage labor, and the system was officially abolished in 1899. Rama V brought slavery to an end by a process begun in 1874 and finished in 1905. The patronage system, too, was dealt a severe blow in the governmental reforms and reorganization of 1891–1892. However, in the very decades during which the Thai masses gradually gained freedom, the growing foreign demand for rice came to be strongly felt in the Thai market, which had been opened to free trade by the Bowring Treaty in 1855. The tremendous expansion in rice cultivation which occurred during the following half century absorbed almost entirely the increase in the Thai population as well as the Thai labor and energy freed by the abolition of the old semifeudal system. The Thai, then, not only had no *inclination* to seek a life divorced from villages and rice cultivation; the wealth of unused land which was theirs for the clearing coupled with the world demand for rice meant that they also had no *necessity* to consider any shift from the traditional livelihood. Meanwhile, as we shall see in a later section, the government came to rely on Chinese labor for the public works formerly built under the corvée system. The net result of the social reform and economic expansion during the reigns of Rama IV and V, then, was to confirm the Thai masses in their preference for rice cultivation and subsistence farming and to strengthen the Chinese hold on commerce, industry, mining, and wage labor.

Specific illustrations, exceptions, and documentation of some of the generalizations presented here will be given in succeeding sections. The purport of this section has been to relate in general terms certain aspects of Thai and Chinese culture and character, society and history to the development of occupational specialization in Siam along ethnic lines. This development cannot go unexplained, since it has overwhelming significance for any attempt to understand contemporary Thailand.

B. Chinese Entrepreneurship

The changes in the Thai economy during the century 1810–1910, taken as a whole, were tremendous in scope and revolutionary in consequences.[13] Almost every one of these changes concerned Chinese entrepreneurs directly or indirectly, but in this section only those developments relating to private, urban entrepreneurship will be discussed. (Tin mining, plantation agriculture, and construction are treated in the following section from the point of view of Chinese labor, while the Chinese entrepreneurial role in activities closely tied to government revenue are discussed in Section D below.) The major developments affecting the private Chinese sector of the urban economy during the century before the First World War include: (1) the expansion of Chinese shipping up to 1840 followed by its rapid decline and almost total eclipse during the new era of free trade, (2) the increase in the absolute volume, if not proportion, of the Chinese import-export business throughout the century, (3) the growth of European import-export houses and of the Chinese-compradore system, (4) the introduction of power rice milling and the Chinese victory over Westerners in this field, (5) the introduction of power sawmilling and its less decisive consequences, (6) the strengthening of the Chinese hold on retail trade, (7) the growth in importance and scope of other middleman functions performed for the upcountry population by the Chinese, and (8) the entry of the Chinese into modern banking.

During the first half of the nineteenth century the Chinese dominated Siam's foreign trade and shipping. Most of the tonnage was carried in Chinese junks, many of which were built by Chinese in Siam.[14] The Chinese also closely co-operated with Thai state trading. They commanded, navigated, and manned most of the king's ships and served as royal factors and warehousemen.[15] At times they even suggested commercial ventures to the king.[16] During Nangklao's reign, certain of the royal trading monopolies were farmed out to Chinese merchants.[17]

It was, in fact, because the Chinese so admirably served the interests of the Thai rulers in expanding trade that they were given special commercial privileges.[18] The Chinese had the venturesomeness and seagoing skills and experience that the Thai lacked; they could call at Chinese ports closed to foreigners; and they never directly challenged government monopolies, but instead supplied products for them and were satisfied with the profits remaining in the trade after the king had taken his cut. Vis-à-vis Westerners, the Chinese had obvious advantages. Duties on junks and their cargoes were small and generally fair, while Westerners were charged higher rates on both imports and exports, and their square-rigged vessels were assessed at exorbitant values.[19] The Chinese were better acquainted with the Thai market and had learned through the centuries how to deal with Thai officials. They had connections with local Chinese retailers which Westerners could never hope to match, and Chinese importers were willing to sell in small quantities direct to consumers, which procedure was unthinkable for Westerners.[20] The Chinese could engage in foreign trade without extensive capital; the king provided funds for many of the larger operations, while the cargo of entirely Chinese junks was financed jointly by the officers and crew, each of whom bought and sold his portion. Finally, the Chinese could buy real estate and travel freely, while Westerners were severely restricted.

For all these reasons, Westerners were unable to compete with the Chinese until they obtained equal commercial rights as well as additional privileges and protection. The treaty of 1855 obtained by the British emissary, Sir John Bowring, secured these desiderata for the first time, and it was followed by similar treaties between Siam and all the major trading states of Europe and America. Thereafter Westerners enjoyed consular protection, extraterritorial privileges, and freedom to trade at all seaports, to buy property and reside in Bangkok, and to travel in the interior (with passes). Above all, the odious measurement duties were abolished and an upper limit of 3 per cent placed on import duties.

The success of British diplomacy in 1855 was achieved in spite of the opposition of Chinese and Thai vested interests and largely because of the realistic and foresighted policies of King Mongkut. The British missions in the 1820's had met with staunch opposition from the Chinese, who represented that the British came with honeyed words of trade but were really planning aggression and seeking political power.[21] Malloch claims that, after King Mongkut came to power, Chinese traders cunningly forged a document purportedly written by the Phrakhlang designed to discourage European hopes of developing a lucrative trade at Siam.[22] Nevertheless, King Mongkut, who recognized the necessity of coming to terms with British power if only to forestall outright intervention or war, in 1852 reduced the measurement duty, legalized the opium trade, and restricted the scope of royal monopoly.[23] The considerable opposition voiced by Chinese merchants was of no avail against the absolute power of a determined and progressive monarch. The Bowring treaty, which had the effect of abolishing royal monopolies, including those farmed out to Chinese by Nangklao, was but the logical extension of Mongkut's policy.[24]

The treaty hardly spelled the doom of Chinese commercial enterprise in Siam, for Chinese merchants had their consolations and recognized the potentialities of free trade. In Bowring's words:

A Chinese merchant of enormous wealth, who held the opium monopoly, with, I was informed, more than ninety other monopolies, had been raised to the ranks of nobility, and was present among the prostrate nobles, dressed in the distinction of mandarin costume, when that article of the treaty was read to them which abolished the whole system of monopoly, and established free trade from the month of April, 1856. Certainly, he bowed his head in silence, but looked as if a hundred thunderstorms were concentrated in that proud, scornful, yet resigned expression. He had been told his doom at a previous conference with the principal 'ministers,' but, as the opium monopoly, the most precious and profitable of all, was preserved to him, he had the sagacity to feign a willing resignation, and to say he would employ his capital for the future in legitimate instead of privileged commerce. Though a small number of the Chinese profited by the farms, the enormous majority expressed their great delight at the emancipation which the treaty provided.[25]

The British, however, had no illusions that the Chinese were not their major adversaries in the struggle for Siamese trade, and they took special pains to have the king's proclamation incorporating the treaty's provisions translated accurately into Chinese and widely distributed in the commercial quarters, Bowring himself undertaking to revise the Chinese translation and have it printed in Hongkong.[26]

At the time of the treaty, the share of Chinese junks in Siam's foreign trade was already on the decline in the face of severe competition from both Thai and Western square-rigged vessels. Within the next few decades, the Chinese share of shipping decreased rapidly. In 1879, total tonnage cleared at Bangkok amounted to about 490,000 tons, of which 242,000 were carried in British ships and only 10,000 in junks, not even all of those being Chinese.[27] By 1882, only 151 Chinese junks entered Bangkok, as opposed to 248 steamers and 160 square-rigged vessels.[28] In 1890, British ships carried 67 per cent of the tonnage of foreign trade at Bangkok and other Western ships 27 per cent; only 128 Chinese junks entered port.[29] In 1892 it was estimated that only 2 per cent of Siam's foreign trade was carried in junks.[30]

The rapid decline in Chinese *shipping* has often been allowed to obscure the fact that the concomitant decline in the Chinese share of the *foreign trade* was considerably less marked; more than half of the greatly expanded foreign trade remained in Chinese hands. In 1890, for instance, the British Consul made a study of duties at Bangkok and concluded that over an eight-month period the approximate percentage of representation in the trade of Bangkok by nationality was: Chinese 62 per cent, British 26 per cent, Indian 8 per cent, and others 4 per cent.[31] In other words, after thirty-five years of Western free-trading enterprise in Siam under privileged conditions, a substantial majority of the foreign trade was still carried for Chinese accounts. Unable to compete in shipping, Chinese merchants had manifestly adjusted to free trade in competition with Westerners.

They could hardly fail to do so because their greatest advantage— intimate knowledge of the market and connections with Chinese retailers and distributors—remained virtually a Chinese monopoly. This monopoly, in fact, gave the Chinese a sizable cut in the Western share of foreign trade. As in China, Westerners found themselves at a loss to gauge the local market and to deal directly with retail merchants. They spoke neither Thai nor Chinese and had limited and indirect sources of trade information. Quite naturally they introduced in Siam the compradore system as evolved in China. Every Western commercial house chose a Chinese merchant of some wealth, Western training,[32] and standing in the Chinese community to serve as the firm's contact man.[33] This compradore invariably spoke Teochiu or Hokkien or both and often other of the south China languages and in addition usually spoke Thai and knew some English. From his familiarity with the local market he advised his employers as to the nature and quality of imports and personally guaranteed their sale by a security deposit with the Western firm. He established sales connections with local dealers and upcountry traders, disposed of the imports on arrival, and was responsible for collecting payment. In many cases, he also handled the firm's day-to-day relations with the Thai government. For his services he got only a small salary but heavy sales commissions. He also usually had the right to hire and fire local personnel, most of whom were naturally Chinese. Compradores of the larger Western firms became men of great power. By the end of Rama

V's reign, they were, along with the largest rice millers, among the prominent Chinese leaders in Bangkok.

Western mercantile houses, faced initially with Chinese commercial dominance, had no choice but to employ Chinese compradores. While the operation of the system ensured predominantly Chinese employment in the firms, the Western merchants would not have had it otherwise, for they preferred Chinese industriousness and know-how to the easygoing work habits of the Thai. Thus Westerners became dependent on their principal competitors. They were cut off from any important role in the retail or internal trade. The Western commercial firms, however, could nonetheless extract large profits with a minimum of concern over petty and messy detail. The Chinese, for their part, had reason to be pleased with developments. The stimulus of Western shipping, the introduction of Western capital and large-scale commercial efficiency, and the world-wide connections of the Western commercial houses led to a tremendous increase in the volume and value of foreign trade. While the solely Chinese proportion decreased somewhat, the absolute increase of the Chinese part of the trade was tremendous, and in addition Chinese were able to secure employment and income from their essential role in the Western trade operations.

The story of the mechanization of rice milling is another crucial chapter in the development of the dominant economic position of the Chinese in Siam. As Ingram has demonstrated, rice was a common item of export from Siam prior to 1855.[34] The output for export, however, came almost entirely from Chinese hand mills.[35] The tremendous growth of rice exports after the Bowring treaty [36] was a golden opportunity for Chinese millers, but it brought with it almost immediate Western mechanization to challenge Chinese interests. The first steam rice mill in Siam was built by an American company in 1858. By 1864 there were three steam mills, and by 1867 five—all Western-owned.[37] But at that figure Western expansion in rice milling stopped. The British Consul reported in 1870 the ominous news that Chinese shippers had ordered several steam mills from England for their own use.[38] And in 1877, the British Consul wrote:

Up till very recently foreigners were the sole owners of rice-cleaning mills, which also until very lately have been highly remunerative. Now however, the indefatigable Chinese were setting up mills, and as they are not only the principal owners of rice milled at the European mills, but likewise enter into arrangements in regard to freight, insurance and other matters with their owners, any change in such transactions must be a loss to the Europeans.[39]

By 1879, there were as many Chinese as Western steam mills, and thereafter the number of Chinese mills in Bangkok and vicinity mushroomed—to 17 in 1889, 23 in 1895, and over 50 in 1912. Meanwhile several Western mills sold out to Chinese millers or burned down and were not replaced, and few new ones were built. By 1912, only three Western mills were in operation.[40]

This striking success of the Chinese was due to many factors. The stakes were so high that the Chinese had every incentive to learn fast. The superiority of steam mills was obvious, and so the Chinese bought them, small ones at first, and hired Western (usually Scottish) engineers to run them. The mechanical genius of the Cantonese eventually obviated direct Western help. By the turn of the century, several Chinese mills employed Cantonese engineers.[41] The father of the most important Cantonese miller in Bangkok today was among the first Chinese rice-mill engineers and is said to have trained over a hundred others. During the first decade of the twentieth century, Cantonese machinists manufactured a complete set of rice-milling machinery, including castings, from their own patterns and crude hand sketches taken from British equipment in a local mill.[42] It was a Chinese who, around 1890, pioneered the process for producing clean, white rice as opposed to the less appealing cargo rice.[43] Within a few years, European mills had copied the Chinese process, and by 1905 almost all Bangkok mills were equipped to produce white rice, which commanded higher prices in foreign markets.[44]

Of equal importance was the simple fact that the whole rice business—buying of paddy, milling, and export—was of one piece. Westerners were in no position to secure their source of paddy, for its collection was in the hands of Chinese middlemen. Chinese millers could easily make arrangements with these itinerant middlemen and, when competition was keen, could send agents into the interior to insure continued supplies.[45] Furthermore, the major foreign markets for Siamese rice were in Singapore, Hongkong, and south China, where the importing firms were largely Chinese. By the 1880's Chinese millers were exporting on their own account to Chinese importers abroad.[46] The lament of the British Consul in 1897 had a frustrated and plaintive ring: "It is impossible under the conditions of trade prevailing in the East for the European to compete with the astute

Chinaman in this particular [the rice] business." [47] The final blow to European rice interests came in 1909, when a Sino-Thai firm with up-to-date mills began selling rice directly in the European markets through London. Prior to that time, British and German rice firms in Bangkok had the export trade to Europe all to themselves. [48]

There are still other factors in the Chinese' success. Their chief weakness vis-à-vis the Europeans was that they ordinarily could not command as much capital. Money from Chinese-held revenue farms made up part of this deficiency, but for the rest Chinese millers interested wealthy members of the Thai elite, though Thai-financed mills were invariably Chinese-managed and operated. [49] Finally, Chinese millers, in the rough and tumble competition that developed after 1880, were willing to run their mills almost continuously to make their investments pay. As soon as electric lights became available, the larger Chinese millers installed them so that the mills could operate day and night and employ two shifts. Western mills were forced to keep up with their Chinese competitors or close. In the end, the pioneering Western mills were abandoned or passed into Chinese hands. Thus did the Westerners lose to the Chinese the biggest prize of all in Siam. The Thai declined to compete.

In sawmilling the Europeans fared better. Prior to the 1880's, teak and other heavy construction timbers were sawed solely by hand in Chinese sheds and used primarily for domestic construction and shipbuilding. The Hainanese in particular engaged in this industry, and some construction timber was exported to Hainan Island. Europeans entered the teak business in earnest only after the Anglo-Thai treaty of 1883, and when operations were under way in North Siam they established steam mills in Bangkok to saw the logs floated down the Jaophraya River. In spite of the Hainanese hold on sawmilling, the first Chinese steam mills were built by Cantonese, presumably because of the latter's mechanical skills. By 1894, there were but three European steam sawmills in Bangkok and one Chinese; [50] by 1908, seven European and four Chinese steam mills. [51] Two of these mills, one Cantonese and one Hakka, are still in operation today. Hand sawmills, largely Hainanese, were still widespread in 1910, both in the north and in Bangkok. The advantage of the European teak sawmillers was simply that they obtained from the Thai government and worked their own extensive forest concessions, thus assuring a steady source of supply. Chinese millers rarely had sufficient capital for both concessions and steam milling equipment.

The retail trade in Siam was dominated by the Chinese both before and after the impact of Western economic influence. During the first half of the nineteenth century, the great Bangkok markets for imported goods were Sampheng and the river itself. On arrival at Bangkok, most of the Chinese junks were converted into retail shops; temporary stalls were built on each side of the deck and the Chinese goods attractively displayed. From February to June (in the 1830's) about seventy junks were moored in the river, forming two lines heading downstream, each crowded with buyers who came shopping by boat.[52] In addition, all year round both sides of the river at Bangkok were lined with floating shops for over four miles. These "houses," some thirty to forty feet square in size and ranged in rows of eight to ten, literally floated on the water, though they were anchored to posts. Each was provided with a covered platform on which was displayed the merchandise for sale—both Chinese imports and local products. They were in effect shop-homes; their Chinese occupants lived in the rear rooms and conducted business in the front. The floating houses were furnished with small canoes for the transport of the tradesmen and their families, and the river in their vicinity was usually crowded with the jostling boats of shoppers.[53] There were also numerous Chinese houseboats, which plied the rivers and canals, usually selling local foodstuffs, especially fresh pork.[54]

In those days Bangkok was indeed an Eastern Venice. Most retail trading was done on the water because the populace lived in houses on stilts at the water's edges. The only road outside the royal city proper was the lane running through the "Grand Bazaar" of Sampheng, built during the third reign. There lived the Chinese not domiciled on the river, and there, according to all accounts, one could buy literally anything. The lane was lined by the distinctive one-story brick houses of Chinese merchants, built not on stilts as were Thai dwellings but still raised somewhat so as to clear the high tide. On the fringes of the quarter were a few Indian craftsmen and retail tradesmen, especially dealers in piece goods; and in food markets at certain waterway intersections Thai women were prominent among the vendors. But, with these exceptions, the retail trade was a Chinese monopoly.

The changes which occurred during the subsequent decades up to 1910 altered details but not the substance of the picture. As foreign trade expanded and Western import houses were established, the Chinese tradesmen added Western manufactured goods to their stocks of Chinese and local products. A few new types of shops developed carrying only European goods. When the first major street outside the royal city—Jaroenkrung or New Road—was built in 1864 to connect the palace with the down-river foreign consulates, Chinese shops soon lined its full two miles. By the 1880's, the city's population was gradually shifting from the banks of rivers and canals to the newly-laid-out roads.[55] The junk bazaar was already a thing of the past, and the extensive road-building program around the turn of the century meant the end of the floating shops as well. The former floating population of Chinese tradesmen moved to the two-story shop-houses built in rows along the new streets.[56] Through it all the Chinese strengthened their hold on the retail trade. The British Consul in 1882 wrote that the "whole trade of the country" was in Chinese hands and that "it would be a difficult matter now to find a Siamese merchant or shopkeeper." [57] By 1889, Chinese had outdistanced Indians in their last stronghold, the piece-goods trade.[58]

The situation in other Siamese ports and gulf towns during the period in question was similar—no essential change in the Chinese dominant position in retailing. In the rural interior, however, the period after 1855 saw a marked extension of the Chinese economic role, both in kind and degree. The major changes wrought in this regard after the Bowring treaty were as follows: (1) The gradual development of an exchange economy following the rapid increase in foreign trade entailed a large increase in the number and kind of middleman functions to be performed, namely, taking the farmers' produce from them and transporting it to the seaports to be sold to processors or exporters, and then buying consumer goods to take back to the farmers.[59] The tremendous growth of rice milling and export, in particular, led to a specialized type of trader in Lower and Middle Siam—the itinerant Chinese paddy dealer, who collected in his boat paddy crops from the individual farmers for transport to the Bangkok mills and then carried back manufactured goods for sale to Chinese tradesmen in the up-country towns. (2) The end of royal trading and the 3 per cent ceiling on import duties stipulated in the Bowring treaty caused the Thai government to introduce new taxes which were most often farmed out to Chinese.[60] The inland traders, therefore, became increasingly the agents of Chinese tax and revenue farmers. (3) The same desire of the government for revenue was seen in the increasing recourse to cash payment in exemption from corvée and other traditional services. Consequently, more cash was needed by the populace to pay the exemptions as well as the new taxes. The growth in demand for goods not locally produced also increased the need for money or credit. So did the expansion of rice cultivation, for the farmer often needed an advance to cover at least the cost of seed rice. Credit and cash for these and other needs came to be provided by the Chinese trader. He became a moneylender, too. (4) Finally, the rapid increase in internal trade, the concomitant loss of village economic self-sufficiency, and the growth of new wants on the part of the Thai peasant made it worthwhile for Chinese retailers to settle in the smaller market towns and even villages throughout the interior.

By the turn of the century, then, Chinese middlemen were virtually ubiquitous in the interior, and their role had developed considerable complexity. They bought paddy and other local produce, advanced credit and supplies, lent money, collected taxes, sold imported goods, and transported merchandise in both directions. As Ingram has pointed out, it would have been impossible to estimate the value of any single function because they were all so mixed together.[61]

The introduction of modern banking in Siam provides yet another example of the interplay of Western and Chinese interests. The growth of European business in Siam led to the establishment of Bangkok branches of three European banks—the Hong Kong and Shanghai Banking Corporation in 1888, the Chartered Bank of India, Australia and China in 1894, and the Banque de l'Indochine in 1897.[62] These banks were founded to finance Western foreign trade and provide foreign exchange, but they soon found it expedient and profitable to deal extensively with Chinese merchants as well. In their business with Western commercial houses, furthermore, they had to deal with the Chinese compradores who were financially responsible for much of the firms' operations. The foreign banks, therefore, were forced to employ Chinese compradores themselves. The system was similar to that already employed in their branches in Singapore, Hongkong, and the Chinese treaty ports. The compradore solicited the banking business of Chinese merchants (and to some extent of foreign firms), and guaranteed loans made on his recommendation by depositing a large sum with the bank. He hired the bank clerks, was responsible for their honesty, and guaranteed the cash balance at the end of each day. As was the case with his counterpart in Western commercial houses, the banking compradore received only a nominal salary but liberal commissions.

The diversion of Chinese business to Western banks and the successful operation in Singapore of solely Chinese banks on Western lines led to the establishment in Bangkok of at least three Chinese banks during the first decade of this century. The first—Yü Sheng Hsing (Jao Seng Heng)—was founded about 1904 and rapidly acquired an important position in financial circles. In 1908, it was reorganized as a corporation with locally subscribed capital of three million baht.[63] In 1905, the smaller Yüan Fa Li (Guan What Lee) Chinese bank was established, and in 1908 the Chino-Siamese Bank was founded, with strong backing from rice millers, in part to finance a new Chinese shipping venture and to provide funds for Sun Yat-sen's revolutionary activities.[64]

It is not possible here to mention other types of Chinese entrepreneurship in the commerce, processing industry, and finance of Siam. Those discussed, however, indicate clearly enough that Chinese merchants and lesser tradesmen, in all their variations, greatly strengthened their position and extended their scope and functions during the one hundred years before 1910. They achieved this broader and stronger hold on the economy unopposed by the Thai and in spite of—or rather, partly because of—Western competition. The expansion of the Thai economy must, in the first instance, be attributed to Western example, innovation, and enterprise, but in general Chinese entrepreneurs outdid Westerners in exploiting the new opportunities.

C. Labor and Artisans

For the first two-thirds of the nineteenth century, the merchant-entrepreneur was the type par excellence of the Chinese immigrant. However, the expansion of the Thai economy after 1855 greatly increased the demand for manual workers and eventually led to the recruitment of Chinese peasants for "coolie" labor in Siam and to the mass migration which began in the 1880's. Even before these developments, there was a steady need for manual labor in mining and agriculture, and Chinese immigrants supplied the bulk of recruits.

Tin mining in South Siam was almost a monopoly of the Chinese throughout the nineteenth century. Their knowledge of the country's mineral resources was supreme, and they kept it secret from both Thai and outsiders.[65] Mining could be carried on individually, and even at the end of the century Smyth found Chinese working a certain type of hill deposits with crowbars—"calmly knocking out the crystals with their hammers one by one." [66] Usually, however, the tin-bearing earth had to be washed, and the pumps and other devices for this purpose required co-operative endeavor. Chinese workings were generally small, but some mines employed as many as nine hundred men.[67] In the larger mines, the workers were organized into one or more kongsi; [68] each group or kongsi lived together in housing provided by the mine-operator, and mined together as a team. The Chinese operators were licensed by the government—often by the local governors (rajahs)—in return for royalties of 10 to 16 per cent on the tin produced.[69] Smelting rights were in some localities farmed out to the highest bidder.

Tin mining was at a low ebb during the first two Jakkri reigns because of the repeated Burmese incursions on the west coast of the peninsula. Recovery was slow in the west during the third reign, but the workings on the east coast began to attract immigrants in increasing numbers direct from China.[70] The real spurt in tin mining came during Mongkut's reign, when enlightened governors took office in several of the key tin provinces. The best tin deposits are in Phuket, and there the new governor encouraged Chinese immigration (primarily Hokkiens via Penang), and furnished them with funds to commence work.[71] Every month brought new immigrants, and the Chinese population grew to 28,000 by 1870 and to over 40,000 in 1884, the great majority of whom labored in the mines.[72]

Labor conditions were not good. The work was arduous, especially the stripping of the overburden preliminary to washing. Miners also took turns manning the pumps and the smelter bellows—the latter at night after up to ten hours of steady labor in the sun and rain. Miners working the hill outcrops fell victim to fevers, and those who lived through them suffered from enlarged spleens and livers.[73] In view of these conditions, wages had to be relatively high, since only free labor was employed. The Chinese mine operators, however, also served as agents for revenue farmers and made additional profits from the gambling, opium, and liquor shops attached to the kongsis. It was calculated in the 1890's that, taking all the farms and taxes into consideration, the government took 40 per cent of the earnings of all the miners in Phuket.[74]

The employment of labor in the tin mines began to decline in the late 1880's for several reasons. Tin prices fell, and the demand increased for manual labor in Lower Siam, where better conditions prevailed. Even more important, however, was the appointment of a Siamese special commissioner to Phuket monthon (where the bulk of the mining was carried on), who apparently had a profound hatred for the Chinese and adopted policies which could not have been better calculated to drive the miners elsewhere. The former immigration turned into a mass exodus, and by 1897 the Chinese population of Phuket island had declined to less than twelve thousand.[75]

The situation in the mining areas of Southwest Siam was far worse. Smyth, in 1898, wrote the following about labor problems in the tin mines of Ratchaburi:

The death-rate among the coolies, who are generally Hainanese imported direct, is large in all the mining districts, which being as a rule in the hill ranges, are the worst for fever and dysentery. The death-rate from these causes among new arrivals has, in many cases, exceeded 60 per cent. Panic accounts for many more, and as new drafts go up-country, the effect produced by the stories they hear is such that bolts and bars cannot keep them. As advances have to be made to all these men, it is a serious matter to lose 70 per cent by desertion before arriving at the mines, and 60 per cent of the remainder in the next rainy season. . . . It is quite impossible to get Chinese who have been any time in the country to go to a mine, even by promises or advances of a most exorbitant kind.[76]

Most of the mining operations in Southwest Siam were abandoned shortly thereafter, but Chinese mining continued in South Siam, though on a greatly reduced scale. British and Australian firms, with dredgers and improved methods developed in Malaya, began operations in Siam only in the first decade of this century. That development will be mentioned in a later chapter.

Chinese agricultural labor on Chinese plantations was of considerable commercial importance during most of the nineteenth century. The general pattern of development, from the records available today, appears to have been as follows: Early in the century Chinese had *settled* in considerable numbers in certain rural areas of Southeast, Lower, and Southwest Siam; they married Thai women and to a large extent recreated peasant life in south China. They grew rice as well as tobacco, pepper, sugar cane, seri leaf, cotton, fruits, and vegetables. It was soon apparent, however, that there was an economic advantage in specialization; those near population centers produced seri leaf and vegetables for the local markets, while others concentrated on the production of pepper and sugar for the Western markets, cotton for the Chinese market, and tobacco for local and Malayan consumption. At the beginning of the nineteenth century, Chinese were already cultivating small pepper and seri-leaf plantations; commercial sugar cultivation began in the second decade of the century, and tobacco plantations were first noted in the fourth decade. Plantation owners were for the most part Chinese who had settled down in the country and their lukjin descendants. At first they hired Chinese or Sino-Thai workers and, in the case of sugar, Thai, but as the plantations prospered the owners came to rely more and more on Chinese immigrants for field labor. Chinese plantations in Siam were most prosperous between 1840 and 1880. Their decline came with the competition of Western-operated plantations in the European colonies of Southeast Asia and rising labor costs due to the heavy demand in Bangkok.

Pepper cultivation, one of the most ancient industries of Siam, provided probably the steadiest employment for Chinese agricultural labor during the period reviewed here (up to 1910). The plantations were concentrated in Southeast Siam, especially Janthaburi and Trat, and on the west coast of South Siam, Trang and Satun in particular.[77] The peak of production was reached in 1890, after which exports declined, planting was restricted, and many plantations failed. The decline was due to low and fluctuating prices on the London market but also, significantly, to rising labor costs.[78] In the first decade of this century, however, it could still be said that pepper was "one of the few agricultural products the cultivation of which employs a considerable amount of Chinese labor."[79]

The most important of the Chinese plantation crops, looking at the nineteenth century as a whole, was sugar. Apparently Teochiu settlers introduced sugar as a commercial crop in Southeast Siam around 1810, and within a decade or so it was a leading Thai export.[80] The largest plantations were located in what are today Chonburi, Chachoengsao, and Nakhǫnpathom jangwats. In mid-century Neale wrote: "Many Chinese who have settled and married in Siam reap immense wealth from sugar plantations they possess in the interior."[81] At the peak of sugar production in the 1850's and 1860's, thousands of Chinese were employed in the cane fields and refineries. Pallegoix counted over thirty refineries in Nakhǫnpathom alone, each employing two to three hundred Chinese workmen.[82] World competition eventually brought an end to Siam's prosperous sugar industry. The Chinese plantations were unable to compete because of the rising costs of labor. Rice cultivation by the Thai was extended at the expense of cane, and Chinese labor flocked to the rice mills where conditions and wages were better.[83] By 1889, sugar exports had ceased; only a few refineries still operated and those primarily in connection with liquor manufacture.[84]

Cotton, which was also grown by the Thai on a small scale during the nineteenth century, was produced for export primarily by Hainanese.[85] During the first half of the century, Southwest Siam was the principal center of production,[86] but, in the 1860's and 1870's, Hainanese were reported as engaging in extensive cotton cultivation in jungle clearings of Middle and North Siam. Siam has no comparative advantage in cotton production, and the industry died out within two decades after the beginning of free trade. The extensive tobacco plantations operated by the Chinese in both Southeast and Southwest Siam also declined after 1875, as the Thai acquired a taste for foreign tobaccos.

Chinese agricultural production for the local market, as distinct from that for export, showed a steady growth throughout the period under review. There developed around Bangkok and other important towns a zone of vegetable gardens, seri-leaf and betel-nut groves, and pigsties, which grew more extensive with the passage of time. The Chinese were, then as today, excellent gardeners. Bradley's description of Chinese gardens back from the river at Bangkok in 1836 applied throughout the century:

The gardens are cultivated very neatly. They may not be termed tasteful, but rich. . . . Beds of peas, . . . lettuce, onions, radishes, turnips, sera-leaf and betel occupy large portions of the gardens. The gardeners live in small dirty huts within their premises, guarded by a multitude of dogs, and a horrible stench of pigsties.[87]

The Chinese used liquid manure for the vegetables and decayed fish to fertilize the seri vines and continually watered the crops by hand from the small ditches laid out between the raised planted strips. Pig breeding was usually carried out in conjunction with gardening so as to utilize both manure and waste vegetable matter. The Thai declined to raise and slaughter pigs because of religious scruples, thus leaving a very lucrative occupation to the Chinese. As of 1910, some three hundred pigs were slaughtered daily in Bangkok alone.[88] By that year, vegetable and seri-leaf gardening and pig raising gave employment to several thousand Chinese in the vicinity of Bangkok.[89]

Gardening aside, however, plantation agriculture began to decline in the 1870's just as the demand for nonagricultural labor in Bangkok and other towns was picking up strongly. Wages were so much better in Bangkok that by 1876 "only the poorest of the Chinese immigrants will in the beginning [of their stay] do field labor and construction work." [90]

As a matter of fact, however, public construction work absorbed

more and more of the newly arrived immigrants right up to the First
World War. The construction of temples, canals, and roads was not
new work for Chinese immigrants. The Chinese built the structures
for the cremation of Rama II in 1824, and they built canals as early as
the third reign. In 1837, for instance, King Nangklao "graciously
ordered" a Thai nobleman "to be the overseer to hire Chinese coolies"
to dig a canal 54 kilometers long from Bangkok to the Bangpakong
river, a task which took three years.[91] King Mongkut regularized the
employment of Chinese labor on public works, at least near the capital,
by decreeing that corvée labor need not be employed for work that
might be done by paid laborers, the latter being almost invariably Chinese.[92] Wage labor came to be recognized as more efficient than conscripted labor, and both Mongkut and Julalongkǫn interpreted their
use of Chinese instead of Thai labor as a benevolent service to their
people. In ordering a canal to be dug from Bangkok to Ayutthaya in
1873, King Julalongkǫn "was graciously pleased to give of his personal
funds enough to pay Chinese workmen" for the work in order to avoid
the "vexation, misery and compulsion" of impressing Thai labor.[93] In
the canal and road construction—the amount of which increased
steadily throughout the century—the Thai bureaucrat responsible
hired Chinese foremen, who in turn hired and oversaw the Chinese
"coolie gangs." [94]

The construction of the main lines of the Thai railway system,
which began in 1892, would, from all accounts, have been impossible
without Chinese labor. The hope was expressed in 1891 that "one of
the best results of making railways would be the development of the
country people into laborers," [95] but it was ill-founded, for the Thai
would work a few days at most and then trudge off to spend their
earnings in the nearest town.[96] Most of the "coolies" employed were
newly immigrated Teochius and Hakkas, some of whom were transported from Swatow specifically for the job, while much of the skilled
labor was Cantonese. The engineers in charge found the Chinese immigrants "enduring and efficient" because they "tended to ignore the
transient nature of life in the rail construction camps" and could "look
forward, at the completion of a labour contract, to settlement in a
country which offered opportunity for people of commercial acumen." [97]

Most of the Chinese labor for the railways was freely contracted
for in Bangkok by the headmen or foremen employed. When construction began in jungle terrain, the mortality from malaria and other

fevers rose to frightening proportions. It became, therefore, "a matter of difficulty to the contractor to engage the necessary coolies, and of even greater difficulty, and one requiring infinite tact on the part of the sectional engineers . . . to persuade them to remain." [98] It is no exaggeration to say that thousands of Chinese lost their lives prior to 1910 on railway construction in Siam.[99] It was recorded that three hundred Chinese laborers were buried in the Phrayafai forest alone, victims of fever while constructing the stretch from Saraburi to Khorat.[100] Under such conditions, contractors had to offer relatively high wages, and even so the labor crews frequently struck for higher pay.[101] During the first year of railway construction (1892) some two thousand Chinese were employed, and thereafter to 1910 the figure was never less and often larger. Turnover was high, however, especially through desertion in the face of what often seemed imminent death. Chinese immigrants who worked on the railways during the first twenty years of construction must be numbered in tens of thousands. By 1909, railroads radiated from Bangkok in all directions extending into North, Northeast, Southeast, and Southwest Siam—a tribute not only to the farsightedness of Julalongkọn and the skill of Western engineers, but also to the gangs of Chinese "coolies" who built the earthworks and bridges and laid the rails.

The heaviest demand for Chinese labor in the period after about 1870 came from private enterprises in Bangkok. The growing city required increasing numbers of workers in the construction and building trades, the booming port absorbed more and more dock workers and lighter crews, and, above all, the mushrooming rice mills and sawmills needed both skilled and unskilled labor in ever greater number. By the early twentieth century it was estimated that Bangkok's rice mills and sawmills employed about 10,000 Chinese laborers.[102] Between 1890 and 1910 Bangkok changed from a city on water to one on land. New roads were constructed in the capital, as well as thousands of new shop-homes, Western-style residences, and government buildings. Hundreds of Chinese construction firms were formed to do the job, each with dozens of apprentice-laborers. The construction business was largely in Cantonese hands, but certain Teochiu firms also played an important part.[103] By 1910, several thousand Chinese workers in Bangkok were engaged in construction of one kind or another.

The labor force directly connected with the ocean trade of Bangkok also came to be very large and important. Prior to the displacement of Chinese junks and Thai square-rigged vessels by Western steamers, thousands of Chinese were employed as mariners alone.[104] After the revolution in shipping, the Chinese of Siam provided few crews for Western steamers, but they became the dock workers and manned the lighters which plied between the port and anchorages below the bar. Smyth, around the turn of the century, gave an amusing if biased account of the port, where, he claimed, there were

no rules but one: "Thou shalt not rebuke or in any way inconvenience a Chinese coolie, whatever he may do." He is the master of the port. He may grapple on to a steamer with his cargo boat as she comes up river and seeks her moorings. He may refuse to cast off when the captain has to change her berth; he may, and probably will, refuse to load the ship in any way but his own, even to the peril of ship and cargo; he may spit and smoke on the poop, and may generally lord it. But he must be allowed his sweet will; and if an officer cuts his rope away, or a quartermaster kicks him over the side, there is a general strike, and the captain is dropped on by the agents. For the Chinaman is a privileged person, and the port is run for his private edification and enjoyment.[105]

The situation caricatured in this passage arose because Chinese immigration failed to keep up with the demand, and labor was in short supply from the 1880's at least up to 1903. It might be worthwhile to reiterate here that the aim of the Chinese laborer was to make and *save* money, either to return to China and raise his family's status there or to begin business on a small capital in Siam in hopes of further gain. He would not have come to Siam in the first place if it were not mathematically possible, in view of prevailing wages and his standard of living, to save at a fairly rapid rate. The Chinese was the best laborer to be found in the East, and he had to be paid accordingly. As early as 1873, it was said that the "most common day laborer [in Bangkok] can save two-thirds of his earnings." [106] The British Consul in 1880 noted "a rise in the price of labour, and often . . . a total want of hands." [107] A few years later it was recorded that the Chinese laborer in Siam could earn wages double those prevailing in south China ports and live both better and cheaper than in his own country.[108] The Consul in 1889, with the horror typical of his class and time, provides the first record of concerted action to obtain higher wages:

Should the majority of the coolie class demand increased wages, they have no hesitation in striking work altogether and boycotting those who continue at the old rate of wages. A strike of this kind happened during the year, lasting for several days, and causing an entire cessation of business. Some steamers were even obliged to leave the port for want of hands to load the cargo.[109]

The labor shortage was chronic between 1898 and 1902, and Western employers were subjected to what apparently seemed the basest sort of labor difficulties.[110] In 1900:

The coolies seem to consider the present a suitable opportunity to agitate for higher pay. The cost of labour has been steadily going up of recent years, but latterly the men's demands have become excessive. Difficulty is now being felt in securing lighters' crews and considerable inconvenience and loss has been caused to some of the firms here.[111]

In 1901, the complaint was made that Chinese laborers were "able to impose their terms upon the employers" and in 1902 that "the demand for labour continues to exceed the supply." [112]

The tremendous influx of Chinese immigrants in 1903 put employers in a somewhat more advantageous position, and thereafter new immigration generally met demands placed on the labor force. Wages for manual labor, however, remained higher in Bangkok than any other port of East Asia. An interesting indication of the rise in relative value of unskilled manual labor in Bangkok is provided by comparing the wages of a mill "coolie" with those of a first-class carpenter in 1850 and 1890. In 1850, the carpenter was paid six times as much as the "coolie," [113] while forty years later he got only one-third more.[114]

The Chinese early became indispensable in the various skilled trades as well as in unskilled labor. Crawfurd wrote in 1830 that "the useful arts practised in Siam are commonly in the hands of Chinese and other strangers," [115] and before long the "other strangers" were out of the picture too. The earliest nineteenth-century visitors to Bangkok remarked specifically that Chinese were dominant among boatbuilders, blacksmiths, tinsmiths, tailors, leatherworkers, and shoemakers. Earl in the 1830's specified that the Chinese "engross all the mechanical employments." [116] In the 1860's, Werner attempted an exhaustive list of the commercial crafts in which any Thai were to be found, and it amounted to brick baking, pottery making, cabinetmaking, masonry, tanning, dyeing, coppersmithing, and rope manufacture. He concluded that practically the entire industry of Siam had passed into Chinese hands.[117] By the 1880's, Chinese were stated to be dominant among carpenters, cabinetmakers, carriage manufacturers and gold- and silversmiths, in addition to the artisan occupations already noted for the early nineteenth century. Thai were still dominant only among potters.[118] At this point, one can share the sentiments of Le May, who in discussing Chinese occupations in Siam at a later date, said he had "no wish to weary the reader with a recitation of almost every craft known to man." [119] The steady advance of Chinese artisans in Siam must be attributed—apart from their conceded industriousness and skill—to the guild organization brought from China. Young men were apprenticed in the craftsmen's shops of Bangkok just as in the cities and towns of south China. The tight guild organization served not only to freeze out non-Chinese but also to restrict certain crafts to various speech groups and even more exclusive groupings. Occupational specialization by speech group was very rigid by the turn of the century, according to the accounts of old-timers in Bangkok today.

The Chinese have been praised and damned for it, but the fact as stated in Ratzel's appraisal in 1876 cannot be denied: "While elsewhere they [the Chinese] make their living mainly as merchants and only secondarily as miners and fishermen, in Siam they control the *entire* economic life and leave to the natives only the cruder . . . aspects of agriculture." [120]

D. The Chinese and Government Revenue

The Chinese role in the various monopolies and farms operated by or under authority of the Thai government in the nineteenth century is remarkable—and complex. A brief description of the system of monopolies in existence prior to the second Jakkri reign will provide a basis for understanding the subsequent development. Royal trading monopolies were of two kinds, import and export. The only import monopolies of any importance were those of arms and ammunition: only the king could import these items and then sell that portion of them not needed by the state. Products for export monopolized by the king were far more numerous, including tin, pepper, saltpeter, sapanwood, ripe areca, hides, cardamoms, and gamboge. They had to be sold to the king's factors, and the king alone could export them or sell them to foreign traders. In the third reign, several of the royal export monopolies were farmed out to Chinese merchants. This meant that the merchant paid a lump sum to the Crown for sole rights to buy locally and export, say, hides; all hides for export had to be sold to the Chinese farmer, and he alone could export them or sell them to foreign traders. It was these export monopolies (as well as the arms and ammunition import monopoly, which had never been farmed out) that were given up after the Bowring treaty of 1855.

During the second and third reigns, that is, before the Bowring treaty, several other kinds of farms had been created. First of all, the collection of certain traditional taxes was farmed out.[121] This meant that the citizen paid his tax to the agent of the farmer at rates stipulated by the government, but that the farmer agreed *before* the tax was collected to pay the government a stipulated lump sum. The government sold each tax farm to the highest bidder, and the amount of profit the farmer made depended on how thoroughly he tracked down every taxpayer and wrung full payment from him. This system was obviously quite a different matter from the government's merely hiring Chinese tax collectors. At first only city taxes, such as the shop and boat tax were farmed out, but later certain of the taxes on agricultural production and land were farmed to Chinese as well.

Second, sole rights to perform certain services, and to manufacture and sell locally certain products—services and products which themselves would otherwise have been or had theretofore been taxed by the government—were farmed out. Chief among these were rights to operate lotteries and gambling establishments and to manufacture and sell spirits and playing cards. In each case, the farmer paid a lump sum to the Crown for rights in a certain area and for a certain period of time. These farms were in effect indirect taxes on the consumer of the goods or services; the government was assured of a fixed revenue, and the farmer assumed the risk—which was, of course, well calculated prior to the bidding. Third, the collection of duties on certain imports and exports was farmed out. This kind of farm, it should be noted, differed from farmed *trading* monopolies in that the farmed product was not—as part of the agreement—bought or sold by the farmer, but merely channeled through him for the collection of duties according to the tariff fixed by the government.

Early in King Mongkut's reign all existent trading monopolies were abolished, but a new kind of monopoly was established which was, among other things, an import trading monopoly. This was the highly important opium monopoly, established in 1852 and confirmed by the Bowring treaty. According to the treaty, opium was to be free of duty but had to be sold to the (Chinese) opium farmers. The latter in buying the farm from the government, in effect, paid the government the duties it could have collected directly and bought sole import rights as well as rights to process and retail the opium locally.

The end of royal trading and of trading monopolies together with the 3 per cent ceiling on import duties constituted important losses of revenue for the state, and at a time when large-scale construction and modernization was being planned. To make up the losses, the government (1) converted the old export monopolies into duty revenue farms, (2) farmed out the collection of duties on almost all other imports and exports, (3) reorganized the collection of other traditional taxes as monopolies, and (4) created new taxes, which were also farmed out. In addition, the opium, spirits, lottery, and gambling farms were allowed to expand to the limits the traffic would bear, and new ones of the same type—e.g., the pork monopoly—were established. Thus, while the Chinese lost some trading monopolies as a result of the Bowring treaty, in the end they gained innumerable revenue farms of far greater aggregate value.

It is significant that four of the most lucrative farms—together providing between 40 per cent and 50 per cent of the *total state revenues* during most of the second half of the nineteenth century—were based essentially on Chinese consumption. These were the opium, gambling, lottery, and spirit farms. It is not unfair to state that while the country depended on Chinese virtues for the expansion of commerce and industry, the government relied on Chinese vices for the expansion of public revenue. These four farms, because of their importance for Chinese society as well as for government finance, deserve closer attention here.

Opium consumption was introduced to Siam probably prior to the beginning of the nineteenth century; Rama II in 1811 issued the first edict against its sale and consumption in the kingdom.[122] The subsequent story is not dissimilar to that of opium in south China, for the demand of the Chinese population and the rapacity of both local merchants and the Western traders combined to increase smuggling and bribery in spite of the contraband. In 1839, while Lin Tse-hsü was taking strong measures against the opium trade in Canton, King Nangklao "pronounced a divine word, a commandment, giving it to be distributed and published abroad, not allowing any person whatever to buy and sell opium."[123] In spite of the dire punishments provided in the edict, smuggling continued apace; interestingly enough, when cases were discovered the local Chinese merchant-recipients were sentenced to death or imprisoned while the foreign traders were usually let off free.[124]

The situation soon got out of hand, and Mongkut in 1852 established the opium farm, taking measures at the same time to restrict opium smoking to Chinese. He ordered that any Thai who smoked opium must wear a queue and pay the Chinese triennial poll tax, on the theory that by picking up the Chinese vice he forfeited all claims to good standing as a Thai.[125] It has been said that opium was virtually a necessity for the laboring Chinese in Siam; it was resorted to most widely by those doing the hardest physical labor—mill and dock workers, rickshaw pullers, and the like. The Thai—whether or not the fact that they ordinarily did not indulge in heavy labor is crucial in this regard—never adopted the habit in any numbers. As the Chinese population and the proportion of laborers in it increased, the value of the opium farm mounted steadily. By 1874, the price of the farm was equivalent to about £100,000, and it rose to £136,000 in 1891.[126]

By the 1880's, the opium farm was such a huge operation that only syndicates of the richest Chinese could make successful bids. In 1890, an additional syndicate of three was formed under the opium farm merely to handle retail sales through the 1,200-odd licensed shops in Bangkok, the person in charge of each shop being a salaried employee of the farm.[127] By 1903/04 the annual revenue from the farm was over seven million baht, and by 1905/06 over ten million, amounting to between 15 per cent and 20 per cent of total government income.[128] The government finally took over control of the opium traffic and abolished the farm in 1907/08 and 1908/09.[129] Revenue from opium *régie* remained high for many decades thereafter, but Chinese entrepreneurs no longer shared in the big profits.

The opium farmer held tremendous power. In order to obtain the monopoly, he had to pay "amazing perquisites" to the high nobles whom he considered to have crucial influence in the government. These officials, once bought, backed him up in any use or abuse of his monopoly rights. He dictated the price of opium and ruthlessly punished anyone who tried to evade his farm. He even had his own agents on the lookout for smugglers, and any caught by the regular police were turned over to him for trial and punishment. It was his abiding desire to increase the consumption of opium, and to this end no ruse, trick, or subterfuge to attract new addicts was overlooked.[130]

The Chinese gambling farm was hardly a more savory institution. The farm dates back to Ayutthayan days but became an important source of revenue only when the Chinese population reached large proportions in the nineteenth century. The games used in gambling houses were originally introduced by Chinese settlers, and their inveterate love of gaming, unlike their fondness for opium, proved to be contagious.[131] Chinese gamblers, however, provided the majority of customers throughout the existence of the farm. The farmer had the sole right to operate or authorize the operation of gambling houses. According to law, the populace could gamble freely without molestation from the farmer for three days each at the Chinese and Thai New Years, but at all other times gambling was permitted only at houses licensed under the farm. Revenue from the farm, a few hundred thousand baht in the third reign, had grown to 5,700,000 baht in 1903/04.[132]

One form of gambling, the Hua-hui (C 42), was reserved as a separate monopoly, the lottery farm.[133] The Hua-hui originated in China and was introduced to Bangkok in 1835. King Nangklao suspected the populace of hoarding coins, and the Chinese spirit farmer suggested the lottery as a means of bringing the money into circulation. The Chinese game was somewhat altered, so that there were thirty-four different characters, each identified by a distinctive picture, Chinese character, and Thai letter. Almost any amount could be staked; winners received thirty times their bet. Bangkok and vicinity were divided into thirty-eight districts each under a manager, who had solicitors and salesmen scattered along the streets and in all public places of his district. In addition to the mass of men thus employed, the farmer required a staff of about two hundred to run the lottery itself. Drawings were held twice daily, and it is said that at drawing times normal business paused until the winning character was bruited through the streets. When the farm was first started the price was 20,000 baht. It soon came to be put up for auction every year, and the price never failed to increase. The figure reached about 200,000 baht in the fourth reign, increased to 2,100,000 in 1903/04 [134] and to its all-time peak of 3,800,000 in 1911/12. Stakes placed *daily* during the last two decades of the lottery's existence averaged 40,000 baht, while the farmer's usual daily payments on winnings were around 10,000, although every year there were a few lucky strikes bringing daily payments to 30,000 baht or more. Clearly the lottery farm was highly profitable to the farmer as well as to the government.

Both Mongkut and Julalongkǫn were aware of the evils of commercialized gambling, especially in the provinces, but farms could not be abolished until substitute sources of revenue were found. The number of gambling houses began to be reduced in 1900, and, in 1906/07, gambling farms in the provinces were abolished.[135] The final abolition of both the lottery and gambling farms in Bangkok came only in 1916/17, thus bringing to an end what Smyth had termed "state aid to ruin with a vengeance." [136]

The spirit monopoly, which carried sole rights to distill and sell rice liquor, was one of the first farmed out to Chinese; by mid-century there were farmers for every part of the country. As with the opium farmer, the spirit farmer's power with regard to his product was absolute. If an unauthorized still was found, there was apparently no limit to the vengeance the farmer could take.[137] Consumption of rice spirits was largely, but by no means wholly, Chinese. Revenue from spirit farms reached the astounding figure of 4,200,000 baht in 1903/04 —over 9 per cent of all national revenues.[138] In 1909, the government began direct collection of the excise duty on locally distilled spirits,[139] but to this day monopoly rights to produce liquor in the various jangwats of Siam are auctioned to the highest bidders.

The various duty and tax farms were gradually done away with during the latter part of Julalongkǫn's reign. By 1910, only a few remained in modified form, that for bird's-nests being the most important. Before the total demise of tax farms, they reached their fullest development in the autonomous principalities of the north; in Chiangmai even the collection of the tax on rice fields was farmed out to a Chinese syndicate.[140] Fortunately for Sino-Thai relations, the system was not adopted elsewhere.

The only direct tax on the Chinese as such was the poll tax payable every three years.[141] The tax was first levied in the second reign and was apparently set first at 1.50 baht payable annually.[142] From 1828 until 1909, the tax was triennial and fixed at 4.25 baht. It was considered payment for exemption from corvée and from personal service to a patron, and payment entitled a Chinese to move freely about the country without molestation. The tax was never raised during the reigns of Rama IV and V, a reflection of their established policy to encourage Chinese immigration. Therefore, in spite of the increase in the number of Chinese, receipts from the tax probably never constituted more than 3 per cent of total government revenues in any year during which the tax was paid. The highest figure recorded— somewhat under a million baht—was for the last year of the tax, 1909.

No review of the role of the Chinese in the economy of any country where they reside would be complete without mention of remittances. Given the general aim of the immigrants—to advance family fortunes— it was to be expected that settlers in Siam would devise ways to send moey to their families even before they could return in person. In the words of Gutzlaff:

A part of . . . [the] hard earnings [of Chinese settlers] is annually remitted to their kindred who are left in their native land; and it is astonishing to see what hardships they will suffer to procure and send home this pittance. . . . If an emigrant can send but a dollar, he will send it. . . . Indeed, he will never send home a letter unless accompanied with some present; he will rather entirely cease writing than send nothing more substantial than paper.[143]

In the heyday of the junk traffic, the letters and money were entrusted when possible to acquaintances from the same district in China but more often to the agents, found on most every junk, whose regular business it was to collect and deliver remittances. During the spring, when junks were in port, a Chinese could easily find a remittance agent from his native district who, for a commission of about 10 per cent, would remit his money.[144]

During the second half of the century remittance shops sprang up in Bangkok to handle the growing business; they sent the money by regular couriers, and some remittance shops established connections with emigration agencies in the south China ports to facilitate distribution to the recipient families. The shops guaranteed delivery and in time included proof of delivery as part of their service; consequently, they charged somewhat higher commissions—up to 20 per cent.[145]

There is no basis for estimating the amount of remittances sent from Siam to China in the early days. According to Gutzlaff there were instances (c. 1830) of junks carrying more than $60,000 (Spanish) in remittances. And for the first decade of the twentieth century a Chinese customs report estimates total annual remittances received in the Teochiu and Hakka emigrant areas served by Swatow at $21,000,000,[146] but not more than a third of this could have come from Siam. It can be said only that remittances from Siam were sizable and growing.

Several interesting, if somewhat speculative, conclusions can be drawn from the material presented in this section. It would appear that revenue was the government's primary concern in expanding farms and monopolies. The system effectively harnessed the Chinese money-making drive in the interests of government revenue, but, it must be admitted, to the detriment of the people's welfare. It should be remembered, however, that the government was hamstrung by the tariff limitations of the Bowring treaty and could ill afford being selective in its revenue methods.

The government's policy also served to attract more Chinese to Siam, to keep more of them there, and to depress remittances to China. The Chinese poll tax, the income from the monopolies, and the amount of remittances were to some extent interdependent variables. A higher Chinese poll tax would have restricted immigration and reduced revenues from the opium, gambling, lottery, and spirit monopolies, which were patronized largely by the Chinese. If, from whatever motives, the government had restricted or prohibited gambling and liquor and opium consumption, then there is every reason to believe that fewer Chinese would have remained permanently in Siam, more would have been able to return after a shorter stay, and remittances to China would have been higher. Few of the nineteenth-century observers failed to note that the savings of the Chinese immigrants were continually being depleted by enticements to gamble, drink, and smoke opium. The average immigrant set himself a certain goal of savings which he hoped to achieve before going back to China; constant victimization at the hands of the farmers and their agents meant not only less money to remit but postponement of the day of final return. As it turned out, the balance of these forces in the second half of the nineteenth century resulted in exactly what the government desired: an increasing supply of the Chinese commercial skill and labor necessary for the expansion of the Thai economy, high revenue indirectly from the Chinese, and low remittances to China. This conclusion, reached only in hindsight, in no way implies that the Thai government, with Machiavellian cunning, devised the country's revenue policy with these interrelations clearly in mind. While there is no evidence that the welfare of Chinese residents in Bangkok was of real concern to Julalongkǫn's government, it is nonetheless probable that, had other revenue sources been available, the government would have restricted gambling, at least, before the turn of the century.

The anomalous conclusion remains, however, that for a period of at least fifty years, during which Siam achieved a modern government, a thriving economy, and entered the world economy and family of nations, almost half of the government's revenues was derived directly or indirectly from the comparatively small Chinese minority. On fiscal grounds alone, the Chinese contribution to Siam's achievement must be given considerable weight.

4

THE

PATTERN OF INSTABILITY:

Chinese Society in Siam from the Third through the Fifth Reign

A. *Intermarriage and Assimilation*

PERHAPS the primary social fact about nineteenth-century Chinese society in Siam was the dearth of Chinese women. Prior to 1893 women almost never emigrated from China; [1] females cannot have exceeded 2 per cent or 3 per cent of the Chinese arrivals during the immigration period 1882–1892.[2] At that time, lineage councils in the emigrant areas of south China never permitted wives to accompany their husbands abroad for fear of losing the family entirely.[3] Emigrants were supposed to make money abroad in the interests of kin-oriented goals and then return to tend to family affairs. It was even more unthinkable for unmarried girls to emigrate, excepting of course those who, because of family poverty, were sold into prostitution. Indeed a sizable proportion of the Chinese women who did emigrate to Siam prior to 1910 were destined for brothels.[4] An analysis made of all burials in the Teochiu cemetery in Bangkok during a five-year period, 1900–1906, showed that only 3 per cent of those buried were women.[5] The significant change in female immigration began in the 1893–1905 immigration period, but even then the proportion of women among arrivals can hardly have been more than 5 per cent. In the 1906–1917 period, female immigration increased still further, perhaps to 10 per cent of the total. These percentages are merely informed guesses, but it is clear that the general picture of an extremely abnormal sex ratio obtained throughout the fifth reign.

During the nineteenth century, then, the alternatives for the great mass of Chinese immigrants were to remain single or marry local women. (Many, of course, had wives in China.) A survey of the nineteenth-century sources indicates the following pattern: [6] The great majority of the mining and plantation laborers did not marry so long as they remained in that occupational status. The same could be said of urban wage earners, though apparently a somewhat larger minority did marry in Siam. On the other hand, Chinese who settled down on the land as farmers or plantation owners almost always got married. Most of the merchants and artisans also married local women, though the rate was presumably lower for shop assistants and apprentices. Wealthy merchants usually had more than one wife, and by the turn of the century some had wives from China. There was, then, a considerable class differential in the marriage rate, low among the more temporary working-class groups, and high among those who were more settled and held higher economic status. Smyth at the turn of the century hazarded the guess that about half of the Chinese immigrants still living after five years in Siam had married local women.[7]

Language and poverty seem to have been the only barriers to intermarriage with Thai women. Immigrants in all occupations other than mining and wage labor usually picked up some Thai language for business reasons, and most of the immigrants after a few years in the country were as well off as the bulk of Thai men. There were no religious scruples on either side, and indeed Chinese men were said to have readily accommodated themselves to the Thai form of Buddhism. There were in fact several positive inducements for Thai women to marry Chinese. Thai women—not their menfolk—were the traders in the indigenous population; they had a certain amount of business know-how and could appreciate the advantages of an industrious Chinese husband. "The Siamese woman is a shrewd, practical person, and is willing to put sentiment in the background for the sake of obtaining a hardworking and not unaffectionate husband who has his little savings and a thriving business." [8] According to Smyth,[9] Chinese could "get the best girls to marry them, for they have more to offer, and treat the ladies with more consideration than do the men of their own nationality." Moreover, to the Chinese man, taking a Thai wife presented certain advantages stemming from her birth. It was convenient for a Chinese merchant to have a wife who could deal with Thai customers, and in the days of slavery it was said that Chinese with local wives could more readily obtain loans.[10] Furthermore, marrying a Thai was a much less expensive proposition than a wedding in China.[11]

In the nineteenth century, then, marriage with Thai women was the rule for Chinese immigrants when occupation and financial status permitted. The next question concerns the offspring of such marriages: was the influence of the father or of the mother supreme? Before attempting to answer this question on the basis of the nineteenth-century literature, it might be well to point up a few general considerations. First of all, there was in Siam no racial barrier to complete assimilation. Differences in physical appearance between Thai and Chinese are not marked, and if anything the Thai showed a preference for certain physical characteristics—fair skin especially—more typical of Chinese than of "pure-blooded" Thai. As early as 1825, it was noted that Siamese chiefs married "daughters of Chinese or fair women of Chinese extraction . . . in preference to their own females." [12]

Lukjin were not a class apart—as were the products of many varieties of mixed marriages in Southeast Asia. In view of their parentage, they almost invariably spoke Thai fluently in addition to their father's language. They could either identify with the Chinese or achieve complete acceptance by the Thai, and they were not constrained by convention to take either course. Differences of dress and coiffure between Chinese and Thai prior to 1910 were clear-cut. Sons and grandsons of Chinese immigrants either wore a queue or did not; daughters and granddaughters wore their hair either in the Thai style or in the Chinese fashion. There was no middle ground in the matter of identification, no Sino-Thai culture with distinct values or outward signs. Government policy also made it necessary for male descendants of Chinese immigrants to identify themselves clearly as Chinese or Thai. Chinese men were subject to the triennial tax and exempt from corvée and personal service, while Thai (and other Asian) males had to be attached to a patron or government master. The Chinese descendant either paid the Chinese poll tax or sought out a Thai patron; it was virtually impossible to do neither.[13] For these reasons, a marginal role midway between the two societies was unusual.

While nothing approaching a stable Sino-Thai culture developed in nineteenth-century Siam, local Chinese culture did undergo some remarkable changes in the direction of Thai culture which, by closing the gap between the two ways of life, facilitated the assimilation of local-born Chinese to Thai society. As Gutzlaff, with his usual sweet temper, noted in the 1830's, the Chinese were "very anxious to conform to the vile habits of the Siamese." [14] It will be most telling, perhaps, to demonstrate acculturation in local Chinese society with religious examples, inasmuch as religion, of all the aspects of culture, is generally affirmed to be the most resistant to change.

As early as 1823, Crawfurd wrote that "the Chinese . . . profess themselves Buddhists as soon as they come into the country." [15] This is amplified in his later work: "Whatever may have been their religion before, or whether they had any or not, [the Chinese adopt] the Buddhist form of worship, visiting the Siamese temples, and giving the usual alms to the priests. A few of them even enter the priesthood, although this mode of life is by no means very congenial to their industrious and active character." [16] Gutzlaff also remarked that the Chinese "are very prone to conform entirely to the religious rites of the [Siamese]." [17]

One type of Thai Buddhist temple in particular came, by a chance similarity of name, to be major places of worship for the Siam Chinese. [18] The leader of the great Ming maritime expeditions, Cheng Ho, had another name, San-pao, and is commonly known as San-pao T'ai-chien (C 44). In Buddhism there is a basic concept of the "Three Treasures," which refers to the three essentials of the faith: the Buddha, the Doctrine, and the Priesthood. The concept of the Three Treasures was literally translated into Chinese, both in China and in Siam, as San-pao (C 45). Although the *pao* in Cheng Ho's small name is written with another character and has quite a different meaning ("protection") from the *pao* of the Buddhist concept, the two words are pronounced exactly the same. It is hardly surprising, therefore, that the largely illiterate Chinese of Siam confused the two homophonous names in their folklore. Cheng Ho was deified in Siam perhaps as early as the seventeenth century, and his name, San-pao Kung, is more often written as "Three Treasures" than as "three-protections." There is an allusion in the Ming History to a "Three Treasures" temple in Siam established by Cheng Ho, [19] and this compounding of errors indicated that during the Ayutthayan period the confusion had already been made between the deified San-pao Kung and the Buddhist concept.

The most famous of the San-pao ("Three Treasures") Buddhist temples is located in Ayutthaya; it was founded by Rama I but may have replaced an earlier San-pao temple destroyed by the Burmese in 1767. In any case, a legend among the Chinese today has it that San-pao Kung himself, i.e., Cheng Ho, established this temple in the Ming dynasty. In the nineteenth century there were at least three San-pao temples especially venerated by the Chinese—at Thonburi, Ayutthaya, and Paetriw. All three temples are in the Thai-style with an image of the Buddha therein. They were worshipped by both Thai and Chinese following the Thai form. San-pao Kung was one of the chief deities of the local Chinese; his veneration in the form of a Thai-style Buddha undoubtedly eased the transition for local-born Chinese to the Thai form of Buddhism.

Quite apart from Buddhism—with the Mahayana form of which most Chinese immigrants were already familiar before they left China —the Chinese in Siam have shown themselves ready to adopt almost any objects worshipped by the Thai and believed to have local power. One nineteenth-century Chinese temple in Chiangmai has a large tablet to the Chiangmai *Wang*, i.e., the ruler of the old principality. Another old Chinese temple in Sukhothai houses a statue believed to be of Phra Ruang, i.e., the old Sukhothai king, Ramkamhaeng. The most remarkable and significant example, however, is the Chinese worship of *lak-mueang*, the "pillar of the State." The Thai *lak-mueang* is derived from the Siva-linga of India, via Cambodia. In ancient Khmer culture, stone Siva-lingas in phallic form came to symbolize royal sovereignty and were enshrined in the capital and viceregal towns, including many in what is now Thailand. Long after the fall of Angkor, almost every city (in the area formerly subject to the Khmer empire) which aspired to independence or autonomy maintained a linga or lak ("pillar") at its symbolic center.[20] By the nineteenth century the laks were in most cases carved from logs and stylized, though their phallic nature remained apparent. In the popular Thai religion, the *lak-mueang* was assimilated to the animistic *phi* or spirits and came to be regarded as the supreme *phi* of the city or state. The Chinese who settled in these cities and towns (e.g., Bangkok, Khorat, Surin, Sisaket, Roi-et, Songkhla) recognized the potency of this locality deity, began worshipping it, and eventually assimilated this descendant of phallic worship to their own religious concepts. *Lak-mueang* was equated with Ch'eng-huang (C 46), the Chinese "god of the walls and moats" found in practically all walled cities in China. Many of the *lak-mueang* were rehoused by the Chinese in new temples, and once again Chinese and Thai found themselves worshipping together the same deity in the same temples.

If any aspect of traditional Chinese culture is inviolate, it is presumably the cult of ancestor worship. Basic to this cult is burial and the whole complex of ceremonials concerning grave placement, care, and worship. Nevertheless, the evidence is incontestable that in nineteenth-century Siam the great majority of Chinese cremated their dead. In the 1820's, it was noted that the Chinese had "sacrificed the practice of burying their dead and erecting costly monuments over them" and were "burning their dead like the Siamese." [21] The oldest public Chinese cemetery in Bangkok was built in 1884, and only by 1900 did each of the five major speech groups have a cemetery. This meant that up until that time the poorer Chinese had no choice but to cremate, for only the rich could send the remains back to China or, alternatively, build graves according to *feng-shui* [22] in the nearest suitable hills (Southeast Siam). In the whole year of 1892, only two hundred Chinese corpses were shipped back to the homeland from Bangkok. In reporting this fact, the British Consul pointed out that "only people who are well off can . . . have this honour paid to their remains. The common Chinese in Siam follow the usual custom of cremation after death." [23] Outside of Bangkok, the oldest Chinese cemeteries date back no further than the first decade of the twentieth century. Informants upcountry are agreed that the majority of Chinese prior to the First World War were cremated on death and that most of the remainder were buried in the precincts of Thai temples.

In adopting cremation even for those born in the home country, the Chinese were influenced not only by considerations of expense but also by the Thai conception of burial as a practice suitable only for those who die unnaturally, of a mishap or accident. The Thai wives of Chinese immigrants undoubtedly also argued for cremation as against burial of their deceased husbands and children. Whatever the cause, the important point here is that in the heart of this Chinese society, not just at its most assimilated fringes, Thai death practices were followed which entailed chanting by Thai priests and cremation in a Thai temple compound.

These illustrations demonstrate that the religious content of local Chinese culture in Siam differed from traditional south Chinese culture through the incorporation of Thai elements. Even aside from this acculturative aspect, the social mingling of Chinese and Thai in Siamese temples and shrines can only have facilitated the assimilation of the lukjin descendants of Chinese immigrants.

The extent and rapidity with which the descendants of Chinese assimilated to the Thai pattern obviously varied from one case to another. Children of mixed families living in the Sampheng quarter of Bangkok or other numerically strong and compact Chinese communities grew up as Chinese more often than did offspring of mixed families in a strongly Thai milieu. Whether the child of a part Chinese family was reared as Thai or Chinese depended also in part on the personalities of the parents. Many immigrants who married eventually returned to China, and they ordinarily left Thai wives and their progeny—especially daughters—behind, in which case the mother's influence on the remaining children automatically became supreme.[24] A differential on the basis of sex was, in any case, quite natural: girls more often than boys copied the mother's pattern and became Thai, while sons more often followed the paternal pattern.

To return now to the question posed earlier about the assimilation of the children of mixed marriages up to 1910, this writer's conclusions from a reading of the contemporary literature is that the lukjin proper —that is, children of China-born Chinese fathers and Thai mothers— more often than not considered themselves Chinese, but that children of a lukjin father—whether his wife was Thai or lukjin—usually considered themselves Thai. However, the range of variation in the observations made by Western writers in this regard is fairly wide, and it will be illuminating to quote the more authoritative statements pertinent to the identification choice made by Chinese descendants.

Gutzlaff in the 1830's:

[Lukjin] frequently cut off their queues and become for a certain time Siamese priests. Within two or three generations, all the distinguishing marks of the Chinese character dwindle entirely away, and a nation which adheres so obstinately to its national customs becomes wholly changed to Siamese. These people usually neglect their own literature, and apply themselves to the Siamese.[25]

In 1838, a missionary resident in Bangkok:

The daughters of Chinese by Siamese mothers assume the dress and adopt the languages, manners and customs of the Siamese.[26]

According to Bowring in 1857:

Though they intermarry with the races among whom they dwell, the Chinese type becomes predominant, and the children are almost invariably educated on the father's model.[27]

Elsewhere, however, Bowring, quoting with approval:

Those children [of Chinese immigrants] who speak only Siamese (and their number is very great) are marked upon the wrist like the Siamese.

The British Consul in his annual report for 1864:

The female [lukjin] . . . are in dress and appearance similar to the Siamese; the males, growing the Chinese tail and dressing similar to their father, are not easily distinguishable from the native Chinaman.[28]

The *Siam Repository* in 1873:

If Chinamen take to themselves women of Siam for wives, and have by them male children, these children, if they retain the paternal costume, can claim the same exemptions as if they had been born in China. It sometimes, though seldom, occurs that their grandchildren claim these exemptions. These as a rule prefer to be considered Siamese subjects, and ignore the costume and habits of the grandfather.[29]

Hallet in 1890:

The grandchildren of Chinese immigrants are classed and registered as Siamese, and are liable to corvee labour as soon as they measure . . . 50 inches to the shoulder, and are marked to one or other Government master.[30]

Smyth in 1898:

Considering the money they [the Chinese] make out of the country, and the freedom of action they enjoy when compared with the native Siamese, it is no wonder that the children of mixed marriages adopt the pigtail when they can.[31]

Annandale, with regard to South Siam, in 1900:

Whereas the son of a Chinese father and a Malay mother often grows a pigtail and calls himself a Chinaman, . . . the son of a Chinese father and a Siamese mother just as often calls himself a Siamese and attempts to lose sight of his paternal ancestry.[32]

Campbell in 1902:

Though often unable to speak any language but Siamese, he [the lukjin] is proud of being a Chinaman and wearing the queue like any other Celestial, and continues to bear his clan and family name. . . . Of course in the second and third generation there is a tendency for him to get lost among the natives of the country.[33]

Raquez in 1903:

The mixed bloods of the third generation sacrifice their pigtails, dress in the Siamese fashion and forsake even the ancestral cult.[34]

P. Thompson in 1906:

The children of this mixed parentage . . . speak Siamese, have no particular reverence for the pigtail, which they as often as not dispense with, and in their sympathies and manners they are entirely Siamese.[35]

The conclusion that third-generation descendants of Chinese immigrants were generally Thai in culture and identification would seem warranted for the period under review. This meant, first of all, that the Thai population was continually being increased by the incorporation of Chinese 'blood' (genes), and that the Thai population of the main immigrant areas was becoming more and more Chinese in physical appearance. The average Thai of Lower Siam and to a lesser extent of all the regions bordering on the Gulf is today fairer skinned and more Chinese in appearance than the Thai of North and Northeast Siam. Few Siamese families whose residence in Bangkok dates back more than one generation do not have a Chinese ancestor.

The comparatively rapid assimilation of Chinese descendants in Siam also meant that the perpetuation of Chinese society there was dependent on continued immigration. The frequent references to the cultural persistence of the Chinese in Siam during the nineteenth century—take, for instance, Bowring's flat statement that "the Chinese . . . preserve their own language, their own nationality, their own costume and religious usages, their own traditions, habits and social organization." [36] —are witness not to a peculiar unchangeableness on the part of Chinese but to the continual reinforcement of Chinese society through immigration.

B. Chinese Society

The social structure of Chinese communities in Siam during the latter part of the nineteenth century was fluid and rather amorphous.[37]

Social stratification was ill-defined, organizations cut across such class lines as did exist, and social mobility was high. Nevertheless, there were distinctions of status and prestige, and the available evidence would seem to indicate that these were functions primarily of wealth and secondarily of commitment to the local Chinese community as opposed to an orientation exclusively towards China.

Those with the highest status and prestige were the merchants who held the larger monopolies and farms. They were the wealthiest individuals in the community and, because of their vested interest in the Thai economy, had the strongest commitment to local Chinese society and to Siam. Close to them at the top was the rising group of mill owners and compradores, whose wealth and local loyalties were likewise extensive. At the bottom of the social scale were hawkers, agricultural laborers, street barbers, actors, rickshaw pullers—people with no capital whatsoever and few ties to the local society. Only slightly above them were the mass of mill and dock workers, whose income was somewhat higher but who seldom put down roots before returning to China or shifting to a higher occupation. Between these extreme positions were the following: the great mass of tradesmen and artisans, the lesser revenue farmers; the shop assistants, craft apprentices, employees of the opium, gambling, and revenue farms, clerks in Western banks and commercial houses; and the few professionals. Within this extensive middle class, other things being equal, self-employment gave added prestige.

Whatever may have been its value in China, education was of little importance in determining social position in the Chinese community of Siam. As early as 1838, an astute observer called attention to "the low estimate in which education is held" [38] in the Chinese community. Scholarship was a luxury indulged in after high status was attained through the accumulation of wealth; it was not a path to upward mobility. Wealthy merchants hired Chinese teachers to give a classical education to their children, and for the rest there were a few small private schools to which other well-off tradesmen sent their children for a few years at most. Real scholars seldom immigrated to Siam, which with most of Nan-yang was considered a cultural wilderness. In fact professionals of any standing were conspicuous by their absence. There were no Chinese lawyers, and the old-style doctors and "tooth-artists" were little respected.

Largely because of fairly rigid occupational specialization, there were important status differentials among the speech groups. Teochius and Hokkiens were of highest status. The great majority of revenue farmers and of rice-mill owners were Teochiu, with Hokkiens in second place, at least among revenue farmers. Teochius also dominated most of the lucrative trades, including rice and other local products, imported textiles, and Western foodstuffs, and they virtually monopolized pawnbroking. Hokkiens were also prominent among merchants and dominated the important tea business in particular. Cantonese, who came next in the prestige ladder, owned several rice mills and sawmills, but above all they were the engineers and mechanics, operated most of the hardware and machine shops, and dominated the construction business. They were also predominant in the silk piece-goods trade and operated most of the hotels and restaurants. An article in the *Siam Repository* of 1870 throws light on the relative position of Teochius and Cantonese: "The Tia Chu people love the almighty dollar. They will do anything to earn an honest penny, and they often become rich and influential; and the Cantonese hate them for the power they possess." [39]

Not all members of these three speech groups had upper- and middle-class standing, however. Teochius constituted a large part of the dock workers and laborers on canal and railway construction, Hokkiens formed a large part of the tin miners in South Siam, and Cantonese laborers were predominant in the building trade. Teochius, in fact, were found in large numbers in all strata; their general high standing rested on the fact that they dominated most of the highest socioeconomic positions.

Hakkas and Hainanese, on the other hand, were almost entirely unrepresented in the occupations of higher standing. Hakkas in particular were the petty tradesmen, especially those dealing in sundry goods; the lesser artisans, including silversmiths, leatherworkers, and tailors; manual laborers, hawkers, and barbers. Hainanese were the hand sawyers, market gardeners, fishermen, domestic servants, waiters, tea-shop operators, and, not infrequently, "coolies," miners, and peddlers. They were the poorest of all the speech groups, and their general low social standing was undisputed.

Upward mobility in this Chinese society was extremely high, especially during the period 1880–1910.[40] Most of the immigrants arrived with a roll of bedding, a few cash, and a determination to make good. With the help usually of kinsmen or those from their native village or hsien, they obtained jobs as shop assistants or apprentices, if possible; as "coolies," if able-bodied; and if all else failed, as peddlers, rickshaw pullers, and the like. A moderate rise in status was almost the rule among those who stayed: the peddler eventually established a permanent stall of his own; the shop assistant became a shop owner; the apprentice established his own machine shop; the laborer became a foreman and eventually set up his own hand sawmill; the petty tradesman became an established merchant. Initially, motivation for upward mobility was based on the desire to acquire enough money to return to China with savings, but after a few years many immigrants wanted to get ahead for reasons congruent with the values and structure of the *local* society. Those who did not rise but were able to save something usually returned to China for good.[41] Those who achieved even a moderate commercial and social success rarely severed their ties to Siam; if they returned to China, then a son or nephew carried on.

Examples of spectacular upward mobility and total success were almost legion. The rags-to-riches story was if anything more common among the Chinese in Siam than among European immigrants in the United States during the same period and arose from a similar expansion of the national economy.[42] There is the case of Chang Ting (C 47), the founder of Chin Ch'eng Li (Kim Seng Li) Company, who came to Bangkok from Ch'ao-an in the 1870's indebted eighteen baht for his passage. He worked first as a cook, then as a rice-polishing "coolie." Next he began operating a sampan ferry across the river at Bangkok, earning three baht a month, after which he became a market gardener making ten baht. Soon he had enough savings to lend money to those even poorer than himself, thus increasing his capital until in 1882 he established a small export business of his own. By this time he was sufficiently affluent to marry into a good family in North Siam, and his mother-in-law, who was friendly with the governor of Lampang, obtained for him an excellent teak forest concession. While his firm expanded, he became a subfarmer of three gambling houses and a spirit-farm operator. By the first decade of the twentieth century, his company owned five rice mills, a sawmill and a dockyard.[43]

Ch'en Tz'u-hung (C 48) provides another example of the possibilities of upward mobility in Bangkok. He arrived in Bangkok about 1865, a penniless Teochiu lad of twenty, and after working as a mariner obtained his own junk which he sailed between Bangkok and China, trading rice for Chinese products. When competition with Western steamers became excessive, he quit shipping and worked as an accountant for another Chinese firm. With the experience thus gained, Tz'u-hung opened his own commercial firm, dealing in the same products he formerly carried in his junk. In 1874, he established the first of the company's rice mills. When he retired to Swatow around the turn of the century, his vast interests in rice and both Chinese and Western imported goods were turned over to his son, Li-mei, born of a Thai mother but educated in China.[44]

Such stories could be greatly multiplied. While the proportion of the population who rose from penniless immigrants to millionaires was small, such instances were sufficiently numerous and well-known to serve as examples for the whole Chinese population.[45] Horizontal class solidarity was largely absent from Chinese society, because almost everyone was striving to achieve a higher status. The laborer was not proletariat-conscious, because his eyes were fixed either on a small shop or mill of his own in Bangkok or on a higher status in his native village. The whole community was sustained by the conviction that anyone could, through hard work and thrifty habits, achieve success and status.

Organizations in this society, fittingly enough, were entirely vertical, each embracing members from different strata. Guilds, organized on occupational lines, included both employers and employees—quite unlike the business associations and labor unions of today. Benevolent, mutual-aid, and regional associations were each restricted to a single speech group at most, and membership was not limited by class.

The Chinese temples were more often symbols of division than of unity. Each speech group had one or more favored deities, who in some cases functioned in a manner reminiscent of Catholic patron saints. The Hainanese Shui-wei Niang and the Hokkien T'ien-hou Sheng-mu have already been cited. The Teochius and Hakkas evolved a new deity, Pen-t'ou Kung (C 49),[46] who was worshipped almost exclusively by them prior to 1910. Pen-t'ou is most likely modeled on Ti-t'ou (C 50), a locality god inferior to Ch'eng-huang and found in most villages of Ch'ao-chou and Chia-ying-chou. The legends told by most Pen-t'ou worshippers relate him to Yen Ch'ing (C 51), one of the Shui-hu bandits who have become Chinese culture heroes. According to the usual version, after failing in a rebellion against the imperial government, Yen Ch'ing fled to Siam, taught boxing to the natives (thus making him the father of Thai boxing), and died in Siam, where he was later deified. Other versions, relating him in some way to Thailand, also attest his local origin. In any case, after 1850 Pen-t'ou temples were built with increasing frequency in the Teochiu-dominated areas of central Siam. What is probably the oldest Pen-t'ou temple north of Paknampho is found in Chiangmai; Pen-t'ou temples in the areas first settled by Hainanese date back beyond 1900 in only one or two cases. Hakkas, in addition to joining Teochius in the worship of Pen-t'ou Kung, had a distinctively prominent role in the establishment of the Chinese Mahayana Buddhist temples in Siam and were dominant among the Chinese Buddhist priests. The Cantonese, always the least "superstitious" and most correct (in the Confucian sense) of the overseas Chinese in religious matters, erected primarily ancestral temples or halls, around which a semblance of clan or lineage organization was maintained.

The religious specializations of Chinese speech groups in Siam were also expressed in death. When cemeteries were built in Bangkok at the end of the nineteenth century, they were restricted in each case to a single speech group. The first public cemetery was Cantonese (1884), and the last of the five speech-group cemeteries was founded by the Teochius in 1899. Even in several of the larger upcountry towns (Khorat and Lampang, for instance), different speech groups founded separate cemeteries.

The nineteenth-century literature on Siam is full of testimony to the division and animosity among the speech groups. In 1837, Earl wrote that "the natives of different [Chinese] provinces are strongly opposed to each other, as much so, indeed, as if they belonged to rival nations." [47] A few years later Malcom observed that "the variety of their dialects drives them to clan-like associations, which not only keep them reserved and cold toward each other, but often engage them in injurious animosities." [48] A perceptive article written in 1870 pointed up the bad feeling of the Cantonese towards Hakkas, whom they looked down on and oppressed, and towards Teochius, whom they hated for their power.[49]

The all-important secret societies also reflected the horizontal disunity of overseas Chinese society. They were organized on the vertical principle of complementary membership from the "elder brother" at the top to the "coolie" and professional criminal at the bottom. The Hung-men (C 52) secret societies [50] were introduced into Siam from China probably in the seventeenth and at least by the early eighteenth century. Their original *raison d'être* was the overthrow of the Manchu dynasty and restoration of the Mings, but in Southeast Asia, as in parts of China, their manifold functions in the local communities came to override the long-range political ends. The real purpose of the societies in Siam was to secure protection and economic advantage for members by extralegal if not illegal means. The societies achieved supreme sociological importance with the growth in value of the revenue farms during the second half of the nineteenth century. In a milieu notable for wide-open gambling, unrestricted opium smoking, and prostitution thriving in an almost all-male ethnic community, the underground methods of the secret societies were especially suitable.

The structure of the societies was strictly hierarchic, with "degrees" and flowery nomenclature not unlike those found in Masonic lodges. The title of first-degree or Great Elder Brother was reserved for the Ming Emperor, so that those holding top political power were the second-degree elder brothers, whose special responsibilities related to the struggle against outsiders. The third-degree elder brothers were responsible for mutual aid and charity within the membership; as a result, they were inevitably drawn from the ranks of the most wealthy Chinese. Any member was bound to help a "brother" in time of need or trouble; he could seek aid in case of sickness or attack, expect to be put up while traveling, and in some cases could count on burial after death. One of the chief functions of the societies was to preserve traditional occupations against intruders; and conversely the expansion of one speech group into a new craft or trade was possible only with society backing. Prostitution and protection rackets were carried on under society auspices. Headmen of "coolie" gangs were able to obtain and maintain rights to supply labor for particular jobs or at certain mills or docks because of society backing. And laborers, in turn, had to belong in order to get jobs. Virtually all the railroad workers from 1892 to 1910 were society members who joined in Bangkok prior to their employment. Informants are agreed that only those who were not in business or employed in any way could avoid joining the Hung-men. By 1902, it was said that "all Chinese belong to one or other of the numerous secret societies." [51]

Leaders of the larger societies were primarily farmers of opium, gambling, and spirits, or merchants wealthy enough to bid for such monopolies. By threatening and terrorizing rival Chinese factions prior to bidding, they used society power to help secure monopolies; and they maintained the full privileges the farms entailed by wreaking vengeance on "poachers." Hatchetmen and professional criminals in the lower ranks of each society did the bidding of their elder-brother bosses. Thus the societies served the ends of the leaders, while providing protection for the mass membership against the very evils the societies fostered.

From the elder brothers down to the tenth-degree recruits, all were sworn to blood brotherhood and secrecy. The ties among members of a given branch or kongsi [52] were cemented by elaborate rituals and involved symbolism. The chief religious symbol was Kuan Kung (C 56), the San-kuo general who has been deified as Wu-ti (C 57), the god of war. Most of the temples in Siam dedicated to Kuan Kung, or Hsieh-t'ien Ta-ti (C 58), one of his titles, are known to have been established by secret societies—for instance, those at Chiangmai, Paknampho, and Khlọngtan. And the presence of altars to Kuan Kung in the Shui-wei Niang and Pen-t'ou temples in several towns of Siam attests the division of the Hung-men movement by speech group. Whether in special kongsi headquarters or in temples, the blood of a cock was shed before Kuan Kung and drunk by all in the name of the Ming Emperor. That done, the members sallied forth for further struggle against their compatriots of other societies.

Far from providing a solid front against Thai or Westerners, secret societies constituted a divisive force within Chinese society. Riots and terrorism were directed against other kongsis for control of plums not sought by either Westerners or Thai.[53] Bangkok by 1889 had at least six different societies of great power,[54] while in Paknampho a decade later there were three distinct kongsis, all in continual conflict. There were also at least two competing kongsis in Phijit, Phitsanulok, Phuket, Trang and doubtless many another of the larger towns in Siam for which the writer has no specific information. Membership was almost exclusively along speech-group lines, and in several cases rival societies of the same speech group fought for supremacy. The Hakka Chi-hsien-kuan, for instance, founded somewhat before 1880 eventually split into two factions—the Ming-shun and the Ch'ün-ying, who "fought both in the open and in secret," until mediation brought an end to the disunion in the first decade of this century.[55]

It was only in the smaller towns or those largely dominated by a single speech group that only one kongsi held complete control. Thus in Khlọngtan and Thalọ there were single kongsis with almost exclusively Hainanese membership, while in Chiangmai the one large kongsi was Teochiu-dominated. The smallest towns could support no kongsi, but often the resident Chinese belonged to a branch in the nearest larger town.

When faced with interkongsi feuding in addition to speech-group animosity, the system of Chinese captains or headmen broke down during the nineteenth century. In Bangkok, by the 1890's, the headman position had been largely converted to a judicial post in the Thai Foreign Office, carrying responsibility for civil cases among the Chinese. The last person who was ever called headman by the Chinese in Bangkok was Phraya Choduek Ratchasetthi, whose duties ended in the first decade of the twentieth century.[56] In many upcountry towns, however, where headmen were appointed as warranted by a growing Chinese population, the classic system persisted intact until the last decade of the nineteenth century. In each of the autonomous principalities of the north—Chiangmai,[57] Lamphun, Lampang, Phrae, and Nan—the Chinese headman was appointed and ennobled by the prince (Jao), while in other towns further south the appointment and title came from the Siamese king via the governors. The Chinese headman—in Thai usually called Hua-na-fai-jin ("the chief concerned with the Chinese") or colloquially as Nai-amphoe-jek ("the Chinamen's district officer")—was responsible to the prince or governor for maintaining peace and order within the Chinese community. He had the power to make arrests and administer corporal but not capital punishment. The headman of Chiangmai in the late nineteenth century, Tu Kuan-sheng (C 59), even had a jail attached to his residence. The prince or governor usually accepted the headman's word that a Chinese criminal would neither repeat his crime nor attempt escape.

With the centralization of the Thai territorial administration and the extension of the direct authority of Bangkok to the northern principalities in the 1890's, Chinese headmen in whatever town were appointed from Bangkok and stripped of all powers except those of mediator and guarantor. Within a few years thereafter, the system died a natural death.

Given the organization of Chinese society in the nineteenth century, the headman system could only work in conjunction with the secret societies. It worked best in communities strongly dominated by a single speech group with only one Hung-men kongsi, whose supreme elder brother was also the headman. In Chiangmai, for instance, Tu Kuan-sheng, a Teochiu, was the Chinese headman and chief of the San-tien society and one of the major monopoly farmers. In Sawankhalok, the Chinese headman, a Hainanese, was also leader of the Lao-hung kongsi and held the gambling farm. The system broke down first in those cities, such as Bangkok and Paknampho, where more than one kongsi held sway.

Chinese society in the nineteenth century, to summarize, was badly divided (vertically) both in structure and function. In Bangkok and the larger towns, there was not a single organization embracing the whole community or even more than one of its major components. Even the few genuine benevolent and mutual-aid societies were restricted to a single speech group. Under these circumstances, there could be no community-wide leadership. Such leadership, to be sure, was hardly necessary in the absence of any organized threat from the outside.

C. The Chinese and the Thai Government

Thai government policy towards the Chinese resident in Siam during the nineteenth century was generally favorable. Many of its positive aspects have already been mentioned: unrestricted immigration, complete freedom of movement, low direct taxation, and a monopoly policy that led to Chinese supremacy. For the rest the policy was one of laissez faire, except when Chinese activities openly thwarted Siamese sovereignty or threatened peace and order. Corruption, vice, even anarchy within nineteenth-century Chinese society were of no vital concern to the government so long as the Chinese continued to foster the country's trade and pay ever larger sums into the treasury in the form of annual tenders for the monopoly farms. Difficulties arose primarily in connection with disturbances of the peace and the Chinese recourse to the protection of Western treaty powers.

During Nangklao's reign, there were several Chinese rebellions and uprisings. Little is known of the motivation behind most, in particular the uprisings at Janthaburi in 1824, at Nakhonchaisi in 1842, and at Langsuan in 1845.[58] The earliest Chinese rebellion described in any detail occurred at Bangplasoi early in Nangklao's reign. It was of secret-society origin and directed against a tyrannical local government. The ringleader escaped but the other rebels were either massacred or imprisoned for life.[59] The year 1848 saw revolution in Siam as well as Europe. The most serious Chinese rebellions in Siamese history occurred in that year, following the imposition of a new, augmented tax on sugar refineries.[60] The first uprising took place in the sugar districts of Lower Siam between Thajin and Nakhonchaisi. The Thai nobleman who was sent from Bangkok with a contingent of police to suppress the riot was mortally wounded, and another much stronger force of soldiers was dispatched under the Phrakhlang, who, in his capacity as Minister of Foreign Affairs, was responsible for the Chinese in the country. In three weeks the rebellion was quelled, three hundred of the rebels put to death, and two hundred more brought to the king's palace in irons. By this time, news of a similar uprising in the sugar districts of Southeast Siam centering at Paetriw (Chachoengsao) reached the capital, and several thousand soldiers were sent under the Phrakhlang's command to recapture the fort occupied by the Chinese and quell the disorder. The fort was easily retaken, though the governor was killed in the process, but the rebellion continued for a month. It was generally reported that ten thousand Chinese were killed in all Chachoengsao, and by the most conservative estimate the figure was at least two thousand. In the course of the uprising thirteen sugar mills and other property to the amount of a million U.S. dollars were destroyed.

The folly of insurrection directed against the local authorities was well borne in upon the Chinese by the ruthless reaction of the court to the 1848 rebellion. During the fourth and fifth reigns, disturbances of Chinese origin were confined largely to feuding and riots among secret societies, which, while not directed at the government, still constituted a challenge to its authority. An upsurge of secret-society activity in Julalongkǫn's reign was heralded by the return to Bangkok of the founder of one of the leading societies, who had previously been banished by King Mongkut.[61] The most important of the riots in Bangkok occurred in 1869, 1883, 1889, and 1895, but lesser disturbances were frequent throughout the fifth reign.[62] It will suffice here to describe only one of these, the riots of 1889. In June of that year a dispute arose between two societies [63] apparently over rights to supply "coolies" for three of Bangkok's largest rice mills. The resulting riots eventuated in the construction of barricades and heavy gunplay in the main road of the city. After thirty-six hours, the police, with the help of a military force commanded by two Danish officers, managed to disperse the rival factions. The sequel (with some revealing gratuitous comments) follows in the words of the British Consul:

The result was most satisfactory and highly creditable to the Siamese. Many headmen of the secret societies were arrested. About 900 Chinese were sent up for trial by a court specially constituted for the purpose, and those proved to have been implicated in the riots were punished either by fines or whippings. The action of the Siamese government on this occasion has certainly given the coolie class a lesson which they will not forget; but, at the same time, one might expect that precautionary measures would have been taken against a recurrence of such outbreaks in future.[64]

By this time, in fact, the establishment of a governmental body to control the Chinese community, analogous to the Chinese Protectorate in the Straits Settlements, was under consideration.[65] Nevertheless, the reorganization of the government on modern lines in 1891 failed to provide for a Chinese protectorate. The riots of 1895 again emphasized the gravity of the situation, and two years later the government promulgated the Secret Societies Act, providing for compulsory registration and police control of all societies as well as heavy punishment for organizing or managing unlawful societies.[66] Secret societies, naturally enough, declined to register, and even legitimate organizations preferred to go underground rather than conform to the law, which was thought to be preliminary to a military draft.[67] When the Bangkok police were reorganized under a British commissioner in 1897, a Chinese branch was set up to handle Chinese problems, and a few years thereafter another special squad to supervise the Chinese pawnshops was organized. In 1907, the police began fingerprinting "professional Chinese criminals" and came to an agreement with Straits police providing for the exchange of information about Chinese deported for criminal activity.[68] None of these measures, however, got at the root of secret-society organization or power.

Another major source of trouble between Chinese and the Thai government arose from the extraterritoriality provided for in the treaties concluded with Britain, France, the United States, Portugal, and the Netherlands by King Mongkut. The British in Malaya and Hongkong, the Dutch in the East Indies, and the Portuguese in Macao all had Chinese under their jurisdiction. When any of these immigrated to Siam, they could, by the terms of the treaties with Siam, claim status as European subjects. Once properly registered with the European consulate in Bangkok, they enjoyed such privileges as consular jurisdiction and exemption from the Chinese poll tax.

Had the matter gone no further than this, no particular problem would have arisen. However, Chinese in no way connected with European colonies quickly perceived the advantages of consular protection and sought registration. Several of the consulates issued certificates of registration on improper or forged accreditation, often unwittingly; and even before the end of Mongkut's reign the American and Portuguese Consulates in particular made an open business of selling certificates to all comers. The American certificates issued by Consul J. M. Hood in 1867 said simply: "Know ye that I . . . have granted the protection of this Consulate to [so and so], a subject of the Chinese Empire . . . [who has] made known to the undersigned that he has no Consul resident of his own nation to assist him in case of need." [69]

Hood's arrogation of authority led to his hasty recall and the end of American "protection." But the practice of issuing certificates to Chinese who were not bona fide European subjects was continued by the Portuguese and to a lesser extent by the British and Dutch off and on for the rest of the century.

It was the French, however, who most consistently and regularly abused extraterritoriality with regard to the Chinese. They interpreted Article 6 of the 1856 treaty as according French protection to all servants and employees of Frenchmen and French firms.[70] After the show of French force in 1893, French protection became very popular among the Chinese of Lower, Southeast, and Northeast Siam, and the French Legation and Consulates registered hundreds of them as "protégés" between 1893 and 1896. French priests in the outlying districts were vested by the Consul with authority over all protégés in their neighborhood, whereupon the popularity of French missions among the Chinese noticeably increased.[71] By this time many of the leading merchants with widespread interests to protect and with reason to fear the application of Siamese law to their activities were seeking consular registration by one means or another, bribery in particular. Registration guaranteed, among other highly desirable privileges, that their premises could not be searched without a warrant from the Consular Court.[72] The proprietor of Chin Ch'eng Li Company, mentioned in the preceding section as a prize example of upward mobility, showed typical opportunism in this matter: he himself was registered at the British legation, while his son was enrolled as a French protégé.[73] In Chiangmai, the gambling and opium farmers as well as the more notorious opium smugglers became French protégés, and the suet-cake monopolist avoided paying taxes by taking out Dutch papers; many of the other prominent merchants and monopoly farmers were British subjects. By 1903 an important "minority of the commercial elite" had registered with European consulates and legations.[74]

Meanwhile as a Thai student of the matter put it:

Siam declined to accept the assumption by the Master-Powers of the right to claim these aliens as their subjects or protégés, with special rights and privileges attached to them on equal footing with their own subjects. And besides this difference, the method of recruiting or admitting protégés used by certain foreign consuls was a cause of considerable worry and annoyance to the Siamese Government.[75]

Judicial reform in the last decade of the nineteenth century gave the Thai government a lever with which to limit and finally abolish the abuses of extraterritoriality resorted to by Chinese and other Asians. Treaties to this end were concluded with Britain in 1899 and 1909, with the Netherlands in 1901, and with France in 1904 and 1907. Chinese claiming status as Portuguese subjects by virtue of actual or alleged birth in Macao, however, enjoyed full consular protection until the late 1920's.[76]

Registration with foreign consulates, as has already been mentioned, was a sure method of evading the Chinese poll tax, but it was only one of many. Domestic servants of foreigners, by wearing a badge or hatband bearing their employer's name, could usually, though illegally, avoid paying the tax. So also could employees of Western firms and those connected with the Presbyterian or Catholic missions. There were even cases of Chinese taking temporary employment or feigning conversion to Christianity in order to avoid the tax.[77] Many tried to evade payment by keeping in retirement until the time for taxation passed.[78]

Money was not necessarily the major consideration in this evasion, for the procedure and signification of tax payment carried an aura of contempt and degradation.[79] The procedure was as follows: Each Chinese was supposed to seek out one of the agents and pay 4.25 baht. On receiving payment, the agent tied around the left wrist of the Chinese a cord, which was knotted and fastened with gum and then stamped with the government seal. An identification certificate was issued at the same time.[80] For the rest of the year, the Chinese had to wear the wrist seal and show the certificate whenever challenged by any policeman or official. There was no dignity or ceremony to the affixation or subsequent examination of the seals. However, the seal could be omitted altogether by the payment of an additional 6.25 baht. The Chinese of any means was thus placed in the awkward position of having to weigh his dignity against his pocket-book. Wealthy Chinese inevitably took advantage of the extra payment to avoid the degradation of the wrist seal. In view of the fact that the certificate alone could suffice, the whole procedure smacked a little of calculated contempt.

After the specified limit for paying the tax had passed, any Chinese who, when challenged, could show no seal on his wrist was arrested. The police were very busy at this time, and it was said that "there is nothing the Siamese policeman so much enjoys as leading some unfortunate Chinaman to pay the tax." [81] In Sampheng in 1900 after the tax-paying period expired, "gangs of about twenty Chinamen, tied by a narrow cord wrist to wrist, under the charge of a Siamese official . . . armed with a big stick, would pass down the street on the way to the lock-up." [82] There they were detained until the tax plus an additional sum for the arrest were paid in full. All in all the triennial tax, in the details of its collection and enforcement, was hardly designed to develop mutual respect between Chinese and Thai.

There were two sides to the coin of Chinese relations with the Thai government. Not only were Chinese an object of government policy; they also participated at the court and in government administration to a surprising degree during the nineteenth century. Certain aspects of this participation were to be expected: the retention of Chinese scholars at court up through Mongkut's reign; the appointment of Chinese as maritime and treasury officials in the days of royal trading; the use of Chinese commanders and artisans in the Thai navy during the third and fourth reigns and on royal yachts during the fifth reign; [83] the employment of Chinese customs officials from the third through the fifth reign; [84] and the incorporation of local-born Chinese into the Chinese Squad of the reorganized police force after 1897.[85]

Only the first two of these examples would seem to require any elaboration. Hsieh Ch'ing-kao (C 61), a Chinese voyager who visited Siam in either the first or second reigns, wrote in his *Hai-lu* (C 62): "They [the Thai] have much respect for Chinese literature, and whenever the King hears of people who are versed in poetry and literature he retains them at court." [86] In the third reign, Tomlin mentioned "an aged and learned Chinese, who has been long in the service, and under the patronage, of the King," [87] and Chinese scholars and translators were also employed during the fourth reign. But after the cessation of tribute missions to China in 1853, interest at court in Chinese scholarship and literature seems to have declined. With regard to other Chinese officials, the *Hai-kuo t'u-chih* (C 43), dated 1842, stated that "the King also chooses the clever ones among them [the Chinese residents] to be officials and administrators of tax-collection and commerce." [88] As early as the second reign, a Western writer called attention to the first place of Teochius among these mercantile and financial officials of Bangkok.[89]

In addition to these unexceptional uses of Chinese talent, the government pursued two related and rather remarkable policies which had the result of drawing portions of the Chinese elite into the Thai nobility. These policies—the employment of Chinese as governors in the gulf regions of Siam and the ennoblement of Chinese leaders— were followed with consistency throughout the nineteenth century. Discussion of these developments would be simplified by a brief review of the rank-title systems of the Thai elite.

There were two such systems, one for the royal aristocracy and one for the bureaucratic nobility. Royal titles,[90] governed by a declining descent rule, were dependent on blood relationship to the king and never bestowed on commoners. The titles of the bureaucratic nobility, however, were completely independent of royal rank and, as we shall see, not infrequently conferred on Chinese. In order of descending rank these were Jaophraya (Chao Phya), Phraya (Phya), Phra, Luang, and Khun.[91] Each title corresponded roughly to rank or status in the bureaucratic system: The title of Jaophraya was held by only a very select few; Phraya by governors, department heads, senior judges, and so on; Phra by division chiefs; Luang by section chiefs or lesser judges; and Khun by those in minor posts. The recipient of a bureaucratic title usually also received a noble appellation to go with it, and so dropped his former name. Titles could often be kept for life, but they were *not* hereditary.[92]

In view of the much-repeated generalization that the Chinese have never had any interest in political power in Southeast Asia, the several cases of Chinese governors in Siam during the nineteenth century are worthy of careful attention. By the beginning of the third reign, the governors (or rajahs, as they were often called locally) of Ranong, Songkhla, Nakhonsithammarat, and Janthaburi were Chinese, as was the Luang-rajah Capitan of Phuket. At one time or another during the fifth reign, there were Chinese rajahs, governors, or commissioners at Pattani, Tomo, Trang, Songkhla, Ranong, Kra, Langsuan, and Paknam. Many of these officials were born locally of Thai mothers, but most still spoke Chinese; and several were immigrants. The stories of enough of these Chinese governors are known to provide a basis for valid generalization.

The Luang-rajah of Phuket achieved his position in the following manner: [93] He was a Hakka named Lin Hai (C 63) (Lim Hoi), who early in the century immigrated from Macao to Phuket, where he became a merchant. In 1821, sailing his own ship, he had gone to Penang on business and while returning sighted a Burmese sailing vessel which aroused his suspicions and caused him to attack. On searching the vessel he found an official letter from the Burmese government to the rajah of Kedah, then tenuously under Thai suzerainty, whereupon he took the ship and crew to Phuket and turned them over to the governor. When the letter was found to be an instigation to rebellion, Lin Hai was rewarded with the appointment in question.[94]

Another example has already been mentioned (see pp. 21–22), namely, the family of Wu Yang, the Hokkien bird's-nests farmer who was made governor of Songkhla by King Taksin. Wu Yang's eldest son, Wen-hui, had no heirs, and on his death in 1812, Wu T'ien-chung (C 64), the eldest son of Wu Yang's second eldest son (Wen-yao), succeeded to the post. He in turn was succeeded by his brother, T'ien-sheng (C 65), who was duly appointed governor with the title of Phraya by Rama II. T'ien-sheng and his cousin Wen-shuang (C 66), also a grandson of Wu Yang through Wen-ch'en (C 67), brilliantly served Rama III, most notably in putting down the revolt of the Malays at Saiburi in 1838–1839. In achieving this victory, Wu Wen-shuang led four overseas-Chinese regiments into battle—probably the only time since Taksin's reign that Chinese military units have fought in the service of the Thai king. Wen-shuang succeeded to the governorship on the death of T'ien-sheng in 1847 and served until he died in 1865. In 1862, he was raised, like his uncle, to Jaophraya, the highest of the bureaucratic titles. Wu Wen-shuang was the fifth "Chinese rajah" of Songkhla. He was followed in turn by T'ien-chung's son, Nai Min (1865–1884); Wen-shuang's son, Nai Som (1884–1888); and Nai Som's son, Nai Chom (1888–1901). Nai Chom, Wu Yang's great-great-grandson, was given a sinecure as inspector-general of Songkhla in 1901, and his descendants were pensioned off by the Crown.[95]

It is interesting to note the progressive Thai-ification of Wu Yang's descendants. His sons all spoke Chinese and were buried in the Chinese style. His grandson T'ien-chung was cremated (1817) but his ashes were buried in an imitation Chinese grave. T'ien-sheng, also a grandson, was a Theravada Buddhist by faith, learned Chinese only as a second language, and was cremated two years after his death in full Thai style. The great-grandchildren spoke no Chinese, did not even have Chinese names, and intermarried within the family and across generations in a fashion that would have appalled their great-grandfather.[96] In 1916, the family adopted the Thai name of Na Songkhla ("Na" in surnames is the Thai counterpart of the German "von" or the French "de"), and various members are prominent today in Thai government and business.

The original Chinese rajah of Ranǫng was a Chang-chou Hokkien like his counterpart at Songkhla, but the story of his family is even more remarkable.[97] As Hsü Szu-chang (C 68) (Kaw Su Chiang), he immigrated to Penang about 1810, owning only a carrying pole and the clothes he wore. Working first as a "coolie," he finally saved enough to begin trading out of Penang; his operations extended to South Siam and attracted the attention of the rajah of Takuapa. Under the rajah's patronage, Hsü expanded his coastal trading to the advantage of both. He eventually founded a company to mine tin near Ranǫng, which at that time was a village of small importance, and made a fortune from the venture. As was the custom he ruled the mining community he created, and his exceptional administrative ability and the growing importance of Ranǫng led the court at Bangkok to appoint him rajah with the title Phra, raised to Phraya in the third reign. When Hsü Szu-chang died in the fifth reign, his eldest son, Sen-kuang (C 69) (Sim Kong), was given the title of Phraya Setthi and appointed his successor. Three other sons of this remarkable man were also ennobled by Julalongkǫn and appointed governors: Sen-te (C 70) (Sim Tek) at Langsuan, Sen-chin (C 71) (Sim Kim) at Kra, and Sen-mei (C 72) (Sim Bee) at Trang.

Hsü Sen-kuang proved to be an enlightened ruler in Ranǫng, and was later appointed Commissioner of Chumphǫn.[98] But neither he nor his two other rajah brothers were the equal of Sen-mei, who, as Phraya Ratsada, ruled Trang long and well. Hsü Sen-mei has been called "the most brilliant administrator that south Thailand has ever known."[99] In 1901, he went to Bangkok and "formally changed his nationality by going through the ceremony of having his queue cut off in the presence of a large gathering of princes and officials at the residence of the Minister of Interior."[100] It is significant that while those of Hsü Szu-chang's grandchildren who returned to Penang remained Chinese, all those who stayed in Siam became Thai. The family adopted the name Na Ranǫng and is prominent today in Thai national life.

The rajah of Tomo got his start in much the same way as Hsü Szu-chang. He began business in the Narathiwat area on "quite a small scale," and eventually began gold mining at Tomo. He came to rule his mining community and "by giving much money to great Siamese men" was recognized by the court.[101] As for his contemporary, the

governor of Paknam, he was said to have started as a bootblack to
a British mariner and, by a process not detailed, to have become owner
of four rice mills in Siam.[102]

This survey accounts for the great majority of the Chinese governors
and rajahs who held power in Siam during the third, fourth, and fifth
Jakkri reigns. The most striking fact which emerges is that none of
these ruling families or individuals was originally of the scholar-official
class. All had humble origins. Furthermore, almost all started in private
business of one sort or another and got into government administration
because of the special nature of their enterprises (i.e., mining in the
south), business success, and exceptional talent. In no case, apparently,
was the original intention to enter political life; none of them started
in government service, as would have been the case with Thai heading
for bureaucratic position. The celebrated Chinese rajahs appear, therefore, to be merely special cases of spectacular Chinese-type upward
mobility. It is significant that once sidetracked, as it were, into the
Thai administration, this Chinese talent became loyal to the Thai government and eventually assimilated to Thai society.

The Thai government's use of Chinese as governors may also be
viewed as a special instance of the general practice of ennobling the
most important Chinese in the kingdom to assure their allegiance
and obtain the use of their talent. The practice was widely and continually resorted to during the first five Jakkri reigns and must be
considered part of a calculated and conscious policy.

Robert Morrison's mention of Chinese serving as officials and nobles
in the second reign has already been quoted. Crawfurd too referred
to "Chinese bearing Siamese titles." [103] Gutzlaff's remarks on the subject with regard to 1831 are worth quoting:

To them [the Chinese] nothing is so welcome as being presented, by the
king, with an honorary title; and this generally takes place when they have
acquired great riches, or have betrayed some of their own countrymen. From
that moment they become slaves of the king; the more so if they are made
his officers. No service is then so menial, so expensive, so difficult but they are
forced to perform it.[104]

Gutzlaff's statement to the effect that titles were conferred on the very
rich Chinese is corroborated for a later period by the fact that Phraya
Phisan, wealthiest Chinese merchant in Bangkok around 1860, bore
the highest title conferred on any Chinese not in government service.[105] Of the twenty-five leading Chinese *merchants* at that time,

there were two Khun and one Luang in addition to Phraya Phisan.[106] Even after King Wachirawut came to the throne, leading Chinese merchants in many towns of upcountry Siam as well as the capital were ennobled as Khun or Luang, usually as a reward for services to the governor, or for exceptionally large contributions to a royal cause, or, in one case known to the writer, for entertaining the king on an official tour. It was also government policy to give titles to most of the Chinese holding revenue monopolies. In the third reign, both the lottery and the gambling farmers were automatically given the title of Khun; by the fifth reign the rank had been raised to Luang.[107] The opium farmer was also given noble rank. By the first decade of this century there were four Phraya among Chinese rice millers alone. One of these was the grandson of Phraya Phisan mentioned above. The family by this time was said to "occupy a high place in *Siamese* social . . . circles." [108]

Chinese headmen were also ennobled and given special titles by the king or local prince. In Bangkok the headman's rank was Phraya, while in other towns it was Phra (e.g., Khorat), Luang (e.g., Chiangmai), or Khun (e.g., Uttaradit). The writer had the good fortune to interview Chan Ts'ai-ch'ing (C 73), probably the only living man who ever served as a Chinese headman in Siam. He held such a post in Uttaradit for several years around 1902 and later became a prominent opium and spirits farmer in several jangwats of the north, whence the noble name he still uses, Luang Sinakharanukun. He himself now lives as a Thai gentleman; most of his children identify as Thai rather than Chinese, and all but two of his thirty-odd grandchildren are growing up as Thai.

Bastian was probably the first to point to the real significance of the government's practice. He termed it a "policy to ennoble every Chinese important because of riches or influence, and thus draw him into the interests of the country." [109] McDonald implied another motivation in her remark that "Chinese of wealth often become favorites with the rulers and receive titles of nobility, and these noblemen in return present their daughters to their majesties." [110] And Raquez adds the final twist: "Siamese politics puts into practice the old maxim, divide and rule: The Siamese have opened to the most fortunate of the Chinese the ranks of their nobility." [111]

The success of the Thai policy was striking. The very Chinese with power to offer serious opposition to the government were at least neutralized. And in the long run the assimilation of their families was pretty well assured. Descendants of the Chinese ennobled during Julalongkɔn's reign are among the leading Thai families today. Some are in business, many in government; all demonstrate complete loyalty to the country and the Thai way of life.

The government's practice of ennobling and utilizing successful and influential Chinese also had significance for Chinese leadership. The very acceptance of a noble title involved a partial commitment to the king and government which precluded wholehearted leadership of the Chinese community as such. To some extent, the government succeeded in skimming off the cream of the Chinese elite to serve *its* ends and not those of Chinese society.

≫ 5 ≪

INTO A NEW ERA:

Transition to Nationalism

and Cohesion

THE YEAR 1910 was a turning point in the history of the Chinese in Siam. It saw the death of King Julalongkǫn, a friend to the Chinese, and the enthronement of his son, Wachirawut, a romantic nationalist and proponent of anti-Sinicism. It also witnessed the calamitous Chinese general strike in Bangkok, which in effect launched the "Chinese problem." Moreover, 1910 marks the mid-point of an approximately fifteen-year transition period notable for several no less significant developments. The events leading up to the Chinese revolution, the establishment of the first Chinese newspapers and community schools, the founding of new kinds of Chinese associations, the abolition of monopoly farms and of the triennial tax, the weakening of secret societies—all of these marked the transition to a new era for the Chinese in Siam.

A. The Rise of Chinese Nationalism

The increase in nationalist feeling among the Chinese in Siam was ✓ as inevitable as it was significant. The tide of Chinese nationalism which swelled after China's defeat by Japan in 1895 was quickly felt in Southeast Asia, and its specific forms—the royalist reform party and the revolutionary movement—were reflected in overseas Chinese society. The center of the revolutionary movement in Nan-yang was at Singapore, where a newspaper popularizing the cause was already being published before Sun Yat-sen arrived there in June 1905.[1] Shen Lien-fang (C 74), one of the first adherents of the movement in Singapore, established a branch of his firm in Bangkok partly to enlist support for the cause.[2] Among those he influenced was Ch'en Yi-ju (C 75)—today one of the "grand old men" of the Chinese community—who proclaimed his conversion by cutting his queue years before the revolution.

The acknowledged leader of the revolutionists in Siam, however, was Hsiao Fo-ch'eng (C 76),[3] whose background singularly suited him for this role. Hsiao's ancestors fought with the anti-Manchu resistance after the fall of the Mings and eventually fled to Taiwan to continue the fight under Koxinga. When the Manchus gained control of Taiwan, Fo-ch'eng's branch of the family fled to Malacca, whence, almost two centuries later, part of the family came to Bangkok. Fo-ch'eng became prominent in Bangkok as a businessman and attorney, and when Malacca friends interested him in the revolutionary movement, he put his full influence and talents to its service.

In the winter of 1905, Hsiao and a few followers contacted a prorevolutionary newspaper in Hongkong, the *Chung-kuo Jih-pao*, for help in starting a mouthpiece for the movement in Bangkok. The following year, Shen Hsing-szu and Ch'en Ching-hua (C 77), together with Hsiao Fo-ch'eng, established the *Mei-nan Jih-pao* (C 78), "Maenam Daily." Ch'en, the editor in chief, was a Cantonese[4] of Hsiang-shan (Sun Yat-sen's native hsien) who had been a district magistrate in Kwangsi before fleeing to Siam.[5] Because of lack of funds, the paper soon floundered and was reorganized under a name of the same meaning but with a different first character (C 81). Shortly thereafter, a Cantonese supporter of K'ang Yu-wei came to Siam and won the support of half the trustees of the *Mei-nan Jih-pao*, whereupon the paper was succeeded by the *Ch'i-nan Jih-pao* (C 82), a proManchu royalist organ. Undaunted, Hsiao and Ch'en in 1907 founded a new paper which proved one of the most successful of the early publishing ventures in Bangkok. It had two editions, the Chinese *Hua-hsien Jih-pao* (C 83) and the Thai *Jinno-sayam Warasap*, edited respectively by Ch'en Ching-hua and Hsiao Fo-ch'eng (and daughter).[6] The Thai edition was described in 1908 as "candid and highly independent,"[7] while the Chinese edition reflected more strongly the revolutionary aspirations of the backers.

In 1907, Dr. Sun sent Wang Ching-wei (C 84) to Siam to establish a branch of the T'ung Meng Hui (Chinese Revolutionary Alliance) along the lines of the first Nan-yang branch, founded at Singapore in 1905. Wang's mission was a success, and at the formative meeting Hsiao, Ch'en, and Shen Hsing-szu were elected president, secretary, and treasurer, respectively.[8] The Chung-hua Association was also set up shortly thereafter as the public front for the underground organization. In the winter of 1908, Dr. Sun himself, accompanied by Hu Han-min, Hu Yi-sheng, Ho K'o-fu, and Lu Chung-lin (C 85), arrived in Bangkok from Singapore. Hundreds of Chinese, including many prominent merchants, welcomed the visitors at a celebration held in the Chung-hua Association headquarters. The next day the Siamese government, warned by the British Legation, notified Dr. Sun that he would have to leave the country within one week. However, the American Minister was prevailed upon to intervene on the grounds that Sun was a resident of Hawaii, and the deadline was postponed one week.[9] During Sun's ten-day stay, which as it turned out was his only visit to Siam, plans were drawn up for future strategy and financing. Thenceforth, most of the money for the cause was sent through remittance shops in Bangkok to Hu Han-min in Kwangtung. The T'ung Meng Hui organization was tightened and regularized as a subbranch of the Nan-yang head branch in Singapore.[10] Within the next three years, small revolutionary cells were organized around private business firms in a few upcountry towns, and the first Shu-pao-she ("book and newspaper societies")—which came to be the usual designation for the front organizations of the Nationalist groups upcountry—were established in South Siam under stimulus from Penang.

Although many recruits to the Bangkok branch of the T'ung Meng Hui had been members of the Hung-men, it was decided not to try to work through the secret societies in Siam. Dr. Sun was reportedly repelled by their unsavory and corrupt character. In some cases, however, attempts were made to reform and reorganize certain Hung-men kongsis into revolutionary organizations. The two rival Hakka groups mentioned earlier (p. 141) were united through the mediation of Yü Tz'u-p'eng (C 86), a member of the T'ung Meng Hui, thus making possible the formation of the prorevolutionary Hakka Association in 1909.[11] In the same year, the Ch'iung-tao Hui-so (Hainan Islanders' Meeting Place) was also founded and served as a front for the T'ung Meng Hui and its successor, the Chung-hua Ke-ming Tang (Chinese

Revolutionary Party).¹² The formation of separate organizations by speech group followed the new line laid down by Hu Han-min at Singapore in 1909.¹³ Hainanese, as the weakest of the five major speech groups in Singapore, were there joined with the Teochius in a single *pang* ("company or group"), but in Bangkok the Hainanese were too strong to go along with such an arrangement. Many of the earliest party activists in Siam were Hainanese.

It appears that the formation in Bangkok of the Chino-Siam Bank in 1908 was not unconnected with the revolutionary cause. It was capitalized primarily by local rice millers and merchants engaged largely in financing the rice trade with Hongkong. It also came to provide funds for the revolution, and its stability was bound up with Sun's success. The loss of confidence in the revolutionaries following the victory of Yüan Shih-k'ai and the flight of Sun to Japan in 1913 led to the complete failure of the Bank, a disaster which harmed the revolutionary movement in Siam and caused a severe financial crisis in Bangkok.¹⁴

The antirevolutionaries remained active in Bangkok until well after the 1911 revolution. The royalist paper, *Ch'i-nan Jih-pao,* died within a year of its birth, but adherents of the Pao-huang Tang (C 88) (Party to Preserve the Monarchy) continued to oppose Sun Yat-sen's movement. In the spring of 1909, Ma Hsing-shun (C 89), a major backer of the *Hua-hsien Jih-pao,* went to Ch'ao-chou on business, and the Chinese royalists in Siam cabled the viceroy at Canton of his arrival there. Ma was arrested and imprisoned as a revolutionist, and Ch'en Ching-hua had to go to Hongkong to arrange for his release.¹⁵ In 1912, the Chinese royalists in Bangkok established the *Chung-hua-min Pao* (C 90), which for several years fought Hsiao Fo-ch'eng's paper tooth and nail.

Chinese national politics thus provided the major impetus to a healthy development of the Chinese press in Thailand. By 1918, Bangkok had seen six or seven Chinese papers come and go. The predominance of revolutionary sentiment was by that time apparent, however, for the three papers then being published—the Cantonese *Hsia Pao* (C 91), *Hua-hsien Jih-pao* and even *Chung-hua-min Pao*— were all giving editorial support to Sun Yat-sen's Nationalist movement.

The first Chinese schools in Bangkok were also established in the interests of Chinese national politics. Between 1909 and 1911 the T'ung Meng Hui, directly or through its front, the Chung-hua Association, established several "study societies" and the Hua-yi school. The royalists countered with their own study societies and the Chung-hua school. Several other schools were established in the next year or two, but the most important of these, Hsin-min, was also founded under T'ung Meng Hui auspices.[16]

The rise of nationalist sentiment on the part of the Chinese in Siam was naturally accompanied by a strengthening of ties with the homeland. The Manchu government, fighting against time for its life, finally took steps in the last years of the dynasty to gain the support of its overseas Chinese. In 1907, an imposing Chinese commercial mission visited Siam escorted by two cruisers,[17] and thereafter attempts were made to negotiate a treaty with Siam. In 1909, the Manchus promulgated the first Chinese Nationality Act, which provided that offspring of a Chinese parent were Chinese nationals—a move designed "to keep natural-born Chinese from falling under foreign domination." [18] The new Ch'ing code in 1910 finally eliminated the emigration ban, long a dead letter but still a source of constant friction between returning emigrants and government officials. These belated gestures on the part of the imperial government, together with the attention shown overseas Chinese by Sun Yat-sen, led the Chinese in Siam to hope for real protection from the Republican government after 1911. For the first time, they looked to a Chinese regime as their home government.

Among the important consequences of the growth of nationalism among the Chinese in Siam, then, were the strengthening of ties with the homeland, the establishment of Chinese newspapers and schools, an increase in Chinese political activity in Thai territory, and a tendency to bridge differences within the local community in the interests of a purely Chinese cause. The overseas community gained a new awareness of its Chinese character and nationality.

B. The Chinese Problem

The Thai, for their part, also developed a spirit of nationalism during the first two decades of the twentieth century. Young members of the Thai elite, in increasing numbers throughout the fifth reign, were educated in Western schools in Siam and sent abroad to study in Europe. They learned not only the meaning of modern nationalism but also its close relation in Western countries with the bigotry of racism. It goes without saying that contact between ethnic groups as different in character as the Chinese and Thai had, in Siam, led to stereotyping that was sharpened by the occupational specialization of the two groups. Chinese tended to regard Thai as "barbarians," while Thai considered the Chinese uncouth.[19] These stereotypes and prejudices took on political importance, however, only as the Thai elite absorbed nationalism from the West. It was from Westerners, for instance, that the Thai gained a full appreciation of their national past: around the turn of the century, the Siamese elite, through contact with Western scholars, learned of their ancestors' migration from China, and of the still earlier struggle for Thai independence from Chinese rule.[20] In Europe they came to appreciate the political dimensions of ethno-centrism and met for the first time the doctrines of anti-Semitism and the Yellow (i.e., Chinese) Peril. Above all, they were exposed in Siam to the European's unfavorable attitude towards the Chinese.

The influence of European anti-Sinicism on the development of Thai nationalism and racism has never been properly appraised. This is not the place to analyze the origins of the Western attitude, which presumably arose from the nature of the contacts Westerners had with Chinese—either as trade competitors or low-status employees.[21] The anti-Chinese bias of the Europeans in Siam might well be conveyed by quoting two of the prominent advisors to the Thai government around the turn of the century. Warington Smyth, a British Director of the Royal Department of Mines, wrote in 1898:

Beyond the very high qualities of which he is undoubtedly possessed—qualities shared perhaps equally by the buffalo—I confess I have no great admiration for the Chinese coolie.

The Chinese . . . are the Jews of Siam; . . . they have on the whole enjoyed an immunity from official interference which they have neither merited nor appreciated. Their only return has been that species of high-handed rowdyism which results from the methods followed by Chinese secret societies elsewhere. . . . By judicious use of their business faculties and their powers of combination, they hold the Siamese in the palm of their hand. The toleration accorded to them by the Government is put down to fear; they bow and scrape before the authorities, but laugh behind their backs; and they could sack half Bangkok in a day.[22]

J. G. D. Campbell, educational advisor to the Thai government, also compared the Chinese to the Jews and was of the opinion that the "quiet-loving [Thai] natives . . . have virtually sold to them [the Chinese] their birthright for a mess of pottage." Of the European attitude, he wrote: "It cannot be said that they [the Chinese] are employed by Europeans on account of any great love inspired by them, but simply because necessity knows no choice; . . . they are only tolerated as a necessary evil." [23]

By the turn of the century, Chinese had been excluded from most of the "Anglo-Saxon" countries, and the Yellow Peril was a very serious concern among Westerners taking the large view. Many were alarmed by the influx of the Chinese into Siam, and they did not fail to voice their fears. In 1903, a Western geographer predicted: "One day will see the Siamese race no longer in existence and the Menam valley peopled only by Chinese." [24] Campbell, too, warned that the Chinese "are more than likely before many years to be the dominating people of Siam . . . and either to swamp the indolent and lethargic natives, or transform them by fusion and intermarriage till they are past recognition." [25] The French were not unconcerned either. An article in the *Revue Indo-Chinoise* predicted that Siam "will be completely absorbed by the Chinese element," [26] and another, provocatively entitled "Bangkok, colonie Chinoise, ou le secret du colosse jaune," [27] pictured the Chinese immigration into Bangkok as part of a grand imperialist design.

The European-educated Thai elite could hardly avoid these Western prejudices and fears. They had attended British, French, and American schools, and they associated socially with the Western commercial and diplomatic set in Bangkok. They read the English newspapers published in Bangkok, and these by no means failed to discuss the local Chinese. [28] Above all, they were, in their official capacity, influenced by European advisers to the Thai government who, like Smyth and Campbell, had very definite opinions about the Chinese which they were wont to share. Smyth once congratulated a Thai special commissioner at Phuket for having adopted anti-Chinese policies, and he advised the Thai to suppress Chinese secret societies as the British had done in Malaya and to tax them more heavily. [29]

It is significant in this regard that the first recorded expression of Thai fears of the Chinese came from a lawyer educated in England. In the last decade of the nineteenth century he started a Thai journal which began to claim that the Chinese were becoming too numerous in Siam. The paper was closed through the intervention of Rama V himself, who considered the subject best left alone. [30]

Julalongkọn's attitude, maintained until the last year of his reign, was expressed clearly in 1907:

It has always been my policy that the Chinese in Siam should have the same opportunities for labor and for profit as are possessed by my own countrymen. I regard them not as foreigners but as one of the component parts of the kingdom and sharing in its prosperity and advancement.[31]

This tolerance was badly shaken, however, as a result of one of the last reforms of Julalongkǫn's reign. In 1899, corvée had been replaced by an annual head tax, and for the next ten years the Thai and other Asians resident in Siam paid from 4 to 6 baht *per year* while the Chinese continued to pay only 4.25 baht *once every three years*. This inequity went unrectified as long as it did probably because of the urgent demand for labor. In March 1909, however, a decree was issued which ended the triennial tax and made the Chinese liable to the regular capitation tax paid by the rest of the population. Whether the tax the Chinese paid in 1909 was the triennial tax—due in that year—or the general capitation tax is not clear, but in any case a tax was expected and no trouble occurred. But when in 1910 the Chinese learned that they had to pay again, considerable opposition was manifest.[32]

It is, of course, true that the change was only fair and that the Chinese were no more entitled to a privileged fiscal status than other Asian aliens in the country. The average Chinese, however, knew only that he had to pay a new tax which upped his annual rate from less than 1.50 baht to 6 baht.[33] He never had the situation officially explained to him in any case,[34] and he protested long and hard. The secret-society leaders, for their part, had to do something for the mass membership in such an emergency, and, faced by a threat from outside the Chinese community, they united for concerted action. A general strike was planned for June 1, and in the last days of May placards in Chinese were distributed throughout the city calling for a complete cessation of work; merchants were warned to close shop if they wanted to avoid pillage and arson. On the appointed day society gangs went through the business quarters repeating and enforcing the threats. All Chinese shops closed, in spite of the fact that Thai police and troops had promised protection to shopkeepers who stayed open. Every Chinese enterprise and service was at a standstill for three days, during which time rice and other food became scarce and very expensive, and business and shipping were paralyzed. Only domestic servants and employees of Western business firms did not take part in the strike. There was no serious rioting, and the police, reinforced by the army, performed well in the emergency. About four hundred arrests were made, some for public brawls but most for threats or provocations to disorder. Some shops reopened the evening of the third day, and by the fifth all was over.

The strike was a failure and a disastrous mistake. For the Chinese it was an indication of the bankruptcy of the old secret-society leadership. It is doubtful whether the strike leaders had decided what to do if the government failed to respond with a retraction of the tax decree. No public gatherings were held, no public demands made, and, if the leaders approached the government behind closed doors, they achieved nothing. Rice millers, who had apparently been forced to close just when the rice trade was particularly active, were hardly pleased by the strike, while the compradores took no part. It was the secret-society leaders—the old monopoly farmers and racket bosses—who bore full responsibility for the strike. Its failure showed that they could not bring their power to bear on the Thai government, however well they could coerce elements within Chinese society. It also demonstrated to the Chinese that the newly reorganized police and army were efficient and strong, and left no doubt that ultimate power in Siam lay with the Thai government.

The average Thai was badly inconvenienced by the whole episode, and his prejudices against the Chinese were intensified. For the Thai nationalists, moreover, the strike bore a lesson of far-reaching consequences.[35] The extent to which the Thai people had become dependent on Chinese trade and business was made apparent. The city was not completely paralyzed only because employees of the streetcar company and power plants were Thai, as well as many food sellers. The moral was obvious: if the Chinese were to extend further their role in the country's economy, then the Thai population would be completely at their mercy. Furthermore, the strike served to demonstrate that the resident Chinese were in Siam only to get what they could out of it—that they were not willing to contribute their share and that they valued money above loyalty, obedience, and justice. The whole fiasco placed the Chinese in an extremely unfavorable light and a very vulnerable position.

King Wachirawut (Rama VI) came to the throne a few months after the Chinese strike. On the occasion of his coronation in 1911, Chinese community leaders made a concerted effort to erase the memory of the events of the previous June. Expensive gifts were presented to the king, and the court was persuaded to route the coronation procession to the Chinese quarter, where a ceremony demonstrating Chinese loyalty was made. The address presented to the king by the Chinese community pointedly referred to the fact that many descendants of Chinese had become Thai nationals and entered the priesthood and government service and then went on to request a continuation of Rama V's policies in these diplomatic words:

In Your Majesty's Dominions, the Chinese have been granted the same privileges as the rest of the people, and have not been subjected to any prejudicial discrimination on account of their race. When we bear this fact in mind, we can only feel extreme satisfaction and a deep sense of gratitude, for we all realize that, in coming to seek our livelihood in Siam, we may confidently expect to be treated exactly as the people of the Great Thai race are treated, enjoying the same privileges and living under the same laws without the slightest distinction.[36]

The last phrases, of course, were designed to express the community's acceptance of the justice of equal taxation.

The new king, however, never forgot nor forgave the Chinese strike. He was, in many ways, typical of the new Thai nationalism. Educated in England from boyhood on, he also included Europeans among his closest friends. He was intelligent, had a flair for the dramatic, and felt called upon to rouse his people to their national destiny through writing, his favorite occupation. He was, to some extent, the philosopher of Thai nationalism, drawing on his wide knowledge of the West to point up Thai shortcomings and potentialities. Among the notable documents allegedly from his pen was *The Jews of the East,* published in 1914.[37] An elaborate comparison of the Chinese with an anti-Semite's caricature of the Jews, it provided a classic statement of the Thai case against the Chinese resident in Siam. A summary of its contents, then, will define the Chinese Problem as seen by Thai nationalists forty years ago.[38]

The Chinese first of all were said to be unassimilable: because of their racial loyalty and sense of superiortiy, they remain always Chinese. They regard residence in Siam as temporary, their only purpose in coming being to make as much money as possible. When they marry Thai women, they force their wives to become Chinese and rear their children as Chinese. Second, they were accused of being opportunistic and two-faced: the Chinese profess Buddhism and political allegiance only for the advantage they get out of it; in fact they are neither loyal nor Buddhist. Their gentle manners towards Thai are an opportunistic deception. In the third place, the Chinese were held to be devoid of civic virtues: they expect all the privileges, but refuse the obligations, of citizenship. Their attitude towards the state is treacherous, secretive, and rebellious. Fourth, the Chinese were said to worship Mammon as their sole god: for money they endure any privation, perform the vilest deeds, cheat, embezzle, rob, and kill. In money matters they know neither morals nor mercy. Finally, they were accused of being parasites on the Thai economy: the Chinese buy little that is produced in Siam for their own consumption, preferring to import clothes and food from China, and they drain off the wealth of the country in the form of remittances to their homeland.

This arraignment was accompanied by a thinly veiled threat: "We try to conduct ourselves like men of good will. But we are only ordinary human beings and there is a limit to our self control. If there should be another incident like the Chinese strike I should not care to be responsible for the outcome." And in view of the supposed authorship, the meaning of the following sentence was equally pointed: "They [the Chinese as described] are likely to be a cause of lively concern to those charged with the offices of government, whose endeavor is so to rule that the people of a country shall be able to maintain their national entity." [39] Wachirawut has been described as a man more given to philosophizing and dramatic gesture than to action. Whether this is just or not, it is remarkable that his reign was marked by only a few, comparatively minor government steps that could be viewed as anti-Chinese. However, his writings alone, voicing so eloquently a nascent chauvinism, did much to arouse fear and distrust between Chinese and Thai.[40] *The Jews of the East* served notice on the Chinese that a new era was at hand in which the Thai were determined to be fully sovereign and supreme in their own land.

Early in the sixth reign (1913/14), the Thai government promulgated the first Nationality Act, which, like the Chinese Nationality Act of 1909 affirmed the principle of *jus sanguinis,* by stating that "every person born to a Thai father on Thai or foreign territory" was Thai. Of more importance to the Chinese, however, the law also claimed as Thai "every person born on Thai territory." [41] A long-lasting dispute over the citizenship of Chinese born in Siam was thereby clearly joined. Several hundred thousand persons, born in Siam of Chinese fathers, became dual nationals, subject to rival claims and divided allegiance.

C. The Evolution of Chinese Society

The period from the turn of the century to the end of the First World War was also one of transition in Chinese social organization in Siam. The major trends, in a word, were those from underground activity toward legitimacy, from division toward cohesion, from informal toward formal organization, from social anarchy toward community responsibility. The changes came in response to new situations both within and without Chinese society, but naturally each development in turn served to condition those in its train.

Among the most notable developments were the decline in influence, authority, and structural importance of the secret societies and the assumption of many of their more legitimate functions by newly established speech-group associations. A Thailand Chinese of the present day has evaluated the rise and fall of secret societies as follows:

When steamships made sea voyages easy, those who came were not necessarily vagabonds and rascals, but it was difficult to find a son of wealth. The strong, the uncouth, the illiterate came in hordes and the gold rush was on. The idea was to make a fortune and go back home. It was a pity that most of them were illiterate and did not know that there were legitimate ways to organize. They joined secret societies and fought each other. How stupid not to use their united forces to develop the means of livelihood instead of killing each other! Living in a strange land, it is difficult enough to exist without any political protection. Killing each other was simply suicidal as well as destructive of what foundation our forefathers had laid. Some wise latecomers realized all this and also knew that the secret societies were hated by the local government. They began to organize legally recognized societies.[42]

The rapid decline of secret societies after 1910 was a result of several factors. The gradual abolition of monopoly farms—a process begun about 1900 and fairly well completed in 1917—knocked the economic props from under the society leaders, brought gambling and opium smoking under control, and ended the intra-Chinese rivalry connected with obtaining the monopolies. Insofar as the societies had political aims, these were obviated by the overthrow of the Manchus in 1911, and any remaining political fervor or patriotic altruism was captured by the Chinese Nationalist movement. It has already been mentioned that the onus of the unfortunate Chinese strike of 1910 fell on the societies because of their key role in its organization. As a result of that strike, the government began a serious campaign of suppression as soon as Wachirawut came to the throne. In any case, traditional secret-society methods had become less efficacious with the modernization of the police and army during the first decade of the century. Thai government policy was also instrumental in neutralizing the influence of important old-time society leaders. The case of Cheng

Chih-yung (C 92) provides a striking illustration. During the first decade of the present century, Cheng headed the most important branch of the Triad (San-tien) Society and was known to members as Erh-ko Feng, i.e., Second-degree Elder Brother Feng. His position was enhanced through registration with the French Consulate. At one time or another, he held both gambling and lottery farms, wherefore he held the title of Luang. Early in Wachirawut's reign, however, he was given the title of Phra and provided with a mansion for the rest of his life. Cheng obligingly settled into his new role as a wealthy Thai nobleman and retired from Chinese community life.

After 1910, some of the secret societies simply became inactive, others were reorganized as legitimate mutual-aid associations, and still others whose members were primarily drawn from the same speech groups patched up their differences or merged, thus paving the way for the establishment of legal speech-group associations. In some up-country towns with a single, entrenched society, its power continued into the 1920's, and not all societies elsewhere became completely defunct. But as a major social force in the community, the societies were finished.

Speech-group and regional associations were founded to meet many needs. They protected the special occupational interests of members; helped new immigrants from the home district or emigrant area to find jobs and get established; built and maintained temples with gods peculiar to the home district and cemeteries for the use of those who could not afford shipment of their deceased to China for burial; provided the locale and occasions for social gatherings of those from the same district or emigrant area, and so on. The first speech-group-wide association in Bangkok was that of the Cantonese, founded in 1877. A Hainanese association was established about 1900, followed by the Hokkien Association a few years later, and by the Hakka Association in 1909. The first Teochiu association was not organized until long after the First World War. This order is significant: the numerically weakest group—the Cantonese—organized first; the three intermediate groups organized within ten years of one another, while the Teochius, who were numerically dominant and in positions of greatest power, found it unnecessary to organize for another two decades. The order, in fact, will be seen to be almost exactly inverse to the power and resources of each speech group, if it is remembered that the Hainanese, in spite of being numerically stronger than either the Hokkiens or Hakkas, were of lower prestige and power, and that Hokkiens, who had higher standing than the Hakkas, were in Bangkok numerically far inferior. It would seem, then, that the speech groups commanding less power and resources felt the need to organize for self-protection earlier. The stone tablet commemorating the establishment of the Cantonese Association bears out this analysis. After pointing out that the other dialect groups were numerically stronger, the account states:

According to the law of evolution, it was feared that our small group could not survive. . . . Our greatest weakness is lack of organization. . . . Therefore, ten of us proposed the establishment of this *Pieh-shu* and numerous supporters gathered around as soon as the news got out.[43]

The earliest of the speech-group organizations did not call themselves *hui-kuan* (C 93), the ordinary term for association, because all regularly established associations were suspect by the government. Thus the Cantonese used *pieh-shu* (C 94), "villa," and the Hainanese *kung-so* (C 95), "public meeting-place." After the Secret Societies Act of 1897 proved ineffective and was forgotten, the first associations came into the open, while the new ones were established as fully legitimate and public organizations with the name Hui-kuan.

The speech-group associations played an important role in the expansion of Chinese education in Siam. Before describing this development, however, a word of background is in order. Western-type education was introduced into Siam by the American Protestant and French Catholic missions.[44] Their first modest schools were in some cases attended largely by Chinese, but the impact of the mission schools on the Chinese community became important only toward the end of the nineteenth century. In particular the French-operated Assumption College,[45] which opened in 1885, and the American-operated Bangkok Christian Boys School (later College), which opened in Bangkok proper in 1901, became popular with Chinese boys hoping to enter Western business houses and banks. English and French were offered as foreign languages, but several of the mission schools had Chinese departments or gave instruction to their Chinese students in Teochiu. About 1910, a Chinese boys school was established in connection with a French Catholic cathedral. However, most of the boys who received any education prior to 1910—and their number was small—attended the private classical schools described in Chapter 4.

Meanwhile, during the first decade of the twentieth century a revolution in education was taking place in the emigrant areas of south China. Mission schools conducted in Chinese were flourishing, and Western-type Chinese schools aiming at "the speedy acquisition of practical knowledge" were established in increasing numbers.[46] The new schooling was given a further boost by the rise of nationalism and revolutionary fervor.

Thus, a new type of Chinese education—based still on rote memorization but modern in content—became available to the Chinese in Siam through contact with local missionary schools and with their home districts. The need for greater literacy in Chinese arose primarily from the increasing size and complexity of business: the usefulness of efficient bookkeeping and filing in large firms, the introduction of banking, the greater reliance on correspondence with Chinese firms in Singapore and Hongkong, and so on. And the practical contents of the new education had far more appeal to a commercially oriented community than did the traditional classics. When, therefore, Chinese nationalists established the first of these new-type schools in Bangkok for propaganda purposes just before the revolution, the new schooling won immediate approval.

Hsin-min, the first community-supported Chinese school, was sponsored originally by all five speech groups. But instruction—which could, after all, be in only one language—was in Teochiu and so attracted primarily Teochiu students and teachers. The administration was soon taken over by Teochiu administrators (the superintendent was Ch'en Yi-ju, mentioned in Section A) and so failed to meet the needs of other speech groups. Consequently, each group established its own school with instruction in its own language. The Hakka Association founded the Chin-te school in 1913, the Cantonese Association the Ming-te school in 1914, and the Hokkien Association the P'ei-yüan school in 1916. Only in 1921 was the first Hainanese school, Yü-min, established. This order, it will be noted, almost precisely parallels the order of speech-group power and resources.

The decline of secret societies and the introduction of modern Chinese education seemed, therefore, to give added importance to speech-group associations. While this development could be interpreted as a divisive trend in the society, a sounder view would see in it primarily a trend toward legitimate, formal, and public organization. For the divisions among speech groups were far more bitter in the heyday of secret societies than they were after the establishment of the four formal speech-group associations. And the first decade of this century saw the establishment of associations which for the first time cut clearly across speech-group lines and embraced the whole community.

In fact, probably the most significant social trend in the transition period under discussion was the development of horizontal, community-wide organizations. The two most important of these were the T'ien-hua Hospital and the Chinese Chamber of Commerce. The Hospital was organized between 1904 and 1906 by representatives of all five speech groups to fill a badly felt community need. A fund of 115,000 baht was solicited from leading merchants in Bangkok to build what was then the finest hospital in the city, with wards accommodating two hundred patients.[47] It was maintained by monthly subscriptions from members, i.e., the more important and public-spirited Chinese firms in town. The organization of this first co-operative venture among the speech groups was cleverly devised. Member firms, represented by their owners or managers, selected annually the governing board consisting of a chairman, a treasurer, and ten regular directors. According to the constitution the chairmanship was to rotate among each of the speech groups in turn, while the treasurer was always a Teochiu. This system gave special weight to the one predominant group but at the same time avoided speech-group competition.

The Chinese Chamber of Commerce was organized in 1908 and registered with the imperial government at Peking. Chinese Chambers had been founded with official blessing in Amoy and Swatow at the turn of the century to help the local authorities regulate the emigration traffic and promote Chinese as opposed to Western trade.[48] In Siam, European businessmen in 1898 had formed the Bangkok Chamber of Commerce, with membership restricted to Western firms. Competition from the growing Western enterprises in shipping, import-export, milling, and banking prompted Chinese merchants in these lines to put aside differences and organize the Chamber for their mutual benefit. Membership was by firm, each represented by its owner or manager. For the first few years, the officers consisted of a president, vice-president, a ten-man executive committee and forty-man "senate," but after the Republic was founded this unwieldy arrangement was replaced by a thirty-man board of directors, headed by a chairman and vice-chairman. The term of office was two years. The constitution provided no restrictions or apportionment according to speech group, but it was understood that the various groups should be represented on the board roughly in proportion to their membership. The chairman was almost always Teochiu in the early years, however, and meetings were conducted in Teochiu.

Within a few years after its establishment the Chamber of Commerce had assumed broader powers and functions than organizations of the same name in Western countries. The most important Chinese organization in Bangkok, it soon became *the* organization representing the Chinese community as a whole. Its chairman spoke on behalf of the whole Chinese community at Rama VI's coronation in 1911. As a formally constituted organization, the Chamber admitted only legitimate and respectable firms. As its prestige in the community rose, its officials became the acknowledged leaders of the Chinese community.

The economic base of the new leaders differed from that of the old: their interests were in the rapidly growing processing mills, banking and insurance, steam shipping as well as import-export. They were not vice-monopoly or revenue farmers and their commitments to secret societies were nominal or nil. For the most part they supported the revolutionary cause. Above all, they were sufficiently enlightened to see the necessity of overcoming the obstacles to Chinese unity. Typical of the young leaders who helped bridge the gaps separating speech groups were Wu Tso-nan (C 96), a Hakka with major interests in sawmilling, Yün Chu-t'ing (C 97), a Hainanese with major interests in import-export and shipping, and Lu Tieh-ch'uan (C 98), a Teochiu with major interests in rice milling. The three became fast friends in their youth and, in such organizations as the T'ien-hua Hospital and the Chamber of Commerce, worked closely together for the whole community.

In the decades following the establishment of the Chamber of Commerce, several other Chinese business associations were formed by the new leaders. The most important of these first associations still in operation today are the Insurance Business Association and the Rice Merchants Association, founded in 1917 and 1919. These associations like their numerous successors founded in the 1920's were horizontal employer-owner organizations in contrast to the traditional guilds.

By the end of the First World War, Chinese society in Bangkok—and the same could be said of that in several of the Siamese towns—could legitimately be called a community. It had its own newspapers, read by all regardless of speech group, and devoted to the same revolutionary cause. It had a welfare institution in the operation of which all five speech groups were effectively co-operating. And above all it had reputable community leaders, in the persons of the Chamber of Commerce officers, who could speak for the Chinese as a whole.

⇉ 6 ⇇

INFLUX AND FLUX:

Demographic Trends, 1918-1955

A. *The Climax and End of Mass Immigration*

FOR most of the years 1918–1955, three independently collected statistical series of Chinese migration to and from Thailand are available: those of the Thai Customs Department (1918/19–1955), the Thai Immigration Division (1928/29–1954), and the Chinese Customs (1918–1928, 1930–1939, 1946). On the whole, the three series not only are compatible but largely corroborate one another, so that it is possible to estimate total arrivals and departures of Chinese for the period with considerable accuracy. Table 6 and Chart 3 present this writer's estimates for total migration of ethnic Chinese (all Thailand, not just Bangkok) by immigration periods, namely the boom period after the First World War (1918–1931), the depression and war years (1932–1945), and the period after the Second World War (1946–1955).

During the first of these periods, Chinese flocked into Siam at an unprecedented rate. Not only were arrivals high, averaging almost 95,000 annually, but departures were relatively low, averaging 62 per cent of arrivals as compared with 78 per cent of arrivals during the preceding migration period (1906–1917). The result was an immigration surplus for the fourteen-year period of approximately half a million China-born Chinese—a surplus larger than that of the three preceding periods together (1882–1917: 451,500) and much larger than that of the subsequent twenty-four years (1932–1955: 252,400). In all prob-

Table 6. Estimated total arrivals and departures (in thousands) of ethnic Chinese, all Thailand, annually and by periods, 1918–1955 *

Year	Arrivals	Departures	Year	Arrivals	Departures	Year	Arrivals	Departures
1918 (¼ yr.)	9.8	9.1	1932 (¼ yr.)	18.7	14.1	1946	86.0	5.8
1918/19	67.9	37.0	1932/33	59.5	44.1	1947	83.8	23.4
1919/20	65.7	43.4	1933/34	25.7	32.6	1948	28.5	22.3
1920/21	70.4	36.8	1934/35	27.0	31.1	1949	20.0	15.8
1921/22	76.5	46.9	1935/36	45.2	36.5	1950	7.6	7.4
1922/23	95.4	65.2	1936/37	48.9	28.0	1951	17.9	13.7
1923/24	115.0	66.4	1937/38	60.0	22.0	1952	9.8	7.3
1924/25	92.7	66.1	1938/39	33.5	30.0	1953	6.4	2.8
1925/26	95.5	60.6	1939/40	25.1	18.8	1954	4.0	4.5
1926/27	106.4	73.7	1940 (¾ yr.)	23.6	19.8	1955	3.8	4.8
1927/28	154.6	76.9	1941	44.8	36.7			
1928/29	101.1	72.8	1942	11.1	17.8			
1929/30	134.1	68.2	1943	20.1	20.7			
1930/31	86.4	62.4	1944	18.1	17.9			
1931 (¾ yr.)	56.1	42.4	1945	12.4	11.2			
Total	1,327.6	827.9	Total	473.7	381.3	Total	267.8	107.8

Period	Total arrivals	Total departures	% Departures of arrivals	Avg. ann. arrivals	Avg. ann. departures	Total surplus of arrivals	Avg. ann. surplus of arrivals
1918–31	1,327.6	827.9	62.4	94.8	59.1	499.7	35.7
1932–45	473.7	381.3	80.5	33.8	27.2	92.4	6.6
1946–55	267.8	107.8	40.3	26.8	10.8	160.0	16.0

* Based on statistics supplied by the Immigration Division and the Customs Department in Bangkok and given in the following serial publications: *China Trade Returns* 1918–1929; *Chinese Customs Decennial Reports* 1912–1921, 1922–1931; *Reports on China Trade* 1930–1948; *Thai Customs Statements* 1917/18–1946; and *Thailand Statistical Year Books* 1924/25–1953.

ability, at least half of the China-born Chinese living in Thailand today first immigrated during the 1918–1931 period.

This mass influx of Chinese resulted, quite simply, from favorable conditions in Siam and unfavorable conditions in south China. The 1920's saw a boom in rubber and tin production in South Siam, further expansion in rice milling and sawmilling, a rapidly expanding foreign trade, and a resumption of railroad construction—all of which contributed to a heightened demand for labor and entrepreneurial skill. As in the prewar years, Siam could boast the highest wage level in the East.[1]

In south China, on the other hand, social order and crop yields reached a new low by the mid-1920's. It will suffice to mention only the more salient instances. The rice crop in Hainan was completely destroyed two years in a row, 1924–1925, by typhoons and droughts.[2] The proportion of cultivable farm land planted to rice in Ch'ao-chou was said to have decreased during the 1920's from 75 to 40 per cent largely because of instability: political unrest, banditry, and military strife.[3] Ch'ao-chou between 1925 and 1927 was the scene of continual fighting in connection with the active phase of the Nationalist revolution, and the insecure living conditions in the interior caused thousands to emigrate from the country districts.[4] Communist activity, said to be a factor leading to increased emigration as early as 1925, took a new turn in 1927 when the Kuomintang-Communist working alliance was violently broken. Thousands of leftists fled the country, and the foraging activities of the Communist groups which formed in the mountainous interior of south China induced others to emigrate.[5] Credner, with good reason, relates the all-time peak of Chinese immigration in 1927/28 to Chiang Kai-shek's attack on Communism in Kwangtung in 1927.[6]

The rapid decline in Chinese immigration to Siam during 1930–1933 was a response primarily to worsening economic conditions in Siam itself. The coming of the world depression brought a collapse in the tin and rubber markets, a contraction in rice milling, and a large drop in the volume and value of imports and exports. Wages dropped, and the demand for labor was adequately met by the immigrants of the previous decade. Other factors in the decline, though much less important, were the more peaceful conditions obtaining in south China after 1930 [7] and the beginning of immigration regulation in Thailand.

The migration period 1932–1945, in contrast to the preceding boom

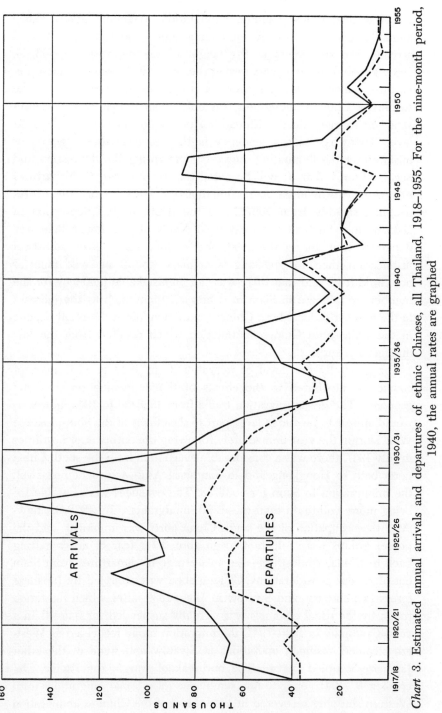

Chart 3. Estimated annual arrivals and departures of ethnic Chinese, all Thailand, 1918–1955. For the nine-month period, 1940, the annual rates are graphed

era, was one of low Chinese immigration, averaging about 33,800 annually, and of relatively high emigration—about 80 per cent of arrivals. For two years at the height of the depression (1933/34, 1934/35), and for two years during the war (1942–1943), Chinese departures exceeded arrivals. For the total fourteen-year period, the surplus of Chinese immigrants was only about 92,000, which was insufficient to maintain the China-born population in Siam at the 1932 level. There has been a tendency in the literature to exaggerate or misinterpret the fluctuating migration rate ruring the depression and Second World War. It will be noted that for no year did departures exceed arrivals by more than a few thousand. Furthermore, departures declined steadily from 1927/28 to the depth of the depression in 1934/35 and fluctuated thereafter at levels always lower than any departure rate during the 1906–1931 period. There is no statistical justification, then, for speaking of a "mass exodus" or "wild flight"; [8] nor could it be said that there was "an unmistakable tendency for the numbers of Chinese in Siam to decrease," [9] inasmuch as the increase in the number of local-born Chinese more than offset the small decline in the China-born Chinese population which resulted from the low immigration surplus.

The generally low level of migration from 1932 to 1937 may, of course, be attributed to the effects of the depression on the Thai economy. The dip in migration traffic from 1938/39 to 1940, however, would appear to be due in large part to the effects of the Sino-Japanese War. During the year immediately following the outbreak of hostilities in July 1937, there was a considerable evacuation from the south China ports both to Hongkong and to Southeast Asia—which helped swell the immigration to Siam for 1937/38. The evacuees were notable for being more well-to-do than the usual immigrants.[10] By 1938/39, however, the occupation of the south China ports was imminent, and the poorer groups were reluctant to go abroad for fear of never getting back to China, while there was an upsurge of departures from Siam out of similar considerations. Ch'iung-chou was occupied by Japanese forces in February, and Swatow in June, 1939, after which migration traffic by the usual channels was virtually suspended for more than a year. Gradually in 1940–1941, the migration traffic recovered as Western steamers resumed operations at Swatow and some of the other Japanese-occupied ports.[11] The outbreak of war in the Pacific, December 8, 1941, ended any semblance of normal migration until Western shipping recovered in 1946. Most of the Chinese immigration to Siam 1942–1945 was by land from Malaya; and the slight peak in 1943 represents in part the import of conscripted labor from the Straits for work on the Japanese-sponsored "Death Railway" to Burma.

The fluctuation in the Chinese migration rate during the 1930's was also influenced by the Thai government's immigration policy. The first Siamese law on immigration had been promulgated in 1927, but it had little practical effect on the migration rate.[12] An immigrant with no passport had to pay a fee of only 4 baht for identification papers, raised to 10 baht in 1928/29. In 1931, an additional fee of 30 baht for a residence certificate was imposed, as well as a 5-baht fee for a return permit. These fees were upped the following year to 100 baht and 20 baht respectively, and were undoubtedly an important factor in suppressing the migration rates from 1932 to 1935. When Chinese immigration increased to the sizable figure of almost 60,000 in 1937/38, the Thai government passed another act raising the residence fee to 200 baht, and requiring immigrants to have an independent income or some other means of support. Thereafter immigration sharply declined. The rise in the departure rate for 1938/39 has also been attributed to the fear instilled in resident Chinese by the passage of the 1937/38 Immigration Act.[13]

Postwar immigration reflects even more clearly Thai government policy. The 200-baht fee for a residence certificate was still in effect after the war, but wartime inflation meant that the fee was roughly equivalent to the pre-1932 20-baht fee.[14] This was no deterrent to immigration, and the war-weary Chinese flocked to Thailand, which had largely escaped the ravages of war and was well on the way to full economic recovery and prosperity. The immigration rates for 1946–1947 were higher than any since 1931, while the emigration rate remained extraordinarily low. The immigration was all the higher in 1946 and early 1947 because of rumors that the government would soon raise immigration fees or impose a quota.[15] The Thai government, in fact, reacted to the tremendous influx by putting into effect a quota system for the first time in May 1947. The annual quota for Chinese immigration was fixed at 10,000, and then reduced, effective at the beginning of 1949, to the same level fixed for other nationalties, i.e., only 200 per year. The Immigration Act of 1950 fixed the upper limit on the immigration quota for any nationality at 200, set the residence fee at 1,000 baht, and provided severe restrictions and controls on immigration. After a brief "readjustment" recovery of the migration rates in 1951, both arrivals and departures steadily declined thereafter to the lowest levels in over a century. Most of the Chinese arrivals in Thailand since 1950 have been former residents re-entering on return permits, temporary visitors, and transit passengers. Chinese mass immigration is, for the time being at least, at an end.[16]

The Thai government's immigration policies had a profound influence on the composition as well as the numbers of Chinese immigrants. During the 1918–1931 period, the great mass of male immigrants were laborers of one sort or another, but the high fees exacted after 1932 reversed the proportion, with businessmen taking the lead. The declared professions of incoming male Chinese aliens were recorded by the Thai Immigration Division for the years 1928/29–1930/31, and 1933/34–1938/39.[17] For the former period—prior to the imposition of high immigration fees—only 31 per cent declared their profession to be commercial, while for the latter period, 75 per cent so declared. With fees after the Second World War low again because of inflation, laborers once more became predominant among immigrants, but the imposition of quotas (creating an increased need for bribery) and of higher fees between 1948 and 1950 has meant, in effect, that in recent years only wealthy Chinese have been able to enter Siam as new immigrants.

Available statistics do not allow any definitive conclusions as to the proportion of the various speech groups among the immigration surplus. However, Table 7, which is based primarily on Chinese customs statistics for Swatow and Hai-k'ou, throws light on the relative importance of Teochius and Hakkas together as against Hainanese. For the 1918–1931 period, there were 4.95 times as many direct immigrants from Swatow (i.e., Teochius and Hakkas) as from Hai-k'ou (i.e., Hainanese), while the immigrants from these two ports together totaled about 83 per cent of all direct immigrants. These figures have only a limited application, however, because there are undoubtedly differentials according to speech group both with regard to indirect migration and to rate of return. Hokkiens, and to a lesser extent Hakkas and Cantonese, travel to Siam more often indirectly via Malaya and Indochina than do Teochius and Hainanese. The figures presented in the lower part of Table 7 would seem to imply that the return rate for Swatow and Hai-k'ou immigrants is higher than that for the Hokkiens and Cantonese combined, but it may simply mean that proportionately fewer Hokkien and Cantonese migrants return to China directly from Bangkok than arrive in Siam directly at Bangkok. There is, however, presumptive evidence that the proportion of the surplus for 1918–1931 of all Chinese arrivals in Siam who originated in Swatow lay between 52.3 and 69.5 per cent, while the Hainanese proportion of the surplus was between 11.6 and 14 per cent.

It is important to note that not only did Swatow provide the majority of immigrants to Siam, but Siam absorbed a majority of all emigrants

Table 7. Direct Chinese migration between Bangkok and Swatow and Hai-k'ou, by periods, 1918–1939 *

	1918–1931		1932–1939	
	Swatow	Hai-k'ou	Swatow	Hai-k'ou
Direct arrivals in Bangkok	817,881	165,331	139,275	46,506
Annual average of arrivals	58,420	11,809	17,409	5,813
% of total direct arrivals by sea at Bangkok	69.5%	14.0%	51.9%	17.3%
Direct departures from Bangkok	590,650	114,940	160,328	34,453
Surplus of direct arrivals over direct departures	227,231	50,391	−21,053	12,053
Average annual surplus	16,231	3,599	−2,632	1,507
% of total surplus of direct arrivals over departures	52.3%	11.6%	—	26.7%

* Compiled from Chinese Customs statistics given in *China Trade Returns* 1918 to 1928; *Reports on China Trade* 1929 to 1939; *Chinese Customs Decennial Reports* 1912–1921, 1922–1931. The percentages are computed on the total figures for arrivals and departures of Chinese aliens collected by Thai Customs and given in *Thailand Statistical Year Book* 1935/36 to 1939/40–1944 (Nos. 18–21). For 1918–1931, the base figure for total direct arrivals at Bangkok is 1,177,050, and for total surplus of direct arrivals over direct departures, 434,550. For 1932–1939, the base figures are 268,600 and 45,100 respectively.

from Swatow. From this writer's calculations on the basis of Swatow customs returns, of the approximately 1,577,000 emigrants from Swatow to all of Southeast Asia during 1918–1931, about 868,000 or 55 per cent immigrated to Siam. It is also clear from these figures that the proportion of all returnees to Swatow who were from Siam was considerably smaller than 55 per cent, though it is not possible to compute the exact figure. In other words, the return rate of Teochius and Hakkas was lower in Siam than in the rest of Southeast Asia together. This meant, in turn, that more than 55 per cent of all the Swatow emigrants who stayed abroad in Southeast Asia were in Siam.

The preference of Teochius and Hakkas for Siam was more clearly marked during 1918–1931 than in any previous immigration period.

The following period, 1932–1945, was much less decisive for the speech-group composition of the Chinese population in Siam because the total immigration surplus for the period was less than 95,000. The figures for 1932–1939 presented in Table 7 show a net loss of Teochius and Hakkas when only direct migration is considered. Whether figures for all migration would still show a deficit is questionable. The conclusion is inescapable, however, that the proportion which Teochius and Hakkas together formed of the China-born population in Siam must have decreased during the 1932–1945 period. The relative proportion of Hainanese, on the other hand, increased. (This is probably also true of Hokkiens and possibly of Cantonese as well.) Not only did proportionately more Hainanese immigrate to Siam (17.3 per cent of the total direct immigration in 1932–1939 as against 14 per cent for the preceding period), but more Hainanese stayed in Siam, so that they constituted over a quarter of the surplus of direct arrivals over direct departures. It is likely that the 26.7 per cent given in Table 7 would be lowered if computations could be made on the basis of indirect as well as direct migration, for Hainanese migrate directly to Bangkok more often than emigrants from Swatow, Amoy, or the Cantonese area. Nevertheless, these statistics indicate that by the 1930's Hainanese were becoming more permanently settled in Siam than ever before, a conclusion borne out by the emigration of Hainanese women and children to Siam in significant numbers after 1927 (see Section C below).

In the postwar period, it would appear that those from Swatow regained their predominant position among immigrants to Siam. The only postwar Chinese customs figures available are those for Swatow for 1946, which may be incomplete. They show 40,875 direct emigrants to Bangkok and 1,090 direct returnees.[18] Direct arrivals and departures of all Chinese by sea in Bangkok were recorded by the Thai Immigration Division at 81,902 and 4,546 respectively,[19] so that immigrants from Swatow constituted at least half of the total while emigrants to Swatow were less than a quarter of the total. There are no other usable postwar statistics pertinent to the immigration of other speech groups, but from accounts in Bangkok it would appear that the Hainanese held their own during 1946–1947, while the increase in Cantonese and Hokkien immigration over the preceding period was disproportionately small.

B. *The Growth of the Chinese Population in Thailand*

Inasmuch as no reliable statistics exist as to the total number of ethnic Chinese in Siam, it will be instructive to review the estimates made during the last thirty-five years by the various authorities and parties concerned. The Chinese government has from time to time made official estimates of the total number of Chinese in Thailand, but only in very round figures. From 1916 to 1934, the official estimate stood at 1,500,000, from 1934 to 1948 at 2,500,000, and since 1948 at 3,500,000.[20] Prewar private Chinese sources have made similar estimates: Chen Han-seng estimated 2,500,000 as of 1930,[21] and Lin Yu estimated 2,500,000 in 1936 and 3,000,000 in 1937.[22] Chinese writers, presumably out of nationalistic bias, have often made unrealistically high estimates and resorted to absurd calculations. Thus Sun estimated the 1926 population of *pure-blooded* Chinese in Siam at 2,500,000 and stated that, if mixed bloods were included in the count, the Chinese would total two-thirds of the entire population.[23] Chen Su-ching managed to arrive at a Chinese population in 1937 of seven million by starting with Rautier's three million estimate for 1888 and adding to it four million immigrants, ignoring deaths and returns to China.[24] Hsieh Yu-jung's estimate of 3,690,000 for 1947 [25] is more than suspect, if only because of the procedure used to reach it. A preliminary government survey in *1927* prior to the 1929 census had shown 3.9 per cent of the sample to be pure-blooded Chinese and 17.4 per cent to be Thai of (unspecified) mixed blood. Hsieh simply added these percentages, and took 21.3 per cent of the total population of Thailand according to the *1947* census to get his figure.

German writers have often been equally freehanded in their calculations. Mosolff, for instance, starting with a statistic for 1921 indicating that 31.6 per cent of the Bangkok population was Chinese, managed to conclude that 25 per cent of the country's population was *pure* Chinese.[26] Credner, a more careful and informed scholar, estimated the total Chinese population of Siam for around 1932 at two million by making the following assumptions and calculations: that the Chinese population was 200,000 in 1900, that the immigration excess during the years 1900–1932 was at least 800,000, and that local-born Chinese of China-born fathers totaled about one million in 1932. By adding these figures together, he arrived at what he considered the maximum figure.[27] "All figures surpassing this [two million] which have appeared in the literature in recent years do not apply." [28] This writer would agree, but on the basis of somewhat more valid calculations. Credner's estimate of the immigration excess would appear to be accurate (according to the figures presented in Table 6, the total excess, 1900–1932 inclusive, was 806,000), and his figure for the Chinese population in 1900, if taken to apply to the China-born only (as his method of addition implies) is not too far off, though certainly smaller than the true figure. His guess for the 1932 population of local-born Chinese is also within the realm of possibility, though in this case probably too large. In ignoring deaths among immigrants who stayed in Siam, however, Credner made a most egregious error and one which almost surely makes of his final figure an overestimate.

Other estimates of the Chinese population of Thailand made by foreign scholars include those of an Indian, Kiliani, who suggested two to three million for 1926; of a Japanese, Tateyania: 2,500,000 in 1941; and of a Frenchman, Mullender: three to four million in 1950.[29] Two scholars with long residence in Thailand and special interests in the Chinese there have made estimates which carry the weight of some authority. Kenneth Landon gave the Chinese population as 1,500,000 in 1939 and 1,600,000 in 1943, while Erik Seidenfaden took issue in 1939 with Credner's earlier estimate of two million, suggesting 2,500,000 as a more nearly correct figure.[30] For reasons suggested above, however, this writer would accept Credner's figure as the maximum for the 1930's. The estimates of Credner and Landon in all probability bracket the true figure.

At this point, it might be well to introduce a probable model of Chinese population growth for the past thirty-five years (see Table 8), similar to that already given in Chapter 2 for the period prior to 1917. There is not space here to give a full defense of this model, whose virtues are merely that it is demographically probable and consistent, conforms with available statistics, and does not violently contradict any reliable estimates. The figures given for the total population of Thailand (column 7) are adjustments to December 31 of statistics supplied by the Central Statistical Office in Bangkok, which in turn were based on the corrected results of the 1919, 1929, 1937, and 1947 censuses. The figures for the China-born population (column 1) were calculated year by year by adding the annual immigration excess to the population living at the beginning of the year, and then applying the annual death rate to that total to obtain the population living at the beginning of the next year. The initial figure for December 31, 1917, 349,000, is the final figure of the earlier model. The death

Table 8. A probable model of the growth of the Chinese population in Thailand, 1917–1955
(estimates as of December 31 in thousands)

Year	1 Est. total of China-born Chinese	2 5-yr. rate of change since previous date	3 Est. total of local-born Chinese	4 5-yr. rate of increase	5 Est. total of all Chinese	6 5-yr. rate of increase	7 Est. total population of Siam	8 % China-born Chinese of total	9 % all Chinese of total
1917	349	%	557	%	906	%	9,232	3.78	9.8
1922	445	35.3	634	13.8	1,079	19.1	10,202	4.36	10.5
1927	600	34.8	733	15.6	1,333	23.5	11,419	5.25	11.7
1932	728	21.3	864	19.2	1,592	19.4	13,087	5.56	12.2
1937	714	−1.9	1,020	18.1	1,734	8.9	14,721	4.85	11.8
1942	689	−3.5	1,187	16.4	1,876	8.2	16,066	4.29	11.7
1947	765	11.0	1,359	14.5	2,124	13.2	17,643	4.34	12.0
1952	727	−5.0	1,524	12.1	2,251	6.0	19,384	3.75	11.5
1955	696	−7.1	1,619	10.4	2,315	4.7	20,480	3.40	11.3

rates used were estimated annually on the basis of data supplied by the Central Statistical Office or presented in the office's publications,[31] and an attempt was made to take into account the age and sex distribution of immigrants and of the total population of Chinese nationals (as given in the 1947 census results; see Section C below), epidemics, changes in health and sanitary facilities, and the wartime conditions bearing on mortality. The actual annual rates used varied from a high of 23.2 (1924) to a low of 14.3 (1947), the average being 18.8. It should be noted that the estimates given for the period since 1937 may be somewhat low inasmuch as illegal immigration was not specifically taken into account. The growth of the China-born population is also graphed in Chart 2.

The remaining set of basic figures—those for the local-born Chinese population (column 3)—is, of course, the least satisfactory, inasmuch as data are simply not available to make reasonable estimates of the birth, death, and assimilation rates pertinent to this population. The series given is merely a plausible one when changes in the size and sex-ratio of the Chinese population of childbearing age are taken into account, and when a death rate similar to that for the total Bangkok population and a steadily decreasing rate of assimilation are assumed. "Local-born Chinese" are here defined as those who were born of a Chinese or lukjin father, who speak a Chinese language (they usually also speak Thai), and who in most social situations identify with Chinese rather than Thai.

Before drawing any conclusions from this model, it should be examined critically in the light of Thai census returns. The Thai government has conducted four nationwide censuses, with results quoted as of April 1, 1919, July 15, 1929, May 23, 1937, and May 23, 1947. Shortcomings with regard to trained personnel and census-taking procedure have led to results far less reliable than those of censuses in Western countries and less satisfactory even than those of the Malayan and Sarawak censuses. Furthermore, the count of Chinese residents in each census was almost certainly less complete and accurate than that of any other special group of the population, with the exception of certain hill tribes. There are many reasons for this. Scholars of Chinese society have repeatedly noted the preference of the mass of the Chinese population for avoidance of direct contact with government functionaries. Centuries of bitter experience had taught the average Chinese to keep his disputes and grievances out of the magistrate's office and to evade government tax collectors and military conscriptors whenever possible. The traditional Chinese suspicion of government officials was, if anything, strengthened in Siam, where there was the additional embarrassment of a language barrier and a growing fear (after 1914) that government policies were discriminatory against the Chinese. It was noted in an early chapter that legitimate Chinese societies declined to register with the government in part because they considered it preliminary to drafting Chinese for military service. Later, when local-born Chinese were conscripted into the army, the suspicion became almost universal that the census takers' forms were made available to the military.

It is an unfortunate coincidence that each of the four censuses closely followed a government action which intensified fear and suspicion among the resident Chinese. At the time of the 1919 census, the Chinese community was up in arms over the government's first attempt to control Chinese education, following the promulgation of a law in January which made the study of Thai compulsory and required examinations and Thai schooling for Chinese principals and teachers.[32] The 1929 census followed an upsurge of anti-Chinese feeling which resulted from the anti-Japanese boycott carried out by Chinese traders in 1928, as well as the increase in 1928/29 of immigration fees. The 1937 census was immediately preceded by the Registration of Aliens Act of 1936/37, which required all aliens over twelve years of age to obtain certificates and provided a fine of 200 baht for failure to produce it on demand.[33] The Chinese were reluctant to register, and those who had not registered avoided the census taker for fear of being requested to show the certificate and pay the 200-baht fine. The 1947 census was preceded a few weeks earlier by the imposition of the first quota on Chinese immigration, which led immediately to fears that a repetition of the 1939 wave of anti-Chinese measures was in the offing. At none of the censuses, therefore, was the Chinese mood one of co-operation with the census takers. Almost every Chinese was motivated to avoid them if possible, and those who could not were often ready to falsify their replies if so doing could be presumed to offer protection from the government.

With these severe reservations in mind, let us now turn to the census results, presented in Table 9 A. It has already been mentioned that the Thai Nationality Act of 1913/14 defined anyone born in Siam as a Thai national (Section 3). The law was in effect until 1953, so that local-born Chinese were ordinarily recorded as Thai nationals. The Nationality Act also provided (Section 4) that "a Siamese woman who marries an alien loses her Siamese nationality if by his national law she has acquired the nationality of her husband." Chinese law would appear to be ambiguous on this point, and in any case the practice of Thai census takers varied from census to census. So far as can

Table 9. Thai census totals, 1919–1947, compared with other estimates

A. Census totals *

Row	Total count of those of:	1919	1929	1937	1947
1	Chinese nationality	260,194	445,274	524,062	476,588
2	Chinese race	—	558,324	618,791	835,915
3	Chinese nationality *and* race	—	—	463,012	476,516
4	Chinese race but Thai nationality	—	113,050	154,119	358,937

B. A comparison of estimates with census totals,
as of census dates (in thousands)

	Census results		Model estimates			Calculations assuming 1919 census count at the start		
Year	Total	Increase	Total	Increase	Census under-count	Total	Increase	Census under-count
	1	2	3	4	5	6	7	8
		%		%	%		%	%
1919	260.2	—	370	—	29.7	260.2	—	—
1929	445.3	71.1	648	75.1	31.3	560	115.4	20.5
1937	463.0	4.0	696	7.4	33.5	620	10.7	25.3
1947	476.5	2.9	750	7.8	36.5	688	11.0	30.7

* Data for the 1919 and 1929 censuses are taken from *Thailand Statistical Year Book* 1933/34–1934/35 (No. 18), 77; those for the 1937 census from *Thailand Statistical Year Book* 1939/40–1944 (No. 21), 59; and those for the 1947 census were obtained from the Division of Census, Ministry of Interior, and from the Central Statistical Office in Bangkok.

be ascertained, the 1919 and 1929 censuses recorded as Chinese nationals only a small number of Thai women married to China-born Chinese. The 1937 census, however, recorded 57,674 such women as Chinese nationals, while the 1947 census recorded a negligible figure.[34] The census count of Chinese nationals (row 1), then, was for the most part limited to Chinese born in China or elsewhere outside Thailand, with the exception of the 1937 figure, which included a sizable number of Thai wives. Happily the 1937 and 1947 censuses also recorded race separately and tabulated race against nationality, so the figures given in row 3 for those of Chinese race and Chinese nationality are roughly comparable to the nationality figures (row 1) for 1919 and 1929.

The practical definition of Chinese race used, however, was peculiar, to say the least. An individual was considered to be of Chinese race if his father was a Chinese national, regardless of the individual's own nationality. This meant that only first- and second-generation Chinese could be recorded as of Chinese race. Furthermore, the question as to the nationality of the respondent's father was asked only if there was some obvious reason to suspect an alien father—only if the respondent spoke Thai with a foreign accent, wore non-Thai clothing, or if his features were atypical. Thus an individual born of a Chinese father and Thai mother who spoke Thai well and looked as much Thai as Chinese might not be asked the question, even though he habitually spoke Chinese and identified himself as Chinese. The difficulty of telling Chinese from Thai in Lower Siam where a large section of the Thai population have Chinese blood is obvious; some of the most "Thai" families are racially up to three-quarters Chinese. It is not surprising therefore that the counts of those of Chinese race but Thai nationality (i.e., those born in Thailand of Chinese national fathers) were unrealistically low (row 4). Row 2 ("Chinese race") actually gives the totals of Chinese born outside Siam and those born in Thailand of Chinese national fathers.

It will be seen that the census definitions of Chinese were rather different from those used in constructing the model presented in Table 8. It is reasonable, however, to compare the estimated total population of China-born Chinese (Table 8, column 1; Table 9 B, column 3) with the census count of Chinese nationals in 1919 and 1927 and of Chinese nationals of Chinese race in 1937 and 1947 (Table 9 B, column 1), for those enumerated in these counts must have been well over 90 per cent China-born. A comparison of rows 1 and 2 with rows 3 and 4, Table 9 B, shows the census counts in each case to be appreciably lower than the model estimates, and to increase at a lower rate. If the model is assumed to be correct, then the percentage of the census undercount of China-born Chinese is that shown in row 5. The fact that the percentage increases steadily with each census would indicate at first glance that the model was based on either excessively low death rates or excessively high immigration surpluses. The immigration surpluses, however, were calculated almost entirely on the basis of

Thai government records and in all probability err in being too low rather than too high. Furthermore, death rates were calculated higher than those for the country's population as a whole (primarily to account for differences in age distribution) even though high infant mortality is not a factor in the China-born population and in spite of the common Chinese practice of returning to China in old age. In short, the model was constructed with minimum probable surpluses and maximum probable death rates, deliberately to obviate this objection.

The reason for the discrepancy, it seems to this writer, must be sought rather in the increasingly valid reasons and increasingly stronger motivation for evasion on the part of China-born Chinese. As will be seen in later chapters, Thai government policy took on a more anti-Chinese cast with the passage of time after 1918. The most plausible explanation of what appears to have been an increasing undercount, then, is simply that a greater proportion of Chinese nationals at each census avoided the census taker or falsified their replies.

Another reasonable objection to the model is that the starting figure was too high. For comparison purposes, then, the growth of the China-born population was calculated assuming 260,194—the 1919 census count of Chinese nationals—as the number of China-born Chinese in 1919. The results for census dates are shown in columns 6–8, Table 9 B. They yield excessively high intercensal increases, but still indicate substantial census undercounts.

As a matter of fact, Thai government officials consider the census results in this regard as entirely unrealistic. In 1940, Phibun estimated the total Chinese population at "more than two million" [35] despite the 619,000 total for Chinese race reported by the 1937 census. Again in January 1952, when an increased alien fee was under consideration, officials of the Police Department and Ministry of Finance issued statements indicating that they placed the number of Chinese aliens in the neighborhood of one million. [36] Their estimate, however, was based on improperly kept alien-registration rolls. Sad experience with inflated budget estimates led the police to inspect the alien rolls and make extensive corrections, including the removal of a few hundred thousand dead and departed Chinese.

The total number of Chinese aliens, according to the corrected police rolls, was given as 765,167 in December 1953. [37] For the same month the estimate yielded by the model of the China-born Chinese population is 719,850. The number of registered Chinese aliens may in fact be larger than that of China-born Chinese alone, because of the common postwar practice by young local-born Chinese males of registering as Chinese and paying the fee in order to avoid military service. In any case, the close similarity of the newly corrected 1953 alien-registration figures to the model estimate for that year lends strong support to the model figures as opposed to the census results. The alien-registration tabulations as of December 1955 showed a drop of only some four thousand to 760,988,[38] while the model estimate for that month is 696,290. The increased disparity indicates nothing more than that the police still have no method for ensuring the removal of dead men from the alien rolls.

If we may now accept the model given in Table 8 as reasonable, perhaps the most surprising conclusion it affords is that notwithstanding extensive Chinese immigration during the period in question, the ethnic Chinese population increased between 1917 and 1952 only slightly faster than did the total population of the country. The national population in 1955 was 2.22 times that of 1917, while the Chinese population in 1955 was 2.56 times that of 1917. Because of the rapid increase in the Thai population (accounted for in small part by the "infusion of Chinese blood" through assimilation to Thai society of Sino-Thais), the proportion of Chinese never surpassed one-eighth, and, in fact, has shown a decline in recent years. It is also interesting to note that the proportion of China-born Chinese in the total population of Thailand was somewhat lower in 1955 than in 1917. While the absolute number of China-born Chinese (column 1) fluctuated during the 1930's and 1940's, with peaks at 1932–1933 and 1947, their proportion of the national population (column 3) showed a steady rise to an all-time high of 5.56 per cent in 1932, after which there was a fairly steady decline to the present time.

It is clear, of course, that in the absence of further significant immigration, an increasingly rapid decline in the China-born population is inevitable. While the total Chinese population will in all probability continue to rise during the next decade, the proportion of the total population formed by all ethnic Chinese may be expected to continue the decline evident since 1947. Even though mortality among the essentially rural Thai is undoubtedly higher than among the more urban Chinese, the fertility rates in many populous and almost exclusively Thai sections of the country (e.g., large parts of the northeast) are extremely high and unquestionably surpass those obtaining in the most Chinese regions (e.g., Bangkok and vicinity). This implies that only if the Chinese assimilation rate were to approach zero could the ethnic Chinese population begin to hold its relative position in the total population. As will become evident in a later chapter, there is no reason to assume that assimilation is even beginning to come to an end. The best prognostication relative to the ethnic Chinese population, then, is that its proportion of the total will continue to decrease in the years to come.

C. Age and Sex Distribution

Perhaps the most significant trend in Chinese migration in the past thirty-five years has been the increase in the number of women immigrating to and staying in Thailand, for its sociological consequence has been the establishment of more and more purely Chinese homes and a rapid decline in intermarriage with the Thai populace. There was some female immigration beginning with the 1893–1905 period, as mentioned earlier, but the immigration of respectable women reached significant proportions only after 1906. Prior to the immigration wave after the First World War, the proportion of women among Chinese immigrants probably never exceeded 10 per cent. The 1919 census showed 21 per cent of Chinese nationals in the country to be women, but the percentage is doubtless too high because some of the women recorded as Chinese nationals were Thai wives of Chinese. It is also probable that proportionately more Chinese men than women evaded the census takers because of taxes applicable only to adult males and fear of military service, which motivated only men. In any case, in the first year for which immigration by sex is recorded, 1921/22, only 15 per cent of the Chinese immigrants were female, while the proportion steadily increased thereafter.[39]

Table 10 summarizes the most reliable of the data for that part of each of the three migration periods after the First World War for which they are available. It can be seen that the proportion of females among immigrants rose steadily period by period. Furthermore, in each period proportionally fewer females than males returned to China, so that the female proportion of the immigration excess was still larger. By the period after the Second World War, females constituted more than a third of the immigration surplus.

Table 11 presents the age and sex distribution of Chinese immigrants to Bangkok for the two periods between the wars for which data are available. It should be noted, first of all, that well over half the immigrants in both periods were males in the prime of life (i.e., aged 15 to 44): 56.5 per cent for 1928–1931 and 55.3 per cent for 1933–1941. The number of children under 15 was constant at slightly less than 19 per cent. The most notable trend is seen in the increase of girls under 15 and of women aged 25–34. Middle-aged and old people (i.e., those 45 and over) were relatively few—less than 10 per cent in both periods. No statistics after the Second World War are

Table 10. Chinese migration by sex, Thailand, 1921–1941, 1945–1949 *

A. By sea only, Port of Bangkok, April 1, 1921 to December 31, 1931

	Male	Female	Total	% female of total
Arrivals	765,265	201,842	967,107	20.87
Departures	489,617	116,586	606,203	
Surplus	275,648	85,256	360,904	23.62

B. By all means of travel, all Thailand, 1932–1941 inclusive

	Male	Female	Total	% female of total
Arrivals	300,799	108,997	409,796	26.60
Departures	232,573	77,432	310,005	
Surplus	68,226	31,565	99,791	31.63

C. By all means of travel, all Thailand, 1945–1949 inclusive

	Male	Female	Total	% female of total
Arrivals	132,337	60,704	193,041	31.45
Departures	36,417	11,031	47,448	
Surplus	95,920	49,673	145,593	34.12

* The original source for A was the Customs Department. Data compiled from *Thailand Statistical Year Book* 1933/34–1934/35 (No. 18), 98. Data for B and C were compiled from statistics supplied by the Immigration Division. The war years, 1942–1945, have been omitted.

available for age distribution of immigrants, but there is some evidence that the proportion of children, as well as of females generally, increased over the prewar percentage.[40]

The data presented in Table 12 show that well over two-thirds of all immigrants aged 15 and over arriving in Siam between the wars were married, and that the proportion of married among immigrants was increasing. Over 95 per cent of the women immigrants in both periods were already married, which demonstrates clearly that the usual way of obtaining a China-born wife was to marry her in China. Unmarried women rarely emigrated from China, even after the Second World War. Thus, there were more than 25 unmarried men for every unmarried woman among the immigrants. Clearly these men—37.9 per cent of all male immigrants in 1928–1931 and 32.3 per cent in 1933–1940—would either have to marry local-born Chinese and Thai women or remain single. In all probability most of these unmarried

Table 11. Chinese alien arrivals, Port of Bangkok, by age and sex, 1928–1931, 1933–1941 *

A. April 1, 1928 to March 31, 1931

Age class	Total recorded cases			Distribution of 1000 immigrants		
	Male	Female	Total	Male	Female	Total
–14	30,051	14,302	44,353	128	61	189
15–24	54,445	14,248	68,693	232	60	292
25–34	51,900	13,870	65,770	221	59	280
35–44	26,373	6,805	33,178	112	29	141
45–54	11,746	4,192	15,938	50	18	68
55–64	4,312	1,732	6,044	18	8	26
65–	752	238	990	3	1	4
Total	179,579	55,387	234,966	764	236	1000

B. April 1, 1933 to December 31, 1941

Age class	Total recorded cases			Distribution of 1000 immigrants		
	Male	Female	Total	Male	Female	Total
–14	26,032	15,686	41,718	117	71	188
15–24	49,947	12,699	62,646	225	57	282
25–34	44,834	16,892	61,726	202	76	278
35–44	27,880	6,043	33,923	126	27	153
45–54	12,681	2,957	15,638	57	13	70
55–64	3,972	1,200	5,172	18	5	23
65–	1,022	270	1,292	5	1	6
Total	166,368	55,747	222,115	750	250	1000

* Data for A compiled from *Thailand Statistical Year Books* 1929/30 (No. 14), 53; 1930/31 (No. 15), 63; 1931/32 (No. 16), 64. Data for B compiled from *Thailand Statistical Year Books* 1933/34–1934/35 (No. 18), 101; 1935/36–1936/37 (No. 19), 69; 1937/38–1938/39 (No. 20), 66; 1939/40–1944 (No. 21), 92–93.

men were laborers, and of these most returned to China within five years without having married in Siam.[41] It is also worth noting that for every 487 married male immigrants in 1928–1931 there were only 205 married female immigrants, while the corresponding proportion for the 1933–1940 period—528:210—was even more extreme. These figures indicate the high frequency with which men migrated to Siam leaving wives behind in China.

Thai census results, presented in Table 13, throw further light on the problem of the Chinese sex ratio and marriage possibilities. The data for Chinese nationals and those of Chinese nationality *and* race (A and C) merely confirm the trend already demonstrated on the

Table 12. Marital status by sex of Chinese alien arrivals aged 15 and over, Port of Bangkok, 1928–1931, 1933–1940 *

A. April 1, 1928 to March 31, 1931

	Total recorded cases			Distribution of 1000 cases		
	Male	Female	Total	Male	Female	Total
Married	92,884	39,091	131,975	487	205	692
Unmarried	56,644	1,994	58,638	297	11	308
Total	149,528	41,085	190,613	784	216	1000

B. April 1, 1933 to December 31, 1940

	Total recorded cases			Distribution of 1000 cases		
	Male	Female	Total	Male	Female	Total
Married	90,339	35,832	126,171	528	210	738
Unmarried	43,045	1,768	44,813	252	10	262
Total	133,384	37,600	170,984	780	220	1000

* Data for A compiled from *Thailand Statistical Year Books* 1929/30 (No. 14), 52; 1930/31 (No. 15), 62; 1931/32 (No. 16), 62. Data for B compiled from *Thailand Statistical Year Books* 1933/34–1934/35 (No. 18), 100; 1935/36–1936/37 (No. 19), 69; 1937/38–1938/39 (No. 20), 66; 1939/40–1944 (No. 21), 92–93.

basis of immigration statistics. It should be noted, however, that the sex ratios for Chinese nationals (A) are lower than was actually the case for reasons mentioned earlier in this section; the ratios for those of Chinese nationality *and* race (C) are doubtless more realistic. The sex ratio for local-born second-generation Chinese (D) is demographically normal, with even a slight preponderance of women. It is to this group (i.e., women of Chinese fathers and either Chinese or Thai mothers) that unmarried male immigrants increasingly turned for wives. The sex ratio for all those of Chinese race (B, i.e., the total of C and D) by 1947 was approaching normality. The actual sex ratio for all ethnic Chinese must have been even lower, i.e., more nearly normal than 1.96 and 1.45, because local-born Chinese, with their normal ratio, were more severely undercounted (by being miscounted as Thai) than were China-born Chinese.

The final set of available statistics pertinent to this section is the distribution by age and sex of Chinese nationals according to the 1947 census, presented in Table 14 for 10,000 individuals to facilitate interpretation. The high sex ratios for ages 45 and above reflect the less frequent immigration of women prior to the mid-1920's. The high

Table 13. Chinese population by sex according to the Thai censuses, 1919–1947 *

	Total	Male	Female	% female	Sex ratio
A. Chinese nationality					
1919	260,194	205,470	54,724	21.0	3.75
1929	445,274	313,764	131,510	29.5	2.39
1937	524,062	335,524	188,538	36.0	1.78
B. Chinese race, i.e., Chinese father					
1929	558,324	—	—	—	—
1937	618,791	409,652	209,135	33.8	1.96
1947	835,915	495,176	340,739	40.8	1.45
C. Chinese nationality *and* race					
1937	463,012	332,471	130,541	28.2	2.55
1947	476,516	319,139	157,377	33.0	2.03
D. Chinese race but Thai nationality					
1929	113,050	—	—	—	—
1937	154,119	76,081	78,038	50.6	0.975
1947	358,937	175,773	183,164	51.0	0.960

* Data for the 1919 and 1929 censuses are taken from *Thailand Statistical Year Book* 1933/34–1934/35 (No. 18), 77; those for the 1937 census from *Thailand Statistical Year Book* 1939/40–1944 (No. 21), 59; and those for the 1947 census were obtained from the Division of Census, Ministry of Interior, and from the Central Statistical Office in Bangkok.

ratios for the 10–19 age group are a consequence of the scant immigration of female children (i.e., families) during the crisis years 1938–1945, and of the low immigration rate of unmarried girls during the two years immediately following the Second World War. The lowest ratios are those for children under 10—a reflection of the high rate of immigration of whole families during the two years immediately following the war. The next lowest ratios are those for ages 20–39; the high proportion of women in the childbearing ages in 1947 is a result not only of the high immigration rate of whole families after the war but also of the high rate of female children immigrants during the 1930's (see Table 11).

From these age-specific sex ratios, one can tentatively conclude that a slight majority of China-born men aged 20–39 in 1947 were married to China-born women, while the remainder either had wives in China or were married to local-born women (or both), or were single. The relatively large group of China-born men aged 15–19 in 1947, however, had much dimmer prospects for marrying China-born

Table 14. Distribution by age and sex of 10,000 Chinese nationals, Thailand, 1947 *

Age class	Male	Female	Total	Sex ratio
– 4	80	59	139	1.36
5– 9	182	115	297	1.57
10–14	316	156	472	2.02
15–19	520	195	715	2.66
20–24	503	272	775	1.85
25–29	615	378	993	1.63
30–34	784	480	1264	1.63
35–39	818	441	1259	1.86
40–44	733	350	1083	2.09
45–49	650	261	911	2.50
50–54	474	195	669	2.43
55–59	395	157	552	2.51
60–64	276	114	390	2.43
65–69	181	67	248	2.71
70–74	104	37	141	2.84
75–	65	27	92	2.43
Total	6,696	3,304	10,000	2.03

* Computed from 1947 census statistics supplied by the Division of Census, Ministry of Interior, Bangkok. Computations were based on a total of 475,809, since the ages of 773 individuals were not recorded.

women (note the ratio 520 men to 195 women). Immigration was reduced to an insignificant figure within a year or two after the 1947 census, and from 1950 on, when these young men were thinking of marriage, it was virtually impossible to go to China to bring back a wife. Many of the male Chinese nationals aged 15–19 in 1947 were marrying in 1951–1955, when this writer was in Bangkok, and the great majority chose local-born Chinese women, often daughters from wholly Chinese homes.

By way of summary, it might be well to trace the marriage prospects and possibilities of the Chinese in Thailand during the first half of the twentieth century. Prior to 1905, only some of the wealthy merchants had brought wives from China to Siam, and most of the other China-born females were prostitutes. Most of the Chinese immigrants and lukjin men married Thai or lukjin women, though there were far from enough of the latter to go around. Lukjin women, as in later decades, were also sought and often won by Thai men of better-off families. The practice of bringing wives from China became less rare during the 1906–1917 immigration period, but it became common only after the First World War. By the late 1920's most of the male im-migrants were married, and over a third of all male immigrants were bringing their wives with them. Immigration of whole families was not uncommon. Unmarried male immigrants and lukjin men could by then more easily find wives among lukjin women, although intermarriage with Thai was still common. Expense was, of course, an important consideration. Landon noted that in the 1930's in South Siam the bride price was 50 to 200 baht for a Thai peasant girl, 100 to 300 baht for a lukjin girl, and 300 to 500 for a Chinese girl.[42] By the late 1930's even more of the China-born men had China-born wives, and daughters of China-born fathers and lukjin mothers were increasingly available as wives for immigrants who were unmarried or had left their wives in China. Intermarriage with Thai women was becoming less common, at least in Bangkok and other centers of Chinese population.

After the Second World War, about half the male immigrants brought wives from China, and other China-born residents returned to China to marry or bring back to Thailand wives they already had there. In the postwar years, a large proportion of young second-generation Chinese had China-born or local-born Chinese mothers. The relatively small number of unmarried men among Chinese im-migrants tended to choose wives from the young women of this generation, while lukjin men could also, for the most part, marry second-generation women from all or three-quarters (i.e., lukjin mother) Chinese homes. The necessity for looking to Thai women for wives has become slight. In recent years, intermarriage between Chi-nese and Thai has been rare, in Bangkok especially.

Before leaving the subject of the Chinese sex ratio and marriage, a word should be said of speech-group differentials in this regard. Gen-erally speaking, marriage with a girl of the same speech group is strongly preferred. Those who marry in China almost always take wives in or near their native hsien of the same speech group, though some of the wealthier men take wives in the more cosmopolitan cities —Hongkong and Canton in particular—so that among the elite one occasionally finds Teochiu or Hokkien men with Cantonese wives. Even when immigrants marry Sino-Thai girls, they prefer descendants of their own speech group. Language is, of course, the chief barrier to intermarriage among speech groups, but differences in customs and tradition also play a part.

Exceptions to the general rule have occurred primarily because of disparate sex ratios among the various speech groups. Proportional to the male population of each group, more Cantonese women came to Siam earlier, so that marriage of Cantonese men with women of other speech groups has been very rare for several decades. The big influx of Teochiu women began only in the early 1920's, while Hakka women began to immigrate about the same time though in proportionately smaller numbers. By 1928, the Customs Commissioner at Swatow could write that "women and children formed a great proportion of the passengers leaving in the early spring." [43] Hainanese women were the last to come to Siam in any significant numbers. According to Chinese Customs reports, the first notable efflux of Hainanese women occurred in 1927, when whole families emigrated to avoid the depredations of Communist bands.[44] It is interesting to note that the Thai representatives to a League of Nations conference on white slavery and prostitution reported that the number of registered Chinese brothels in Siam had decreased between 1929 and 1936 from 137 to 63, and the number of inmates from 646 to 326. In explaining the change, the representative stated: "In past years the majority of those who frequented brothels were Chinese from Hainan whose women seldom migrated with their men. The number of Hainanese female immigrants who have become more domestic in their habits has increased. This is believed to have an indirect effect on the traffic." [45]

During the late 1920's and early 1930's, then, Cantonese had the most nearly normal sex ratio, followed by Teochius, Hakkas, and Hainanese, in that order.[46] Hainanese immigrants, as the speech group of least prestige, power, and wealth, remained unmarried in Siam more often than immigrants of other speech groups. Nevertheless, because those who did marry usually had to seek non-Hainanese women, the most common type of inter-speech-group marriage has been that between Hainanese men and local-born women of Teochiu fathers. Cantonese women, because of their head start in Siam as well as their reputation for beauty and "culture," have not infrequently been taken as wives by Teochius and Hokkiens, the two dialect groups of highest prestige. In the postwar period, the sex ratios of all speech groups have approached normality, especially when local-born Chinese are taken into account. At the present time, at least four out of five marriages involving Chinese or those of part Chinese ancestry on both sides still stay within a single speech group. However, an increased freedom in the choice of marriage partners, greater opportunities for intimate contact with those of other speech groups, especially in schools open to children of all speech groups, and the growing importance of Thai, Teochiu, and Kuo-yü as *linguae francae* in the Chinese community are all leading to more and more speech-group intermarriage.

D. Geographical Distribution

The expansion of Chinese settlement into the upcountry regions of Thailand, given impetus by the construction of railroads prior to the First World War, continued at an accelerated pace in subsequent decades. The process can be measured in the period under review by comparing the results of successive censuses. Table 15 presents the distribution by region of Chinese nationals according to the four censuses from 1919 to 1947. Table 16 apportions the model estimates of the China-born Chinese population for each census year according to the regional distribution of Chinese nationals. From these tables, it is possible to note changes not only in the regional distribution of the Chinese population, but also in the relative proportion of the Chinese within the total population of each region.

It should be noted first of all that the three inland regions were still extremely sparsely settled with Chinese immediately after the First World War, and that the Chinese population increased far more rapidly between the wars in these regions than elsewhere in the country. Between 1919 and 1937, the Chinese population in the north more than tripled in the wake of a rapid development in overland transportation facilities, most notably the construction of the railroad on through Lampang and Lamphun to Chiangmai by 1921, and of highways from Lampang to Chiangrai in the 1920's and from Phrae to Nan around 1930. In the northeast, the growth in the China-born Chinese population was even more spectacular (almost fourfold), as might be expected from the fact that most of the railroad construction in Siam between the wars was done in this region. The Khorat-Ubon line was completed during the late twenties, and the Khorat-

Table 15. Distribution by region of Chinese nationals, according to the Thai censuses, 1919–1947 *

Region	1919		1929		1937		1947	
	Number	% dist.	Number	% dist.	Number	% dist.	Number	% dist.
North	3,626	1.4	6,989	1.6	11,625	2.3	6,179	1.3
Northeast	6,226	2.4	14,933	3.4	24,457	4.9	21,535	4.5
Middle	8,267	3.2	18,318	4.1	29,339	5.9	24,847	5.2
Lower	152,601	58.6	289,882	65.1	280,503	56.5	310,650	65.2
Southeast	21,261	8.2	36,057	8.1	43,205	8.7	34,513	7.2
Southwest	30,110	11.6	25,426	5.7	37,024	7.5	28,250	5.9
South	38,103	14.6	53,669	12.1	70,176	14.1	50,614	10.6
Total	260,194	100.0	445,274	100.1	496,329	99.9	476,588	99.9

* Data for 1919 Thailand Statistical Year Book 1923/24 (No. 8), 26; for 1929 from Thailand Statistical Year Book 1933/34–1934/35 (No. 18), 82–83; for 1937 from Thailand Statistical Year Book 1939/40–1944 (No. 21), 52–53; and for 1947 from statistics supplied by the Central Statistical Office in Bangkok. The 1937 figures are not entirely comparable inasmuch as they include 57,674 Thai wives of Chinese and exclude the 27,733 Chinese national children aged 10 and under. The regional distribution, however, is probably not greatly affected by this discrepancy.

Udọnthani line was built during the thirties. The railway system in the northeast was supplemented in the thirties by feeder highways, most notably the road from Banphai on the Udọnthani line through Mahasarakham and Rọi-et to Ubon. In Middle Siam, too, large areas were opened up to modern transport as a major highway was built south from the rail spur at Sawankhalok to Sukhothai and on west to Tak, and another road was constructed from Paknampho through Kamphaengphet to Tak. In consequence, the China-born population of Middle Siam more than tripled between the wars to 41,000 in 1937. In that year the China-born population formed about 4 per cent of the total population of the region. By 1937, over 13 per cent of the Chinese population in Siam lived in the three inland regions as against only 7 per cent in 1919.

Of the four gulf regions, Southeast Siam had the most rapid increase in the Chinese population between the wars. There the China-born population doubled between 1919 and 1937, in part because of the extension of the eastern rail line from Paetriw on to the Cambodian border at Aranyaprathet. The least attractive region to the Chinese during the interwar period was the southwest, where a decrease in the China-born population occurred in the twenties, followed by only a moderate increase in the thirties. This must be due in large part to the fact that no new areas in the southwest were supplied with improved transportation during the twenties, in contrast to other regions of the country. Perhaps the declining importance of commercial agriculture—which had been the mainstay of the Chinese population in Southwest Siam around the turn of the century—was also a factor.

After the First World War, South Siam supported a gradual growth in the Chinese population, which continued unabated during the depression years in spite of the reliance of South Siam's economy on tin and rubber. This was possible because economic conditions were poorer in Malaya than in South Siam while Thai rubber and tin quotas were comparatively favorable, thus stimulating immigration of Chinese from Malaya.[47] Although the major towns of the South achieved rail communications with Bangkok between 1910 and 1917, they were at the same time linked to the Malayan railway system. Consequently, it continued to be more convenient for Chinese immigrants to travel to Songkhla or even Nakhọnsithammarat via Penang than via Bangkok.

A clear majority of the Chinese population in each census year resided in Lower Siam, but the percentage was high in 1929 compared

Table 16. Model estimates of the population of China-born Chinese by region, according to the distribution of Chinese nationals in the Thai censuses, 1919–1947

Region	1919 Total	1919 China-born Chinese	1919 % of total	1929 Total	1929 China-born Chinese	1929 % of total
North	1,341,936	5,200	0.39	1,549,390	10,200	0.66
Northeast	3,092,117	8,800	0.28	3,887,275	21,700	0.56
Middle	762,245	11,800	1.55	1,089,922	26,600	2.44
Lower	1,729,187	217,000	12.55	2,235,934	421,900	18.87
Southeast	557,230	30,200	5.42	677,965	52,500	7.74
Southwest	471,143	42,800	9.08	579,357	37,000	6.39
South	1,253,497	54,200	4.32	1,486,364	78,100	5.25
Total	9,207,355	370,000	4.02	11,506,207	648,000	5.63

Region	1937 Total	1937 China-born Chinese	1937 % of total	1947 Total	1947 China-born Chinese	1947 % of total
North	1,917,548	16,300	0.85	2,023,510	9,700	0.48
Northeast	4,952,288	34,300	0.69	6,210,279	33,900	0.55
Middle	1,457,889	41,100	3.99	1,790,163	39,100	2.18
Lower	2,751,680	393,400	14.30	3,395,689	488,900	14.40
Southeast	843,235	60,600	7.19	1,039,628	54,300	5.22
Southwest	699,729	51,900	7.42	822,618	44,500	5.41
South	1,841,736	98,400	5.34	2,160,800	79,600	3.68
Total	14,464,105	696,000	4.81	17,442,687	750,000	4.30

with both 1919 and 1937. The explanation is simple enough, inasmuch as the great mass of immigrants entered Siam at Bangkok. The 1929 census was taken just past the peak of the greatest Chinese immigration wave in Thai history, while the 1919 and 1937 censuses followed two periods (the First World War and the depression years) of low immigration, during which earlier immigrants to Lower Siam dispersed to outlying regions faster than new immigration could fill their places. Thus, while the proportion of Thailand's Chinese population living in every other region increased during the 1929–1937 period between censuses, it declined in Lower Siam (see Table 15).

The intercensus period which included the Second World War showed precisely the reverse pattern. There was a rapid increase in the proportion of China-born Chinese who lived in Lower Siam but a decrease in every other region. It is clear that the 1946–1947 immigration rush had not yet begun to spread out to other regions. The decline in the Chinese position between 1937 and 1947 was most rapid in the north and the south, the two regions most remote from Bangkok and thus least affected by the 1946–1947 immigration. Even more important was the fact that for a period beginning in 1943 four of the six jangwats in the north were prohibited to aliens, while in the south the rubber and tin industries were adversely affected by the war and had only begun to recover by the time of the 1947 census. The decrease in the Chinese population of Middle and Northeast Siam was minimal during the war in spite of the fact that three areas within these regions were prohibited to aliens from 1941 to 1945. Unlike the north, the larger part of both Middle and Northeast Siam was not closed to aliens, so that most Chinese refugees from Uttaradit, Khorat, and Ubon-Warinchamrap (the three prohibited areas in question) went to nearby towns in the same regions. Middle Siam was also the area of maximum development during the war, when highways were constructed from Phitsanulok to Sukhothai and from Taphanhin to Phetchabun. The wartime prohibited areas in the southeast (Prajinburi jangwat and Satthahip) and the southwest (Kanjanaburi jangwat) bordered on Lower Siam and were more extensive than those in Middle and Northeast Siam, so that many Chinese refugees left these regions and moved to Lower Siam. In consequence, the Chinese population of these two regions showed a sharp decline during the 1937–1947 intercensus decade.

The geographical distribution of the Chinese in Thailand as of 1947 is shown in Map 6. An index of concentration was computed for each amphoe (or combinations of amphoes where the areas of single units are too small to show up on the map) taking into account both the density of Chinese population and the Chinese proportion of the total population. The heavy concentration of the Chinese around the upper Gulf is immediately apparent from a glance at the map. Other areas of Chinese concentration in Lower Siam are centered at Ayutthaya and Saraburi. The Chinese distribution northward into Middle and North Siam follows the Yom-Nan River system and the railroad, with chief concentrations at Paknampho and Phitsanulok (and the Nan River area in between) and at Lampang and Chiangmai. East from Saraburi, the Chinese distribution follows the rail line to Khorat and on east to Ubon, and north from Khorat to Udonthani, with the chief concentrations in the northeast at Khorat and Ubon. The pattern of Chinese concentration in the southern peninsula is more complex, but the chief centers for Chinese at Phuket, Suratthani, and Hatyai stand out clearly. Other centers of Chinese population can be seen in the jangwats of Pattani, Yala, and Narathiwat in the far southeastern tip, and in and around the towns of Trang, Nakhonsithammarat, Ranong, Chumphon, and Prajuapkhirikhan.

The geographical concentration of Chinese at the head of the Gulf emphasizes the importance of Bangkok for the Chinese of Thailand. The capital is not only the main port of entry for Chinese, but the communications hub for the whole country. Map 5 (p. 85) shows clearly how all the country's railroads radiate from Bangkok and especially how well they serve the area of Chinese concentration at the upper Gulf. The same pattern is characteristic of the country's extensive system of canals, while most roads either begin in Bangkok or take off from one of the rail lines beginning in Bangkok. Approximately half of the Chinese in Thailand live within fifty miles of Bangkok, and at least one-fifth of the total reside in the capital itself. It is not surprising, then, that the Chinese organizations in Bangkok function to a large extent on a nationwide basis and that the community leaders of the Chinese in Bangkok can speak for the whole Chinese population of the country.

Bangkok has often been used loosely by Western writers. The capital's metropolitan area includes parts of two jangwats: Phranakhon east of the river, and Thonburi on the west bank. Technically two municipalities are involved, Krungthep or Bangkok proper in Phranakhon and Thonburi in the jangwat of the same name. It is an error to quote the population figures of Phranakhon or of Phranakhon and

Thonburi jangwats together as those of "Bangkok," because both jangwats contain fairly extensive areas that are part of neither municipality and rural in ecological fact.

The amphoe offices in both municipalities register the population in each amphoe (or *khwaeng*, "municipal ward," where these differ from amphoes) by nationality. There is unfortunately considerable room for error in the registration of nationality, because proof of citizenship is not always required by amphoe officials and in any case can often be successfully forged. It is not uncommon for China-born Chinese to attempt registration as Thai nationals in order to avoid payment of alien fees, and for young local-born Chinese men to try to pass themselves off as Chinese nationals in order to avoid military conscription. The resulting errors tend to cancel one another out, however, and the figures for Chinese nationals are probably as accurate as those for Thai nationals. Another error arises from the lack of a good system to ensure the removal from the registration lists of those who die or leave the city. This factor, however, affects all nationals alike, so that while the total figures are somewhat inflated, the relative proportion of the various nationalities is probably a good approximation of the true picture.

Figures for the municipality of Krungthep are available for four years, covering a six-year period:

Year	Total population	Chinese nationals	% of total
1950	757,636	214,743	28.3
1952	845,374	218,288	25.8
1954	951,965	224,060	23.5
1955	1,024,502	235,227	23.0

Although Bangkok has been growing rapidly ever since the war, the rate of growth is undoubtedly less than that shown above because of the inflationary bias of registration procedures, as elaborated earlier. Similarly the China-born population of the city, which undoubtedly increased from 1946 to 1948, has in all probability been decreasing since 1950. The apparent absolute increase shown above can only be a function of the same fault in the registration system. Since the deficiencies apply to all nationals, however, it is safe to use the percentages given and conclude that the proportion of Chinese nationals in Krungthep declined from a high in 1948 of approximately 30 per cent to about 25 per cent in 1952, and that the decline is continuing at the present time. This fairly rapid change results from a steady internal migration of Thai to the city, from the dispersal of recent Chinese immigrants from Bangkok to the outlying regions, and from a death rate among the China-born Chinese higher than the rate of immigration from China.

Registration figures by nationality for Thonburi municipality are available only for 1954–1955. They indicate that in August 1954, 17.2 per cent of the population consisted of Chinese nationals, while by December 1955, the proportion had decreased to 16.1 per cent (46,497 out of 288,467).

Table 17 presents a slight reworking of the registration figures for both municipalities as of August 1954. The figures have been grouped into three zones in which the Chinese element is differently represented. The first of these (A in Table 17) is the heart of the city and includes the major business and shopping centers for Thai, Chinese, and Westerners. It lies along the east bank of the river in Krungthep. The second zone (B) almost completely surrounds the central business zone and includes all other municipal areas to the east and south. The third zone (C) consists of the outlying areas in the north of Krungthep and the north and west of Thonburi.[48] For each zone, the registered figures for Chinese nationals and the total for nationals of countries other than China and Thailand are given without change. The registration figures for Thai nationals, however, have been split in an attempt to estimate the number of local-born Chinese of Thai nationality. On the basis of over three years' residence and research in Bangkok, a careful survey of each of the three zones, and an inspection of the registration rolls in several instances, this writer has estimated that approximately 65 per cent of the Thai nationals in zone A are ethnic Chinese (i.e., still speak a Chinese language and identify in most social situations as Chinese), and that the corresponding proportions for zones B and C are approximately 30 per cent and 10 per cent, respectively. Consequently, the appropriate portion of the registered residents of Thai nationality are shown in Table 17 as local-born Chinese. The figures have not been rounded, so as to preserve the original statistics intact. The number of registered Thai nationals as supplied by the municipal governments can be had by simply adding the figures in the second and third rows together in each case. Because of the unbalanced sex ratio characteristic of the China-born population, the number and proportion of female ethnic Chinese is lower than that for males. To save space, however, only the figures for males and for the total of both sexes are given in the table.

In the central business area, over two-fifths of all males are Chinese nationals (i.e., almost entirely China-born immigrants), while in the surrounding zone the proportion is less than one-quarter, and in the outlying sections of the city only one-tenth. For the population of both

Table 17. The registered population of Bangkok (the combined municipalities of Krungthep and Thonburi) by nationality, August 1954 *

	A. Central business area				B. Surrounding area			
	Male only		Both sexes		Male only		Both sexes	
	No.	%	No.	%	No.	%	No.	%
Chinese nationals	77,370	42.7	130,730	38.5	60,944	23.9	104,047	21.2
Local-born Chinese of Thai nationality	66,652	36.8	134,711	39.6	57,277	22.5	114,828	23.4
Others of Thai nationality	35,890	19.8	72,536	21.3	133,646	52.4	267,932	54.5
Other nationals	1,439	0.8	2,090	0.6	2,970	1.2	4,524	0.9
Total	181,351	100.0	340,067	100.0	254,837	100.0	491,331	100.0
All ethnic Chinese	144,022	79.4	265,441	78.1	118,221	46.4	218,875	44.5
Others	37,329	20.6	74,626	21.9	136,616	53.6	272,456	55.5
Total	181,351	100.0	340,067	100.0	254,837	100.0	491,331	100.0

	C. Outlying areas				D. All of both municipalities			
	Male only		Both sexes		Male only		Both sexes	
	No.	%	No.	%	No.	%	No.	%
Chinese nationals	19,820	10.0	33,229	8.8	158,134	24.9	268,006	22.2
Local-born Chinese of Thai nationality	17,890	9.0	34,251	9.1	141,819	22.3	283,790	23.5
Others of Thai nationality	161,014	80.9	308,260	81.9	330,550	52.0	648,728	53.7
Other nationals	417	0.2	619	0.2	4,826	0.8	7,233	0.6
Total	199,141	100.1	376,359	100.0	635,329	100.0	1,207,757	100.0
All ethnic Chinese	37,710	18.9	67,480	17.9	299,953	47.2	551,796	45.7
Others	161,431	81.1	308,879	82.1	335,376	52.8	655,961	54.3
Total	199,141	100.0	376,359	100.0	635,329	100.0	1,207,757	100.0

* Original statistics supplied by the Municipal Offices of Krungthep and Thonburi.

sexes, the proportion of Chinese nationals is in each case a few percentage points smaller. When estimates of the number of local-born Chinese of Thai nationality are added to the registration figures for Chinese nationals (see the last two rows of Table 17), it will be noted that ethnic Chinese greatly outnumber ethnic Thai in the central business area (about 80 to 20), while in the outlying areas ethnic Thai outnumber the Chinese to an even more extreme degree. In the inter-mediate zone (B), the two ethnic groups are represented more equally, but with a decided edge in favor of the Thai. For the entire municipal area on both sides of the river (see D in Table 17), these computations indicate that some 45.7 per cent of the total population are ethnic Chinese. Because of factors already mentioned above with regard to the China-born population as well as of continuing assimila-tion on the part of the local-born population, this proportion may be expected to decrease in years to come.[49]

The degree to which municipal registration figures are inflated is indicated by the results of the 1954 Economic and Demographic Survey, completed in the two municipalities in April 1955. According to this survey, the populations of Krungthep and Thonburi were 824,600 and 232,680 respectively, giving a total population for the combined municipalities of 1,057,280.[50] If this is assumed to be the true figure, then the registered total is an overcount of 14.2 per cent. Accordingly, the size of the ethnic Chinese population in all of Bang-kok may be estimated at 483,000 (45.7 per cent of 1,057,280).

The Economic and Demographic Survey was conducted according to an admirable sampling design. There were several aspects of its execution, however, which in this writer's opinion reduced its accuracy with regard to the Chinese population. First, the enumerators were exclusively Thai and spoke no Chinese. This had two unfortunate consequences: a bias in favor of avoiding households where only Chinese was spoken and a loss of accuracy when interviewing Chi-nese heads of households. Second, the enumerators were of low educa-tional background and received inadequate training. Their ability to handle the rather finely pointed questions on nationality and mother tongue is consequently questionable. Third, the survey was con-ducted at a time when strong pressures favored misrepresentation in a single direction. From January 1953 to August 1955, Thai citizens born of alien fathers were exempted from military conscription. Furthermore, from 1952 through 1955, the annual alien fee was set at 400 baht, an unreasonable level and all-time high. All but a small proportion of the 1954 registered Chinese population (see Table 17) had been entered in the municipal rolls prior to 1952–1953, i.e., at a time when alien fees were lower and local-born Chinese were sub-ject to conscription. At the time of the Survey, however, fear of conscription was removed as a motivating factor in misrepresentation, while fear of the alien fee was intensified. In consequence, there was strong motivation for China-born Chinese to give their place of birth as Thailand and their nationality as Thai, but no balancing motivation for local-born Chinese to falsify their responses in favor of a Chinese birthplace or Chinese nationality. For these reasons, the writer considers the Survey's figures with regard to nationality, place of birth, and mother tongue biased in favor of Thai, Thailand, and the Thai language, respectively.

For what they are worth, however, these figures indicate that in Krungthep only 18.5 per cent of the males and 15.9 per cent of both sexes are of Chinese nationality, the corresponding figures for Thonburi municipality being 12 and 9.9 per cent. (The proportions of the population shown to have been born in China are virtually identical with those relating to nationality.) The proportion of the Krungthep population whose mother tongue was Chinese is given as 39.2 per cent for males and 37.9 per cent for both sexes; the corresponding figures for Thonburi are 25.8 and 23.7 per cent. The Survey's total of those whose mother tongue was Chinese (both municipalities) is 367,600. This figure would in any case exclude many bilingual ethnic Chinese, and in view of the circumstances described above, it cannot be taken as even a minimal approximation of the population of ethnic Chinese. The figure mentioned earlier, 483,000, is undoubtedly closer to the actual size of the ethnic Chinese population in Bangkok.[51]

It remains to define the geographical distribution of the various Chinese speech groups. Thai censuses, unlike those conducted in most other Southeast Asian countries, have never recorded the speech group of Chinese residents. For Bangkok, the writer resorted to several types of data in estimating speech-group proportions. These include calculations based on emigration from the various south China ports, comparative membership of the speech-group associations, official estimates of the speech-group associations' staffs, the number of burials in the five speech-group cemeteries, and the opinions of various key informants. As far as can be determined, the proportion of the major groups is approximately as follows: Teochiu 60 per cent, Hakka 16 per cent, Hainanese 11 per cent, Cantonese 7 per cent, Hokkien 4 per cent, and others 2 per cent.

The writer has personally surveyed most of upcountry Thailand, and in every town made inquiries and gathered data pertinent to speech-group proportions. In the case of South Siam, however, estimates are based on descriptions of Chinese communities found in the Chinese press and other local publications, and on data from informants who have traveled or resided there.

The northeast has a higher proportion of Teochius in the Chinese population than any other sizable area in the country. Except for jangwats Loei, Chaiyaphum, and the part of jangwat Khonkaen in between, Teochius on the average form about 70 per cent of the Chinese population, with Hakkas in second place (about 15 per cent). This situation is related to the fact that the northeast was the last region of the country to be opened up by railroads and highways. Not being accessible from Bangkok by any waterway, its settlement by Chinese in any numbers awaited the construction of the railways in the 1920's and 1930's. Thus most of the Chinese population of the northeast dates back to the 1918–1931 immigration wave, which, more strongly than any previous body of immigrants, was dominated by those from Swatow.

An influx of Teochius and Hakkas into Middle and North Siam also followed the construction of railroads and motor roads, wherever they were constructed. For instance, the Teochiu-Hakka majority at Lampang dates back no further than the coming of the railroad, the Hakka preponderance at Nan goes back only to the construction of a connecting road to the railway, and the Teochiu plurality at Sukhothai only to the arrival of the road from the rail spur at Sawankhalok. As a result of Teochiu-Hakka inroads, only in the smaller towns along the northern tributaries of the Jaophraya do Hainanese still form a plurality of the Chinese population. The largest of the towns still dominated by Hainanese are Phichai, Khlongtan, and Thalo, although in Lampang and Lamphun the Hainanese are about on a par with the Teochius and with the Hakkas. In all the old area of Hainanese settlement, including the countryside as well as the towns, the Hainanese today form only 25 to 30 per cent of the total Chinese population. There is one area of upcountry Thailand where the Hainanese form a majority of the Chinese population, namely, the malarial and relatively inaccessible districts north and east of Phetchabun jangwat, including Chaiyaphum, Loei, and amphoe Chumphae (jangwat Khonkaen) in between those two jangwats. Informants cite fear of fevers as the main reason for the Teochiu avoidance of this region. The Hainanese may soon lose out even in this area, however, inasmuch as a new highway from Lomsak to Loei was just completed in 1955.

There is also one region of upcountry Thailand where Hakkas are the dominant speech group, namely jangwats Nan and Chiangrai and most of jangwats Phrae and Lampang. The Hakka preponderance in this area, again, came about only as each district was opened up by the railroad or highways, which for the most part occurred in the 1920's. Hakkas greatly outnumbered Teochius among the new arrivals in this area because the man who played the leading role in the economic development of these four jangwats was a Hakka from Feng-shun, Chan Ts'ai-ch'ing. Mr. Chan held the liquor and opium concessions in Phrae consistently for over thirty years beginning in 1902 (before the railway reached Denchai) and obtained liquor concessions in jangwats Lampang (1918), Chiangrai (1920), and Nan (1925), in each case before or just as the jangwat capital was reached by the railroad or highway. He built markets, rice mills, and distilleries throughout the area. At one time, he operated three distilleries each in jangwats Phrae and Lampang and four each in jangwats Chiangrai and Nan. In all of his operations, he tended to favor the employment of those from his own native hsien, and even though he gave up all of his concessions in 1935, Feng-shun Hakkas are today still dominant everywhere in these jangwats. The only notable exception is Lampang town, and even there the number of Hakkas is perhaps not quite matched by either Teochius or Hainanese.

Outside of the areas of Hakka and Hainanese predominance already mentioned, Teochius are the major speech group everywhere in upcountry Siam. Their proportion of the whole ranges from over 80 per cent in Nongkhai and Kanlasin in the northeast to about 70 per cent in Tak, 60 per cent in Chiangmai, 50 per cent in Uttaradit, 45 per cent in Sukhothai, and 40 per cent in Phitsanulok. In every town and region of upcountry Thailand, Teochius, Hakkas, and Hainanese are the three main speech groups in one order or another. In fourth place everywhere come the Cantonese, with only a sprinkling here and there of Hokkiens and Chinese of other speech groups.

In South Siam, the picture is more varied and complex. Towns and districts can be found in which each of the five major speech groups constitutes a plurality. To give a few examples: In Yala town, Teochius are the largest group, followed in order of numerical importance by Hakkas, Hokkiens, and Hainanese.[52] In Betong, however, also located in Yala jangwat, Cantonese and Kwongsais [53] predominate, followed by Hokkiens, Teochius, and Hakkas.[54] To the east in Narathiwat, Hainanese are the dominant group, followed by Hakkas and Hokkiens.[55] In Pattani, farther north, Hokkiens are dominant, while if any one group is dominant in jangwat Songkhla, it is the Hakkas. In Trang town the Hokkiens predominate, but in Huaiyǫt, also in Trang jangwat, Hainanese are the dominant group.[56] In Phuket, the major port on the west coast, Hokkiens are in the great majority; the speech-group pattern there, in fact, would seem to be a replica in miniature of that in Penang, farther south on the same coast. In general, Hokkiens are dominant all along the west coast from Ranǫng south to Trang, while Hainanese have their strongest concentration at scattered localities on the east coast from the island of Samui on south to Narathiwat. Teochius and Hakkas are found throughout the region, the former concentrated somewhat in the north and along the east coast, and the latter in the central part of the peninsula from Suratthani on south through Thungsong and Hatyai. A reasonable estimate for all of South Siam gives Hokkiens 32 per cent, Teochius 20 per cent, Hakkas 20 per cent, Hainanese 13 per cent, Cantonese 11 per cent and others 4 per cent. These estimates show some resemblance to the proportions of the speech groups in the three west-coast states and settlements just south of Thailand in Malaya, as shown in the 1947 census: Hokkiens 37.8 per cent, Teochius 22.5 per cent, Cantonese 21.8 per cent, Hakkas 11.2 per cent, Hainanese 3.4 per cent, and others 3.4 per cent.[57]

There are several guesses in the prewar literature as to the order of the speech groups in all of Thailand. In 1937, Lin Yu wrote that "Swatow people are the most numerous; next come the Cantonese, then the Hakkas and the Ningpo people [i.e., Southern Mandarin], with Fukienese, who were among the earliest Chinese settlers in Siam and have long been absorbed by the Siamese, coming last." [58] Landon, in his book *The Chinese in Thailand*,[59] states that Teochius are the dominant group in Thailand, Cantonese the second largest group, and implies that Hainanese, Hokkiens, and Hakkas follow in that order. Both of these writers have lived in Siam, and it is difficult to see how, aside from reporting the obvious fact of Teochiu dominance, they could so completely misjudge the situation. It is true, of course, that while no Cantonese in Siam would maintain that his speech group was numerically superior to Hakkas or Hainanese, many will claim that Cantonese are the second most *important* group of Chinese in the country. The Japanese scholar Tateyania came much closer to a realistic estimate in 1941: Teochius 60 per cent, Hainanese, Cantonese, and Hokkiens 10 per cent each, Hakkas 8 per cent, and others 2 per cent.[60] Hsieh Yu-jung in his first gazetteer of 1949 accepted Tateyania's figures, but revised them in 1953 by reversing the figures for Hakkas (from 8 to 10 per cent) and Hokkiens (from 10 to 8 per cent).[61] In an earlier survey of the Chinese in Southeast Asia, this writer made the following estimates: Teochiu 60 per cent, Hakka 12 per cent, Hainanese 12 per cent, Cantonese 10 per cent, Hokkien 3 per cent, and others 3 per cent.[62]

On the basis of more detailed research and in particular the surveys of upcountry Thailand made by the writer, it is now possible to make a more detailed and accurate estimate. The proportions of the speech groups separately estimated for each special area or region of the country, when combined in accordance with the proportion of the entire Chinese population in each area or region, yields the following estimates for the country as a whole (1955):

Speech group	Proportion of total Chinese population	Number
	%	
Teochiu	56	1,297,000
Hakka	16	370,000
Hainanese	12	278,000
Cantonese	7	162,000
Hokkien	7	162,000
Other	2	46,000
Total	100	2,315,000

＊ 7 ＊

CONFLICTING INTERESTS:

Chinese Life in

Thai Society to 1938

A. *Chinese and the Thai Economy*

RICE, timber, tin, and rubber are the four major products of Thailand, accounting during the period under review (1910–1938) for from 85 to 90 per cent of the country's total exports.[1] It might be well, therefore, to summarize first the changing role of the Chinese in the economic processes surrounding each of these major products.

In rice milling the Chinese strengthened their position. By 1919, the European-owned mills had been either sold to Chinese or closed down.[2] In that year all but ten of the sixty-six large rice mills in the country were Chinese-owned, and those ten were Chinese operated.[3] During the following decade the number of large rice mills in Bangkok alone had risen to seventy-one, some of which were powered by electricity and gasoline motors rather than the usual steam engines.[4] Perhaps the most significant development in rice milling during the period under review, however, was the establishment of smaller mills outside Bangkok in the rice-producing areas themselves. This expansion of rice milling in the provinces was facilitated by the construction of railways and roads into areas not served by the major commercial waterways. This permitted shipment to Bangkok for export, but the higher cost of overland transport compared to river shipping made it economically advantageous to reduce weight and volume prior to shipment by milling the paddy near to the source of supply. This development was stopped by the depression; its magnitude prior to the thirties can be seen in Table 18. These provincial mills for the most part had a daily capacity of 30 to 40 tons of paddy, compared with the 100- to 200-ton capacity of the larger Bangkok mills. They were at least 80 per cent Chinese owned. In 1930, a Japanese source estimated Chinese capital investment in rice milling in Siam at fifty million baht.[5]

Table 18. Growth in the number of rice mills, all Thailand exclusive of metropolitan Bangkok, 1919–1929 *

Region	Established before 1919	Established 1919–1925	Established 1926–1929	Total mills, 1929
Lower	37	107	95	273
Southeast	5	37	54	102
Middle	2	28	49	80
Southwest	3	13	57	73
South	7	5	14	28
Northeast	2	3	22	27
North	0	5	5	10
Total	56	198	296	593

* Source: *Commercial Directory for Siam* 1929, 92. The last column includes 43 mills whose date of establishment is unknown.

Even before the expansion of milling capacity in the late 1920's, the number of mills was excessive in terms of Thailand's total paddy production. In 1929, overexpansion led to the failure of several mills and to more aggressive steps on the part of millers' agents to secure supplies from Chinese paddy dealers. The price of rice for export, which had averaged 7.20 baht per picul during the 1925–1929 quinquennium, fell to an average of 3.50 baht per picul during 1930–1934,[6] thus further aggravating an unfavorable situation. Closures of mills were frequent during the depression, and the total milling capacity in operation was somewhat lower in 1937 than in 1929. For some reason Cantonese millers were hardest hit; by 1937, only four Cantonese milling firms remained in Bangkok, the business having become virtually a Teochiu monopoly. The fall in world rice prices also put the squeeze on Chinese paddy dealers, whose economically complex operations in the 1930's became the object of popular discontent and government concern.

With regard to timber, there was little significant change between

1910 and 1938. European firms continued to dominate the forest operations and to employ local non-Chinese labor in them. Of the nine
large modern sawmills in Bangkok in 1924, three were Chinese; by
1940, one Chinese mill and one European mill had gone out of business.[7] Labor in all sawmills was almost exclusively Chinese, however.
The numerous small mills operated by Hainanese in Bangkok and in
North Siam began to introduce steam-powered saws during the 1920's.
Retailing of timber by the 1930's was virtually a Teochiu monopoly,
however, and Cantonese dominated the relatively small Chinese share
of the teak export trade. European firms continued to control the export of teak for Western markets.[8]

The introduction of dredges into tin mining in South Siam seriously
affected the Chinese position in that industry. The first dredge was
put into operation by an Australian firm in Phuket in 1907; by 1921,
there were thirteen dredges in operation and by 1937, thirty-nine.[9]
While Chinese miners lacked the capital to purchase dredging equipment and so stuck to the opencast or gravel-pumping system, they
nonetheless maintained or expanded output during the 1920's and
1930's. Around 1929 the production of Western dredging firms surpassed that of small Chinese mines for the first time, and by 1937/38
the output of Western firms was about 1.7 times that produced by non-
dredging methods in Chinese-owned mines.[10] Labor for all mines,
Chinese and Western, remained predominantly Chinese. The 1937
census showed 7,551 Chinese nationals and 8,966 Thai nationals engaged in mining in Siam; [11] the great majority of the latter, however,
were almost certainly ethnic Chinese. Most of the miners were Hokkiens and Hakkas, although mine laborers of other speech groups,
Cantonese in particular, were found in certain localities. The merchants who bought and exported the ore produced in Chinese mines,
however, were exclusively Hokkien and Hakka. In 1907, about half
the total output was smelted locally by Chinese, but fifteen years
later the smelting industry was almost defunct in the face of competition from Malayan smelters. By 1930, all Thai exports were in
the form of ore, and over 90 per cent went to Malaya direct.[12] The
period as a whole, then, saw the introduction of Western capital far
in excess of Chinese capital in tin mining, an expansion in total
mining operations with consequent increased employment of Chinese
labor, and the complete demise of the Chinese tin-smelting industry.

Rubber, which by the end of the period under review was Thailand's
third largest export (after rice and tin), was produced in Thailand for

the first time during the First World War.[13] Unlike tin during the same period, rubber was a predominantly Chinese industry at all levels. In the 1930's there were only two plantations controlled by Western companies,[14] and the bulk of the production came from Chinese small holdings. Production was begun by Chinese immigrants from Malaya, where conditions in the rubber industry were less favorable. Production responded roughly to world price changes, dropping after the First World War, picking up in the boom of the 1920's, declining with the onset of the depression, and recovering after 1933. Between 1935 and 1939, rubber accounted for 12.9 per cent of the total value of Thai exports.

Most of the planters and tappers, whose total number in the late 1930's is estimated at 70,000, were Hakkas, but with important representation by Teochius and Hokchius (immigrants from Foochow and hinterland). Chinese holdings in the 1930's were ordinarily smaller than 3,000 trees, but even so, the average holdings of the ethnic Chinese were larger than those of the ethnic Thai or Malay planters. Small holders usually sold their rubber in the form of raw rubber sheets to rubber merchants, who did the smoking on a large scale, but some of the larger Chinese planters did their own smoking as well. The rubber merchants, whether they bought raw or smoked sheets, also sorted, graded, packed, and exported them. They were from the beginning almost entirely Hokkiens.

By the late 1930's, then, the ethnic division of labor with regard to Thailand's four major products was as follows: The Thai produced virtually all the paddy, provided a small part of the labor in tin mines, engaged (together with Malays) in some rubber planting and tapping, and (together with Burmese and certain hill peoples in North Siam) provided the forest-working labor. Western capital and entrepreneurial skill were most important in teak, where Western firms held over four-fifths of all forest concessions and owned most of the big sawmills, and in tin, where they held mining concessions producing well over half of the total production. Chinese capital and entrepreneurial skill, however, were overwhelmingly dominant in the transport, processing, retailing, and export of rice and in the production, processing, and export of rubber, and were important in the processing, retailing, and export of timber and in the production and export of tin. Chinese also supplied the overwhelming majority of labor for tin mining and rubber production, for the processing of rice, timber, and rubber, and for the handling of all four products at the wharves for export.

Aside from rice, several of Thailand's other major food products were produced and marketed in large part by Chinese in the period under review as in the decades preceding it. In this category fall pork, fish and fish products, market vegetables, and sugar. Pork, the meat staple of Chinese and Thai alike, was produced, slaughtered and retailed almost exclusively by Chinese right up to 1938. The Thai aversion to taking life operated to deter their entering the pork business, and as of 1938 the government had taken no steps to this end. By the 1930's, coastal fishing was operated largely by Chinese entrepreneurs who supplied the boats and equipment but hired Thai and Malay as well as Chinese crews. Chinese merchants bought the fish, sold them fresh locally, or salt-dried them for export and upcountry sale. The annual commercial fish production was estimated in the late 1930's at twenty-five million baht, salt-fish exports alone in 1936/37 being valued at over two million baht.[15] Fish sauces and condiments of all kinds were also produced almost entirely by Chinese. Market gardening remained in Chinese hands and continued to expand to meet the demands of the ever increasing urban populations. The most significant development in food production during the period under review was the revival of the sugar industry in Chonburi jangwat after the First World War. In the early 1920's, the output of cane sugar was approaching half that of the peak nineteenth-century year, 1859.[16] In 1927, a specific import duty was applied to sugar and was increased in 1931 and 1936. The newly protected industry expanded steadily during the 1930's. Most of the cane was grown on Chinese plantations and processed in small, crude, Chinese-owned mills.[17]

During the three decades following 1910, Chinese provided between 60 and 75 per cent of all skilled and unskilled, nonagricultural labor in Thailand. The remainder was supplied—hill tribes working in forest concessions aside—by middle-aged Thai men, Thai women, and young Thai men in that order.[18] The major types of Chinese unskilled labor were millworkers (rice, timber, rubber, sugar), dock workers (including lighter crews), miners, construction workers (roads, railways, buildings), man-power transport workers (rickshaw and cart pullers, carrying-pole runners, river-boat polers), and domestic servants. Unskilled Chinese laborers prior to the depression earned about one baht (approximately 44¢ U.S.) for an eight- to nine-hour day, but the rate fell to 0.80 baht during the 1930's. Weekly hours varied from fifty to fifty-four. When on a piecework basis, Chinese "coolies" would often work even longer hours and could earn in a month several times the wages of a day laborer. Generally the wage scale compared favorably with that of neighboring countries.[19] However, the work was hard and labor conditions very poor; many of the unskilled Chinese laborers were driven to opium for relief from pain and exhaustion.

Chinese skilled laborers—the mechanics, carpenters, craftsmen, artisans of all kinds, foremen, and office workers—generally worked shorter hours (as low as forty-four and a half hours weekly for the last) and were better paid. Representative wages are given in Table 19.

Table 19. Representative wages of Chinese skilled laborers, 1930–1937 *

	Average rate per day in baht		
	1930/31	1933/34	1936/37
Sailmakers	1.25	1.00	1.00
Carpenters	2.00	1.45	1.45
Blacksmiths	3.00	2.52	2.45
	Average monthly salaries in baht		
Head coolies	90.00	70.00	71.00
Steersmen	35.00	31.50	31.50
Office clerks	95.00	71.00	64.87

* "Wages in Siam, 1930–31" 1933, 951; "Labor Conditions in Thailand" 1944, 1174.

Only in very recent times has Thailand seen anything that could be called a labor movement or a government labor policy. After the labor shortage at the turn of the century was rectified about 1903 and before the depression was felt in Siam in the early 1930's, strikes were rare and usually settled without government intervention. One of the few attempts of the Thai government to control labor prior to the end of absolute monarchy in 1932 came in 1913, when measures were enacted to regulate rickshaw pullers, whose large numbers and freewheeling operations created a nuisance on the streets of Bangkok. They were obliged to register and to pay a fee of 0.03 baht for a license, which was granted only to those physically fit, aged eighteen to forty, who knew enough Thai to follow directions.[20]

Luang Pradit Manutham (later known as Pridi Phanomyong) and his copromoters of the 1932 coup d'état, once in power, found themselves in something of a dilemma with regard to labor. The left wing of the People's Party, under Luang Pradit, might under ordinary circumstances have been expected to champion the cause of labor. One of the planks of the Party's platform, however, was the improvement of economic conditions for the Thai people (as opposed to aliens), and the Party committed itself in the initial manifesto to solving the unemployment problem. The unemployed were mainly Thai, because Chinese unable to find work generally returned to China. The new government, then, desiring to find work for unemployed Thai, and, in the long run, to replace Chinese labor in certain industries with Thai, could hardly act to strengthen Chinese labor. The issue came to a head in the two years immediately following the coup, for the Party's lavish promises of economic betterment and the deteriorating economic conditions precipitated a wave of strikes involving Chinese labor.

The first of these came in August 1932, when Bangkok's rickshaw pullers united to demand of the rickshaw contractors better treatment and lower rentals. Both parties to the grievance were Chinese, and mediation by the Chinese Chamber of Commerce led to a compromise with only nominal government intervention. Another strike in the same month—of Chinese women dyers—was settled on the strikers' terms because further work stoppage would have caused the (Chinese) employers considerable loss through spoilage of the berries used as dye.[21] Other strikes during 1932 and 1933 were, like the two just mentioned, solely Chinese matters, or else solely Thai. However, early in 1934 two strikes were staged that forced the government to show its hand.

In the largest rice-mill strike in Thai history, the millworkers demanded a higher end-of-(Chinese)year bonus, solicited government interference, and appealed to public opinion with a statement couched in patriotic platitudes. The government intervened, but moved too slowly to prevent the outbreak of violence, and in time the passage of the Chinese New Year obviated the immediate cause of the disturbance. While the strike was on, the few Thai among the mill workers petitioned the government to guarantee the employment of a certain percentage of Thai workers in rice mills.[22] In the end the strike was broken, and the government deported seven of its organizers to China. The following year a law was passed requiring rice mills to employ a 50 per cent minimum of Thai workers.[23]

Before the mill strike was settled, employees of the government-owned railroads struck for better working conditions and less arbitrary methods on the part of management. The strikers, who were mixed Thai and Chinese, demanded government intervention and guarantees by Premier Phraya Phahon himself. Phraya Phahon appointed military officers to run the railroads for an interim period and set up a committee to study the strikers' grievances. Work was resumed. The most significant outcome of the strike was the gradual replacement of many of the Chinese laborers—especially the strike leaders—by Thai nationals. Two other Chinese strikes failed, that of taxi drivers in Bangkok for higher wages in December 1934 and of two hundred miners in Yala to obtain restoration of a 10 per cent wage cut in August 1936. A few years later a law was passed restricting taxi driving to Thai nationals.[24]

As early as 1934, it was patent to the Chinese that the government's concern with labor was primarily nationalistic. It was not only the government's handling of the strikes involving Chinese which led to this conclusion; the gist of the government's long-range program to oust aliens from their dominant position in the Thai economy was by that time common knowledge. In consequence, there were few Chinese strikes during the remainder of the 1930's, and Chinese workers never again appealed to the government for intervention. It goes without saying that government policy militated against the formation of labor unions cutting across ethnic lines. Labor legislation to improve and standardize working conditions, furthermore, was hardly urgent from the Thai point of view as long as the majority of the labor force was Chinese. A comprehensive labor law introduced to the Assembly early in 1938 was rejected by the surprising vote of 62 to 28.[25]

The nationalistic premises of the Phahon government (1933–1938) became equally apparent in its regulation of the commercial sector of the country's economy. Developments since 1910 had, if anything, strengthened the Chinese hold on Thai commerce, and by the 1930's, Chinese were estimated to constitute 85 per cent of the "commercial class" and to hold in their hands 90 per cent of the country's commerce and trade.[26] This situation was strongly resented by Thai nationalists. Many of them, in fact, had personal reason for bitterness. Unable to advance in government service or even dismissed outright as a part of King Prachathipok's economy drive in the late 1920's, they had tried to enter business and more often than not failed in the face of Chinese competition and restrictive practices. In spite of its strong desire to establish Thai in commercial lines, however, the group of nationalists that seized political power in 1932 had to go slow. The first concrete portent of things to come was the establishment in 1934 of another Bangkok Chamber of Commerce, the membership of this one being open only to Thai firms. Interestingly enough, many if not most of the member firms were owned by Thai nationals of Chinese extraction. Then in November 1936, the Business Registration Act was promulgated with the object of bringing commercial activities under government control. The Act required registration of business firms under penalty of fines up to 500 baht, and required that every commercial signboard carry a Thai name or at least the transliteration into Thai of the foreign language name. The registration forms called for information as to the merchants' race as well as nationality.[27]

Chinese commercial activities upcountry took on special importance in the view of Thai nationalists as the impact of the depression was felt by the peasantry. It became generally accepted that Chinese merchants, paddy dealers, and other middlemen exploited the peasants by taking excessive profits on imported merchandise sold in the interior, by lending money at exorbitant interest rates, and by taking unfair advantage of the peasants' impecunious condition in paddy buying—in short that "most of the troubles of the Siamese farmer and debtor are to be ascribed to the baleful influence of Chinese money-lenders and middlemen." [28] As Jacoby has pointed out,[29] the literature on this problem is very contradictory. Zimmerman, who carried out an extensive economic survey in rural Siam in 1930–1931, stated the problem with regard to paddy marketing as follows:

The local padi dealers usually possess a number of granaries for holding supplies of padi which are sold to millers or padi dealers when the market prices at Bangkok rise. This gives an opportunity for speculating the rice prices. Oftentimes they lend money to the farmers and take padi as interest instead of money. . . . As a rule farmers do not know any rice prices except that offered by the local dealers. . . . Through ignorance of the farmers regarding the market prices, the middlemen are often able to buy at prices which leave them a large margin of profit (in those farm districts which are far away from the market). The chronic impecuniosity of some farmers often compel them to sell their crop as soon as it has been reaped, and in such cases the middlemen tend to buy lower in comparison with Bangkok prices. *Peasants have not developed a method of self-defense.*

On the other hand there is another side to the situation. The industry of padi buying is very competitive. There are hundreds of padi buyers and they all want to profit as much as they can. They can only do this by buying large quantities of rice and by selling it at a profit. So they compete with each other and drive down the profits of the business. Since the cost of doing business is very low, the ordinary padi dealer can afford to buy on low margins. The padi dealer and his family generally live on the boat and all of the members work. It does not cost much to operate a boat. Consequently the padi dealer is generally forced by competitive bidding to pay good prices for padi in relationship to Bangkok prices. Further, the dealer may buy when prices are high and be forced to sell when prices are low. He has money invested in buying padi, and this money required a heavy interest payment, probably averaging not less than 10 to 12 per cent. *So the padi dealer also has no method of self-defense.*[30]

The Second Rural Economic Survey of Siam was conducted in 1933–1934 by Andrews under the joint auspices of the Thai government and Harvard University. He found, as was to be expected, that shop-keeping in rural Siam and interregional trade were generally carried on by Chinese.[31] His conclusions pertinent to the Chinese role in rural credit and paddy marketing are worth extensive quotation:

The Chinese have been found by this Survey to be primarily businessmen and, very secondarily, creditors. The Chinese appears to prefer business transactions on a strictly cash basis: he does, however, sell goods on credit in regions where this practice is well established, and he sometimes lends money when the farmer is well-known to him and cannot obtain funds elsewhere. If the farmer is of good reputation, he is allowed to borrow from the Chinese at interest rates well below the legal limit and, even in a number of cases where it was very evident that the farmer was not a man of good reputation, the interest rates were still below the legal limit. The Siamese farmer, and especially his wife, is much more given to money-lending with the hope of high profits than is the Chinese. When he does lend money, the Chinese is businesslike about it and insists on a written contract, security and interest, but he does not ask for illegal rates of interest as often as the Siamese. On the other hand, both Chinese and Siamese often lend to close friends and relatives without asking for any interest at all.

The Chinese paddy-dealers and buyers probably do, on some occasions, make more than a strictly legitimate profit on their transactions; but it must be remembered that their business calls for very hard labor in transporting the paddy and requires an ability to quote prices, without recent knowledge of Bangkok rice values, which will meet competition on the part of other middlemen and still leave them a profit. It is inevitable that such transactions should sometimes result in more than a fair gain, but such occurrences appear not to be very frequent, and it was found, in a number of cases, that the farmer had beat the middleman A farmer who has dealt for some years with the same paddy buyer often borrows rice for food from the buyer at a time when prices are high and pays it back without interest after harvest when prices are lower.[32]

Jacoby has criticized the findings (as quoted) of both these surveys. With regard to Zimmerman's point, Jacoby held that the Thai farmer is in no position "to take advantage of competition among middlemen and thus raise the selling price of rice, as long as the competition among farmers for higher cash advances is greater than the competition among the rice buyers." As for Andrews' study, Jacoby doubted that it met squarely "the real problem: the advance payment by the Chinese rice dealer to the Siamese peasant and the subsequent dictation of the final price":

The combination of credit and purchase in the advance sale—often five months ahead of the harvest—is unfavorable to the distressed peasant producers, and presents the real problem of indebtedness. It is much more important than the isolated money-lender business. . . . The marketing problem is intimately related to the cash problem. As long as the farmer is in urgent need of cash, and consequently indebted, he will be at the mercy of any middle man, regardless of nationality. The middle man, who in Siam, happens to be a Chinese, is nothing but a function of the prevailing conditions, and his continued existence is favored by the very same conditions which—as is generally agreed—can scarcely be tolerated any longer.[33]

During the period under review, the Thai government took the reasonable position that the "intolerable conditions" prevailing in rural trade and credit could be remedied only through long-range economic planning. To break the network of trade beginning with the upcountry Chinese trader and paddy dealer and ending with the Chinese rice importers in Singapore and Hongkong, the government proposed to dredge the bar at the mouth of the Jaophraya River and develop the port of Bangkok to accommodate large ocean-going steamers. It was felt that this development would provide opportunities for young Thai businessmen to enter the rice trade at Bangkok and enable them eventually to expand their operations upcountry. Work on this project was begun during the 1930's, but it was far from completion by the advent of the Second World War. To give young Thai the know-how to enter trade both in Bangkok and in the provinces, the government proposed an extensive expansion and revision of the educational system with emphasis on vocational and commercial training. Considerable progress was made during the 1930's along these lines, but the effect was little felt in the commercial world prior to 1938.

Third, to solve the problems of agricultural credit—including tenancy, debt, and interest rates—the government put its faith in the co-operative movement.[34] The first credit co-operative had been founded in 1916, but the movement made little progress under the absolute monarchy: in 1932 there were only one hundred and fifty societies in the country. Through government initiative after the 1932 coup, however, the movement expanded rapidly in the 1930's until there were 2,851 credit societies in 1941. They were financed almost entirely with funds supplied by the government—an arrangement which, incidentally, militated against the mobilization of local capital. In particular, the careful selection of members—usually limited to owner-farmers—meant that tenant farmers and the poorer and impecunious peasants generally did not benefit from the movement. On the whole, the government's long-range steps to alter the patterns of rural trade and credit had little effect on the role of the Chinese prior to the Second World War.

The question of Chinese remittances to China was yet another economic problem that caused the Thai government serious concern in the 1930's. Remittances had been sent regularly to China since long before the turn of the century, but full cognizance of their significance for the Thai economy came only with the advent of the depression and the coming to power of the Thai nationalist revolutionary government. Throughout the period under review, Chinese sent remittances primarily through special shops or bureaus in Bangkok and other major towns. The individual wishing to remit money to his family in Ch'ao-chou, say, handed over the sum in baht to the remittance shop or remittance bureau of a bank or business firm, along with a letter to the recipient which mentioned the amount of the remittances. At intervals (from a week to a month), the shop mailed the accumulated remittance letters together to Swatow, and transmitted the sums received, less fees, to its branch in China, usually in the form of Hongkong dollars or Chinese currency. The gross profits of the remittance shop came from fees, from interest on the sums entrusted to it prior to the actual transmission of money, and sometimes from fluctuations in the exchange rate.[35] Remittance bureaus connected with import-export houses often converted the money received into goods—usually rice—and sent the money to Swatow in that form. Once the letters and money or goods were received in Swatow by the branch of the Bangkok remittance shop, agents were sent out to the various towns and villages of Ch'ao-chou to deliver the letters and cash. The recipient of the remittance then wrote acknowledging receipt of the amount, and this reply was transmitted to Bangkok by the remittance firm and delivered to the original remitter.

It is important to realize that Thailand-born Chinese who had never been to China very seldom sent remittances. Regular remitters were usually China-born immigrants who had not been away from their native place for more than a decade or so. Particularly up to the 1930's, most local-born Chinese were in the process of assimilation, and ties to their native places were tenuous. Probably the number of regular remitters to China never exceeded 150,000 during the period under review. Most remittances, of course, contributed to the support of families in China, and, when more substantial, to the expansion of family landholdings or to the education of younger kinsmen. Merchants with business connections in China also remitted money for a variety of reasons: capital investment in China, the purchase of goods to be shipped to Siam, safekeeping as deposits, and so on.[36]

The total amount of Chinese remittances from Siam during the prewar years can probably never be known with any accuracy. The earliest estimate mentioned in the literature is that of "a well-known writer on Eastern affairs" for 1912/13: twenty-six million baht. A later Financial Adviser to the Thai Government, Sir Edward Cooke, however, in connection with balance-of-payments calculations, decided that the earlier estimate was an exaggeration even of the true amount for 1925/26.[37] A Thai estimate for 1916 of thirty million baht [38] must be even more inflated. Remer's estimate of HK twenty million dollars (fifteen to sixteen million baht) for 1930 [39] is probably a better indication of the true magnitude. Doll, the Financial Adviser in the late 1930's, wrote in 1939 [40] that it was "difficult to see, having regard for the importance of other foreign interests in Siam, how Chinese remittances, despite the room for an important increase in the last two years, can on the average exceed a figure well below Baht 20 millions a year."

The three sets of Chinese estimates available for parts of the 1926–1935 decade relative to remittances transmitted to or via Swatow are given in Table 20. These figures were obtained originally from Chinese in the remittance or banking business in Swatow.[41] Liu's figures for all remittances from Southeast Asia to Swatow (last column) are given to indicate the degree to which the other series may be inflated. The estimates of Remer and Doll mentioned above make sense only in terms of Liu's series. The great majority of remittances sent from Siam to China pass through Swatow, and such comparative figures as are available indicate that the portion of total remittances arriving in Swatow that originated in Siam never exceeded 40 per cent.[42]

All in all, it would appear likely that total Chinese remittances from Siam during the period under review never exceeded twenty to twenty-five million baht in any one year, and probably averaged considerably less than twenty million baht annually. The trend in the volume of remittances is much clearer than their absolute size. After the First World War, remittances from Siam in baht showed a gradual rise to a high in 1928–1930, followed by a sharp decrease during the depression to a low in 1935, after which their volume picked up again.

Table 20. Estimates of remittances via Swatow, 1926–1935 [*]

	Remittances in millions Siam to Swatow				Remittances in millions all Southeast Asia to Swatow
	Chen		Hsieh		Liu
	HK$	Baht	HK$	Baht	HK$
1926	—	—	—	—	$19.03
1927	$15.5	17	—	—	19.65
1928	34.6	38	—	—	19.80
1929	34.2	34	—	—	23.04
1930	33.2	24	$40	28	29.61
1931	19.9	12	35	22	17.84
1932	16.8	11	32	21	12.13
1933	14.9	11	27	20	—
1934	—	—	20	18	—
1935	—	—	15	14	—

[*] See note 41 for sources.

It is obvious from the brief description given here of the Chinese position in the Thai economy that a large share of the money income of the nation must have accrued to them. Just what proportion the Chinese spent in Siam, invested in Siam, contributed to national revenues, or remitted abroad is impossible to determine. But a few comparisons are enlightening. Government revenue from opium *régie* alone, 1910 to 1938, varied from eight to twenty-three million baht annually, with an average of 14,900,000 baht.[43] It seems clear, then, that the total Chinese contribution to the government revenue—when other fees and taxes are taken into account—must have at least equalled their remittances to China. Callis estimated the investments of alien Chinese in Siam at 100 to 120 million U.S. dollars, or approximately 220 to 270 million baht.[44] Ingram put the matter simply in the following words:

Much of the capital invested in Thailand arose from profits re-invested there. Especially was this true of Chinese-owned capital. Remittances cannot be considered as a net drain, therefore, because if they had not been permitted, the investments would not have been made.[45]

In all probability, by far the greater part of the money income of the Chinese remained in Thailand.

B. Chinese Education

The new type of Chinese community schools, whose beginnings were described in Chapter 5, became increasingly popular after the First World War. The number in all Siam had risen to 48 in 1925, to 188 in 1928, and to 271 in 1933.[46] In 1932, there were 7,726 Chinese pupils in Chinese schools.[47]

This expansion, while rapid enough, resulted in an extremely poor showing when compared with Chinese education in other countries. In 1931, there were in the Dutch East Indies about 600 Chinese schools with over 30,000 pupils while the Chinese community of Malaya in 1933 supported over 370 Chinese schools with an enrollment of almost 25,000 students.[48] Basing calculations on the best available estimates for the Chinese populations of these countries in 1931–1932 [49] approximately one out of 43 Chinese in the East Indies and one out of 68 Chinese in Malaya were in Chinese schools, while the corresponding figure for Siam was only one out of about 200.

Several reasons for the relatively poor development of Chinese education in Siam up to the early 1930's suggest themselves. First of all, in 1931 approximately 68 per cent of the Chinese in Malaya were China-born, while the corresponding figure for Siam, assuming the model presented earlier to be correct, is about 46 per cent,[50] and a Chinese education is quite naturally considered more desirable by China-born than by local-born parents. Second, there is considerable evidence that the Chinese in Malaysia during the first decades of this century were more progressive and revolutionary than those of Siam. Living in European colonies, they were subject to stronger Western influence, and it was the Chinese of Malaya and the Indies who had supplied the major support among overseas Chinese for Sun Yat-sen's revolutionary movement. Inasmuch as Cantonese were the revolutionists par excellence and were generally regarded as more advanced in the acceptance of Western ways than other speech groups, it is perhaps significant that they formed a much higher proportion of the Chinese in Malaya and the Indies than in Siam. It is certainly true that the Malaysia Chinese began the new schools earlier and extended them more rapidly.[51] Third, and probably of most importance, the Thai government controlled and restricted Chinese schools far more severely than did the colonial governments in Malaysia prior to the early thirties.

The first Thai legislation to affect Chinese education was the Private Schools Act promulgated in January 1919. The Act and its subsequent ministerial regulations stipulated that all schools established by aliens must register with the Ministry of Education, that principals of such schools must be educated to the standards set by the Ministry for the second year of secondary school, that all alien teachers must study Thai and pass examinations in the language six months and one year after they begin teaching, and that the Thai language must be taught at least three hours each week.[52] The regulations did not single out Chinese schools and in fact were aimed at mission schools as well, but they nonetheless shocked the Chinese and led to considerable protest and agitation in the Chinese press; the law was, in fact, unprecedented in all Nan-yang. Lax supervision, however, allowed the furor to cool, at least until the passage of the Compulsory Education Act of 1921. This law required all children aged 7 (in some cases 8, 9, or 10) to 14 to attend primary school for at least four years. They could meet the requirements of the law only by attending government schools or private schools which followed the regular Thai course of study and used books approved by the Ministry of Education.[53] The law, however, was to be put into effect gradually in various jangwats according to the government's financial ability to provide free schooling. Under the absolute monarchy, the law was never applied in Bangkok and certain other centers of Chinese population, so that its main effect up to 1932 was to limit the growth of Chinese education in selected outlying regions.

In 1928, King Prachathipok made formal visits to the schools operated by the four major speech-group associations in Bangkok,[54] and also toured South Siam, where he was impressed with the problem of controlling Chinese schools. In consequence, existing laws were more rigidly enforced and a decree issued that made it impossible for anyone to teach—even for six months—without having passed a Thai language examination. Theretofore, teachers for the local Chinese schools had usually come direct from China, but this practice on any scale was no longer feasible. It was on the basis of this decree that several Chinese schools were closed by the government in 1930/31.

Really serious difficulties for Chinese education came only after the

1932 revolution. The new government was determined that all children should receive a Thai education to prepare them as useful citizens of the country. To this end, the Educational Policy promulgated in March 1933 emphasized national values, the provisions of the Compulsory Education Act were applied for the first time to Bangkok, and inspection of Chinese schools became overnight extremely strict and unyielding. These moves meant that Chinese schools throughout the country could teach Chinese only as a foreign language and for a maximum of seven hours a week. The reaction of the Chinese community was immediate and vigorous. Nine community leaders drew up a petition signed by over six thousand parents and several hundred business firms, requesting more time for teaching Chinese and greater lenience in licensing Chinese teachers.[55] The government remained firm, and the issue became a *cause célèbre* among Chinese nationalists all over the Far East. There can be little doubt, in retrospect, that the Thai government was unduly strict and uncompromising in executing its policies and that certain of its education officials and inspectors deliberately antagonized the Chinese. On the other hand, Chinese nationalists, in Siam and China, irresponsibly exaggerated the injustices perpetrated, reported rumor as fact, and generally acted so as to harden Thai intransigence.[56]

In order to conform to the law, Chinese schools could either accept only students under 10 and over 14 years of age and operate according to the provisions of the 1919 Act, or they could comply with the rigid restrictions of the Compulsory Education Act of 1921 and operate as ordinary primary schools. In order to maintain their student bodies, most schools did both,[57] and in the process tried to evade the letter of the law at every turn. It was reported that between March 1933 and August 1935 some seventy-nine Chinese schools were closed for infractions of the law,[58] many being the only Chinese school in their respective towns or communities. Enforcement of the law was relaxed somewhat in 1936, and the government took steps to soothe popular feeling and regularize the situation.[59] Luang Pradit published a statement in July 1936 which said in part:

Any misunderstandings between China and Siam are built mainly on ignorance of the facts and on prejudice. . . . The Primary Education Law in Siam was enacted years ago, but efficiency in its enforcement is more recent. What the Ministry of Education insists on enforcing is that a certain number of hours per week be devoted to the teaching of the Siamese language in Chinese and in other foreign-owned and foreign-managed schools. When

Chinese immigrants choose to settle down in Siam, it is but natural that their children should be afforded the educational background which will qualify them for their social and political status and responsibilities as sons of the soil.[60]

In 1936/37, a new Private Schools Act was promulgated which defined the government's position more consistently, but otherwise did not aggravate the situation. From 1936 to 1938, there was an uneasy truce in the campaign to Thai-ify Chinese education.

The most striking result of the government's campaign was the sharp reduction in the number of Chinese schools and students between 1933 and 1934. In 1933/34, there were 271 Chinese schools with over 8,000 students.[61] Thereafter the yearly changes according to Hsieh [62] were as follows:

Year	Schools	Teachers	Students
1934/35	193	291	4,742
1935/36	191	311	7,562
1936/37	224	482	9,124
1937/38	233	492	16,711

The year, 1937/38, marked the prewar peak development of Chinese education in Siam.

Prior to the late 1920's, Chinese schools in Siam were largely limited to a single speech group. In Bangkok, those that were not operated by one of the speech-group associations were controlled by school boards limited to the speech group whose language served as the medium of instruction. Towns that could support only a single Chinese school were often rent by disputes over the language to be used and over speech-group representation on the board. In Pattani, for instance, the Cantonese principal in 1923 sided with those of his speech group on the Chung-hua school board, thereby precipitating such high feelings among the speech groups that fighting broke out, and the government was moved to close the school.[63] In towns dominated by a single speech group, its members usually ran the school and dictated the language to be used for instruction; in consequence, parents of other groups often declined to send their children to school at all.

In several of the larger towns, speech-group antagonism led to the establishment of two or more schools. In Chiangmai, the Hua-ying school was established in 1917 with Teochiu the teaching medium, but in the mid-twenties a controversy arose as to the language of instruction which ended in 1927, when the Hainanese and Hakkas broke off to establish the Hua-ch'iao school teaching in Kuo-yü. In Uttaradit, it was the Hainanese who established the first school, Ch'i-ming; after a similar argument in 1927–1928 the Teochius established their own school, Ch'ung-wen, teaching partly in Teochiu and partly in Kuo-yü. Lampang and Phitsanulok both saw the establishment of separate Teochiu and Hainanese schools prior to 1928. In Khorat, the community school, Lin-hua, was dominated by Teochius, and both Hakkas and Cantonese, frustrated with regard to the language problem, established their own separate schools.

In the late twenties, the rifts among school supporters were exacerbated in some cases by Chinese national politics. Several of the organizations sponsoring the schools were Kuomintang subbranches, and while most of these remained loyal to Chiang Kai-shek after the 1927 purge of Communists in China, the teachers in their schools did not necessarily go along. As one Chinese writer put it in 1928: "Although there are many Kuomintang members among the teachers of the overseas Chinese schools in the Siamese capital, there are also Communists among them." [64] Almost all Chinese considered politics in the Chinese schools to be a natural concomitant of patriotism. The question concerned the brand of politics to be propagated, and arguments in this regard were detrimental to the development of sound Chinese education in many communities.

The early schools charged tuition from the start, but fees were seldom high enough to cover expenditures. The chief financial support came from prominent businessmen or from the funds of the sponsoring association. In several towns, an informal business tax was collected for the school treasury. In Chiangmai after 1921, Chinese businessmen paid a sum to the school for every railway car rented. In Pattani, an ad valorem surtax was levied on imports and exports of Chinese merchants. Some schools obtained subsidies from the Overseas Chinese Affairs Commission in China, but their number was limited by the Commission's rather stringent regulations for registration.[65]

The earliest Chinese schools in Thailand were for boys only. K'un-te, established in 1917 by the Cantonese, was the first Chinese girls school. Bangkok could boast six Chinese girls schools by 1920, but few Chinese communities outside the capital could afford to set up a second school for girls.[66] Real progress in female education had to await the acceptance of coeducation a decade later. Few Chinese schools in Siam offered instruction beyond the fourth or the sixth grade. Not until the mid-twenties did several schools in Bangkok open junior middle-school departments with courses up to the eighth or ninth grade.

The general level of Chinese education was poor up to 1928. A letter written by a Chinese principal in a Bangkok Chinese school in that year pointed out that the standards of the few Chinese junior middle schools were little better than those of higher primary schools in China, while higher primary schools in Siam were equivalent only to the better lower primary schools in the homeland. "Since the standard of education is low, there is no position [for educators] to speak of in the community. The overseas Chinese are not aware of the importance of education." [67]

The consolidation of the Chinese Nationalist revolution in 1928 and Thai government control after 1933 led to considerable changes in the nature of the schools. Between 1928 and 1930 several conferences on overseas Chinese education were held in China and attended by representatives from Siam.[68] They were followed by a noticeable increase in the nationalist content of instruction; Sun Yat-sen was revered in the schools, and chauvinist textbooks were introduced from China. This trend was of course most objectionable to the Thai government and contributed to the virulence of their restrictions on Chinese education after 1933.

At about the same time the movement to use Kuo-yü, the national language based on northern Mandarin, as the language of instruction received a strong impetus. In almost every town, it was the minority speech groups who applied pressure for using Kuo-yü in the schools. Some leaders of the dominant speech group also went along for patriotic reasons—Kuo-yü being a symbol of, and a means to, Chinese national unity. Most communities with a single school, including even such large towns as Ubon, Phitsanulok, and Paknampho, had by 1930 adopted Kuo-yü as the language of instruction. In Lampang, the Hainanese and Teochiu schools were merged in 1932 to form the new Yü-hua school teaching in Kuo-yü. Even the schools established by speech-group associations in Bangkok began teaching Kuo-yü, if not actually using it for instruction.

Another trend evident after 1930 was the increasing acceptance of the new education for girls. By 1934/35, 39 per cent of the students in Chinese schools were girls.[69] This progress was possible only because of an increasingly widespread conversion to coeducation. By the late thirties, Chinese schools restricted by sex were an oddity in Siam. The

1930's also saw a rapid expansion into secondary education. Inasmuch as the restrictive Thai laws were mainly concerned with primary schools, their strict enforcement indirectly stimulated the establishment of Chinese middle schools. No separate middle schools were established anywhere in Thailand until the early thirties, when three were opened in Bangkok. The largest of these was Chung-hua, founded in 1934 by the Chinese Chamber of Commerce. During the same period, several Chinese primary schools in the larger upcountry towns started junior middle-school sections.

The Thai government restrictions necessitated a much greater reliance on local-born Chinese and Thai teachers. By the end of the period under review most Chinese schools employed more Thai than Chinese teachers. Nationalist teachings had to be toned down or carried on *sub rosa*. The standard of Chinese reached in four years of lower primary school had to be reduced in accordance with the limited number of hours devoted to its instruction. The enforced change in the nature of the Chinese schools after 1933 made them far less attractive to Chinese businessmen, who thereafter were less generous with their support. As a result, many schools found it necessary to increase tuition. This factor, as much as anything else, accounts for the relatively meager development of Chinese education during the 1930's.

It is apparent from the total enrollment in Chinese schools, even in the peak year of 1937/38, that a small minority of Chinese children attended them. There were of course other ways of getting a Chinese education. Wealthy merchants often hired tutors for their children or sent them to small tutorial classes. Classes of under seven students were by law not considered schools, and many teachers unable to meet government requirements for employment in private schools turned to tutoring small classes. It is also true that China-born parents who could afford it often sent their offspring, especially sons, back to their native places in China for education. Upcountry, a very few of the wealthier merchants sent their children to the relatively unregulated Chinese schools across the border in Burma, Laos, or Cambodia, while for Chinese in South Siam the Chinese schools of Penang and Singapore were the chief attraction. Especially after 1933, children of the rich were sent in increasing numbers to Chinese schools in Malaya and Hongkong. These opportunities, however, were never available to the majority of Chinese children in Siam.

The only other alternatives considered by Chinese parents in Siam were the government schools and Thai- or mission-operated private schools, but very few of these offered Chinese even as a foreign language after 1933.[70] Mission schools, in spite of the fact that they were subject to the same governmental restrictions as the Chinese schools, were popular with Chinese parents because of the opportunity to learn Western languages, the high quality of instruction, and the strict discipline; in addition, several offered excellent instruction in commerce. In spite of the rapid expansion of Thai government schools, they were never adequate even for the needs of the Thai population. Few children of first-generation parents attended government schools, and the many more third- or fourth-generation children who did generally already identified themselves as Thai. In all probability, the majority of Chinese children took no formal schooling in Thailand prior to the end of the Second World War.

The tragedy of education for the Chinese in Thailand during the period under review lay simply in the inability of the Thai government to effect its not unworthy ends. The government aim was to educate Chinese children as Thai—to encourage assimilation. The logical way to do this would have been to supply attractive, useful, and inexpensive alternatives to education in Chinese schools, that is, a sufficient number of government schools offering instruction in Chinese language and history as well as the usual Thai curriculum. This course was rendered unthinkable, however, by the limited financial resources made available for education, the lack of trained personnel, and a hypernationalist temper in government circles. Instead the Ministry of Education tried to remake the schools financed by the Chinese themselves into agencies of forced assimilation. The net result was a strong intensification of ill feeling and suspicion between the Thai elite and the Chinese, a strengthening of Chinese in-group sentiment which retarded assimilation, and an emasculated education of limited value or no education at all for the children of Chinese parentage. There was more than a grain of truth in the widespread feeling during the 1930's that Chinese children schooled in Siam learned to be good citizens neither of China nor of Thailand.

C. Chinese Press and Politics

The post-revolution hopes of the Chinese in Siam for protection by the republican government at Peking were not met because of internal dissention and weakness in China. The issue came to a head after the passage of the first Thai Private Schools Act. In April 1919, leading Chinese individuals and organizations in Siam addressed a petition to Hsü Shih-ch'ang (C 99), President of the "legitimate" Chinese government controlled by northern warlords. The petition complained of high taxes and lack of protection from Thai police and officials, as well as of the unprecedented restrictions on Chinese education; it requested the President to open negotiations with the Thai government with a view to redressing their grievances.[71] Since 1912 Chinese diplomats had several times attempted negotiations with Thai representatives in Tokyo and various European capitals without success. In 1919–1920, President Hsü, whose government was rapidly weakening, was powerless even to attempt aid to the Siam Chinese, whose consequent disillusionment with Peking was matched by increasing support for Sun Yat-sen's hitherto abortive movement.

When Dr. Sun was elected President of the southern government at Canton in 1921, he was supported by the entire Chinese press in Bangkok, which incidentally was mainly in Cantonese hands. (Even Hsiao Fo-ch'eng's *Hua-hsien Jih-pao* was edited by Cantonese.) From then on, press opinion and political organization closely reflected developments in China. The period of the working alliance between the Communists and the Kuomintang in China was marked in Siam by the establishment of two leftist newspapers, the Teochiu *Lien-ch'iao Pao* (C 100) and the Cantonese *Ch'iao-sheng Pao* (C 101).[72] By 1925, organization of Kuomintang branches in Siam was already well advanced, and the extreme left wing of the party was reported to have over four hundred members.[73] The major pro-Communist organization in Bangkok was known as the Li-ch'ing Shu-pao-she (C 102). Moderates and radicals were united in support of the May 30th Movement (1925), which resulted in an anti-British boycott in south China. By October 1925, the Chinese in Siam had raised a fund of 700,000 baht for the relief of the Canton strikers,[74] and it is said that only the personal intervention of King Prachathipok prevented the declaration of a formal boycott.[75] On account of inflammatory statements in connection with the May 30th Movement, both the orthodox nationalist *Hua-hsien Jih-pao* and the leftist *Lien-ch'iao Pao* were closed by the Thai government, and shortly thereafter *Ch'iao-sheng Pao*, the other leftist paper, was closed for publishing an article condemning Western imperialism.[76] The Thai government, of course, was in no position to risk offending the British.

The success of the southern revolutionaries in China was readily apparent in the increasing proportion of Kuomintang flags flying in Bangkok. On the Double Tenth (October 10, the Chinese national day) in 1925, only about a fifth of the flags flown were those of the southern Kuomintang revolutionaries, the majority being the old five-barred flag of the Peking regime. A year later, the proportions were reversed, and by New Years 1927, only a few five-barred flags were to be seen in Bangkok. The new flag was flown everywhere when news was heard of the fall of Hankow and Shanghai to the Kuomintang armies.[77]

The Chinese of Siam sent delegates to the first and second National Congresses of the Kuomintang in 1924 and 1926 respectively. The most notable of these representatives were Lin Po-ch'i (C 103) and Hsiao Fo-ch'eng. The latter was elected to the Party's Central Executive Committee in January 1926, where he pressed for a vigorous policy on overseas Chinese affairs.

On the wave of the victories in China, a new strongly pro-Kuomintang Bangkok paper was founded in 1927, the *Kuo-min Jih-pao* (C 104), which immediately took the Chinese Chamber of Commerce to task for its legalistic persistence in flying the old five-barred flag. Meanwhile both the *Hua-hsien Jih-pao* and *Lien-ch'iao Pao* were allowed to reopen, and the *Ch'iao-sheng Pao* was succeeded by a paper of similar policies, the *Li Ch'ing Pao* (C 104). The Communist-Kuomintang split in China was followed by a vigorous press war in Bangkok, with the *Li Ch'ing* and *Lien-ch'iao* dailies supporting the Communists against the pro-Chiang Kai-shek policies of the other papers. As in China, the Kuomintang view prevailed. Circulation of the *Li Ch'ing Pao* fell, as one Chinese writer delicately put it, "because its editorials were not in keeping with the times," [78] and its editor was expelled in 1928 by the Thai government on political charges. *Lien-ch'iao Pao* also folded shortly thereafter.

The Kuomintang emerged as the most powerful force in the Chinese community. It was not open in its operations, but used existing organizations and underground branches. The Chung-hua Association and the Ch'iung-tao Hui-so (Hainanese Association), both of which had been founded prior to the Chinese revolution by the T'ung Meng Hui, were the major front organizations in Bangkok. By the beginning of 1928, regular Kuomintang membership was estimated at about twenty thousand, organized into thirty-eight "cells" in Bangkok and about a hundred more in the rest of the country.[79] Factions within the Kuomintang organization were a major problem. A few were still controlled by Communists, and there was a perennial split between the progressive and orthodox wings even of the purged party. Equally troublesome were the differences among speech groups, sharpened on occasion when they paralleled ideological differences. By this time the Chung-hua Association realized the danger inherent in Hu Han-min's organizational model stipulating "companies" for each speech group, and the Party was making every effort to unify the speech groups in or under a single organization. In Phijit, for instance, the KMT cell fronted by the Ch'iung-ch'iao Shu-pao-she (Hainan Over-seas Chinese Book and Newspaper Society) was at loggerheads with the town's Teochiu faction, which was thereby alienated from the Kuomintang. In 1925, Hsiao Fo-ch'eng sent a Cantonese to Phijit to heal the breach. He succeeded in starting a new organization sup-ported by all, the Ch'in-mien ("diligent effort") Shu-pao-she, which shortly thereafter established a community-wide school teaching in Kuo-yü. A few Chinese communities remained split to the bitter end of crisis and suppression in 1939: the Kuomintang supporters in Chiang-mai, for instance, were divided into two antagonistic groups, one subbranch being almost exclusively Teochiu and the other comprising those from other speech groups. But most upcountry localities had by 1928 a single, united Kuomintang organization under cover of a Shu-pao-she. The authority of the main Kuomintang branch in Bangkok in political matters came to be recognized by most Chinese associa-tions throughout the country.

Political developments in the Chinese community in the late twen-ties quite naturally caused alarm in Thai government circles. The or-ganization of an underground party in Siam, the growing strength of leftist elements 1925–1927, the influx of Communists from China 1927–1928, organized movements aimed at the British, and the intro-duction of the hypernationalist and anti-Western doctrines of Sun Yat-sen into Chinese schools—all contributed to a flare-up in anti-Chinese feeling among the Thai elite. In August and September of 1927, rumors circulated that in some places in Siam Chinese riots were planned.[80] As noted previously, the government reacted to all this with stricter enforcement of the education laws and the passage of an immigration act which specifically excluded those "who are of bad character or are likely to create disturbances or to endanger the safety of the public or the Kingdom of Siam." [81] In 1927 also, the treason and riot laws were broadened, and a more stringent press law was promulgated. The latter stipulated that licenses to operate news-papers would be denied those who had not been steady residents of Thailand and that a license could be revoked at any time for reasons of public security or for the publication of articles tending to under-mine relations between Siam and the governments with which it had treaties.[82]

The Thai government's worst fears were realized in the anti-Japanese boycott of 1928, which also gave the newly purged and reorganized Kuomintang an opportunity to prove its patriotism, militancy, and effectiveness. Japan's trade with Siam had grown steadily since the First World War and was handled to a large extent by Chinese merchants in Bangkok. The boycott had been repeatedly employed in China as a weapon of international politics, but earlier talk of boycotts by the Chinese in Bangkok had never been effectively implemented. In 1928, however, following the Sino-Japanese incident at Tsinan in May,[83] the main Kuomintang branch in Siam declared a boycott and formed a Committee to enforce it.[84] Merchants trading in Japanese goods were circularized and fined, but it became necessary to deal more drastically with those importers and retailers specializing in Japanese merchandise who were reluctant to co-operate. In June the T'ieh-hsüeh T'uan (C 105), or Iron and Blood Corps, began ter-rorizing Japanese merchants and Chinese breaking the boycott. Threatening letters with the Corps's symbol of a red heart pierced by two daggers were freely distributed, and several individuals were mobbed, kidnapped, or shot at. Chinese dock workers refused to handle cargo to or from Japan, and when questioned by the Thai authorities, they said their lives were at stake. In the latter part of July it was noted that "the position of the ordinary Japanese shops here has become grave indeed." [85] Somewhat later the Bangkok man-ager of the Mitsui interests claimed that most of the prominent Chinese merchants were connected with the T'ieh-hsüeh T'uan and lamented that the Corps's hold was "so strong on all Chinese merchants that few dare to do any business with us." [86] Although Hsiao Fo-ch'eng publicly denied that the "merchant class" had anything to do with the boycott, the Minister of Interior in August was moved to set up a committee to investigate charges that Hsiao and eleven other Kuo-mintang members formed a committee enforcing the boycott.[87] The government took other steps as well. It closed the *Chung-hua-min Pao* for two weeks on grounds that it had encouraged bad feeling between Chinese and Japanese—a clear warning to the rest of the Chinese press. It arrested and deported several of the terrorists and, in Septem-ber, convicted the gunman involved in the most sensational of the assassination attempts and sentenced him to life imprisonment. Thai workers under police protection were used on the docks as early as August, and the boycott was finally broken in October 1928. During the year, the Chinese in Siam collected a fund of $600,000 to aid the Chinese victims of the Tsinan incident.[88]

Between 1928 and 1931, the government occasionally took legal action against Chinese editors and publishers, but the revocation of Chinese newspaper licenses under the 1927 press law became frequent only after the Japanese invasion of Manchuria in September 1931. By that time, the major Chinese papers were the *Hua-hsien Jih-pao, Chung-hua-min Pao, Kuo-min Jih-pao, Hua-ch'iao Jih-pao* (C 106), and *Ch'en-chung Jih-pao* (C 107), the last two founded in 1928. All were pro-KMT, with *Ch'en-chung Jih-pao* representing the progressive wing of the Party. Hakkas, as well as Cantonese, Teochius, and Hokkiens, were among publishers and editors; only Hainanese had no part in the Chinese press. All Chinese newspapers attacked Japan vigorously in 1931–1932. To evade closure by the Thai government, the papers resorted to double registration. Thus, when the *Kuo-min Jih-pao* was ordered to close, it continued publication almost without a hitch under its other registered name, *Min-kuo Jih-pao* (C 108). Several of the smaller papers, however, were closed permanently by the government, and the *Hua-hsien Jih-pao*—the oldest of the papers—ceased publication in 1932.[89]

Popular indignation with Japan in the Chinese community of Siam was no less pronounced between 1931 and 1933 than it had been in 1928. The local Chinese were so eager for good news that when word reached Bangkok on March 6, 1932, that a Japanese general had been captured in Shanghai, a spontaneous celebration broke out in the Chinese quarter. The afternoon and evening of March 7 produced another episode in the series marking a steady deterioration of Sino-Thai relations.[90] Thai police trying to restrain the riotous demonstration were openly resisted, and the mob turned to a Japanese drugstore. The Japanese Embassy demanded protection, and police reinforcements made about one hundred and seventy arrests. Thereupon a crowd of over two thousand protesting Chinese assembled at the Samyaek police station. Pleas from high-ranking police officers were of no avail, and finally at 9 P.M. fire-fighting equipment was brought up to dispel the crowd with water so that Their Majesties could proceed to a command performance of a play nearby. The chairman of the Chinese Chamber of Commerce tried to make amends next day, and in the end only five of the arrested Chinese were deported.

The Chinese in Siam were somehow unable to translate this heady exuberance into effective help for China's cause. The depression made it impossible to provide economic aid on the 1928 scale: when the Chamber of Commerce organized a committee for the relief of war refugees in Shanghai, it collected a fund of only 21,000 baht.[91] An anti-Japanese boycott was halfheartedly sustained by certain Chinese groups until early 1933, but the Japanese trade with Siam actually increased considerably between 1931 and 1933.[92]

No sooner had the anti-Japanese furor begun to die down than the government's actions regarding Chinese education precipitated a new political crisis. The Chinese community split on how to deal with the new emergency. The most radical Chinese nationalists called for direct retaliation against the Thai government, but the great majority followed the more moderate course, staked out by the Chamber of Commerce, of petitioning and persuasion. The essential failure of this course to reach a *modus vivendi* satisfactory to the Chinese strengthened the hand of the radicals, who by 1934 had also enlisted the support of public opinion in China. The extreme nationalists finally mapped out a plan for the application of an embargo in China on the import of Thai rice. They enlisted the support of civic organizations and chambers of commerce in Canton, Swatow, and Shanghai, and when closures of Chinese schools by Siamese authorities continued unabated into 1935, the Overseas Chinese Association of Shanghai in May formally petitioned the Chinese Ministry of Foreign Affairs to declare an embargo on Thai rice.[93] It goes without saying that Chinese rice millers and exporters were something less than lukewarm about the proposal, and the Chinese government, in part out of consideration for the livelihood of the several thousand Chinese employed in the Thai rice business, declined to proclaim the ban. Nevertheless, several civic organizations in China supported the embargo, as did public opinion generally in the major port cities.[94] Some Chinese writers claim that the boycott reduced China's share of Thailand's rice exports by about 15 per cent in 1935, and that this economic pressure was responsible for the relaxation in the enforcement of the education laws in Siam.[95] However, it is difficult if not impossible to determine cause and effect in such a complex matter.

Through all these developments the Nanking government was not unconcerned with the problems of the overseas Chinese in Siam. Its major efforts were directed toward securing a treaty with the Thai government and establishing diplomatic relations. Four leading officials of the Kuomintang government were successively charged with undertaking negotiations with Siam: Ch'eng Yen-sheng (C 109) in 1928, Hsiao Fo-ch'eng himself in 1929, Dr. Wu Ch'ao-ch'ü (C 110) in 1930, and Chu Hao-hsiang (C 111) in 1932. All were put off by the Thai on one basis or another.[96] Finally the Chinese Minister to Tokyo succeeded in reaching an agreement with Thai representatives for the stationing of an official Chinese Commissioner of Commerce in Bangkok. In confirming the arrangement, the Thai Ministry of Foreign Affairs stated:

It must be understood, however, that the special envoy of the Chinese Government to be stationed in the Capital of Siam shall have only the power of signing consular invoices and shall not have the power of any diplomatic or consular representatives.[97]

The Chinese government appointed Ch'en Shou-ming (C 112), the chairman of the Chinese Chamber of Commerce, as its Commissioner.[98]

In the fall of 1933, the Chinese government dispatched another mission to Siam, including Hsiao Fo-ch'eng once again, with the aim of soothing Sino-Thai relations while at the same time gathering information on the current status of the overseas Chinese.[99] Nanking had few legal grounds for complaint to that Thai government, whose measures against the Chinese were technically nondiscriminatory in the sense that they applied to all aliens. Faced by an intransigent Thai attitude regarding the question of diplomatic relations, and by growing Chinese demands in 1935–1936 for a Sino-Thai treaty, the Nanking government could devise nothing better than a Goodwill Mission to Siam in June 1936, composed of high-ranking government and Kuomintang officials. By this time, Thai authorities were anxious to smooth over the tense situation, and they gave the Mission a warm reception; even the Thai Chamber of Commerce entertained the Mission. The subject of diplomatic relations was broached, but the Thai pointed out that a general revision of Thailand's foreign treaties was under way and that a temporary postponement of the "inevitable" Sino-Thai treaty would yield better results.[100] The Mission also investigated the problem of Chinese education, but apparently made no specific proposals in the matter. Its main instructions were economic—the development of Sino-Thai trade and the establishment of a Sino-Thai bank and steamship line; and in this regard, too, the Mission achieved few tangible results.[101] However, the Goodwill Mission did succeed in raising the morale of the Thailand Chinese—who were gratified by the high rank of its members and their careful and thorough investigation in Siam—and provided ample occasion for bringing Thai and Chinese together in mutual expressions of friendship. The public statements of Dr. Ling Ping (C 113), the Mission head, served to indicate to the local Chinese that their plight was not as bad as they made out and to demonstrate to the Thai nationalists the Chinese government's reasonable attitude. At the suggestion of the Mission, Sino-Thai Friendship Associations were subsequently promoted in both countries, with respective headquarters in Bangkok and Shanghai.[102] For over a year (1936–1937), Sino-Thai relations were at their most nearly cordial since the mid-twenties.

In the meantime, Siam had since the 1932 revolution set out on the road to parliamentary democracy. Several local elections as well as elections of jangwat representatives to the (non-appointive half of the) People's Assembly were held in the thirties, and it is important to note the legal provisions affecting Chinese political rights. The Electoral Law of 1932/33 stipulated the following requirements for voters and candidates in elections for tambon (commune or ward) representatives:

(1) He must be of Thai Nationality in accordance with the law; but
  (a) if his father is an alien, irrespective of whether the father and mother are legally married or not, he must have studied the Thai language till he has obtained a certificate for Matayom 3 [third year of lower secondary school], or must have completed his service under the Military Conscription Law or have been in the permanent service of the Government from the position of a salaried clerk upwards for a period of not less than five years,
  (b) if he is a naturalized Thai, he must possess one of the qualifications prescribed in (a) or must have resided in the Kingdom of Siam continuously for a period of not less than ten years from the date of his naturalization.[103]

These stipulations were repeated almost without change relative to the election of jangwat representatives in the Act of 1936/37.[104] Second-generation Chinese were thus second-class citizens. Few could meet the qualifications for the franchise or candidacy, but significantly enough even fewer cared. The Chinese community was never incensed over these restrictions, and at no time did the Chinese government or its representatives raise the matter with the Thai government. In the thirties, local Chinese manifested no desire to participate in Thai democratic processes. Their political interest was centered on China.

By 1936, the Kuomintang in Siam was a well-established and orderly organization whose existence, though illegal, was knowingly tolerated by the Thai government. After *Ch'en-chung Jih-pao* was forced to close in 1935, *Min-kuo Jih-pao* became the official party organ. *Hua-ch'iao Jih-pao* and *Chung-hua-min Pao*, each with sister papers, were only slightly more critical of orthodox Kuomintang policy. In 1936, the *Hua-ch'iao Jih-pao*, which in this period was the finest example of journalism Bangkok had ever seen, sparked a fierce competition among the Chinese newspapers. Subscription rates were halved, the coverage of both the local scene and China was improved, and special editions and pictorial supplements were added. The more cutthroat of these practices were brought to an end in June 1937 through the mediation of Ch'en Shou-ming, the Chinese Commissioner of Commerce.[105] On the eve of the Sino-Japanese War, the Chinese community in Siam was relatively composed and politically united.

The outbreak of war in China in July 1937 galvanized the Chinese nationalists in Siam. Their efforts to aid the homeland took three forms: propaganda in Thailand, the collection of funds for the China war chest, and the enforcement of another anti-Japanese boycott.

When the war broke out, Thai papers depended for foreign news solely on Japanese and German news services, plus English and Italian radio broadcasts. To counteract the influence of these sources, the *Hua-ch'iao Jih-pao* requested permission of the government to furnish Thai papers with translated dispatches of the Chinese Central News Agency. In October, however, the Thai Deputy Police Chief suggested in an informal meeting of reporters that the scheme might infringe upon Thailand's international relations. Frustrated in this direction, the *Hua-ch'iao Jih-pao* promoted a plan to send mixed Chinese and Thai correspondents to the China war fronts; three Thai newspapers co-operated in the project, which was a novel departure in Thai journalism.[106] In October 1938, the militantly anti-Japanese cause was further strengthened by the establishment of the *Chung-kuo Jih-pao* (C 114), financed by four of the most active Teochiu leaders in Bangkok, including Yi Kuang-yen (C 115), the chairman of the Chamber of Commerce. Closed by the government for its aggressive stand, the paper continued as the *Chung-yüan Pao* (C 116), another paper registered by the publishers in expectation of just such an emergency.

In the matter of soliciting contributions the Chinese were handicapped by a law promulgated in 1937 which expressly prohibited the collection of money for war purposes.[107] By October 1937, contributions had reached the equivalent of $600,000, which, however, was much smaller than the amounts collected by overseas Chinese in Malaya ($6,000,000), Philippines ($3,600,000) and the East Indies ($1,200,000).[108] By mid-1938, several Chinese leaders had been imprisoned for their part in collecting money for China.

The anti-Japanese boycott declared by the Siam Chinese was extremely effective. The value of the Japanese trade with Siam decreased from 6,300,000 yen in September 1937 to 2,700,000 yen in April 1938. As was the case with the 1928 boycott, the Kuomintang organized a committee to run it and an underground strong-arm organization to enforce it. This organization, known as the Hua-k'ang (Chinese Resistance),[109] whose activities were illegal on several counts, was closely connected with several of the most reputable Chinese community leaders and under the direct control of the Chinese Chamber of Commerce.

The movement to help China and resist Japan was a dangerous and precarious business in Siam. As of late 1938 anything could happen, and the following year practically everything did.

D. Thai Policy toward the Chinese

Any attempt to assess the motivation of the Thai government's policy toward the Chinese subsequent to the First World War runs into the paradoxical fact that many of the most anti-Chinese government officials were of Chinese extraction. Luang Pradit Manutham (Pridi Phanomyong), the leading figure in the 1932 coup and the man primarily responsible for the "Thailand for the Thai" economic policies, was the son of a Teochiu father from Ch'eng-hai; his Chinese name is Ch'en Chia-lo (C 117).[110] Luang Pradit's brother, Lui Phanomyong, who as a department head in the Ministry of Education in 1933 ardently supported the Thai-ification of Chinese schools, was himself educated as a boy in his native hsien in China. Phraya Phahon Phalaphayu, Premier of Siam 1933–1938, also had a Chinese father,[111] as did Luang Wijit Wathakan, the cultural leader of the Thai revolution, who in 1938 publicly intimated that Siam's Chinese problem was comparable to that of the Jews in Germany. But there is no need to labor the point. In 1928, King Prachathipok in an address to the Chin-te School, stated that: "Thai high officials, both past and present, are mostly Chinese descendants." [112] If this was true before 1932, the only change in this regard wrought by the revolution was an increase in the anti-Chinese sentiments of this elite of Chinese extraction. [113]

China-born Chinese and Chinese nationalists generally were not a little resentful of those considered to have turned against "the voice of their blood." One Chinese writer in the thirties [114] asserted bitterly that "one can, without hesitation, hold them [Thai of Chinese extraction] responsible, in part at least, for the recent measures which have thrown consternation among the Chinese." Another went so far as to say that "the most violently anti-Chinese elements [in Siam] have closest blood relationship with the Chinese," and to speak of "hatred" between "the Siamised Chinese and the Chinese who remain Chinese." [115] Tsan maintains that a Chinese who was appointed Director-General of the Police Department in the late 1920's was "the incidental factor which went direct to the root" of the growing Sino-Thai conflict:

It was this Chinese who not unwittingly and yet not expressly or intentionally, diverted the undercurrent of the feeling of the nationalistic Chinese in Siam into one searching wave of bitterness, suspicion, fear and almost hate against the Siamese, that is the Siamese Government.

Although this man's mother might have in her Siamese blood, . . . his father was pure Chinese. He looks an absolute Chinese. He used to go about under a Chinese name and he speaks Chinese like a real Chinese. . . .

[He] was a self-made man, . . . exceedingly ambitious, . . . astute, courageous, purposeful. . . . He was one of those who have the make-up of a despot, and he prided himself in being one. And so . . . he liked to be feared or to be pleased, and he took good care that the Chinese either feared or pleased him. . . . The privileged few did please him, but the rest of the Chinese feared and hated him, and in fearing and hating him, they feared and hated the Siamese Government. [116]

What particularly irked the Chinese nationalists was the pattern so frequently followed by government spokesmen in explaining away measures opposed by the Chinese: "The Chinese and Thai are blood brothers. Most government officials are of Chinese extraction. I myself am of Chinese origin. So I cannot be accused of anti-Sinicism when I say . . ."

The explanation of the paradox is not difficult. Local-born Chinese at all social levels assimilated freely prior to the early twenties, and the government practice of conferring Thai noble titles on the Chinese elite facilitated the process in the upper strata. With their economic interests primarily in Siam, many perceived that the road to greater prestige, status and power pointed toward identification with the Thai elite. Precisely because of their origin a display of *complete* identification was advantageous. It has been observed in many heterogeneous societies that individuals making a new group identification overcompensate for their background by stressing those values and prejudices, if you will, of the new group most sharply distinguished from those of the old. To take extreme examples from Western society, many officials of part Jewish extraction in Hitler's Germany were more anti-Semitic than their "Aryan" colleagues. And it is not uncommon to find a Jew converted to Catholicism less tolerant of the Jewish religion than his fellow Catholics of long standing. The Thai elite after the First World War adhered to increasingly nationalistic values, which in Thailand inevitably took an anti-Sinitic coloring. It was not surprising, then, that a member of the Thai elite who had himself or whose father had recently been identified with Chinese society should be more anti-Chinese than many of his "pure Thai" colleagues. This does not imply that each such individual consciously decided to parade anti-Chinese sentiments; rather, in most cases, the individual came to look on the Chinese through the eyes of the Thai elite—to see them as uncouth, selfish, and materialistic—so that acting on anti-Chinese prejudices would not seem consciously hypocritical. Most of the wealthy Chinese who assimilated to the Thai elite had, after all, been only poorly educated in Chinese; they had never moved in elite circles in China. Once they broke through the Chinese definition of Thai as "barbarians," it was more than reasonable—comparing Thai elite society with general Chinese society in Siam—to reverse the stereotype.

In many cases, moreover, the blindly ethnocentric assumption of superiority on the part of Chinese kinsmen bitterly antagonized Siamborn Chinese aspiring to position and prestige. In the perceptive words of Lin Hsi-ch'un, writing in the mid-thirties:

Because of the old moral teaching, those who remained in China often looked down upon those who left their ancestors' tombs behind for, as it were, a "mess of pottage." Their offspring were often regarded as "wild seeds," or as "barbarous sons." So when oversea Chinese in their old age did bring their families back, they often were ill-treated and abused. Their foreign-born sons, before they were reinstated by the clan, had no share in the sacrificial feast and meat. Even the ancestral hall they were not allowed to enter. The ceremony for the reinstatement into the clan consisted of a feast to the members of the clan and a money present to the clan varying from $50 to $500 to be agreed upon during the feast. After this such foreign-born sons became members of the clan nominally, but in reality inequality still exists. And because of their lower status in the clan girls were not willing to marry them, unless they were able to make a money present twice the usual amount to the girls' parents. As a result of this, unless they were well educated, they usually returned to the land of their birth with an ingrained hatred for the China-born Chinese.[117]

This version may be somewhat hyperbolic as a general statement, but there are many case histories which indicate the importance of such experiences in China. One of the most instructive of these is supplied in the anti-Sinitic tract, *The Jews of the East,* summarized in Chapter 5. The author repeats a story told him by a lukjin "who strangely enough, hates the Chinese":

He told me how, when he was still quite young, he had gone to China with his father, who was Chinese. One day a Chinese nobleman came to call upon his father at his home. The nobleman said to his father: "Now that you have amassed a considerable fortune in Thailand, why don't you return to China to live?" His father replied that he stayed on in Thailand because he had a family there. The nobleman then said: "Well, what of that? Do you have to be considerate of a wife who is nothing but a barbarian? Bring her along and let her be the slave of your Chinese wife. Your barbarian children will make handy house servants." These words of the Chinese nobleman were spoken in front of my friend, who was favored with not so much a glance. It certainly is not strange that, after having heard them, he determined in his heart that from that day forward he would be a Thai and a true one.[118]

At this point it might be well to summarize briefly the events and developments during the period under review that contributed to the measures directed against the Chinese by the nationalistic Thai elite. For one thing, the unprecedented magnitude of Chinese immigration during the 1918–1931 period contributed in no small part to fear on the part of Thai that they would be "swamped" in their own country. It is perhaps no accident that the first across-the-board government measures directed at the Chinese came in 1927/28, the year when over 150,000 Chinese poured into Siam, and that the intensification of these measures in 1932/33 came when the China-born Chinese population was at its all-time peak before the Second World War. Considerations of international power were also important in understanding Thai government actions relative to the Chinese. China was relatively weak throughout the period under review, while Britain was the dominant power in Southeast Asia during the twenties, though challenged by the growing strength of Japan in the thirties. When Chinese nationalism was at its most anti-Western (especially anti-British) phase, 1925–1928, and Kuomintang dogmas were being propagated in Siam, it was precisely the British with whom the Thai had to be most concerned. As anti-Japanese activities came in the thirties to dominate Chinese politics in Siam, Japanese power was in rapid ascendancy, and the Thai—whether admiration for the Japanese example played a part or not—had to be especially careful not to offend Dai Nippon.

On the domestic scene the most offensive developments from the Thai point of view were the introduction of the Kuomintang apparatus and the propagation of Chinese nationalist dogmas through Chinese organizations and schools. The 1928 boycott, executed and enforced by Chinese nationalists, brought violently to the attention of the Thai elite the almost absolute economic power of the Chinese along certain lines and the extent to which they constituted a state within a state. Radicalism, lawlessness, and virulent nationalism—so evident in the Chinese community of 1927/28—forced the Thai to end what one observer has called its "policy of drift" in dealing with the Chinese.[119] The frustration of young educated Thai in their attempts to enter commercial life during the five years or so prior to the 1932 coup reinforced the determination of the Thai nationalists who took over power in 1932 to end the Chinese grip on Siam's economy.

Within a few years after the new government came to power, yet another factor came into play. The early pronouncements of the left wing of the People's Party encouraged visions of rapid economic improvement, but Luang Pradit's comprehensive economic plan was rejected as such on grounds of impracticality and radicalism by the more conservative elements in the coup party, and it was necessary to count on long-term programs for the eventual solution of such rural problems as tenancy and agricultural credit. The Chinese middleman, though in fact only a part or function of the total economic system, was the most visible reason for the misery and indebtedness of the Thai pleasantry.[120] It became advantageous, therefore, for the Thai government to divert attention from the limited results of its economic policies by pointing to the Chinese middleman as the *cause* of rural problems. The Chinese, as a visible minority without political rights, were admirably suited for the scapegoat role.

Finally, it should be noted that in this regard the influence of British opinion on the Thai nationalists was no less marked in the period under review than it had been prior to the World War. For instance, prior to the 1932 revolution, the Governor of the Straits Settlements, Sir Hugh Clifford, paid an official visit to Bangkok as a guest of the Thai government:

Following the completion of his mission in this country, Sir Clifford commented on the political and economic situation in Thailand thus: "Everything about this country is nice. Food is abundant; the country peaceful. The only shortcoming is that the Chinese are allowed too full a living. If the Siamese Government does not resort to any limitation, it will face trouble in the future." [121]

This remark still serves as ammunition for Thai nationalists; in fact, this excerpt is from an editorial in a recent Thai newspaper on "The Chinese Problem." Another even more significant example occurred in 1937.[122] In 1935, the British Financial Adviser to the Thai government had resigned in a huff because he refused to condone a tremendous deal in contraband opium in which Finance Ministry officials were implicated. England, anxious at that time to retain Thai friendship unimpaired, ignored the opium transaction and appointed William Doll as the new Adviser with instructions that, as Landon put it, "may well be imagined." Doll's first annual report, published in 1937, was just what the Thai extremists ordered. It stated that "nearly all the profits of internal trade are remitted and not retained in the country," that the estimate by a Chinese banker in 1932 of Chinese remittances at thirty-seven million baht was "probably not far short of the truth," and recommended "any measure or series of measures the object of which is the retention of a larger share of the country's earnings." Two years later, Doll virtually admitted that the figure of thirty-seven million baht was about 100 per cent too high, but the retractions, cautions, and pleas to go slow in his report for 1938/39, published as it was after Thai economic nationalism had begun to harm British interests, carried considerably less weight with the Thai.

What were the aims of Thai government policy during this period? The most obvious were the encouragement of assimilation and the gradual loosening of the Chinese grip on the country's economy. There is no question that assimilation was the major conscious motive behind the government's educational policies. In 1929, for instance, a prominent Thai author wrote:

Without a doubt, compulsory education in Bangkok, where most Chinese congregate, is one means of assimilation. In compulsory education lies an

instrument which is infinitely useful for our purposes. . . . [It] would ensure that the second generation of Chinese will to all intents and purposes be
Siamese.[123]

Similarly the restrictions on immigration were designed in large part
to facilitate eventual assimilation, and by imposing literacy requirements in the thirties the government hoped to reduce the proportion of
women and thus reverse the trend toward all-Chinese homes.[124] To
this end also, the Thai government took steps to weaken Chinese ties
with China. Much of the reluctance of Thailand to enter into diplomatic relations with the Chinese government stemmed from fears
that a Minister from Nanking would help perpetuate the Chineseness
of the local community and might try to reorganize local Chinese
society on a Kuomintang model. It is also significant with regard to
assimilation that the earlier laws on naturalization and nationality were
left unchanged during the period under review. Thus a local-born
Chinese was automatically a Thai citizen, and a Chinese "of good
character and in possession of sufficient means of support" who had
resided five years in Siam could apply for naturalization. No restrictions of any kind were placed on the freedom of Chinese to travel and
reside in Siam or to own or rent land. Theoretically at least, Chinese
were equal to Thai before the law and its enforcement officers.

These are the major aspects of Thai policy aimed at assimilating the
Chinese. The steps aimed at weakening the Chinese hold on the
economy, discussed in Section A, need no further elaboration, except
to point out that the government's handling of strikes and its imposition of literacy and wealth requirements for immigration in part
aimed at replacing Chinese labor with Thai.

There is good reason for attributing another major aim to the Thai
policies regarding the Chinese—namely, the maintenance and increase of government revenue. During the period under review the
government made no serious effort to decrease Chinese consumption
of opium, and revenue considerations underlay this negative policy.
The gradual decline in opium *régie* from 1927/28 to 1933/34 was
largely a function of the falling world price of opium and of increasing
financial disability to buy it on the part of the Chinese, rather than of
conscious government policy. Immigration policy, too, must also have
been based partly on revenue considerations. In 1928/29, the first full
year during which immigration fees were charged, revenue from this
source, 114,119 baht, amounted to less than 0.4 per cent of total gov-

ernment revenues. But fee increases during the thirties caused government income from this one source to increase fairly steadily to 2,931,825 baht in 1937/38 or about 2.7 per cent of all government revenues.[125]

It is unrealistic to expect complete consistency in the policies of any government because of the multitude of considerations which must be taken into account. Nevertheless, it may be worthwhile to point up a few of the major contradictions in Thai policy toward the Chinese during the thirties, not by way of criticism but in hopes of understanding the changing bases of government action. The three major aims suggested above are in themselves logically inconsistent. In immigration policy, for instance, the assimilation aim called for immigration by sex-specific quotas, the economic Thai-ification aim called for immigration restriction by occupation-specific quotas, and the revenue aim called for immigration restricted only by the amount of the fees. In opium control, the assimilation aim suggested steps to decrease Chinese opium addiction (by cultural definition, a good Thai does not indulge), while the revenue aim argued for unlimited consumption with control only of production and smuggling. In commercial policy, the assimilation aim suggested measures to make Thais of Chinese merchants and middlemen and entrepreneurs, the economic Thai-ification aim called for the gradual replacement of these Chinese by Thai, while the revenue aim suggested leaving them well enough alone except for heavy taxes and business fees. In education policy, as suggested in Section B, the assimilation aim called for the provision of a school system which limitations of revenue precluded.

In these and other matters of policy, then, the Thai government effected a compromise of different and sometimes conflicting aims. In addition, however, there were already indications prior to 1938 of a more negative aspect of policy, that of containment or restriction per se. It rested on the whole range of Thai prejudices and stereotypes about the Chinese but in particular on the belief succinctly stated by the author of *The Jews of the East:* "No matter where they live, what nationality they assume, Chinese remain essentially Chinese." [126] Lacking confidence that any complex of policies would result in the eventual assimilation of the Chinese, proponents of the policy of containment were willing to restrict any Chinese activity offensive in Thai eyes, without consideration of sociological or psychological consequences. Prior to 1938, what is here called the containment policy could be seen primarily in the methods used by certain officials in the control of education—in Landon's words, "The whole course of changes could hardly have been handled in a way more calculated to antagonize" [127]—and in smaller degrees, of immigration and commerce. However, the policy was destined for greater prominence in the period to follow.

Finally, it should be pointed out that during the period up to 1938 at least, relations between the Chinese in Siam and the mass of the Thai people were far less hostile than this survey of elite attitudes and government policy might imply. Occasions when friction did occur between Thai and Chinese can often be traced back to the attitude of the government and intelligensia. The differences between Thai and Chinese labor in Bangkok, most noticeable during 1928–1934, clearly resulted from government policy during the 1928 boycott and the wave of strikes following the 1932 revolution. Concern over the exploitation of Chinese middlemen in upcountry Siam during the thirties was far more pronounced among the Bangkok elite than among the Thai peasants themselves, who would have been chagrined indeed to have been deprived of the services of Chinese traders. The only serious outbreak of violence between Chinese and Thai during this period was an incident at Betong (South Siam) in October 1933, arising from a misunderstanding between police and a Chinese shoemaker. The Chinese and his son were arrested for reasons unknown to the other Chinese residents of the town, who gathered at the police station to protest. Police thought the station was being mobbed and after some altercation opened fire and killed several Chinese. Sixteen arrests were made, and most of the remaining Chinese population fled to Malaya. It is significant here that the non-Chinese population did not interfere and that the arrested Chinese were fairly tried; after appeal to a higher court all but one of the sixteen were set free.[128]

It is perhaps also worth noting that responsible leaders of the Chinese community missed no opportunities during the period under review of expressing their loyalty to the Crown and the government in power.[129] Chinese groups were prominent in the ceremonies connected with Wachirawut's cremation and Prachathipok's coronation. On his tours of upcountry and South Siam in 1927–1928, the King was well received and entertained by Chinese delegations and organizations. After the 1932 revolution, the goodwill of the Chinese community was demonstrated at the celebration of the promulgation of the new Constitution in December 1932:

The parade included the leading merchants of Bangkok, the leaders of the Chinese Chamber of Commerce, the leaders of various Chinese clubs, and the children and teachers from several Chinese schools. They marched for five hours through the streets bearing standards inscribed in Chinese characters which told of their goodwill toward Thailand in general and the new constitutional government in particular. The parade ended at the club-house of the People's Party where it massed to hear speeches by some of the leading government officials. The Chinese community then offered a programme of entertainment, and made a financial donation to the Thai cause.[130]

Thereafter, at the annual celebration of Constitution Day and at the mixed banquets of the Chinese and Thai elite, which were ordinarily held on occasions when Chinese support was solicited for a Thai cause, the attempt was made by both sides to smooth over differences. In part, at least, the platitudes expressed—"Our two peoples are congenial, kind and generous . . . [which] is perhaps the reason for the happy mingling of our people socially as well as commercially" [131] —reflected the sincere desire of both sides to live together in harmony and peace.

E. Social Change, 1918–1938

One of the effects of Thai government policy during the decades following the First World War was the intensification of in-group feeling among the Chinese—a turning inward in search of strength through unity. This tendency was reflected in two of the major trends within Chinese society between the wars—retarded assimilation and increased organizational activity.

Assimilation was slowed for several reasons. The sheer mass of Chinese immigration during the 1918–1932 period meant that Chinese communities everywhere in Thailand were larger and that the proportion, and consequently the influence, of the China-born within them was high. Even more important was the increasing numbers of Chinese women and of whole families among the immigrants, and the consequent decline of intermarriage between Chinese and Thai. Because of these developments, documented in Chapter 6, fewer of the new generation of local-born Chinese were born of Thai mothers or had other close Thai relatives. Proassimilationist influences within the home were everywhere decreased.

At the same time, the growth of Chinese schools during the period under review meant a rapid increase in the number of local-born children obtaining a Chinese education. While the number of local-born Chinese less than doubled between 1917 and 1937, Chinese educational facilities more than tripled. From 1918 to the outbreak of the Sino-Japanese War in 1937, travel to and from China was discouraged neither by war, nor by high fares or shipping shortages, nor for those resident in Siam by any but the most routine restrictions. Thus it was easy for Chinese parents to send their children back to China for study, and the practice was more common than it might otherwise have been because such a trip enabled boys to avoid conscription in Thailand.

The impetus to nationalist fervor and patriotism provided by the unification of China and Japanese aggression also drew local-born Chinese closer to Chinese society. Against this background, the growth of prejudice and Thai government policy—especially those measures discriminating against Thai nationals with alien fathers—further decreased the proportion who made a complete identification as Thai.

While Chinese assimilation was slowed, it was in no wise stopped. Fewer children of Chinese immigrants had Thai mothers, to be sure, but many had lukjin mothers whose commitment to the Chinese way of life and Chinese society was often limited. And in spite of educational progress, probably a majority of local-born Chinese children had no opportunity for formal Chinese schooling. Especially after 1933, fewer and fewer local-born children ever got back to their ancestral villages.

Furthermore, after 1910 it was no longer necessary to choose consciously between identification with Chinese or Thai society. Identification of the Chinese as Chinese was decreased by the abolition of the triennial tax (for the Chinese no longer had to wear wrist tags), by the abandonment of the queue after the Chinese revolution, and during the twenties by the gradual adoption by both Chinese and Thai men, especially in the upper social strata, of Western-style haircuts and clothing. Women were more conservative in matters of dress, but by the late thirties younger women of both ethnic groups were adopting permanent waves and a modified dress. Thus, while new pressures were mostly in the direction of commitment to Chinese society, few local-born Chinese were forced consciously to reject Thai society. In any case, the increasing tendency for Chinese to remain Chinese was coupled with growing permanence of settlement in Siam.

The Chinese reaction to the depression and the government's economic Thai-ification policies involved two developments of importance to the social structure. On the one hand, hard times led shopkeepers and merchants in almost every trade to organize. The T'ung-yeh-hui ("same business association") became the most widespread type of Chinese formal organization. Through them, businessmen in the same line could exchange information, formulate concerted action in the face of government regulation, operate to avoid excessive competition, and restrict entry of new entrepreneurs into the trade. The other Chinese response took a more sinister form—the recrudescence of secret societies in the old Hung-men tradition, complete with religious hocus-pocus and sworn brotherhood. They were organized along speech-group lines with the primary aim of preserving each group's share in the rapidly diminishing economic plums. The legitimate trade associations were established almost exclusively in Bangkok, while secret-society activity was up to 1937 largely restricted to the provinces, especially South Siam.[132]

Outside of the south, few provincial Chinese communities could any longer afford the luxury of speech-group division. Only in Chiangmai and Khorat, the two largest towns outside Bangkok, did formal Chinese organizations reflect speech-group cleavages. Elsewhere unity was achieved or maintained out of dedication to the Chinese Nationalist cause and the common danger perceived in Thai government policies. In many upcountry towns, the only formally constituted Chinese association was the Kuomintang Shu-pao-she, on which devolved responsibility for the Chinese school, temples, and cemetery. It is indicative that all upcountry Chinese cemeteries established during the thirties were community-wide undertakings supported by all speech groups.

As for speech-group power and prestige, the situation did not change radically from that obtaining just before the First World War. In the late thirties Teochius were still the most prestigeful and powerful group in Bangkok and northern Siam generally, while Hokkiens were of highest status in most parts of the south. The standing of Cantonese, whose general social and occupational position was second only to that of the Teochius by the early 1920's, declined somewhat during the late twenties and thirties when they lost considerable ground in such high-prestige occupations as rice milling, banking, and insurance. The standing of both Hakkas and Hainanese rose steadily. By the 1930's, there were several prominent and wealthy Hakkas among the community leaders of Bangkok, as well as a few Hainanese. The general trend, then, was in the direction of a leveling off in prestige differentials among the speech groups.

One of the most notable developments in Chinese formal organization during the period under review was the rapid increase in the number and scope of mutual-help and welfare associations. The Thai government, even after the 1932 revolution, was slow in extending public social welfare facilities. Its activities were primarily limited to general sanitation measures and the provision of free medical care at hospitals and clinics of inadequate capacity in Bangkok and the larger towns. The government took no measures that could be interpreted as providing social security, and labor welfare legislation was consistently defeated precisely because the bulk of nonagricultural labor was Chinese. In these circumstances the Chinese community utilized its own resources to provide these services, the need for which was increasingly felt after the First World War. Even in China, of course, it was traditionally not the government but private organizations and philanthropists who financed and organized welfare activities.

In fact, the very nature of local Chinese society fostered intra-community self-help. Poor Chinese still counted on raising their occupational status; upward mobility remained relatively high up to the depression, and the social values of the average laborer were not radically different from those of the elite. His employer was often his model, and his fellow workers his competitors in the struggle to get ahead. This was anything but fruitful grounds for the development of a class-conscious labor movement aiming to achieve welfare measures by militant means. Nevertheless, the poor were still poor and inadequately provided for. The elite, for their part, could achieve full prestige according to Chinese values only through generous philanthropy, morally motivated. The *ch'iao-ling* (C 118) or overseas Chinese leader was defined as a wealthy man who utilized part of his wealth in public service. A Chinese rice miller, who might show signs of apoplexy at the thought of increasing the daily wages of his mill "coolies" by two satang, would in all mellowness contribute the annual total of such an increase to a Chinese hospital or benevolent society. Chinese society warmly rewarded charity, but deprecated softness, or what in other times and places has been called enlightenment, in business. This peculiar paternalism and highly sanctioned philanthropy formed the foundation of most of the Chinese associations founded or expanded during the twenties and thirties.

Several of the smaller organizations in Bangkok were founded on surname lines. Unlike organized lineages in China, actual kinship was unimportant, and considerations of generation and age in the selection of leaders were entirely subordinate to those of wealth and standing in the local community. Most surname associations, however, were restricted to members from a particular hsien or even village in China, and none cut across speech-group lines. One of the major functions was usually the provision of funeral expenses for poor members and of memorial services for the more prominent members. Other mutual-aid associations were founded on a hsiang or hsien basis, with membership open only to natives of a particular district in China. The most important of these was the Ch'ao-an Mutual Aid Society, founded in 1927.

Another type of welfare organization which became prominent in Bangkok during the period under review was the *shan-t'ang* (C 119) or benevolent society—a type found all over China and especially well developed in Ch'ao-chou. Several small benevolent societies were founded in the nineteenth century on strict speech-group lines, but by the early 1920's, one of them, the Pao-te Shan-t'ang, became recognized as *the* benevolent society in Bangkok. Based on highly eclectic (Confucian, Buddhist, and Taoist) religious sanctions, its major activities were the collection and burial of corpses found on the streets and of unclaimed dead from the T'ien-hua Hospital, the provision of free coffins and burial to destitute families, and the organization of relief to victims of fires and floods. It maintained a free cemetery on the outskirts of town.

Yet another type of essentially mutual-aid organization was the Buddhist society. The most important of these, Chung-hua, Lung-hua, and Yi-ho, were founded in 1930, 1932, and 1935 respectively. Aside from contributions from wealthy members, the societies relied on regular monthly or annual membership dues. On the death of a member, a Buddhist society contributed substantially toward his funeral expenses and held religious services designed to secure the early release of his soul from limbo.

The T'ien-hua Hospital continued to be the mainstay of medical service in the Bangkok Chinese community. Originally founded to provide Chinese-style treatment, it expanded into Western medicine in the 1930's, when a modern medical department was added through the generous contribution of Wu Tso-nan, the most prominent of the Hakka leaders.[133] Another medical organization, the Chung-hua Charitable Clinic, was established in 1921 by Teochiu leaders to supplement the services of the Hospital. An out-patient clinic, it has always provided free (old Chinese-type) treatment, and, with the exception of the initial years and the depth of the depression, free drugs as well. It operated on the basis of the contributed services of some thirty Chinese doctors and regular subscriptions from supporting members.[134]

Speech-group associations also expanded their welfare activities during the period under review. The Cantonese Association was the most advanced in this regard. It had founded a cemetery in 1884 and a clinic in 1903. The exhaustion of the old cemetery led to the purchase and construction of a new Cantonese cemetery between 1931 and 1934, and at about the same time the old Cantonese clinic was reorganized as a hospital with both out-patient and in-patient departments.[135] In 1928, the Hakka Association took over the Hakka cemetery, founded originally in 1890. The Hainanese and Teochiu cemeteries, however, continued under separate auspices. Local Chinese cemeteries generally took on new importance as the Chinese population became more permanently settled. For lack of space, it became necessary to disinter remains from the "free graves" every few years and cremate them en masse—a practice unthinkable in China.

Another significant trend in Chinese formal organizations was evident between 1927 and 1938—the strengthening and reorganization of the major community associations, i.e., the Chamber of Commerce, and the speech-group associations. The intense reorganizational activity which characterized this period was a response to the increased pressure put on the Chinese by the Thai government. The community felt the need of more effective organizations, properly registered with the government, and of leaders with solid organizational backing who could deal directly with Thai officials. Protection from extreme government action became one of the most important functions expected of Chinese leaders.

The Hakka Association was the first to reorganize. A new constitution was drawn up in 1927, membership was regularized, and the Association was registered. In 1932 began a series of further changes which replaced the manager system with a committee system. By the mid-thirties, the executive and supervisory committees were regularly elected by the full association membership, and other committees— for education, publicity, athletics, and so on—were appointed by the chairman of the executive committee, i.e., the chief officer of the Association.[136]

The Chinese Chamber of Commerce also underwent significant

changes during this period. During the boom years of the late twenties, membership expanded and construction of a new and imposing headquarters was begun. The new buildings, occupied in 1930, were located not in the Chinese quarter but in the legation and consular district. As a matter of fact, the Chamber functioned by this time as something of an unofficial Chinese legation, negotiating with the Thai government on behalf of the local Chinese. This role was strengthened and the Chamber's standing enhanced in the community when the Chinese government appointed its chairman to be the new Chinese Commissioner of Commerce. Thereafter the Chamber issued consular invoices acceptable all over the Far East. Y. H. Tsan, the legal advisor to the Chamber of Commerce during the period of reorganization, has even compared the Chamber to a Magistrate's office in China:

In the old days, every "yamen" in Swatow had an official notice-board hung on either side of its gate. On the one was inscribed "instant arrest," and on the other "severe punishment." . . . Beside either board was hung an ear-like bamboo stick that was used for striking the posterior with. Now, on either side of the gate of the Chinese Chamber of Commerce was hung the official notice board and the bamboo stick—a regular Chinese "yamen" in Siam.[137]

These remarks, significantly, were made with the intention of imputing presumptuous ambitions to the Chamber leaders in Bangkok, with whom Tsan had fallen out.

The activities of the Chinese Chamber of Commerce were, in fact, all encompassing. In the year 1932–1933, for instance, it organized relief for the Shanghai war refugees, arranged for an exhibition in Bangkok of Chinese products, mediated the rickshaw-pullers' strike, arranged for the return to China of girls abducted to Bangkok for immoral purposes, assumed full responsibility to the Thai government for several hundred Chinese immigrants detained for failure to meet immigration requirements and eventually secured their legal entry, and founded and operated the biggest and best Chinese middle school in the country.[138] In 1933, the Chamber tightened its organization according to a new constitution, which provided for an executive committee of fifteen members and a supervisory committee of seven, to be elected by the full membership, and for the election by the committee members of the chairman, secretary, and treasurer.

The Cantonese Association underwent a complete reorganization after 1930. Still known at that time as the Kuang-chao Pieh-shu

(Cantonese Villa), it depended for operating expenses solely on contributions. Financial difficulties led initially to the appointment of a presidium to raise funds for the hospital, school, and cemetery, and when over a thousand regular supporters had been enlisted, it was decided in 1932 to reorganize as the Kuang-chao Tsung Pan-shih-ch'u (Cantonese General Office), with executive and supervisory committees elected every two years by the supporters. Finally in 1936, the organization succeeded in registering with the Thai government as a Hui-kuan (Association) and thereafter accepted members on a regular dues-paying basis.[139]

It was not until 1936 that the first steps were taken to organize the Teochiu Association in Bangkok. Prior to that time, unofficial headquarters for local Teochius were located in the buildings of one of the Teochiu schools, designated by a sign reading Ch'ao-chou Kung-so (Teochiu Meeting Place). Official histories of the Association indicate that the main motive of the fifty-five prominent Teochius who met in that year to set up a preparatory committee was the need to meet more effectively the unfavorable measures of the Thai government: "[At that time], overseas Chinese lived under increasingly hard conditions in their host country. . . . Unless they organized into a strong group, their existence was in danger." [140] The chairman of the preparatory committee was Yi Kuang-yen, chairman of the Chamber of Commerce and the chief leader of the strongly anti-Japanese elements. When the Sino-Japanese war broke out, the preparatory work was speeded up, and by February 1938 the Association was formally registered and fully organized according to what had by then become the standard system among Chinese associations: an executive committee of active leaders from whom were selected the chairman, secretary, and treasurer, and a supervisory committee of older and more experienced leaders. Within a few months of its establishment, the Teochiu Association was recognized as the most important Chinese organization next to the Chamber of Commerce itself. With the establishment of a speech-group-wide association for the Teochius, the Bangkok Chinese community as of 1938 was thoroughly and efficiently organized along modern lines.

⫸ 8 ⫷

CRISIS, WAR, AND RESPITE:

The Second World War

and Its Aftermath

A. *The Phibun Era, First Round*

IN DECEMBER 1938, the government of Phraya Phahon was forced to resign by a no-confidence vote in the Assembly, and he was replaced as Premier by Luang Phibun Songkhram, leader of the militaristic right-wing of the original People's Party and exponent of hyperna-tionalism. Luang Phibun kept the Interior portfolio himself and appointed Luang Pradit as Minister of Finance. It was a combination that promised radical changes in the areas of national life most affect-ing the Chinese. An event earlier in the year not unconnected with the change in government had, in fact, already given the Chinese an indication of what to expect. In July, Luang Wijit Wathakan, Director of the Fine Arts Department, gave an address in which he compared the Jewish problem in Germany to the Chinese problem in Thailand and implied that the Nazi solution might be applicable. The speech, in the nature of a trial balloon, aroused a vigorous political controversy during which Luang Wijit was defended by appointive Assemblymen of rightist persuasion. The whole episode contributed to the split between appointive and elective Assemblymen which brought about the fall of the Phahon cabinet.[1]

During its first year the new administration carried out an intensive program of economic Thai-ification and firmly adhered to the policy of containment in its dealings with the Chinese.

The new emphasis on Thai-ification of the economy became immediately apparent. In December 1938, the government formed the Thai Rice Company by buying out several Chinese mills in Bangkok.[2] The Company, 51 per cent of whose shares were held by the government, was given preferential rates by the state-owned railways for the transport of paddy and soon received heavy orders from Japan and Germany. Co-operative societies for the sale of rice were created in five localities, and in succeeding years the Company worked out close relations with co-operatives for the direct purchase of paddy. It was made explicit that the aim of the company was to free the Thai rice industry from Chinese control.[3]

In January 1939, a law was promulgated which reserved bird's-nests concessions, previously given to Chinese firms, for governmental development. In the same month, the Ministry of Education ordered all government schools and offices connected with the Ministry to permit only Thai food hawkers on their premises, and within a few months most of the other government Ministries had issued similar orders. Thousands of Chinese vendors were deprived, without warning, of their usual means of livelihood.[4]

In March and April came a spate of legislation that seemed to knock the economic props right out from under the Chinese. The Salt Act, passed in secret session March 22 and enforced eight days later, established firm government control over the production of salt and levied a heavy tax on the commodity. Most of the salt producers in Thailand were Chinese as were the five leading companies engaged in salt export. Enforcement of the law was so sudden and inefficient that many firms were forced into bankruptcy.[5] The Tobacco Act, passed at the same time and under the same circumstances, established similar controls and excise duties on tobacco production and manufacture. Three Chinese cigarette factories sold out to the government.[6] (Two years later, the Thai Tobacco Monopoly was established with exclusive rights concerning Virginia-type tobacco and the manufacture of modern-type cigarettes.) A few days after the passage of these two laws came the Act for the Slaughter of Animals for Food, aimed specifically at the replacement of Chinese by Thai as pig slaughterers and pork wholesalers. Under the provisions of the new law, Thai men for the first time in history began slaughtering and butchering pork in November 1939.[7]

The new Revenue Code passed by the Assembly on March 29 was designed to effect a 40 per cent increase in government income, in general by taxing the commercial class more heavily. It provided in particular for an income tax and shop tax—both of which would be borne primarily by alien merchants—and for increased fees for gambling, opium-den, and other operating licenses. The revised code was acclaimed by Thai public opinion as a move to help the poor Thai and put the financial burden of the country on the rich, especially the Chinese. To prevent merchants from passing on their new burden to the consumer, the Anti-Profiteering Act promulgated the previous December was strictly enforced.[8]

Another bill, passed that March and put into effect with the beginning of the new Thai year on April 1, hit hard at the pride if not the pocketbooks of Chinese merchants. It was the Signboard Act, which taxed signs according to area, but at rates ten times higher for boards more than half of which were devoted to non-Thai lettering. Overnight most of the large and handsome Chinese signboards were replaced by tiny plaques lettered in Thai as well as Chinese.[9]

The next move in the Thai-ification campaign was aimed at Chinese taxi drivers. According to amendments of the Vehicles Act effective April 10, persons of non-Thai nationality were no longer eligible to secure licenses to operate taxicabs.[10] The same day another law was promulgated—the Thai Vessels Act—which adversely affected the jobs of an even larger number of Chinese. According to this Act, all fishing and trading vessels over a specified gross tonnage operating in Thai territorial waters had to be registered by the following October as the property of Thai nationals or of corporations 70 per cent of whose capital was owned by shareholders of Thai nationality.[11] Even before the Thai Vessels Act went into effect, another law was passed which quite simply forbade the issuance of fishing licenses to aliens.[12]

The last of the Thai-ification laws passed in the fateful March and April of 1939, the Liquid Fuels Act, was indirectly one of the most disastrous for the Chinese. The Act strictly regulated the import, distillation, and marketing of petroleum, and at the time of its passage the government was already building an oil refinery with capacity output of gasoline in excess of the country's normal requirements. The two Western firms which had theretofore supplied all petroleum products could not accept the new terms and withdrew from the country in August. The firms' employees, most of whom were Chinese, were dismissed on a month's notice. Even more important, the entire distribution network of Chinese agents and subagents was largely by-passed as the petroleum industry passed into Thai hands.[13]

In May, the government announced that it would shortly begin mining operations in South Siam, and within a year it had successfully begun experimental mining with Thai labor on Samui and Pha-ngan islands.[14] In the fall of 1939 regulations were issued requiring both public and private industry to employ at least 75 per cent Thai national labor,[15] though the government made no real attempt to enforce them in the absence of Thai labor to replace Chinese nationals. The increasingly vigorous attempts to bring Thai into commercial and industrial life were put on a patriotic basis by the promulgation November 1 of the fifth Ratthaniyom (Cultural Mandate of the State) by Luang Phibun himself. It called on Thai patriots to eat food derived only from Thai produce by Thai manufacture, to wear clothing manufactured by Thai preferably of Thai cloth, and to assist one another in entering trade and industry.[16]

The government's program of economic Thai-ification, so intensively pursued during the twelve months beginning December 1938, completely stunned the Chinese community. After a few protests and petitions, the Chinese kept their own counsel and tried to devise ways of coming to terms with the rapidly deteriorating situation. All the restrictions were on the basis of nationality, not race, and so did not directly affect the great majority of local-born Chinese; China-born Chinese, however, by the end of 1939 were circumscribed in their economic activities to a degree largely unforeseen and, so it seemed to them, unjustified. It should be made clear that the legislation reviewed above scrupulously avoided singling out the Chinese; restrictions applied to all aliens of whatever nationality and were generally enforced without favoritism.

The new accent on Thai nationalism was manifested during the same period by a concerted campaign to contain Chinese nationalist and community activities within strict limits defined by the Thai government. As indicated in the previous chapter, Chinese illicit activities, both political and economic, were on the increase well before Luang Phibun came to power. The severe economic restrictions in 1938–1939, which primarily affected the Chinese, inevitably fostered a wave of smuggling, protection and extortion rackets, and other illegal money-making schemes. For the most part, these crimes were perpetrated by the revived secret societies, which appealed to patriotism with increasing persistence after the Sino-Japanese war began.

By the time Phibun came to power, there were several new kongsis in Bangkok, but their activities were designed as much to fight one another as to help China's cause. Kidnapping for ransom and prostitution protection accompanied violence against those conducting business activities which might help the Japanese.[17]

More important than the secret societies, however, were the political-action organizations established in 1937–1938 to aid the Chinese war effort. Their specific aims were the enforcement of the anti-Japanese boycott and the collection and remittance of funds for the Chinese national war fund. Activity to either end was illegal. The Thai government, eager to conciliate Japanese power, forbade the collection of funds for war purposes and considered the boycott a conspiracy in restraint of trade. Chinese patriotic organizations, therefore, had to operate underground or by subterfuge. The chief political-action group was the Hua-k'ang, organized by the Chinese Chamber of Commerce and, in keeping with the united-front policies in China, enjoying both Kuomintang and Communist support. In persuading Chinese merchants to make contributions and to refrain from handling Japanese goods, the Hua-k'ang increasingly resorted to force. Bombings, shootings, and kidnappings occurred with increasing frequency after the fall of 1938.

Within a few weeks after the change of government, the Thai police cracked down on all illegal Chinese activities. Arrests of Chinese leaders and political workers were stepped up early in January 1939, and while the Chinese were preoccupied with the celebrations and ceremonials of the Chinese New Year, the police conducted a series of raids on the headquarters of illicit Chinese societies.[18] Two centers of the Hua-k'ang were exposed and anti-Japanese circulars seized; one of the secret societies was raided while conducting an initiation ceremony. The Thai press carried the stories in full detail, and Thai public opinion was further crystallized when a member of the Hua-k'ang who had bombed a Chinese store selling Japanese merchandise was captured by the police and "confessed all."

To collect funds for China's war effort in spite of government bans, the Chinese community resorted to subterfuge on a grand scale. The Teochiu Association founded the Ch'ao-chou Controlled-Price Rice Company as a means of getting aid to Swatow in the form of donated rice. The Ch'ao-an Mutual Aid Society organized a fund-raising drive for famine relief in Ch'ao-an. Many collections were also made clandestinely. In Chiangmai, the Chiu-kuo Hou-yüan Hui (Association for Backing National Salvation) secretly collected a monthly subscription from almost all Chinese businessmen. In 1939, however, the financial help Chinese in Thailand could render to their homeland was greatly curtailed as a result of police action. The responsible officers of the Ch'ao-an Mutual Aid Society—two of the chief Chinese community leaders in Bangkok—were imprisoned on grounds that any relief for a country at war is *ipso facto* for war purposes. Over thirty Chinese leaders and businessmen in Chiangmai were arrested when the police uncovered the subscription system there. Mass deportations were avoided only because one leader took on full responsibility for the campaign and convinced the courts that a one-man operation could hardly be a society, illegal or otherwise, and that the monies collected were for Yellow River flood relief. The Teochiu Association's scheme had to be discontinued when Swatow fell to the Japanese in June 1939.

Meanwhile the new administration had tightened its control of Chinese schools and newspapers. In March 1939, the President of the Assembly warned, with regard to the bills directed at the Chinese then under consideration by the Assembly, that "if wrong reports were published or important news interpreted in such a way that any harm might occur, he would be obliged to withdraw Press permits issued to the newspapers concerned." [19] In April, the Ministry of Education issued new orders that students in the compulsory age limits (seven to fourteen) could study Chinese language only two hours a week and that all other subjects must be taught in Thai. Strict inspections were resumed, and during the months of April through July, twenty-five Chinese schools were closed by the authorities.[20]

During the same period the government adopted measures with regard to the capitation tax that brought the tortuous history of that levy around the full circle. It will be recalled that, between 1899 and 1910, Chinese paid the triennial tax but were exempt from the larger capitation tax levied on the Thai. This injustice had been rectified in 1910 by the elimination of the triennial tax and the extension of the capitation tax to all regardless of nationality. In March 1939, however, the capitation tax was abolished by the passage of the new Revenue Code, while a tax of similar magnitude was levied on non-Thai nationals in the form of an "alien-registration fee." By July 7 all Chinese nationals had to pay the first annual four-baht fee or risk arrest.[21] It was now the Chinese' turn to complain of subjection to a tax not levied on the Thai.

The grand climax in the government's containment policy came in a series of police raids beginning the third week of July and extending through August.[22] Schools, printing presses, newspaper offices, and Chinese association headquarters were searched, pamphlets and documents seized, and several hundred arrests made. Evidence was gathered to show that Chinese schools, newspapers, and banks worked in close alliance with the undercover societies. For instance, the Oversea Chinese Bank was found to hold disguised deposits of 800,000 baht from merchants and societies presumably destined for China's war chest; the printing press publishing the *Kuo-min Jih-pao* was discovered to house the meeting hall of the Kuomintang; and several Chinese schools were found to be actively distributing Hua-k'ang and Kuomintang literature.[23] One of the raids in late August yielded a membership list of the Kuomintang with over ten thousand names.[24] The position of the Chinese was not helped by the disclosure by Bangkok newspapers in August that the Thailand Chinese had contributed $2,400,000 to the Chinese war cause between November 1938 and April 1939.[25] Of those arrested, many were sentenced to imprisonment, while some of the most prominent—including the managers of the Bank of Canton and the Oversea Chinese Bank, as well as a score of illegal society leaders—were deported.

Far more disastrous consequences of the raids were the permanent closure in July and August of all Chinese newspapers, large and small, with the sole exception of the *Chung-yüan Pao,* and the closure in August and September of all the larger important Chinese schools.[26] The Chinese community was stunned by these drastic measures. As a Thailand Chinese writer later put it: "The overseas Chinese in Siam were in a desperate situation. Their cultural achievements were almost all destroyed, and their economic position was tottering." [27]

The Chinese had yet to sustain another blow during that first year of the Phibun administration. On November 23, Yi Kuang-yen, the chairman of the Chinese Chamber of Commerce and treasurer of the Teochiu Association, was assassinated in a daring crime that attracted nationwide interest. The police arrested two Chinese who later confessed to the murder, explaining that the assassinated man was head of the Hua-k'ang itself and identifying previous murders and terrorist acts carried out by the organization.[28] The episode caused the Thai government to regard the Chamber of Commerce and the other main legitimate Chinese associations with undisguised suspicion and weakened the ranks and prestige of the Chinese community leaders just as their services were most needed.

These events during 1939 caused increasing concern in other parts of Southeast Asia and in China. In April, the First People's Assembly of China passed a resolution requesting the Ministry of Foreign Affairs "to start treaty negotiations with Siam in order to improve Sino-Siamese relations and to protect the overseas Chinese in Siam." [29] To meet mounting criticism from abroad, the Thai government in August 1939 sent an official communiqué to foreign governments pointing out that the recent actions against the Chinese were designed solely to maintain public order and in no way impaired the country's traditional foreign policy of equal friendship for all. This was followed by broadcasts in the Chinese language—for the first time in the history of the government radio station—justifying the government's actions for the benefit not only of local Chinese but of those in Malaya, Hongkong, and China.[30] In September, Chinese leaders were invited to a party well attended by Thai officials, at which friendly speeches were once again exchanged.[31] And in November, the Premier himself broadcast to the local Chinese an extended justification of government policy.

At the end of November, when full reports of the events of the previous August had been studied in Chungking, President Chiang Kai-shek telegraphed Premier Luang Phibun requesting

that the Government of Thailand give full protection to the lives and property of Chinese citizens residing in your country and permit them to engage in their lawful pursuits without molestations as heretofore. Measures of protection accorded by your Government to Chinese residents at this time of our national trial will be the more appreciated by the Chinese government and people and will result in the mutual benefit of Thailand and China.[32]

This elicited a prompt reply from Luang Phibun which stated in part:

Thailand gives full protection to the lives and property of all foreigners residing in this country and permits them to engage in their lawful pursuits on the same footing of equality.The Chinese residents, through their agelong traditional friendship with the Thai people, are also regarded with a fraternal feeling of friendship, and I may assure Your Excellency, therefore, of the constant care with which His Majesty's government afford protection to the lives and property of the Chinese residents in this country, as well as permit them to engage in their lawful pursuits throughout the Kingdom.[33]

It has been suggested by some Chinese writers, and not unreasonably, that the Thai government moderated its policy toward the Chinese in September 1939 because the unexpectedly stout resistance of China and the declarations of war against the Axis in Europe convincingly demonstrated the power and determination of the democratic Allies.[34]

It may also be that certain of the administration's recent measures were too extreme for some of the more liberal Thai nationalists in the "coup" group of government leaders.

In any case, the most active phase of the anti-Chinese campaign was over for the time being. The government nonetheless held firmly to its containment policy. In January 1940, Luang Phibun told a press conference that one newspaper should suffice for the Chinese community, since the Western community was served by only one Western-language paper and inasmuch as over half the Chinese in Thailand could read Thai.[35] At the same press conference, the Premier indicated that the government had abandoned assimilation as an aim of Thai policy toward the Chinese. He said that it would be better for the nation if civil officials refrained from marrying aliens; and for "the average citizen who lived in close proximity to the Chinese" he proffered the advice that Thai should marry Thai for their greater happiness.[36] In February 1940, a brother of Hsiao Fo-ch'eng broadcast in Siamese from Chungking urging that Thailand agree to the establishment of diplomatic relations with China, but the Thai government ignored the appeal.[37] In March, Phibun issued the seventh Ratthaniyom, in which he exhorted every able-bodied Thai person "to establish himself securely in some form of economic endeavor" [38]—an attempt to get the Thai into the occupations vacated by Chinese as a result of the 1939 legislation.

In education too, the line was firmly held. A few of the Chinese schools closed in August and September 1939 were allowed to reopen as compulsory private schools, with instruction entirely in Thai and only a few hours of Chinese language instruction per week. Many of the largest Bangkok schools, however, were refused registration as Chinese schools; some changed their names and registered as regular Thai private schools, teaching no Chinese whatsoever.[39] In June 1940, Phibun issued the ninth Ratthaniyom, which extended the Thai culture program to the areas of language usage. In essence it required all Thai nationals to know and use the Thai language.[40] It was aimed specifically at local-born Chinese (and Malays), who had never learned or did not habitually use Thai. The ninth Ratthaniyom was the signal for a mass closure of Chinese schools, on one pretext or another, throughout the country. By the end of 1940, there were no Chinese schools as such in operation outside of Bangkok. In the capital itself, the number was reduced to two by 1941.[41]

Vigilance was also maintained in the political realm. A new wave of arrests began in February 1940.[42] The local Chinese were by no means completely cowed, however, and activities to help the cause of China and resist the Japanese advance continued. The steady infiltration of Japanese merchants was hindered by Chinese opposition, occasionally mounting to violence. The Chinese hospitals in Bangkok continued training nurses to be sent to China for service with the army, but this practice was stopped in 1940, and the superintendent of the Hua-ch'iao Hospital [43] and the chairman of the T'ien-hua Hospital were both deported to China. Funds were still sent to Chungking via Hong-kong and Malaya. In the spring of 1941, representatives of several Chinese associations in Thailand attended the conference of Nan-yang Chinese held at Singapore. The message which the gathering cabled to Chungking was a great morale booster for the Thailand Chinese. It read in part:

The conference of delegates of Chinese in the South Seas, including the Philippines, Malaya, Dutch East Indies, Thailand and Indo-China, was held on March 29 at Singapore. . . . We wish to pledge the fullest support of the National Government, our Generalissimo, Chiang Kai-shek, and also the national policy of resistance and reconstruction. This firm resolve will not compromise or change, but will remain firm. We will lead all Chinese over-seas to continue such efforts.[44]

As Thailand drew closer to Japan during 1941, the number of Chinese arrests and deportations on grounds of anti-Japanese activity in-creased. By the outbreak of the Pacific war, several thousand Chinese —nationalists of all political colorings—had been deported by Phibun's regime as undesirable aliens.[45]

Even before the Pacific war began, Phibun found it necessary to forget the earlier assurances to Generalissimo Chiang that his govern-ment would permit Chinese residents "to engage in their lawful pur-suits throughout the Kingdom." On May 23, 1941, a royal decree was issued naming Lopburi jangwat, Prajinburi jangwat, and the district of Sattahip in Chonburi jangwat as strategic "prohibited areas." Aliens were thereafter forbidden to enter, and those already residing in these areas were forced to leave within ninety days.[46] Lopburi and Sattahip were, according to Phibun's master plan, being developed as Thailand's main military base and naval base, respectively, while Prajinburi, on the Cambodian border, contained Thailand's only through rail connection with Indochina. When some opposition to this decree was expressed in the Assembly, an enabling act was pushed through in July approving the designation by decree of areas prohibited to aliens.[47] On September 19, 1941, presumably because army bases were located there, the three amphoes which included the municipalities of Khorat, Ubon, and Warinchamrap (across the river from Ubon) were also named as prohibited areas. All aliens had to evacuate these areas by December 17.[48]

The hardships borne by Chinese aliens in the six areas prohibited to them in 1941 were great indeed.[49] There was a delay of weeks in some cases before the local authorities were officially notified, and much more of the ninety-day period of grace was eaten up before the local Chinese knew the full details of their fate. Some Chinese aliens had local-born children or relatives who could look after their shops and property, but a majority had to sell out or at least close up shop before evacuating. In most cases the Chinese could take very little with them because the government refused to allocate extra freight cars to the prohibited areas. Hundreds of shops sold their entire inventories to Thais at a fraction of their value. The Cantonese Association of Khorat was forced to sell the premises of its school, Ming-yi, for a ridiculously small sum. While this case was not unique, most Chinese schools and associations in the prohibited areas persuaded second-generation Chinese to stay behind and take responsibility for their real property. Any alien who wanted to enter the prohibited areas to clear up personal or business matters prior to the ninety-day deadline had to obtain written permission from the Ministry of Interior. Those who entered the areas in ignorance of the ban were often arrested by zealous police. During 1941, hundreds of refugees arrived in Bangkok, but most of the alien evacuees descended on nearby jangwat and amphoe towns which had no facilities to handle the influx.

The 1941 prohibitions could have been worse—and would have been immeasurably so had they applied to Thai citizens of alien descent as well as to aliens. In this sense, the regulations which affected the Chinese in Siam were far more just than those applying to Japanese in the United States shortly after Pearl Harbor. Nevertheless, the treatment accorded the Chinese in 1941 was "a far cry from the traditional tolerance and humanity of the Thai."[50] There is considerable evidence, in fact, that the government consciously had to prepare public opinion in advance of its extreme measures against the Chinese during 1938–1941, and that Thai opposition to the administration's policies was relatively slight only because the militarist clique in power could appeal to a feeling of national, military emergency. A

Chinese businessman who visited Siam in June 1939 wrote that the whole anti-Sinitic movement in Thailand "appeared to have had an artificial origin—it lacked the character of a general feeling against the Chinese." [51] Ill feeling toward the Chinese was rapidly spreading from the elite to the common people, however. By 1940, numerous instances were reported in Bangkok of violence between Chinese and Thai on grounds of ethnic animosity. [52]

B. The Japanese Occupation

On December 8, 1941, Japanese troops landed in Thailand, and under the circumstances the government decided to co-operate with the Japanese forces. The next day arrests of Chinese in any way connected with the Chungking regime began. The important Chinese leaders in Bangkok met varying fates. A few fled the capital and made their way overland to Burma and China; others went into hiding upcountry. The majority, however, remained in Bangkok; of these the openly pro-Chiang individuals were arrested, and many of the others enticed to co-operate in the pursuit of "Co-prosperity."

By the end of January 1942, the ranks of the old Chinese leaders were sadly depleted. The most prominent of the prewar Teochiu leaders, Yi Kuang-yen, had already been assassinated, and three of the other top leaders arrested or deported before the Japanese occupation. In December 1941 and January 1942, the chairman and three executive-committee members of the Teochiu Association were arrested after refusing collaboration and sentenced on one charge or another to long imprisonment. At least three other prominent Teochiu leaders fled upcountry to avoid arrest. The Hainanese had been similarly stripped of their top leadership. Their three most important leaders had been deported prior to December 1941, and in that month the chairman of the Ch'iung-tao Hui-so (Hainanese Association) was arrested by the Japanese. Leadership of the other speech groups was also weakened, but to a lesser degree.

Most of the smaller Chinese associations ceased operation during the occupation, but the Chamber of Commerce and the major speech-group associations elected to continue on whatever basis proved possible. These decisions were made in hopes of forestalling confiscation or requisition of association properties as well as of continuing efforts to protect Chinese interests. Accordingly new elections were held by several associations in 1942 to replace arrested or "compromised" officers; in some cases individuals thought to be in a position which would facilitate effective dealings with Japanese authorities were deliberately elected. The difficulties of Chinese associations were compounded by the freezing of bank deposits of Chinese nationals on December 10, 1941. Lack of funds forced the Cantonese Association, for instance, to abandon the Western medicine and obstetrics departments of its hospital.[53]

The Japanese initially sought to win the support of the Chinese population by refraining from discriminatory action against Chinese as such, by acts symbolic of Sino-Japanese friendship, through control of the Chinese press, and by holding out economic favors for merchants who could see their way to co-operate. In Thailand there was no parallel to the mass executions of Chinese which occurred in Malaya. When the Japanese Commander arrived in Bangkok, he called on the chairmen of the leading Chinese associations. At the Pao-te Benevolent Society, he made obeisances to the Society's patron deity and contributed 1,000 baht. Having arrested most of the directors and driven the editor into hiding with a price of 100,000 baht on his head, the Japanese took over the *Chung-yüan Pao*, the only Chinese newspaper licensed by the Thai, and ran it as a propaganda organ for the duration of the occupation. Under a Chinese editor, the paper attained a certain amount of respectability and, widely read because of its commercial and local news, maintained some of its preoccupation influence. Few Chinese could afford complete and open opposition to Japanese commercial interests, for it involved economic ruin if not imprisonment. A few of the merchants who responded wholeheartedly to Japanese advances made fortunes during the war.

The Japanese pose of benevolence toward the local Chinese was badly shaken, however, by the treatment accorded forced Chinese labor on defense and communications projects in Thailand. The largest of these was the railway constructed from Banpong to the Burmese border, begun at the end of the 1942 monsoon and completed in October 1943. In December 1942, Kanjanaburi jangwat, through which most of the railroad was to pass, was designated a prohibited area, but in this case aliens were given only seven days to evacuate. At this point in the occupation, the Japanese were more considerate of the Chinese than were the Thai, and Japanese trucks and boats were put at the disposal of Chinese aliens to move families and belongings. In keeping with their "Asia for the Asiatics" propaganda line, the Japanese used only Western prisoners of war as laborers during the first months of railroad construction.[54] But early in 1943, the need for additional labor became so acute that tens of thousands of Asian workers were recruited in Malaya, Indonesia, and South Siam and sent up past Banpong for work on the line. Most of them, attracted by wages of three dollars a day, had signed a three-month contract for "engineering work," but many others had been forcibly recruited. Several tens of thousands of Chinese laborers—the other Asian workers were primarily Tamil, Malay, and Javanese—were employed, the bulk of whom were Hokkiens from Malaya. It is conservatively estimated by Allied personnel that 50 per cent of them died before the year was out. Working conditions of the Asian labor were "unspeakably terrible," and it was believed by medical authorities that more than half of the lives lost could have been saved by relatively trifling expenditures for drugs and food. As John Coast summed it up, the Japanese "regarded their fellow Asiatics as machines pure and simple, and utterly failed to regard them as men—as human beings." [55] When cholera hit the Asian workers' camp, the European Medical Officer was forbidden to waste time in treatment. Aside from cholera, the main killers were dysentery, malaria, dietary deficiencies, and tropical ulcers. The project became known in all languages as the Railroad of Death. Other Japanese installations in Siam used conscript labor, part of which consisted of Chinese from south China as well as Malaya. Chinese also worked on construction projects at Phetchabun after that isolated town was selected by Phibun to be the wartime capital.

Defence considerations not unrelated to the Japanese campaign in Burma caused the Thai government in late January 1943 to apply its prohibited-areas policy in the north. Six whole jangwats—Chiangmai, Lamphun, Lampang, Chiangrai, Phrae, and Uttaradit—were declared out of bounds for aliens, and thousands of Chinese had to evacuate by April. In several jangwats the Chinese were given only seven weeks effective notice. The hardships experienced by the northeastern Chinese in 1941 were not only repeated but compounded by the fact that such a vast and contiguous area was banned all at once. Chinese in the areas served by railroad stations below Lampang invariably found all cars filled to overflowing with refugees from farther north, and freight cars were almost impossible to obtain. The panic was increased by a widespread rumor—in some jangwats never effectively denied by responsible authorities prior to the April deadline—that wives of aliens, even when they were Thai citizens, had to evacuate with their husbands. In order to maintain property and avoid forced sales of shop inventories, some Chinese legally divorced their Thai wives. It should be pointed out, however, that certain of the jangwat governors were extremely benevolent in enforcing the regulations. The governor of Chiangmai, for instance, exempted pregnant women, the disabled and aged, and those whose children were serving in the Thai army or in government service.

Some of the evacuees from Phrae went to Nan—Nan and Maehǫng-sǫn, both remote and underdeveloped jangwats, were not included in the prohibited area—but most went on south, especially to Phitsanu-lok, Sawankhalok, and Bangkok. Many of the refugees who poured into Bangkok in April 1943 were induced to sign contracts for work on the Railway of Death. Recruitment was carried on by Japanese and Thai authorities through the Chinese Chamber of Commerce.

The expulsion of Chinese aliens from Lopburi, Khorat, and Ubon in 1941 had been followed by economic paralysis and acute food short-ages in those towns. To prevent a repetition of this situation, the authorities of most of the prohibited jangwats in the north, either before the April deadline or within two months thereafter, exempted such alien industrialists as rice millers, sawmillers, and ice-plant opera-tors, and such key food producers as market gardeners, pig slaughterers, and duck raisers. Even merchants could get back to their homes by becoming suppliers for the Japanese troops or taking jobs with the Japanese commercial firms which were expanding their operations at this time. Others were allowed to return for short periods to dis-pose of real property or take care of urgent business. By midyear it was made clear that aliens who applied for naturalization could reside in prohibited areas even while their applications were pending. More than 5,000 Chinese aliens were able to return to their homes in the north by this means. (During the six years 1935–1942, applications by Chinese for naturalization had averaged less than 170 annually, but in 1943 no less than 6,086 Chinese took out papers, of whom 2,761 were granted naturalization.) [56] By the end of 1943, so many exemptions had been made that the ban was void for all practical purposes. In hindsight, many Chinese in the north feel that military security was only the ostensible reason for prohibiting the northern jangwats to aliens and that the real purpose was economic Thai-ification. If this is true, the Japanese gained as much as the Thai, for most of the larger economic plums lost by the Chinese in the north in 1943 fell to Japanese firms rather than to Thai enterprise.

Direct measures toward economic Thai-ification were not neglected during the occupation. Price-control measures were strengthened in

1942 and heavy penalties fixed for profiteering and hoarding; in consequence, Chinese merchants experienced a severe cost-price squeeze
as the inexorable inflation progressed.[57] By a royal decree issued in
June 1942, the Thai government reserved for Thai nationals the pursuit of twenty-seven different occupations and professions.[58] Aliens
were allowed three months to stop the manufacture (and in a few
cases, the sale) of lacquer and nielloware, dolls and toys, umbrellas,
women's hats and dresses, fireworks, certain kinds of wickerware,
bricks, firewood, charcoal, and torches. They were given a year to
cease hairdressing and the practice of law. Two of the reservations
had a special nationalistic twist: aliens were forbidden to manufacture or sell images of the Buddha, or to work as typesetters using
Thai letters. In 1942, the government also passed the Occupational
and Professional Assistance Act, which provided that by royal decree
factories could be required to employ a minimum percentage of Thai
citizens.[59] The newly created Ministry of Industry, however, never
felt up to coping with the disruption which would have followed
such a decree. As it was, the government experienced difficulty in
securing Thai to fill the positions left vacant by these and earlier
reservations. A Bangkok radio broadcast in April 1943 complained:
"The Government has done its utmost to urge Thais to sell rice and
pigs, but they refused and the Chinese are holding the whole trade.
Schools were opened to teach Thai hairdressing, but no pupils appeared." [60]

Of even greater long-term significance to the Chinese than the occupational reservations was the passage of a bill in 1943 which effectively prohibited Chinese nationals from buying land in Siam. The
Land Pertaining to Aliens Act (B.E. 2486) denied aliens not protected
by special treaties the right to purchase immovable property, though
it did not require them to dispose of land already owned. Thus two
of the basic economic freedoms traditionally underlying Chinese assimilation in Thailand—the rights to reside anywhere in Siam and
to own property without restriction—were severely impaired during
the war years.

By 1943, there were several well-organized underground groups
operating against the Japanese in Thailand. The Free Thai movement,
headed in the country by the Regent, Luang Pradit, was by far the
most important of these, and several Chinese underground organizations worked in more or less close co-operation with it. The Chungking government had sent special agents into Thailand in 1941 in

expectation of a Japanese advance into the country,[61] and espionage contacts were quickly established between the local Kuomintang leaders and Free China. The Kuomintang underground published several small newspapers during the occupation, perhaps the most influential of which was *Ching Pao* (C 120), issued fairly regularly from 1942 until after V-J Day. Chinese Communists—whose united-front alliance with the Kuomintang had been in abeyance since before the Japanese landed—organized their own underground, under Major Ch'iu Chi (C 121). During part of the occupation they published a newspaper in Bangkok called *Chen-hua Pao* (C 122).[62] Both groups relied on contributions and exactions from local Chinese merchants. One of the strangest enterprises of the war years was the *T'ai-hua Shang-pao* (C 123), a full-sized Chinese paper which began publication only semiclandestinely early in 1943. It was published in conjunction with a Thai newspaper whose responsible person was Phraya Pricha, a son-in-law of Phibun. The paper was Thai-owned, but, while it was backed by such Free Thai leaders as Luang Adun Detcharat and employed several of the most anti-Japanese Chinese newspapermen, it reportedly operated with the full knowledge of Phibun himself! The *T'ai-hua Shang-pao* was published regularly until early 1946.

It is impossible to estimate the amount or degree of "collaboration" on the part of Chinese leaders in Thailand, much less to pass judgment. Many of those who pursued "business as usual" with the Japanese provided a continual stream of funds for the undergound. Moreover, without their leadership and support the Chinese associations which did so much to alleviate distress of the local Chinese during the war would have floundered. In the case of the Hakkas, for instance, their chief leader continued operation of his extensive businesses, but functioned simultaneously as "treasurer" for the Chungking agents. Another prominent Hakka who worked openly for the Japanese nonetheless contributed 75,000 baht to be split between the Free Thai and the Kuomintang underground, and another, less openly pro-Japanese, also donated large sums. One Hakka businessman made a fortune in Japanese textiles during 1942–1943, but ended up soliciting funds for the Chungking cause and supplying khaki cloth for underground troop uniforms. All of these men kept the Hakka Association functioning during the war—one served as chairman, two others as executive committee members. They helped maintain the Association's free clinic, cemetery, and even school (on a purely Thai-language basis), and organized relief during emergencies.

On the whole the major Chinese associations served the community well during the occupation. In the fall of 1942, Bangkok suffered one of the most disastrous floods in its history, and the most effective relief provided in the city was organized by the Chinese Chamber of Commerce and the major Chinese speech-group and charity associations. Rice was distributed to over 160,000 persons, Thai as well as Chinese. When Chinese from the upcountry "prohibited areas" arrived in Bangkok early in 1943, the Teochiu Association devoted its major energies and funds for several months to solving problems of their adjustment.[63] When, in the latter part of 1943, Allied bombings of Bangkok became more severe, the Chinese associations formed a standing committee to organize first-aid and disaster relief. The Pao-te Benevolent Society did an excellent job of collecting the wounded and dead in the Chinese districts of the city during air raids and administering treatment or providing burials.[64]

For the last year of the occupation, pressure on the Chinese from the Thai government relaxed at the same time that the Japanese persecution grew more ruthless. In July 1944, the Phibun government was ousted by parliamentary means, and Free Thai leaders took over the administration even as the Japanese looked on. Relations between the Free Thai and Chungking were strengthened at the top level,[65] and in the underground, Kuomintang, Free Thai, and Allied agents worked closely together. One KMT leader in Bangkok during 1944–1945 worked for Khuang Aphaiwong's government, served as chief of liaison with the Chinese regarding the secret airports being prepared for Allied use, and even shielded two Allied airmen from the Japanese. The new Khuang government, on its part, reduced the number of occupations reserved for Thais from twenty-seven to four in November 1944 and soft-pedaled other anti-Chinese policies inherited from Phibun. A week after the Japanese surrender, a royal decree reopened all prohibited areas to aliens.[66] The Chinese in Thailand had reason to hope that the postwar era would find a friendly government in power, able and willing to effect a lasting reversal of the hated policy of containment.

C. Sino-Thai Relations, 1945–1948

Within a month or two after V-J Day, it appeared that peace was as disruptive of Sino-Thai friendship as war. Both the Chinese, as nationals of one of the Big Five powers, and the Free Thai were wont to exaggerate their role in the Allied victory over Japan. The numerous Thai and Chinese celebrations held during August and September touched off continual disputes, often involving the Thai police. One of the sore points was the Chinese inclination to fly Chinese flags in conjunction only with those of the other Big Five powers, in spite of the Thai insistence that any foreign flags flown in Siam must be accompanied by the Thai colors as well. On September 21, one of these disputes developed into a serious clash between Chinese and Thai, both police and armed civilians, on Yaowarat Road in the center of the Chinese quarter.[67] Leaders of the Chinese associations had been invited by Allied military authorities to attend a special military film that evening at the principal theater on Yaowarat Road. Before the showing could commence, gunfire on the street outside disrupted the gathering; instead of a military newsreel, they witnessed firsthand a display of Thai military power such as had seldom been seen during the war.

The police at one point attempted to break up a hostile Chinese demonstration with a bayonet charge and machine-gun fire, and Thai troops in full battle array were dispatched to the scene. Fighting and sniping continued unabated through the twenty-second, when seven dead were counted. By this time the whole Chinese quarter had been barricaded off by Thai military authorities, and a 7 P.M. curfew proclaimed. Armed cars and tanks patrolled the streets; soldiers, police, and even student cadets armed with rifles and machine guns occupied air-raid shelters which doubled as pillboxes. Chinese snipers operated from the upper floors and roofs of the Chinese buildings lining the street. During the three days of confusion and anarchy which followed, scores of shops and homes were looted, and armed robbery was common.

Responsibility for the so-called Yaowarat Incident has never been officially fixed, but it is clear that extremists on both sides share the blame. There is considerable evidence that extreme elements in the KMT supported the Chinese gunmen [68] and that the Thai militarists used harsher tactics in suppression of the riots than had been authorized by the responsible government leaders. M. R. Seni Pramot, the Free Thai leader in America during the war, had taken office as Premier only three days before the incident, and his control of the situation was unavoidably incomplete.

In August, the five major Chinese speech-group associations plus the Chiang-che Association had formed a joint organization to provide over-all leadership in the postwar period.[69] Representatives of this organization managed to get around the barricades for a meeting on the morning of September 23 to seek a solution to the crisis. They formed an inter-speech-group Public Relations Committee, which proceeded to contact both Thai and Allied military authorities. On the twenty-fourth, the Committee was received by Premier Seni, who assured the Chinese that the incident was as unexpected as it was deplorable. The Committee requested that the military blockades be removed and the army and special police withdrawn to avoid further bloodshed. The Premier complied, traffic was resumed, and some shops opened. When robberies and looting of Chinese shops and homes continued unabated the night of the twenty-fifth, practically all Chinese stores closed again, and the Chinese Committee determined to see Luang Pradit, then a popular Thai hero but without actual portfolio in the government. He could do no more than promise to forward the Committee's wishes to the proper authorities. On the twenty-sixth, Committee representatives approached the Thai Director of the Publicity Department—who had been to China during the war as a Free Thai emissary and there been well treated by Thailand Chinese in exile—in hopes of calming the Thai press. The Director promised to screen carefully all news releases to avoid inflammatory statements. But incidents continued and business was still at a standstill, so the Committee, on the twenty-seventh, approached the British Major-General in charge of Allied troops and requested his protection. The General explained that he had no power to interfere with the Thai administration and that he could do nothing unless the Chinese government persuaded General MacArthur to issue specific orders. It is difficult to know just how much these activities of the Chinese Committee contributed to the improvement of the situation which was noticeable after the twenty-seventh. In any case, Thai police had robberies under control by the twenty-ninth, and on the thirtieth normal business was resumed in the Chinese quarter.

In the succeeding weeks, leaders of both the Thai government and the Chinese community were agreed that co-operative measures should be taken to prevent the recurrence of such unfortunate incidents, and on the government's suggestion a Sino-Thai Security Corps was formed in October to enforce the "peace." Representatives of all major Chinese associations met and elected sixteen men to a Security Corps committee. Most of the sixteen were civilian business leaders, but also included were Colonel Liu K'un (C 124), who had served with the Chinese Army during the war, and Major Ch'iu Chi, the

Chinese Communist wartime leader. A Thai rear admiral served as Commander of the Corps, with Colonel Liu as his assistant. Other Corps officers were provided fifty-fifty by Thai Military Police and the Chinese committee. Several hundred Corps members, Chinese and Thai in equal numbers, were recruited by the two sides and provided with special uniforms. For over four months the Corps, whose headquarters were in the Teochiu Association buildings on Songwat Road, patrolled and stood guard in the major Chinese districts, with authority to arrest other military and police personnel as well as civilians. Several hundred cases were successfully handled by the Corps in one of the most convincing demonstrations of Sino-Thai co-operation ever seen in Thailand. Expenses for the Chinese half of the Security Corps, amounting to over 100,000 baht, were met entirely by the Chinese associations.

Meanwhile, the reaction in Chungking to news of the Yaowarat Incident threatened to exacerbate the difficult situation in Bangkok and posed a knotty problem for the Thai government. During the war, many Kuomintang nationalists in Free China came to regard Thailand as an enemy country. In 1943, Professor Yüan Chen, a member of the Chinese People's Political Council, wrote for Western consumption that "for a limited number of years, some sort of international supervision should be exercised over the affairs of Thailand." [70] The Chinese attitude was spelled out more completely in 1945 by Chen Su-ching of the National Southwest Associated Universities in Kunming:

As for Thailand, undoubtedly her guilt is too obvious to be excused. . . . While Thailand may retain her territorial rights, she should not be allowed to do those things which she was free to do before the Japanese invasion. In other words, after the war, some sort of external guidance is necessary not only in her foreign conduct but also in her internal affairs, for at least a certain length of time. . . .

Concerning China's relations with Thailand, it would seem a matter of course that, first of all, the latter should abolish all the restrictions or discriminations solely or mainly against the Chinese, and that at least the conditions concerning the Chinese before 1930 should be restored. Any wrongs done to the Chinese as a result of these restrictions or discriminations . . . should be redressed. It is needless to add that those who have been responsible for these acts should be severely punished, for their guilt is no less than the war criminals in Germany or in Japan.

Moreover, Thailand should no longer refuse the exchange of diplomatic envoys between herself and China. . . . Under the control of Japan, . . .

Thailand is compelled to accept the diplomatic agents of the Chinese puppet government. This being the case, she has no reason to refuse Chinese diplomatic agents after the war.

Every Chinese should be left free to choose his or her own citizenship regardless of whether or not he was born in Thailand . . . [and the Chinese] should have a voice in the politics of Thailand so that at least their economic and other interests may be guaranteed.[71]

Given this set of attitudes and expectations, even the most moderate of Chinese nationalists were incensed by the news that Thai army tanks had taken action against Chinese in Bangkok with no interference from Allied authorities. Demands were made in China that the Thai government be forced to go through a surrender ceremony, that Chinese troops occupy the country, and so on.[72] In view of public opinion in Chungking, the protests of the Chinese government were mild indeed. The Chinese Ambassador in Washington was instructed to ask the Thai Minister there for an explanation of the incidents and to demand measures to prevent recurrence as well as compensation for the Chinese victims.[73]

The Thai assurances were something less than satisfactory to the Chinese Foreign Office, but it decided to press for diplomatic relations even without prior settlement of the Yaowarat Incident and other outstanding problems. The Thai government had managed to avoid a treaty with China for forty years, and the Chinese had no intention of letting the psychological moment pass in quibbling over details. For its part, the Seni administration needed regular relations with China to forestall a possible Chinese veto of Siam's application for membership in the United Nations. Accordingly, both governments tried to ease popular feeling in their countries during the last months of 1945, while an attempt was made to reach agreement. Hsiung Chün-ling (C 125), chairman of the Hakka Association, went to Chungking with instructions from Premier Seni and from the joint organization of Chinese speech-group associations. He returned with an official Chinese Mission, which entered into negotiations with the Thai. On January 23, 1946, the Siamese-Chinese Treaty of Amity was signed, providing for the exchange of diplomatic and consular representatives and affirming "perpetual peace and everlasting amity" between the two countries and peoples.[74]

Li T'ieh-cheng (C 126), the head of the Chinese Mission which negotiated the Treaty, was appointed the first Chinese Ambassador to Thailand and arrived in Bangkok September 6. The ensuing year saw the formal opening of Chinese consulates in Bangkok, Chiangmai (North), Paknampho (Middle), Khorat (Northeast), and Songkhla (South). Ambassador Li and his staff had a host of problems to take up with the Thai government, the most chronic of which dealt with immigration and education.

Ambassador Li arrived in Bangkok just as immigration was becoming a matter of serious public concern. The Thai were worried not only about the magnitude of the influx—though the immigration was termed an "invasion"—but also about conditions on the immigrant ships and of the health of the passengers:

Many Chinese did not shrink from suffering the tortures on heavily over-loaded ships which had no proper food, water and sanitary facilities; disease-ridden and half-dead, thousands eventually disembarked after their night-marish trip (during which several riots were also staged), to be placed under quarantine. The Bangkok public has cried out against these outrages.[75]

Soothing statements were made to the public, but the government was already considering immigration quotas.[76] Li T'ieh-cheng and M. R. Seni Pramot had discussed the immigration problem at length during the negotiations for the Sino-Thai treaty. The treaty itself (Article IV) stipulated:

The nationals of each of the High Contracting Parties shall be at liberty to enter or leave the territory of the other under the same conditions as the na-tionals of any third country, in accordance with the laws and regulations of the country applied to all aliens.

M. R. Seni's statement on the Treaty, in his capacity as Foreign Min-ister, included this elaboration:

In order to avoid any misunderstanding on the subject of immigration, His Majesty's Government wish to make their intentions clear:

a) In the event of a quota system being enforced by either High Contract-ing Party for the regulation of immigration, the basis to be adopted for fixing the annual quota of immigrants, being Nationals of the other High Contract-ing Party, will be that which is usually adopted for the same purpose in other countries, for instance, taking into account the size of the population con-stituted by the nationals of the other High Contracting Party in the country concerned.

b) The entrance fee to be paid by immigrants is to be a fee in the true sense of the word. It will not be made substantially a tax nor will it be al-lowed to become prohibitive. Non-immigrants being nationals of the other High Contracting Party, who come into the country without the intention of establishing themselves therein, will not be required to pay the entrance fee.

c) It is not contemplated by the Government of either High Contracting Party to apply the educational or literacy test to immigrants from the territory of the other.

These assurances, while not formally incorporated in the Treaty, were something of a diplomatic victory for Mr. Li, and his role as Ambassador was in this regard confined to making representations to the Thai government as to the size and effective date of the Chinese quota and to pressing his home government for stricter control of the quality of emigrants destined for Siam. In April 1947, the Thai government formally announced an annual Chinese quota of ten thousand retroactive as of the beginning of 1947, and the following November the Overseas Chinese Affairs Commission of the Chinese government promulgated regulations requiring that all emigrants to Siam be able to read Chinese, be free from drug addictions and contagious diseases, and be capable of earning a living. The Thai government's immigration control during 1947 and 1948 was, on the whole, both lenient and fair. Exemptions from the quota were extended to Chinese students over fifteen years of age enrolled in accredited schools, teachers and their dependents, and those who had previously entered as immigrants.[77]

With regard to education, the Treaty of Amity (January 1946) provided only that "the nationals of each of the High Contracting Parties shall have . . . the liberty to establish schools for the education of their children . . . in accordance with the laws and regulations of the country" (Article VI). However the Declaration issued by M. R. Seni, in his capacity as Minister of Foreign Affairs, "for the purpose of clarifying the intentions of His Majesty's Government in certain matters concerning the application of the Treaty" stated:

Chinese schools in Siam will likewise receive treatment not less favorable than that given to schools of any other nationality. In schools for primary education, which is compulsory in Siam, all children have to learn the Siamese language: it is however the intention of His Majesty's Government to afford appropriate opportunity and the necessary number of hours for the teaching of a foreign language in such schools. His Majesty's Government have no intention of imposing restrictions on the teaching of foreign languages in secondary schools.

The local Chinese, however, hoped for a thoroughgoing revision of the primary-school regulations, and on the occasion of Children's Day,

April 4, 1946, the Chinese launched an attack on the Thai education laws. In that month also, a Chinese Students Association was organized in Bangkok "to encourage contact among Chinese students in Siam and to promote unity and solidarity." [78] In June it was reported that a fund of a million baht was being raised by the Chinese community in Bangkok to get local schools on their feet. Meanwhile the government indicated a relaxation of the containment policy in education by announcing in May that the Chinese language would again—after an eight-year lapse—be taught in government schools as an optional subject.

Within ten months after V-J Day, Chinese schools in Thailand had been reopened in numbers which surpassed the prewar peak. The growth was most spectacular in the more recently settled regions upcountry. In Chiangrai jangwat, for instance, which before the war had only a single school, four additional schools were founded in 1946 in the minor towns of Maejan, Chiangkham, Phayao, and Phan. Many if not most of the Chinese schools upcountry taught only Chinese during 1945–1946, in contravention of the prewar education laws, which remained on the books even though they were not enforced. In November 1946, Ambassador Li launched a plan to expand Chinese education still further and to organize a Chinese school system in Thailand under the control of the Embassy's cultural officer. At the same time, however, the Thai government began to enforce the existing private-school regulations, including those provisions limiting the hours of Chinese to be taught and requiring registration with the Ministry of Education. [79] In a misguided display of national pride, many of the largest Chinese schools refused to register, some students went out on strike, and there was talk of closing Chinese shops as a further protest. When the government closed three Chinese schools, Ambassador Li intervened and secured from the Minister of Education a promise that modifications of the laws affecting Chinese schools would be made within three months. In the negotiations conducted during the spring of 1947, the Ambassador secured several concessions concerning Thai examinations for Chinese teachers, the selection of textbooks, the use of Chinese in teaching geography and history, and so on. The government, however, strictly adhered to the principles of compulsory education for all and fixed qualifications for private-school teachers. [80]

In April, the Nanking government offered scholarships to nine Thai students for study at a Chinese university and allocated a sum of over

US$300,000 for Chinese education in Siam—which, however, was never actually forthcoming. By the end of 1947, even without substantial assistance from the Embassy, Chinese schools in Siam numbered over four hundred. In January 1948, the Minister of Education wrote to Ambassador Li confirming that the concessions made by the government before the November 1947 coup would be respected.[81] The same month, however, Chinese resentment was aroused when the government began rigid enforcement of the regulation that in all schools the Thai flag must be flown and the Thai national anthem sung every morning.

Two of the Ambassador's other important problems in the field of Sino-Thai relations concerned compensation to Chinese nationals for casualties and losses during the Yaowarat Incident and participation of local Chinese in China's national elections. Neither matter was allowed seriously to strain relations with the Thai government. The compensation issue was the subject of increasingly successful negotiations in October 1947,[82] but these were interrupted by the coup of November 8 and never seriously raised again. In September 1947, the Chinese Consulates in Siam were proceeding with plans to supervise the voting of local Chinese nationals in the Chinese general elections scheduled for October.[83] The proposed voting was denounced by the Thai Foreign Minister as a "direct violation of Siamese sovereignty," and on October 15, Ambassador Li officially informed the Minister that his government had withdrawn authorization for the vote in Siam in the interests of good will.[84]

Friendship between the two peoples was a constant theme of the Embassy, and in fact Sino-Thai relations were unusually amicable during 1947. In April, a Sino-Thai Friendship Society was organized with Pridi prominent among the Thai members and Chinese Chamber of Commerce officers among the Chinese.[85] It actually engaged in joint activities—benefit shows and lectures—that enhanced co-operation and understanding between the two elites. In August, Ambassador Li returned from Nanking with a number of decorations conferred by Chiang Kai-shek on prominent Thai officials.[86] On the occasion of Double Tenth, 1947, both the Chinese and Thai press were moved to new heights in the expression of Sino-Thai friendship.

Developments in the field of labor 1945–1947 were also encouraging from the point of view of relations between the two peoples. May Day, 1946, saw one of the first gatherings of Bangkok workers united in terms of class interest regardless of ethnic group. Under the auspices of M.C. Sakon Worawan, advisor to the pro-Pridi Sahachip Party and organizer the previous August of a Sino-Thai Cultural Association, both Thai and Chinese workers attended a meeting devoted to furthering labor's rights.[87] In the fall of 1946, there was evidence of Sino-Thai co-operation in strikes, and on January 1, 1947, the first labor federation in Thai history was formally inaugurated and registered. The Saha Achiwa Kamakǫn, usually known in English as the Central Labor Union, comprised over fifty unions by midyear with a membership of several tens of thousands. The leadership, primarily provided by pro-Pridi liberals, was largely Thai, but two-fifths of the membership was Chinese at the start, and the Chinese proportion increased as organization proceeded.[88] By 1948, the great majority of *organized* Chinese labor was affiliated with the interethnic Central Labor Union.

The government's handling of strikes, 1945–1948, gave no evidence of a deliberate attempt to drive a breech between Thai and Chinese labor; there was little Thai strike-breaking of Chinese strikes, and no resort to deportation of Chinese labor leaders. The nature of the strikes during that period, however, suggested that Chinese laborers were more concerned with China's political struggle than with a joint labor movement with the Thai. During 1946–1947, there were 173 strikes in Siam, 28 being of major importance.[89] Probably the most significant of the major strikes were those carried out by Chinese rice-mill workers.[90] The first was called in November 1945 for higher wages and at its peak involved some four thousand men. It was settled by a compromise reached by representatives of the laborers, mill-owners, and government. Chinese political motivation, alleged to have been a factor in the November work stoppage, was more evident in the next two major strikes which began in April and June 1946. In the April strike, workers demanded assurances that the rice they were loading on ships destined for China be honestly distributed among the famine-stricken civilian population and not be used for KMT troops. The strikers in June listed as a condition for the resumption of work that future rice shipments to China be handled solely by the Overseas Chinese Famine Relief Committee of Siam (see Section D below).

From the Thai point of view, the whole question of rice was perhaps the sorest aspect of Sino-Thai relations. The strikes of Chinese "coolies" and smuggling, hoarding, and bribery by Chinese rice merchants were considered especially damaging to the recovery of Thailand's economy and international standing. In January 1946,

Siam agreed to supply 1,500,000 tons of rice free of charge to the Allies as a sort of indemnity for her wartime role.[91] The low prices offered by the Thai government in conjunction with local inflation led to widespread hoarding of paddy. The January commitment was modified by a Rice Agreement the following May which called for the delivery of 1,200,000 tons at prices averaging less than £16 per ton—when world prices were at a level of about £40 per ton. Later in the year, prices of uncontrolled rice in Malaya reached as high as £500, while subsequent adjustments in the official prices paid under the Rice Agreement were still unrealistic in terms of the black market rates.

With such prices and with a huge demand in neighboring Malaya, the incentive to the rice trader to smuggle out his rice, instead of selling it officially, was enormous. His extra profit was, on the average something like £200 per ton of rice smuggled. He could afford to pay—and did pay—such huge bribes that few of the poorly-paid administrative, police, and customs officials could resist co-operating. The result was, as competent observers estimated, that exports of smuggled rice in 1946–7 were at least equal to the legal exports: the fabulous sum of £100 million sterling of extra profits went into the pockets of the rice merchants of Siam, a proportion of these profits being paid in bribes to the officials in Siam and Malaya.[92]

Thai government steps to remedy this situation were unfortunately both productive of ill feeling between Chinese and Thai and ineffective in obtaining the amount of rice for export needed to meet international commitments. The adverse economic effects of the Rice Agreement (even after its termination in August 1947) and the smuggling and corruption which it fostered were prominent among the factors underlying the November 1947 coup d'état. To the extent that Chinese merchants contributed to corruption and inflation, they share responsibility for the downfall of the Thai administration which, of all administrations since the 1932 revolution, had been most consistently friendly to the Chinese.

   The November 8 coup, engineered by Phibun's military clique and certain conservative civilians, was followed by a five-month period during which democratic forms were re-established and recognition of the foreign powers secured. The Chinese Ambassador publicly warned Chinese nationals in Siam that the coup was an internal affair and that they should take no part in any political activities prejudicial to good relations between China and Siam.[93] And in fact the administration of Khuang Aphaiwong made no significant changes in the government's policies towards the Chinese. In the first week of April 1948, however, the Army, whose Commander in Chief was Luang Phibun, presented an ultimatum to Premier Khuang stating that if he wanted to regain the confidence of the army he must form a new cabinet which, among other things, would "exert closer control over foreigners in Siam (meaning the Chinese)." [94] The Khuang cabinet resigned, and Phibun resumed the premiership. The reaction of local Chinese was an almost visible, collective shudder.

D. *Chinese Community Organization, 1945–1948*

On August 16, 1945, two days after V-J Day, the chairman of the Chinese Chamber of Commerce, Ch'en Shou-ming, was assassinated by an unknown hand. [95] It is generally assumed that the crime was committed by members of a left-wing Chinese underground organization resentful of Mr. Ch'en's leadership during the Japanese occupation. The murder was starkly symbolic of the political controversy that was to plague the Chinese community throughout the postwar period. Its disruptive consequences were almost immediately apparent: the Chamber of Commerce was immobilized; other leaders with records similar to Mr. Ch'en's declined to take positions of responsibility; and several important organizations became entirely inactive. To provide emergency leadership in this anarchic situation, representatives of the five major speech-group associations plus the Chiang-che Association met on August 23 and formally organized the Six Speech-group Associations' Temporary Joint Office, with the chairmanship rotating every week among the six member associations. [96]

During the remainder of 1945, this joint organization assumed the major burden of responsibility for all problems of pressing concern to the Chinese community. It staged a reception for the Allied military authorities in Bangkok, handled the negotiations immediately consequent on the Yaowarat Incident, took over responsibility for aiding and repatriating conscripted Chinese laborers, and initiated famine relief for China. These last two activities warrant some extended description.

By the end of August several hundred Chinese laborers brought to Siam during the war had arrived in Bangkok, destitute, ill or starving in many cases, and penniless. [97] The Cantonese Association immediately mobilized staff and equipment to handle the refugees, who were given housing in the Association's premises and treatment in its Hospital. By the first week in September, the number of refugees needing help had swollen to over seven hundred, and their care was taken over by the Joint Office. Under the brilliant leadership of several Cantonese, of whom Liang Jen-hsin (C 127) and Li Hua-Hui (C 128) may be singled out for special mention, the project thus begun was carried through to its final stage. Help in securing food and housing was enlisted from the Thai government, the International Red Cross, and Allied military authorities. But the bulk of the expense and all of the administration of a major relief project was borne by the Chinese community. Over two thousand refugees were taken in between August and November. The Pao-te Benevolent Society provided rice gruel in the initial stages, Chinese merchants contributed clothing and bedding, Chinese doctors and dentists volunteered their services, Chinese barbers gave free haircuts, Chinese publishers provided free newspapers, Chinese theater-owners free movies, and so on. A standing committee of one representative from each of the six associations daily inspected the major camp of the refugees.

Meanwhile the Cantonese managers arranged with the British authorities for the repatriation of the Chinese from Malaya, and for the return of a portion of the Chinese troops to their division which was then stationed in Indochina. Beginning in late October, twelve hundred of these refugees were repatriated to neighboring countries. In March 1946, permission was obtained from the Thai government for return to their homes of the several hundred refugees from South Siam; they were given rail fares and accompanied home by the Hokkien member of the joint standing committee. In May, the remainder of the troops was sent to China to rejoin their division, while in June about two hundred of the refugees desiring repatriation to China were sent by ship to Canton and Swatow. Their full expenses were borne by the local Chinese; they were accompanied by members of the joint committee; and the chairman himself flew ahead to arrange for their reception in China. Many of the captive laborers originally brought from China elected to stay in Thailand; some even got married through the match-making services of the Cantonese Association.

An equally thorough and even more extensive humanitarian job carried through by the Chinese in Thailand was the provision of famine relief for south China. In this undertaking the executive officers were mainly Teochiu. After preliminary meetings in October 1945, under the auspices of the Joint Office, a relief committee was formally organized in November. The Thai government was persuaded to permit a fund-raising campaign, and eventually over twenty million baht were collected. This sum was used almost entirely to buy rice; the committee was able to arrange for the necessary supply of gunny sacks and transportation through UNRRA. Distribution of the relief rice in China was, however, something less than satisfactory. Reports of irregularities reached Bangkok almost immediately, and early in 1946 the committee's chairman, Cheng Wu-lou (C 129), went to China to supervise distribution. It was found that a considerable part of the rice had been sold for the private benefit of certain officials, or diverted to troops for whom it was not intended. Even the more public-spirited officials in Swatow proposed selling part of the rice in order to build a memorial to the relief project! Before the project was concluded, over ten Bangkok leaders each spent months in China trying to ensure free and equitable distribution of the relief rice.

News of the corruption of certain KMT officials in China with regard to famine relief added new fuel to the flames of political controversy within the Chinese community in Siam. Immediately after the war, the Chinese underground groups came into the open and pressed forward with the organization of more or less legitimate associations to further their aims. Special attention, quite naturally, was paid to education and newspapers. The Chinese Communists, it is said, got off to a good financial start by exacting heavy sums from Chinese merchants whose wartime records were stained by collaboration with the Japanese. Many of the schools organized in 1946 and 1947 were under Communist influence. The wartime *Chen-hua Pao* was continued as a weekly under the management of Ch'iu Chi, and on October 10, 1945, the Communist daily, *Ch'üan-min Pao* (C 130), began publication.[98] The Chinese Communist Party of Siam was also active in labor organizations and co-operated in the establishment of the Central Labor Union. Ch'iu Chi, in an interview with Virginia Thompson and Richard Adloff, stated that the Party's only concern was with the situation in China itself, but the Thai Communist Party program for Thailand significantly called for an extremely pro-Chinese government policy.[99] The Chinese Communists appealed to local Chinese on the basis of a radical domestic program (i.e., the abolition of electoral restrictions, of the alien registration fees, of immigration fees, and of all restrictions on private schools) which the Kuomintang could not espouse with equal ardor in view of the real world in which the Kuomintang government's Ambassador had to work.

The Kuomintang, however, remained the chief political force in the Chinese community until 1948. The Chung-hua Association was revived, political workers from China arrived to help reorganize the underground party, and a branch of the San Min Chu-yi Youth Corps was founded, along with several schools. Organization upcountry proceeded apace under stimulus and guidance from the five Chinese consulates. In a few towns—Khǫnkaen, Phijit, and Bangmunnak (jangwat Phijit), for instance—the Shu-pao-she was revived as a KMT organization, while elsewhere, as in Chiangmai and Nǫngkhai, branches of the Chung-hua Association were founded. Wherever possible, however, the Kuomintang line called for the establishment of a single, united Chinese association dedicated to support of the Nanking government. In many upcountry towns, the Party achieved success.

The Kuomintang was the first to get a full-sized daily newspaper into the field after the war—the *Chung-kuo-jen Pao* (C 131), which began publication September 21, 1945. On January 1, 1946, the *Min-sheng Jih-pao* (C 132) appeared under Youth Corps auspices, and the *Cheng-yen Jih-pao* (C 133), first published on the same day, eventually fell under Kuomintang control.[100] The Party's operations in Siam were quite naturally facilitated by the opening of the Chinese Embassy, where Party functions could be held and from which underground activities could be organized and financed with impunity. It was reported that the Chinese Military Attaché in Bangkok headed the Party's secret service in Siam.[101]

Disillusionment with the Kuomintang was partly responsible for the establishment in early 1946 of the Siam Branch of the China Democratic League. In May of that year its first press organ, *Min-chu Hsin-wen* (C 134), began publication as a weekly. The League increased its support during the following year, largely on the basis of its courageous record in China at that time. By April 1947, several of its important members were able to finance the establishment of the daily, *Man-ku Shang-pao* (C 135), which became one of Bangkok's most respected newspapers.[102]

The Chinese press in Bangkok, however, was by no means confined to party organs. Between 1945 and 1948, the all-time peak of Chinese journalism in Siam, a dozen independent papers were established. Perhaps the two most important of these were revivals of prewar papers. The *Chung-yüan Pao* was resumed in October 1945, under its pre-occupation editor, and half a year later the *Hua-ch'iao Jih-pao* reappeared with something of its prewar zeal. These and other papers, most notably *Kuang-hua Pao* (C 136), established in October 1945, represented the large body of neutral or Siam-centered opinion concerned above all with peace in China and the welfare of the local Chinese community. The overwhelming majority of the Chinese in Siam supported the 1946 truce efforts in China and deplored the resumption of the Civil War. In January 1947, some 346 Chinese associations in Siam associated themselves with a resolution calling for a truce in China, which was cabled to both Chiang Kai-shek and Mao Tse-tung.[103] Nevertheless, the Civil War was fought in the Chinese press of Siam as in China, and on occasion the war of words erupted into physical violence.[104]

Political machinations in several cases severely complicated the reorganization of Chinese associations after the war. Only the most notable example will be outlined here. Since 1909 there had been two Hainanese regional organizations: (1) the Ch'iung-tao Hui-so, founded by Sun Yat-sen with a specific political purpose and (2) the Ch'iung-chou Kung-so, which had been organized more as the usual speech-group association and operated Yü-min, the main Hainanese school. The former, headed by a local KMT official, managed to keep in operation during the occupation and was the organization that took part in the Six Speech-group Associations' Temporary Joint Office in 1945. In the fall of 1945, a group of Hainanese leftists and non-KMT merchants founded the Ch'iung-yai T'ung-hsiang-hui, secured registration with the Thai government, and even got Li T'ieh-cheng, then in Bangkok negotiating the Sino-Thai treaty, to write the new association's signboard. Around the turn of the year, however, a KMT special commissioner arrived from China and after a little investigation, branded the Ch'iung-yai T'ung-hsiang-hui as pro-Communist, and insisted that the Ch'iung-tao Hui-so be reorganized as the only Hainanese association. This suggestion was poorly received by the Ch'iung-chou Kung-so, whose chairman was also a prominent KMT leader, but which had never registered with the Thai government; as the oldest Hainanese organization in Siam, it refused to cede priority. So a new organization, the Hai-nan Hui-kuan, was founded in 1946 incorporating both the Ch'iung-chou and Ch'iung-tao associations and organized in accordance with the regulations of the Chinese government. It took over administration of the Yü-min school and claimed full legitimacy. Meanwhile the moderates were scared out of the Ch'iung-yai T'ung-hsiang-hui, and when the latter organized a rival school, Ch'i-kuang, in 1946, it appointed a Communist as principal. Thus the Hainanese community was split in half, and much of its energy during succeeding years was dissipated in political feuding. The Ch'iung-yai

T'ung-hsiang-hui declined in importance after 1946, but the Hainanese Association proper (Hai-nan Hui-kuan) never carried the weight in community affairs warranted by the number of Hainanese in Bangkok.

The other speech-group associations managed to avoid any open breeches on political lines after the war. The Cantonese Association had been most successful in maintaining an efficient organization without significant collaboration during the occupation, and it emerged after the war as the strongest and most influential of all community organizations. The Hakka Association, somewhat less successful in these regards, attained full effectiveness only after new elections early in 1946. The Teochiu Association was handicapped right after the war by a dearth of active and proved leaders. The two former Chamber of Commerce chairmen assassinated in 1939 and 1945 were Teochius, and most of the prewar Association leaders imprisoned during the war were reluctant to resume top offices. The Association's chief officers in 1945 were preoccupied with the reorganization of the Chamber of Commerce after Ch'en Shou-ming's assassination in August. By the turn of the year, however, the Association was well established under the leadership of the two young men primarily responsible for the success of the famine relief campaign. When, however, the association adopted a somewhat cool attitude toward the Kuomintang in 1946–1947—in part as a result of experiences with Party officials in China—the Party actively assisted in the organization of four or five associations (*t'ung-hsiang-hui,* "same-native-place associations") for natives of the chief hsiens in Ch'ao-chou, to counter the influence of the main Teochiu Association. In October 1945, the Taiwan Association was formally organized, and in spite of the small number of Taiwan natives in Bangkok it soon achieved full standing alongside of the five major speech-group associations and the Chiang-che Association. This move constituted local recognition of China's postwar reincorporation of Taiwan.

In large towns upcountry some interest was shown in establishing separate speech-group associations after the war. A strong Hainan Association was formed at Phitsanulok in 1945, and a much weaker Hakka Mutual-Aid Society was launched in Khorat. In Chiangmai, preparations were made for three speech-group associations (Hainanese, Hakka, and Cantonese) and two Teochiu hsien associations (Ch'eng-hai and Ch'ao-yang), but in the end none achieved government approval or permanent tenure. The Chinese in Chiangmai were formally split on political lines, however, by the establishment and registration of the Hsin-sheng Mutual-Aid Society, a pro-Communist organization opposed to the Chung-hua Association. Aside from school boards, however, pro-Communists were for the most part either unsuccessful or uninterested in establishing formal organizations outside of Bangkok. In fact, the pattern that emerged most clearly for provincial Thailand in the immediate postwar period was that of a single community organization enjoying the support of all speech groups and either dominated by the Kuomintang or nominally loyal to the Nanking government. The organizations had different names, but they were everywhere similar in structure and function. In the northeast as of 1946–1947, there were Hua-ch'iao Shang-hui (chambers of commerce) in Nongkhai, Udonthani, Khonkaen, Sakonnakhon, Nakhonphanom, Surin, and Buriram; and Hua-ch'iao Kung-so (public meeting places) in Roi-et and Mahasarakham. In Middle Siam, to take another region, there was a Hua-ch'iao Kung-hui (association) in Uttaradit, and Hua-ch'iao Hsieh-hui (alliances), in Phitsanulok, Phetchabun, Lomsak (jangwat Phetchabun), Thalo, and Taphanhin (both in jangwat Phijit).

The Chinese Chamber of Commerce in Bangkok, however, never did achieve the unity, much less the political unanimity, considered desirable by the Chinese Embassy. Largely inactive during the last months of 1945 because of the assassination of its chairman, the Chamber first elected a Hainanese as its head—one of the "grand old" Chinese Nationalists. This gentleman resigned in May 1946 to serve as the chief overseas delegate from Siam to the Chinese National Assembly at Nanking, and his place was taken by Lin Po-ch'i, another old and respected leader. Before the end of the year, however, internal political wrangling led to Mr. Lin's resignation and the election of a new slate of officers. Eight of the fifteen newly elected executive-committee members were Teochius, and the chief officers were practically identical with the Teochiu Association officers of the previous term. The elected officers included individuals of all political coloring, from Communist through Democratic League to Kuomintang. Effective control, however, remained in the hands of Teochiu middle-of-the-roaders—independents and Democratic League members.

An issue arose late in 1947 which pointed up political differences within the Chamber and forcibly raised the question of the role of the Chinese (Kuomintang) Embassy in local community affairs.[105] The Overseas Chinese Affairs Commission of the Nanking government, in order to exert control over Chinese communities abroad, held that overseas Chinese organizations of all kinds should conform as closely as local conditions permitted to the Chinese regulations on chambers of commerce, "peoples" associations, schools, and so on. One of the duties of the Chinese Embassy and consulates in Siam was to bring Chinese associations in line, and, with most of the newly formed organizations after the war as well as the speech-group associations, the Chinese diplomats achieved a large measure of success. In the case of the Chinese Chamber of Commerce, however, the Embassy was frustrated.

The Chamber of Commerce had registered, under the constitution revised in the 1930's, with both the Thai government and the Chinese government. That constitution provided for the membership not only of business firms and trade associations, but of individuals and speech-group associations as well. In 1947 it had some three thousand members in these latter categories. This arrangement was considered only natural because the Chamber's responsibilities were in fact not limited to commercial matters but covered the whole range of Chinese community affairs. On November 21, 1947, the Chamber issued a notice stating that the regular general meeting would be held December 4 to elect new officers for the 1948–1949 term. But on November 28, Sun Ping-ch'ien (C 137), the Chinese Consul-general in Bangkok, ordered the Chamber to revise its constitution prior to another election in accordance with the Revised Regulations on Commercial Organizations of the Nanking government. Those Regulations stipulated that regular membership of commercial organizations be restricted to commercial firms and business associations.

The motivation of the Consul-general was indicated in a statement handed to the press on December 3: "In order to live up to its name, the Chamber should be organized by overseas Chinese commercial groups and shops so that the organization will not be too mixed in its elements and political complications may be avoided." [106] Mr. Sun obviously desired to purge the organization of anti-Kuomintang members, most of whom belonged as individuals rather than firms. The majority of Chamber members, however, disapproved of his peremptory tactics. The meeting was held as scheduled, and after a warm discussion of the revision question, the members present passed a resolution affirming the legality of the Chamber constitution and calling for immediate elections, which were in fact promptly held. The following day, Consul-general Sun issued another statement charging election irregularities and stating point-blank:

It is evident that the so-called election was manipulated by Chinese Communist and Democratic League elements. In order to fool the legitimate merchants, they purposely put in a few greatly respected overseas Chinese leaders who are thus exploited by them. But I am sure that these leaders will not be willing to be used. Since the purpose of this kind of election was to ignore Government orders and to fool overseas Chinese merchants, the results . . . will not be recognized.

Mr. Sun also wrote personal letters to most of the men elected asking their opinion of the "obnoxious disobedience" and inquiring whether they would take office.

The battle thus joined raged for four months. In effect, Sun's intransigence facilitated the formation of a working alliance between Communist, Democratic League, and independent elements within the Chamber. The organization officially kept a discrete silence, while the Overseas Chinese Affairs Commission tried to determine the facts and effect a mediation. Ambassador Li T'ieh-cheng took a personal hand in the dispute. Meanwhile the cause of local independence from Nanking was championed most vociferously by the Democratic League and Communist press, while the Kuomintang organs argued the matter in terms of legality and loyalty to the home government. The Democratic League organ, *Man-ku Shang-pao*, took the offensive in the press war, openly attacking the Consul-general, who replied through the Kuomintang press with equal vigor.

Not until the end of March 1948 was a formula reached for resolving the dispute. On the recommendation of the Overseas Chinese Affairs Commission, the Embassy gave permission to proceed with organization of the Chamber on the basis of the December elections. To save face for the Consul-general, the Chamber requested his permission to proceed with the election of a chairman and other officers, after which they would attend to the revision of the constitution. Permission was granted, and on April 10 the committees met and elected officers. The previous chairman, treasurer, and secretary were re-elected. All members of the newly elected standing committee were Teochiu; one of them was a Communist. The revision question died a natural death. The entire episode not only affirmed local autonomy; it was a blow to the local prestige of the Kuomintang and to the community standing of the Chinese Embassy from which neither fully recovered.

The Chamber of Commerce dispute was settled the very week that Luang Phibun resumed the Thai premiership. The Chinese community entered the second Phibun era with a façade of unity that poorly concealed the undercurrent of political friction.

REPRESSION

AND RECONSIDERATION:

Chinese under the Second Phibun

Administration, 1948-1956

A. *Chinese Social Structure*

DURING the last half-century, Chinese society in Siam has become much less sharply distinguished from the larger Thai society. By 1950, it had already been forty years since social reforms under royal auspices wiped away the basic administrative distinctions between Chinese and Thai. During that period, the social visibility of the Chinese decreased vis-à-vis the Thai, and the identification choice of the local-born Chinese became relative and situational. At the turn of the century, the Chinese had to make a clear-cut choice: he either wore a queue, acknowledged the jurisdiction of the Chinese headman, paid the triennial tax, and was marked on the wrist, *or* he clipped his hair, paid an annual capitation tax, and established client relations with a Thai patron. When these components of the choice were removed, a clear decision was no longer forced, and the whole range of inter- mediate statuses between the core of Chinese immigrant society and Thai society could be explored with no necessary end position as a goal. As mentioned earlier, the public dress of both Chinese and Thai was modified during the twenties and thirties in the direction of West-

ern models. During the Second World War, Phibun decreed the whole-
sale adoption of Western dress in the country, and this particular part
of his "culture movement" was never repudiated. In Thailand, both
the Chinese gown and the Thai *phanung* (the traditional lower gar-
ment) are anachronisms for men, who prefer Western clothing for
public wear. Women of both ethnic groups have adopted the permanent wave with equal enthusiasm and determination, and Western
dresses are increasingly preferred by the prestige-conscious upper
classes.

With the removal or weakening of social pressures forcing un-
equivocal ethnic identification, the possibility arose that a local-born
Chinese society, intermediate in culture between Chinese immigrant
society and Thai society, might develop in Siam. Insofar as this writer
can read the signs, however, such a development, permitted by the
objective situation, has not in fact occurred. There are thousands of
intermediate individuals who identify as Chinese in some social situations and as Thai in others, who have both a Chinese and a Thai
name, either of which is used according to suitability, and who can
speak Thai and Chinese with equal fluency. But such individuals are
not developing relationships *among themselves* that are more frequent
and enduring than the social interaction which they have with those
who are unequivocally members of Chinese or of Thai society. Their
private relations may be largely with Chinese and their public relations largely with Thai. Or their relations with elders may be largely
Chinese and those with age-mates and juniors largely Thai. But even
these generalizations suggest a neater pattern than characterizes any
given individual. The larger society in Thailand's cities and towns is
still polarized, with separate Thai and Chinese nuclei. No society has
grown up consisting of those of Chinese extraction who eschew
identification with either nucleus and interact more frequently among
themselves than with "real" Thai or "real "Chinese.

This point is labored here because the developing social structure
in some other Southeast Asian countries has eventuated in just such an
intermediate society—that, for instance, of the Straits Chinese in
Singapore and Penang and of the Peranakan Chinese in Java. The
Chinese in these societies interact among themselves more often
than with immigrant Chinese, have indeed a different set of values
strongly influenced by the West, and reject identification or merger
with the indigenous society. Perhaps the major determinant of the
different social development in Thailand lies in the fact that *the* elite

in Siam has always been Thai. This indigenous elite has always possessed power, prestige, enlightenment, and (with qualifications)
wealth to a higher degree than any other major group. This was
manifestly not the case in colonial societies. Upward mobility—and
we assume here that the descendants of all Chinese aspire to it—in
Java meant movement in the direction of Dutch and Eurasian society
rather than toward the low-status indigenous society, and in the
Straits in the direction of British society. Full assimilation in those
directions, however, was impossible because of colonial attitudes and
obvious physical differences. In Thailand, on the other hand, upward
mobility carried the Chinese in the direction of Thai society, and the
absence of sharp differences in physical appearance between Chinese
and Thai and the modification of the cultural overlay distinguishing
the two ethnic groups made full assimilation possible. Social movement toward Thai society, however much it was retarded during the
twenties, thirties, and forties, has never met with a dead end. The
highest statuses in the society remained Thai and their achievement
has never been out of reach for the descendants of Chinese.

It will, therefore, be helpful to look briefly at the whole society in
postwar Thailand in order to describe the Chinese position in it. And
this description can best be made in terms of core Chinese and Thai
groups, with the realization that individuals rather than social groups
are intermediate between them.

The firmest clues to the relative social positions of Chinese and
Thai are to be had in available statistics on occupational distribution.
Table 21 represents an attempt to wring full sociological significance
from the 1947 census data on occupations of the employed labor force
in jangwat Phranakhǫn. The figures have been adjusted to apply to
Krungthep only and to accord with the registered population as of the
end of 1952. Krungthep was chosen for this analysis because, as the
chief urban concentration of both Chinese and Thai, it brings the
occupational specializations of the two ethnic groups into sharpest
focus. It was assumed that one-third of the population of Thai nationals
within Krungthep are in fact local-born ethnic Chinese. The allocation of this portion of the population to each occupation class was
calculated according to a formula which reflects the fact that ethnic
Chinese of Thai nationality tend to concentrate in the same occupations
as Chinese nationals.[1] The grouping of occupation classes into four
major status categories roughly portrays the prevailing evaluation of
these occupations in Bangkok—according to prestige, income, and

Table 21. Occupational stratification, Krungthep, Thai and
Chinese ethnic groups only, 1952 *

| Occupation class | Estimated occupied population | | | | | |
| | Male | | Female | | Total | |
	Ethnic Chinese	Ethnic Thai	Ethnic Chinese	Ethnic Thai	Ethnic Chinese	Ethnic Thai
Highest status						
1. High-ranking gov't officials	0	6,080	0	50	0	6,130
2. Large business owners, mgrs.	2,890	470	1,500	1,340	4,390	1,810
3. Highest-status professionals	280	1,020	10	110	290	1,130
4. High-ranking office staff	620	860	30	180	650	1,040
Total	3,790	8,430	1,540	1,680	5,330	10,110
Mid-high status						
5. Lower-ranking gov't officials	10	18,220	0	150	10	18,370
6. Smaller business owners, mgrs.	54,900	8,980	28,560	25,500	83,460	34,480
7. Lesser & semi-professionals	2,340	4,040	530	3,590	2,870	7,630
8. Government clerks	20	16,290	0	2,840	20	19,130
9. Business clerks	5,070	1,920	310	910	5,380	2,830
10. High-status industrial staff	380	720	20	50	400	770
Total	62,720	50,170	29,420	33,040	92,140	83,210
Mid-low status						
11. Carpenters & furniture makers	7,230	1,160	80	10	7,310	1,170
12. Repairmen, machinists, etc.	4,050	2,880	30	10	4,080	2,890
13. Auto, bus, & truck drivers	1,380	4,330	0	10	1,380	4,340
14. Metal workers (base metals)	3,060	440	110	80	3,170	520
15. Miscellaneous technicians	3,620	1,550	1,810	740	5,430	2,290
16. Tailors & dressmakers	1,850	70	2,130	2,550	3,980	2,620
17. Jewelers; gold-, silversmiths	2,880	220	480	270	3,360	490
18. Miscellaneous craftsmen	2,170	340	530	610	2,700	950
19. Cooks, bakers, food processors	1,720	130	1,280	2,610	3,000	2,740
20. Market sellers (in stalls)	4,390	290	400	450	4,790	740
21. Weavers & dyers	2,420	30	6,070	250	8,490	280
22. Hairdressers	0	0	50	1,120	50	1,120
23. Shoemakers	1,640	30	240	50	1,880	80
24. Hotel & restaurant employees	3,210	150	420	330	3,630	480
25. Workers in building trades	1,140	180	30	70	1,170	250
Total	40,760	11,800	13,660	9,160	54,420	20,960

* The data on which this table is based are the 1947 census statistics, "Occupational Classification by Nationality, Phranakhǫn" (supplied by the Central Statistical Office in Bangkok), and the amphoe registration figures for Krungthep municipality as of December 31, 1952 (supplied by the Krungthep Municipal Office). See note 1, pp. 415–416, for the procedure followed in constructing this table.

Table 21 (continued)

Occupation class	Estimated occupied population					
	Male		Female		Total	
	Ethnic Chinese	Ethnic Thai	Ethnic Chinese	Ethnic Thai	Ethnic Chinese	Ethnic Thai
Lowest status						
26. Farmers & fishermen	10	2,120	0	1,950	10	4,070
27. Market gardeners	1,300	920	1,040	1,720	2,340	2,640
28. Actors	1,830	100	100	310	1,930	410
29. Sailors & ships' crews	460	190	0	0	460	190
30. Low-status domestic & serv- ice	2,830	5,110	1,490	7,390	4,320	12,500
31. Barbers	1,020	330	0	0	1,020	330
32. Hawkers, petty market sel- lers	1,880	120	170	230	2,050	360
33. Unskilled laborers	30,200	20,240	3,900	7,370	34,100	27,600
Total	39,530	29,130	6,700	18,970	46,230	48,100

Summary

Occupations of:	Estimated occupied population							
	Male only				Both sexes			
	Ethnic Chinese		Ethnic Thai		Ethnic Chinese		Ethnic Thai	
	No.	%	No.	%	No.	%	No.	%
Highest status	3,790	2.6	8,430	8.5	5,330	2.7	10,110	6.2
Mid-high status	62,720	42.7	50,170	50.4	92,140	46.5	83,210	51.3
Mid-low status	40,760	27.8	11,800	11.8	54,420	27.5	20,960	12.9
Lowest status	39,530	26.9	29,130	29.3	46,230	23.3	48,100	29.6
Total	146,800	100.0	99,530	100.0	198,120	100.0	162,380	100.0

skill. It can be no more than approximate, however, since each occupation class includes a more or less broad range of individuals when
ranked according to these values. Table 21, it will be noted, is so organized as to compare ethnic Thai and ethnic Chinese, and leaves
both Westerners and other Asians out of consideration.

Before analyzing Table 21 as it stands, it might be well to present
certain data given there in somewhat different form. When the occupation classes of Table 21 are regrouped, socio-occupational status
aside, into broad occupational categories, the results are as in Table 22.
This grouping presents in the broadest terms prevailing ethnic occupational specialization: the Thai preference for (and dominance
in) government, the professions, and agriculture, and the Chinese
preference for (and dominance in) commerce and finance, and industrial and artisan occupations.

Table 22. Ethnic occupational specialization by major categories, Krungthep, 1952

Occupation category	Ethnic Chinese		Ethnic Thai	
	No.	%	No.	%
Government	30	0.02	43,630	26.87
Professions	3,160	1.59	8,760	5.39
Commerce and finance	100,720	50.84	41,260	25.41
Industry and artisan	38,450	19.41	9,880	6.08
Domestic and service	19,310	9.75	24,540	15.11
Agriculture	2,350	1.19	6,710	4.13
Unskilled labor	34,100	17.21	27,600	17.00
Total	198,120	100.01	162,380	99.99

The more specific listing in Table 23, however, points up the danger inherent in using extremely general categories. There it can be noted that within the large categories generally dominated by one ethnic group, the other ethnic group is nonetheless strongly represented in certain subclasses. Thus while most business clerks are Chinese, most *female* business clerks are Thai, and most of the higher-ranking office staff are Thai. And while agriculture generally is dominated by Thai, the majority of male market gardeners are Chinese. Hairdressers are predominantly Thai; barbers predominantly Chinese. The great majority of chauffeurs, bus and truck drivers are Thai, and Thai are heavily represented among repairmen and mechanics, even though such technical and mechanical occupations are in most other cases overwhelmingly Chinese.

To return now to Table 21, perhaps the most striking phenomenon it portrays is the tendency for Chinese to concentrate in occupations of mid-low status and the complementary tendency for Thai to concentrate in occupations of highest status. Of the ethnic Thai 6.2 per cent but of the ethnic Chinese only 2.7 per cent are in occupational positions of highest status, while 27.5 per cent of the Chinese but only 12.9 per cent of the Thai are in occupational positions of mid-low status. These differentials are still sharper when only males in the two ethnic groups are compared. The distribution of the ethnic groups is more nearly equal in occupations of mid-high and of lowest status, with Chinese slightly outnumbering Thai in the former and Thai slightly outnumbering Chinese in the latter.

This over-all occupational distribution can easily be placed in historical context. The sharpest division within premodern Thai society was that between the elite and the masses, and the tendency of

Table 23. Occupational classes, Krungthep, arranged according to ethnic-group dominance *

Occupational classes in which:	No. of ethnic Chinese per ethnic Thai		
	Male	Female	Total
Chinese nationals are a majority			
Weavers & dyers	80.7	24.3	30.3
Shoemakers	54.7	4.8	23.5
Hotel & restaurant employees	21.4	1.3	7.6
Jewelers; gold-, silversmiths	13.1	1.8	6.9
Carpenters & furniture makers	6.2	—	6.3
Market sellers	15.3	.84	6.2
Metal workers (base metals)	7.0	1.4	6.1
Actors	18.3	.32	4.7
Workers in building trades	6.3	.43	4.7
Barbers	3.2	—	3.2
Miscellaneous craftsmen	6.4	.87	2.8
Business owners & mgrs.	6.1	1.1	2.4
Sailors & ships' crews	2.4	—	2.4
Miscellaneous technicians	2.3	2.5	2.4
Ethnic Chinese are a clear majority			
Business clerks	2.6	.34	1.9
Tailors & dressmakers	26.4	.84	1.5
Repairmen, machinists, etc.	1.4	—	1.4
Unskilled laborers	1.5	.53	1.2
Ethnic Chinese & Thai are about equally represented			
Cooks, bakers, food processors	13.2	.49	1.09
Market gardeners	1.4	.60	.89
Ethnic Thai are a clear majority			
High-ranking office staff	.72	.17	.63
High-status industrial staff	.51	—	.52
Lesser & semi-professionals	.58	.15	.38
Low-status domestic & service	.55	.20	.35
Auto, bus, & truck drivers	.32	—	.32
Highest-status professionals	.27	.09	.26
Hairdressers	—	.04	.04
Farmers & fishermen	.01	.00	.00
Government clerks	.00	.00	.00
Government officials	.00	.00	.00

* This table is based entirely on Table 21; the ethnic ratios are computed from the absolute figures given there. When the total of one sex in a given category is less than 100 (as occurs several times for females and once for males), the ratio between Chinese and Thai would be next to meaningless and unreliable; such cases are indicated by a dash in the table.

ethnic Thai in present-day Bangkok to polarize at the extreme ends of the socio-occupational status scale may be seen as a natural outcome of nineteenth-century social structure. In premodern society, the Chinese were outside of the elite-masses dichotomy characteristic of the majority society, performing economic functions necessary for both the Thai elite and the Thai masses but congenial to neither. As Chinese rose to positions of higher status, they were in large part drawn out of Chinese society into the Thai elite by virtue of the deliberate government policy described above (Chapter 4, Section C). Thus there are relatively few ethnic Chinese in positions of highest occupational status. The general upward mobility characteristic of Chinese society in Bangkok prior to the depression meant that many of the immigrants and their descendants who came in the two main waves of Chinese laborers before and after the First World War have since raised their occupational status to mid-low or mid-high, thus reinforcing the nineteenth-century specialization of Chinese in middle-status occupations. Meanwhile the demand for unskilled and low-status labor has been met by Chinese immigrants of the short-term postwar immigration wave, and increasingly by Thai from upcountry. While Chinese immigration decreased rapidly after 1947 to a negligible quantity, in-migration of Thai to Krungthep proceeded at a minimum rate of 37,800 annually between 1947 and 1954.[2] In consequence Thai have come to equal Chinese in callings of lowest status.

The relatively strong representation of Thai in occupations of mid-high status implies the occurrence of considerable social mobility in Thai society during the past half-century. In broad terms, it would appear that the growth of the Thai "middle class" is based primarily on upward mobility through education of descendants of former free-men and on assimilation of descendants of nineteenth-century Chinese immigrants, and only to a much smaller degree on downward mobility from the old aristocratic and bureaucratic classes. It is clear, in any case, that Thai have strongly preferred occupations of mid-high status—as being more similar to those of the old Thai elite (i.e., more congruent with Thai values)—to occupations of mid-low status. With the possible exception of chauffeurs and drivers, dressmakers, cooks, and hairdressers, most of the relatively few ethnic Thai in mid-low status occupations are assimilated descendants of Chinese of similar occupational position.

It is not yet possible to make a case that Bangkok presents a "true" class-organized society. According to Goldschmidt, such a society is:

one in which the hierarchy of prestige and status is divisible into groups each with its own social, economic, attitudinal and cultural characteristics and each having differential degrees of power in community decisions. Such groups would be socially separate and their members would readily identify.[3]

The social groups Goldschmidt conceives of are more or less identifiable and they differ—though they are not always sharply separated —in regard to most of the stipulated characteristics. In this sense, Bangkok society can be said to approach a class system. Especially with regard to identification, social groups in Bangkok are often ambiguously oriented or seem so to the objective observer. If, however, we utilize the idea of core Chinese and Thai groupings, with the understanding that there are many local-born Chinese intermediate, a discussion of social structure in terms of class can profitably be made. The aim is not to turn up a fixed number of distinct classes nicely named and categorized, but rather to suggest probable or apparently emerging class alignments in the form of hypotheses subject to the test of further research.

The most clearly defined group at the top of the social system is a traditional elite class composed chiefly of royal aristocratic and old-time bureaucratic families. It is characterized by wealth based primarily on real estate, high enlightenment (educational attainment), respect or prestige in high degree and of long standing, and high "culture," i.e., a devotion to the old elite traditions. Self-identification on the basis of these interests is manifest; and social access to the traditional elite by members of other classes is strictly limited. The class in general deplores open involvement in commercial, financial, or industrial enterprise, but economic pressure is forcing its members increasingly to seek salaried employment or at least to lend the prestige of their names to the boards of important enterprises in consideration of emolument. Aside from the *rentier* elements (presumably not included in the occupied population according to the Thai census), its membership is based on the top three occupation classes in the highest status category, ethnic Thai columns, as presented in Table 21. While many are in positions of governmental authority, they do not as a class possess political power in high degree; their political role is more that of councilorship, sponsorship, and guidance. They are limited to ethnic Thai, though many are at least partially of Chinese ancestry. Typically they live in large and old houses serviced by a flock of loyal servants, with whom they maintain a relationship of paternalistic patronage. In this class are found the relatively few Thai who continue to wear the traditional court apparel, especially on ceremonial occasions. The class exemplar is the king.

The other major high status social grouping which may reasonably be considered a class is the new elite. Its core is made up of descendants of the premodern bureaucratic class but with important accretions from the premodern royal aristocratic class, freeman class, and Chinese business class. It is characterized by wealth based on business enterprise and the state coffers, political power of highest degree, high enlightenment, and high homage (respect by virtue of power position). The bulk of the occupied membership of this class consists of government officials and business entrepreneurs, with an important professional element and a sprinkling of high-status office personnel. It is thus drawn from all occupation groups listed in Table 21 as being of highest status. It is also suggested here that this emerging class, consisting primarily of high-status ethnic Thai, also includes important ethnic Chinese elements, perhaps as much as one-fifth of the ethnic Chinese listed in occupations of highest status (as given in Table 21). In other words, government bureaucrats, military brass, certain elements of leading Chinese businessmen and financiers, and many high-status professionals are held to be increasingly united in common interests—by the high valuation and possession of wealth-through-power and power-through-wealth, and by considerable Westernization of culture. Evidence for this class alignment can be seen in the military's remarkable role in governmental politics and business, the bureaucracy's entry into business in alliance with leading Chinese merchants, and social intercourse among these groups through cosmopolitan clubs, private parties, mutually used schools, and so on. A *nouveau riche* coloring clearly distinguishes this class from the traditional elite. The class symbol of status par excellence is the big American automobile. In housing and attire, the new elite is more modernized and Westernized than any other grouping in Bangkok society.

Underneath these upper classes there are what appear to be two middle classes, or at least two major middle-class groupings—the Chinese and the Thai. They overlap for the most part in stratification, but the mean status of the Chinese middle class is appreciably higher. The latter consists of most ethnic Chinese in occupations of highest and mid-high status, i.e., occupations of relatively high income which involve no manual labor. The backbone and exemplar of the class is, of course, the Chinese businessman, and the major class interests are commercial wealth and the maintenance of the Chinese way of life. It is this class which supports and fights for the system of private Chinese schools and which maintains the closest ties with China and Chinese communities elsewhere in Southeast Asia. To some extent, it takes upper and middle-class Hongkong society as a model—thoroughly Chinese and yet oriented to the modern world. In contrast to the Thai middle class, well-being (standards of housing, apparel, diet, comfort) is less highly valued than wealth or even enlightenment. It is this class from which most members of Chinese community associations are drawn. Its concern with power is limited, on the one hand, to intraclass self-control, and on the other, to mitigating the force of Thai political power.

The Thai middle class, consisting mainly of those in mid-high status occupations (government employees, small entrepreneurs, teachers, newspapermen, clerks, secretaries, and so on), is white-collar in flavor and almost literally in attire. Its ethos is typically middle-class, with perhaps unusually accentuated nationalism. It is oriented more to the new elite than to the traditional. Few members of the Thai middle class would not aspire to high or higher government positions, and the jobs of most of them are dependent on the continued favor of the new elite. In consequence, interest is focused on political developments and the doings of men of power; and connections with members of the new elite are a source of additional prestige and informal power within the class. Enjoyment of life, especially of leisure-time activities, is diligently pursued, and well-being in its various facets is highly valued.

Another discernible grouping which seems to meet most criteria of class is that of Chinese artisans, mechanics, and craftsmen—the Chinese artisan class. Its occupied membership consists essentially of ethnic Chinese in occupations of mid-low status (see Table 21). Skill appears to be the value held in highest esteem, and a higher possession of skill, wealth, and respect help distinguish the class from others below it. The orientation is again Chinese, but in this regard it differs from the Chinese middle class in having limited access to Chinese schools and much less contact with Chinese in other countries. Consisting of manual laborers for the most part, the class is also sharply distinguished from the Chinese middle class in terms of prestige.

Nonetheless the major external interest of the Chinese artisan class is centered on activities and developments in the Chinese middle class.

The writer would tend not to accord separate class status to ethnic Thai in occupations of mid-low status, on the grounds that there is no evidence of class identification and that the grouping is numerically small. Rather, many Thai in occupations of mid-low status—chauffeurs and drivers, technicians, hairdressers, and so on—appear to identify with the Thai middle class, while others of Chinese extraction tend to identify with fellow workers in the Chinese artisan class. Those of lower status within the category may, on further research, be found to identify with the lower class.

There is, in fact, considerable evidence that a Thai lower class is emerging with common interests and some class consciousness. Low in possession of most values important in Bangkok society, the class is primarily concerned with basic well-being, i.e., the health and safety of the organism. Some elements within the class, pedicab drivers for instance, are formally organized for the attainment of group interests, while others—domestic servants and market gardeners for example—are informally organized. The class has been wooed by some Thai politicians in hopes of support at the polls. The fact that a large proportion of this class consists of recent immigrants from upcountry, especially Northeast Siam, provides a natural basis for some working arrangement with Assemblymen representing the jangwats in question.

Whether low-status Chinese laborers should be considered a separate class is another question which can only be decided by further research. The answer would appear, on the basis of limited evidence, to be in the affirmative. Chinese hawkers, actors, and barbers are each fairly well organized and conscious of intergroup common interests; to some extent they are united by the fact that all are held in low esteem by the Chinese population. Unskilled Chinese laborers have also shown some solidarity in the numerous postwar strikes for better wages and working conditions. On the other hand, there is evidence that, ethnic antagonism aside, many Chinese in lower-status occupations identify or advocate identification with Thai laborers of similar status. The history of organized labor between 1948 and 1954, however, tended to abort the promise of an interethnic labor movement manifested in 1947. But the last year or two has seen developments reinforcing the common interests of Chinese and Thai laborers. It is also significant that a large section of unskilled Chinese laborers is characterized by a mental set toward upward social mobility—from all indications this is truer of Chinese than of Thai labor. By way of tenuous prediction, it would appear that low-status Chinese laborers will eventually either assimilate to the Thai lower class or rise in the stratification system to the Chinese artisan class. With further replenishment of Chinese labor through immigration no longer possible, on the one hand, and a surplus Thai population steadily coming into Bangkok from upcountry Thailand, on the other, it would appear that lower-class Chinese as a whole may continue in the historical trend towards upward mobility, with the void at the bottom being filled in the future by unskilled Thai labor.

The foregoing discussion, admittedly impressionistic and unverified, is nonetheless felt by the writer to provide some insight into the structure of Bangkok society as a whole. It is probably worth drawing specific attention to the fact that Bangkok society is not a caste system along ethnic lines; class boundaries are by no means coterminous with ethnic-group dimensions, and Chinese and Thai groupings show only a limited tendency to stratify. In this respect, too, models of social structure and functioning which have proved useful in the social analysis of other Southeast Asian countries—notably Furnivall's concept of plural society [4]—seem to be only most imperfectly approached by Bangkok (and Thailand) society. In Bangkok the manifestly non-exclusive role of Westerners, far less crucial than that in Southeast Asian countries with a colonial history, the overlapping economic function and socio-occupational status among Thai and Chinese, and the large number of individuals intermediate between Chinese and Thai societies, all render the plural society concept of limited value for analysis. Thailand society may in several respects be pluralistic—government for instance is almost exclusively a Thai preserve—but the ethnic divisions if anything tend to be vertical rather than horizontal and, in Bangkok at least, fail to coincide with differences of economic function.

In each major city and town of Thailand a geographical core of Chinese society is easily distinguishable. In Bangkok it is still the Sampheng area (known administratively as amphoe Samphantha-wong), and, as indicated in Chapter 6, the Chinese concentration thins out in all directions from this Chinese quarter. Samphanthawong is a mixture of the traditional and the modern, of provincialism and cosmopolitanism, but in essence it is all Chinese. The flavor of old

China is met most strongly along Sampheng Lane, the first road ever built outside the royal city, and in the area between it and the river. There traditional-type shops, traditional business practices, and to a large extent the traditional Ch'ao-chou way of life persist, and there it is possible for a Chinese to live for years almost devoid of significant contact with the Thai. The modern cosmopolitan flavor is most pervasive along Yaowarat and Ratchawong roads, wide thoroughfares cut through the Chinese quarter in recent decades. Along these streets are found the big Chinese department stores, modern cinemas, and the imposing façades of Sino-Thai banks.

Throughout the area of major Chinese concentration, the streets are usually lined with Chinese shop-houses in row buildings, ordinarily two to three stories tall. The interiors of the big blocks are packed with crowded tenement-type housing, on the whole in ill repair and poorly ventilated. Even in the predominantly Thai areas of the city, Chinese shop-houses line the major streets. While Thai society has no single geographical core comparable to amphoe Samphanthawong, Thai government offices, the grandest Thai temples, and other symbols of Thai culture and the Thai state are located principally in amphoe Phranakhon, the old royal city, and in the area to the northeast of it. Unlike the usual Chinese pattern of combining residence with place of business, the Thai tend to reside in separate and more spacious housing outside of the main business centers. In general, the pattern of Chinese concentration in the business centers surrounded by residential areas largely occupied by the Thai is found in all provincial towns.

Nevertheless, residence patterns are rapidly changing away from any ghetto-like distribution. As local-born Chinese acculturate, they show enhanced concern with well-being, in particular an appreciation of the value of less crowded, separate housing. Throughout the new residential suburbs of Bangkok—especially to the east, but also north, south, and, across the river, west of the central areas—Chinese are found residing among the Thai in a random arrangement which shows no sign of neighborhood segregation. Even families headed by Chinese immigrants have moved to such suburbs in the postwar period. This changing pattern facilitates the development of social intercourse between the Chinese and Thai elites.

In family life, as with residential arrangements, a core Chinese pattern is distinguishable from the Thai. Parental arrangement of marriages is much more strictly adhered to by first-generation Chinese than by Thai parents. Elopement is a common actual if not ideal pattern among the Thai, while for first-generation Chinese it is rare indeed. Divorce, too, is not only common but casual among the Thai, while immigrant Chinese take a strict view. The ideal of a large family is kept alive by Chinese immigrants, while the Thai tend to settle on a lower preferred number of children. Polygamous arrangements within the same household are still favored by Chinese much more than by Thai, who prefer to set up minor wives in separate

Table 24. Number of ordinary households, Krungthep, by size and mother tongue of household head, 1954 *

| Size of household | All households † | | Households the mother tongue of whose head is: | | | |
| | | | Thai | | Chinese | |
	No.	%	No.	%	No.	%
1	8,160	6.1	5,400	7.2	2,480	4.2
2	11,680	8.7	7,600	10.2	3,760	6.5
3–4	33,080	24.5	19,720	26.4	12,760	21.9
5–6	33,600	24.9	17,640	23.7	15,560	26.8
7–9	31,320	23.2	15,520	20.8	15,480	26.6
10–14	14,160	10.5	7,200	9.7	6,800	11.7
15–	2,840	2.1	1,480	2.0	1,320	2.3
All sizes	134,840	100.0	74,560	100.0	58,160	100.0

* Taken from *Economic and Demographic Survey 1954*, 1st Series, Table 17.
† Includes 2,120 households the mother tongue of whose head is a language other than Chinese or Thai.

residences. In consequence of these differences, the size of the Chinese household is larger than that of the Thai. Table 24 summarizes the results for Krungthep of the 1954 Economic and Demographic Survey in this regard. Six is the mean size of households headed by those whose mother tongue is Chinese, while five is the mean for households headed by those whose mother tongue is Thai.

But with regard to family as well as most other aspects of life in Thailand, there is a wide variety of arrangements intermediate between the Chinese and Thai patterns followed by local-born Chinese in process of assimilation. The crowded quarters where Chinese tend to live often force a local-born Chinese son to set up a separate household even though his parents would prefer to have him and his family under their own roof. Marriage customs are greatly modified from the Chinese ideal. Even when both parties are second-generation

Chinese, the wedding ceremony is often in the Thai style; for the Chinese elite, weddings are frequently the occasion for Sino-Thai social events, and a high-status Thai as often as not officiates at the ceremony. Many local-born Chinese of wealth keep Thai mistresses or secondary wives in conformity with the Thai pattern; outright polygamy of the traditional Chinese type is not well regarded by them. Local-born Chinese generally value well-being more strongly than their parents, and they are more often prepared to limit family size in the interests of higher living standards. Local-born Chinese women usually refuse to tolerate the subordinate role in which Chinese immigrant mothers-in-law would cast them.

In religious matters, too, Chinese and Thai core patterns are clear-cut and distinctive. The Thai worship at Buddhist *wats* (the religious precincts housing sanctuaries, preaching halls, rest houses, monastic quarters, and so on), the immigrant Chinese at their own deity temples. The Thai cremate in their *wats* or crematories; the Chinese bury in their cemeteries. The Thai have no ancestral duties; the Chinese are duty-bound to maintain and honor graves at Ch'ing-ming and the New Year and to maintain ancestral shelves or shrines in their homes. The Thai consider temporary service in the monastic order as an ideal for all men, while the Chinese make monastic service in their Buddhist temples a lifelong career for a negligible minority.

Local-born Chinese, however, effect a selective combination of the two traditions. Few of them have not worshipped in Thai *wats;* fewer still maintain ancestral shrines or tablets in their homes. Perhaps the only traditional Chinese custom adhered to by all Thailand-born persons who still consider themselves Chinese is that of honoring ancestors at the time of the Chinese New Year. Traditional Chinese days of worship are the first and fifteenth of the lunar months, while holy days for the Thai come weekly at the phases of the moon. The two calendars are often one day apart, however, and it is not uncommon for the same individual to worship at a Thai *wat* one day and at a Chinese temple the next. In most of the Thai temples in the Indian or animistic tradition, local-born Chinese worship as frequently as the Thai; this is true for the rural shrines to native spirits and other types of *phi* as well as for the urban *lak-mueang* temples. Even second-generation Chinese, especially when they have Thai mothers, serve in the Thai Buddhist priesthood; in many upcountry towns, service for seven days at least is the rule rather than the exception for local-born Chinese sons. The writer was not surprised to find a second-generation Chinese who had studied at Amoy University serving the Buddhist Lent in the monastery of a Thai *wat* in his father's town of Rọi-et.

With regard to funerals and death practices, the patterns followed by local-born Chinese show almost infinite variety. Few funerals even in Chinese cemetery buildings fail to include chanting by Thai Buddhist priests. The most traditional of Chinese funeral processions often end up in a Thai *wat* for Theravada Buddhist ceremonies prior to cremation. A majority of local-born Chinese are eventually cremated rather than permanently buried. Elaborate compromise patterns are followed, one of the most common being burial, followed after two or three years by disinterment and cremation, and placement of the ashes either in a mock Chinese grave, or in a Thai-style memorial tomb in the precincts of a *wat,* or behind a statue of the Buddha in a *wat* sanctuary, or on the Chinese ancestral shelf. It is not considered bizarre to couple cremation with the traditional Chinese seventh-day and one-hundredth-day observances. One can scarcely imagine a combination of Chinese and Thai death practices that has not been followed by some local-born Chinese in Thailand.

With regard to formal social and recreational organizations, the situation is not dissimilar. The Chinese core society has its own organizations in profusion. The speech-group, hsien, and surname associations all have social functions catering especially to Chinese immigrant members. Chinese clubs, formally registered as "friendship societies," provide opportunities for legalized gambling, and also serve as places where leading Chinese merchants congregate, read the newspaper, listen to music, and discuss business and community problems. While the Thai are in general less avid joiners than the Chinese, they also have formal social organizations, ranging from alumni associations to sports clubs to *wat* lay committees. Local-born Chinese, on the other hand, have no organizations of their own. They are members alongside of immigrants in the Chinese organizations, and at the same time join Thai and Sino-Thai associations. They are found among the membership of such Thai elite organizations as the Dusit Golf Club and the Silom Club, or in such organizations as Rotary, the Turf Club, and the Cosmopolitan Club. There are also general clubs whose membership is deliberately inclusive of both Thai and Chinese. The most important of those in Bangkok is the Samosọn Sahamit, in which scores of prominent local-born Chinese find recreation alongside of an equal number of ethnic Thai. In addition, the active alumni associations of the major mission schools (Assumption College, Bangkok Christian College, and so on) include in strength both local-born Chinese and Thai.

It is clear, then, that while immigrant Chinese and Thai have distinct societies in Thailand, second- and third-generation Chinese can move in either according to personal choice. Their way of life is in general intermediate between the norms for the two core societies, but they are not welded into a separate social grouping or class or society.

Among the ethnic Chinese in postwar Thailand, speech-group distinctions remain the most important social divisions after the socio-economic factors discussed above in terms of class. But the significance of speech-group differences has greatly altered since the turn of the century. Historical events of the twentieth century have had the effect of minimizing differences among speech groups: the growth of Chinese nationalism, and not of Teochiu, Cantonese, and Hainanese nationalisms; the unification of China under the Kuomintang; the development of a popular Chinese national literature and the promotion of Kuo-yü as a Chinese national language; and in Thailand the increase of anti-Chinese sentiment and measures, which (as outlined in Chapter 5 above) forced a certain degree of unity in Chinese society. Ethnic Chinese are today indisputably Chinese first and Teochiu, Cantonese, or whatever second.

Nevertheless it remains a fact that social relations are far more frequent within speech groups than among them. This can be seen in the occupational structure, the formal organizational structure, and to a lesser extent in patterns of education, religion, and recreation.

Within the occupational structure, marked speech-group specializations occur more often than not. For instance, within industrial and artisan fields in Bangkok, about 97 per cent of rice millers are Teochius, 85 per cent of sawmillers Hainanese, 98 per cent of leather-workshop proprietors Hakkas, and 50 per cent of machine-shop proprietors Cantonese. Examples of specialization in service occupations in Bangkok include a disproportion of Teochius among old-style druggists (92 per cent), of Hakkas among tailors (90 per cent), of Hainanese among barbers (50 per cent), and of Cantonese among restaurant operators (50 per cent). In commercial occupations, salient instances of specialization include those of Hokkiens among rubber exporters (87 per cent) and Teochius among pawnbrokers and rice merchants 'almost 100 per cent in each). A list of the more important occupational specializations of each speech group in Bangkok is given in Table 25. Often specialization is seen to be more extreme when the categories are more narrowly defined. Thus, when silversmiths are subdivided according to the type of work done, basin and belt makers turn out to be 90 per cent Hakka, chain and ornament makers over 60 per cent Teochiu, and Chinese nielloware makers (many if not most nielloware makers are Thai) over 50 per cent Hainanese. The jewelry field also provides a prize example of occupational specialization by native hsien: all of the 243 individual members of the Gold and Jewelry Merchants Association are Teochius, and for 235 of them Ch'ao-yang is the native hsien.

It is quite clear that traditional occupational specializations have been in the process of breaking down since before the turn of the century. The major changes have resulted from the steady advance of Teochius into occupations traditionally the specialization of other speech groups. This trend, of course, is the natural consequence of the changing patterns of immigration to Bangkok outlined above in Chapters 2 and 6. Particularly notable is the rapid decline of Cantonese in a series of important occupations during the past thirty years. Cantonese entered rice milling only around the turn of the century, but by the 1920's operated eleven large mills in Bangkok and vicinity. Competition from Teochius mills in the depression years had reduced this number to four by 1937, none of which were revived under Cantonese ownership after the war. Thirty years ago Cantonese had a virtual monopoly in the machine-shop line, but the steady advance of Hainanese and Teochius has since reduced the Cantonese share to about half. Cantonese likewise held first place in the printing business and publishing, but have since lost out to Teochius and Hakkas. In 1930, over half of the hardware stores were Cantonese, but now of these only two of any importance remain in Bangkok. The insurance business, begun in Bangkok by Cantonese in 1914 and dominated by them until 1928, had by the Second World War passed into other hands, mainly Teochiu. The last of the two Cantonese insurance companies re-established after the war was closed in late 1952. In thirty years' time, also, the proportion of Cantonese hotels has decreased from over half to less than 5 per cent. When questioned about this trend, Cantonese today sometimes mention the proportional decline in Cantonese immigration, but more often they stress competition from other speech groups, and in particular the industriousness,

Table 25. Occupational specialization by Chinese speech group, Bangkok *

Teochiu	Hakka
Bankers	Sundry-goods dealers
Rice merchants & exporters	Newspapermen
Insurance brokers	Tobacco manufacturers
Gold and jewelry merchants	Tailors
Hardware merchants	Silversmiths
Textile merchants	Leather workshop proprietors
Liquor merchants	Shoemakers
Pawnbrokers	Shirtmakers
Canned-goods & grocery dealers	Barbers
Local-products dealers	
Timber merchants	
Rubber manufacturers	**Cantonese**
Book and stationery dealers	Printers
Chinese (type) doctors	Machine-shop proprietors
Chinese (type) druggists	Silk piece-goods dealers
Pork butchers	Tailors
Actors	Restaurant proprietors
Rice-mill laborers	Machinists
Dock workers	Auto repairmen
	Beef butchers
Hainanese	Construction workers
Western (type) pharmacists	Furniture makers
Sawmillers	
Ice-plant proprietors	
Hotel proprietors	**Hokkien**
Remittance-shop proprietors	Rubber exporters
Tailors	Tea merchants
Machine-shop proprietors	
Contractors	
Coffee-shop proprietors	**Mandarin**
Furniture makers	Teachers
Goldsmiths	Furniture dealers
Hotel and restaurant employees	Furniture makers
Domestic servants	Chinese (type) doctors
Actors	
Ship caulkers	
Fishermen	**Taiwanese**
Barbers	Tea merchants
Lighterage "coolies"	Japanese-goods importers
Sawmill laborers	

* Occupations are listed only when the proportion of the speech group in question in the occupation is, at the .01 level, significantly greater than the proportion of the speech group in the total population. Significance, where not obvious, was computed by the difference-of-percentages method. The original statistics were collected by the Cornell Research Center in Bangkok, in 1952–1953.

venturesomeness, sharpness, and penurious habits of the Teochius.

The Cantonese decline was accompanied by a marked expansion of Teochius into occupations at all status levels, an expansion which affected even Hakkas and Hainanese. Teochius have taken over more and more of the sundry-goods trade, once primarily a Hakka preserve. And the field of Western medicine, which Hakkas once dominated by virtue of the happy circumstance that a disproportionate number of the early missionary hospitals were established in Hakka regions of Kuangtung, is now rather more than shared with Teochius. As for the Hainanese, their earlier monopoly of coffee shops has in part given way to Teochiu competition, though even in Teochiu shops the head-man who grinds the coffee and brews the tea is invariably Hainanese. On the whole, however, Hakkas and Hainanese have not only held their own in occupations traditionally followed but expanded into other fields of higher status, generally at the Cantonese' expense.

The situation in Bangkok today with regard to occupational special-ization is still fluid, but the rapid changes of the past decades will not likely be repeated now that mass immigration has ceased. The special-ization pattern, of course, casts considerable light on the relative social status of the speech groups. A perusal of Table 25 will show that Hainanese and Teochius, more than any others, specialize in low-status occupations, followed by Hakkas and Cantonese in that order. At the other extreme, Teochius, who are very strongly represented in finance (banking, insurance, pawnbroking, gold business) and the more lucrative commercial trades, together with the smaller speech groups (Hokkiens, Mandarin-speakers, and Taiwanese) specialize in high-status occupations more than the others. In the middle range, Cantonese, Hakkas, and Hainanese are the specialists, with Teochius and Mandarin-speakers following in that order.

From this generalized pattern of occupational specialization it can be seen that Teochius are disproportionately represented in the Chi-nese middle class and in the Chinese lower class, that Cantonese and Hakkas are most strongly represented in the Chinese artisan class, and that Hainanese are disproportionately represented in the Chinese artisan and lower classes.

Other evidence of the continued vitality of speech-group differences is seen in the fact that next to the two old community-wide organiza-tions—the Chinese Chamber of Commerce and the T'ien-hua Hos-pital—speech-group associations are the most important of the formal organizations in Chinese society. Every Chinese in Bangkok is presumably eligible to belong to one or more of the seven speech-group associations. Only in the case of the Hakka Association, however, are membership requirements expressed in terms of language. For the others, the principle is territorial. Thus, any natives or descendants of natives from Ch'ao-chou can belong to the Teochiu Association, from Fukien province to the Hokkien Association, from Kuang-chou and Chao-ch'ing to the Cantonese Association, from Hainan to the Hainanese Association, and so on. Any Chinese whose native place lies outside of Kuangtung, Fukien, or Taiwan is eligible for membership in the Chiang-che Association. In point of fact, however, association members are effectively restricted to those who speak the language of the dominant speech group. Thus few Hakkas belong to the Teochiu Association or the Hokkien Association, and those who do can speak Teochiu or Hokkien as the case may be. Since the seven speech-group associations together are considered to represent all the sub-groups within Chinese society, complete community-wide representation is ordinarily achieved by convening meetings of these organizations, usually under Chamber of Commerce leadership. The more important of the speech-group associations operate schools, hospitals or clinics, and cemeteries. It is indicative of the decline in rigidity of speech-group differences, however, that in the postwar period the speech-group clinics and hospitals have been opened to all patients regardless of background, and that the schools operated by the speech-group associations in Bangkok have large minorities of students from other than the sponsoring group.

In religious matters, too, the differences among speech groups are rapidly declining in the postwar era. Most of the temples in Bangkok are under the custodianship of one or another of the speech groups, but the worshippers are not necessarily even primarily from the sponsoring groups. In Bangkok shifting proportions and distributions of the speech groups have left Hokkien deity temples in largely Teochiu and Hakka neighborhoods, and their body of worshippers has changed accordingly. In upcountry Thailand, the Pen-t'ou temple has become *the* Chinese temple, with worshippers from all speech groups. While the priests in the Chinese Buddhist temples are still disproportionately Hakkas, the worshippers in them are indiscriminately of all speech groups.

In the Chinese community of Bangkok, the overall socio-political structure is dominated by the formal Chinese associations. The importance of these associations derives in part from the fact that the ethnic Chinese of Bangkok play no direct role in the Thai government. Chinese who do not hold Thai citizenship are perforce disenfranchised, and the Electoral Law of 1951 provided that those born in Thailand of an alien father (completely second generation) can vote only if they have been educated in Thai to the Matayom 6 level (equivalent to the tenth grade) or have served in government employ for at least five years. The same law requires candidates for political office to have been born of a Thai father, i.e., to be at least completely third generation.[5] With no weight in Thai politics, then, ethnic Chinese understandably have few champions in government councils and representative bodies. When government policies run counter or threaten to run counter to Chinese interests, the community's need is great for protection from this outside government and for the application of pressure to it. These diplomatic functions are performed, insofar as they can be, by the larger community associations.

The welfare functions of Chinese associations are as important in the fifties as they were in the thirties (see Chapter 6). Government schools and hospitals make virtually no concessions to the special needs or aspirations of the Chinese population. No comprehensive labor code has yet been enacted by the Thai government, and the beginnings of a social security program in 1955 were aborted by popular opposition. At the same time, profit-making enterprises cannot begin to fill Chinese needs in this regard. In this situation, the Chinese must provide their own welfare facilities on a nonprofit community basis through formal associations.

The need for social control and mediation within the community, obviously important for any large group, is likewise intensified by the peculiar position of ethnic Chinese in the larger society. Disorder, social unrest, or open conflict within the Chinese community inevitably brings stricter control and repression from the "outside" government. The more effective the intracommunity self-control, the less interference from the Thai. In the village environment in which most of the Chinese or their immediate ancestors found themselves in China, social control was largely effected within lineages and informally by gentry and village elders. In the urban setting of Bangkok, however, lineages are nonexistent or relatively ineffective in a sea of non-kin. In consequence, social controls operate much more at the extrafamilial associational level.

The protective and diplomatic, welfare and control functions are performed by formal associations rather than informally structured groups, because Thai law and its enforcement are such that only formal organizations can operate with any effectiveness. Regulations of both the Police Department and the National Culture Institute require registration of any association or grouping collecting monies or recruiting members. In order to comply with the requirements of registration, the association must be formally organized with responsible officers and a written constitution. Beginning in 1949, police investigation and supervision have made it extremely difficult for non-registered and clandestine groups to function at all. Thus it is that the associations through which major community functions are performed are formal and official rather than informal or illegal.

The Chinese community organization for Bangkok and the whole country remains the Chinese Chamber of Commerce, which functions as the chief diplomatic and protective agency of the entire community. The Chamber has always striven for proportional representation of the various speech groups among its elected officers. An analysis of the elected committees from 1946–1957 (six two-year terms) shows that 61 per cent of the offices have been filled by Teochius, 11 per cent by Hakkas, 10 per cent by Cantonese, 9 per cent by Hainanese, 4 per cent by Hokkiens, 3 per cent by natives of Mandarin-speaking areas, and 2 per cent by Taiwanese—in fact a fairly close approximation of speech-group distribution in the total population.

The other major community-wide organization, the T'ien-hua Hospital, is constitutionally required to include representatives from each speech group in specified number: eight Teochiu, three each of Hakka, Hainanese, and Cantonese, two Hokkien, and one each of Taiwanese and Mandarin-speakers. This stipulation dates back to 1941, when it replaced the original requirement that the chairmanship must rotate among the five main speech groups, while the treasurer must always be a Teochiu. Since the reform, which also increased the term of office to two years, Hakkas, Hainanese, and Cantonese have disproportionately held highest offices.

These two organizations still, in 1956 as in 1910, serve to integrate the various speech groups into a single structure, and their function in this regard was supplemented in the late forties by such cross-speech-group school boards as that of Huang-hun in Bangkok. Through interlocking officerships on the part of elected leaders, each of the five main speech-group associations is tied to the central structure. An even more elaborate system of interlocking directorates in the major Chinese corporations of Bangkok unites the same formal leaders into a web of economic power relationships. Fewer than two hundred Chinese leaders are crucial to the leadership structure of the Chinese community.[6] Stability throughout the postwar period has been enhanced by the culmination of lines of control and decision-making power in the hands of the same man. Chang Lan-ch'en (C 138), a Teochiu, has been re-elected to the chairmanship of the Chinese Chamber of Commerce every term since 1946. He almost always serves as an officer of several other major community organizations, including the T'ien-hua Hospital and the Teochiu Association. In business his position is no less prominent. In recent years he has been chairman of the boards of more than twenty industrial, financial, and commercial enterprises, and serves on the boards of over fifty other corporations in Bangkok. He has received heads of official foreign missions and leading Thai politicians, is an intimate of several top officials, and has been decorated by both the Thai King and the President of China. Insofar as the Chinese of Thailand constitute an *imperium in imperio* he is the undisputed head of state.

All the co-ordination that structural unity could afford and more was needed by the Chinese community to cope with the policies followed by the Thai administration from 1948 to 1954, and with the political dissension within the Chinese community itself. In the following section, we will focus attention on the complex political developments since Phibun's return to power.

B. The Chinese Response to the Shifting Political Climate

The second Phibun administration took over the Thai government just as the swing in overseas Chinese sentiment in favor of the Chinese Communists began to gain momentum. From the spring of 1948 to the summer of 1950, the prestige and local power of Communist elements among the Chinese in Thailand steadily increased. As the People's Liberation Army won repeated victories against the Chinese Nationalists and gained control of the entire mainland, the patriotism and hopes of the Thailand Chinese were visibly quickened. With the establishment of the new central government in Peking on October 1, 1949, Communist organizers in Thailand could appeal to all Chinese for the first time in terms of loyalty and nationalism. The Chinese

Communist Party of Thailand, which had been operating semiopenly as well as underground since 1946, became a major political force in the Chinese community, its progress seemingly hindered only by the Thai government's policies. In July 1948, Phibun himself estimated the number of Chinese Communists in the country at about fifty thousand,[7] though the core of full-fledged members probably never exceeded five thousand.

Communist progress within the formal Chinese organizational structure was apparent first in labor unions. The leadership of the Central Labor Union (Saha Achiwa Kamakọn) was clearly under Communist control by 1948, and membership drives were pressed forward in 1948–1949 among Chinese laborers in a wide variety of callings. In February 1949, the Central Labor Union affiliated with the World Federation of Trade Unions and in November sent delegates to the Federation Conference in Peking. By 1950, the total membership of the Central Labor Union was in the neighborhood of fifty thousand. The Kuomintang-sponsored union, by contrast, never even became a mass organization.[8]

Communist progress was also apparent in the Chinese schools, whose teachers, like the young intellectuals of China, in general constituted a vanguard in the acceptance and propagation of New Democracy. One by one, the formal Chinese associations assumed a neutralist and then a pro-Peking pose. By 1949, the auditorium of the Chinese Chamber of Commerce was no longer available for celebrating the Nationalists' Double Tenth anniversary. With the increasing polarization of the struggle in China, the stand of the China Democratic League became less and less distinguishable from that of the Chinese Communists and its activities no less objectionable to the Thai government. After the Chinese Nationalists were driven from the mainland to Taiwan, they found it necessary to close the four upcountry consulates, and after 1950 their mission to Bangkok was headed only by a chargé d'affaires or minister. Yi Mei-hou (C 139), a Teochiu member of the Standing Committee of the Chamber of Commerce, and Chou Cheng (C 140), chairman of the Ch'iung-yai (Hainanese) Association, both went to Peking to serve as members of the Communists' Commission on Overseas Chinese Affairs. Other Chinese leaders less anxious to leave Thailand were more circumspect about their political inclinations, but the general trend was unmistakable. In February 1950, a Thailand loyalty mission made up of second-rank Chinese leaders went to Peking. The delegation released a laudatory report which was printed in June in the Bangkok Communist press.[9]

The changing temper of the Chinese in Thailand was clearly reflected in their newspapers.[10] In April 1948, there were six major dailies: three independent papers with neutral policies and one organ each of the Communists, Democratic League, and the Kuomintang. In June 1948, the Democratic League's *Man-ku Shang-pao* was raided and subsequently suspended. In November, the Kuomintang paper, *Cheng-yen Jih-pao*, closed after large financial losses, and its successor, *Man-ku Kung-pao* (C 141), was moribund from the start. During 1949, the *Hua-ch'iao Jih-pao* adopted an increasingly pro-Communist editorial policy, which precipitated a split in the staff and the eventual departure of pro-Nationalist employees. The *Chung-yüan Pao* also began a shift towards pro-Communism after October 1948, when it put out an evening edition with a somewhat more leftist editorial policy. *Ch'üan-min Pao,* the official Communist organ, doubled its circulation in the eight months from July 1948 to March 1949 and continued to grow until the new *Hsing-hsien Jih-pao* (C 142) with its evening edition *Hsing-t'ai Wan-pao* (C 143) entered the field in January 1950. These papers were the latest additions to the "Star" newspaper chain of Aw Boon Haw (Hu Wen-hu) (C 144), and in keeping with the then views of its backer, it too took a pro-Peking line. In the spring of 1950, the most right-wing of the Chinese newspapers was *Kuang-hua Pao*, whose policy was slightly left of neutral, the Nationalist regime being referred to merely as the "Taiwan Government."

During the same two-year period, the policies of the Phibun administration were directed toward a firm control of all Chinese activities, but with no special emphasis on anti-Communism. The first move was aimed at Chinese education. The general disdain of the letter of the Private Schools Act encouraged by the Chinese Embassy and consulates and permitted by lax enforcement on the part of preceding administrations gave Phibun ample legal justification for a series of school raids and closures during May and June 1948. Arrests of teachers and principals were made, for the most part, on the grounds that public subscription even for educational purposes was illegal without special permission. Nor were Chinese associations overlooked. The morning of June 14, 1948, residents in the major Chinese areas of Bangkok (Samphanthawong, Bangrak, and part of Thonburi) awoke to find roads closed to traffic and extensive police raids in progress.

Sixty Chinese were arrested in three days, including labor leaders, newspapermen (from *Man-ku Shang-pao* and *Ch'üan-min Pao*), teachers, and directors and staff members of various Chinese associations. A report on the work of the Communist Party was seized, and police announced they had scotched a plot to create disorders similar to those already begun by the Chinese terrorists in Malaya. Chinese labor and youth organizations and the Ch'iung-yai (Hainanese) Association were charged with fronting for subversive activities.[11] The raids precipitated charges in the Communist weekly, *Chen-hua Pao*, that Kuomintang partisans were acting as informers for the police.[12] Major Ch'iu Chi of that paper was soon sought by the police and later turned up in Peking as a delegate of the Thailand Chinese to the People's Political Consultative Conference and the World Federation of Trade Unions Conference in Peking. Nationwide raids in early August 1948 rounded up about two hundred Chinese charged with membership in unregistered societies allegedly extorting money from merchants.[13]

Any thought that the Phibun administration held a kinder view of Kuomintang activities than of the Chinese Communist movement was dispelled early the following year by events upcountry. The pro-Nationalist Ch'ing-hua school in Chiangmai was closed, and some sixty of the town's most prominent pro-Kuomintang citizens were arrested for irregular solicitation of funds, while the pro-Communist Hsin-sheng school was not molested. In Nọngkhai, neutralist and pro-Communist elements informed the police that the hotel where the Chung-hua Association's signboard hung was an illegal political headquarters, whereupon the organization was effectively crushed.

The significance of these moves went far beyond any erratic favoritism, however. Every one of the leaders holding a responsible official position with the Ch'ing-hua school in Chiangmai was included among those arrested; several of them were sentenced to deportation, and only four of the most prominent were able to secure commutations to exile in Phetchabun jangwat. As the implications of these developments dawned on Chinese leaders elsewhere, a rush to resign from responsible positions on Chinese school boards and associations could be observed all over upcountry Thailand. In Lampang the executive committee of the Hua-ch'iao Club and the school board of Yü-hua were dissolved when word of the Chiangmai developments was received. On hearing of the consequences of school-funds solicitation from the Chiangmai merchants who arrived in Phetchabun for their exile, the Ta-chung school there was voluntarily closed by the directors. The threat from the government plus the growing dissension between left and right led, between 1949 and 1951, to the demise of the Chinese Chambers of Commerce in Khǫnkaen, Surin, Buriram, and Sakon-nakhǫn, of the Hua-ch'iao Associations in Uttaradit and Thalǫ, and of both the schools and Hua-ch'iao Kung-so in Rǫi-et and in Mahasa-rakham. Dozens of Chinese communities were left with no formal organizations and no leaders willing to accept responsibility for community endeavors.

In other moves, Phibun tried to lure Thai workers away from Chinese and Communist influence. Shortly after he came to power the Thai Labor Union was launched, and the raids of 1948–1949 against Chinese-dominated unions were designed to expose their alien loyalties and connection with political subversion.[14]

In March 1949, Phibun minimized the Communist threat and expressed belief that the government's press censorship and policy of deporting Chinese for illegal organizational activities constituted "a sufficient check on Communism or other alien penetration." [15] In a radio message to the Chinese in Thailand on October 2, 1949, the Premier took a plague-on-both-your-houses stand: "If the Chinese should decide to split into two groups . . . Siam and the Siamese people would certainly not interfere, as this is a domestic matter. But the Siamese Nation would regret it very much if the Chinese . . . forget that they live in Siam and start fighting among themselves." He asked "all Chinese 'in Siam, whatever their political convictions may be," to remember that violation of Thai laws would not be tolerated. With regard to flying the new Communist flag, he reminded them that Thailand had not recognized the new Peking regime.[16] In October of that year, Chinese leaders co-operated with Thai police by going through the Chinese districts urging shop owners to pull down Communist flags in the interests of peace. Only a few of the most courageous merchants flew the Nationalist flag on Double Tenth in the face of rumors that the "Chiang flag" would be greeted with hand grenades.[17] In October 1949, the government sponsored the creation of a Sino-Thai committee to improve relations between the two peoples in Thailand, but it soon became evident that the Chinese leaders serving on it were heavily weighted with pro-Communists, and the project was dropped.

The potentialities of New China's role vis-à-vis the Chinese minority in Thailand were brought forcibly to the attention of the Thai administration in January 1950, when Peking Radio accused the government of oppressing local Chinese, protested police cruelties and unjust deportations, and demanded assurances that such treatment would not be allowed to recur. This move, which followed the receipt of complaints from Chinese prisoners in Bangkok awaiting deportation, was the signal for activating the entire network of political parties and mass organizations in China on behalf of "the suffering Chinese" of Thailand. The Revolutionary Committee of the Kuomintang offered its condolences to the "hundreds of thousands of local Chinese" who "lost their means of livelihood" through legal action of "the Phibun clique" against Chinese commerce and industry, and to the "approximately 200,000 Chinese youths" who "have been deprived of their education" by action of Phibun politicians. Another coalition party in Peking, the Conservatives, pledged "to help those suffering Chinese to the last in order to enable them to maintain their justified rights." The China Democratic League in a statement addressed to the Chinese of Thailand deplored the severe punishment and beatings which allegedly resulted in the deaths of more than ten Chinese in Bangkok prisons and declared that "with the rise of the New China, the Government of the People's Republic will never allow such oppression to be resorted to against our fellow countrymen." [18] In Thailand, the comparatively moderate *Chung-yüan Pao* commented: "The demonstration by the Central Government of China of its interest in the justified rights, welfare, and security of Chinese lives and properties overseas has been welcomed with pleasure and gratitude by the Chinese community in this country." [19]

Alarmed by this turn of events, the Thai government gradually took a more serious view of Chinese Communism in the country. Vigorous anti-Communism was, of course, in keeping with Phibun's international commitments to American Far Eastern policy made during 1950. A series of agreements with the United States for educational exchange, technical assistance, and military aid were followed by Thailand's support of United Nations intervention in Korea in the form of badly needed rice and an expeditionary force. With Thailand participating in the Korean campaign, Phibun stated that "there is a status of undeclared war between this country and Communism." [20] In September 1950, ten wealthy Chinese businessmen, including several pro-Communists, were pressured into contributing 20,000 baht each to the families of the Thai expeditionary soldiers. Government officials in upcountry towns carefully explained to Chinese merchants how they could make monetary contributions to the fight against Communism in Korea.[21] Throughout 1950–1951, attempts were made to stamp out Communist influence in Chinese schools, and the Communist infiltration of Chinese associations was hindered by strict control of the solicitation of funds.

The government also paid special attention to reducing liaison between the local Chinese and the Communist-controlled mainland. In November 1950, the Ministry of Interior announced that a Thailand-born Chinese over 18 years of age desiring to study in China would be allowed to return only if a "native Thai" guaranteed him to the amount of 5,000 baht, and only if his return was made before he reached the age of 21 (i.e., before passing the conscription age).[22] Chinese youths under 12 were allowed to travel to China only when accompanied by their parents, while those aged 12 to 18 could leave only with parental permission. Students attempting to sail for China without such permission were removed from the ships. In several such cases, the students revealed that Communist headquarters had arranged for their departure.[23] Meanwhile the Police Director-General announced that the authorities would not allow anyone to remit money (to China) for purchasing arms to fight United Nations troops in Korea. And in December 1951, the Bank of Thailand took the first steps toward control of the remittance of money abroad.

The period from June 1950 to the end of 1951, which saw a strengthening of anti-Communist measures on the part of the government, was for the Chinese populace one of political readjustment and reconsideration. Pro-Peking fervor was somewhat cooled by the Communist reverses in Korea and the international disapproval of Chinese Communist intervention. More important, news from the emigrant areas of south China, which had been relatively rosy from the arrival of the People's Liberation Army in 1949 on through 1950, took on a more ominous tone in 1951. In Chieh-yang and P'u-ning, two of the Teochiu emigrant hsiens, land reform was completed in 1951, and it was begun during that year in most other areas. Overseas Chinese who learned of the division of their land, acquired by hard work and frugality over decades, were not pleased, while many more disapproved of the cruel treatment of landlords.[24] Hundreds of Chinese in Bangkok could tell of the imprisonment or execution of relatives and friends. Peking insisted that "the majority of families of overseas Chinese and those who have returned from abroad" considered the land-reform policy "fair and reasonable," and claimed that "the land holdings of an average overseas Chinese family in Chieh-yang hsien had been doubled by land reform." [25] But the Chinese in Thailand were at least equally impressed by what appeared to be attempts at extortion on the part of Communist authorities. From April to November 1951, Teochius and Hakkas in Thailand received desperate appeals from relatives in China urging more and more remittances. One Bangkok merchant got a demand for ten million JMP (roughly 10,000 baht) to be paid his mother-in-law in Swatow. [26] The attitude of the local Chinese toward these demands stiffened following the case of a Chinese wholesaler who sold his business in Bangkok to supply the money demanded by Communist authorities in Canton for the release of his mother, only to learn of her death, a few days after leaving prison, from tuberculosis contracted there. One prominent Hakka leader received a letter telling him that his wife would be tortured and executed if he did not send 300,000 baht. [27] Such persons were thrown into torments of doubt as to the best course to follow, but whatever their decisions, all found their enthusiasm for Communism dimmed. In February 1951, Bangkok money-market circles reported a decline in remittances to China, while by October, a survey of Chinese remittance shops in Bangkok indicated a reduction in the average size of monthly remittances to less than HK$40. Many Chinese feared that larger remittances could cause the Communists to take their families and relatives for "rich peasants" or subject them to heavier taxes. [28]

These second thoughts were reflected in a trend towards neutralism on the part of most Chinese newspapers. *Ch'üan-min Pao,* the Communist organ, showed no change, but *Hua-ch'iao Jih-pao*'s former pro-Communist zeal had dropped almost to the zero point by October 1951, when it ran an "objective" series of articles on Communist rule which were strongly adverse to the new regime. In the same month *Chung-yüan Wan-pao* still referred to Peking as New China, but the number of favorable articles about mainland conditions was on the decrease. The morning edition of *Chung-yüan* was already neutral in its editorial policy and called the competing regimes simply Peking and Taiwan. In the fall of 1950, Aw Boon Haw's papers became lukewarm towards the Chinese Communists following the confiscation of his Tiger Balm factory at Canton earlier in the year. By the end of 1951, *Hsing-hsien Jih-pao* could be described as neutral, with only the slightest favoritism shown the Peking regime over that of Taipei.

The policies of *Kuang-hua Pao* showed a slight rightward movement between early 1950 and the end of 1951, in that it carried less favorable news about the mainland, even publishing some Central News Agency reports about conditions in Communist China. In March 1951, a rightist paper, *Min-chu Jih-pao,* was successfully launched with financial and other help from Taiwan and American sources. As of the end of 1951, however, it was still the only Chinese daily which referred to the Nationalist regime as "our government."

The year 1952 was critical for the Chinese in Thailand. As it dawned, the Chinese Chamber of Commerce was in the throes of the most serious crisis in its history, split wide open between the pro-Communists and the pro-Nationalists. With both a Kuomintang and a Communist organ in the press field, the war of words during 1952 reached a new peak of bitterness. In almost every Chinese organization a relentless political struggle proceeded throughout the year between the two opposing factions. While the Chinese were thus divided, the Thai government once again reverted to a full-scale policy of containment towards the Chinese. Following the "insiders" coup of November 29, 1951, which brought Police Director-General Phao Siyanon into political prominence, the administration launched broadside attacks against the Chinese on almost every front.

The first of the attacks, an increase in the alien registration fee, had serious political repercussions.[29] It will be recalled that the fee was set at four baht per annum in 1939. In 1946, the government increased the figure to eight baht and in 1949 to twenty baht; it was now proposed to up the fee to several hundred baht. From the point of view of the new administration, a sharp fee increase had the simultaneous advantage of increasing government revenues without raising the tax rates of the voting population, and of capitalizing on anti-Sinitic prejudice. It seemed such a good idea to the Assembly (hand-picked by the militarists who carried off the November coup) that they upped the ceiling figure of the Ministry of Finance's original proposal from 200 baht to 400 baht in the legislation passed in January 1952. The level of the fee within the limits established by the new legislation was to be set by ministerial decree, and Police General Phao, Deputy Minister of Interior, held out for the maximum sum. On learning of the impending increase, the Chinese in Thailand were thrown into a paroxysm of protest. While the legislation was under consideration, however, the Chinese Chamber of Commerce was paralyzed by the earlier resignation of chairman Chang Lan-ch'en over a political issue involving the celebration of the previous Double Tenth, by the post-ponement of the election of new officers due to machinations to stuff the ballot, and by the arrest in late December of the chief secretary of the Chamber on charges of Communist espionage. By the time elections for the chair officers of the Chamber were successfully held on February 23 and Chang Lan-ch'en returned to the chairmanship, the government position had hardened. From February to August, the major efforts of the Chinese leaders were directed toward obtaining a reduction in the fee, but they succeeded only in wringing minor ex-emptions and concessions from the administration. The fee was officially set at 400 baht annually, a twenty-fold increase over the former figure.

The efforts to secure a fee reduction were hindered at every turn by Kuomintang-Communist antagonism. The Chinese chargé d'affaires claimed that the increase in the fee would "provide opportunities for Communist propaganda and subversive activities." [30] Peking protested the fee increase via radio, most vigorously in the broadcast of February 29. The Communists in Thailand accused the Kuomintang and their American friends of only token opposition to the increase and pro-ceeded to capture the mass movement of protest. By May, organized bands of poor Chinese were calling at the residences and offices of Chinese leaders, Thai administrative offices, Thai Assemblymen be-lieved to be somewhat sympathetic, and Thai politicians of liberal or monarchist persuasion. The mass movement reached its climax on the evening of June 13, when over ten thousand poor Chinese gathered in the heavy rain near a restaurant where Chang Lan-ch'en on behalf of the Chamber of Commerce was entertaining over three hundred Thai officials. The crowd demonstrated for a fee reduction and dis-persed only after the Governor of Phranakhǫn, the Metropolitan Police Inspector-General, and several Chinese leaders spoke to them. Shortly thereafter a few more concessions were made by the police in return for a notice signed by the Chinese Chamber of Commerce and the seven speech-group associations pleading for lawful and orderly conduct.

Nonetheless, several of the organized bands of poor Chinese were planning a mass march on the National Assembly Hall scheduled to coincide with the opening of the Assembly on June 24, the Thai Na-tional Day. *Min-chu Jih-pao* printed this information as early as June 19 and implied that Communists planned to incite riots. The Chinese Deputy Minister of Foreign Affairs in a note to the Thai chargé d'affaires at Taipei pointed out that the Nationalist government disapproved the June 24 parade. In addition the Nationalist Embassy sent a note to the Phayathai police station requesting special police protection.[31] These developments gave the Thai police an opportunity for a full show of force. Fire-brigade units and guards with tear-gas bombs were posted on the boulevard leading to the Assembly Hall, and police bren-gun carriers were stationed along Yaowarat and upper Jaroenkrung roads in the Chinese quarter. Chinese were barred from the park surrounding the Assembly Hall, and Chinese approaching the area were stopped and searched for weapons. The day passed without incident. Two days later, however, a crowd of about two hundred Chinese approached the Chinese Embassy to appeal for help in effecting a fee reduction. Police details prevented their entering the Embassy compound and arrested three of the leaders, who were taken to the Nationalist chargé d'affaires to be questioned.[32] Chinese "neutralists" and the Communist press naturally took a dim view of the Kuomintang's role in these events.

The Thai government attempted to bring the furor and controversy over the alien-fee increase to a close on July 22, when the Thai Foreign Ministry sent replies to the formal protests which had been lodged by the Chinese Embassy and five other diplomatic missions. The administration refused to give further consideration to a fee reduction. In the years to come, it was faced with passive resistance and nonpayment on the part of thousands of Chinese who were unable to meet such a high tax.[33]

Early in March, at the peak of the alien-fee controversy, a disastrous fire in the Saphan Lueang district of Bangkok destroyed the houses of almost twenty thousand people, the great majority ethnic Chinese. As usual in such cases the Chinese benevolent societies and other associations organized a brilliant job of emergency relief and collected over three million baht for long-term rehabilitation relief. In this case, however, the Provisional Relief Committee set up was rent by disputes, and the whole affair deteriorated into a political struggle that strained the Chinese community almost to the breaking point.

Contributions to the relief fund were solicited by the five Chinese newspapers (*Hua-ch'iao Jih-pao* had closed for financial reasons in the spring of 1952), which, with the Pao-te Benevolent Society, formed the Provisional Relief Committee. Since the sums collected gave proportionate weight to the respective papers within the Committee and heightened prestige with the public, press rivalry was intense. On the political scale from Communist to Kuomintang in order, the funds in baht collected by the Chinese newspapers up to May 15 were as follows: *Ch'üan-min,* 720,000; *Chung-yüan,* 825,000; *Hsing-hsien,* 575,-000; *Kuang-hua,* 185,000; *Min-chu,* 155,000.[34] (These proportions are probably the best estimate of political sentiment in the Chinese community at the time: i.e., about 30 per cent pro-Communist, 7 per cent pro-Kuomintang, and the remainder "neutralist.") This put *Min-chu Jih-pao,* the only pro-Nationalist member, in the weakest position. After the allocation of emergency relief funds to the fire victims, the neutralists put forward a plan to distribute three hundred baht in cash to each victim, to set aside one million baht to lease the razed area of the fire from its owners for the construction of new housing, and to allocate the remaining funds for future fire relief. This plan was accepted only over the protests of *Min-chu Jih-pao* to the effect that such a long-term plan should be adopted only if a permanent committee were organized, failing which all funds collected should be distributed to the fire victims immediately. Kuomintang partisans feared that at best the "neutralists" and pro-Communists would so distribute the funds as to gain maximum credit for themselves and at worst would put some of the funds at the disposal of Communist partisans; the Pao-te Society, furthermore, was anything but sympathetic to the Nationalists. Immediate distribution of the funds would minimize the political effect which the "neutralists" could wring from the relief. A reorganization of the Committee, too, would mean the inclusion of several pro-KMT associations and the admission of pro-KMT leaders into the executive councils, thus ending *Min-chu's* political position as a minority of one. *Min-chu's* plans, however, were completely rejected.

Unable to influence the Committee, much less control it, *Min-chu Jih-pao* resigned and launched a campaign to wreck it. The four Communist and neutralist papers were charged with embezzling a million baht, and even *Kuang-hua Pao* was accused of being a Communist agent. Only Aw Boon Haw's papers managed to remain somewhat aloof from the controversy. Each side in the press war organized and interviewed the fire victims to "prove" intimidation by the other. By the end of May, *Min-chu Jih-pao* named a Communist agent as the originator of the plan adopted by the Committee and claimed that the original plot called for only one million baht to the fire victims, the other two million to be split between the Communist Party and the Pao-te Society.

By early July, the Provisional Relief Committee, under pressure, had distributed just over two million baht, leaving somewhat over one million baht on hand. At this point negotiations with the owners (Julalongkǫn University) for lease of the razed land broke down, and the Thai police approached the relief committee for a contribution of 320,000 baht for the purchase of fire engines, later upped to 800,000. When Kuomintang partisans favored a contribution, a member of the Pao-te staff claimed that the request was a result of *Min-chu*'s attacks, which had drawn the attention of the police to the Committee's finances. The Committee resisted compliance with the police request throughout August, but in early September the editors and managers of the Chinese newspapers were summoned to police headquarters for minute cross-examination about the Committee's finances. The next day the Pao-te Society staff member who had opposed the fire-engine donation was picked up by the police and detained for questioning. With this, even *Ch'üan-min Pao* granted that for the sake of promoting good relations with the Thai the Committee should accede to the police request. A few days later, the Committee handed over a 320,000-baht check to the accompaniment of the high public praise of police officials. By the end of the month, the Provisional Relief Committee was dissolved amid anguished cries from the *Ch'üan-min*, *Chung-yüan*, and *Kuang-hua* newspapers that *Min-chu Jih-pao* and its Kuomintang backers had sabotaged the relief effort.

With the bitter taste of the Saphan Lueang fire episode still on the public tongue, the opposing factions next made preparations for the "political month" of October, in which fall the Peking regime's National Day on the first, the Nationalists' National Day on the tenth, and Chiang Kai-shek's birthday on the thirty-first. Official celebrations on October 1 were out of the question because of police vigilance, while lack of support from the formal Chinese organizations limited the Kuomintang observances to Embassy functions. Kuomintang forces, however, made a supreme effort in connection with the conference which the Nationalist Overseas Chinese Affairs Commission announced would be convoked in Taipei on October 21 for all non-Communist overseas Chinese irrespective of party affiliation. The aim of the Nationalist partisans in Bangkok was to persuade as many of the influential leaders as possible to visit Taiwan during the month in one capacity or another. Since negotiations to this end were delicate, to say the least, Communist strategy was to expose to merciless publicity every move of the Kuomintang and to badger every leader approached

by Party workers. Communist success was evident in the final composition of the loyalty mission, which included none but die-hard
Kuomintang partisans. In particular, the attempt to enlist Chang Lan-
ch'en as head of the mission failed.

The Communist success, however, was short-lived, for on November
10, the Thai police under the direction of General Phao staged a series
of mass raids and arrests which inaugurated a three-month roundup
of leftists. The police claimed the existence of a wide-ranging Communist plot to overthrow the government, involving not only many of
the important Thai political opponents of the administration but the
Communist Chinese government and thousands of local Chinese as
well. Between November 10, 1952 and January 24, 1953, when the
last major raids occurred in Bangkok, over two hundred and fifty
Chinese were arrested and over one hundred and fifty Chinese firms
were raided as well as a score or more of Chinese associations and
schools in Bangkok. Among the associations raided were the Ch'iung-
yai (Hainanese) Association and the Teochiu Association, while the
raided schools included several of the most important: Huang-hun,
P'ei-ying, P'u-chih, and Chin-te. The responsible officers of all these
organizations were busy for weeks bailing out teachers and staff, or
otherwise securing their release. Several influential Chinese leaders
were summoned by the police in connection with the investigation of
the arrested Chinese. The firms of over a dozen important Chinese
leaders were among those raided. Two prominent Teochiu leaders
were arrested, and two others emplaned for Hongkong. For months,
the operations of several associations were paralyzed, and many
schools closed for reorganization and reconsideration of staff.

Three days after the first raids, an anti-Communist bill was sub-
mitted to the Assembly by General Phao, rushed through all three
readings, and promulgated as the Un-Thai Activities Act of B.E. 2495
—all in one day. It prescribed imprisonment of from five to ten years
for, among other persons:

Those who incite, advise, coerce others to act as communists or propagate
communism, associate or rally, or are accomplices of communists, or prepare
to do something communistic, or those who know someone is going to com-
mit a crime under this act but conceal and fail to report it to the authorities
concerned . . . (Section 5)

Those who support any communist organization or support members of
any communist organization in the following manners: (a) give them lodg-

ings or a meeting place; (b) persuade others to be members of any communist organization; (c) finance the organization or provide any other aid . . . (Section 9)

Those who are found guilty of assaulting or threatening to assault persons, property, honour, reputation or to detain others or act in any way to cause fear in order to make others act in accordance with instructions of a communist organization or are found guilty of activity in accordance with the purpose of that organization . . . (Section 11) [35]

The Act further provided (Section 10) that if any crimes under the Act are committed by a Communist organization, "those who are leaders, managers or officials attached to that organization or members who used to attend meetings held by that organization will be penalized in the same manner as if they themselves had committed the crime."

Little question was left in anybody's mind that this sweeping Act was aimed primarily at the Chinese. In November, General Phao estimated that there were only 2,000 Thai but over 10,000 Chinese Communists in Thailand.[36] At a December meeting of the pro-government party, he announced that many alien (Chinese) associations were Communistic, and stated that if the government were to arrest all the Chinese who had violated the Un-Thai Activities Act, the number would run to 100,000 or even 200,000. In making similar arguments to the National Assembly later in the month he cited as an example that Communists had been making use of the Pao-te Benevolent Society to carry out their activities and of its charity funds to finance their propaganda.

In December 1952, the *Ch'üan-min Pao* was ordered to close, while *Nan-ch'en Pao*, a Communist evening paper begun only six months earlier, was closed the following month. The police also began an investigation of those on *Ch'üan-min Pao*'s list of dealers and subscribers, and on December 23 a roundup of *Ch'üan-min Pao* distributors began upcountry.

It is difficult to judge the Chinese role in the so-called Communist plot against the Thai government because only four of the Chinese suspects were ever given a trial. Of the Chinese held in February 1953, most were never even brought before the public prosecutor but sentenced to deportation without hearing. Almost all of the Chinese suspects released by the public prosecutor on insufficient evidence were also ordered deported and returned to jail. The trial of the 43 (eventually increased to 54) alleged conspirators, including the four Chinese, began in February 1953 and lasted until March 1955. In the course of the hearings, police witnesses testified that, prior to the 1952 arrests, money for the Communists in China was sent through the Andar Company and the Farland-Thai Company in Bangkok via Hongkong business houses, that local Chinese Communists connected with the *Ch'üan-min Pao* in 1951–1952 tried to train saboteurs and armed units in various rice mills and plantations; and that the Chinese Communist Party had organized a clandestine Chinese Women's Association, which trained and indoctrinated teachers and nurses.[37]

Meanwhile arrests of Chinese under the provisions of the Un-Thai Activities Act continued throughout 1953–1954. The major mass arrests of Chinese in Bangkok occurred in late April 1953 (36 suspects) and mid-June 1954 (25 suspects),[38] while during 1954 an average of 8 to 10 Chinese Communist suspects a month were picked up in the jangwats bordering Malaya. After some public disagreement, Phibun and Phao agreed in mid-1954 on an estimate of 5,000 known Chinese Communists still at large in the country. The public was told that police would act only against those obviously engaged in activities threatening the security of the country.[39]

During this period, the Thai police showed every willingness to cooperate with Kuomintang Chinese in the campaign against Communism. In January 1953, a systematic inquiry was begun among "local Chinese residents loyal to Generalissimo Chiang Kai-shek" to obtain information about the movements of Chinese Communists.[40] In March, the administration announced a plan to enlist and train an anti-Communist volunteer corps of local Chinese citizens which would be dispatched under police command to border regions to assist in the Communist-suppression campaign.[41] Enabling regulations were drafted, but the project eventually came to naught. When the Taipei government announced plans in 1954 to form an infantry division of overseas Chinese volunteers, the Thai Minister of Interior stated that the path would be cleared for Chinese nationals to enlist in the division and leave Thailand for Taiwan.[42]

The anti-Communist campaign also led to a brief revival of the wartime prohibited-areas policy. In 1954, British progress in the fight against jungle terrorists in Malaya forced up to one hundred and fifty Communist guerrillas to take refuge on the Thai side of the border. To prevent resident Chinese from giving aid to the terrorists, the Thai government ordered all aliens to leave selected areas of amphoes Betong and Sadao (in jangwats Yala and Songkhla, respectively) by

September 28, 1954. But when tin mining and rubber tapping came to a virtual standstill as Chinese moved out, the policy was reconsidered, and on October 15 the cabinet rescinded the order.[43]

In the new political climate created by the Thai government's vigorous anti-Communist campaign, the Kuomintang staged an impressive revival in Thailand. Late in 1952, it began sponsoring public "sacrifices-from-afar" to honor relatives of Thailand Chinese said to have died by Communist persecution in China. The full and harrowing story of each victim was widely publicized, and maximum official participation in the impressive public ceremonies was arranged. In addition, the full apparatus of Chinese Buddhism in Thailand was enlisted in the commemorative services. Before they were closed, *Ch'üan-min Pao* and *Nan-ch'en Pao* gave quite a different version of each case, but this distraction was removed by January 1953. These services, held not only in Bangkok but also in Phitsanulok and Banpong, were effective in stimulating emotional rejection of the Peking regime.

The Kuomintang was also able to trade on the public passion for sports in building up popular support. In October 1952, pro-Nationalists in Bangkok organized basketball teams and financed their participation in the President Chiang Birthday Tournament in Taiwan. This move was repeated the following year, and, to the enhancement of its propaganda effect, the leader of the team was a prominent Teochiu considered in 1950–1952 to be an ardent pro-Communist. In November 1953, the crack K'e-nan basketball team of Taiwan arrived in Thailand for regional matches, which it handily won. Twice in 1954 Thailand was host to basketball teams from Taiwan, and in March 1955, the Free China tennis team came to Bangkok to play local champions.

As part of the Kuomintang offensive, Taiwan also sent a series of prominent officials and delegations to boost and publicize the Nationalist cause. Members of the Overseas Chinese Affairs Commission from Taiwan visited Bangkok in May 1953 and September 1954.[44] Seven anti-Communist ex-prisoners of war toured Thailand in April 1954, and a representative of the Chinese Anti-Communist Alliance made a visit in March 1955.[45]

During 1953, Kuomintang progress was clearly evident in the formal Chinese associations. The most dramatic change occurred in the Hakka Association, which in 1952 had pointedly refrained from observing Double Tenth and had refused to participate, much less cosponsor, the sacrifices-from-afar held on behalf of Hakka families.

But with land reform underway in Mei hsien, an increasing number of Hakkas in Bangkok learned of personal tragedies which embittered Hakka opinion toward the Communist regime. Many Hakka leaders were also worried because the principal of Chin-te, the Hakka Association school, had disappeared during the anti-Communist raids of late 1952. Against this background, Kuomintang elements in the Association engineered a coup at the annual meeting held in February 1953, ousted the officers a year before their terms were to expire, and in special elections chose a chairman so rightist in his views as to be considered a fascist by his moderate opponents. Thereafter the Association played a steadfastly pro-Kuomintang role in the Chinese community.

The Chamber of Commerce was also cleansed of pro-Communist elements during the year. As early as February 1953, the Chamber joined as an official sponsor of a Kuomintang function. In April, its most pro-Communist officer was arrested by the Thai police, and in July the secretary-general of the Bangkok branch of the Kuomintang was appointed chief secretary of the Chamber. Beginning with Double Tenth in 1953, the Chamber made its auditorium available for all Nationalist holidays and celebrations. The Chamber elections of December 1953 returned the most strongly pro-Nationalist slate of officers since 1946. Chairman Chang Lan-ch'en thereafter functioned as one of the major spokesmen of the Kuomintang in Thailand. In May 1954, he headed a loyalty mission to Taiwan.

During 1953–1954, the other major Chinese associations were also forced to show some interest in Kuomintang activities, if only to take out "anti-Communist insurance." The vice-chairman of the Hokkien Association played a publicly pro-Kuomintang role on behalf of that organization. After holding out firmly against any commitment, the Teochiu Association finally broke down in September 1953, and joined other speech-group associations and the Chamber of Commerce in a declaration that the Overseas Chinese Conference soon to be convened in Peking would include no delegation of any kind from Thailand.[46] In 1953 and 1954, the presidium of the Double Tenth celebration in Bangkok included leaders from all the major Chinese associations.

With the Communist newspapers no longer publishing, *Min-chu Jih-pao* was allowed to close by its subsidizers in July 1953. By that time, the two most important Chinese newspapers, *Chung-yüan Pao* and *Hsing-hsien Jih-pao*, were both vigorously pro-Nationalist (Taiwan, for instance, had become "Free China"). Their rush rightward—

stimulated by the arrest in 1953 of twelve Chinese newspapermen for May-day editorials allegedly favorable to Communism [47]—left *Kuang-hua Pao*, with its slightly right-of-center editorial policy, the most leftist Chinese daily in Bangkok. All three newspapers put out special issues for Double Tenth and themselves observed this Nationalist holiday, both in 1953 and 1954. The circulations of the three dailies in 1953 indicated the changed temper of the community. The strongly pro-Nationalist papers, *Hsing-hsien* and *Chung-yüan*, had the largest circulations (about 11,000 each), compared with *Kuang-hua*'s 5,000. By October 1954, however, both *Kuang-hua Pao* and *Chung-yüan Pao* had shifted slightly leftward. In that month, *Chung-yüan* had the largest circulation (12,000), followed by the staunchly pro-Nationalist *Hsing-hsien* (10,000), while *Kuang-hua* had increased its circulation somewhat to over 6,000.

In February 1955, Chang Lan-ch'en, in a public message to the SEATO conference in Bangkok, stated that "a great majority of Chinese in Thailand . . . are strongly supporting the Government of the Republic of China with its temporary seat in Taiwan." [48] While this was an overstatement, it would be safe to say that in the spring of 1955 most of the politically conscious Chinese in Thailand were in some degree opposed to Communism and the Peking regime. Although there was little sincere enthusiasm for the Taipei government and practically no serious expectation of a Nationalist return to the mainland, the Kuomintang represented the only focus around which the more serious anti-Communist elements could rally. The political alignments of the Chinese in Thailand were influenced, of course, by the fact that the power of the Peking regime was never effectively felt in Thailand, in particular because of the presence of the American Navy in China waters, because of American pressure to prevent any substantial trade between the Chinese mainland and Southeast Asia, and because of American intransigence with regard to admitting Communist China to the family of nations. As a loyal international protégé of the United States, and now as an ally in SEATO, Thailand has consistently opposed recognition of the Peking regime or its admission to the United Nations. Thus Peking's potential role as protector of the overseas Chinese in Thailand, apparently ominous in 1950, was not actualized up to 1955.

Against this background, the Asian-African Conference which convened in Bandung in April 1955, was an eye opener for the Chinese in Thailand. It was Peking's first representation at a big international forum, and the general acceptance of Chou En-lai as a sane and moderate statesman of a great Asian power put the mainland regime in something of a new light. The agreement reached between China and Indonesia concerning overseas Chinese raised the intriguing possibility of real protection should the Chinese in Thailand ever be recognized as citizens of the People's Republic. The fact that the foreign ministers of Thailand and Red China attended the same conference was significant in itself, but that Prince Wan conferred with Chou En-lai on the status of the Chinese in Thailand caused a flurry of speculation and mental readjustment in Thailand. To offset the effect of Bandung on the overseas Chinese, Taiwan sent a deputy chairman of the Overseas Chinese Affairs Commission to Bangkok. He conferred with the leaders of the major Chinese associations and used the dinner parties in his honor as forums for Taiwan's rebuttal of Chou En-lai's case.[49] On April 5, Chang Lan-ch'en and Yün Chu-t'ing, a long-time KMT leader, issued a joint statement warning the free nations of Asia and Africa of the Communist threat to world peace.[50] By May 1955, the Chinese Communists' trade offensive was felt in Thailand, commodities worth some seventy million baht from the mainland having been imported from China indirectly via Hongkong and Singapore.[51] The favorable prices of this merchandise gave the Chinese merchants who handled it a competitive advantage in Thailand's markets.

A readjustment in Chinese political inclinations away from anti-Communism was also stimulated during 1955–1956 by events within Thailand. The judgment of the "Red-plot" case of November 1952 to January 1953 was finally read by the court in March 1955.[52] Three of the four Chinese on trial were convicted and sentenced to twenty years imprisonment, but the court's judgment treated the Chinese role in the "Red conspiracy" so lightly that Police General Phao's anti-Communist campaign appeared slightly ridiculous. Forty-six of the 49 convicted, after all, were Thai. And if among even the four Chinese against whom the police had a strong enough case to risk trial there was one innocent man, what about the hundreds of other Chinese arrested in 1952–1953 and deported to China or exiled to Phetchabun? In anticipation of such reasoning the Ministry of Interior, in April 1955, released some 128 Chinese who had been exiled to Phetchabun since 1949 in lieu of deportation. Then, in July 1955, after an extensive trip abroad, Phibun announced a plan to strive for Full Democracy in Thailand. In a series of rapid moves in August, Police Director-General Phao, the high priest of anti-Communism and the politician most closely identified with the anti-Chinese policies of 1952–1954, was shorn of several political and governmental positions. In October, Phibun specifically reassigned duties of the two Deputy Ministers of Interior so that General Phao was relieved of responsibility for Chinese affairs. A week later Phao himself had to explain to a press conference that the Government's new policy toward the Chinese was one of "closer relations with friendly aliens." [53]

The real harbinger of political freedom in Thailand for Thai and Chinese alike was the abolition of both direct and indirect police press censorship on August 31 and the appointment of the governor of Phranakhǫn as press officer in place of General Phao.[54] This was followed within a week by the passage of legislation legalizing and facilitating the formation of political parties. It now became possible to advocate closer political and economic relations with mainland China, and several of the newly formed opposition parties took this line. Ethnic Chinese of Thai nationality were free to join any political party.

The influx of inexpensive Chinese goods became a flood by October 1955, and pressure from merchants—Thai as well as Chinese—on the Thai government to relax barriers against direct trade with mainland China continued to mount.[55] It was argued that China had now solved its economic problems and could assist Thailand by supplying not only cheap goods which would lower the cost of living but also technicians to help build her industry. These arguments, put forth by Thai politicians, were music to the long-injured pride of the local Chinese. Early in 1956, a Thai Assemblyman returned from a trip to Communist China with glowing reports for his countrymen. His arrest by the Thai government only strengthened political pressures to reconsider Thailand's policy toward Communist China.[56] By September 1956, the major Thai officials concerned had indicated that merchants could trade directly with Communist China.

Greater flexibility in the Thai government's China policy was shown in another significant development. In September 1956, Phibun announced that on request of the Cambodian Embassy the Thai government would welcome and accord protection to an official economic mission from Communist China to Cambodia, scheduled to stop overnight in Bangkok. The Thai police then arranged that the Chinese Chamber of Commerce would assume responsibility for greeting and accommodating the mission. In fact, an official delegation of the Chamber went to the airport to greet the mission, which, however, changed its plans and arrived three days later (September 21) for a stopover of only an hour and a half. Several hundred Chinese were on hand to greet the mission with applause.

The police favoritism shown the KMT during 1952–1954 was specifically disavowed in 1956. A new Thai-Chinese Association organized under police auspices in June included some twenty-seven Chinese leaders among its officers, about half of whom were leftists. In October, Police Brigadier-General Rat stated that the Thai police would never allow aliens to carry on political activities in Thailand—Kuomintang as well as Communist. In November, Police Director-General Phao told reporters that the police were keeping close watch on a newly organized secret KMT organization which was soliciting funds to buy weapons for Taiwan and Chinese troops in Burma. This development moved Phibun to express open annoyance with the KMT at his November 16 press conference: "The Kuomintang causes too much trouble: they trade in opium and cause Thailand to be blamed in the United Nations." [57]

In consequence of these developments, the year and a half since the Bandung Conference has seen a progressive shift in Chinese political opinion in Thailand towards neutralism and pro-Peking attitudes. This is increasingly possible as memories of the excesses of land-reform enforcement and Peking's ill-advised extortions from overseas Chinese merchants fade into history. Each of the old-time newspapers began in 1955 to print more news about mainland China, and *Chung-yüan Pao* and especially *Kuang-hua Pao* have moved to a left-of-center position with no illusions about Taiwan and a new-found respect for Peking. In July 1955, a new Chinese daily, the *Shih-chieh Jih-pao* (C 145), was launched by several prominent Chinese leaders under the sponsorship of Police Director-General Phao, and for two months it followed a pro-Nationalist course. But a reorganization within the paper in October led to the resignation of the anti-Communist editor and the discharge of many other pro-Nationalists on the staff. The new editorial writer is an adherent of the Third Force, who from his neutralist vantage point finds much to recommend the Peking regime. In January 1956, yet another Chinese daily, *Chung-kuo Jih-pao*, began publication, with the help of the first editor and several staff members of the *Shih-chieh Jih-pao*. Its policy to date is unequivocally pro-Nationalist and anti-Communist. From right to left the order of the Chinese daily press (in mid-1956) is as follows: *Chung-kuo* (3,500 circulation), *Hsing-hsien* (7,000), *Shih-chieh* (3,500), *Chung-yüan* (8,000), and *Kuang-hua* (6,000). Thus, with a more balanced and varied newspaper fare, a slight concentration of readership at the leftist end of the political spectrum is discernible.[58]

To check the deterioration of its position in Thailand, the Nationalist government in Taiwan was spurred to new action in mid-1956. In June, Foreign Minister Yeh Kung-ch'ao led a goodwill mission to Thailand to "strengthen the traditional friendship" between the Thai and Chinese governments and peoples, to exchange opinions with leaders of the Thai government, and to "bring the love and comfort of the mother country to the overseas compatriots." [59] In September, Taipei sent Dr. Hang Li-wu as its new head of mission to Bangkok, the first in six years to hold ambassadorial rank. The Nationalists' diplomatic offensive was coolly received by the Thai government. Foreign Minister Yeh expressed his hope to Phibun that all dealings between resident Chinese and the Thai government be handled by the Chinese Embassy. At a subsequent press conference, the Premier discreetly pointed out that inasmuch as resident Chinese are so closely related to Thais and have long had direct contact with the Thai government, it is difficult for the government to end direct relations with them. When Ambassador Hang stated at his first Bangkok press conference in October that despite existing friendly relations between Bangkok and Taipei there remained some outstanding problems, Phibun was quick to reply that the relationships between Chinese and Thai were so close and cordial that he could not see what problems remained. This repartee took on a sharper turn in November 1956, when the Thai government accused the Kuomintang of illegal solicitation of funds for arms and ammunition—an allegation vigorously denied by the Chinese Embassy.

During the same period, the local Kuomintang had somewhat more success in bucking the prevailing trend. Pro-Nationalist elements gave the new ambassador a rousing welcome and came through the "political month" of October with flags bravely flying. A fairly strong loyalty mission was sent to Taipei for the Double Tenth celebrations, led by Chang Lan-ch'en, chairman of the Chamber of Commerce. The thirty members of the delegation included eight top-ranking Chinese community leaders (and the wives of three of them), six second-rank leaders, and eight local newspapermen.

As of late 1956, there are no signs that the Thai government will accord recognition to Peking short of a similar American action, but there is every indication that the new ambassador from Taiwan will have a difficult role to play and that the local Kuomintang partisans face an uphill fight to maintain their influence in the Chinese community.

C. New Forces in the Thai Economy

Thailand's major exports in the postwar period continue to be rice, rubber, tin, and timber, in that order. In 1951, these four commodities accounted for 86.5 per cent of the country's total exports.[60] In recent years, the position of the Chinese in the economic processes involving these major products has changed in several important respects. Particularly is this true of rice, Thailand's major item of production, consumption, and export.

Since 1946, the number of rice mills in Thailand has rapidly increased. By 1950, the number stood at 925 and at the present time is estimated at 960. If the increase in milling capacity which occurred in the twenties was largely outside the Bangkok area, the postwar increase has been entirely so. Not a single rice mill has been built in Bangkok since the war and several of those operating in the twenties and thirties have been permanently closed. As of 1956, there are only about fifty rice mills in the Bangkok area, of which five or six are not in operation. The new upcountry mills are located for the most part along the roads and railroads built since 1930, when the last major expansion of rice-milling capacity came to an end. The upcountry mills are relatively small, the great majority having a daily capacity of between 20 and 85 tons of paddy, with 30 to 40 usual. The mills in the Bangkok area range from 60 to 550 tons of paddy in daily capacity, with 200 to 220 about average.

This expanded plant is still largely owned and operated by ethnic Chinese. Only one independent mill in the Bangkok area plus the seven mills of the Thai Rice Company are owned by ethnic Thai. The shares in the Thai Rice Company are held by Thai Farmers Co-operatives (74 per cent) and individual Thais (26 per cent). The general manager and six of the seven mill managers of the Thai Rice Company, however, are ethnic Chinese of Thai citizenship. All other Bangkok mills, including the one Thai-owned independent mill, are Chinese operated. Upcountry, too, less than 15 per cent of the rice mills are owned by ethnic Thai, and all but a small fraction are operated by ethnic Chinese.

In Bangkok, rice-mill entrepreneurship is almost entirely Teochiu, only five of the smaller mills being owned and operated by Hainanese or Cantonese. Upcountry, Teochius are generally dominant, but in some regions, Hainanese, Cantonese, and Hakkas are well represented. The proportion of China-born among rice-mill owners and managers, however, has been steadily decreasing for many years. In Bangkok, less than three-fifths of Chinese owners and operators are China-born, while upcountry the proportion is probably somewhat less than one-half. Many upcountry mills operated by local-born Chinese have adopted Thai instead of Chinese names and are coming to be considered Thai rather than Chinese enterprises.

Major changes have taken place in the composition of the rice-mill labor force in the postwar period. Only in Bangkok is ethnic Chinese labor still extensively employed, and even there unskilled machine tenders are now predominantly Thai. Other unskilled labor in the Bangkok mills is for the most part supplied by Teochiu immigrants of the 1946–1948 wave, but upcountry, "coolie" labor is largely supplied by non-Chinese. In Bangkok mills the engineer or mechanic, ironworker, and carpenter are almost always Cantonese, but upcountry the Cantonese in these highly skilled positions are gradually being replaced by Thais. The office staffs of almost all rice mills, however, consist of first- and second-generation Chinese.

The labor force of the Ta-cheng mill, with a daily capacity of 200 tons of paddy, is typical of Bangkok: The manager and office staff are entirely Teochiu, while the three highly skilled maintenance positions are filled by Cantonese. The 33 other machine tenders are all Thai, while the 32 indoor and 45 outdoor unskilled laborers are all Teochiu, about 80 per cent China-born. Thai Isan mill number 2 in Khonkaen, with a capacity of about seventy tons of paddy, is typical of upcountry mills: There the manager and office staff are Teochiu, mostly local-born, while all the skilled and unskilled labor, indoor and outdoor, are Lao (i.e., Northeastern Thai). Although Chinese laborers are generally considered more industrious and efficient by management, they have been replaced upcountry by local peoples because of sharp wage differentials. Chinese will seldom work for less than four or five hundred baht per month, while for Thai, Lao, Cambodian (in the southern jangwats in the northeast), and Kamuks (widely employed in the rice mills of North Siam), monthly wages begin at 200 baht. For the country as a whole a substantial majority of all rice-mill workers (of whom there were 12,837 in 1949) [61] are no longer ethnic Chinese.

This Thai-ification of the rice-mill labor force has its counterpart in the co-operative marketing arrangements that have developed since the war between millowners and "Thai enterprises." In this process, the Thahan Samakkhi (since 1955 known as the Saha Samakkhi), one of the corporations under the Thai War Veterans Organization, has played a major role. In 1946, Wang Mu-neng (C 146), a Chinese rice miller in Udǫnthani, started organizing Chinese rice millers in Northeast Siam. The millers were finding the transport of rice to Bangkok very difficult; in order to obtain the use of freight cars they had to bribe railroad officials, and with the various mills competing with one another, the size of the bribes was skyrocketing. In his bid for greater power in the rice business, Mr. Wang met opposition from rice millers and merchants in Bangkok, as well as from certain Thai politicians. After a year of struggle he finally organized twenty millers into an embryo Northeast Rice Millers Association. Needing some power behind the new organization, Mr. Wang approached Colonel (now Field Marshal) Phin Chunhawan, head of the Thahan Samakkhi, suggesting a possible merger. Colonel Phin, whose veterans' organization was then primarily in the soft-drink business and doing rather poorly, recognized the possibilities, and the Thahan Samakkhi was reorganized in 1947–1948 with the members of the Northeast Rice Millers Association as shareholders. The veterans in the old organization were happy to get into the lucrative rice trade, while the millers got the backing of powerful military figures in their struggle to market and transport their rice. The union was, in fact, most successful. By 1949, seventy rice mills in the northeast had joined the Association and become shareholders of the Thahan Samakkhi corporation. The corporation soon got full control of freight cars on the northeast railway line; squeeze was regularized and allocated among the millers. Rice-mill shareholders of the corporation were required to sell at least half their output to the Thahan Samakkhi, which in turn sold to the government and exported to meet government commitments. In 1952, rice millers in North Siam were organized into the Northern Rice Millers Association under Thahan Samakkhi auspices. By the end of that year, 132 rice mills in both regions were shareholders in the Thai corporation. As a leader of the November coup of 1951, Field Marshal Phin became one of the half-dozen most powerfully placed Thai politicians. Since that time, the Thahan Samakkhi has co-operated fully with the Thai administration, and its board of directors and advisory boards are laden with important military personnel and government officials. It regularly receives financial assistance from the government; in 1952, for instance, it obtained a government loan of forty million baht.

In January 1954, the formal connections between rice millers and governmental officials were tightened by the organization of syndicates in two important rice-producing areas. Practically all the millers in jangwats Udǫnthani, Nǫngkhai, Sakonnakhǫn, and Nakhǫnphanom were organized into a syndicate capitalized by the mills and the Thahan Samakkhi at ten million baht. At the same time, 29 of the 30 rice mills in jangwats Chiangmai and Lampang formed another syndicate capitalized at fifteen million baht. The syndicate's fifteen-man board of directors is made up almost entirely of Thais and headed by General Sarit Thanarat, a member, along with Field Marshal Phin and Police General Phao, of the powerful triumvirate who came into prominence with the November coup of 1951. Each of the member mills (all but seven being Chinese-owned) has contributed to the syndicate's capitalization along with the Thahan Samakkhi, and all also have shares in the latter corporation. The Thahan Samakkhi helps the syndicate in many ways, most notably in obtaining the use of railway cars from the government's Railway Organization and arranging for sale of rice to meet the government's export commitments.

At the close of the Second World War, the Thai government declared a monopoly on the rice trade in order to meet its commitments to foreign governments and to control domestic retail prices. Under this arrangement, which persisted through 1954, the government was able to appropriate a large part of the high prices received for rice exports.[62] The government bought rice from the miller ex mill and immediately sold it to exporters ex mill at a price about 20 per cent higher. By taking advantage of the difference between the official and the open market exchange rates (i.e., 12.5 baht official versus 21 baht open-market per U.S. dollar in 1951) and by expressing the export price in foreign exchange, the government was able to secure a tremendous potential profit. The government did not control the price of paddy, but the prices it paid for rice were fixed for long periods, so that the farmers had a better idea than formerly of the price they should get for paddy. Although this was an excessively low price in terms of prevailing rates in the world market, farmers were in a position to hold their paddy for better prices vis-à-vis the Chinese middleman, whose margins were consequently reduced. The postwar expansion of rice milling in the rice-producing areas themselves has also tended to eliminate the paddy middleman in many parts of upcountry Thailand, where farmers deliver paddy directly to the mill. It is generally agreed that "both millers and middlemen now receive a much smaller share of the export proceeds than they used to." [63] According to Ingram, the government's monopoly of the rice trade, which lasted through 1954, had the effect of increasing the number of Thai middlemen and exporters:

The fixed buying price of the Rice Office introduced a degree of stability into the paddy market and enabled Thai middlemen to compete with the Chinese. Formerly, the price of paddy fluctuated wildly from place to place and from month to month because of the variety of measures used in buying it, because of seasonal variations, and because of the many transactions involving merchandise or loans. Thai middlemen did not have the working capital, the experience, or the trading ability to compete with the Chinese under those conditions. But when the millers' buying prices became fixed within narrow limits for long periods, the middleman function was greatly simplified. No doubt other factors were involved, but people in the rice trade consider the greater stability of prices to be of major importance in the rise of Thai middlemen. [64]

During 1954, the Thai government found it increasingly difficult to sell its rice at advantageous prices through governmental agencies, and at the end of the year it declared an end to the government's monopoly on the rice trade. Under the new arrangement, effective January 1, 1955, exporters paid a premium of from 200 to 400 baht per ton to the Ministry of Economic Affairs and surrendered an amount of foreign exchange to the Bank of Thailand varying according to grade from US$14 to US$84 per ton. Beginning August 13, 1955, the premiums were raised to 1,050 and 400 baht for whole and broken rice, respectively (935 and 380 baht as of March 1956), and exporters were henceforth allowed to sell all their foreign exchange at the free-market rate. The net effect of this freeing of the rice trade has been to increase competition among Chinese millers and rice merchants. Deprived of special privileges and the assurance of fairly steady paddy prices, Thai middlemen and exporters have suffered.

Nevertheless, there is a persistent tendency for Chinese rice exporters, faced with the need for endless governmental licenses and permits, to seek out co-operative arrangements with Thai governmental officials. Two Bangkok rice firms established in 1953 exemplify the trend. While the capital and management of both are Chinese, the chairman and several members of the boards are Thai police and army officers. It can be seen, too, in the attempt of the six major rice organizations in Bangkok, on the advice of Police General Phao, to organize a Thailand Rice Exporters Association. The Association was formally organized in July 1955, bringing together three Chinese associations (Bangkok Rice Millers, Rice Merchants, and North-line Rice Millers) and three "Thai enterprises" (Thai Rice Company, Thahan Samakkhi, and the Bangkok Trading Company). The chief officers are prominent Chinese merchants, while the advisers are prominent Thai, headed by Police Colonel Phansak Wisetphakdi. Whether the Association will prove viable is highly questionable, but it is illustrative of the Sino-Thai business co-operation which has flourished in recent years.

The production of rubber in Thailand has expanded since 1947 to levels far higher than those obtaining prewar. The proportionate share of the Chinese in the total production, however, is on the decrease. In 1949, there were 7,610 rubber holdings registered with the Rubber Division as the property of Chinese nationals.[65] While these constituted less than 10 per cent of the number of holdings, the *area* of rubber holdings owned by Chinese nationals amounted to 25.8 per cent of the total. Chinese rubber holdings in 1949 averaged 61.7 *rai* each as against only 17.9 *rai* for those owned by Thai nationals. It is estimated that between one-third and one-half of the holdings registered by Thai nationals are in fact owned by ethnic Chinese.

Comparable figures as of January 1, 1954 (the latest available), indicate that the Chinese position among rubber holders is decreasing. The number of holdings owned by Chinese nationals (7,618) remained virtually unchanged, but an increase in the number of holdings owned by Thai nationals reduced the proportion of Chinese holdings to 7.5 per cent of the total. The area under the ownership of Chinese nationals likewise decreased to 20 per cent of the total, and the average size of the holdings owned by Chinese nationals fell to 42.3 *rai* in 1954. This proportionate Chinese decline has resulted from the large-scale entry of Thais and Malays into rubber small-holding operations under impetus of high postwar prices, especially those prevailing during the Korean-war boom of 1950–1953. Ethnic Chinese are still dominant among owners of plantations and large holdings, however. In 1954, 42 per cent of all holdings of fifty *rai* (about twenty acres) or larger were owned by Chinese nationals alone. The role of Westerners in rubber production has remained negligible.

Some 60,000 tappers are employed in rubber production in Thailand,[66] and of these the majority are ethnic Chinese. But the Chinese proportion of the total decreased considerably during the Korean-war boom, which occurred after Chinese immigration had virtually ceased. High wages attracted both Malays and Thais, some of the latter from upcountry, to employment as rubber tappers. Indigenous ethnic groups, however, have not seriously encroached on the Chinese position in the operation of crepe factories and smokehouses or in the export of processed rubber. While Hakkas predominate among tappers and planters, Hokkiens are dominant both in processing rubber and in trading of the processed product.

The Chinese position in Thailand's tin industry has somewhat declined in the postwar period. Over half of the capital invested in tin mining is European, mostly British and Australian. No Chinese company has as yet begun dredge mining; of the twenty-five companies employing dredges in 1950, three were Thai and the remainder European. Of the approximately three hundred mines operating by non-dredging means in 1950, however, the great majority were Chinese-owned and operated.[67] As in the 1930's, output of the European and Thai mines far surpassed that of the Chinese-owned mines. In 1950, the differential was about the same as in 1938 (i.e., about 70 per cent more from the non-Chinese mines), but it has almost certainly widened since, to the disadvantage of the Chinese.[68]

No postwar statistics are available comparable to the 1937 census figures on nationality of mineworkers. Observers agree, however, that the proportion of ethnic Thai among miners has increased to one-fourth of the total in some areas. There is some evidence that a majority of the ethnic Chinese miners are by now local-born Chinese of Thai nationality.[69] Even today there is still strong speech-group specialization by area in South Thailand's mining labor force. In Phuket it is estimated that approximately two-fifth of all miners are Hokkiens, that in amphoe Thungsong (jangwat Nakhǫnsithammarat) and jangwat Songkhla the majority of tin miners are Hakkas, and that in jangwat Yala, about two-thirds of the miners are Kwongsais. The number of Chinese tin miners employed in South Siam is by now probably just about equal to the prewar peak.

In recent years no tin smelting whatsoever has been done in Thailand. In 1954, however, the Thai government announced plans for construction of a tin smelter to which the entire output of the country is to be directed.[70] This industry will exclude Chinese. The biggest new tin-mining venture of recent years is the Chiang Phra Mining Company, a joint Japanese-Thai corporation with heavy investments from the Mitsubishi Company.[71] Chinese capitalists are increasingly unable to compete with foreign investors and semigovernmental Thai enterprise in the tin industry.

In sawmilling, on the other hand, Chinese interests have made considerable progress vis-à-vis European in the postwar period. In 1956, there are thirteen teak mills with a daily production of 20 cubic meters or more, and of these ten are Chinese. It is of course true that the two largest teak mills in Bangkok (and Thailand) are European-owned, namely those of the British company, Bombay-Burmah, (capacity 200 cubic meters), and of the Danish company, East Asiatic (capacity 100 cubic meters). The third largest teak sawmill is the Thai Timber Company, a government-owned enterprise with a daily capacity of about 50 cubic meters. The output of the ten largest Chinese mills (about 275 cubic meters), however, is almost always greater than that of the European and Thai sawmills together. In addition, there are in Bangkok about sixty Chinese teak mills with daily capacities of between 8 and 20 cubic meters each. It is clear that teak output from Chinese mills far surpasses that of all others combined.

In all of Thailand there are over nine hundred sawmills, processing a variety of timbers.[72] Of the total, approximately 130 are in Bangkok. The great majority of mills throughout the country are owned by ethnic Chinese, although precise figures are not available. The specialization of Hainanese in this field has not been significantly altered in Bangkok. While only four of the ten largest Chinese teak mills are Hainanese, 80 to 85 per cent of the smaller mills in and around the capital are Hainanese. In many parts of upcountry Thailand however, Teochiu sawmills are now about equal in number to those operated by Hainanese.

As is the case with rice mills, the labor force in sawmills has become increasingly Thai in recent years. Upcountry, a majority of unskilled sawmill laborers are no longer ethnic Chinese. Indigenous labor—Thai and Lao, Kamuk, and Cambodian—is used even by Chinese owners because of the shortage of Chinese and the higher wages they ask. In Bangkok, the smaller Chinese mills employ largely Chinese labor, of whom about half are local-born. The larger Chinese mills, however, hire as many Thai unskilled workers as Chinese. For instance, of the 54 unskilled workers employed by the largest Chinese teak mill, 30 are ethnic Thai, 10 ethnic Chinese of Thai citizenship, and 14 China-born Chinese. In the European and Thai sawmills, less than a third of the unskilled workers are ethnic Chinese, and most of these are local-born. Nevertheless, Chinese still predominate all over the country among skilled laborers, foremen, and office workers. Only in the Thai- and European-owned mills do ethnic Chinese hold a minority of the higher paid positions.

In general, the office staff in a Chinese sawmill is drawn from the same speech group as the owner. In the case of skilled laborers and foremen, however, there is a tendency for non-Hainanese mill-owners to rely on Hainanese talent. Thus in one Teochiu mill in Bangkok (capacity 25 cubic meters), the manager and six of the eight skilled laborers are Hainanese. In the largest Hakka mill (capacity 30 cubic meters), all of the skilled laborers are Hainanese, while in the largest Cantonese mill, six of the twelve skilled laborers are Hainanese.

Aside from sawmilling proper, there have been few changes in the timber industry in Thailand. The Chinese role in forest operations, both entrepreneurial and labor, remains negligible. With regard to marketing, Chinese dominate the export trade to the Far East as well as domestic distribution and retailing. The overwhelming majority of timber merchants, in contrast to millers, are Teochius.

The Chinese position with regard to Thailand's four major commercial products, then, may be summarized as follows. In the actual production of the raw commodities, Chinese labor is unimportant with respect to paddy and timber logs, but Chinese supply a slight majority and easy majority, respectively, of the labor force producing raw rubber and tin ore. In the processing of these raw products, Chinese supply somewhat less than half the labor force in rice milling, about half the labor force in sawmilling, and well over half the labor engaged in rubber processing. Chinese capital and entrepreneurship play no role with regard to paddy production, only a minor role in the production of timber logs, an important but minority role in the production of tin ore, and a major role only with regard to raw-rubber production. In the processing of these raw commodities, the position of Chinese capital and entrepreneurship is a majority one in rice milling, sawmilling, and rubber processing, in decreasing order of predominance. As for marketing, Chinese predominate in the domestic distribution of rice and timber and play a major role in the export of all four products.

If we now look at recent economic developments in Thailand from the point of view of the government's role, economic nationalism stands out as one of the major themes of the administration since 1948. The campaign to Thai-ify the economy was revived shortly after Phibun returned to power, gained momentum up to 1952, reached a climax in 1953, subsided in 1954, and was consciously relaxed in 1955. The major components of the campaign were (1) economic assistance to, and vocational education for, ethnic Thais; (2) economic restrictions on aliens; (3) an expansion of the state's role in industry; and (4) encouragement of semigovernmental "Thai enterprises" in commerce and finance.

The administration's positive policies to encourage greater participation by ethnic Thai in the national economy were for the most part a continuation of the long-term planning laid down in the thirties by the People's Party. To reduce indebtedness to Chinese traders and paddy merchants, the government gave every encouragement to the co-operative movement. In 1952, the Department of Co-operatives was elevated to a Ministry with an expanded budget. During the first five years of Phibun's second administration, the number of credit societies alone increased from 5,358 (with 96,700 members) to 8,856 (with 166,200 members).[73] As part of the plan to break the Chinese hold on the rice trade, it was proposed in the thirties to develop rice-marketing co-operatives. And it was reasoned that dredging the bar at the mouth of the Jaophraya River would channel all rice exports through the government-operated Port of Bangkok at Khlong Toei, thus ending the lightering of rice (under Chinese control) for loading at Sichang island. Considerable progress was made along both these lines after 1948. The membership in rice and vegetable marketing co-operatives—separate figures are not available—increased from 2,700 to 42,000 between 1947 and 1952.[74] In August 1953, the administration decided to grant a big loan to co-operative societies to open rice-marketing outlets with a co-ordinating agency in Bangkok.[75] In February 1954, the newly completed Jaophraya channel, deep enough to accommodate fully loaded 10,000-ton ships, was officially opened.[76] As it happened, the rapid postwar growth of rice mills in the paddy producing areas and the more stable prices consequent on the government's monopolization of the rice trade were probably of greater importance in reducing the role of the Chinese paddy merchant and stimulating the entry of Thai into the rice trade than either of these measures.

To give Thai the know-how necessary to compete with Chinese in artisan, industrial, and commercial enterprise, the government put special emphasis on the development of vocational education. The number of students in vocational schools increased fourfold between

1947 and 1954 (from 9,625 to 40,093).[77] In 1953, a Technical Institute with well-equipped shops and laboratories was opened in Bangkok to train advanced students and graduates from the Thai secondary schools.

Another government measure to assist Thai vis-à-vis aliens was the establishment in March 1953 of the Food Trade Promotion Committee, headed by the Minister of Economic Affairs, with the aim, among others, of encouraging the "formation of trade associations by Thai which will take over from alien-controlled bodies." [78] In the same year a plan was developed to move Thai businessmen into the Chinese business quarters of Bangkok; the Cabinet appointed a committee headed by the Minister of Interior to ensure that Thais be given first chance and good terms in renting newly built shop-houses.[79] After years of discussion, the administration proposed and the National Assembly passed, in February 1956, a comprehensive Thai Employment Assistance Act. By its provisions, any class of firms or business organizations employing ten or more persons may be required by royal decree to employ up to 50 per cent Thai nationals, the required proportion to be reached by filling all vacancies which occur with Thai citizens. To date, no decrees have been issued under this enabling legislation.

These various positive measures of the administration were accompanied by a much more thoroughgoing set of restrictions on alien economic activities. In February 1949, a new Occupational Restriction Act was promulgated barring aliens from ten occupations, including barbering, salt manufacture, metal inlaying, and the driving of buses and of pedicabs and motor tricycles for hire.[80] In August 1951, six more occupations were closed to aliens, including taxi driving and the manufacture of charcoal, umbrellas, and the accouterments of monastic service.[81] In 1952, by the simple expedient of refusing to renew their licenses, aliens were barred from operating private wharves and commercial fishing. In November of that year, Police General Phao reported to the National Assembly that "at present 100% of the fishermen in Thailand are Thais." [82] In September 1952, another Occupational Restriction Act was promulgated, in this case providing for the progressive elimination of aliens from women's haircutting and hairdressing and dressmaking. In December 1952, the National Assembly passed the Fresh Fish Jetty Act, with the aim of excluding aliens from the marketing of fresh fish. These were the chief occupational reservations as such actually promulgated and enforced, but a listing of them only suggests the touch-and-go atmosphere surrounding the livelihood of Chinese aliens in 1952–1953. For at one time or another, National Assemblymen proposed, or the administration considered, restrictions barring aliens from such lines as rice milling, rice wholesaling, sawmilling, rubber production, mining, pig slaughtering, pork marketing, and the ownership of barbershops and opium dens. No Chinese alien could be sure that his means of livelihood would not be threatened.

Another series of administration decisions affected Chinese domestic trade. Steps were taken during 1952 to deny aliens the right to hold agencies for wholesaling Maekhong liquor produced in government distilleries and cigarettes produced by the government's Tobacco Monopoly. Plans were also made during that year to eliminate aliens from the retailing of cigarettes, refined sugar, oils, matches, umbrellas, cloth, cotton yarn, hats, shoes, and so on. Not all of these proposals, however, were effectively implemented.

The third approach of the administration to economic Thai-ification was government participation in industry and transport. The railway and telecommunications systems had been government-owned for years, and in 1950 the government acquired the Bangkok Electric Works, whose assets included the city's major power plant and the tramway system.[83] Various government agencies or government-owned companies also monopolized the manufacture and import of Virginia cigarettes, the manufacture of opium and of both Thai and Chinese playing cards, internal aviation, and most of the Thai-flag shipping.[84] The activities of the Ministry of Industry, created during Phibun's first administration, were expanded after 1948. By 1953, the Ministry operated sixteen distilleries and six sugar refineries throughout the country, plus a weaving mill, a tannery, and two paper mills.[85]

In January 1953, the Minister of Industry opened a new glass factory in Thonburi designed to make Thailand self-sufficient in regard to bottles.[86] In February, plans were laid for the establishment of two gunny-sack factories as "Thai enterprises," the larger to be built in the northeast and operated by the Ministry, and the smaller to be built in jangwat Saraburi and operated by the semigovernmental War Veterans Organization.[87] In 1953, the administration also unveiled a large-scale industrialization program drafted by the Ministry of Industry. As of May 1954, elaborated plans called for the construction of an iron and steel smelter, alum factory, pottery plant, chemical works, wood-distillation plant, rope factory, margarine plant and the enlargement of the Ministry's paper factory and weaving mill.[88] Later in 1954, the government announced plans to build and operate a pin factory and an ice and cold-storage plant in Bangkok.[89] Stymied by lack of capital for effecting many of these industrial projects, the cabinet gave its blessing—and in fact enrolled almost en masse in its board of directors —to a giant industrial corporation capitalized at fifty million baht to promote Thai enterprise. The Thai Economic Development Company, Ltd., soon obtained a government-secured loan of two hundred million baht from the Bank of America and proceeded with plans for building big gunny-sack and sugar factories and with more distant plans for paper and rubber factories.[90]

Government advance in the transport business was made through its wholly owned agency, the Express Transport Bureau. In June 1953, the Bureau took over all trucking at the Port of Bangkok; it allowed Thai drivers to join with it, but excluded the alien truckers who had been working out of the Port.[91] A month later, the Bureau took over the major bus routes in Bangkok. Private Thai bus owners who thereby lost their concessions then organized a joint company to apply for route concessions elsewhere; alien owners were expressly excluded.[92] In December 1953, the National Assembly approved a bill to give the Transport Department full control of transport vehicles and vessels after Police General Phao explained that it would "help the Government to take control of the services from Chinese hands and place it in Thai hands." [93]

The fourth major aspect of the government's program to Thai-ify the economy was the attempt to monopolize various sectors of commerce and finance by forming, and giving special privileges to, semi-governmental financial and trading corporations. The commercial offensive was launched soon after Phibun's return to power. The Government Purchasing Bureau, which had access to foreign exchange at official rates, was reorganized in 1948 and its activities broadened. Jangwat trading companies were also revived to distribute the Bureau's presumably less expensive products in competition with Chinese merchants upcountry.[94] All government departments were eventually instructed to obtain their requirements through the Bureau. In 1953, the Bureau answered criticism that it was selling goods to governmental agencies at higher than prevailing market prices by stating that, as a government organization, it could not practice the "wiles and ruses" of ordinary merchants which make it possible for them to sell at lower prices.[95] Nevertheless, when the Ministry of Economic Affairs announced, in May 1955, a further expansion of the network of jangwat trading companies, it cited "assistance to the rural population in their fight against increased living costs" as an aim along with recovery of the economy from alien hands. At that time, such trading companies were operating in thirty jangwats, all under supervision of the Ministry of Economic Affairs.[96]

The War Veterans Organization has, along with its subsidiary corporations, been the chief recipient of governmental assistance and privileges in commercial fields. In 1948, its director outlined a plan for the Organization's participation in "all aspects of Siam's economic life," [97] and within the next seven years this aim was virtually attained. At one time or another, the War Veterans Organization and its related corporations held monopoly rights for the distribution of the Mae-khong liquor and cigarettes produced by government factories, the sole agency for refined sugar, a monopoly on the marketing of pigs and pig butchering, and a monopoly on the export of livestock to the Philippines. Special privileges also put the Thahan Samakkhi, the major veterans' corporation, in a favorable position to engage in rice marketing and the import and retailing upcountry of foreign goods.

In January 1953, the National Assembly passed a law which provided the government with authority to convert semigovernmental business organizations such as the Government Purchasing Bureau into full government organizations, and which empowered the administration to set up new business organizations by merely announcing their existence through royal decrees without Assembly approval. In introducing the bill, General Phao claimed that the measure was required "to restore national commerce to its proper owner." [98] Questioned shortly thereafter on the extent of the government's role in business, Phibun told the press that his government was "only temporarily engaged in business as a step towards bringing control of Thailand's commerce from foreign into Thai hands." The government's only purpose, he said, is "to show the way." Inasmuch as "foreigners, mainly Chinese, are keeping a tight hold on the business of the country," it is not possible for Thai private businessmen to take over at once. Government policy, therefore, is to bring together Thai financial resources and "with official aid" promote "organizations like the Thai Financial Syndicate." [99]

In fact, the Thai Financial Syndicate, a combine of government and semigovernment banks set up in 1952, was only the first in a series of commercial and financial syndicates organized under government auspices in 1952–1953. Next came the Thai Gold Syndicate, then the Pork Syndicate, and then the Remittance Syndicate. In November 1953, the cabinet established the Economic Co-ordination Council, headed by Field Marshal Phin, to assist the expansion of private trade by Thai nationals. It requested the semigovernment Monthon Banks to provide Thai traders with low-interest loans and asked the Railway Organization to give priority to Thai in conveying products to markets. Its chief aim, however, the promotion of all-encompassing Thai syndicates in such lines as import-export, rice, rubber, and tin, has not been attained.[100] In April 1955, the Public Welfare Department opened two government-financed pawnshops, one each in Krungthep and Thonburi, to break the Chinese monopoly in that field. As welfare organizations backed by a revolving fund of several million baht, the government pawnshops were able to offer somewhat better terms than Chinese shops and thus attract their clients.[101]

It is not proposed here to evalute the effect on the Thai public of the administration's measures to promote economic nationalism. In many ways, real assistance was rendered Thai nationals, while the effect of many other measures was simply to give government officials a middleman's profit or expediter's cut, thereby raising the purchase price of consumer goods. One of the important consequences to Chinese was that the expanded government role in business encouraged bribery, while the restrictive measures aggravated the opportunities for extortion. In 1954, a scandal developed in the Ministry of Economic Affairs with regard to extensive corruption in the granting of rice-export permits.[102] As the representative of the Chinese Chamber of Commerce delicately put it at a meeting called by Field Marshal Phin: "If a merchant knows officials of the Ministry of Economic Affairs well, he gets a number of import permits relatively easily; if he does not know the officials well he is less likely to get permits; and if he is not personally acquainted with the officials at all, there is no chance whatsoever of his getting a permit." [103] The behavior expected of Chinese merchants was spelled out clearly in an administration statement in October 1954, that acceptance of gifts by government officials is *not* considered by the government to be a practice leading to corruption.[104] Without giving details, the possibilities of police extortion can be suggested by quoting from an article published in an independent Thai newspaper after police censorship was ended in August 1955:

Any person hearing merchants relate the actions of some groups of police-men, who use the influence and authority they possess to bleed these Chinese in a barefaced and shameless manner, would be simply aghast. . . . It is the easiest thing in the world to bleed Chinese in our country. Merely preferring a charge of being a communist or having communist tendencies is more than sufficient for members of the police to obtain huge sums of money from them as they please. But the police are not able to use such tactics with Indian or western merchants, because their Governments are capable of protecting the rights and property of their citizens. . . . Chinese shops are apt to receive invitations or letters from influential members of the Police requesting advertisements or else asking for free gifts, and such letters are received by them without end. Should anyone refuse to pay these "bribes," he is practically certain to be in for trouble in the not very distant future.[105]

The consequences of the government's economic Thai-ification program, however, go far beyond the facts of limited Chinese retreat, sporadic Thai advance, and increased corruption. Of greater significance than any of these is the alliance which it stimulated between Chinese merchants and the Thai ruling class. In one of the most intriguing paradoxes of Thai history, militant economic nationalism has resulted not in the defeat of the enemy but in co-operation between the antagonists.

To put the matter in simplest terms, governmental pressure on Chinese businessmen forced them to seek security among those able to offer protection—government officials, police, and army officers. For their part, the Thai militarists and politicians who came to power with Phibun in 1948, and especially those who achieved political prominence in the coup of November 29, 1951, lacked an economic base to bolster their political and military power and enable them to bid for higher prestige. Inexperienced in business, they could not simply appropriate the economic structure without its deteriorating in their hands. In this situation, three developments took place: (1) Chinese merchants reorganized their major commercial and financial corporations to include on the boards of directors top government officials and other members of the Thai elite with "good connections." (2) Most of the major new corporations in Thailand established since the coup d'état of 1951 have been co-operative Sino-Thai ventures with Chinese supplying the capital and entrepreneurial skill and Thai officials supplying "protection" for the Chinese, official privileges, and in some cases government contracts. (3) The semigovernmental business and financial organizations utilized the managerial skill and commercial acumen of local-born and naturalized Chinese by bringing them into their boards and staffs. These developments, well underway in 1952, had by 1954 evolved into a consistent system. The system functioned imperfectly because of rivalries within the Thai ruling group; one political clique could not always offer Chinese merchants allied with it protection from Thai politicians in one of the other cliques. But in general, the Thai ruling group found in the new Sino-Thai alliance a satisfactory and legitimate source of wealth and economic power, while Chinese merchants profited from the political protection and special privileges the alliance afforded.

In support of these generalizations, one can cite the fact that the boards of directors of 20 of the 33 major insurance companies in Bangkok include members of the Thai elite as well as Chinese businessmen, as do 8 of the 10 major non-Western banks and trust companies. Seventeen of the 27 major import-export and shipping companies—excluding Western firms—manifest the same interethnic co-operation at the formal level alone. All of the big new cinema theaters in Bangkok are Sino-Thai ventures. As for the semigovernmental "Thai enterprises," the Saha Samakkhi (formerly Thahan Samakkhi), whose chairman is the Deputy Minister of Culture, includes four prominent Chinese on its board. The boards of the two new gunny-sack factories (headed respectively by Field Marshal Phin and General Sarit), of the Chiangrai-Lampang Rice Mill Syndicate (headed by General Sarit), of the Thai Financial Syndicate, and of the Thai Economic Development Company (whose promoters include Field Marshal Phin, General Phao, and General Sarit), all include two or three prominent Chinese businessmen as members. The Thai Gold Syndicate, the Pork Syndicate, the Udọn Rice Mill Syndicate and the Remittance Syndicate, all founded with the support of the Thai government and the councilorship of its top officials, are predominantly Chinese organizations. Even in the two government pawnshops, the managers are Chinese. As of October 1955, no less than sixty of the one hundred most influential Chinese leaders had formal business relations with Thai government officials and other powerful members of the Thai elite.[106]

Since Phibun's return from his round-the-world tour in June 1955, the business as well as political climate has improved, at least from the Chinese point of view. Governmental pressure on Chinese businessmen has resumed normal proportions, and the excesses of the government's involvement in business are being checked. The role of government officials in private business concerns has also come under censure, both by Phibun and by the public.[107] To what extent these developments will remove the basic determinants of the Sino-Thai business alliance that has developed since 1948 cannot yet be ascertained. Many government officials have resigned from managing directorships of private firms while retaining their formally less responsible positions and shares in such businesses.[108] A check of Sino-Thai corporations in November 1955, revealed that the system of alliances noted above had barely been touched. The writer's guess is that short of a renunciation of economic nationalism and the appearance on the scene of some alternative economic base for the Thai ruling class, the top-level Sino-Thai business alliance will remain a permanent feature of Thailand's socio-economic structure. There is no questioning the fact that many Chinese businessmen have gone so far in coming to terms with Thai officials as to have an interest in the continued power of the present Thai ruling group.

It remains to discuss the major changes with regard to Chinese remittances and the Chinese contribution to government revenue. Remittances from Thailand to the Chinese mainland picked up after the war at a rate appreciably higher than the prewar figure, even when inflation is taken into account. It was concluded in Chapter 7 that Chinese remittances during the twenties and thirties probably averaged considerably less than twenty million baht annually. In terms of the inflated postwar baht, this would mean a figure of approximately 150,000,000 annually, or 12,500,000 monthly. Remittance circles in Bangkok, however, estimate the average monthly remittances from Bangkok to China during 1946–1948 at twenty-five to thirty million baht. The increase reflects a rush to contribute to families neglected during the war and also the great influx of new immigrants during those years—recent immigrants being the most diligent remitters. Inflation in Nationalist China, the increasingly unrealistic exchange rate set by the Central Bank of China, and the approach of the Communist armies to the emigrant areas of south China, all contributed to a reduction in Chinese remittances during 1948–1949.

After the Communist take-over of south China in the fall of 1949, remittances revived somewhat in spite of initial administrative confusion at the China end, and the monthly rate stabilized at between ten and twelve million baht according to remittance circles in Bangkok. Remittance shops continued to mail at weekly intervals a large package containing the letters written by all remitters, to its corresponding agency in China, while the money, equivalent to the total described in the letters, was remitted through any channel to the Communist Bank of China in Hongkong. The Communist authorities then gave the shop's agency in China the equivalent of the remitted sum in JMP, the local currency.

As mentioned earlier, the reaction among the Chinese in Thailand to Communist policy and practice in China led to a decrease in remittances in 1951. Concerned by the alarming decline in remittances from both Southeast Asia and the Americas, the Communists appealed to overseas Chinese for greater confidence. In September 1951, Ho Hsiang-ning, Director of the Overseas Chinese Affairs Commission in Peking, broadcast a glowing report of the new life of overseas Chinese families in south China, together with an appeal to overseas Chinese to shoulder their "duty in national reconstruction":

Overseas Chinese and their dependents have many advantages in taking part in national construction. Firstly, we have our own government, the People's Government, and its departments, which offer all-out assistance and guidance to overseas Chinese and their dependents, in particular in production and investment. Secondly, natural resources in the provinces along the coast are extremely rich, and it will be much more profitable than working abroad if efforts are directed to their development. Thirdly, overseas Chinese have acquired land and other materials for production following on implementation of land reform. Fourthly, the government is granting all facilities to overseas remittances. They will not be affected by the devaluation of foreign currencies. If these remittances are deposited in a bank, they will get an attractive interest.[109]

Within the next nine months, Communist authorities virtually admitted their previous errors in trying to force remittances from overseas and instituted thoroughgoing reforms. By the second half of 1952, Chinese remittances from Bangkok began to increase once again. It is estimated that the monthly rate, which gradually fell during 1951 to a low of only five million baht, had revived to about seven million baht by the fall of 1952.

The Thai government began to apply serious pressure on the remittance business in 1952. The first measure in a series which eventually led to syndication came in January, when the Bank of Thailand informed the Chinese Remittance Shops Association that each remittance must be reported to the Bank on a form bearing full particulars and the seal of the shop. In March, a limit of two thousand baht per family per month was placed on remittances sent abroad, and the Bank of Thailand required remittance shops to obtain foreign exchange licenses even though the shops as such did not function as exchange brokers. The latter move forced a suspension of the entire business for one month, during which the very practice of sending remittances to family members in Communist China came under attack not only from Thai circles but also from the Overseas Chinese Affairs Commission in Taiwan. While this particular crisis was resolved by compromise with the Ministry of Finance, another arose in June when the Ministry imposed a censorship on remittance letters to China. The *coup de grâce* of the old remittance system was administered in January 1953: The managers of five remittance shops were arrested on charges of having Communist connections, and two consignments of remittance letters, over twenty thousand in all, were detained by the police for screening. Once again business operations were suspended.

After free-for-all maneuvers involving two of the major Sino-Thai business cliques, all remittance shops in Thailand became agents of one of three licensed concerns, organized into a syndicate with sole authorization to remit money to China.[110] Since April 1953, all shops accept remittances at the rate fixed by the syndicate and hand the money received over to the syndicate once a week. The money is then sent through the Asia Trust Company in Bangkok to China via the Communist Bank of China in Hongkong.[111] Since 1953, remittances from Thailand have averaged seven to eight million baht monthly. Up until 1955, there was little remitting of money for purposes other than family support, but with the Communists' commercial offensive, increasingly large sums have been remitted to pay for commodities imported from China indirectly via Hongkong and Singapore. It is estimated that such remittances during the last five months of 1955 totaled about sixty million baht.

From the best available estimates, then, it would appear that Chinese remittances to China since the Communist take-over have averaged less than one hundred million baht annually—a rate far below that of 1946–1948 and, in all probability, considerably below the prewar average in terms of comparable currency.

Without making any attempt to estimate the Chinese contribution to Thai government revenues, one can demonstrate that it must exceed the total amount remitted abroad by the Chinese in Thailand. In 1955, the government revealed that its annual income from the opium monopoly approximated 117,000,000 baht, including 67,200,000 from the sale of opium to licensed dens and 47,300,000 in tender bids for den licenses.[112] The overwhelming majority of den operators in Thailand are Chinese, while considerably more than half of the smokers are ethnic Chinese. The government's expenditures in operating the monopoly are not known, but they cannot be more than a fraction of the total income, inasmuch as opium supplies are largely met by stocks confiscated from smugglers, and operating expenses of the dens are paid by their operators. The direct contribution of Chinese to government revenues in connection with the opium monopoly probably approximates 75,000,000 baht annually and is in any case not less than 50,000,000 baht.

The upward revision in the alien registration fee in 1952 resulted in a sizable increase in the direct Chinese contribution to Thai government revenues. The income from this source was 116,000,000 baht in 1953 and 136,000,000 baht in 1954, while the amount for 1955 was budgeted at 180,000,000 baht.[113] According to government statistics, Chinese form over 93 per cent of all aliens residing in Thailand,[114] so the Chinese portion must have been at least nine-tenths of the total. On this assumption, Chinese aliens probably paid at least 104,000,000 baht in 1953, and 122,000,000 baht in 1954, i.e., annual sums larger than the probable total of Chinese remittances. In view of these relative figures, Chinese remittances abroad in recent years cannot reasonably be considered a serious drain on the national economy.

D. The Decline of Chinese Education

During his first administration, Phibun virtually eradicated the system of Chinese schooling through which some 17,000 students were being educated in 1938. But when he became premier for the second time, he found a completely revived and far more formidable network of Chinese schools, with an enrollment of over 175,000. Whereas in 1937/38 only about one out of a hundred ethnic Chinese was enrolled in a Chinese school, in early 1948 about one out of every twelve ethnic Chinese of all ages was attending a Chinese school. This situation was not pleasing in the sight of the new administration, and between April and June the new Minister of Education, General Mangkọn Phromyothi, took drastic steps to reverse the trend.

Chinese schools that had failed to register according to law were not allowed to open for the new academic year (which begins in Thailand around the end of April). In particular, the applications for registration of all Chinese middle schools were rejected, and ever since May 1948, Chinese secondary education has been limited to elective courses in one or two Thai middle schools plus a handful of Chinese evening schools in Bangkok. Registered Chinese schools, compelled for the first time since the war to adhere to every provision of the private-school regulations, were thrown into administrative chaos. Curricula had to be rearranged to limit instruction in Chinese to two hours per day. Even more appalling to the Chinese was the Minister's plan, announced on May 13, whereby the total number of Chinese schools in the country was to be reduced to 152, i.e., eight in jangwat Phranakhǫn, three each in jangwats Thonburi, Chiangmai, Nakhǫn-ratchasima (Khorat) and Ubon, and two each in all remaining jangwats. The reduction was to be effected by closing schools permanently for infractions of the regulations and by refusing to permit any new schools to open. As the implications of this plan were digested by Chinese educators, most of the intractable boards proceeded to register their schools in a proper fashion and comply with the letter of the regulations.

These moves laid the basis for a struggle between the Ministry of Education and the Chinese schools that proceeded without letup until 1955—a struggle given singleness of purpose by the fact that the same men served as Minister and Undersecretary of the Ministry for most of the seven-year period. The government's policies emphasized three categories of interrelated measures—those designed to cleanse Chinese schools of political influence, to Thai-ify their staffs and curricula, and to limit their financial base.

The police raids on two Chinese schools in mid-June 1948 were but the first of a series aimed at eliminating the use of schools for political ends and for political instruction. By about April 1950, fourteen Chinese schools had been irrevocably closed on charges of political activity.[115] In mid-May 1950, three of the largest Chinese schools in Bangkok were raided and Communist propaganda and letters showing connections with the Chinese Communist Party seized.[116] Beginning in 1951, the Ministry began making systematic use of the Thai principals (which all private schools had to employ by law) for thought control within the schools. On August 1, 1951, the chief of the Private Schools Division summoned the Thai principals of Chinese schools in Krungthep and Thonburi to a meeting, gave them a list of twenty-two banned Chinese books, and instructed them to keep close watch on the political ideology and activities of the Chinese faculty and students in their schools. The next month Chinese schools all over the country were prohibited from possessing or allowing students to read the banned books. In October 1952, the Ministry decreed that only Thai principals could call student assemblies and give didactic speeches and that no gatherings could be held in the absence of the Thai principal. In December 1952, the police notified Chinese schools that in engaging teachers, special attention should be paid to the "thought" of the candidates; the directors or principals who hired a teacher found to be leftist would be held fully responsible.

The anti-Communist drive begun by the police in November 1952 did not neglect Chinese schools. The principal and eleven teachers of one Bangkok Chinese school and twenty Chinese teachers of another were taken into custody in the first raid. On December 23, at least eight Chinese schools in Bangkok were raided, including the largest community school, Huang-hun, and the schools operated by the Teochiu and Hakka Associations. In January 1953, the Chief of the Private Schools Division required the raided schools to send on to the Division for examination all printed matter received by the schools.[117] In the same month, the Chinese schools in Chiangrai and Singburi were ordered closed on account of Communist activity.[118] Following the promulgation of the Un-Thai Activities Act, education authorities began investigating the so-called "underground Chinese schools"— tutorial groups of no more than seven students and consequently not covered by the private-school regulations. Beginning in January 1953, the Private Schools Division required that before engaging new teachers, Chinese schools must submit a report on the candidates' "antecedents and thought" and await the Division's approval. In March, the Division increased its staff of inspectors so that every Chinese school in Bangkok could be visited at least once a month. At the same time, police inspection of Chinese schools began.[119] In December 1953, the Minister of Education told principals of Chinese schools that they were responsible for seeing that no students brought Communistic books to school.[120] The new private-school regulations passed in March 1954 provided for C.I.D. screening of all private-school teachers not of Thai nationality, and for the appointment to each Chinese school of an educational supervisor, whose duty it was to prevent Communist subversive activities.[121] By October, such supervisors, mostly retired police officers, had been appointed to 28 Chinese schools.[122] In July 1954, the Ministry of Education ordered Bangkok Chinese schools to discharge 152 teachers blacklisted for alleged Communist sympathies.[123] In October 1954, anti-Communist indoctrination meetings were arranged for the Chinese teachers of Bangkok.[124] In January 1955, Chinese schools were asked to transfer to the Ministry-appointed supervisor the duties of the Thai principal, the latter to become the supervisor's assistant.[125]

Paralleling the implementation of this system of thought control and political cleansing, the Ministry forced through a series of measures designed to Thai-ify the curricula and administration of the Chinese schools. Up through 1950, attention was concentrated on compliance with existing regulations, which limited class time for Chinese instruction to ten hours per week and required Chinese teachers to pass an examination in Thai at the fourth-grade level. Between 1948 and 1950, some thirty schools were closed for slighting regulations of this kind.[126] During 1951, the Thai-ification campaign was considerably stepped up. In February, Chinese schools were ordered to follow the grade system consistently by having students studying Chinese at the level of a given grade also study Thai at the same level. This regulation, enforced at first only for the first and second grades but later at all levels, was designed to make certain that all students would possess a knowledge of Thai at least on a par with their knowledge of Chinese. During the same year, the system of subsidies was expanded in such a way as to induce Chinese schools to reduce the number of hours devoted to Chinese; the regulations provided that only schools teaching less than six hours of foreign language per week could receive a subsidy. Many schools in desperate financial plight, especially those upcountry, were constrained to change their curricula so as to qualify for the subsidy.

In April 1951, the Ministry of Education decreed that uniform Chinese textbooks be used in Chinese schools throughout the country, and a committee of ten Bangkok Chinese schools took on the task of writing new books which would stress orientation and loyalty to Thailand. The approved revisions were compulsory for all Chinese schools after May 1952. In that month, too, Chinese schools were ordered to have the Thai national anthem sung every morning at the flag-raising ceremony. In September 1952, the Private Schools Division decreed that music and physical education were Thai courses and should be taught by Thai teachers exclusively. In December, it was pointed out that writing Chinese on the blackboard in other than Chinese classes or explaining Thai or even arithmetic lessons in Chinese was strictly against regulations.[127]

In August 1953, authorities of the Private Schools Division announced plans to raise the Thai proficiency requirement for foreign-language teachers to the level of the third year of secondary school. But in the face of the critical shortage of teachers, this requirement was relaxed in July 1954.[128] At the same time the Ministry proceeded with plans to reduce the maximum hours for Chinese lessons to one a day. In April 1954, the Thai Minister of Foreign Affairs formally notified the Chinese Embassy of the proposed cut.[129] Diplomatic pro-tests that the move violated the letter and spirit of the 1946 Treaty of Amity delayed the issuance of a formal order to Chinese schools, but in June 1955, schools were instructed to cut the time devoted to Chi-nese to five and one-half hours per week for first-grade students.[130]

By this time the authority and responsibility of the boards of Chinese schools had been reduced to a formalistic level. In May 1952, Chi-nese schools were reminded that the Thai principal had full ad-ministrative responsibility, not the so-called "Chinese principal," and Chinese schools were ordered to pay Thai teachers according to the salary scale for Chinese teachers. In the same month, the Ministry in-sisted that, in the interests of stability, it would not tolerate changes in the teaching staff of schools following new elections of the school board or sponsoring organization. The new regulations concerning engagement of teachers, already mentioned above, effectively removed responsibility for hiring and firing from the hands of the Chinese principal or board. As one Ministry official said in consoling the Chi-nese educators, the police and not the school's authorities would hence-forth bear responsibility for the activities of its teachers.[131] With the appointment of educational supervisors to Chinese schools, the decision-making power of Chinese principals and school-board direc-tors was subject to so many vetoes as to be nullified.

Chinese associations running schools were thus expected to finance their operation but were denied control over them. Schools operated by registered Chinese associations, however, at least had a steady and legal source of income in the form of dues paid to the sponsoring or-ganization. It was the schools run by unregistered associations and boards or operating without formal boards which faced the greatest difficulties under the second Phibun administration. Most of the educa-tors arrested in the 1948 raids in Bangkok were charged with soliciting funds illegally, and the celebrated Ch'ing-hua school closure in Chiang-mai in 1949 made it even clearer to Chinese educational circles that soliciting funds for the operational expenses of Chinese schools was asking for trouble. In any case, few Chinese were willing to contribute freely to schools that were very nearly Chinese in name only. Faced with insolvency, most of these schools increased tuition to a point beyond the capacity or willingness of many Chinese parents to pay. With Chinese teachers leaving the profession because of the government's stiff language requirements and political restrictions, and with practically no new teachers arriving from China, the salaries of Chinese teachers at the same time rose beyond the ability of many schools to pay. Probably more schools closed voluntarily for financial reasons between 1950 and 1954 than were ordered closed by the government for political activities or failure to conform to other regulations.

The net result of the Ministry of Education's policies was disastrous to the cause of Chinese education. Between 1948 and 1956, the total number of Chinese schools in Thailand decreased from over 430 to about 195.[132] The plan announced by the Ministry of Education in 1948 seemed incredible to the Chinese at the time, but in many respects its goals have already been attained. It called for a reduction in Chinese schools outside the Bangkok area to 141, and by 1956 the number had been reduced to about one hundred and thirty. The plan allowed Chiangmai, Ubon, and Nakhonratchasima three Chinese schools each, and in 1956 the number of Chinese schools in these jangwats was only two, three, and one, respectively. Whereas almost every jangwat had at least one Chinese school in 1948 and all were to be allowed by the Ministry's plan to have at least two, in 1956 at least twenty jangwats had no Chinese school whatsoever.

Furthermore, in the remaining schools, enrollments have on the average dropped to between a half and a third of the 1947 levels. The number of students in every upcountry Chinese school is far below that permitted by the Ministry of Education. For instance, in North Siam in 1955 there were eight Chinese schools in operation with a combined permitted enrollment of 2,056 students, but these eight schools in fact had only about 1,400 students. In 1955–1956 there were only 22,000 students in all Chinese schools outside the Bangkok area. This meant that the average provincial Chinese school had only 168 students, and that only one out of every 75 ethnic Chinese was in a Chinese school.

In the Bangkok area, the reduction in Chinese educational facilities was less drastic. The number of schools in jangwats Phranakhon and Thonburi has fallen from somewhat over 100 to 63 in the past eight years. The total enrollment as of early 1956 was about 27,000, that is, one student in Chinese schools for approximately every 23 of the total ethnic Chinese population. Even so, in the entire country, the decrease in the number of students in Chinese schools in eight years—from over 175,000 to less than 50,000—represents a change of tremendous importance to the future of the Chinese in Thailand.

The decline is even more dramatic when the altered content of the education offered by the Chinese schools is considered as well. Every Chinese school in the kingdom has more Thai than Chinese teachers. The stark fact is that, aside from the best schools in Bangkok and a few of the larger towns, only a fraction of those who finish four years in a Chinese school have acquired a real speaking knowledge of Kuo-yü much less a solid foundation in written Chinese. In one school after another all over Thailand, Chinese teachers and principals told the writer that not only could their students read, write, and understand Thai far better than Chinese, but they also learned practically nothing of Chinese culture, or Chinese history and geography. Even when ten hours per week can be devoted to Chinese lessons, there is not enough time to cover the simplified and revised Chinese textbooks in the four-year program. The absence of any formal Chinese secondary schooling for eight years has meant that very few of the local-born Chinese now entering adulthood have any suspicion of the richness and traditional grandeur of Chinese culture.

Once again, as in the prewar days, most of the children of ethnic Chinese are not even exposed to Chinese schooling. In contrast to the prewar period, however, an interlude of study in China is virtually out of the question. At the same time, the educational facilities of Thai schools have, since the war, grown more rapidly than the ethnic Thai population. Consequently, more and more Chinese parents can send their children to Thai primary schools, where tuition is free or lower than in Chinese schools. The great majority of third-generation Chinese children are today educated exclusively in Thai schools, while even of second-generation children, at least as many attend Thai schools as attend Chinese schools. The Chinese elite, on its part, has shown an even stronger preference for mission and foreign schools than before the war. A study of Chinese leaders in Bangkok in 1952 showed that they utilized Chinese schools less frequently than other available schooling. Of the children of 135 prominent leaders, 290 were educated wholly or in part in non-Chinese schools affiliated with Christian missions, as against only about 150 children who had some or all of their education in local Chinese schools.[133]

Since 1955, there have been signs of a softening in the Thai administration policies concerning Chinese education. After five years of fruitless negotiations between the Ministry of Education and the Chinese Chamber of Commerce, the Ministry finally agreed to permit the Chamber to operate a secondary school in the quarters of its former Chung-hua middle school; but the new Hua-shang middle school, which opened in May 1955, was not permitted to teach any Chinese, at least for the first year.[134] In May, the Private Schools Division relaxed its restrictions on tuition levels.[135] In the same month, police circles presented a plan which would allow the operation of Chinese higher-primary and middle schools, with the aim of combating Communist influence among Chinese youth. It was felt that the provision of attractive—and firmly controlled—Chinese secondary education would help control the small "underground classes" operated by pro-Communist private teachers and cut off the steady trickle of youths going to China for their schooling (and for possible training for subversive work in Thailand).[136] This plan met with strong opposition in the Ministry of Education,[137] and although Phibun has been reported to favor the reopening of Chinese middle schools, nothing has come of it to date. In the meantime, in hopes of eventual permission to teach Chinese and in order to relieve the shortage of secondary school facilities of any kind for Chinese students, four more Thai middle schools (in addition to Hua-shang of the Chamber of Commerce) were established in Bangkok by Chinese educators, two in 1955 and two in May 1956. In October 1955, Phibun, in keeping with his program toward Full Democracy, expressed his opposition to the use of ex-police officers as educational supervisors in Chinese schools.[138] The system has since been dropped entirely on the guarantee of the schools involved that there would be no political activity.

It is unlikely, however, that these straws in the wind portend any basic change in the government's aims with regard to Chinese education. The school-reduction plan of 1948 is still an official blueprint. No Thai government can be expected willingly to acquiesce in Communist infiltration of the schools or in a reversal of the successful Thai-ification policy. A less extreme system of controls is undoubtedly in the offing; minor relaxations, however, can hardly revive Chinese education in Thailand from its increasingly moribund state.

E. *The Changing Order of Sino-Thai Relations*

During the ten years since the close of the Second World War, Thai policy toward the Chinese has run the full gamut from tempered

benevolence to harsh containment. The laissez-faire policy of 1945–
1947 was stiffened somewhat in late 1947 and early 1948, and replaced
during the first years of Phibun's administration by a policy of firm
control. After the coup d'état of November 1951, governmental policy
hardened to one of full containment. The first signs of a relaxation in
anti-Chinese fervor came in 1954, and during the second half of 1955
the government virtually repudiated anti-Sinicism as a political instrument. In 1956, a benevolent policy designed to integrate the Chinese
into Thai society is apparent.

The major political, economic, and educational dimensions of the
Phibun administration's increasingly anti-Chinese policies up to 1953–
1954 have been explored above. Any discussion of these aspects alone,
however, cannot convey the all-pervasive quality of the Thai policy of
containment. In terms of shock effect on the Chinese in Thailand,
1952 and 1953 were comparable to the black years of 1939 and 1940.
The new era of containment was ushered in by the increase of the
alien fee from twenty to four hundred baht annually in January 1952.
In the same month, the new cabinet made a basic decision to reserve
land (and any buildings thereon) in the vicinity of railway stations,
important bridges, and new highway intersections for Thais and to
evict all aliens residing there. The Ministries of Agriculture, Communications, and Interior were charged with implementing this
decision.[139] The Ministry of Communications and the Railway Organization drew up plans in February to refuse renewal of leases for
·alien-owned granaries, to force alien merchants to move off land belonging to the Railway Organization, and to prevent Thai leaseholders
of Railway-owned land from subletting to aliens.[140] Chinese were
almost the only aliens affected, the installations of Western oil companies being specifically excepted.

Several considerations combined to cause the government to soft-
pedal these plans, even though orders to execute them were in fact
issued between May and August. The government's financial in-
capacity to take over Chinese granaries, the questionable legal grounds
for the Railway Organization's orders, the paralysis of trade which
would have resulted from barring alien merchants from the area around
railway stations, the indifference of the Thai public to their new commercial opportunities, vigorous radio denunciations from Peking, and
official protests from the Nationalist Chinese Embassy—all led to a
retraction of the more severe parts of the plan in September 1952. In
the end, Chinese were required only to remove Chinese signs from

shops on the Railway Organization's lands, while aliens near other strategic installations were required only to transfer title to Thai citizens.[141] The fear so prevalent in 1952 that Chinese were in a position to resort to sabotage left its mark in one piece of permanent legislation. The Emergency Administration Act, passed in March, provided that once an Emergency is declared the government "shall have the power by public notice to forbid aliens to enter into any place required to safeguard the stability or safety of the Kingdom or any strategic point." [142]

During 1952, the administration also introduced into its land policy elements of discrimination against Thai citizens of Chinese extraction. In January, the Ministry of Interior ordered jangwat authorities to examine every case of lease or purchase of land and to withhold approval if it involved the money of aliens—this in order to prevent aliens from obtaining land through their relatives of Thai citizenship. In August, jangwat authorities were ordered to enforce a cabinet decision that only "pure" Thais or ex-servicemen of Thai citizenship be allowed to lease Crown land. Later that month, the authorities were instructed to prevent Thai nationals born of alien fathers and still using alien surnames from acquiring rights to land in any form.

In the first two months of 1953, new legislation unequivocally repudiated the traditional system whereby children born in Thailand of whatever parentage were not discriminated against but encouraged to assume their duties and responsibilities as full Thai citizens. The Military Service Act promulgated on January 27, 1953, added "persons' born of an alien father" to those who shall not be called into active service. Thus did the government publicly declare its lack of confidence in the loyalty of the second-generation Chinese among its citizens. An amendment to the Nationality Act promulgated on February 3 repealed the long-standing provisions that "any person born within the Kingdom" is a Thai subject by birth and substituted "any person born of a Thai father . . . [or] of a Thai mother inside the Kingdom." [143] Thus children both of whose parents were Chinese citizens were denied Thai citizenship by birth. Police General Phao's remarks to the Assembly when the amendment was being considered typify the spirit with which it was passed. Since Chinese nationality laws regard all persons born of Chinese parents anywhere as Chinese, he said, why not "let Chinese born here of Chinese parents be regarded as Chinese straight-away, so that there would be only pure Thai." [144]

In 1952, legislation had already been passed to discourage naturalization: the residence requirement was upped from five years to "an uninterrupted period of not less than ten years," and "knowledge of the Thai language as prescribed by Ministerial Regulations" was imposed as an additional requirement.[145] In June 1953, the Ministry of Interior requested jangwat authorities to send in detailed reports of their reasons if and when they permit aliens to use Thai names. The Ministry's stated purpose was to prevent aliens from using Thai names to facilitate naturalization in order to take up occupations reserved for Thais.[146] Legal assimilation of the Chinese could not have been more thoroughly checkmated. During 1953–1954, progovernment newspapers recalled the Yaowarat Incident of 1945, "when a great many naturalized Thai citizens turned their backs on hospitable Thailand." This "unforgettable episode in the Nation's history," the newspapers wrote, should serve as a reminder that "there is nothing more difficult in the world than an effort to relegate into oblivion one's original nationality."[147] In November 1953, Phao affirmed before the National Assembly "the impossibility of absorbing" Chinese aliens.[148]

No detail was overlooked during the peak of the anti-Chinese campaign in 1953. In January, the Krungthep Municipal Office issued regulations giving Thai nationals priority in getting new water mains, to cut off "those with money, the aliens."[149] In June, the Ministry of Interior ordered an end to the use of amplifiers for advertising in foreign languages, it being "likely that communist propaganda may infiltrate into the advertising business."[150] Later that month the cabinet decided "to prohibit or control residence by aliens, particularly Chinese, in areas gutted by fires."[151] In December, the Chief of the Metropolitan Police banned Chinese opera performances in public places within Krungthep municipality.[152]

These examples will certainly suffice to establish the government's persistent and consistent adherence, in the years following the 1951 coup, to policies designed to antagonize and alienate first- and second-generation Chinese, to discourage Chinese assimilation, and to check any Chinese activities considered undesirable regardless of consequences. But why? What motivated the administration to pursue such a strongly anti-Chinese course? Fear of Communism and of a war with Communist countries was certainly an important factor. Communist victories first in China and then in Vietnam, the continued presence of armed Communist groups in Burma and Laos and of armed Communist terrorists in Malaya and in the border jungles of South Siam itself all contributed to an awareness of military insecurity on the part of the country's leaders. A Communist advance on the domestic scene, furthermore, would have threatened the power of the ruling group itself. Since most Communists within the country were Chinese and since China was the major Communist power in Asia, the Chinese residing in the country were feared both as a potential political force and as a potential fifth column for Peking.

Given these fears, however, the administration could have sought security from the Communist threat by more enlightened measures. It did not, it would appear, for two reasons. First of all, the oligarchy which came to power in the November coup of 1951 consisted largely of military officers who were veterans of several coups, i.e., specialists in force. They were inexperienced in politics and ignorant of statesmanship. In their inexperience and with their background, forceful suppression was the most natural weapon at hand. Secondly, anti-Communism and anti-Sinicism could be used to political advantage within the country. Under Police General Phao's leadership the two issues became as inextricably mixed as did anti-Bolshevism and anti-Semitism under the Nazi regime. Like their counterparts in Germany, they were admirable tools for suppressing political opposition and useful rationalizations for the maintenance of militarized undemocratic rule. Prejudice against the Chinese had, if anything, increased since 1938. The level of its intensity in Bangkok, for instance, is considerably higher than that of anti-Semitic prejudice in New York City. Bangkok, after all, has never witnessed any official encouragement of ethnic brotherhood nor seen any concerted efforts to improve "race relations" at a sophisticated, practical level. And Bangkok's Thai-language press, with few exceptions, wears its anti-Sinitic bias on its sleeve. An administration seeking support can, therefore, count on the efficacy of anti-Chinese measures to rally popular enthusiasm. Measures that can be given an anti-Sinitic twist are less critically received. Thus, the administration's attack on the leftist Thai National Peace Council was linked with the campaign against *Chinese* Communists. Even the economic alliance formed with the Chinese business elite was pursued in the name of the fight to wrest control of the economy from Chinese. The sheer mass of measures with an anti-Chinese label of itself ensured considerable popular assent to the regime's policies.

It should also be noted that the Thai administration was able to play politics with anti-Sinicism to such an extreme degree because of the peculiar international situation. After 1949, the Nationalist Chinese government was powerless to provide any real protection to the Chinese in Thailand, while at the same time a protective American umbrella shielded the administration from the impact of Peking's power. In general, the dim view Americans took of the administration's anti-Chinese containment policy was brightened by their vision of its anti-Communist Siamese twin.

The first danger signals for the administration's containment policy came as early as 1953, when a small group of opposition Assemblymen began voting with some consistency against the anti-Chinese bills presented by the progovernment Legislative Study Group. The beginnings of governmental relaxation of that policy, however, came only the following year. In June 1954, a new Alien Division was established by the Police Department, and among its stated objectives was the provision of assistance in naturalizing aliens considered "desirable as Thai subjects" and of assistance to aliens "in all affairs concerning them, in seeking justice, in earning a livelihood, in disputes with officials who may be trying to oppress them or trying to extort money from them." [153] In October 1954, the Police Department requested the Minister of Interior to cancel orders to deport 110 of the Chinese who had been exiled to Phetchabun,[154] and in April 1955, 128 Chinese were released from their confinement there. In May 1955, the police sponsored a plan to allow the operation of Chinese middle schools.

If these police moves represented some fence-mending on the part of Phao, he was soon far outdistanced by Phibun. Within a week of his return in June 1955 from his extensive tour abroad, Phibun found some kind words for the local Chinese.[155] At his press conference on July 15, he announced that the administration planned to give to the Chinese rights as nearly equal to those of Thai nationals as possible, to encourage Chinese assimilation, and to reduce the alien registration fee.[156] This pronouncement marked the beginning of a new era in the administration's treatment of the Chinese. Containment was repudiated and proassimilationist policies revived. In July, it was announced that aliens desiring naturalization would not even have to be fluent in the Thai language. In August, Phibun advised Chinese with Thai wives and children to naturalize.[157] By September, the Ministry of Interior was virtually begging Chinese aliens born of Thai mothers to apply for naturalization.[158]

Before legislation was promulgated to effect the new policies, Phibun explained to the Thai public that since the Chinese in Thailand could go neither to Taiwan nor to Red China, they found themselves in a difficult predicament; in consequence they deserved considerate treatment, the sympathy of the Thai people, and "all possible assistance" from the government.[159] On August 26, an amendment to the Military Service Act was promulgated restoring the equality of all Thai nationals regardless of ancestry with regard to conscription.[160] In September, it was announced that the government would lower the immigration fee in 1956, probably to half of the current level (1,000 baht).[161] In October, regulations were promulgated whereby six broadly defined classes of aliens could apply for exemption from payment of the alien fee.[162] At his press conference on October 14, Phibun reported the administration's intention, "in conformity with the Government's liberal policy towards the Chinese," of amending the Nationality Act so that all persons born in Thailand are automatically Thai citizens.[163] On October 19, in his capacity as Minister of Interior, Phibun

instructed all authorities concerned to render as much convenience as possible to [aliens]. . . . The Premier viewed these authorities' past action as overwhelming Aliens with a remarkable amount of inconvenience which impeded them from coming to pay their registration fees. The Premier stressed that these authorities should behave themselves properly not only to Thai people, but also these aliens, so that no difference might be observed.[164]

In January 1956, decrees were promulgated officially reducing the alien registration fee from 400 to 200 baht and waiving the collection of unpaid back fees under certain liberal conditions.[165] In March 1956, a new Electoral Law was promulgated giving Thai nationals born of alien fathers and naturalized Thai citizens the basic right to stand for election to the National Assembly. A liberalization of legislation closely affecting Chinese is still in process. In July the Cabinet instructed the Ministry of Interior to consider amendments to the Nationality Act permitting Thailand-born children of aliens to obtain Thai citizenship. In August the Ministry revealed that it will propose new naturalization requirements which reduce the fee from 4,000 to 2,000 baht and which abolish formal educational requirements. In September 1956, the Cabinet approved a draft Deportation Act which provides for a fifteen-day interval between formal notification of a deportation order and its execution and which guarantees the right of appeal.

As a reflection of this policy reversal, the progovernment press was swept by a breath of fresh air with regard to the Chinese problem. In an editorial prompted by the Sino-Indonesian agreement on citizenship reached at Bandung, the progovernment *Bangkok Tribune* startled its readers by identifying the Chinese in Thailand as "a minority which has made an exceptional contribution to the commercial progress of the nation," and stating, "it is a compliment to our land that they choose to cast their lot and spend their talents here." [166] Ever since, the progovernment press has in general adhered to the administration's policy of "closer relations with friendly aliens," and since August 1955, the opposition press has been comparatively free to attack the excesses of the government's former policies and prod it toward fuller realization of its new aims.

The new course taken by the Thai administration in its Chinese policy cannot be entirely understood apart from the program toward Full Democracy personally sponsored by Premier Phibun following his round-the-world tour of April to June 1955. After this trip, his public stance was barely distinguishable from that of a newly elected reform governor in the United States. Most observers interpret the change as a bid for popular support to recover the power assumed in 1951–1952 by members of the 1951 coup clique. According to this view, Phibun was impressed in America and several European and Asian countries by the tremendous political power genuine popularity can give a national leader. If the beneficent Eisenhower approach yields greater political security and international prestige than the repressive Franco way can hope to achieve, why not give it a try? These observers noted in this connection that the tour was Phibun's first trip abroad since the late 1920's. Whatever the reasons for the Premier's conversion to a more democratic rule might be, the new approach inevitably spelled less malevolence toward the Chinese, because a large part of the measures adopted to restrict the liberties of the Thai people had been taken in the name of anti-Sinicism and anti-Chinese Communism.

But there are other, more specific reasons for the change in the administration's Chinese policy. In 1955, the chances of a Far Eastern war involving Thailand seemed more remote than at any time since 1950. The fighting was over in Vietnam, Communist China gave every assurance at Bandung that military adventures were not contemplated in the future, and Thailand herself achieved a sense of security in SEATO. Thus fears of Chinese Communist subversion and fifth-column activities were diminished. The Bandung Conference in April 1955 influenced the Thai government in several other ways. It brought the Thai delegation face to face with the majority Asian view of Communist China as a great new Asian power; Prince Wan himself was impressed by the diplomatic skill of Chou En-lai. The conference left most observers with the distinct impression that admission of the Peking government to the United Nations and recognition of that regime by almost all the countries of Europe and Asia were inevitable. The citizenship agreement between Indonesia and Red China and the Communist trade offensive both served notice on the Thai government that a long-term policy of containment toward the Chinese was perilous, to say the least. A new awareness of the potential power of Communist China in Southeast Asia was coupled with an appreciation of the fact that a period of peaceful competition for the loyalty of the Chinese in Thailand was in the offing—and that Thailand's future and the tenure of the present administration might be strongly conditioned by the results of that contest. Nothing short of a concerted attempt to assimilate and integrate local Chinese into Thai society held promise of success. Finally, the growth of neutralist sentiment among the Thai public, based on a nationalistic resentment of the administration's dependence on the United States, plus a welling up of popular disgust with the excesses of the administration's economic Thai-ification program forced a policy change inevitably affecting the Chinese.

It is now possible to assess the effect of postwar developments on Chinese assimilation in Thailand and to point to the factors which will likely determine its future course. There is every indication that the rate of Chinese assimilation reached its all-time nadir in 1946–1947. Not only did second- and third-generation Chinese consider themselves Chinese in almost all situations; there were even cases of great-grandchildren of Chinese immigrants assuming a Chinese name, studying the Chinese language, and identifying on occasion as Chinese. The depression of Chinese assimilation in the immediate postwar period was a response to several concomitant developments. Phibun's containment policies of 1938–1944 had effectively killed the desire of many second-generation Chinese to assimilate, while the laissez-faire policies of the various administrations from 1945 to 1947 gave the Chinese free reign to indulge their antiassimilationist desires. Specifically, unrestricted Chinese immigration allowed the proportion of China-born Chinese within the Chinese community to increase sharply and permitted a new influx of China-born women, to the discouragement of ethnic intermarriage. The government's relaxation of pressure on Chinese education led to an increase in the number of children in Chinese schools to ten times the prewar peak. Of equal importance was the new international position of China as one of the victorious Big Five powers and the establishment of Chinese diplomatic and consular offices in Thailand.

In spite of the fluctuations since 1948 in Thai policies toward the Chinese, they have been consistently proassimilationist in several respects. A negligible Chinese immigration quota has been maintained ever since 1949, while unremitting pressure on Chinese schools has played a major part in the decline of Chinese education. The importance of immigration and education to Chinese assimilation in Thailand can hardly be overstressed. In the absence of replenishment from China, the ethnic Chinese population of Thailand is becoming increasingly dominated by the Thailand-born, who for the most part have little or no firsthand experience in China. The Thai-ification of Chinese schools together with the reduction in their number has greatly restricted the opportunity to learn written Chinese and become better acquainted with the rudiments of Chinese history and traditions. The importance of a Chinese education in this regard is brought out by two conclusions reached by the writer after several years of working among the Chinese in Thailand: The only third-generation Chinese who identify in most social situations as Chinese are those educated in Chinese schools, in Thailand or abroad. The only fourth-generation Chinese who *ever* identify as Chinese are likewise Chinese-educated. The implication is clear that *without a Chinese education* grandchildren of Chinese immigrants at the present time become Thai.

So far as the writer can determine, the Thai containment policy of 1952–1954 had a selective effect on Chinese assimilation. In general it strengthened the in-group solidarity of first- and second-generation Chinese and crushed the inclination of most second-generation Chinese to assimilate. With regard to third-generation Chinese, however, probably most were encouraged to hasten the assimilation process and thereby escape the impact of anti-Chinese virulence and government policy. This effect, as already pointed out above, was also noticeable among those Chinese—of whatever generation—who had most at stake in Thailand, the leading businessmen. It is an interesting feature of Thai psychology that no matter how strong the prejudice against "those Chinese," the Thai are never inclined to reject anyone of Chinese ancestry who speaks and behaves like a Thai.

At the present time, the Thai government's policy is consistently proassimilationist in almost every respect. Educational and economic policies are characterized by firm but moderate pressure on the Chinese. The legal disadvantages of alien citizenship as contrasted with Thai citizenship are still apparent, while, by contrast, legal discrimination against citizens of alien extraction has been eliminated. Even in labor policy a new proassimilationist approach is apparent. The Free Workmen Association of Thailand, promoted by Thai politicians and Chinese businessmen jointly in 1954, has encouraged interethnic solidarity from the start. Its present membership of approximately 18,000 workers is about two-thirds Chinese and one-third Thai. The administration has also announced plans to discontinue its opium monopoly and close the 1,090 licensed opium dens by January 1, 1957.[167] If the government is successful in its plans to cure opium addicts, an important divisive factor between the ethnic groups will have been eliminated; for most Thai regard opium smoking as a Chinese vice and hold Chinese in contempt for indulging.

In historical perspective, one can conclude that the chief factors influencing the rate of Chinese assimilation in Thailand—taking Thai and Chinese cultures and Thai social structure as given—are the content and amount of Chinese schooling available to local-born Chinese; the sex ratio among ethnic Chinese; the proportion of China-born Chinese in the ethnic Chinese population; the nature and extent of the differential in treatment and legal status between Thai nationals and aliens, firstly, and between Thai nationals of immediate alien extraction and other Thai nationals, secondly; the scope and ability of Chinese agencies to promote Chinese nationalism; and the effective influence in Thailand of the government of China.

All of these factors can be influenced to some degree—many to a crucial degree—by Thai governmental policy. The position and role of the People's Republic of China is the most important of the relevant factors outside Bangkok's control. The situation may very well develop in which Thailand has no choice but to recognize Peking and allow the establishment of Communist Chinese diplomatic and consular offices in Thailand. This development or any general victory of Communism in Southeast Asia would certainly retard Chinese assimilation. For the rest, however, the Thai government has it within its power to bring closer the day when descendants of Chinese immigrants will be fully assimilated and completely loyal citizens. The indications in 1956 are that Thailand may choose to handle the Chinese Problem by attempting to obviate it through a moderate and liberal program designed to integrate the Chinese into Thai society.

Notes

Chapter 1

1. Poujade 1946, 1678.
2. Mosolff 1932, 331; Credner 1935, 360; Helbig 1949, 163.
3. Briggs 1951, 247.
4. Graham 1924, II, 92.
5. Nunn 1922, 80.
6. "Mining" 1930, 107.
7. Credner 1935, 360; Helbig 1949, 163.
8. E.g., Graham 1924, I, 27.
9. Gerini 1905; Blythe 1947, 65.
10. Hsieh 1949, 45.
11. The precise dates and composition of these late 13th-century embassies is questionable. The Northern Thai Annals state that Ramkamhaeng himself went to China in 1294 and 1299–1300, but the Yüan history nowhere mentions that the Hsien King had an audience with the Emperor. It has also been suggested that Ramkamhaeng went no further than Kwangtung, but Briggs places no reliance on any version stating that the King went to China. See Briggs 1951, 242; Hsieh 1949, 45–46; Landon 1941, 4.
12. Hsieh 1949, 45–46.
13. See 1919, 36.
14. Prince Damrong, however, equates Lo-hu with the principality of Uthǫng, the predecessor of the kingdom of Ayutthaya, rather than with Louvo. Hsieh 1949, 45–47. Lo-hu sent a tribute mission to Peking in 1289.
15. King Baromarat I (1370–1388) was so invested by the first Ming Emperor. Hsieh 1949, 275.
16. The second voyage, probably 1407–1409, clearly extended to Siam, and while Ayutthaya is not mentioned by name, the geographical description of the approach to "the country" given in Ma Huan's *Ying-yai sheng-lan*

(C 8) leaves no doubt that the destination was Ayutthaya. In 1412, the eunuch Hung Pao was sent by the imperial court on a mission to Siam, presumably to conduct the son of the Thai king back to Ayutthaya. Fei Hsin lists Siam among the countries he personally visited, and his stop-over was probably made en route to or from Bengal in 1412–1414 or 1415–1418. Ayutthaya sent tributary envoys to China with Cheng Ho's suite when it returned from the sixth voyage (1421–1422), so that Siam may have been among the countries which Cheng Ho personally visited on that trip. On the return from the seventh voyage in 1433, the expedition put in for a day or two at some port on the Gulf of Siam. See Duyvendak 1939, 363–366, 374, 386; and Ch'en Y. T. 1940, 57–58.

17. Ma Huan, *Ying-yai sheng-lan*, 1416, and Fei Hsin, *Hsing cha sheng-lan* (C 9), 1436. The pertinent passages from both works are given in Hsieh 1949, 275.

18. Literally "offspring of Chinese."

19. *Hai-yü* (C 10), 1537. The pertinent passage is quoted in Hsieh 1949, 275. In regard to this passage, it should be noted that the Thai adopted surnames only in the 20th century.

20. Spinks 1956, 66–71. To account for the marked differences between the wares of Sukhothai and Sawankhalok, Spinks posits the immigration of two distinct companies of Chinese potters: one around 1300 from Tz'u-chou (south of Peking) to Sukhothai, and one about fifty years later from Lung-ch'üan (Chekiang) to Sawankhalok.

21. Le May 1925.

22. Hsieh 1949, 275.

23. Hsieh 1949, 48.

24. Hsieh 1949, 49.

25. Yü Yung-ho, *Hai-shang chi-lüeh* (C 15). The pertinent passage is quoted in Hsü 1946, 118. Several other 17th-century sources mention that Lin Tao-ch'ien became a king on an island in the Southeastern Sea or in Po-ni (Brunei). But since Po-ni and Ta-ni were badly confused in the Chinese literature, these provide no basis for deciding that Lin went elsewhere than to Pattani, especially in view of the traces of Lin in Pattani folklore. The problem is carefully discussed by Hsü 1946, 111–120.

26. The passage occurs in vol. 325 of the *Ming shih* in the section entitled "Po-ni chuan (Annals of Brunei)," but according to Hsü it most likely relates to Pattani.

27. Hsü 1946, 120.

28. One Teochiu version, in fact, has Lin Tao-ch'ien going to Ayutthaya and marrying the King's daughter, but this cannot be taken seriously. See Hsü 1946, 118.

29. Hsü 1946, 121–122.

30. The number of missions is based on Hsieh's perusal of the *Ming shih*, the Twenty-four Histories, and the Encyclopedia of Imperial Dynastic Records. Hsieh 1949, 46–50.

31. Fairbank and Teng 1941, 204.

32. Hsieh 1949, 49.

33. Wood 1926, 97.

34. Campos 1940, 22–25. During the 16th century, the Portuguese provided the chief competition to Chinese traders. There were supposedly about 300 Portuguese in Ayutthaya in the mid-16th century. Their junks, however, transported Siamese goods south and west to Nakhǫnsithammarat, Pattani, and Malacca, rather than east to China, which trade was largely carried by Chinese and Siamese junks.

35. Hsü 1946, 107.

36. Hsü 1946, 110.

37. Anderson 1890, 80. See also Hale 1909, 197, 205, 207, for further details on the Chinese in Pattani and vicinity, 1600–1605.

38. *Tung-hsi-yang k'ao* (C 21), 1617. Translated from the quotation in Hsieh 1949, 275.

39. Quoted in Giles 1938, 277.

40. Anderson 1890, 80.

41. Vliet 1638, 93.

42. *Tung-hsi-yang k'ao*, 1617. Quoted from Sun 1931, 15.

43. Giles 1938, 175.

44. Vliet 1638, 51. The Chincheeu, Chincheo, or occasionally Chinseeuw, of early Portuguese and Dutch traders has been shown by Boxer to refer in most cases to the area of the Bay of Amoy and only occasionally to Chang-chou or Ch'üan-chou as specific ports. In any case, Chincheeu designated trading areas in the Hokkien-speaking coastal region of southern Fukien. See Boxer 1953, Appendix "Chincheo."

45. Giles 1938, 281–303.

46. Anderson 1890, 253.

47. Vliet 1638, 68.

48. Vliet 1638, 90, 93.

49. Vliet 1638, 92.

50. Giles 1938, 212–221, 304; Nunn 1922, 82–83.

51. Vliet 1638, 51.

52. Anderson 1890, 42, 426.

53. Vliet 1638, 89, 92.

54. Vliet 1638, 51.

55. Hutchinson 1940, 34.

56. Giles 1938, 323.

57. Giles 1938, 324.

58. Gervaise 1688, 29; Tachard 1686, 365.

59. Quoted in Anderson 1890, 426.

60. Gervaise 1688, 29; Tachard 1686, 365; other details of the Chinese trade are given in Anderson 1890, 422–423.

61. Hutchinson 1940, 191; Thompson V. 1941, 209.

62. Sarasas 1942, 49.

63. These will not be detailed for lack of space. See MacNair 1926, 3; Vliet 1638, 51.

64. Ling 1912, 79; Helbig 1949, 157. According to Sun (1931, 15), the *Hai-kuo wen-chien-lu* (C 22), completed in 1730, states that "after the

Manchus invaded Shanhaikuan, many Chinese streamed to Siam." But this writer has been unable to locate this passage in the original.

65. The dates of missions have been derived from Hsieh 1949, 50–52, and from Fairbank and Teng 1941, 193–194.

66. The factor of royal security with relation to the frequency of tribute missions is, for this period, difficult to assess because most of the reigning Thai kings were usurpers or came to the throne by means of violence and murder. Early in their reigns, therefore, most of the reigning kings sat insecurely on their thrones, while throughout the period the legitimacy of the Ayutthayan government as such was never challenged. The factor of royal security, in consequence, may be considered roughly constant during the period.

67. Loubère 1693, 11, 112.

68. Hutchinson 1940, 12, 181.

69. E.g., Crawfurd 1823, 104; Malcom 1839, 139; Malloch 1852, 9; Ratzel 1876, 161; Gottwaldt 1903, 75; Frankfurter 1904, 9; Mosolff 1932, 331; Thompson V. 1941, 104; Hsieh 1949, 279; Purcell 1951, 112.

70. The major Chinese settlements in Siamese territory during the 17th century were at Ayutthaya, Paknampho, Bangplasoi, Paetriw, Thajin (literally "Chinese wharf"), Bandǫn, Nakhǫnsithammarat, Songkhla, Pattani, and on the island of Phuket. It is probable that the Chinese had also settled at Janthaburi, Bangkǫk, Maeklǫng, Phetchaburi, Ratchaburi, Chaiya, Langsuan, and Trang, though there is no specific documentation.

71. Sun (1931, 15) quotes a modern Japanese source as estimating the Chinese population of Siam in the 17th century at 1,400,000, an absurd figure which may be taken either as a hyperbolic statement meaning "very many" or as a misprint for 14,000. De la Loubère (1693, 11) estimates the country's total population at 1,900,000—not 900,000, as Purcell (1951, 115) states. However, as Burney (1826, 51) points out, de la Loubère's estimate may have been exclusive of certain Malay and Lao principalities. Even if de la Loubère's figure be taken at its face value, then the Chinese would have had to number 19,000 to have formed 1% of the total population.

72. Chaumont 1686, 109; Hutchinson 1940, 14; Choisy 1687, 217; Kaempfer 1727, 42.

73. See the maps in Loubère 1693, and Kaempfer 1727.

74. Chaumont 1686, 109; Loubère 1693, 112 and map.

75. Vliet 1638, 66.

76. Loubère 1693, 112; James 1922, 587.

77. Chaumont 1686, 80.

78. Vliet 1638, 103.

79. Choisy 1687, 241; Loubère 1693, 47.

80. Loubère 1693, 62.

81. Pallu 1668, 121; Anderson 1890, 228–229.

82. Letter quoted in Giles 1938, 276–277.

83. Vliet 1638, 51.

84. Quoted from Giles 1938, 316.

85. Pallu 1668, 126.
86. Forbin 1689, 508.
87. Quoted in Anderson 1890, 426. There spelled "Vphrah Sivepott."
88. Choisy 1687, 316.
89. Kaempfer 1727, 38. There spelled "Peja Jummeraad."
90. Fairbank and Teng 1941, 168.
91. Chen T. 1940, 51.
92. Ratzel 1876, 64.
93. Chen. T. 1940, 51; Hsüeh 1894, 138; MacNair 1926, 4.
94. Chen T. 1940, 57.
95. Ch'en H. M. 1754, 128.
96. Ch'en H. M. 1754, 129–130.
97. Translated from the quotation in Hsieh 1949, 51.
98. Translated from the quotation in Hsieh 1949, 51; see also Bowring 1857, I, 77–78.
99. Translated from the quotation in Hsieh 1949, 51.
100. Bowring 1857, I, 78; Hsieh 1949, 52.
101. Hsieh 1949, 52.
102. Section 225 of the *Ta-ch'ing lü-li* (The Legal Code of the Great Ch'ing), compiled during Ch'ien-lung's reign. Quoted from Staunton 1810, 543.
103. Fairbank and Teng (1941, 194–195) failed to list in their table the missions for 1722, 1729, 1762, 1765, and 1766, all documented in Hsieh 1949, 51–52.
104. Graham 1924, II, 94–95.
105. *Huang-ch'ing wen-hsien t'ung-k'ao* (C 23), vol. 297, 1747. Quoted in Hsü 1946, 105.
106. Gerini 1905, 32.
107. Quoted in Gerini 1905, 31–32.
108. Gerini 1905, 39–41.
109. Wood 1926, 232.
110. *Hai-kuo wen-chien-lu*, 1731. Translated from the passage quoted in Hsieh 1949, 276.
111. Bowring 1857, I, 65–66.
112. Turpin 1771, 161, 64.
113. Hutchinson 1940, 14, 273.
114. The major theories and views on Phraya Tak in Western literature are those of the French historian Turpin (1771, 117); King Mongkut himself, whose manuscripts on Phraya Tak have been translated in part and published in the *Siam Repository* (1869, 258) and the *Bangkok Calendar* (1871, 86); Parker (1897, 117–118); Gerini (1898, 158–159); and Landon (1941, 6–7). The forms given by Landon ("Hai Hong") and Gerini ("Yong") are transliterations of the Thai based on the Teochiu pronunciation of Hai-feng and Yung, respectively. Many writers who have based their conclusions only on Thai sources misinterpret the personal name "Hai Hong" as being the place in China from which Taksin's father came. Chinese sources, however, make

it perfectly clear that Cheng Ta's native place was Ch'eng-hai and not Hai-feng. See Ch'en Y. T. 1941, 269. According to King Mongkut, Phraya Tak was born in the town of Tak, but no other documents support this view.

115. What happened to Taksin's father is not related in any of the sources, but he probably died or returned to China prior to 1767 inasmuch as he is not mentioned as having been given a royal title. Nang Nok-iang was given a title in 1768 and died in 1774.

116. According to Gerini, an unlucky omen a few days after the birth of Phraya Tak caused his father to want to dispose of the child, to which the mother was opposed; the resulting fracas attracted the nobleman, who solved everything by taking the child as his own. According to London, the child early showed unusual promise and so attracted the nobleman's attention.

117. Sarasas (1942, 100), in what can only be considered a position motivated by supernationalism, maintains that Taksin was pure Thai and that the "extravagant assertion" to the contrary was a political fabrication given credence by the fact that Taksin as a boy lived in the midst of a Chinese colony.

118. Credner 1935, 193, 361.

119. Turpin 1771, 9.

120. Crawfurd 1823, 103.

121. *Bangkok Calendar* 1871, 86.

122. Launay 1920, Documents Historiques II, 267–269. The translated passage is from M. Corre's letter to M. le Fiscal of Malacca dated Nov. 1, 1769.

123. This material is taken from the Annals of Songkhla, as compiled and analyzed by Hsia Ting-hsün. Hsia 1953, 40–51.

124. Translated from the quotation in Hsieh 1949, 53.

125. Taksin is commonly said to have been "very fastidious about his court, being absolutely in the good old Mandarin style." Tsan 1935, 12.

126. Translated from the quotation in Hsieh 1949, 53.

127. "Chao" is probably derived from the Thai title he used, "Jao." In Siam Taksin's Chinese surname is usually spelled Tae or Tay, according to the Teochiu pronunciation, whence "Tay Cheow," as given by Landon 1941, 6.

128. Seidenfaden 1928, 67.

129. Parker 1897, 118.

130. Parker 1897, 118.

131. Fairbank and Teng 1941, 172.

132. Translated from the quotation in Hsieh 1949, 54.

133. *China and Siam*, an unpublished manuscript referred to in Landon 1941, 7.

134. Hsieh 1949, 54.

135. Hsieh 1949, 54–56. Rama II as Cheng Fo (C 34), Rama III as Cheng Fu (C 35), Rama IV as Cheng Ming (C 36).

136. Cf. King Mongkut's account published in the *Siam Repository* 1869, 66–67, 111.

137. Finlayson's letter of June 15, 1882, quoted in Finlayson 1826, xvi.

138. Fairbank and Teng 1941, 199.

139. Fairbank and Teng 1941, 170–173.

140. Parker 1897, 118.

141. For numerous instances, see Hsieh 1949, 54–56.

142. Fairbank and Teng 1941, 206.

143. Quoted in Bowring 1857, I, 65–66.

144. The high royal title of Taksin's Queen was rescinded by Rama I after King Taksin was put to death, and she was left with the name Mǫm Suan. It seems unlikely that she was Rama I's daughter, since he would hardly have degraded his own child and a first-generation princess to such a lowly rank. See Ch'en Y. T. 1941, 270.

145. The genealogy of the Thai royal family is presented in detail in Smith 1944.

146. McDonald 1884, 146.

147. Smith 1944, 152; Smith 1947, 51.

Chapter 2

1. Lattimore 1937, 125.

2. Cf. Zelinsky 1950.

3. Goodrich 1943, 198–199. Corn was also introduced, but its cultivation was not advantageous in south China, at least by comparison with certain other regions of the country.

4. In the 150 years since 1800, Siam's population has quadrupled, while that of south China has in all probability less than doubled. Yet even today, Siam is greatly underpopulated (in terms of current productivity) when compared with Fukien and Kwangtung.

5. *Swatow Consular Report* 1872.

6. Ch'en S. C. 1945, 6.

7. Richard 1908, 344.

8. See MacNair 1926, 16–17; Sun 1931, 41.

9. Chen T. 1923, 16–17.

10. For an intelligent discussion of the dialect-language distinction with reference to China, see De Francis 1950, 192–198. Professor George Kennedy has suggested that "two forms of speech the mutual intelligibility of which amounts to at least seveny-five per cent be considered as dialects and any having a lower proportion be considered as separate languages" (*ibid.*). On this basis, Hainanese must be considered a separate language, though such writers as De Francis and Y. R. Chao apparently consider it a dialect of Hokkien-Teochiu (Amoy-Swatow).

11. These statements say nothing, of course, about the historical or genetic relations among these various languages and dialects. In fact, for instance, Northern Min (Foochow), Hokkien-Teochiu, and Hainanese form a single linguistic subfamily, genetically speaking; by the criterion of mutual intelligibility, however, they are distinct languages. Cf. Forrest 1948, 227. The statements above also say nothing about writing; all Chinese languages and dialects can be written in much the same system.

12. Forrest 1948, 213.

13. The so-called *szu-yi* ("four counties"), namely Hsin-hui, T'ai-shan or Hsin-ning, K'ai-p'ing, and En-p'ing; and the *san-yi* ("three counties"), namely Nan-hai, P'an-yü (including Canton itself), and Shun-te. (See Map 2 for names in Chinese.) The dialects of these two popular groupings of hsien are quite distinct from each other.

14. Just as Cantonese, as used here, is not to be literally interpreted as people from the city of Canton or as people from the province of Kwangtung (but rather as natives of certain areas in and west of the Pearl River delta where the Cantonese language is spoken), so Hokkien, as used here, is not to be literally interpreted as people from the province of Fukien, inasmuch as there are Hakkas and Northern-Min-speaking peoples who have just as much right to the name Fukienese as the Hokkiens.

15. Some writers indicate that Teochius settled in number in Ch'ao-chou before the Hakkas, and that it was the Teochius who dubbed the newcoming Hakkas *k'e* or "guests." Others argued just the reverse case, that the Hakkas got there first and named the newly arrived Teochius *fu-lao* or "people of Fukien." This matter can probably be cleared up by a careful study of the older gazetteers from the area. Kulp (1925, 79) is almost certainly wrong in interpreting Hoklo as "rich people," with the rationale that the Hakka immigrants were poor and found the Teochiu natives rich by comparison. Cf. Forrest 1948, 219.

16. Again, Teochiu, as used here, should not be literally interpreted as people from the prefecture of Ch'ao-chou, for a sizable part of the population of that former prefecture consists of Hakkas, while large numbers of Teochius live in the coastal regions of Lu-feng and Hai-feng hsiens to the south in Hui-chou prefecture. How to classify emigrants from Chao-an hsien in Fukien is a problem. The dialect of this hsien is closer to that of Ch'ao-chou than to that of Chang-chou, and the hsien is closer to Swatow than to Amoy, so that Chao-an people have usually emigrated via Teochiu ports rather than Hokkien ports, though this varies according to comparative fares. The Chao-an immigrants in Bangkok, however, join the Hokkien rather than the Teochiu regional association.

17. Namely Ch'ao-an (formerly Hai-yang and, under the Empire, Ch'ao-chou-fu), Ch'ao-yang, Ch'eng-hai, P'u-ning, Chieh-yang, and Jao-p'ing. (See Map 3 for the Chinese characters.)

18. Forrest 1948, 219.

19. This was certainly true for Malaya, Java, and the Philippines, as well as Siam.

20. Cf. Gutzlaff 1840, 173–174.

21. Cf. Freeman 1938, 15.

22. Gutzlaff 1840, 88–89.

23. Crawfurd 1830, II, 163–165; Neale 1852, 173–176; Ingram 1955, 26. As Ingram suggests, the sailing range of the junks may have contributed to the development of Bangkok's role as an entrepôt. There is the further consideration that, following the decline of Macao as an important port and prior to the rise of Hongkong, there was no other major port *whose traders were mainly Chinese* so near to the south China ports; prior to 1842 only Chinese

could trade in Chinese ports other than Canton. Bangkok lost its entrepôt function shortly after the establishment of Hongkong.

24. Crawfurd 1830, II, 160; Crawfurd 1820, 173.

25. Note especially Canton, Chiang-men, Ch'ao-chou, Chieh-yang, Jao-p'ing, and Chang-chou, all ten to thirty miles inland. See Maps 2 and 3.

26. Donnelly 1924, 115.

27. *China Trade Returns* 1879.

28. Ruschenberger 1838, 73.

29. Cort 1886, 34.

30. Cort 1886, 34.

31. Werner 1873, 269.

32. Cf. Bock 1884, 1.

33. *Siam Repository* 1870.

34. *Siam Repository* 1873, 1874, *Siam Consular Report* 1876–1877.

35. Passenger steamers began running between Swatow and the Straits Settlements as early as 1862. *Chinese Customs Decennial Report* 1902–1911.

36. *China Trade Returns* 1871, 1875.

37. *Swatow Consular Reports* 1882, 1883.

38. See Malloch 1852, 65; Crawfurd 1823, 120.

39. Hainanese junks did go south along the Malay peninsula as far as Singapore, for it was possible to keep in sight of land the whole way.

40. Crawfurd 1830, II, 30, 155. It was usually the first Hainanese junk (in Jan.) from whom the Siamese court astronomers got the Chinese almanac each year. They then prepared the Siamese calendar for the Thai year which commenced around the beginning of April.

41. Gutzlaff 1840, 99. *Kiungchow Consular Report* 1877.

42. *Kiungchow Consular Report* 1877.

43. The name, however, had since been changed to Scottish Oriental Company.

44. *Kiungchow Consular Report,* 1886.

45. *Kiungchow Consular Report* 1886, 1888, 1889, 1892, 1909.

46. Ch'en S. C. 1945, 22.

47. Wright and Breakspear 1908, 139.

48. Leckie 1894, 652. A sharp decline in Siamese-flag shipping with China commenced in 1876, and the Thai role in the China trade was insignificant by 1888. Yang and Hau 1931, 133.

49. Donnelly 1924, 115.

50. Crawfurd 1830, II, 177.

51. "Monograph on Sugar in Siam" 1922, 6.

52. Gutzlaff 1840, 71.

53. Siah 1848, 286.

54. Gutzlaff (1840, 163), for instance, wrote that sugar was a stable article of export from Ch'ao-chou to north China ports in the 1830's. See also almost any issue of the *Swatow Consular Reports* and *China Trade Returns* during the 19th century.

55. *Siam Repository* 1870, II, 1; *Siam Consular Report* 1864.

56. Yang and Hau 1931, 133.

57. "Hui-kuan ti-ch'an shih-lüeh" (Brief History of Cantonese Association Property) 1947, 1.

58. *China Trade Returns,* 1866–1901.

59. *China Trade Returns* 1879.

60. The percentages given pertain to all emigration from Swatow, not just that to Siam. Inasmuch as the Hakkas were well established in West Borneo, Bangka, Billiton, and parts of Malaya while the Teochius were proportionately much more strongly established in Bangkok than were the Hakkas, it is probable that proportionately more of the Hakka emigrants went to the Indies and Malaya and proportionately fewer to Bangkok. The percentage of Hakkas among the total emigrants going to Bangkok from Swatow may, therefore, have been 25% or less.

61. *China Trade Returns* 1869–1882.

62. Unger 1944, 200.

63. Only two sailings from Amoy to Bangkok were recorded by Chinese customs prior to 1890: one in 1883 with 85 passengers and one in 1889 with 20 passengers. *China Trade Returns* 1875–1890.

64. It is interesting to note that in the dialect of T'ung-an hsien, whence many Hokkiens in Siam come, small dried shrimp are named *Ta-ni* for Pattani and larger dried prawns are designated after Songkhla, thus attesting long-standing trading relations between T'ung-an and these Siamese ports. See Hsü 1946, 106–107.

65. Smyth 1898, I, 286–287.

66. Cf. *Amoy Consular Report* 1890.

67. Chen T. 1923, 84.

68. Raquez 1903, 434.

69. Quoted from "Hui-kuan ti-ch'an shih-lüeh" (Brief History of Cantonese Association Property) 1947, 2.

70. Crawfurd 1830, II, 155.

71. Chen T. 1923, 13.

72. Crawfurd 1830, II, 162.

73. Gutzlaff 1840, 146.

74. Crawfurd 1830, II, 161–162.

75. Gutzlaff 1840, 145–146.

76. *China Trade Returns* 1870; *Swatow Consular Report* 1863.

77. *Swatow Consular Report* 1864; see also the reports for 1863 and 1872.

78. Thomson 1875, 286–288; *Swatow Consular Report* 1872.

79. Translated from the French. *China Trade Returns* 1870.

80. Chen T. 1940, 261.

81. *Siam Repository* 1870.

82. *Siam Repository* 1873, 118.

83. *Siam Repository* 1873, 118.

84. Gottwaldt 1903, 22.

85. *Swatow Consular Report* 1885, 99.

86. *Siam Consular Report* 1884.

87. *Swatow Consular Report* 1888. For the Regulations, see Gottwaldt 1903, Appendix.

88. *Swatow Consular Report* 1890, 9.

89. Mosolff 1932, 179.

90. Mosolff 1932, 189–190; *Swatow Consular Report* 1913.

91. *Swatow Consular Report* 1903.

92. Mosolff 1932, 19.

93. Smyth 1898, I, 286.

94. Crawfurd 1830, II, 162–163.

95. Burney 1826, 79

96. Malloch 1827, 223.

97. Malloch 1852, 8. The figure refers to the time when Malloch was in Bangkok, in the late 1820's.

98. Malcom 1839, 139.

99. Malloch 1852, 6.

100. It is not possible in this brief survey to mention *all* relevant factors. Thus, if in a given year immigration from Hainan decreased by 1,000 because of a good crop year on Hainan, but immigration from Swatow increased by 15,000 because of cheap fares and a poor crop year, only the latter factor would be mentioned, because of its overwhelmingly important effect on the total immigration rate.

101. *Siam Consular Report* 1882.

102. *China Trade Returns* 1883, 1884.

103. *Kiungchow Consular Report* 1890; *Swatow Consular Report* 1884; *Siam Consular Report* 1884.

104. *Swatow Consular Report* 1884. This constitutes further evidence that the estimates of a sustained Chinese immigration to Siam at annual rates of 15,000 and more for the decades prior to 1882 are unrealistically high.

105. *Swatow Consular Report* 1888; *Kiungchow Consular Report* 1890.

106. *Swatow Consular Report* 1889, 1890. The years 1888–1889 in the Hainan traffic corresponded to 1882–1883 in the Swatow traffic, the period of the initial rush by steamer.

107. *Swatow Consular Report* 1891; *Siam Consular Report* 1891.

108. *Swatow Consular Report* 1893, 1894; *Siam Consular Report* 1893; *Kiungchow Consular Report* 1894.

109. Mosolff 1932, 171.

110. *China Trade Returns* 1896.

111. *Swatow Consular Report* 1897; *Siam Consular Report* 1897, 1898, 1899.

112. *Kiungchow Consular Report* 1898, 1899.

113. *Swatow Consular Report* 1900; *Chinese Customs Decennial Report* 1892–1901.

114. *Siam Consular Report* 1900, 10.

115. *Chinese Customs Decennial Reports* 1892–1901, 1902–1911; *Swatow Consular Report* 1901; *Kiungchow Consular Report* 1904; *Siam Consular Report* 1902.

116. *Swatow Consular Report* 1903, 5.

117. *Swatow Consular Report* 1906, 1907, 1908; *Siam Consular Report* 1906, 1907.

118. *Chinese Customs Decennial Report* 1902–1911.

119. *Siam Consular Reports* 1908/09, 1909/10, 1910/11; *Swatow Consular Reports* 1908, 1909, 1910, 1911.

120. Sun 1931, 41.

121. *Chinese Customs Decennial Report* 1912–1921.

122. *Kiungchow Consular Report* 1914.

123. *Chinese Customs Decennial Report* 1912–1921.

124. *Chinese Customs Decennial Report* 1912–1921.

125. The writer obtained a series of estimates from the Central Statistical Service in 1953 which differ only slightly from those given in the *Thailand Statistical Year Book* (no. 18) 1933/34–1934/35, 66; and (no. 21) 1939/40–1944, 50.

126. Crawfurd 1830, II, 221–222. Italics supplied by G. W. S.

127. With the possible exception of those too old to work.

128. Malloch 1852, 71–72.

129. Ratzel 1876, 173.

130. Graham 1912, 110.

131. Landon (1941, 21) quotes Rautier's figure of three million Chinese without comment, while Ch'en S. C. (1945, 9) makes the wildest possible use of both Pallegoix's and Rautier's exaggerations. Purcell (1951, 107), leery of Rautier's figures, nonetheless accepts Rosny's as reasonable.

132. Gordon 1891, 288–289.

133. Campbell 1902, 268.

134. Taken from an official Thai memorandum on the 1904 census published in 1905. Quoted from *Directory for Bangkok and Siam* 1907, 110.

135. Carter 1904, 140; Collet 1911, 84.

136. Some of the data used in estimating death rates are to be found in: Angier 1908, 98; Crosby 1945, 42; Gordon 1891, 289; Gottwaldt 1903, 43; Mosolff 1932, 223; Norman 1907, 423; Pelzer 1941, 35; Purcell 1951, 121; Smith 1947, 15–21; Smyth 1898, I, 301, and II, 66; Thompson P. 1906, 49; Werner 1873, 259; Wright and Breakspear 1908, 133; and Wu 1928, 544.

137. This statement has one notable exception, namely the Chinese pottery kilns in North and Middle Siam prior to the 15th century.

138. So far as can be determined now, no permanent Yunnanese settlements were made in Siam prior to the mid-19th century, when Hǫ villages were established in Maejan and Chiangmai. The Hǫs were reluctant to spend the rainy season in the low-altitude Thai towns for fear of contracting malaria and other fevers.

139. Tomlin 1844, 182–184.

140. Crawfurd 1823, 64.

141. Malloch 1827, 232.

142. Finlayson 1826, 212–213.

143. Crawfurd 1830, II, 221.

144. Malloch 1852, 70.

145. *Bangkok Calendar* 1871, 129.

146. Malcom 1839, 139.

147. Malloch 1852, 70.

148. Pallegoix 1854, I, 60.
149. Malcom 1839, 140.
150. Ruschenberger 1838, 7.
151. These developments occurred in the 1830's. McFarland 1928, 11.
152. *Bangkok Calendar* 1871, 129.
153. Gutzlaff 1840, 71–72.
154. Quoted in Bowring 1857, I, 396.
155. Quoted in Bacon 1892, 162–166.
156. Gutzlaff 1840, 72.
157. Malloch 1852, 71–72.
158. Khorat, Nangrong (now in jangwat Buriram), Surin, Sangkha (now in jangwat Surin), Sisaket, and Roi-et.
159. Ratzel 1876, 172.
160. Bacon 1892, 290; McCarthy 1902, 3; *Siam Free Press* as quoted in "L'émigration Asiatique" 1907, 490.
161. Carter 1904, 111.
162. Collet 1911, 63.
163. Graham 1912, I, 110; Basso 1913, 45.
164. Garnier 1911, 232.
165. Raquez 1903, 434.
166. The program and sequence of railroad construction in Siam is described in Stamp 1942, 216–217.

Chapter 3

1. Cf. Benedict 1943, 34.
2. The order of the four main groups is traditionally given as scholar-officials, farmers, artisans, and merchants.
3. With regard to the Southern Sung period, e.g., see Eberhard 1950, 234–235.
4. Gerini 1904, 19.
5. Pelzer 1935, 58.
6. Phenix village in Ch'ao-an hsien. Kulp 1925, 44–50.
7. This characterization is based primarily on Wales 1934, 21–68, and Graham 1924, 229–249.
8. Prior to Taksin's reign the period was 6 months; during the latter part of the 19th century it was again reduced, to 3 months. See Wales 1934, 54.
9. Thompson V. 1941, 600.
10. See Lasker 1950, 102–103.
11. Perhaps the best statement of the favored position of the Chinese in Siam is that given in "Triennial Tax" 1873, 330.
12. Ingram 1955, 56.
13. See especially Ingram 1955.
14. Malloch 1852, 65; Crawfurd 1823, 117.
15. Crawfurd 1823, 118; McDonald 1884, 147.
16. Crawfurd 1820, 186.
17. E.g., sugar in 1844. Moore 1914–1915, 29.

18. Yü 1951, XIX, 18–19.

19. Burney 1826, 177; Crawfurd 1830, I, 269.

20. Neale 1852, 174.

21. Malloch 1827, 225; Crawfurd 1830, I, 138.

22. Malloch 1852, 27–29.

23. Frankfurter 1904, 6.

24. See Malloch 1852, 26–27.

25. Bowring 1857, I, 87–88.

26. Mongkut 1856, XXI, 28.

27. *Siam Consular Report* 1879, 1.

28. Cort 1886, 35.

29. *Siam Consular Report* 1890, 34.

30. *Siam Consular Report* 1892, 2.

31. *Siam Consular Report* 1890, 32–33.

32. A large proportion of the compradores for Western firms during the period under review had received some Western education in Malaya or Hongkong.

33. *Siam Consular Report* 1870, 2.

34. Ingram 1955, 22–24.

35. See Werner 1873, 263; for an excellent description and pictures of hand rice mills, see Wright and Breakspear 1908, 186.

36. See Ingram 1955, 37–43.

37. *Siam Consular Reports* 1864, 217; 1867, 318.

38. *Siam Consular Report* 1870, 2.

39. *Siam Consular Report* 1876–1877, 2.

40. Leckie 1894, 651–652, *Siam Consular Reports* 1889, 3; 1895, 2; *Directory for Bangkok and Siam* 1912, 280–281.

41. Campbell 1902, 284.

42. Wright and Breakspear 1908, 187.

43. Leckie 1894, 651–652.

44. *Siam Consular Report* 1905, 5.

45. Collet 1911, 103–104.

46. *Siam Consular Reports* 1885, 2; 1897, 3.

47. *Siam Consular Report* 1897, 3.

48. *Siam Consular Report* 1909, 13.

49. Leckie 1894, 651–652; see also the listings of rice mills given in *Directory for Bangkok and Siam* 1890, 200–201; 1901, 175–176.

50. Leckie 1894, 653.

51. Wright and Breakspear 1908, 171–181.

52. Dr. Bradley's journal for 1836 reproduced in the *Bangkok Calendar* 1871, 90, 115; Neale 1852, 173–174.

53. Finlayson 1826, 115–116; Dr. Bradley's journal in the *Bangkok Calendar* 1871, 111.

54. Finlayson 1826, 115–116.

55. *Siam Consular Report* 1883, 5.

56. *Bangkok Calendar* 1871, 150–151; *Siam Consular Reports* 1883, 5;

1900, 13; *Directory for Bangkok and Siam* 1901, 97; *Siam Repository,* 1872, 199, 399.

57. *Siam Consular Report* 1882, 2.
58. *Siam Consular Report* 1889, 9.
59. Ingram 1955, 37.
60. Wales 1934, 206.
61. Ingram 1955, 72.
62. Wright and Breakspear 1908, 118–119.
63. Wright and Breakspear 1908, 118.
64. Cf. Wright and Breakspear 1908, 157, 165.
65. Malloch 1852, 22.
66. Smyth 1898, I, 325.
67. Smyth 1898, I, 323.
68. *Kung-szu* (C 41), "company, public organization, office."
69. Ingram 1955, 99.
70. Smyth 1898, II, 129.
71. Bradley 1870, 44–45.
72. Bradley 1870, 45; Smyth 1898, I, 317–319.
73. Smyth 1898, II, 66, 133.
74. Smyth 1898, I, 319, 328.
75. Smyth 1898, I, 317–320; Gerini 1905, 52.
76. Smyth 1898, I, 301.
77. Graham 1924, II, 22–24; Mouhot 1864, I, 41–42; *Siam Consular Report* 1906.
78. Smyth 1898, II, 176, 299.
79. Carter 1904, 167
80. Crawfurd 1830, II, 177.
81. Neale 1852, 68–69.
82. Cited in Bowring 1857, I, 203.
83. "Monograph on Sugar in Siam" 1922, 7.
84. *Siam Consular Report* 1889.
85. *Siam Repository* 1870, II, 1; *Siam Consular Report* 1864.
86. Bacon 1892, 217; Richardson 1839–1840, IX, 5.
87. Quoted in *Bangkok Calendar* 1871, 113.
88. Barnett 1910, 37.
89. Cf. Carter 1904, 167.
90. Ratzel 1876, 171.
91. Translated from the Thai of Nuprapath 1941, 133.
92. Thompson V. 1947, 215.
93. *Siam Repository* 1873, 61–65.
94. Cf. *Siam Repository* 1870, 379.
95. Gordon 1891, 298.
96. Thompson P. 1906, 289.
97. "Some Aspects of the Situation of the Chinese Minority in Thailand" 1952, 528.
98. *Siam Consular Report* 1892, 6.

99. *Siam Consular Report* 1900, 11.

100. McCarthy 1902, 25.

101. *Siam Consular Report* 1903, 9.

102. Carter 1904, 264.

103. "Hsien-lo kuang-chao-shu-chih chien-chu-yeh" (The Construction Business of the Cantonese in Siam) 1947, 12–13.

104. Crawfurd (1823, 120), e.g., estimated that the trade with China alone gave employment to 8,000 Chinese sailors.

105. Smyth 1898, I, 10.

106. *Siam Repository* 1873, 482.

107. *Siam Consular Report* 1880, 1.

108. *Siam Consular Report* 1883, 4.

109. *Siam Consular Report* 1889, 19.

110. *Chinese* employers left no record of their attitude.

111. *Siam Consular Report* 1900, 10.

112. *Siam Consular Reports* 1901, 15; 1902, 11.

113. Fifteen baht per month as against 2.5 baht per month. Malloch 1852, 68.

114. Two shillings per day as against shilling sixpence for the "coolie." *Siam Consular Report* 1890, 38.

115. Crawfurd 1830, II, 28–29.

116. Earl 1837, 169.

117. Werner 1873, 268.

118. Bock 1884, 41–43, 393–394; Laseur 1885, 67.

119. Le May 1930, 166.

120. Ratzel 1876, 168.

121. It is said that the idea of tax-farming was suggested by an English emissary. Pallegoix 1854, I, 304.

122. Sarasas 1942, 116.

123. Quoted from the edict of 1839 as given in Bowring 1857, II, 368–369. It is also interesting to note that while the mandarins in China had the confiscated opium destroyed, Nangklao "graciously granted to have [requisitioned opium] taken away and sold in some foreign place."

124. Senah Body 1843, 95.

125. Frankfurter 1904, 14.

126. *Siam Consular Reports* 1874, 1; 1890, 29. This was the cost of only the main farm centered in Bangkok; there were separate opium farms in South and North Siam.

127. *Siam Consular Report* 1890, 29.

128. Carter 1904, 140; Ingram 1955, 179.

129. *Thailand Statistical Year Book* 1933–1935, 298–299.

130. See especially, *Siam Repository* 1869, 21–23; 1870, 26, 114.

131. It was said as early as 1836 that Thai aristocrats and nobles, whose dignity forbade gambling publicly, were in the habit of playing by proxy. *Bangkok Calendar* 1871, 119.

132. Crawfurd 1830, II, 122; Carter 1904, 140.

133. This account of the lottery farm is based largely on Cartwright, 1924, except where otherwise noted.

134. Carter 1904, 140.

135. *Directory for Bangkok and Siam* 1901, 213; *Thailand Statistical Year Book* 1933–1935, 303.

136. Smyth 1898, II, 256.

137. Pallegoix 1854, I, 305–306.

138. Carter 1904, 140.

139. *Siam Consular Report* 1909, 13.

140. *Siam Consular Report* 1892, 20.

141. Certain social and political aspects of the triennial tax will be considered in Chapter 4.

142. See Wales 1934, 201; Crawfurd 1823, 122, 132; Ruschenberger 1838, 25.

143. Gutzlaff 1840, 145.

144. Gutzlaff 1840, 145–146; Siah 1847, 35–36.

145. *Siam Consular Report* 1885, 4.

146. *Chinese Customs Decennial Report* 1902–1911, 130–131.

Chapter 4

1. Cf. "The Second Annual Report of the Morrison Educational Society" 1838, 309.

2. Cf. Chen T. 1923, 84; *Kiungchow Consular Report* 1892; Gottwaldt 1903, 44–49.

3. Eickstedt 1944, 463.

4. Gottwaldt 1903, 44–49.

5. "Yi-shan-t'ing shih-hua" (History of the Teochiu Association Public Cemetery) 1951, 8.

6. See especially Bradley's journal entries of 1835, quoted in Bacon 1892, 162; Crawfurd 1830, II, 221; Bowring 1857, I, 395; Tomlin 1844, 149; *Hai-kuo t'u-chih* (C 43), quoted in Hsieh 1949, 276; McDonald 1884, 146.

7. Smyth 1898, I, 296.

8. Campbell 1902, 274.

9. Smyth 1898, I, 237.

10. Chinese with families in Siam were considered less likely to abscond than single men. Moreover, in case of default, Chinese with local families could in the last resort sell their wives and children into slavery in order to meet their debts. See "Triennial Tax" 1873, 331.

11. Ch'en S. C. 1945, 14.

12. Burney 1825, 217.

13. Hallett 1890, 461.

14. Gutzlaff 1840, 72.

15. Crawfurd 1823, 137.

16. Crawfurd 1830, II, 220.

17. Gutzlaff 1840, 72.

18. See Ch'en Y. T. 1940, 58–59; *Hua-ch'iao Hsin-yü,* 10 (Sept. 10, 1953), 20–21.

19. Ch'en Y. T. 1940, 58.

20. Cf. Graham 1924, II, 283–284.

21. Crawfurd 1823, 72; Crawfurd 1830, II, 221.

22. *Feng-shui* ("wind and water") refers to the geomantic placement of graves and other structures, taking into account the slope and contour of the land, surface and underground water flow, prevailing winds, compass orientation, etc. A grave can never be well placed according to *feng-shui* in a level, poorly drained area.

23. *Siam Consular Report* 1892, 11.

24. Legatus 1929, 283.

25. Gutzlaff 1840, 72.

26. "The Second Annual Report of the Morrison Education Society" 1838, 309.

27. Bowring 1857, I, 84, 395.

28. *Siam Consular Report* 1864, 216.

29. "Triennial Tax" 1873, 331.

30. Hallett 1890, 461.

31. Smyth 1898, I, 285.

32. Annandale 1900, 517.

33. Campbell 1902, 274.

34. Raquez 1903, 435.

35. Thompson P. 1906, 76.

36. Bowring 1857, I, 84.

37. Unless otherwise stated, this description refers primarily to Bangkok around 1890.

38. An anonymous Western missionary literate in Chinese and concerned with Chinese education in Bangkok, whose report is given in "The Second Annual Report of the Morrison Education Society" 1838, 308–309. Other remarks on Chinese education in the 19th century are also based on this source.

39. "The Chinese" 1870, 507.

40. Credner 1935, 196.

41. See Credner 1935, 196, and "Une grève de Chinois à Bangkok" 1910, 324. The complete failures either could not afford to go back or, as frequently happened, were staked to their return passage by friends or relatives.

42. In fact, the Chinese in Siam were sometimes compared to Americans and called the "Yankees of the East." See *Siam Repository* 1870, 423.

43. Chang Ting's personal history is given in Garnier 1911, 233; and his business described in Wright and Breakspear 1908, 161. Both accounts have been supplemented and corrected by informants in Bangkok.

44. Ch'en Tz'u-hung's story was obtained from his grandson and great-grandson; his business interests in 1908 are described in Wright and Breakspear 1908, 169.

45. Lasker 1945, 75.

46. Pen-t'ou is usually given a wife; the two deities together are called Pen-t'ou Kung Ma.

47. Earl 1837, 170.
48. Malcolm 1839, 139.
49. "The Chinese" 1870, 506–507.
50. The usual name for the anti-Manchu secret-society movement was Hung-men, and in Siam Hung-tzu (C 53) and Lao-hung (C 54) were also used. San-tien (C 55), "triad," was used in Siam to refer to a particular branch of the society.
51. McCarthy 1902, 3.
52. *Kung-szu* (see note 68, Chapter 3).
53. There are persistent reports that some Thai, including government officials, joined the societies, but specific details are wanting.
54. McCarthy 1902, 3.
55. "Pen-hui tsu-chih yen-ke" (History of the Organization of the [Hakka] Association) 1947, 1.
56. Cf. Wright and Breakspear 1908, 155–156.
57. It is noteworthy that the Hǫ community in Chiangmai had a headman distinct from that of the overseas Chinese.
58. McFarland 1928, 37.
59. Gutzlaff 1840, 72.
60. See Bowring 1857, I, 87. The account given here is based primarily on "Rebellion" 1849, 336–337. Bowring's version appears to be hopelessly jumbled.
61. *Siam Repository* 1869, Appendix, 6.
62. Ratzel 1876, 178; *Siam Consular Report* 1883, 1; McDonald 1884, 149; Thompson V. 1941, 106–107. Dr. Thompson seems to have confused the 1889 and 1895 riots.
63. One of these, the Yi-hsing (C 60) (Yee Heng, Ghee Hin, Nghee Hunge) was also of special importance in Malaya and the United States.
64. *Siam Consular Report* 1889, 18.
65. Thompson V. 1941, 107.
66. The full text of the Act is given in the *Directory for Bangkok and Siam* 1902, 33–35.
67. Campbell 1902, 277; Thompson V. 1941.
68. Wright and Breakspear 1908, 107–110.
69. *Siam Repository* 1874, 209–211.
70. Niel 1907, 25.
71. Niel 1907, 46–47; Pinya 1901–1902, XIII, 97. The same phenomenon had been observed in 1867, when Consul Hood's issuance of certificates "resulted in a period of Christian popularity among the Chinese." McFarland 1928, 64.
72. Wood 1935, 30.
73. Garnier 1911, 233.
74. Raquez 1903, 435.
75. Nathabanja 1924, 125.
76. James 1922, 595–601; Nathabanja 1924, 125–129; Sayre 1927, 683.
77. "Marking the People" 1870, 364.
78. McDonald 1884, 150.

79. Frankfurter 1904, 14; *Siam Repository* 1873, 347.

80. This account is based on "Marking the People" 1870; "Notification on the Subject of the Triennial Taxation of the Chinese of Siam" 1870; and Pallegoix 1854, I, 295.

81. Young 1898, 10.

82. McCarthy 1902, 3.

83. Neale 1852, 43–45; Beauvoir 1870, 286.

84. Bock 1884, 4; Hsü 1946, 125–126.

85. Wright and Breakspear 1908, 107, 284.

86. Translated from the passage quoted in Hsieh 1949, 276.

87. Tomlin 1844, 189.

88. Translated from the passage quoted in Hsieh 1949, 276.

89. Robert Morrison, writing in Chinese in the *China Monthly Magazine*, published in Malacca between 1815 and 1821, said that "only Swatow people [among the Chinese of Bangkok] become officials and nobles, administrators and comptrollers of finance and taxes." Translated from the passage quoted in Hsieh 1949, 276.

90. Namely Somdetjaofa (Somdetch Chao Fa), Phraongjao (Phra Ong Chao), Momjao (Mom Chao), Momratchawong (Mom Rajawong), and Momluang (Mom Luang).

91. There was still another title in this system, Somdetjaophraya (Somdetch Chao Phya), which was in practice reserved to royalty.

92. Reeve 1951, 32; Haas 1951.

93. After Gerini 1905, 82–83.

94. The Rajah of Nakhonsithammarat at about the same time was a posthumous son of Taksin, and may have received his post in compensation for wrongs done his family by Rama I. Burney 1826, 143. As for his contemporary, the Governor of Janthaburi, it is known only that he was "of Chinese extraction." Finlayson 1826, 257.

95. Hsia 1953, 45–50. The account in Graham (1924, I, 31) is badly distorted.

96. Hsia 1953, 40–50.

97. This account follows Landon (1941, 11–15) unless otherwise noted.

98. Smyth 1898, II, 27–28.

99. Landon 1941, 14.

100. Campbell 1902, 276.

101. Annandale 1900, 519.

102. Norman 1907, 408.

103. Crawfurd 1830, II, 121.

104. Gutzlaff 1840, 72.

105. An obituary of Phraya Phisan, who died in 1862, called him "a Chinese of extraordinary business powers, standing at the head of all his countrymen here as well as the Siamese, in commercial affairs, the sole owner of a large portion of the Siamese shipping, by which he had accumulated a fortune of six or seven millions of dollars." *Bangkok Calendar* 1863, 111.

106. *Bangkok Calendar* 1862, 39.

107. Cartwright 1924, 222; *Siam Repository* 1874, 250.

108. See the survey of rice millers in Bangkok in Wright and Breakspear 1908, 151–169. Italics supplied by G. W. S.

109. *Die Völker des östlichen Asien* 1867, III, 68. Quoted in Ratzel 1876, 176.

110. McDonald 1884, 146.

111. Raquez 1903, 435.

Chapter 5

1. Huang 1954, 63–64.

2. Much of this chapter is based on data obtained from participants still living in Siam.

3. Usually known to Westerners as Seow Hood Seng, a romanization of his name based on the Hokkien pronunciation.

4. Cantonese were the pioneers in newspaper publishing in Bangkok. The only papers of which there is any record published earlier than the *Mei-nan Jih-pao*—namely, the *Han-ching Jih-pao* (C 79) and the *T'ung-ch'iao Pao* (C 80)—were Cantonese ventures.

5. Huang 1954, 76.

6. This account is based primarily on Hsieh 1949, 283–284, 301–302. Hsieh's version of newspaper developments up to 1918 is more accurate than those in Li 1948, 8; Feng T. Y. 1946, 52–53; or Huang 1954, 75–76. Clearly, some of these writers have confused the founding of *Mei-nan Jih-pao* with that of *Hua-hsien Jih-pao*.

7. Wright and Breakspear 1908, 295.

8. Huang 1954, 75–76. See also Feng T. Y. 1946, 52–53.

9. Huang 1954, 75–76.

10. Some accounts (e.g., Feng T. Y. 1946, 52–53) say that the T'ung Meng Hui was not formally established until Sun's visit in 1908.

11. "Pen-hui tsu-chih yen-ke" (History of the Organization of the [Hakka] Association) 1947, 1.

12. The membership cards issued in Siam in 1910–1911 were called Chung-hua-kuo kuo-min-chün p'ing-p'iao (C 87), "certificates of the National Army of China."

13. Huang 1954, 69–72.

14. Cf. Wright and Breakspear 1908, 165; *Siam Consular Reports* 1909, 11; 1913, 13; Graham 1924, 343.

15. Feng T. Y. 1946, 53.

16. Hsieh 1949, 294.

17. Thompson V. 1941, 108.

18. Tsai 1910, 407.

19. See Landon 1941, 20–21.

20. Cf. Parker 1897, 114–115; Sarasas 1942, 167.

21. Of the Westerners in Siam, the British seem to have displayed the most, and the Americans the least, antagonism toward the Chinese. This differential must be due in large part to the fact that resident British were almost all businessmen in competition with the Chinese, while most resident

Americans were missionaries who found in the Chinese perhaps the most re-warding field for their labors.

22. Smyth 1898, I, 320, 285–286.

23. Campbell 1902, 270–274.

24. Mury 1903, 58.

25. Campbell 1902, 12–13.

26. "Les Chinois au Siam" 1907.

27. Garnier 1911.

28. An article in the *Siam Free Press* of Sept. 27, 1906, e.g., accused the Chinese of crowding Thai out of trade and industry, of degrading the Thai with their gambling, of being the Jews of Siam, etc. See Thompson V. 1941, 107.

29. Cf. Smyth 1898, I, 286, 321.

30. Child 1892, 231.

31. *Bangkok Times* Feb. 21, 1936. Quoted from Thompson V. 1941, 108.

32. "Une grève de Chinois à Bangkok" 1910. Details of the strike in sub-sequent paragraphs are also based on this eyewitness account.

33. 4.5 baht in outlying provinces.

34. Julalongkǫn did not have his decrees published in Chinese, and no absolute Thai king ever felt compelled to explain, much less popularize, his edicts.

35. Cf. Landon 1941, 33.

36. Quoted from "Sino-Siamese Miscellany" 1949.

37. He usually published under pseudonyms. See Landon 1941, 34.

38. The document has been translated and analyzed in Landon 1941, 34–47.

39. Quoted from Landon 1941, 41–42.

40. Cf. Sarasas 1942, 136: "It was due to him [Wachirawut] that the Thai and Chinese became disunited."

41. Nationality Act of B.E. 2456, Section 3.

42. Translated from Lan 1949, 6.

43. "Hui-kuan ti-ch'an shih-lüeh" (Brief History of Cantonese Association Property) 1947, 2.

44. See Jumsai 1951, 17; McFarland 1928.

45. Following European terminology, mission schools in Bangkok offering instruction from primary through secondary levels are often called colleges.

46. *Chinese Customs Decennial Report* 1902–1911, 127–128, 246.

47. Cf. Wright and Breakspear 1908, 134.

48. Gottwaldt 1903, 8.

Chapter 6

1. Standing 1924, 764–765; Dulyachinda 1949, 472.

2. *Chinese Customs Decennial Report* 1922–1931, 313.

3. *Chinese Customs Decennial Report* 1922–1931, 158.

4. *China Trade Returns* 1927, 5; *Chinese Customs Decennial Report* 1922–1931, 313.

5. Cf. *China Trade Returns* 1928, 5.

6. Credner 1935, 363.

7. *Report on China Trade* 1930, 75.

8. See Lin Y. 1937, 1249; Landon 1941, 213; Lasker 1945, 74.

9. Chen H. S. 1937, 140.

10. *Reports on China Trade* 1937, 104; 1939, 125.

11. *Reports on China Trade* 1939, 125; 1940, 110.

12. The Act of 1927/28 prohibited immigration of persons suffering from certain diseases (notably trachoma), those not vaccinated against smallpox, and those "who are of bad character or are likely to create disturbances or to endanger the safety of the public or the Kingdom of Siam." Quoted from Landon 1941, 205. See also Mosolff 1932, 338. The Act also empowered the Minister of Foreign Affairs to fix a quota on immigrants of any nationality and to fix an amount of money which an alien entering Siam must have in his possession, but the Minister never utilized these powers.

13. Landon 1941, 213.

14. In terms of the current exchange rate with the U.S. dollar, the 200-baht fee was the equivalent of $88.10 in 1938, but only $8.30 in 1947.

15. Purcell 1951, 197.

16. It is impossible to estimate with any assurance the amount of illegal immigration. Illegal immigration to avoid fees became a problem only after 1932 and was effectively controlled by about 1938. The Immigration Division was unable to tell this writer whether or not it recorded all the enforced immigration of Chinese labor during the Second World War; unquestionably much of this immigration was properly recorded by immigration authorities, though not by customs officials. Illegal immigration became serious once more in 1947 but was effectively checked in 1950. This writer would judge that unrecorded immigration was never more than a few thousand in any one year and that unrecorded Chinese emigration has been negligible ever since the First World War. Because the writer's estimates are not adjusted to account for illegal immigration, the surpluses given for the 1932–1945 and 1946–1955 periods may be too low by as much as 10,000 each.

17. Given in the *Thailand Statistical Year Books,* 1929/30, 54; 1930/31, 64; 1931/32, 64; 1933/34–1934/35, 102–103; 1935/36–1936/37, 70; 1937/38–1938/39, 67.

18. *Report on China Trade* 1946.

19. Figures supplied by the Immigration Division in Bangkok.

20. *China Year Book* 1916, 1921–1922; *Report on China Trade* 1934, 1945; "Chinese in Southeast Asia" 1952, 13.

21. Chen H. S. 1937, 140.

22. Lin Y. 1936, 191; Lin Y. 1937, 1249.

23. Sun 1931, 43–44.

24. Chen S. C. 1945, 9.

25. Hsieh 1949, 242.

26. Mosolff 1932, 332.

27. Credner 1935, 361–362.

28. Credner 1935, 362.

29. Kiliani 1926, 148; Tateyania 1941, 469; Mullender 1950, 230.

30. Landon 1943, 112; Seidenfaden 1939, 96.

31. *Thailand Statistical Year Book* 1939/40–1944, 96–97; *Bulletin of Statistics,* 1, no. 3 (Aug. 1952), 1–4.

32. Lin Y. 1936, 194.

33. Landon 1941, 209.

34. It was after the 1937 census, in Feb. 1939, that a Thai official for the first time announced that Thai women married to Chinese need not register as aliens because "according to Chinese law they would become Chinese only by applying to the Chinese Ministry of Interior." Landon 1941, 61.

35. *Sayam-nikǫn* Jan. 20, 1940. Quoted from Landon 1941, 231.

36. *Chung-yüan Pao* Jan. 25, 1952; *Ch'üan-min Pao* Jan. 20, 1952. In 1951, official alien-registration figures gave 1,147,084 Chinese aliens in Thailand. *Thailand Statistical Year Book* 1953, 135.

37. Figures supplied by the Alien Division of the Police Department in Bangkok.

38. Figures supplied by the Alien Division in Bangkok.

39. *Thailand Statistical Year Book* 1933/34–1934/35, 98.

40. Cf. Purcell 1951, 197–198.

41. Credner 1935, 361.

42. Landon 1941, 55.

43. *China Trade Returns* 1928, 5.

44. *China Trade Returns* 1927, 1.

45. *League of Nations Bulletin,* July 1936. Quoted from Landon 1939, 198.

46. This writer has no specific data on Hokkien female immigration, which was never numerically great in Bangkok because the earlier Hokkien immigrants had so extensively intermarried with Thai. The Hokkien ratio, however, was certainly more nearly normal than that of Hainanese and possibly similar to that of Teochius.

47. Landon 1941, 199–200.

48. Zone A refers to khwaengs Samphanthawong, Pǫmprap, and Bangrak, all in Krungthep. Zone B refers to khwaengs Thonburi and Khlǫngsan in Thonburi municipality and khwaengs Pathumwan, Phranakhǫn, and Yannawa in Krungthep. Zone C refers to khwaengs Dusit and Phayathai in Krungthep and khwaengs Bangkǫkyai, Bangkǫknǫi, Bangkhunthian, Phasijaroen, and Talingchan in Thonburi.

49. The German writers, Legatus and Credner, writing of Bangkok at the peak of or shortly after the 1918–1931 immigration wave, estimated the Chinese portion of Bangkok's population at 65% and 60%, respectively. See Legatus 1929, 282; Helbig 1949 (which quoted Credner's article, "Hinterindien"), 164. One would expect that the proportion showed a tendency to decline after 1932, reaching a low of less than 50% in 1945; that it increased again after the war to a high of about 55% in 1948–1949, after which a decline set in which is still under way.

50. All figures quoted from the Survey are found in *Economic and Demographic Survey 1954,* 1955, 1st and 2nd series, 1955, Tables 4 and 5.

51. All statistics and estimates given pertain to the municipal areas as of 1954. In 1955, Krungthep was enlarged to include an additional 51.3 square kilometers, but registration figures even up to Dec. 1955 pertain only to the former municipal area, as do the results of the Economic and Demographic Survey.

52. *Chung-yüan Pao* Feb. 25, 1952.

53. Kwongsai is the name given to immigrants from Kwangsi province, usually south of the West River, who speak a dialect of Cantonese and migrate from the port of Pei-hai (Pakhoi) in south Kwangtung.

54. *Chung-yüan Pao* March 3, 1952.

55. *Min-chu Jih-pao* Dec. 27, 1951.

56. Landon 1941, 202.

57. Computed from Del Tufo 1949, Table 36, 292–295.

58. Lin Y. 1937, 1250.

59. Landon 1941, 201–202.

60. Tateyania 1941, 469.

61. Hsieh 1949, 293; Hsieh 1953, 309.

62. Skinner 1951, 80.

Chapter 7

1. Ingram 1955, 94.

2. Great Britain. Foreign Office. *Report on the Commercial Situation in Siam at the Close of the Year 1919*. London 1920, 18–19. Cited in Ingram 1955, 71.

3. MacNair 1926, 48.

4. *Commercial Directory for Siam* 1929, 90–115.

5. Quoted in Hsieh 1949, 26.

6. Ingram 1955, 38.

7. Graham 1924, II, 89–90; Callis 1942, 66.

8. Cf. Ingram 1955, 107–108.

9. Ingram 1955, 100; Landon 1941, 254.

10. See *Thailand Statistical Year Book* 1935/36–1936/37 (no. 19), 488.

11. *Thailand Statistical Year Book* 1939/40–1944 (no. 21), 75.

12. Ingram 1955, 101–102; "Mining" 1930, 115; Tateyania 1941, 470–471.

13. Ingram 1955, 105. This discussion of rubber is based primarily on Ingram 1955, 101–105.

14. Landon 1941, 256–257.

15. Landon 1941, 236.

16. Ingram 1955, 125.

17. Ingram 1955, 126.

18. See Andrews 1935, 187; Kanchananaga 1941, 104; Thompson V. 1947, 228.

19. "Labor Conditions in Thailand" 1944, 1173–1175; "Wages in Siam, 1930–31" 1933, 950–51; Thompson V. 1947, 231–234.

20. Thompson V. 1947, 229.

21. See Thompson V. 1947, 239.

22. Lin Y. 1936, 196.

23. "Labor Conditions in Thailand" 1944, 1176; Thompson V. 1947, 240–242; Thompson V. 1941, 115.

24. See Thompson V. 1947, 240; Landon 1941, 231.

25. Narasimhan 1948, 174.

26. Kanchananaga 1941, 82; Landon 1941, 144.

27. Business Registration Act of B.E. 2479, Sections 6, 7, 10, 13, 22.

28. Andrews 1935, 311.

29. Jacoby 1949, 238 (footnote).

30. Zimmerman 1931, 176–177.

31. Andrews 1935, 167–175.

32. Andrews 1935, 332–333.

33. Jacoby 1949, 237–239.

34. Ingram 1955, 68–69. The following remarks on co-operatives also follow Ingram.

35. See Chen T. 1940, 79.

36. Chen T. 1940, 81.

37. Report of the Financial Adviser 1938/39, 39–40. Quoted in Landon 1941, 166.

38. See Ingram 1955, 204 (footnote).

39. See Callis 1942, 69.

40. Report of the Financial Adviser 1938/39, 41. Quoted in Landon 1941, 167.

41. The first set of figures is taken from Chen C. P. 1935, 442; the second from Hsieh 1949, 291; the third from Liu 1935, 86. Conversions into baht are approximate only, based on contemporary exchange rates.

42. *China Critic* June 6, 1935, 236.

43. *Thailand Statistical Year Book* 1937/38–1938/39 (no. 20), 277.

44. Callis 1942, 70.

45. Ingram 1952, 461.

46. Hsieh 1949, 298; *Thailand Statistical Year Book* 1933/34–1934/35 (no. 18), 418.

47. Chen T. 1940, 276.

48. Chen T. 1940, 275–276.

49. Namely, 1.3 million in the East Indies, 1.6 million in Siam, and 1.7 million in Malaya. The 1931 Malayan census gave 1,704,452 Chinese (Del Tufo 1949, 75), and the less complete 1930 Indonesian census gave 1,-233,000 (Purcell 1951, 443), while the model of the Chinese population proposed in Chapter 6 for Siam yielded 1,592,000 for 1932.

50. See Del Tufo 1949, 85. On the other hand, the percentage of China-born Chinese in Indonesia was lower than in Siam, about 34%.

51. In 1908, there were already 75 Chinese schools with 5,500 pupils in the Indies (Chen T. 1940, 276), while at the same time in Siam there were only a few small, old-style Chinese schools.

52. Hsieh 1949, 299.

53. Landon 1941, 265–266; Hsieh 1949, 299.

54. "Hsien-wang ts'an-kuan hua-ch'iao hsüeh-hsiao chih ching-kuo yü so-yin" (The Visits of the Siamese King to Overseas Chinese Schools and Their Implications), 1928.

55. Landon 1941, 271; Hsieh 1949, 299.

56. A reading of the frequent articles on overseas Chinese education in the *China Critic*, a highly nationalistic journal published by Chinese in Shanghai, from 1933 to 1936 is especially illuminating in this regard.

57. Hsieh 1949, 300.

58. Chen C. P. 1935, 438.

59. The Chung-hua school in Pattani, for instance, which had been closed by the Ministry of Education in Nov. 1934, was reopened on the initiative of the Thai jangwat governor in July 1936. Hsü 1946, 127–128.

60. *Siam Today*, July 1936. Quoted from Purcell 1951, 187.

61. *Thailand Statistical Year Book* 1933/34–1934/35 (no. 18), 418.

62. Hsieh 1949, 299.

63. Hsü 1946, 127.

64. "Hsien-wang ts'an-kuan hua-ch'iao hsüeh-hsiao chih ching-kuo yü so-yin" (The Visits of the Siamese King to Overseas Chinese Schools and Their Implications) 1928, 200–201.

65. Cf. Hsü 1946, 128.

66. Hsieh 1949, 294.

67. "Kuan-yü nan-yang hua-ch'iao chiao-yü ti t'ao-lun" (Discussions of Overseas Chinese Education in Southeast Asia) 1928, 77–78.

68. See Chen C. P. 1935, 435.

69. *Thailand Statistical Year Book* 1933/34–1934/35 (no. 18), 420–421.

70. Landon 1941, 277.

71. Chang 1940, 154.

72. Hsieh 1949, 303.

73. Legatus 1929, 287.

74. The funds were taken to China by Lin Po-ch'i, a prominent Teochiu leader in Bangkok right up to his death in 1956.

75. Legatus 1929, 289.

76. Hsieh 1949, 303.

77. Legatus 1929, 287.

78. Hsieh 1949, 303.

79. Legatus 1929, 287.

80. Legatus 1929, 289.

81. Landon 1941, 205.

82. Lagatus 1929, 292.

83. In early May 1928, Japanese troops, sent to Shantung to protect the interests of their nationals, clashed in bloody and prolonged fighting at Tsinan with the Kuomintang army heading for Peking. In south China the boycott reached its peak effectiveness in the fall of 1928 and ended only in May 1929, when the Tsinan incident was finally settled by negotiation between the Chinese and Japanese governments. See Remer 1933, 137–154.

84. This account is based primarily on the daily reports in *Kan-mueang,* July 5, to Aug. 24, 1928. See also Mosolff 1932, 335–336; Credner 1935, 364; Thompson V. 1941.

85. *Kan-mueang* July 21, 1928.

86. *Kan-mueang* July 31, 1928.

87. *Kan-mueang* Aug. 22, 1928.

88. Lin Y. 1937, 1258.

89. Hsieh 1949, 303–304.

90. This account follows that in *Hua-ch'iao Jih-pao* March 7–8, 1932, March 27, 1932.

91. *China Critic* Oct. 27, 1932, 1130.

92. Thompson V. 1941, 129.

93. "Les négociations entre la Chine et le Siam" 1935, 40.

94. Ong 1935, 356; "Les Chinois du Siam" 1935, 328.

95. E.g., Yang 1936, 12.

96. "Les négociacions entre la Chine et le Siam" 1935, 38–39.

97. *China Critic* Oct. 27, 1932, 1130.

98. Hsieh 1949, 285.

99. *China Critic* Jan. 5, 1933, 13.

100. Hsieh 1949, 286.

101. *China Critic* Nov. 11, 1937, 73.

102. *China Critic* Nov. 12, 1936, 162; "Sino-Siamese Relations" 1937, 4. In Bangkok the chairman was a Thai, with Ch'en Shou-ming as vice-chairman.

103. The Electoral Law of B.E. 2475, Section 4.

104. Amendment Act (No. 3) of B.E. 2479 relative to the Electoral Law of B.E. 2475, Sections 13, 14, 16.

105. Hsieh 1949, 304.

106. Hsieh 1949, 304–305.

107. Landon 1941, 31.

108. *China Critic* Nov. 11, 1937, 73.

109. Abbreviated from Hua-ch'iao K'ang-jih Chiu-kuo Lien-ho-hui (Overseas Chinese Alliance for Resistance to Japan and National Salvation).

110. Lin H. C. 1936, 8; *China Critic* April 23, 1936, 90.

111. Lin H. C. 1936, 8.

112. "Pen-shu hsüeh-hsiao yen-ke (History of [Hakka] Schools)" 1947, 13.

113. Lapomarède (1934, 256) went so far as to say that the revolution was "largely due to the Sino-Siamese officials, lawyers and officers who gave it its first political orientation." He also found that of the 57 members of the Thai Senate in 1934 whose origins were known, 21 had Chinese blood. His linking of the "Chinese racial origin" of the revolutionists with the similarities between the Peoples Party program and Sun Yat-sen-ism is, however, misleading at best. And he errs in implying that Luang Pradit is the son of a Hainanese.

114. "Les Chinois du Siam" 1935, 335.

115. Lin H. C. 1936, 8.

116. Tsan 1935, 13.
117. Lin H. C. 1936, 9.
118. Quoted from Landon 1941, 38.
119. Legatus 1929, 290.
120. See Jacoby 1949, 24, 247–248, 257.
121. Translated from *Thammathipat* Feb. 7, 1950.
122. This account follows Landon 1941, 164–167.
123. Sreshthaputra 1929, 120–121.
124. See Landon 1941, 207.
125. *Thailand Statistical Year Book* 1937/38–1938/39 (no. 20), 280.
126. Quoted from Landon 1941, 35.
127. Landon 1941, 279.
128. *China Critic* Oct. 3, 1935, 18. It is also interesting to read the wildly exaggerated version of the incident earlier published in the same periodical under the provocative title, "Siam Massacres Chinese" (*China Critic* March 1, 1934, 208).
129. Legatus 1929, 286; Landon 1941, 268.
130. Landon 1939, 108.
131. Address delivered by the Thai Minister of Economic Affairs, June 8, 1936. Quoted from "The Chinese Goodwill Mission in Siam" 1936, 42.
132. Cf. Landon 1941, 150, 153.
133. Hsiao 1950, 10.
134. Chou 1950, 1–3.
135. T'an 1937.
136. "Pen-hui tsu-chih yen-ke" (History of the Organization of the [Hakka] Association) 1947, 1–2.
137. Tsan 1935, 14.
138. *China Critic* Oct. 27, 1932, 1130; May 18, 1933, 502.
139. Feng S. W. 1937.
140. "Pen-hui-kuan shih-lüeh" (Historical Résumé of the [Teochiu] Association) 1951, 6.

Chapter 8

1. Cf. Thompson V. 1941, 98–99; Landon 1941, 167–168.
2. The manager of the new company was perforce a Chinese, since no Thai had experience in rice milling. The man selected was the leading Cantonese miller, a former chairman of the Chinese Chamber of Commerce, who sold his own three mills to the company (for ten million baht) and was granted a speedy naturalization.
3. Cf. Landon 1941, 244–250.
4. Landon 1941, 219–223.
5. Landon 1941, 224–227.
6. Landon 1941, 227–229.
7. Landon 1941, 231–232.
8. Landon 1941, 146–147, 182–185.
9. Landon 1941, 229–230.

10. Landon 1941, 230–231.

11. Landon 1941, 232–235.

12. Landon 1941, 237.

13. Landon 1941, 237–241.

14. Landon 1941, 255.

15. Landon 1941, 242, 255.

16. Waithayakon 1944, 137; Landon 1941, 181.

17. Cf. Landon 1941, 150–153.

18. *Si-krung* Jan. 24–27, 1939; *Prachamit* Jan. 26–27, 1939.

19. *Siam Chronicle* March 15, 1939. Quoted from Landon 1941, 286.

20. Landon 1941, 277.

21. See Landon 1941, 185.

22. In the largest of these raids, which began at midnight, Aug. 12, thirty police parties in trucks and taxis descended simultaneously on Chinese headquarters. *Si-krung* Aug. 13, Aug. 19, Aug. 29, Sept. 1, 1939. See also Landon 1941, 277–278.

23. Landon 1941, 278, 288; Thompson V. 1941, 122.

24. *Si-krung* Aug. 27, 1939.

25. Landon 1941, 288.

26. Hsieh 1949, 300, 306; Landon 1941, 278, 285–286.

27. Hsieh 1949, 286.

28. Landon 1941, 153.

29. Quoted in Hsieh 1949, 288.

30. Landon 1941, 192.

31. Cheng T. N. 1940, 208.

32. Quoted from Landon 1941, 193.

33. Quoted from Landon 1941, 194.

34. E.g., Cheng T. N. 1940, 208.

35. Landon 1941, 286.

36. Landon 1941, 64–65.

37. See Landon 1941, 194.

38. Quoted from Landon 1941, 181. See also Waithayakon 1944, 137.

39. "Pen-shu hsüeh-hsiao yen-ke" (History of [Hakka] Schools) 1947, 14–15.

40. Waithayakon 1944, 137; Landon 1941, 194.

41. *Thailand Statistical Year Book* 1937/38–1944 (no. 21), 127.

42. Chang 1940, 154.

43. A Western-type Chinese community hospital founded in 1938.

44. "Chinese in the South Seas Area Pledge Support in War of Resistance" 1941, 223. See also Chen C. K. 1941, 463.

45. Thompson and Adloff 1950, 58.

46. *Government Gazette* May 23, 1941.

47. Act Approving Naming by Decree of Prohibited Areas for Aliens of B.E. 2484. In the *Government Gazette* July 8, 1941.

48. *Government Gazette* Sept. 19, 1941.

49. This account is based primarily on information from Chinese inform-

ants in the region, but also on *Chung-yüan Pao* May 23, May 30, June 7, June 15, June 16, June 20, Aug. 19, Sept. 21, Oct. 11, Oct. 13, Oct. 20, 1941. See also Landon 1943, 116.

50. Landon 1943, 116.

51. Chang 1940, 154.

52. Landon 1941, 46–47.

53. "Shih-nien-lai-chih hui-kuan shih-lüeh" (Brief History of the [Cantonese] Association for the Past Ten Years) 1947, 2.

54. This account is based largely on Fisher 1947, and Coast 1946, 127, 129–130, 147, 163.

55. Coast 1946, 130.

56. Statistics supplied by the Ministry of Foreign Affairs in Bangkok.

57. Cf. "Labor Conditions in Thailand" 1944, 1177.

58. *Government Gazette* June 2, 1942.

59. Occupational and Professional Assistance Act No. 2 of b.e. 2485, Section 4.

60. Quoted from Pramoj 1943, 207.

61. "Chungking's Fifth Columnists Arrive in Thailand" 1941, 120.

62. Cf. Thompson and Adloff 1950, 58; Hsieh 1949, 306.

63. Su 1948, 9.

64. An interesting commentary on the Chinese commercial spirit even in adversity is provided by Smith and Clark (1946, 281), who quoted Luang Adun, head of the Thai C.I.D. as saying in 1945: "A large number of Chinese have lost their lives in the various air raids, . . . but we have observed at headquarters that very few identification cards of the dead have been turned in, as the law requires. We investigated and now it turns out that the families of those killed have been coining money selling their cards to Japs, . . . [who] use them as passports—take them with them to other districts of Siam where they set themselves up as Chinese."

65. In Nov. 1944, a special representative from Luang Pradit arrived in Chungking. See Smith and Clark 1946, 193.

66. *Government Gazette* Aug. 22, 1945.

67. This account is based on information from informants and on Liang 1947. Other accounts may be seen in MacDonald 1949, 202–203 and Purcell 1951, 190–191.

68. Cf. Thompson and Adloff 1950, 58.

69. This account closely follows Liang 1947, 5–9.

70. "What the Chinese Think about Postwar Reconstruction" 1943, 225.

71. Ch'en S. C. 1945, 51–52.

72. *New York Times* Sept. 25, Sept. 30, Oct. 20, 1945; Purcell 1951, 190.

73. *New York Times* Sept. 29, 1945.

74. Article I. The text of the treaty and attached protocols as quoted in this Section can be found in the *Siam Directory* 1948, B 93–97.

75. "The Economic and Political Position of Siam" 1947, 195.

76. Alexander MacDonald (1949, 204), an American editor in Bangkok, has written that shortly before Aug., 1946, he suggested to Pridi that

quotas be set for all foreign nationals, more liberal in the case of the Chinese to avoid offence, and that this proposal was received enthusiastically by Pridi.

77. "Emigration of Chinese Nationals to Siam" 1948, 91.

78. *Democracy* April 13, 1946. Quoted in Thompson and Adloff 1948, 41. The remainder of this account of Chinese education 1946–1948 is based primarily on Thompson and Adloff 1948, 41–42.

79. Hsieh 1949, 300. Thompson and Adloff suggest that the stiffening of Thai policy at the end of 1946 was not unrelated to Thailand's success in gaining admission to the United Nations, which removed Thai fears of a Chinese veto.

80. Hsieh 1949, 300.

81. *Standard* Jan. 10, 1948.

82. See the *Siam Directory* 1948, B 174.

83. *Standard* Sept. 13, 1947.

84. See Purcell 1951, 200–201.

85. *Siam Directory* 1948, B 156.

86. *Standard* Aug. 16, 1947.

87. Thompson V. 1947, 248; Thompson and Adloff 1950, 240.

88. Thompson V. 1947, 247, 261–262.

89. "Business Information on Thailand" 1950, 262.

90. The rest of this paragraph is based on Thompson V. 1947, 245–248.

91. This discussion is based on Reeve 1951, 69–72, 75–77; and Ingram 1955, 87–90.

92. Reeve, 1951, 70. Reeve's £100,000,000 figure is probably hyperbole.

93. *Standard* Dec. 6, 1947.

94. *Standard* May 1, 1948.

95. Two and a half years later, on March 17, 1948, the Police Department announced the arrest of several men alleged to have been responsible for the assassination (*Standard* March 20, 1948). Whether they were, in fact, convicted of murder is not known to this writer.

96. Liang 1947, 5–6.

97. This account is based on "Shou-jung pei-fu t'ung-pao chi-hsiang" (Detailed Account of Receiving Captured Fellow Countrymen) 1947.

98. Hsieh 1949, 306; Li 1948, 9.

99. Thompson and Adloff 1950, 60–62.

100. Hsieh 1949, 306.

101. "The Economic and Political Position of Siam" 1947, 195.

102. Hsieh 1949, 307.

103. *Siam Directory* 1949, B 151.

104. See "The Economic and Political Position of Siam" 1947, 195.

105. This account is largely based on "Ts'ung kai-hsüan tao chiu-chih" (From Election to Office Taking) 1947.

106. *Chung-yüan Pao* Dec. 4, 1947.

Chapter 9

1. The 1947 census recorded occupations in 82 classes grouped into nine major categories. These have been completely regrouped and combined to give an economical listing of maximum sociological significance, as shown in Table 21. The grouping of occupational classes into social-status categories was made according to local valuations. It should be noted specifically that all business proprietors and managers are included in classes 2 and 6, and not in the line of business owned or managed. Thus proprietors and managers of jewelry shops are not included in class 17, which consists almost entirely of the individuals actually doing the artisan labor in workshops not on public view. The Chinese and the Thai evaluate certain occupations somewhat differently, and in such cases the evaluation of the ethnic group most strongly represented in the occupation class is the criterion for placing the class. Three of the more inclusive classifications have been split between status categories, namely, "Government Officials" (1 and 5), "Business Owners and Managers" (2 and 6), and "Market Sellers" (20 and 32). The ratio of high to low status members of each class was based on estimates of informants and the writer's observation; each sub-category (by sex and ethnic group) of an occupation class was split in the same proportion as the whole class.

Four basic assumptions were made in constructing Table 21. The first was that the ratio of occupied to total population for each major segment of the population (e.g., males of Chinese nationality) was the same in 1952 as five years earlier. The relative size of these major segments, however, was made to accord with the 1952 registration figures. The second assumption made was that the proportions of the various occupational classes in the jangwat of Phranakhǫn and in the less inclusive municipality of Krungthep are equivalent except for the two classes, "Farmers and Fishermen" and "Other Agriculturalists" (market gardeners). This assumption follows from the fact that, aside from Krungthep proper, Phranakhǫn consists only of six largely rural amphoe. It was assumed that 95% of Phranakhǫn farmers and fishermen and 75% of Phranakhǫn market gardeners resided outside the municipal limits. In this regard, it might be noted that most of the gulf fishermen supplying Bangkok are not residents of Phranakhǫn at all, but of Samutprakan, Samutsakhǫn, and other jangwats directly on the Gulf. The third assumption made was that one-third of the registered Thai nationals in Bangkok in 1952 were in fact local-born ethnic Chinese. The assumptions used in Table 17 to divide the registered population of Thai nationals by ethnic group and area yielded a percentage for Krungthep alone of 35.9% ethnic Chinese of Thai citizenship. If anything, then, the split made in constructing Table 21 underestimates the proportion of ethnic Chinese among Thai nationals. The fourth basic assumption was that these local-born ethnic Chinese were distributed among the various occupation classes according to the formula

$$x = \frac{ab}{a+b}\, c,$$

where $x =$ the number of local-born ethnic Chinese of Thai nationality in the occupation class, a the total census population of Thai nationals in the occupation class (a includes x), $b =$ the total census population of Chinese nationals in the occupation class, and c is the constant required to bring Σx up to $\frac{1}{3}\Sigma a$. Then, in the case of each occupation class, x was subtracted from a and added to b, to give the estimated total of ethnic Thai and ethnic Chinese respectively. The formula used describes known facts far more closely than $x = \frac{1}{3}a$. It would have been absurd, for instance, to estimate that one-third of the Thai nationals listed by the census as being government officials are ethnic Chinese. The social fact which the formula reflects is that ethnic Chinese of Thai nationality tend to concentrate in the same occupations as Chinese nationals.

The procedure followed, then, was rigorous but based on several assumptions which have not been rigorously verified. The general validity of the assumptions and procedure seems to be attested by the close approximation of the results to data secured from the most knowledgeable informants in Bangkok. The head of the Barbers Union, for instance, estimated on the basis of his records that there were 1,100 ethnic Chinese barbers and well over 100 ethnic Thai barbers in Krungthep, while the application of the above-mentioned assumptions to the 1947 census figures gives 1,020 ethnic Chinese barbers and 330 ethnic Thai barbers. In any case, Table 21 is presented only to make more explicit the basis for statements and conclusions on socio-economic status given in the text, and in lieu of a long series of space-consuming statements on ethnic occupational specialization. It does not presume to have the validity of the results of a properly designed and executed census.

2. *Economic and Demographic Survey 1954*, 1st series, 1955. Tables 15–16.

3. Goldschmidt 1950, 491–492.

4. Furnivall 1948.

5. Electoral Law of B.E. 2494, Sections 14 and 16.

6. The writer's forthcoming monograph, *Leadership and Power in the Chinese Community of Thailand* (Monographs of the Association for Asian Studies, 1957), analyzes the formal Chinese organizational structure in some detail.

7. *New York Times* July 25, 1948.

8. Skinner 1951, 4.

9. Skinner 1951, 12–13.

10. See Hsieh 1953, 321; Skinner 1951, 9–11.

11. *Liberty* June 16–19, 1948; *Bangkok Post* June 16–18, 1948.

12. *Liberty* June 26, July 2, 1948.

13. *New York Times* Aug. 18, 1948.

14. Thompson and Adloff 1950, 65; *Liberty* June, 17–19, 1948.

15. Thompson and Adloff 1950, 60.

16. *Standard* Oct. 8, 1949, 6.

17. *Standard* Oct. 14, 1950 (describing the situation the previous year).

18. *Si-krung* Jan. 25, 1950; *Kiattisak* Feb. 1, 1950; *Maitri-san* Jan. 31, Feb. 4, 1950.

19. *Chung-yüan Pao* Jan. 30, 1950.

20. "Political Alarms in Bangkok" 1952, 66.

21. Bangkok Radio, Thai Home Service, Dec. 2, 1950.

22. *Bangkok Times* Nov. 1, 1950.

23. *Liberty* Feb. 24, 1951.

24. *Ch'ao-chou Yüeh-pao* March 1951, 16.

25. NCNA, English Morse from Peking, Jan. 11, 1952.

26. *Bangkok Post* July 16, 1951.

27. *Bangkok Post* Nov. 14, 1951.

28. *Bangkok Post* Feb. 16, Oct. 17, 1951.

29. Cf. "Some Aspects of the Situation of the Chinese Minority in Thailand" 1952, 528–529.

30. *Bangkok Post* Feb. 6, 1952.

31. *Hsing-t'ai Wan-pao* July 10, 1952; *Kuang-hua Pao* June 27, 1952.

32. *Kuang-hua Pao* June 27, 1952.

33. According to revenues received, only about 290,000 aliens in 1953, and 340,000 aliens in 1954 paid the alien-registration fee. *Bangkok Post* Aug. 25, 1955.

34. *Chung-yüan Pao* April 10, May 19, 1952.

35. Quoted from the text as translated in the *Bangkok Post* Nov. 14, 1952.

36. *New York Times* Nov. 30, 1952.

37. *Bangkok Post* May 19–20, 1953, Feb. 1, 1954.

38. *Bangkok Tribune* April 25, April 29, 1953; *Bangkok Post* June 21, 1954.

39. *Bangkok Post* June 21, June 30, 1954; *Bangkok Tribune* July 1, 1954.

40. *Bangkok Post* Jan. 28, 1953.

41. *Bangkok Tribune* March 29, 1953; *Bangkok Post* March 30, 1953.

42. *Bangkok Post* Oct. 27, 1954.

43. *Bangkok Post* Aug. 5, Aug. 16, Sept. 13, Oct. 1, Oct. 15, 1954.

44. *Min-chu Jih-pao* May 27, 1953; *Hsing-t'ai Wan-pao* Sept. 3, 1954.

45. *Kuang-hua Pao* April 11, 1954; *Hsing-hsien Jih-pao* March 1, 1955.

46. *Hsing-hsien Jih-pao* Sept. 3, 1953.

47. *Min-chu Jih-pao* May 2, 1953.

48. *Bangkok Post* Feb. 25, 1955.

49. *Chung-yüan Pao* April 16, 1955; *Hsing-hsien Jih-pao* April 20, 1955.

50. *Hsing-hsien Jih-pao* April 25, 1955.

51. *Thai-mai* May 27, 1955.

52. *Bangkok Post* March 15–16, 1955.

53. *Bangkok Post* Oct. 7, Oct. 14, 1955.

54. *Bangkok Tribune* Sept. 1, 1955.

55. *Bangkok Post* Oct. 17, 1955.

56. *New York Times* March 3, 1956.

57. *Bangkok Post* Nov. 16, 1956.

58. For several years, another Chinese daily, *Hsin Pao,* has been published in Bangkok. But as simply the most successful of the yellow Chinese journals, it does not deserve treatment along with the serious Chinese press.

59. *Hsing-hsien Jih-pao* June 26, 1956.

60. Ingram 1955, 94.

61. *Thailand Statistical Year Book* 1953, 400.

62. The government's role in the rice trade, as of the 1945–1954 period, is described and carefully analyzed in Ingram 1955, 87–92.

63. Ingram 1955, 89, footnote.

64. Ingram 1955, 92.

65. Statistics as to registered rubber holdings by nationality for 1949 and 1954 were supplied by the Rubber Division of the Department of Agriculture in Bangkok.

66. Cf. Ingram 1955, 104.

67. Ingram 1955, 100.

68. In 1950, 114,000 piculs of tin metal were produced by dredge as against 64,240 by other means (Ingram 1955, 100). Tin-ore production increased from 14,509 metric tons in 1950 to 22,240 metric tons in 1954 (*Bulletin of Statistics* Oct.–Dec. 1954, 37).

69. Cf. Ingram 1955, 101.

70. *Bangkok Post* March 3, Dec. 14, 1954.

71. *Bangkok Tribune* April 8, 1955.

72. According to the *Thailand Statistical Year Book* (1953, 400), Thailand had 908 sawmills in 1949, and 925 in 1950.

73. *Thailand Statistical Year Book* 1953, 326–329.

74. *Thailand Statistical Year Book* 1953, 326–329.

75. *Chung-yüan Pao* Aug. 22, 1953.

76. *Bangkok Post* Feb. 24, 1954.

77. *Bulletin of Statistics* Oct.–Dec. 1954, 10.

78. *Bangkok Post* March 17, 1953.

79. *Bangkok Tribune* March 31, May 23, 1953.

80. The others were: making or casting images of the Buddha, printing in Thai, making bamboo utensils, and farming (except for orchards and truck gardens).

81. The others were: driving pedicabs for other than hire, and collecting dammar.

82. *Kuang-hua Pao* Feb. 29, 1952; *Hsing-t'ai Wan-pao* Nov. 27, 1952.

83. "Business Information on Thailand" 1950, 261.

84. "Foreign Investments in East Asian Countries: Thailand" 1952, 487.

85. *Thailand Statistical Year Book* 1953, 388–391.

86. *Bangkok Post* Jan. 14, 1953.

87. *Bangkok Tribune* Feb. 21, 1953.

88. *Bangkok Tribune* Jan. 30, 1953, May 16, 1954.

89. *Bangkok Tribune* Sept. 23, 1954; *Bangkok Post* Nov. 30, 1954.

90. *Bangkok Post* Nov. 6, Dec. 29, 1954.

91. *Min-chu Jih-pao* May 29, 1953; *Bangkok Post* June 1, 1953.

92. *Chung-yüan Wan-pao* July 1, 1953; *Bangkok Post* July 1, 1953.

93. *Bangkok Post* Dec. 24, 1953.

94. "Economic Reports from Siam" 1948, 330.

95. *Bangkok Post* April 3, 1953.

96. *Bangkok Tribune* May 13, 1955.

97. "Economic Reports from Siam" 1948, 330.

98. *Bangkok Tribune* Jan. 18, 1953; *Bangkok Post* Jan. 21, 1953.

99. *Bangkok Post* Feb. 26, 1953.

100. *Bangkok Post* Nov. 9, 1953.

101. *Bangkok Tribune* June 20, 1953; *Bangkok Post* Jan. 31, 1955; *Bangkok Tribune* May, 3, 1955.

102. *Bangkok Tribune* Feb. 3, 1954; *Thammathipat* July 21, 1954.

103. *Bangkok Post* Feb. 15, 1955.

104. *Bangkok Tribune* Oct. 12, 1954.

105. *Sathiraphap* Aug. 31, 1955.

106. This material is presented in detail in the writer's forthcoming monograph, *Leadership and Power in the Chinese Community of Thailand.*

107. See in particular: *Bangkok Post* July 19, Aug. 9, Aug. 11, Oct. 7, Oct. 13, 1955; *Siam Rath Weekly Review* July 21, Oct. 6, Oct. 13, 1955.

108. E.g. *Siam Rath Weekly Review* Oct. 20, 1955.

109. Peking Radio Voice in Kuo-yü, 2045 hours, Sept. 15, 1951.

110. See in particular: *Kuang-hua Wan-pao* Feb. 5, Feb. 6, Feb. 21, 1953; *Hsing-hsien Jih-pao* March 5, March 27, 1953.

111. The monopoly of the Remittance Syndicate was ended by the Finance Ministry in Sept. 1956, on grounds that it had been exploiting the Chinese remitters. Licenses were granted to eleven companies formed by the remittance shops. Remittance rates began to fall as soon as the prospective end of the monopoly became known.

112. *Bangkok Post* Aug. 4, 1955.

113. *Bangkok Post* Aug. 25, 1955.

114. As of 1953, 819,496 aliens were registered in Thailand, and of these 765,167 were Chinese nationals. Figures supplied by the Alien Division of the Police Department in Bangkok.

115. *Bangkok Post* April 10, 1950.

116. *Liberty* May 22, 1950; *Phim Thai* May 23, 1950; *Sayam-rat* Aug. 11, 1950.

117. *Hsing-t'ai Wan-pao* Jan. 28, 1953.

118. *Min-chu Wan-pao* Jan. 29, 1953; *Min-chu Jih-pao* Feb. 4, 1953.

119. *Hsing-hsien Jih-pao* March 19, 1953; *Chung-yüan Pao* March 20, 1953; *Min-chu Wan-pao* March 24, 1953; *Hsing-t'ai Wan-pao* March 31, 1953.

120. *Kuang-hua Pao* Dec. 25, 1953.

121. *Hsing-hsien Jih-pao* July 3, 1953.

122. *Chung-yüan Wan-pao* March 11, July 1, July 5, July 10, Aug. 9, 1954; *Hsing-t'ai Wan-pao* Sept. 15, Oct. 16, 1954.

123. *Chung-yüan Pao* July 24, 1954; *Hsing-hsien Jih-pao* Aug. 1, 1954.

124. *Hsing-t'ai Wan-pao* Oct. 4, 1954.

125. *Kuang-hua Wan-pao* Jan. 14, 1955.

126. *Bangkok Post* April 10, 1950.

127. *Chung-yüan Wan-pao* Dec. 30, 1952.

128. *Hsing-t'ai Wan-pao* Aug. 7, 1953; *Kuang-hua Wan-pao* July 9, 1954.

129. *Hsing-hsien Jih-pao* May 2, 1954.

130. *Kuang-hua Wan-pao* June 30, 1955.

131. *Chung-yüan Wan-pao* Jan. 22, 1953.

132. The statistics on Chinese education given for 1955–1956 are based on extensive on-the-spot surveys of Chinese schools in upcountry Thailand and Bangkok made by the writer in 1955, plus official statistics on Chinese schools in Thailand as of March 1956, supplied by the Private Schools Division of the Ministry of Education in Bangkok.

133. The role of leaders in relation to Chinese schools is elaborated in the writer's forthcoming monograph, *Leadership and Power in the Chinese Community of Thailand.*

134. *Hsing-hsien Jih-pao* Jan. 19, 1955; *Hsing-t'ai Wan-pao* May 17, 1955.

135. *Sayam-rat* May, 12, 1955.

136. *Bangkok Post* May 28, 1955.

137. *Chung-yüan Wan-pao* May 23, 1955; *Hsing-hsien Jih-pao* July 16, Sept. 9, 1955.

138. *Chung-yüan Pao* Oct. 17, 1955.

139. *Chung-yüan Pao* Jan. 23, 1952; *Min-chu Jih-pao* Feb. 9, 1952.

140. *Ch'üan-min Pao* Feb. 20, 1952; *Hsing-hsien Jih-pao* Feb. 23, 1952.

141. *Chung-yüan Pao* Sept. 9, 1952; *Hsing-t'ai Wan-pao* Sept. 20, 1952; *Hsing-hsien Jih-pao* Dec. 26, 1952.

142. Emergency Administration Act of B.E. 2495, Section 12.

143. Nationality Act of B.E. 2496, Section 7.

144. *Bangkok Post* Jan. 10, 1953.

145. Nationality Act of B.E. 2495, Section 9.

146. *Bangkok Tribune* June 13, 1953.

147. For representative press treatment, see *Bangkok Tribune* Jan. 6, Jan. 11, 1953; Feb. 26, 1954.

148. *Bangkok Post* Nov. 30, 1953.

149. *Bangkok Tribune* Jan. 24, 1953.

150. *Bangkok Tribune* June 4, 1953.

151. *Bangkok Post* June 16, 1953.

152. *Bangkok Post* Dec. 24, 1953.

153. *Bangkok Post* April 23, June 11, 1954.

154. *Bangkok Tribune* Oct. 17, 1954.

155. *Bangkok Post* July 1, 1955.

156. *Bangkok Post* July 15, 1955.

157. *Bangkok Post* Aug. 20, 1955.

158. *Bangkok Post* July 15, 1955; *Bangkok Tribune* Sept. 29, 1955.

159. *Bangkok Tribune* Aug. 20, 1955.

160. Military Service Act (No. 2) of B.E. 2498, Section 3.

161. *Bangkok Post* Sept. 30, 1955.

162. *Government Gazette* Oct. 11, 1955.

163. *Chung-yüan Pao* Oct. 14, 1955.

164. *Bangkok Tribune* Oct. 20, 1955.

165. *Government Gazette* Jan. 12, 1956.

166. *Bangkok Tribune* April 28, 1955.

167. *Bangkok Post* Aug. 22, Aug. 26, 1955.

Reference Bibliography

THIS listing includes only those publications cited in the notes. Entries for authored works are headed by the author's surname (plus initials when necessary to distinguish) and date of publication (or completion) of the book or article; the full bibliographical citation begins after the dash. Serial publications are listed here just as given in the notes; in cases where an abbreviated form of the title has been used, the full catalogue citation is given after the dash. The dates given in newspaper citations merely span the issues consulted; they do not imply that the newspaper was published only during those years.

Amoy Consular Report—Great Britain, Foreign Office, *Annual Diplomatic and Consular Reports on the Trade of Amoy, 1862–1893* [Composite title]. London: Harrison and Sons, 1863–1894.

Anderson 1890—John Anderson, *English Intercourse with Siam in the Seventeenth Century*. London: Kegan Paul, Trench, Trübner and Co., 1890.

Andrews 1935—James M. Andrews, *Siam; 2nd Rural Economic Survey, 1934–1935*. Bangkok: Bangkok Times Press, 1935.

Angier 1908—A. Gordon Angier, *The Far East Revisited*. London: Witherby & Co., 1908.

Annandale 1900—Nelson Annandale, "The Siamese Malay States." *Scottish Geographical Magazine*, 16 (1900), 505–523.

[Reference Bibliography]

Bacon 1892—George B. Bacon, *Siam, Land of the White Elephant,* rev. ed. New York: Scribner's, 1892.

Bangkok Calendar (English-language periodical). Bangkok: Press of the American Missionary Association, 1859–1872.

Bangkok Post (English-language evening newspaper). Bangkok, 1946–1956.

Bangkok Times (English-language daily newspaper). Bangkok, 1950.

Bangkok Tribune (English-language morning newspaper). Bangkok, 1952–1956.

Barnett 1910—J. C. Barnett, *Report of the First Annual Exhibition of Agriculture and Commerce.* Bangkok: Ministry of Agriculture, 1910.

Beauvoir 1870—Ludovic, marquis de Beauvoir, *Java, Siam, Canton,* 4th ed. Paris: Henri Plon, 1870.

Benedict 1943—Ruth Benedict, *Thai Culture and Behavior,* an unpublished war-time study dated Sept. 1943, Data Paper no. 4, Southeast Asia Program, Cornell University. Ithaca: Department of Far Eastern Studies, 1952.

Besso 1913—Salvatore Besso, *Siam and China,* tr. from the Italian by C. Matthews. London: Simpkin, Marshall, Hamilton, Kent and Co., [c. 1913].

Blythe 1947—W. L. Blythe, "Historical Sketch of Chinese Labour in Malaya." *Journal of the Royal Asiatic Society, Malayan Branch,* 20 (June 1947), 64–114.

Bock 1884—Carl Bock, *Temples and Elephants.* London: Sampson Low, Marston, Searle, and Rivington, 1884.

Bowring 1857—Sir John Bowring, *The Kingdom and People of Siam, with a Narrative of the Mission to that Country in 1855,* 2 vols. London: John W. Parker and Son, 1857.

Boxer 1953—C. R. Boxer, ed. *South China in the Sixteenth Century,* Hakluyt Society Publications, 2d s. No. CVI. London: Hakluyt Society, 1953.

Bradley 1870—Daniel B. Bradley, "Poket," an article which first appeared in 1870 in the *Bangkok Advertiser. Journal of the Siam Society,* 3 (1906), 44–47.

Briggs 1951—Lawrence Palmer Briggs, "The Ancient Khmer Empire." *Transactions of the American Philosophical Society,* n.s. 41 (Feb. 1951), 1–295.

Bulletin of Statistics—Thailand, National Economic Council, Central Statistical Office, *Bulletin of Statistics* [Title varies], vols. I–III, 1952–1954.

Burney 1825—Captain H. Burney, "Report of the Mission to the Phraya of Salang and the Chiefs on the Isthmus of Kraw," April 2, 1825. In *The Burney Papers,* 2, 197–222. Bangkok: Vajiranana National Library, 1910.

Burney 1826—Captain H. Burney, *The Burney Papers,* 4 vols. Bangkok: Vajiranana National Library, 1910. (All references are to vol. II, part 4, containing material written in 1826.)

[Reference Bibliography]

"Business Information on Thailand." *Far Eastern Economic Review,* 9 (Aug. 31, 1950), 257–262.

Callis 1942—Helmut G. Callis, *Foreign Capital in Southeast Asia.* New York: Institute of Pacific Relations, 1942.

Campbell 1902—J. G. D. Campbell, *Siam in the Twentieth Century.* London: Edward Arnold, 1902.

Campos, 1940—Joaquim de Campos, "Early Portuguese Accounts of Thailand." *Journal of the Siam Society,* 32 (Sept. 1940), 1–27.

Carter 1904—A. Cecil Carter, ed., *The Kingdom of Siam.* New York: G. P. Putnam's Sons, 1904.

Cartwright 1924—B. O. Cartwright, "The Huey Lottery." *Journal of the Siam Society,* 18 (1924), 221–239.

Chang 1940—C. C. Chang, "Anti-Chinese Campaign in Thai." *China Weekly Review,* 92 (March 30, 1940), 154–155.

Ch'ao-chou Yüeh-pao (C 147) (Chinese-language monthly). Bangkok, May 1950 to Dec. 1951.

Chaumont 1686—Alexandre, Chevalier de Chaumont, *Relation de l'ambassade de Monsieur le Chevalier de Chaumont à la Cour du Roy.* Amsterdam: Pierre Mortier, 1686.

Chen, C. K. 1941—Chen Chia-keng, "A 'South Seas' Chinese Reports on the Burma Road." *Pacific Affairs,* 14 (Dec. 1941), 463–468.

Chen, C. P. 1935—Chen Chun-po, "Chinese Overseas." In *The Chinese Year Book 1935–36,* 428–455.

Ch'en, H. M. 1754—Ch'en Hung-mou, "Notice Reminding Merchants Trading Overseas that they are free to return Home, 1754." In Thomas F. Wade, *Wên Chien Tzŭ Erh Chi, a Series of Papers Selected as Specimens of Documentary Chinese,* and *Key to the Tzŭ Erh Chi.* London: Trübner, 1867. Original, 128–131; tr. in the *Key,* 33–34.

Chen, H. S. 1937—Chen Han-seng, "The Present Prospect of Chinese Emigration." In Isaiah Bowman, ed., *Limits of Land Settlement.* New York: Council on Foreign Relations, 1937, 137–154.

Ch'en, S. C. 1945—Ch'en Su-ching, *China and Southeastern Asia.* Chungking and New York: China Institute of Pacific Relations, 1945.

Chen, T. 1923—Chen Ta, *Chinese Migrations with Special Reference to Labour Conditions.* Washington: U.S. Dept. of Labor, Bureau of Labor Statistics, Bulletin no. 340, 1923.

Chen, T. 1940—Chen Ta, *Emigrant Communities in South China,* a study of overseas migration and its influence on standards of living and social change. New York: Institute of Pacific Relations, 1940.

Ch'en, Y. T. 1940—Ch'en Yü-t'ai, "Cheng ho t'ung-shih t'ai-kuo k'ao" (C 148) (Research on Cheng Ho's Missions to Thailand). In *T'ai-kuo yen-chiu* (C 149), I. Bangkok, 1940, 57–58.

[Reference Bibliography]

Ch'en, Y. T. 1941—Ch'en Yü-t'ai, "Cheng wang tsu-hsi" (C 150) (The Genealogy of King Cheng). In *T'ai-kuo yen-chiu* (C 149), III. Bangkok, 1941, 269 ff.

Cheng, T. N. 1940—Cheng Tze-nan, "Chinese Want Thai Friendship." *Asia*, 40 (April 1940), 207–208.

Child 1892—Jacob T. Child, *The Pearl of Asia*. Chicago: Donohue, Henneberry and Co., 1892.

China Critic (English-language weekly). Shanghai, 1928–1940.

China Trade Returns—China, Inspectorate-General of Customs, *Trade Reports and Returns 1864–1928* [Title varies], Statistical Series No. 3. Shanghai, 1865–1929.

China Year Book, 1912, 1916, 1923. London: George Routledge, 1912, 1916; Tientsin: Tientsin Press, 1923.

"The Chinese." *Siam Repository*, 2 (1870), 505–507.

Chinese Customs Decennial Report—China, Inspectorate-General of Customs, *Decennial Reports on the Trade, Navigation, Industries, etc., of the Ports open to Foreign Commerce in China, 1892–1931*, Statistical Series No. 6. Shanghai, 1894–1933.

"The Chinese Goodwill Mission in Siam." *China Critic*, 14 (July 9, 1936), 42.

"Chinese in South East Asia." *Far Eastern Economic Review*, 13 (July 3, 1952), 13.

"Chinese in the South Seas Area Pledge Support in War of Resistance." *China Weekly Review*, 96 (April 19, 1941), 223.

"Les Chinois au Siam." *Revue Indo-Chinoise*, n.s. 5 (Jan. 15, 1907), 63–64.

"Les Chinois du Siam." *Revue Nationale Chinoise*, 22 (1935), 327–338.

Choisy 1687—François T., abbé de Choisy, *Journal du Voyage de Siam Fait en 1685 et 1686*. Paris: Chez Sebastien Mabre-Cramoisy, 1687.

Chou 1950—Chou Hung-chün, "Pen-so-chih hui-ku yü chan-wang" (C 151) (The Past and Future of the [Chung-hua Charitable] Clinic). *T'ai-ching chung-hua tseng-yi-so san-shih-liu chih san-shih-chiu nien-tu pao-kao-shu* (C 152) (Report of the Chung-hua Charitable Clinic of Bangkok for 1947–1950). Bangkok, 1950, 1–3.

"Chungking's Fifth Columnists Arrive in Thailand." *Far Eastern Survey*, 10 (June 2, 1941), 120.

Chung-yüan Pao (C 116) (Chinese-language morning newspaper). Bangkok, 1941–1956.

Chung-yüan Wan-pao (C 116) (Chinese-language evening newspaper). Bangkok, 1950–1955.

Ch'üan-min Pao (C 130) (Chinese-language morning newspaper). Bangkok, 1948–1952.

Coast 1946—John Coast, *Railroad of Death*. London: Commodore Press, 1946.

Collet 1911—Octave-J-A. Collet, *Étude Politique et Économique sur le Siam Moderne*. Bruxelles, Hayez, 1911.

Commercial Directory for Siam—Thailand, Ministry of Commerce and Communications, *Commercial Directory for Siam, 1920–1929*. Bangkok, 1920–1929.

Cort 1886—Mary L. Cort, *Siam, or the Heart of Farther India*. New York: Anson D. F. Randolph and Co., 1886.

Crawfurd 1820—John Crawfurd, *History of the Indian Archipelago, Containing an Account of the Manners, Arts, Languages, Religions, Institutions, and Commerce of Its Inhabitants*, 3 vols. Edinburgh: A. Constable, 1820. (All references are to vol. III.)

Crawfurd 1823—John Crawfurd, "Report to George Swinton, Esq.," April 3, 1823. In *The Crawfurd Papers*. Bangkok: Vajiranana National Library, 1915.

Crawfurd 1830—John Crawfurd, *Journal of an Embassy from the Governor-General of India to the Courts of Siam and Cochin-China*, 2d ed., 2 vols. London: Henry Colburn and Richard Bentley, 1830.

Credner 1935—Wilhelm Credner, *Siam, das Land der Tai*. Stuttgart: J. Engelhorns, 1935.

Crosby 1945—Sir Josiah Crosby, *Siam, the Crossroads*. London: Hollis and Carter, 1945.

De Francis 1950—John De Francis, *Nationalism and Language Reform in China*. Princeton: Princeton University Press, 1950.

Del Tufo 1949—M. V. Del Tufo, *A Report on the 1947 Census of Population: Malaya. Comprising the Federation of Malaya and the Colony of Singapore*. London: Crown Agents for the Colonies, 1949.

Directory for Bangkok and Siam. Bangkok: Bangkok Times Press, annually 1890–1912.

Donnelly 1924—Ivon A. Donnelly, *Chinese Junks and Other Native Craft*. Shanghai: Kelly and Walsh, 1924.

Dulyachinda 1949—Medhi Dulyachinda, "The Development of Labor Legislation in Thailand." *International Labour Review*, 60 (1949), 476–486.

Duyvendak 1939—J. J. L. Duyvendak, "The True Dates of the Chinese Maritime Expeditions in the Early Fifteenth Century." *T'oung Pao*, 34–35 (1939), 341–412.

Earl 1837—George Windsor Earl, *The Eastern Seas, or Voyages and Discoveries in the Indian Archipelago in 1832–33–34*. London: W. H. Allen, 1837.

Eberhard 1950—Wolfram Eberhard, *A History of China*. Berkeley: University of California Press, 1950.

Economic and Demographic Survey 1954—Thailand, Central Statistical Office, *Economic and Demographic Survey 1954*, 1st Series (Municipality of Bangkok), 2d Series (Municipality of Thonburi), 1955.

[Reference Bibliography]

"The Economic and Political Position of Siam." *Far Eastern Economic Review,* 2 (April 23, 1947), 195–196.

"Economic Reports from Siam." *Far Eastern Economic Review,* 5 (Sept. 29, 1948), 329–330.

Eickstedt 1944—Egon Freiherr von Eickstedt, *Rassendynamik von Ostasien, China und Japan, Tai und Kmer von der Urzeit bis Heute.* Berlin: Gruyter, 1944.

"L'émigration Asiatique." *Revue Indo-Chinoise,* n.s. 5 (April 15, 1907), 490–492.

"Emigration of Chinese Nationals to Siam." *International Labour Review,* 58 (July 1948), 91.

Fairbank and Teng 1941—John K. Fairbank and S. Y. Teng, "On the Ch'ing Tributary System." *Harvard Journal of Asiatic Studies,* 6 (June 1941), 135–246.

Feng, S. W. 1937—Feng Shao-wen, "Liu-shih-nien-lai-chih kuang-chao hui-kuan yü ch'i shih-yeh" (C 153) (The Cantonese Association and its Undertakings during the Past Sixty Years). *Hsien-ching kuang-chao hui-kuan liu-shih chou-nien chi-nien-k'an* (C 154) (Sixtieth Anniversary Publication of the Cantonese Association of Bangkok). Bangkok, 1937.

Feng, T. Y. 1946—Feng Tzu-yu, *Hua-ch'iao ke-ming k'ai-kuo shih* (C 155) (History of the Overseas Chinese Revolution to Open Up the Country). Chungking, 1946.

Finlayson 1826—George Finlayson, *The Mission to Siam and Hué, the Capital of Cochin China, in the Years 1821–2.* London: John Murray, 1826.

Fisher 1947—Charles A. Fisher, "The Thailand-Burma Railway." *Economic Geography,* 23 (April 1947), 85–97.

Forbin 1689—Comte de Forbin, *Mémoires de Comte de Forbin, Première Partie, 1675–1689.* (Michaud et Ponjoulat, eds. *Nouvelle Collection des Mémoires pour servir à l'histoire de France,* vol. IX.) Paris, 1839.

"Foreign Investments in East Asian Countries: Thailand." *Far Eastern Economic Review,* 5 (Sept. 29, 1948), 329–330.

Forrest 1948—R. A. D. Forrest, *The Chinese Language.* London: Faber and Faber, 1948.

Frankfurter 1904—O. Frankfurter, "King Mongkut." *Journal of the Siam Society,* 1 (1904), 191–207.

Freeman 1938—T. W. Freeman, "Recent and Contemporary Chinese Migrations." *Comptes Rendus du XVe Congrès International de Géographie,* 1938, 2, 11–22.

Furnivall 1948—J. S. Furnivall, *Colonial Policy and Practice.* London: Cambridge University Press, 1948.

Garnier 1911—Charles M. Garnier, "Bangkok, colonie chinoise, ou le secret du colosse jaune." *Revue du Mois,* 12 (Aug. 10, 1911), 231–236.

[Reference Bibliography]

Gerini 1898—G. E. Gerini, "Shan and Siam." *Imperial and Asiatic Quarterly Review*, 3d s. 5 (Jan. 1898), 145–163.

Gerini 1904—G. E. Gerini, "On Siamese Proverbs and Idiomatic Expressions." *Journal of the Siam Society*, 1 (1904), 11–168.

Gerini 1905—G. E. Gerini, "Historical Retrospect of Junkceylon Island." *Journal of the Siam Society*, 2 (1905), 1–107.

Gervaise 1688—Nicolas Gervaise, *The Natural and Political History of the Kingdom of Siam, A.D. 1688*, tr. from the French by H. S. O'Neill. Bangkok, 1928.

Giles 1938—Francis H. Giles, "A Critical Analysis of Van Vliet's Historical Account of Siam in the 17th Century." *Journal of the Siam Society*, 30 (1938), 155–240, 271–380.

Girard 1860—M. D. Girard, *Le Commerce de Siam*. Paris: La Société Orientale, 1860.

Goldschmidt 1950—Walter Goldschmidt, "Social Class in America—A Critical Review." *American Anthropologist*, 52 (Oct.–Dec. 1950), 483–498.

Goodrich 1943—L. Carrington Goodrich, *A Short History of the Chinese People*. New York. Harper, 1943.

Gordon 1891—Robert Gordon, "The Economic Development of Siam." *Journal of the Royal Society of Arts*, 39 (March 6, 1891), 283–298.

Gottwaldt 1903—H. Gottwaldt, *Die Überseeische Auswanderung der Chinesen und ihre Einwirkung auf die weisse und gelbe Rasse*. Bremen, 1903.

Government Gazette—Thailand, Office of the Presidency of the Council of Ministers, *Royal Thai Government Gazette*, published at irregular intervals. Bangkok, 1941–1956. (Tr. based on those rendered by International Translations, Bangkok.)

Graham 1912—W. A. Graham, *Siam: A Handbook of Practical, Commercial and Political Information*. London: Alexander Moring, 1912.

Graham 1924—W. A. Graham, *Siam*, 3d ed., 2 vols. London: Alexander Moring, 1924.

"Une grève de Chinois à Bangkok." *Asie Française*, 1910, 324–325.

Gutzlaff 1840—Charles Gutzlaff, *Journal of Three Voyages along the Coast of China in 1831, 1832, and 1833, with Notices of Siam, Corea, and the Loo-Choo Islands, to Which is Prefixed an Introductory Essay on the Policy, Religion, etc., of China*, by the Rev. W. Ellis, 3d ed. London: Thomas Ward and Co., [1840].

Haas 1951—Mary R. Haas, "The Declining Descent Rule for Rank in Thailand: A Correction." *American Anthropologist*, 53 (Oct.–Dec. 1951), 585–587.

Hale 1909—A. Hale, *The Adventures of John Smith in Malaya, 1600–1605*. Leyden: E. J. Brill, 1909.

[Reference Bibliography]

Hallett 1890—Holt S. Hallett, *A Thousand Miles on an Elephant in the Shan States*. Edinburgh and London: William Blackwood and Sons, 1890.

Helbig 1949—Karl Helbig, *Am Rande des Pazifik, Studien zur Landes- und Kultur-kunde Sudostasiens*. Stuttgart: Kohlhammer, 1949.

Hoeylaerts 1892—Hoeylaerts, *Le royaume de Siam*. Bruxelles, 1892.

Hsia 1953—Hsia Ting-hsün, "Min-ch'iao wu yang chi ch'i tzu-sun" (C 156) (The Hokkien Overseas Chinese Wu Yang and his Descendants). *Hua-ch'iao Hsin-yü* (C 157), nos. 11–12. Bangkok, 1953, 40–51.

Hsiao 1950—Hsiao Sung-ch'in, "Ti-szu-shih-yi-chieh tung-shih-hui kung-tso chien-t'ao" (C 158) (Review of the Work of the Forty-first Board of Directors). *T'ai-ching t'ien-hua yi-yüan ti-szu-shih-yi-chieh tung-shih-hui pao-kao-shu* (C 159) (Report for the Forty-first Term of the Board of Directors of the T'ien-hua Hospital of Bangkok). Bangkok, 1950, 10–13.

Hsieh 1949—Hsieh Yu-jung, *Hsien-lo kuo-chih* (C 160) (Siam Gazetteer). Bangkok: Nan-hai t'ung-hsün-she, 1949.

Hsieh 1953—Hsieh Yu-jung, *Hsin-pien hsien-lo kuo-chih* (C 161) (Revised Siam Gazetteer). Bangkok: Yi pao-she, 1953.

"Hsien-lo kuang-chao-shu-chih chien-chu-yeh" (C 162) (The Construction Business of the Cantonese in Siam). In *Hsien-ching kuang-chao hui-kuan ch'i-shih chou-nien chi-nien t'e-k'an* (C 163) (Seventieth Anniversary Publication of the Cantonese Association of Bangkok). Bangkok, 1947.

"Hsien-wang ts'an-kuan hua-ch'iao hsüeh-hsiao chih ching-kuo yü so-yin" (C 164) (The Visits of the Siamese King to Overseas Chinese Schools and Their Implications). In *Nan-yang yen-chiu* (C 165), II. Shanghai, Dec. 1928, 199–202.

Hsing-hsien Jih-pao (C 142) (Chinese-language morning newspaper). Bangkok, 1950–1955.

Hsing-t'ai Wan-pao (C 143) (Chinese-language evening newspaper). Bangkok, 1950–1955.

Hsü 1946—Hsü Yün-ch'iao, *Pei-ta-nien shih* (C 166) (History of Pattani). Singapore: Nan-yang Book Company, 1946.

Hsüeh 1894—Hsüeh Fu-ch'eng, "Chinese Emigrants Abroad," Memorial to the Emperor, tr. from the Shen Pao. *China Review*, 21 (1894), 138–141.

Hua-ch'iao Hsin-yü (C 157) (Chinese-language fortnightly). Bangkok, 1953.

Hua-ch'iao Jih-pao (C 106) (Chinese-language newspaper). Bangkok, 1928–1939.

Huang 1954—Huang Fu-luan, *Hua-ch'iao yü chung-kuo ke-ming* (C 167) (Overseas Chinese and the Chinese Revolution). Hongkong, 1954.

"Hui-kuan ti-ch'an shih-lüeh" (C 168) (Brief History of [Cantonese] Association Property). *Hsien-ching kuang-chao hui-kuan ch'i-shih chou-nien chi-nien t'e-k'an* (C 163) (Seventieth Anniversary Publication of the Cantonese Association of Bangkok). Bangkok, 1947.

Hutchinson 1940—E. W. Hutchinson, *Adventures in Siam in the Seventeenth Century.* London: Royal Asiatic Society, 1940.

Ingram, 1952—James C. Ingram, *Economic Change in Thailand, 1850–1950* (Doctoral dissertation). Ithaca: Cornell University, 1952.

Ingram 1955—James C. Ingram, *Economic Change in Thailand since 1850.* Stanford: Stanford University Press, 1955.

Jacoby 1949—Erich H. Jacoby, *Agrarian Unrest in Southeast Asia.* New York: Columbia University Press, 1949.

James 1922—Eldon R. James, "Jurisdiction over Foreigners in Siam." *American Journal of International Law,* 16 (Oct. 1922), 585–603.

Jumsai 1951—M. L. Manich Jumsai, *Compulsory Education in Thailand* (UNESCO Studies on Compulsory Education VIII). Paris: UNESCO, 1951.

Kaempfer 1727—Engelbert Kaempfer, *The History of Japan, Together with a Description of the Kingdom of Siam, 1690–92,* tr. by J. G. Scheuchzer, F.R.S. First published as translated from the original manuscript in 1727. Glasgow: James MacLehose and Sons, 3 vols., 1906.

Kanchananaga 1941—Thuan Kanchananaga, comp., *Report on Commercial and Economic Progress of Thailand, 1939–40.* Bangkok: Sataman Publishing House, 1941.

Kan-mueang (Thai-language daily newspaper). Bangkok, 1928.

Kiattisak (Thai-language daily newspaper). Bangkok, 1950.

Kiliani 1926—Richard Kiliani, "Die Auslandchinesen in Südostasien." *Ostasiatische Rundschau,* 7 (Aug. 1926), 148–151.

Kiungchow Consular Report—Great Britain, Foreign Office, *Annual Diplomatic and Consular Reports on the Trade of Kiungchow, 1876–1914* [Composite title]. London: Harrison and Sons, 1877–1916.

Kuang-hua Pao (C 136) (Chinese-language morning newspaper). Bangkok, 1949–1955.

Kuang-hua Wan-pao (C 136) (Chinese-language evening newspaper). Bangkok, 1949–1955.

"Kuan-yü nan-yang hua-ch'iao chiao-yü ti t'ao-lun" (C 169) (Discussions of Overseas Chinese Education in Southeast Asia). In *Nan-yang yen-chiu* (C 165), I. Shanghai, June 1928, 77–87.

Kulp 1925—Daniel Harrison Kulp, *Country Life in South China.* New York: Bureau of Publications, Teachers' College, Columbia University, 1925.

"Labor Conditions in Thailand." *Monthly Labor Review,* 58 (June 1944), 1169–1177.

Lan 1949—Lan Wei-pin, "Ts'ung ch'ao-an wen-wu shuo-tao lü-hsien ch'ao-an t'ung-hsiang-hui-chih ching-shen" (C 170) (Discussion of Ch'ao-an Culture and the Spirit of the Ch'ao-an Association in Siam). *Lü-hsien ch'ao-an t'ung-hsiang-hui erh-shih-yi chou-nien chi-nien t'e-k'an* (C 171)

(Twenty-first Anniversary Publication of the Ch'ao-an Association in Siam). Bangkok, 1949, 6–7.

Landon 1939—Kenneth P. Landon, *Thailand in Transition*. Chicago: University of Chicago Press, 1939.

Landon 1940—Kenneth P. Landon, "The Problem of the Chinese in Thailand." *Pacific Affairs*, 13 (1940), 149–161.

Landon 1941—Kenneth P. Landon, *The Chinese in Thailand*. New York: Institute of Pacific Relations, 1941.

Landon 1943—Kenneth P. Landon, "Thailand." *The Annals of the American Academy of Political and Social Science*, 226 (March 1943), 112–119.

Lapomarède 1934—Baron de Lapomarède, "The Setting of the Siamese Revolution." *Pacific Affairs*, 7 (Sept. 1934), 251–259.

Laseur 1885—M. F. Laseur, "L'émigration Chinoise." *Société de Géographie de Lille, Bulletin*, 4 (1885), 62–82.

Lasker 1945—Bruno Lasker, *Asia on the Move*. New York: Holt, 1945.

Lasker 1950—Bruno Lasker, *Human Bondage in Southeast Asia*. Chapel Hill: University of North Carolina Press, 1950.

Lattimore 1937—Owen Lattimore, "The Mainsprings of Asiatic Migration." In Isaiah Bowman, ed., *Limits of Land Settlement*. New York: Council on Foreign Relations, 1937, 119–135.

Launay 1920—Adrien Launay, *Histoire de la Mission de Siam, 1662–1811*, 1 vol. plus *Documents Historiques*, 2 vols. Paris: P. Tequi, 1920.

Leckie 1894—Charles Stuart Leckie, "The Commerce of Siam in Relation to the Trade of the British Empire." *Journal of the Royal Society of Arts*, 42 (June 8, 1894), 649–662.

Legatus 1929—Legatus, "Die Chinesen in Siam; ein Ausschnitt aus dem chinesischen Problem der Gegenwart." *Preussische Jahrbücher*, 215 (1929), 281–294.

Le May 1925—Reginald S. Le May, "A Visit to Sawankalok." *Journal of the Siam Society*, 19 (1925), 63–82.

Le May 1930—Reginald S. Le May, *Siamese Tales Old and New*. London: Noel Douglas, 1930.

Li 1948—Li P'iao-p'ing, "Hsien hua hsin-wen shih-yeh hsiao-shih" (C 172) (Short History of the Chinese Newspaper Business in Siam). *Hsien-lo hua-ch'iao yin-shua t'ung-yeh kung-hui ch'eng-li erh-chou-nien chi-nien t'e-k'an* (C 173) (Second Anniversary Publication of the Overseas Chinese Printers Association of Siam). Bangkok, 1948, 8–9.

Liang 1947—Liang Jen-hsin, "Ts'an-chia liu-shu hui-kuan lin-shih lien-ho pan-shih-ch'u ching-kuo" (C 174) (Participation in the Temporary Joint Office of the Six Speech-group Associations). *Hsien-ching kuang-chao hui-kuan ch'i-shih chou-nien chi-nien t'e-k'an* (C 163) (Seventieth Anniversary Publication of the Cantonese Association of Bangkok). Bangkok, 1947, 5–12.

Liberty (English-language daily newspaper). Bangkok, 1948–1952.

Lin, H. C. 1936—Lin Hsi-chun, "Causes of Anti-Chinese Movement in Siam." *China Critic*, 12 (Jan. 2, 1936), 8–11.

Lin, Y. 1936—Lin Yu, "Twin Loyalties in Siam." *Pacific Affairs*, 9 (June 1936), 191–200.

Lin, Y. 1937—Lin Yu, "The Chinese Overseas." *The Chinese Year Book*, 1937, 1245–1261.

Ling 1912—Pyau Ling, "Causes of Chinese Emigration." *Annals of the American Academy of Political and Social Science*, 39 (1912), 74–82.

Little 1903—Archibald Little, *The Far East*. Oxford: Clarendon Press, 1903.

Liu 1935—Liu Hsing-hua, "The Importance of the Overseas Chinese to China." *China Critic*, 10 (July 25, 1935), 84–86.

Loubère 1693—Simon de la Loubère, *A New Historical Relation of the Kingdom of Siam*, tr. from the French by S. P. Gen. R.S.S., 2 vols. London: Theodore Horne, 1693. (All references are to vol. I.)

McCarthy 1902—James McCarthy, *Surveying and Exploring in Siam*. London: John Murray, 1902.

MacDonald 1949—Alexander MacDonald, *Bangkok Editor*. New York: Macmillan, 1949.

McDonald 1884—Mrs. Noah A. McDonald, "The Chinese in Siam." In [Mary Backus, ed.] *Siam and Laos as Seen by Our American Missionaries*. Philadelphia: Presbyterian Board of Publications, 1884, 145–161.

McFarland 1928—George B. McFarland, ed., *Historical Sketch of Protestant Missions in Siam, 1828–1928*. Bangkok: Bangkok Times Press, 1928.

MacNair 1926—Harley F. MacNair, *The Chinese Abroad, Their Position and Protection: A Study in International Law and Relations*. Shanghai: Commercial Press, 1926.

Maitri-san (Thai-language daily newspaper). Bangkok, 1950.

Malcom 1839—The Rev. Howard Malcom, *Travels in South-Eastern Asia, Embracing Hindustan, Malaya, Siam, and China, With Notices of Numerous Missionary Stations, and a Full Account of the Burman Empire*, 2 vols. London: Charles Tilt, 1839. (All references are to vol. I.)

Malloch 1827—D. E. Malloch, "Private Journal," 1827. In *The Burney Papers*, 2, 221–232. Bangkok: Vajiranana National Library, 1910.

Malloch 1852—D. E. Malloch, *Siam, Some General Remarks on Its Productions*. Calcutta: Baptist Mission Press, 1852.

"Marking the People." *Siam Repository*, 2 (1870), 363–364.

Min-chu Jih-pao (C 134, first two characters) (Chinese-language morning newspaper). Bangkok, 1951–1953.

Min-chu Wan-pao (C 134, first two characters) (Chinese-language evening newspaper). Bangkok, 1951–1953.

"Mining." In *Siam, Nature and Industry*. Bangkok: Department of Commercial Intelligence, 1930.

[Reference Bibliography]

Mongkut 1856—His Majesty King Mongkut, "The English Correspondence of King Mongkut," G. Coedes, ed. *Journal of the Siam Society*, 21 (1927), 3–35, 127–177; 22 (1928), 1–18.

"Monograph on Sugar in Siam." *The Record* (English-language quarterly, published by the Ministry of Commerce). Bangkok, Jan. 1922, 6–17.

Moore 1914–1915—R. Adey Moore, "An Early British Merchant in Bangkok." *Journal of the Siam Society*, 11 (1914–1915), 21–39.

Mosolff 1932—Hans Mosolff, *Die chinesische Auswanderung*. Rostock: Carl Hinstorffs, 1932.

Mouhot 1864—Henri Mouhot, *Travels in the Central Parts of Indo-China* (Siam), *Cambodia and Laos*, 2 vols. London: John Murray, 1864.

Mullender 1950–Philippe Mullender, "L'Évolution récente de la Thailande." *Politique Étrangère*, 15 (April/May 1950), 213–233.

Mury 1903—Francis Mury, "Bangkok." *Revue de Geographie*, 52 (Jan. 1903), 39–58.

Narasimhan 1948—P. S. Narasimhan, "A Review of Labour Legislation in South-East Asia." *India Quarterly*, 4 (1948), 48–60, 165–178.

Nathabanja 1924—Luang Nathabanja, *Extraterritoriality in Siam*. Bangkok: Bangkok Daily Mail, 1924.

Neale 1852—Frederick Arthur Neale, *Narrative of a Residence in Siam*. London: Office of the National Illustrated Library, 1852.

"Les négociations entre la Chine et le Siam." *Revue Nationale Chinoise*, 22 (June 14, 1935), 38–40.

New York Times. New York, 1945–1956.

Niel 1907—Clément Niel, *Condition des Asiatiques, Sujets et Protégés Français au Siam*. Paris: Sirey, 1907.

Norman 1907—Henry Norman, *Peoples and Politics of the Far East*. London: T. Fisher Unwin, 1907.

"Notification on the Subject of the Triennial Taxation of the Chinese of Siam." *Siam Repository*, 2 (1870), 417.

Nunn 1922—William Nunn, "Some Notes upon the Development of the Commerce of Siam." *Journal of the Siam Society*, 15 (1922), 78–102.

Nuprapath 1941—Chao Phya Wongsa Nuprapath, *History of the Ministry of Agriculture* [in Thai]. Bangkok, 1941.

Ong 1935—S. G. Ong, "Sino-Siamese Problem and Its Solution." *China Weekly Review*, 74 (Nov. 9, 1935), 356–357.

"Overseas Chinese Remittances to China." *Far Eastern Economic Review* (March 17, 1948). 251–254.

Pallegoix 1854—Mgr. Pallegoix, *Déscription du Royaume Thai ou Siam*, 2 vols. Paris, 1854.

Pallu 1668—François Pallu, *Relation abrégée des missions et des voyages des évesques français, envoyez aux royaumes de la Chine, Cochinchine, Tonquin et Siam.* Paris: Denys Bechet, 1668.

Parker 1897—S. H. Parker, "Siam." *Imperial and Asiatic Quarterly Review,* 4 (July 1897), 112–119.

Pelzer 1935—Karl J. Pelzer, *Die Arbeiterwanderungen in Südostasien, eine wirtschafts und bevölkerungsgeographische Untersuchung.* Hamburg, 1935.

Pelzer 1941—Karl J. Pelzer, *Population and Land Utilization.* Shanghai: International Secretariat, Institute of Pacific Relations, 1941.

"Pen-hui tsu-chih yen-ke" (C 175) (History of the Organization of the [Hakka] Association). In *Hsien-lo hua-ch'iao k'e-shu tsung-hui erh-shih chou-nien chi-nien-k'an* (C 176) (Twentieth Anniversary Publication of the Overseas Chinese Hakka Association of Siam). Bangkok, 1947.

"Pen-hui-kuan shih-lüeh" (C 177) (Historical Résumé of the [Teochiu] Association). *Ch'ao-chou Yüeh-pao* (C 147) 10 (Feb. 1951), 6.

"Pen-shu hsüeh-hsiao yen-ke" (C 178) (History of [Hakka] Schools). In *Hsien-lo hua-ch'iao k'e-shu tsung-hui erh-shih chou-nien chi-nien-k'an* (C 176) (Twentieth Anniversary Publication of the Overseas Chinese Hakka Association of Siam). Bangkok, 1947.

Phim Thai (Thai-language daily newspaper). Bangkok, 1950.

Pinya 1901–02—Pinya, "A History of the French Mission to Siam." *Imperial and Asiatic Quarterly Review,* 3d s., 11 (1901), 331–343; 12 (1901), 120–133; 13 (1902), 91-105.

"Political Alarms in Bangkok." *World Today,* 8 (Feb. 1952), 60–71.

Poujade 1946—Jean Poujade, *Les Jonques des Chinois du Siam.* Paris: Gauthier Villars, 1946.

Prachamit (Thai-language daily newspaper). Bangkok, 1939–1940.

Pramoj 1943—M. R. Seni Pramoj, "Thailand and Japan." *Far Eastern Survey,* 12 (Oct. 20, 1943), 204–208.

Purcell 1951—Victor Purcell, *The Chinese in Southeast Asia.* London: Oxford University Press, 1951.

Raquez 1903—A. Raquez, "Comment s'est peuplé le Siam." *L'Asie Française,* no. 31 (Oct. 1903), 428–438.

Ratzel 1876—Friedrich Ratzel, *Die chinesische Auswanderung.* Breslau: I. U. Kern's, 1876.

"Rebellion." *Bangkok Calendar* (1849). Reprinted in *Siam Repository,* 1 (1869), 336–337.

Reeve 1951—W. D. Reeve, *Public Administration in Siam.* London: Oxford University Press, 1951.

Remer 1933—C. F. Remer, *A Study of Chinese Boycotts.* Baltimore: Johns Hopkins Press, 1933.

Report on China Trade—China, Inspectorate-General of Customs, *Reports on the Trade of China, 1929–1946.* Statistical Series No. 1. Shanghai, 1930–1948.

Richard 1908—Louis Richard, *Comprehensive Geography of the Chinese Empire and Dependencies.* Shanghai: Tu-se-wei Press, 1908.

Richardson 1839–1940—Dr. D. Richardson, "Journal of a Mission from the Supreme Government of India to the Court of Siam." *Journal of the Asiatic Society of Bengal,* 8 (1839), 1016–1036; 9 (1840), 1–30, 219–250.

Rosny 1885—Léon de Rosny, *Le peuple siamois ou thai.* Paris: Libraires de la Société d'Ethnographie, 1885.

Rousset 1878—Léon Rousset, "Les Chinois hors de chez eux." *Le Correspondant,* 112 (July 10, 1878), 92–113.

Ruschenberger 1838—W. S. W. Ruschenberger, *A Narrative of a Voyage Round the World, during the Years 1835, '36 and '37, including a Narrative of an Embassy to the Sultan of Muscat and the King of Siam,* 2 vols. London: Richard Bentley, 1838. (All references are to vol. II.)

Sarasas 1942—Phra Sarasas, *My Country Thailand.* Tokyo: Maruzen, 1942.

Sathiraphap (Thai-language newspaper). Bangkok, 1955.

Sayam-rat (Thai-language daily newspaper). Bangkok, 1950–1955.

Sayre 1927—Francis Sayre, "Siam's Fight for Sovereignty." *Atlantic Monthly,* 140 (Nov. 1927), 674–689.

"The Second Annual Report of the Morrison Education Society." *Chinese Repository,* 7 (Oct. 1838), 301–310.

See 1919—See Chong Su, *The Foreign Trade of China.* New York: Columbia University, Longmans, Green & Co., 1919.

Seidenfaden, 1928—Erik Seidenfaden, *Guide to Bangkok, with Notes on Siam,* 2d ed. Bangkok: Royal State Railways of Siam, 1928.

Seidenfaden 1939—Erik Seidenfaden, "An Analysis of 'Das Land der Tai.'" *Journal of the Siam Society,* 31 (March 1939), 79–100.

Senah Body 1843—Chowe Peeah Praklang Senah Body, "Letter of S. G. Bonham, Governor of Penang," 1843. *The Burney Papers,* 4, 95–103. Bangkok: Vajiranana National Library, 1910.

"Shih-nien-lai-chih hui-kuan shih-lüeh" (C 179) (Brief History of the [Cantonese] Association during the Past Ten Years). *Hsien-ching kuang-chao hui-kuan ch'i-shih chou-nien chi-nien t'e-k'an* (C 163) (Seventieth Anniversary Publication of the Cantonese Association of Bangkok). Bangkok, 1947.

"Shou-jung pei-fu t'ung-pao chi-hsiang" (C 180) (Detailed Account of Receiving Captured Fellow Countrymen). *Hsien-ching kuang-chao hui-kuan ch'i-shih chou-nien chi-nien t'e-k'an* (C 163) (Seventieth Anniversary Publication of the Cantonese Association of Bangkok). Bangkok, 1947.

Siah 1847—[Siah U Chin] "Annual Remittances by Chinese Immigrants in Singapore to Their Families in China." *Journal of the Indian Archipelago and Eastern Asia,* 1 (1847), 35–37.

Siah 1848—Siah U Chin, "The Chinese in Singapore." *Journal of the Indian Archipelago and Eastern Asia*, 2 (1848), 283–290.

Siam Consular Report—Great Britain, Foreign Office, *Annual Diplomatic and Consular Reports on the Trade of Siam, 1864–1913* [Composite title]. London: Harrison and Sons, 1865–1914.

Siam Directory 1947–1953. Bangkok: The Thai Company, annually 1947–1953.

Siam Rath Weekly Review (English-language weekly). Bangkok, 1952–1956.

Siam Repository (English-language periodical). Bangkok: S. J. Smith's office, 1869–1874.

Siam Trade Statistics—Thailand, Customs Department, *Statistics of the Import and Export Trade of Siam, Port of Bangkok*, 1899–1906. Bangkok, 1900–1907.

Si-krung (Thai-language daily newspaper). Bangkok, 1939, 1949–1951.

"Sino-Siamese Miscellany." *Standard* (Bangkok), no. 145 (Oct. 8, 1949), 12–13.

"Sino-Siamese Relations." *China Critic*, 17 (April 1, 1937), 4.

Skinner 1951—G. William Skinner, *Report on the Chinese in Southeast Asia, December 1950*, Data Paper No. 1, Southeast Asia Program, Cornell University. Ithaca: Department of Far Eastern Studies, 1951.

Smith 1944—Malcolm Smith, "The Families of the Kings of Siam of the House of Chakri." *Annals of Eugenics*, 12 (1944), 151–157.

Smith 1947—Malcolm Smith, *A Physician at the Court of Siam*. London: Century Life, 1947.

Smith and Clark 1946—Nicol Smith and Blake Clark, *Into Siam, Underground Kingdom*. Indianapolis and New York: Bobbs-Merrill, 1946.

Smyth 1898—H. Warington Smyth, *Five Years in Siam*, 2 vols. London: John Murray, 1898.

"Some Aspects of the Situation of the Chinese Minority in Thailand." *Far Eastern Economic Review*, 13 (Oct. 23, 1952), 528–529.

Spinks 1956—Charles Nelson Spinks, "Siam and the Pottery Trade of Asia." *Journal of the Siam Society*, 44 (1956), 61–111.

Sreshthaputra 1929—So Sreshthaputra, "Assimilation." *Bangkok Daily Mail*, Sept. 17, 1929. (Reprinted in So Sreshthaputra, *In Retrospect*. Bangkok: Krungdeb Barnagar Press, 1939, 118–121.)

Stamp 1942—L. Dudley Stamp, "Siam Before the War." *Geographic Journal*, 99 (1942), 209–224.

Standard (English-language weekly). Bangkok, 1947–1951.

Standing 1924—Percy Cross Standing, "Progress in Siam." *Contemporary Review*, 125 (June 1924), 762–768.

"Statistik der Chinesen im Auslande." *Deutsche Rundschau für Geographie und Statistik*, 30 (1907–1908), 277.

[Reference Bibliography]

Staunton 1810—George Thomas Staunton, tr., *Ta Tsing Leu Li, Being the Fundamental Laws . . . of the Penal Code of China.* London: T. Cadell and W. Davies, 1810.

Su 1948—Su Tsung-tse, "Pen-hui-kuan shih-lüeh" (C 181) (Historical Sketch of the [Teochiu] Association). *Hsien-lo ch'ao-chou hui-kuan ch'eng-li shih-chou-nien chi-nien t'e-k'an* (C 182) (Tenth Anniversary Publication of the Teochiu Association of Siam). Bangkok, 1948, 9.

Sun 1931—Sun Fang Si, *Die Entwicklung der chinesischen Kolonisation in Südasien (Nan-yang) nach chinesischen Quellen.* Jena, 1931.

Swatow Consular Report—Great Britain, Foreign Office, *Annual Diplomatic and Consular Reports on the Trade of Swatow, 1862–1914* [Composite title]. London: Harrison and Sons, 1863–1916.

Tachard 1686—Père Guy Tachard, *Voyage de Siam des pères Jésuites envoyés par le Roy aux Indes et à la Chine.* Paris: Daniel Horthemels, 1686.

T'ai-kuo hua-ch'iao kung-shang-yeh ch'üan-mao (C 183) (Survey of Overseas Chinese Industry and Commerce in Thailand). Bangkok: Kung-shang chou-pao she, Dec. 1951.

T'an 1937—T'an Chin-hung, "Kuang-chao yi-yüan chi fen-ch'ang" (C 184) (The Cantonese Hospital and Cemetery). *Hsien-ching kuang-chao hui-kuan liu-shih chou-nien chi-nien-k'an* (C 154) (Sixtieth Anniversary Publication of the Cantonese Association of Bangkok). Bangkok, 1937.

Tateyania 1941—Y. Tateyania, "A Japanese View of Thailand's Economic Independence." *Pacific Affairs,* 14 (Dec. 1941), 469–472.

Thai Customs Statement—Thailand, Customs Department, *Annual Statement of the Foreign Trade and Navigation of the Kingdom of Thailand, 1906/07–1946* [Title varies]. Bangkok, 1908–1950.

Thai Mai (Thai-language daily newspaper). Bangkok, 1954–1955.

Thailand Statistical Year Book—Thailand, Department of the Secretary-General of the Council of Ministers, Central Service of Statistics, *Statistical Year Books of Thailand 1916–1953* [Title varies], vols. 1–21, n.s. 1–2. Bangkok, 1917–1954.

Thammathipat (Thai-language daily newspaper). Bangkok, 1950–1954.

Thompson, P. 1906—Peter A. Thompson, *Lotus Land, Being an Account of the Country and the People of Southern Siam.* London: T. Werner Laurie, 1906.

Thompson, V. 1941—Virginia Thompson, *Thailand, the New Siam.* New York: Macmillan, 1941.

Thompson V. 1947—Virginia Thompson, *Labor Problems in Southeast Asia.* New Haven: Yale University Press, 1947.

Thompson and Adloff 1948—Virginia Thompson and Richard Adloff, *Cultural Institutions and Educational Policy in Southeast Asia.* New York: Institute of Pacific Relations, 1948.

Thompson and Adloff 1950—Virginia Thompson and Richard Adloff, *The Left-Wing in Southeast Asia*. New York: Sloane, 1950.

Thomson 1875—J. Thomson, *The Straits of Malacca, Indo-China, and China*. New York: Harper, 1875.

Tomlin 1844—Jacob Tomlin, *Missionary Journals and Letters, Written During Eleven Years' Residence and Travels among the Chinese, Javanese, Khassians, and Other Eastern Nations*. London: J. Nisbet, 1844.

"Triennial Tax." *Siam Repository*, 5 (1873), 330–331.

Tsai 1910—Chutung Tsai, "Chinese Nationality Law." *American Journal of International Law*, 4 (1910), 404–411.

Tsan 1935—Y. H. Tsan, "Chinese in Siam." *China Press Weekly*, 1, no. 4 (Aug. 25, 1935), 13–14; no. 5 (Sept. 1, 1935), 11–12.

"Ts'ung kai-hsüan tao chiu-chih" (C 185) (From Election to Office-taking). In *Hua-shang* (C 186) (Chinese Commerce). Bangkok: Hsien-lo chung-hua tsung-shang-hui (Chinese General Chamber of Commerce of Siam), 1947, 111–135.

Turpin 1771—M. Turpin, *History of the Kingdom of Siam*, pub. originally at Paris in 1771 and tr. from the French by B. O. Cartwright. Bangkok: American Mission Press, 1908.

Unger 1944—Leonard Unger, "The Chinese in Southeast Asia." *Geographical Review*, 34 (1944), 196–217.

Vliet 1638—Jeremias van Vliet, "Description of the Kingdom of Siam," tr. by L. F. von Ravenswaay. *Journal of the Siam Society*, 7 (1910), 1–108.

"Wages in Siam, 1930–31." *Monthly Labor Review*, 37 (Oct. 1933), 950–951.

Waithayakon 1944—Prince Wan Waithayakon, "Thai Culture." *Journal of the Siam Society*, 35 (Sept. 1944), 135–145.

Wales 1934—H. G. Quaritch Wales, *Ancient Siamese Government and Administration*. London: Bernard Quaritch, 1934.

Werner 1873—Reinhold Werner, *Die Preussische Expedition nach China, Japan und Siam 1860–62*. Leipzig, 1873.

"What the Chinese Think about Postwar Reconstruction." *Foreign Policy Reports*, 19 (1943).

Wood 1926—W. A. R. Wood, *A History of Siam*. London: Fisher Unwin, 1926.

Wood 1935—W. A. R. Wood, *Land of Smiles*. Bangkok: Krungdebarnagar Press, 1935.

Wright and Breakspear 1908—Arnold Wright and Oliver T. Breakspear, eds., *Twentieth Century Impressions of Siam: Its History, People, Commerce, Industries and Resources*. London: Lloyd's, 1908.

Wu 1928—C. C. Wu, "Chinese Immigration in the Pacific Area." *Chinese Social and Political Science Review*, 12 (1928), 543–560.

Yang 1936—Yang Hsin, "Siam's Anti-Chinese Measures and China's Boycott." *China Critic,* 12 (Jan. 2, 1936), 11–13.

Yang and Hau 1931—C. Yang, H. B. Hau, and others, *Statistics of China's Foreign Trade during the Last Sixty-five Years.* Monograph No. 4, National Research Institute of Social Sciences, Academia Sinica, 1931.

"Yi-shan-t'ing shih-hua" (C 187) (History of the [Teochiu Association] Public Cemetery). *Ch'ao-chou Yüeh-pao* (C 147), 19 (Nov. 1951), 7–8.

Young 1898—Ernest Young, *The Kingdom of the Yellow Robe.* Westminster: Archibald Constable and Co., 1898.

Yü 1951—Yü Chin, "Hsien-lo shang-yeh shih-hua" (C 188) (Commercial History of Siam). *Ch'ao-chou Yüeh-pao* (C 147), 16 (Aug. 1951), 10–11; 19 (Nov. 1951), 18–19; 20 (Dec. 1951), 15–16.

Zelinsky 1950—Wilbur Zelinsky, "The Indochinese Peninsula: A Demographic Anomaly." *Far Eastern Quarterly,* 9 (Feb. 1950), 115–145.

Zimmerman 1931—Carle C. Zimmerman, *Siam, Rural Economic Survey,* 1930–1931. Bangkok: Bangkok Times Press, 1931.

CHINESE CHARACTER
REFERENCE LIST

① 周達觀
② 暹
③ 羅斛
④ 鄭和
⑤ 馬歡
⑥ 歡
⑦ 洪保
⑧ 費信
⑨ 瀛涯勝覽
⑩ 星槎勝覽
⑪ 海語
⑫ 陳宜中
⑬ 何八歡
⑭ 謝文彬
⑮ 道乾
⑯ 郁永河著海上紀畧
⑰ 李桂林
⑱ 隱麟
⑲ 許松許楠許棟許椊
⑳ 何亞八林
㉑ 鄭宗興
㉒ 東西洋考
㉓ 海國聞見錄
㉔ 清文獻通攷
㉕ 華富
㉖ 海豐鑪
㉗ 皇
㉘ 吳陽
㉙ 西興
㉚ 文耀
㉛ 文輝
㉜ 鄭昭
㉝ 天右
㉞ 華佛
㉟ 福
㊱ 明
㊲ 福佬
㊳ 客家
㊴ 天后
㊵ 聖母水尾娘
㊶ 公司
㊷ 花會
㊸ 張丁
㊹ 志字
㊺ 三保太監
㊻ 三點
㊼ 城隍
㊽ 燕青
㊾ 陳慈黌
㊿ 老洪
51 本頭公
52 地頭
53 洪字
54 老洪
55 三點
56 關公
57 武帝
58 洪門
59 協天大帝
60 杜關勝
61 義興
62 謝清高
63 海籙
64 林海
65 天鍾
66 天生
67 文爽
68 臣
69 許泗章
70 森廣
71 森德
72 森金

美
⑦⑶ 詹采卿
⑺⑷ 沈聯芳
⑺⑸ 陳繹如
⑺⑹ 蕭佛成
⑺⑺ 沈荇思陳景華

美南
⑺⑻ 美南
⑺⑼ 漢境
⑻⓪ 同僑
⑻① 湄南
⑻② 華暹
⑻③ 華暹
⑻④ 汪精衛
⑻⑤ 胡

漢民胡毅生何克夫盧仲琳
⑻⑥ 余次彭
⑻⑺ 中華國國民軍憑票

⑻⑻ 保皇黨
⑻⑼ 馬興順
⑼⓪ 中華民
⑼① 俠
⑼② 鄭志勇
⑼③ 會館
⑼④ 別墅

⑼⑤ 公所
⑼⑥ 伍佐南
⑼⑺ 雲竹亭
⑼⑻ 盧岵川
⑼⑼ 徐世昌
⑩⓪ 聯僑
⑩① 僑

聲
⑩② 演生
⑩③ 林伯岐
⑩④ 國民
⑩⑤ 鐵血團
⑩⑥ 華僑
⑩⑺ 晨鐘
⑩⑻ 民國

⑩⑼ 程演生
⑪⓪ 伍朝樞
⑪① 朱鶴翔
⑪② 陳守明
⑪③ 凌冰
⑪④ 中國蟻
⑪⑤ 民國

光炎
⑪⑥ 中原
⑪⑺ 陳加樂
⑪⑻ 僑頡
⑪⑼ 善堂
⑫⓪ 警
⑫① 邱及
⑫② 真話
⑫③

泰華商
⑫④ 劉焜
⑫⑤ 熊均靈
⑫⑥ 李鐵錚
⑫⑺ 梁任信
⑫⑻ 利華輝
⑫⑼ 鄭

午樓
⑬⓪ 全民
⑬① 中國人
⑬② 民聲
⑬③ 正言
⑬④ 民主新聞
⑬⑤ 曼谷商

光華
⑬⑥ 光華
⑬⑺ 孫秉乾
⑬⑻ 張蘭臣
⑬⑼ 蟻美厚
⑭⓪ 周錚
⑭① 曼谷公星
⑭② 曼谷商

暹
⑭③ 星泰
⑭④ 胡文虎
⑭⑤ 世界
⑭⑥ 王慕能
⑭⑺ 潮州月報
⑭⑻ 陳毓泰

著鄭和通使泰國考
⑭⑼ 泰國研究
⑮⓪ 鄭王族系
⑮① 周鴻鈞著本

所之迴顧與展望
⑮② 泰京中華贈醫所三十六至三十九年度
⑮④ 暹京

報告書
⑮③ 馮少文著六拾年來之廣肇會館與其事業

廣肇會館六十週年紀念刊
⑮⑤ 馮自由著華僑革命開國史

⑯ 夏鼎勳著閩僑吳陽及其子孫

⑰ 華僑新語

⑱ 蕭松琴著第四十一屆董事會工作檢討

⑲ 泰京天華醫院第四十一屆董事會報告書

⑳ 謝猶榮著暹羅國志

㉑ 謝猶榮著新編暹羅國志

㉒ 暹羅廣肇屬之建築業

㉓ 暹京廣肇會館七十週年紀念特刊

㉔ 暹羅王參觀華僑學校之經過與索隱

㉕ 南洋研究

㉖ 許雲樵著北大年史

㉗ 黃福鑾著華僑與中國革命

㉘ 會館地產史畧

㉙ 關於南洋華僑教育討論

㉚ 藍渭濱著從潮安文物說到旅暹潮安同鄉會之精神

㉛ 旅暹潮安同鄉會紀念特刊

㉜ 李飄萍著暹華新聞事業小史

㉝ 暹羅華僑印刷臨時聯合辦事處經過

㉞ 梁任信著參加六屬會館同業公會成立二週年紀念特刊

㉟ 本會組織沿革

㊱ 暹羅華僑客屬總會二十週年紀念刊

㊲ 本會館史畧

㊳ 本屬學校沿革

㊴ 十年來之會館史畧

㊵ 收容被俘同胞紀詳

㊶ 蘇宗澤著本會館史畧

㊷ 暹羅潮州會館成立十週年紀念特刊

㊸ 泰國華僑工商業全貌

㊹ 譚金洪著廣肇醫院及墳場

㊺ 從改選到就職

㊻ 華商義山亭史話

㊼ 義山亭史話

㊽ 俞瑾著暹羅商業史話

Index

Acculturation, Chinese, 129-134, 150-151, 299-300, 311-315
Agriculture:
  plantation, 46, 83-84, 111-113
  subsistence, 91, 97-98, 111, 303
Aid for China from Thailand Chinese:
  May 30th Movement, 235
  postwar, 290-291
  Shanghai incident, 240
  Sino-Japanese War, 243-244, 265-266, 270
  Tsinan incident, 239
Alien-registration fee, 266, 330-332, 365-367, 377-380, 417n.33
American Far Eastern policy, 327-328, 340
Americans in Thailand:
  anti-Communism, 377
  attitude toward Chinese, 403n.21
  Christian missions, 83, 168, 401n.71
  consular protection of Chinese, 145-146
  intervention for Sun Yat-sen, 107
Amoy, 31, 36(map), 40, 42-43, 47-50, 170
Amphoe, vii
  Chinese concentration by, 202(map)
Ancestor cult and worship, 32, 92-93, 139, 314
Anti-Chinese movement, *see* Anti-Sinicism
Anti-Communism, 324, 327-328, 335-336, 338-340, 362, 366-368, 375-377
Anti-Japanese movement, 185, 238-240, 243-244, 248, 264-266, 270

see also Underground, wartime
Anti-Sinicism, 160-161, 163-165, 185, 261, 330, 376-377, 381
  among Thai of Chinese ancestry, 244-247
  European influence in, 160-161, 271-272
Aristocracy, Thai royal, 96
  titles of, 149, 402n.90
  see also Elite, Thai
Artisan trades, 218
  Chinese dominance of, 117-118, 301-304
  social position of those in, 135, 306-310
  speech-group specialization in, 136, 314-318
  Thai discouraged in, 96
Asian-African Conference at Bandung, 340-341, 379-380
Assimilation, Chinese:
  as government policy, 249-251, 269, 377-382
  education and, 234, 249-250, 253-254, 381-382
  ethnocentrism and, 246-247
  factors favoring, 300, 381-383
  factors retarding, 253-254, 269, 276, 375, 381
  in the Ayutthayan period, 3, 5
  in the 19th century, 71, 128-134, 150-154
  in the 20th century, 189-190, 244, 247, 253-254, 300, 310, 313, 380-382
Assumption College, 168, 315

[Index]

Hainanese (*cont.*):
  leaders, 272
  miners, 111, 136
  occupational specialization of, 47, 86, 113-114, 136, 315-319
  political division among, 293-294
  poverty, 86, 136
  prostitution and marriage, 197
  reasons for numerical strength in Siam, 47-48, 49
  resistance to malaria, 86, 209
  sawmillers, 86, 105, 136, 215, 315, 353
  social position of, 86, 136, 255, 318
  schools, 230-231
  temples, 84, 138
Hainanese speech-group associations:
  Ch'iung-chou Kung-so, 167, 293
  Ch'iung-tao Hui-so, 157, 236, 272, 293
  Ch'iung-yai T'ung-hsiang-hui, 293-294, 323, 325, 335
  Hai-nan Hui-kuan, 293-294
  in Phitsanulok, 294
Hakka Association, 157, 167, 169, 258, 277, 282, 294, 319, 338
Hakkas:
  as railroad construction workers, 111
  emigrant area, 36(map), 37-39
  expansion upcountry with railroad, 88-89, 209-210
  immigrants and settlers in Siam, 41, 52, 178-180, 209-212, 392n.60
  in Bangkok, 83, 208
  in China, 31, 37-38, 390n.14, 390n.15, 390n.16
  in rubber industry, 216, 351
  in tin mining and export, 215, 351
  leaders of, 277
  occupational specialization of, 136, 315-318
  proportion among Swatow emigrants, 48
  reasons for numerical strength in Siam, 47-49
  religion of, 138-139
  schools, 231
  secret societies, 141
  sex ratio and marriage of, 197
  social status of, 136, 255, 318-319
Hang Li-wu, 344
Hatyai, ii(map), 211
Haw, *see* Họ
Head tax, 162, 266
  see also Alien-registration fee *and* Triennial tax
Headmen, Chinese, 14, 141-142

Highway construction:
  effect on Chinese settlement, 198, 200, 209-210
  effect on rice milling, 213-214
Hoihow, *see* Hai-k'ou
Hokchius, 216
Hokkien Association, 167, 169, 319, 339
Hokkiens:
  as laborers on Railroad of Death, 274
  as rubber merchants, 216, 316, 351
  emigrant area, 36(map), 37
  immigrants and settlers, Ayutthayan period, 4, 12, 15, 40
    19th century, 41, 51, 83, 86-87, 110
    20th century, 52, 180, 210-212, 274
  in Bangkok, 83, 208
  in China, 37, 390n.14
  in tin mining and export, 215, 351
  mercantile, seafaring orientation, 84
  occupational specialization of, 135, 216, 316-318
  reasons for immigration decline, 47-49
  sex ratio and marriage, 197-198, 406 n.46
  social status of, 135, 255, 317-318
  temples of, 84, 138, 319-320
Hongkong, 31, 34(map), 42
  as educational center, 233
  as model for Chinese in Thailand, 308
  emigration traffic via, 43, 47, 49, 51
Household size, Chinese contrasted with Thai, 312-313
Housing, Chinese, 13, 106-107, 311-313
Họ, 80-81, 394n.138, 401n.57
Hsia Pao, 158, 440
Hsiang-shan hsien, 34(map), 42, 156
Hsiao Fo-ch'eng, 156, 157, 158, 236, 237, 238, 241, 269, 440(C76)
Hsien (Chinese counties), vii
Hsien (Kingdom), *see* Sukhothai, Kingdom of
Hsien-lo, *see* Ayutthaya, Kingdom of
Hsing-hsien Jih-pao, 324, 329, 333, 340, 343, 440(C142)
Hsin-hui hsien, 34(map), 390n.13
Hsin-min School, 159, 169
Hsü Sen-chin, -kuang, -mei, *and* -te, 151, 439-440(C69-72)
Hsü Szu-chang, 151, 439(C68)
Hu Han-min, 157, 158, 237, 440(C85)
Hua-ch'iao Jih-pao, 239, 243, 292, 324, 329, 332, 440(C106)